THE ODES OF PINDAR

LCL 56

THE ODES OF PINDAR

INCLUDING
THE PRINCIPAL FRAGMENTS

WITH AN INTRODUCTION
AND AN ENGLISH TRANSLATION BY

SIR JOHN SANDYS

HARVARD UNIVERSITY PRESS
CAMBRIDGE, MASSACHUSETTS
LONDON, ENGLAND

First published 1915
Second and revised edition 1919
Reprinted 1924, 1927, 1930
Revised and reprinted 1937
Reprinted 1946, 1957, 1961, 1968, 1978, 1989

ISBN 0-674-99062-5

Printed in Great Britain by St. Edmundsbury Press Ltd,
Bury St. Edmunds, Suffolk, on wood-free paper.
Bound by Hunter & Foulis Ltd, Edinburgh, Scotland.

CONTENTS

INTRODUCTION

I.—THE LIFE OF PINDAR

PINDAR, the greatest of the lyrical poets of Greece, was a native of Boeotia. He was born at Cynoscephalae, about half a mile to the west of Thebes. He has himself recorded the fact that the date of his birth coincided with the celebration of the Pythian festival at Delphi,[1] a festival that always fell in the third of the four years of the Olympic period. According to the lexicographer Suïdas, the poet was born in the sixty-fifth Olympiad. Ol. 65, 3 corresponds to 518 B.C., and this date has been widely accepted.[2] The most probable alternative is Ol. 64, 3, that is 522 B.C.[3] In support of this earlier date, it is urged that all the ancient authorities described the poet as " flourishing," that is, as being about forty years of age, at the time of the Persian war of 481–479 B.C. Had Pindar been born in 518, he would have been only 37 at the beginning, and 39 at the end of the war. Had the date of his birth

[1] Frag. 193 (205).
[2] *e.g.* by Christ, Wilamowitz, and Schröder.
[3] Accepted by Boeckh and Gaspar.

been 522, he would have been forty in 482, the year preceding the expedition of Xerxes.[1]

The poet was proud of his Theban birth and his Theban training.[2] He was the son of Daïphantus and Cleodicê. From his uncle Scopelinus he learnt to play the flute, an instrument which held an important place in the worship of Apollo at Delphi, and was perfected at Thebes, where it was always more highly esteemed than at Athens. At Athens he was instructed in the technique of lyrical composition by Agathocles and Apollodôrus, and probably also by Lasus of Hermione, who brought the dithyramb to its highest perfection. During his stay in Athens he could hardly have failed to meet his slightly earlier contemporary, Aeschylus, who was born in 525 B.C.

On returning to Thebes, he began his career as a lyrical poet. In his earliest poem he is said to have neglected the use of myths. This neglect was pointed out by the Boeotian poetess, Corinna; whereupon Pindar went to the opposite extreme, and crowded his next composition with a large

[1] Gaspar, *Chronologie Pindarique*, Bruxelles, 1900, p. 15 f. The uncertainty between the dates 522 and 518 for the birth of Pindar is due to the corresponding uncertainty between 586 and 582 as the beginning of the Pythian era. If Pindar was born at the 17th Pythiad, the date of his birth would be 522, if we reckon from 586 ; or 518, if we reckon from 582. The latter of the two dates for the Pythian era is now known to be right, and this is a presumption in favour of 518 as the date of the poet's birth.

[2] Frag. 198ᵃ.

LIFE OF PINDAR

number of mythological allusions.[1]   He soon received from his critic the wise admonition: "One must sow with the hand, and not with the whole sack."[2] He is said to have subsequently defeated the poetess Myrtis, who was reproached by Corinna for competing with Pindar.[3]

The poet has generally been regarded as claiming descent from the aristocratic family of the Theban Aegeidae.[4]   However this may be, he was connected closely with the Dorians, and was an admirer of the Dorian aristocracy.   He was an oligarch, but, "in politics," he "deemed that the middle state was crowned with more enduring good"[5]; and his objection to "the raging crowd" of Sicilian revolutionaries[6] is consistent with his appreciation of the reasonable democracy of Athens.[7]   It was from the powerful family of the Thessalian Aleuadae that he received in 498 his first commission for an epinician ode (*P.* x).

In September, 490, the Persians were defeated by Athens at Marathon.   A few days before the battle, Xenocrates, the younger brother of Thêrôn of Acragas, won the chariot-race in the Pythian games.   The official ode was composed by Simonides, then at the height of his fame, while Pindar's extant poem was

---

[1] Frag. 29 (5).   [2] Plutarch, *De gloria Atheniensium*, c. 4.
[3] μέμφομαι δὲ καὶ λιγυρὰν Μυρτίδ' ἰώνγα, ὅτι βανὰ φῦσ' ἔβα Πινδάροι ποτ' ἔριν. Corinna, Frag. 21 Bergk ; Smyth's *Greek Melic Poets*, pp. 69, 339.
[4] Cp. note on *P.* v 75
[5] *P.* xi 53.   [6] *P.* ii 86.   [7] *P.* vii 1.

a private tribute of admiration for the victor's son, Thrasybûlus, who probably drove his father's chariot (*P.* vi). At the same festival, the prize for flute-playing was won by Midas of Acragas, and was celebrated by Pindar (*P.* xii). The poet was doubtless present at this Pythian festival.

During the Persian wars he may well have been perplexed by the position of his native city. He alludes to the crisis in the affairs of Thebes, when the oligarchs cast in their lot with the invading Persians.[1] During these years of glory for Greece, and disgrace for Thebes, Pindar composed more odes for Aeginetans than for any others, and he probably resided in Aegina for part of this time. One-fourth of his epinician odes are in honour oɪ athletes from that island. The first of these (*N.* v), that on Pytheas, has been assigned to the Nemean games of 489. The earliest of the Olympians (*O.* xiv) celebrates the winning of the boys' foot-race in 488 by a native of the old Boeotian city of Orchomenus. In August, 486, Megacles the Alcmeonid, who had been ostracised by Athens a few months earlier, won at Delphi the chariot-race briefly commemorated in the seventh Pythian.

To 485 we may assign the second, and the seventh, of the Nemean Odes. The second Nemean is on the victory in the pancratium won by the Athenian Tîmodêmus; the seventh on that in the boys' pan-

---

[1] Frag. 109 (228), quoted by Polybius, iv 31.

cratium won by Sôgenês of Aegina. (This had been
preceded by the sixth Paean, in which Pindar had
given offence to certain Aeginetans by the way in
which he had referred to the death of Neoptolemus
at Delphi.) Either 484 or 480 may be the date of
the contest in the pancratium won by Phylacidas of
Aegina (*I.* vi), and 478 that of similar victories
gained by Melissus of Thebes (*I.* iv), and Cleander
of Aegina (*I.* viii). In 477 the chariot-race at Nemea
was won by Melissus, and was briefly commemorated
in the third Isthmian, which was made the proëme
of the fourth Isthmian written in the same metre in
the previous year.

After the defeat of the invasion of Xerxes, in 479,
the poet rejoices in the removal of the intolerable
burden, " the stone of Tantalus " that had been hang-
ing over the head of Hellas [1]; he celebrates the
battles of Artemisium,[2] Salamis,[3] and Plataea,[4] and
hails Athens as " the bulwark of Greece." [5]

The Olympian festival of 476 marks a most impor-
tant epoch in the poet's life. No fewer than five
Olympian odes were inspired by victories gained at
that festival. The first Olympian celebrates the
horse-race won by Hieron of Syracuse ; the second
and third, the chariot-race won by Thêrôn of Acragas.
The prize for the boys' wrestling-match, carried off
in the same year by Hâgêsidâmus of the Western
Locri, was promptly eulogised beside the Alpheüs in

---

[1] *I.* viii 10.   [2] Frag. 77 (196).   [3] *I.* v 49.
[4] *P.* i 77.   [5] Frag. 76 (46).

the eleventh Olympian, and was afterwards commemorated in the tenth, which was performed at the victor's home in the West.

If the fifth Isthmian, in honour of Phylacidas of Aegina, is as late as 476, it was composed while the poet was still in his native land. It was probably in the autumn of 476 that Pindar left for Sicily. At Acragas he must have taken part in the production of the second and third Olympian odes in honour of the victory in the chariot-race, lately won by Thêrôn. He also wrote an encomium on Thêrôn,[1] and a song for Thêrôn's nephew, Thrasybûlus.[2] At Syracuse he produced his first Olympian ode in honour of the horse-race won by Hieron's courser, Pherenîcus, and his first Nemean on the victory in the chariot-race won in the previous year by Chromius, whom Hieron had appointed governor of the newly-founded city of Aetna.

Probably in the spring of 475 Pindar returned to Thebes. It was at Thebes that the chariot of Hieron gained a victory celebrated in the "second Pythian," conjecturally assigned to 475. The same is the date of the third Nemean, on the victory of Aristocleides, a pancratiast of Aegina.

In 474 Pindar was once more present at Delphi. After the Pythian festival of that year he commemorated in the third Pythian the victories won in the Pythian festivals of 482 and 478 by Hieron's steed, Pherenîcus, who had since won the Olympic

[1] Frag. 119.   [2] Frag. 124.

race of 476. He also celebrated in the ninth
Pythian the race in full armour won in 474 by
Telesicrates of Cyrene, and, in the eleventh, the
victory of Thrasydaeus of Thebes in the boys' foot-
race. 474 is the conjectural date of the victory in the
chariot-race, won at Sicyon by Chromius of Aetna.
To the spring of 474 has been assigned the dithy-
ramb in praise of Athens.[1]

The fourth Nemean, on Timasarchus of Aegina,
the winner of the boys' wrestling-match, is assigned
to 473. 472 is the probable date of the sixth
Olympian, on the mule-chariot-race won by Hâgêsias
of Stymphâlus and Syracuse, and also of the twelfth,
on the long-race won by Ergoteles of Himera. It
was apparently in this year that the Isthmian victory
in the chariot-race, achieved in 477 by Xenocrates of
Acragas, was privately commemorated by the victor's
son (*I.* ii).

The victory of Hieron's chariot in the Pythian
games of 470 was celebrated in a splendid ode, the
first Pythian. In 468 the wrestling-match at Olympia
was won by Epharmostus of Opûs, a Locrian town
north of Boeotia (*O.* ix). In 464 the famous boxer,
Diagoras of Rhodes, gained the victory celebrated in
the seventh Olympian; and, in the same year, at
Olympia, the foot-race and the pentathlum were
won on the same day by Xenophon of Corinth,
a victory nobly celebrated in the thirteenth

[1] Frag. 76 f.

Olympian.[1] The success of Alcimidas of Aegina, in the boys' wrestling-match, is the theme of the sixth Nemean, assigned to 463, and the same is probably the date of the tenth, on the wrestling-match won by Theaeus of Argos at the local festival of Hêra. 463 is the conjectural date of the second and the ninth Paeans, the former composed for Abdera; the latter, for Thebes, on the occasion of an eclipse of the sun.

The victory in the chariot-race won in 462 by Arcesilas, king of Cyrene, gives occasion to the longest, and one of the finest, of all the odes, the fourth Pythian, which is composed, to propitiate the king, at the request of a Cyrenaean exile. The fifth Pythian was performed at Cyrene, on the return of the victorious charioteer and his horses. Alcimedon of Aegina, the boy-wrestler of 460, is celebrated in the eighth Olympian; another Aeginetan, Deinias, the winner of the foot-race about 459, is lauded in the eighth Nemean; and Herodotus of Thebes, who probably won the chariot-race in 458, is the theme of the first Isthmian, which was soon followed by the fourth Paean, written for the island of Ceôs. A second Theban, Strepsiades, won the pancratium, probably in 456 (*I.* i).

Psaumis of Camarina won the chariot-race in 452, and the mule-race, probably in 448; these two victories are sung in the fourth and fifth Olympians.

Among the latest of the odes is the eighth Pythian,

[1] The same victory is also the theme of Frag. 122 (87).

on the victory gained in 446 by the boy-wrestler, Aristomenes of Aegina. The same is the conjectural date of the eleventh Nemean, an installation ode in honour of Aristagoras, the president of the council of Tenedos. He is probably the elder brother of Theoxenus of Tenedos, a favourite of Pindar, in whose praise he wrote a poem,[1] and in whose arms he died at Argos. The poet is said to have attained the age of eighty. If so, the date of his death would be either 442 or 438, according as we accept the date 522 or 518 as the date of his birth.

His daughters conveyed his ashes to Thebes; and, nearly eight centuries later, his countryman, Pausanias, tells us of the site of the poet's tomb, and adds some of the legends relating to his life :—

Passing by the right of the stadium of Iolaüs (outside the Proetidian gate), you come to a hippodrome in which is the tomb of Pindar. In his youth he was once walking to Thespiae in the heat of noon-day, and, in his weariness, he laid him down a little way above the road. While he was asleep, bees flew to him, and placed honey on his lips. Such was the beginning of his career of song.

When his fame was spread abroad from one end of Greece to the other, the Pythian priestess . . . bade the Delphians give to Pindar an equal share of all the first-fruits they offered to Apollo. It is said, too, that in his old age, there was vouchsafed to him a vision in a dream. As he slept, Proserpine stood beside him and said that, of all the deities, she alone had not been hymned by him, but that, nevertheless, he should make a song on her also, when he was come to her. Before ten days were out, Pindar had paid the debt of nature. . . .[2] Crossing the Dirce we come to the ruins of Pindar's house, and to a sanctuary of Mother Dindymene

---

[1] Frag. 123 (88).   [2] Cp. Frazer's *Pausanias*, ix 23, 2–4.

dedicated by Pindar.[1] At Delphi, not far from the hearth where Neoptolemus was slain, stands the chair of Pindar. It is of iron, and they say that, whenever Pindar came to Delphi, he used to sit on it and sing his songs to Apollo.[2]

Pindar was a devout adherent of the national religion of Greece, and his Paeans give proof of his close connexion with the worship of Apollo at Delphi. Reverence for the gods is a prominent characteristic of his work. " From the gods are all the means of human excellences." [3] " It is the god that granteth all fulfilment to men's hopes; he bendeth the necks of the proud, and giveth to others a glory that knoweth no eld." [4] The poet rejoices in recounting the old heroic legends, especially when they are connected with Castor and Pollux, or Heracles, or the Aeacidae. " My heart cannot taste of song without telling of the Aeacidae." [5] But he resolutely refuses to ascribe to the gods any conduct which would be deemed unseemly if tried by a human standard. If a legend tells that, when the gods feasted with Tantalus, they ate the flesh of his son Pelops, Pindar refuses to represent the gods as cannibals.[6] " It is seemly," he says, "to speak fair things of deities." [7] " To revile the gods is a hateful effort of the poet's skill." [8]

[1] *ib.* ix 25, 4.   When Thebes was taken by Alexander,

> " The great Emathian conqueror bid spare
> The house of Pindarus, when temple and tower
> Went to the ground."

(Milton's 8th *Sonnet*), Pliny, vii 109.

[2] Pausanias, x 24, 5.   [3] *P.* i 41.   [4] *P.* ii 49.
[5] *I.* v 20.   [6] *O.* i 52.   [7] *O.* i 35.   [8] *O.* ix 37.

THE STYLE OF PINDAR

II —THE STYLE OF PINDAR

Writing in Rome in the age of Augustus, Dionysius of Halicarnassus, after quoting a dithyramb of Pindar,[1] expresses an opinion, which (he says) will be accepted by all readers of literary taste :—

> " These lines are vigorous, weighty and dignified, and are marked by much severity of style. Though rugged, they are not unpleasantly so, and though harsh to the ear, are only so in due measure. They are slow in their rhythm, and present broad effects of harmony ; and they exhibit, not the showy and decorative prettiness of our own day, but the severe beauty of a distant past." [2]

In the same age, Horace describes Pindar as inimitable. He is " like a river rushing down from the mountains and overflowing its banks." " He is worthy of Apollo's bay, whether he rolls down new words through daring dithyrambs " ; or " sings of gods and kings," or of " those whom the palm of Elis makes denizens of heaven " ; or " laments some youthful hero, and exalts to the stars his prowess, his courage, and his golden virtue." " A mighty breeze " (he adds) " uplifts the Swan of Dirce." [3]

About 88 A.D. Quintilian tells us that " of lyric poetry Pindar is the peerless master, in grandeur, in maxims, in figures of speech, and in the full stream of eloquence." [4]

---

[1] Frag. 75 (45).
[2] *De Compositione Verborum*, c. 22 ; cp. p. 217 of Prof. Rhys Roberts' translation.
[3] Horace, *Carm.* iv 2.   [4] x i 61.

Our own poet, Gray, in his ode on the *Progress of Poesy,* has sung of the "pride," and the "ample pinion,"

> "That the Theban eagle bear
> Sailing with supreme dominion
> Through the azure deep of air."

Pindar's style is marked by a constant and habitual use of metaphor. To describe the furthest limits of human achievement, he borrows metaphors from the remotest bounds of travel or navigation, the "pillars of Heracles" in the West,[1] the Phâsis and the Nile in the East,[2] and the Hyperboreans beyond the North.[3] The victor's merits are "countless as the sand." [4] Olympia is the "crown," or the "flower" of festivals; it is peerless as water, bright as gold, and brilliant as the sun.[5]

His similes for poetic effort are apt to be drawn from the language of the particular form of athletic skill which he is commemorating, whether it be the chariot-race,[6] or leaping,[7] or throwing the javelin.[8] He has "many swift arrows in his quiver" [9]; he approaches the holy hill of Elis with "shafts from the Muses' bow." [10] The poet's tidings bear abroad the victor's fame "faster than gallant steed or winged ship" [11]; "sounding the praise of valour,"

---

[1] *O.* iii 44 ; *N.* iii 21 ; *I.* iv 12.   [2] *I.* ii 41 f.
[3] *P.* x 30.   [4] *O.* ii 98, xiii 46.   [5] *O.* i 1 f, ii 13, v 1.
[6] *O.* vi 27.   [7] *N.* v 19.   [8] *P.* i 43.
[9] *O.* ii 83.   [10] *O.* ix 5.   [11] *O.* ix 23.

the poet will "mount the flower-crowned prow."[1]
His province is "the choice garden of the Graces"[2];
he tills the field of the Graces, or of Aphrodîtê.[3]
For a digression he finds an image in the parting of
the ways between Thebes and Delphi.[4] But his
metaphors are sometimes mixed, as when he bids his
Muse "stay the oar and drop the anchor," "for the
bright wing of his songs darts, like a bee, from
flower to flower."[5] He fancies he has on his lips a
whetstone, which "woos his willing soul with the
breath of fair-flowing strains."[6] He also compares
the skilful trainer to the whetstone, "the grinding
stone which gives an edge to bronze."[7]

In describing his art, he resorts to familiar and
even homely comparisons. Poets are "the cunning
builders of song."[8] An ode is sent across the sea
"like Tyrian merchandise."[9] The poet's mind is a
register of promised songs, in which a particular
debt can be searched out[10]; praise that has been long
deferred may be paid with interest.[11]

The trainer, entrusted with the words and the
music of the ode, is "a scroll-wand of the Muses,"
"a mixing-bowl of song."[12] Among homely metaphors
we have that of the shoe :—"let him know that in
this sandal he hath his foot"[13]; and that of the
seamy side :—"ills can be borne by the noble, when

---

[1] *P.* ii 62. [2] *O.* ix 27. [3] *P.* vi 1.
[4] *P.* xi 38. [5] *P.* x 51 ; cp. *N.* iii 79, *I.* vii 19.
[6] *O.* vi 82. [7] *I.* vi 72. [8] *P.* iii 113. [9] *P.* ii 67.
[10] *O.* xi 1. [11] *ib.* 9. [12] *O.* vi 91 f. [13] *O.* vi 8.

they have turned the fair side outward." [1] The
poet compares himself to " a cork that floats above the
net, and is undipped in the brine." [2] An inglorious
youth has " hidden his young life in a hole " [3]
or is a " chanticleer that only fights at home." [4]
The victor in a boys' wrestling-match has " put off
from him upon the bodies " of his defeated rivals
"the loathsome return, and the taunting tongue,
and the slinking path." [5] Lastly, by an image
derived from the action of running water on the
basements of buildings, a city is described as " sink-
ing into a deep gulf of ruin." [6]

The metaphors and similes of Pindar are, in fact,
derived from many sources. From common life, as
from awakening and thirst, from a debt, or a drug,
or a spell; from the wine-cup, and the mixing-bowl,
the physician, or the pilot. Or, again, from the
natural world, as from flowers and trees, root and fruit,
gardens and ploughed fields, nectar and honey; from
the bee; the cock, the crow, and the eagle; the fox,
the wolf, and the lion; from a star, from light and
flame, winds and waters, breeze and calm, fountain
and flood, wave and shingle, sailing and steering. Or
from the arts, such as weaving or forging, or cunning
workmanship in gold and ivory and white coral;
gates, or nails, or keys; the wheel or the whetstone;
a foundation, a flight of stairs, a bulwark, a pillar or
tower. Lastly, from manly exercises, from the

[1] *P.* iii 83.   [2] *P.* ii 80.   [3] *I.* viii 70.
[4] *O.* xii 4.   [5] *O.* viii 68.   [6] *O.* xi 37.

chariot, or the chase, or from wrestling, or from flinging javelins, or shooting arrows.[1]

One of his main characteristics is splendour of language, as in the opening of the first Olympian: "Peerless is water, and gold is the gleaming crown of lordly wealth. . . . Look not for any star in the lonely heavens that shall rival the gladdening radiance of the sun, or any place of festival more glorious than Olympia." In the sixth Olympian the new-born babe is "hidden in the boundless brake, with its dainty form steeped in the golden and deep purple light of pansies."[2] This splendour includes swiftness of transition from image to image, from thought to thought. "The blossom of these hymns of praise flitteth, like a bee, from theme to theme."[3]

Another characteristic is the dexterous way in which the poet links the athletic life of the present with the martial exploits of the heroic past. The athletes of the day have their earliest exemplars in the mythical heroes, in Heracles, in Telamon and Ajax, in Peleus and Achilles.

A third is the element of counsel. The odes are frequently interspersed with religious precepts and moral maxims: "If any man hopeth to escape the eye of God, he is grievously wrong."[4] "Trial is the test of men."[5] Few have gained pleasure without

[1] For references, see the Index to Gildersleeve's and to Fennell's *Olympian and Pythian Odes*, s.v. *Metaphors.* Schröder considers Pindar "rude and unrefined" in his use of metaphors.

[2] *O*. vi 54 f.   [3] *P*. x 53 f.   [4] *O*. i 64.   [5] *O*. iv 18.

toil." [1] "Wealth adorned with virtues is the true light of man." [2] Sometimes a touch of satire is added: "The prosperous are deemed wise,—even by their fellow citizens." [3]

The great games of Greece arouse in the poet a lofty imagination that knows no local limitations, but is Panhellenic in its range. The victor whom he celebrates may be the ruler of some Sicilian colony far from the mother-land, but that ruler belongs to the Hellenic world, and the poet who praises him is himself eager to be foremost, not merely within the limits of the land of Hellas, but "among the Hellenes everywhere." [4]

III.—The National Festivals

The national festivals of Greece were among the most important means for awakening and fostering the national spirit. No Barbarian was permitted to take part in them. [5] They were open solely to citizens of Greece, or of the Greek colonies; and on these occasions the colonies were eager to assert their sense of union with the mother-land. Hence the festivals were attended by visitors and competitors from every part of the Greek world, from Rhodes and Cyrene, and from the Greek cities of "Greater Hellas" and of Sicily. The national

---

[1] *O.* xi 22.   [2] *O.* ii 53 f.
[3] *O.* v 16. A hundred further examples of moral maxims are collected in Donaldson's *Pindar*, pp. xxviii–xl.
[4] *O.* i ult.   [5] Herodotus, v 22.

xxii

festivals attained their highest splendour during the time when the national spirit was roused by the conflicts with the Barbarians, which began about 500 and ended in 479 B.C.

On the approach of the festal occasion a sacred truce was proclaimed by heralds sent to all the Greek States. Any soldier in arms entering Elis during the Olympian festival was treated as a prisoner of war, who could not return to his own State until he had been ransomed.[1]

The earliest of the Greek festivals for holding athletic contests had their origin in funeral ceremonies. Such were the prehistoric games held in memory of Patroclus [2] and Oedipus,[3] and the Nemean and Isthmian games. Of the many local assemblies there were four which, in course of time, became of national importance. Of these four, the earliest and the latest, the Olympian and the Nemean, were in honour of Zeus, while the Pythian was connected with Apollo, and the Isthmian with Poseidon. But, in their original form, the Nemean games were founded by the " Seven against Thebes " in memory of the untimely death of the infant Opheltes, the son of the Nemean king, Lycurgus; while the Isthmian games were instituted by Sisyphus, king of Corinth, in commemoration of his nephew, the ill-fated Melicertes, who was washed ashore to the East of the Isthmus, and was afterwards worshipped as a sea-god under the name of Palaemon.

[1] Thucydides, v 49. [2] Il. xxiii passim. [3] Il. xxiii 679.

INTRODUCTION

The Olympian festival was held once in every four years, and the Pythian always fell in the third year of the Olympian period. Both of these were held in August, and each of them was followed by a Nemean and an Isthmian festival, the Nemean taking place in July of the first year, and the Isthmian in April of the second year, after each Olympian or Pythian festival. It is here assumed that the order of the festivals in the age of Pindar was the same as that in 220 to 216 B.C. for which we have definite details.[1] On this assumption, the following table shows the sequence in and after 476 B.C.

April 476	...	...	*Ol.* 75, 4	... ...	Isthmia
August 476	...	...	*Ol.* 76, 1	... ...	Olympia
July 475	...	...	*Ol.* 76, 2	...	Nemea
April 474	...	...	————	... ...	Isthmia
August 474	...	...	*Ol.* 76, 3	... ...	Pythia
July 473	..	...	*Ol.* 76, 4	...	Nemea
April 472	...	...	————	... ...	Isthmia
August 472	...	...	*Ol.* 77, 1	.. ...	Olympia
July 471	...	...	*Ol.* 77, 2	... ...	Nemea
April 470	...	...	————	... ...	Isthmia
August 470	...	...	*Ol.* 77, 3	... ...	Pythia
July 469	...	...	*Ol.* 77, 4	... ...	Nemea
April 468	...	...	————	... ...	Isthmia

The four festivals formed a circuit, or περίοδος, and one who had gained a victory in all is described in Greek inscriptions as a περιοδονίκης.

The Olympian festival is said to have been founded by Heracles.[2] The legend also told that Oenomaüs, king of Pisa, the ancient capital of Elis,

---

[1] G. F. Unger, *Philologus*, xxxvii 1 ff.
[2] *O.* ii 3 f. ; iii 21 f. ; xi 64 f.

compelled the suitors of his daughter to compete with him in the chariot-race, and slew all whom he vanquished. He was at last overcome by Pelops, who thus became the prototype of all Olympic victors. It was near the tomb of that hero that the games were held.

The first definite fact in their history is their reorganisation by Iphitus, king of Elis, in 776 B.C. This date marked the beginning of Greek chronology, and, from 776 B.C., we have a complete list of the winners in the Olympian foot-race for nearly 1000 years, down to 217 A.D. Originally the prizes were tripods or other objects of value; but, in the seventh Olympiad, the crown of wild olive was introduced on the advice of the Delphic oracle.

Olympia, the scene of the festival, lies on the right bank of the river Alpheüs, at the point where it is joined by the torrent of the Cladeüs. To the north is the hill of Cronus, a tree-clad eminence 403 feet in height. In 776 B.C. the only building in the Olympian precinct was the wooden structure of the Hêraeum. Among the treasures of this temple was the disc recording the names of Iphitus and Lycurgus as " founders " of the Olympic festival, and the table of ivory and gold on which the crowns for the victors were placed. There was also an altar of Zeus built up of the ashes of the victims slain in each successive festival. The excavations begun in 1874 have revealed the walled precinct known as the *Altis*, 750 feet long by 570 feet broad, with many remains of important buildings; also the site of the stadium, 630 feet in length, with the start and the finish of the race marked by slabs of stone about 18 inches wide extending across the breadth of the course, each slab divided at intervals of about four feet.[1] Between the stadium and the river lay the hippodrome, with a circuit of eight stades, or nearly one mile, but the actual course traversed was six stades. The four-horse chariots ran twelve times round this course, so that the race extended to 72 stades, or nine miles.

In historic times, certainly in the age of Pindar, the festival lasted for five days,[2] and the day of the full moon was probably the central day of the five. The festival began with a sacrifice, and ended with a feast, and the intermediate time was reserved for the athletic contests. The order of the official record of the events in the fifth century was as follows :—

(1) Single stadium foot-race ; (2) double stadium foot-race ; (3) long race ; (4) pentathlum, or competition in five events, foot-race, long jump, throwing the discus, hurling the javelin, and wrestling ; (5) wrestling ; (6) boxing ; (7) pancratium, a combination of boxing and wrestling ; (8), (9), (10) boys' foot-races, wrestling, and boxing ; (11) race in armour ; (12) chariot-race ; (13) horse-race.[3] There was also a mule-chariot-race, which was discontinued after 444 B.C.

The order in the official record was not the order

---

[1] Reproduced in E. Norman Gardiner's *Greek Athletic Sports and Festivals*, 1910, p. 253.

[2] *O.* v 6.

[3] Cp. *Oxyrhynchus Papyri*, ii (1899), pp. 85–95.

adopted in the actual contests. We know that the boys' contests were completed before the men's; that all the foot-races fell on the same day; that a single day was devoted to the wrestling, boxing, and pancratium; that the horse-race was succeeded by the pentathlum; and that the last of all the events was the race in armour. The morning was reserved for the races, and the afternoon for the boxing, wrestling, pancratium, and pentathlum. The following has been suggested as a probable programme for the period beginning 468 B.C.

Second day.—Chariot- and horse-races, and pentathlum.
Third day.—Boys' events.
Fourth day.—Men's foot-races, wrestling, boxing, and pancratium; and race in armour.[1]

The Pythian Festival.—In 582 B.C. the local musical festival, held every eight years at Delphi, was transformed into a Panhellenic festival, held every four years under the presidency of the Amphictyons.[2] The chief event in the musical programme was the Hymn celebrating Apollo's victory over the Python. This was sung to the accompaniment of the lyre. In 582 two competitions were added, (1) singing to the flute, and (2) the solo on the flute. A victory in the latter event is commemorated in the twelfth Pythian. Playing on the lyre was added in 558. Next in

---

[1] Cp. E. Norman Gardiner's *Greek Athletic Sports and Festivals*, p. 200.

[2] 582 is the date maintained by Bergk, in agreement with the Scholia to Pindar, and in preference to Boeckh's date, 586 B.C., supported by Pausanias (x 7, 3), but now given up.

importance to the musical competitions were the chariot- and horse-races. The athletic programme was the same as at Olympia, with the addition of a double-stadium and long-race for boys. The last of all the events, the race in armour, was introduced in 498.

In Pindar's time the athletic competitions took place, not on the rocky slopes of Delphi, but on the Crisaean plain below; and the horse-races were never held anywhere else. But, about 450, a new stadium for the other events was constructed on the only level ground that was available north-west of the precinct of the temple of Apollo. Pausanias[1] says that the stadium was "in the highest part of the city." This stadium is conspicuous among the remains of Delphi. "A more striking scene for the celebration of national games could hardly be imagined."[2]

The precise duration of the Pythian festival is unknown. It probably began with the musical competitions; these may have been followed by the athletic events; and, finally, by the chariot-race and the horse-race. The prize was a wreath of bay-leaves plucked by a boy whose parents were still alive. The chief religious ceremony was the procession which passed along the Sacred Way to the temple of Apollo.

The Isthmian festival, held near the eastern end of the Isthmus of Corinth, was probably the most

[1] x 32, 1. [2] Frazer's *Pausanias*, v 394.

largely frequented of all the Panhellenic assemblies. This was due to the fact that it was very near to a great city, and was easily reached from all parts of the Greek world. It was only a few hours' journey from Athens, by land or sea.

The ancient local festival in honour of Poseidon was apparently reorganised as a Panhellenic festival in 581. The sanctuary of Poseidon, where the games were celebrated, has been excavated. It was a small precinct surrounded by an enclosure, the northern side of which was formed by the great military wall guarding the Isthmus. Traces have been found of the temples of Poseidon and Palaemon. The sanctuary was lined on one side by a row of pine-trees, and on the other by statues of victorious athletes. The stadium, about 650 feet long, lay in a ravine which had once been the course of a stream. The festival began with a sacrifice to Poseidon, and, in Pindar's day, included athletic and equestrian competitions.

The Isthmian crown was, at that time, made of celery (σέλινον),—dry celery (as the scholiast explains) to distinguish it from the fresh celery of the Nemean crown.[1]

The Nemean festival, the latest of the four, was first organised as a Panhellenic assembly in 573. The scene was the deep-lying vale of Nemea, "beneath the shady hills of Phlius."[2] The neigh-

---

[1] Schol. on Pindar, O. xiii 45, and iii 27.   [2] N. vi 45.

bouring village of Cleônae [1] held the presidency of the games until 460, when this privilege was usurped by the Argives. At Nemea there was no town, but there was a hippodrome, and a stadium, the site of which is still visible in a deep ravine. There was also a sanctuary of Zeus, of which three pillars are still standing, while the grove of cypresses, which once surrounded it, has disappeared. The programme, like that of the Isthmian festival, included numerous events for boys and youths. Most of the competitors came from Athens, Aegina, and Ceôs, and from the Peloponnesus; few from Italy or Sicily.

IV.—THE STRUCTURE OF PINDAR'S ODES

Of the seventeen works ascribed to Pindar,[2] only the four books of the Epinician Odes have come down to us in a nearly complete form. Each of these Odes is prompted by a victory at one of the Panhellenic festivals. The contest itself is not directly described, but it colours the metaphors and similes used in the Ode.[3] The poet also dwells on the skill, the courage, or the good fortune of the victor, and on the previous distinctions won by himself, or his family; but even the enumeration of these distinctions, generally reserved for the end of the ode, is saved from monotony by touches

[1] Cp. *N.* iv 17; x 42.
[2] For the list, see Introduction to the Fragments, p. 510.
[3] *O.* vi 27; *P.* i 43; *N.* iv 93, v 19.

of the picturesque.[1] The athlete's crown brings credit to his home, to his city, and his country; it is therefore open to the poet to dwell on any topic connected with the local habitation of his hero.

In every ode the poet mentions the god in whose honour the games were held, or the festival at which the ode was sung, and introduces some ancient myth connected (if possible) with the country of the victor. Thus, in the odes for Aeginetan victors, we have the glorification of the Aeacidae. Syracuse, although it has its point of contact with the legend of Arethusa, has no mythical heroes. Hence, in the first Olympian, the place of the myth is taken by the legend of Pelops and the founding of the Olympic games.

The myth is generally placed in the middle of the ode, and each ode has necessarily a beginning, a middle, and an end, with transitions between the first and second and the second and third of these portions. Thus an ode may have five divisions, and there is a technical term for each:—the beginning (ἀρχά) is followed by the first transition (κατατροπά), which leads up to the centre (ὀμφαλός), succeeded in its turn by the second transition (μετακατατροπά), and by the conclusion (ἐξόδιον). By placing a prelude (προοίμιον) just before the true beginning and another subdivision (σφραγίς, or "seal") just before the end, we obtain seven divisions corresponding to those of the "nome" of Terpander

[1] e.g. O. vii 82–86; xiii 29–46.

προοίμιον

(*fl.* 700 B.C.), which has been supposed to be the model on which the Odes of Pindar are constructed.

It is further pointed out by some editors of Pindar that, in every poem, he "repeats one or more significant words in the corresponding verses and feet of his strophês, and that in these words we must look for the secret of his thought"; that this repetition is found in 38 out of the 44 extant Odes, while the other six are of very narrow compass, and that "these repeated words served as cues, as mnemonic devices." [1]

In the earlier lyric poetry of Greece, every stanza was in the same metre, was sung to the same music, and accompanied by the same movements of the dance. Such were the stanzas of Sappho and Alcaeus, imitated in the Sapphic and Alcaic Odes of Horace. Traces of a three-fold division have, however, been found in a recently discovered poem of Alcman (*fl.* 657), in which two symmetrical stanzas of four lines are followed by a stanza of six in a different metre. These three divisions may be regarded as an anticipation of the Strophê, Antistrophê, and Epôdos usually ascribed to Stêsichorus of Himera (632–556). The theory that the choral Epode was added by Stêsichorus depends on the interpretation of a proverb applied to ignorant persons, οὐδὲ τὰ τρία

---

[1] Mezger's ed. (1880), pp. vi f, 36–41 (criticised by Gildersleeve, in *A. J. P.* ii 497 f). Bury regards these verbal responsions as aids to tracing the argument, while Fennell considers them without significance.

Στησιχόρου γινώσκεις. By some of the late Greeks
this was referred to the choral " triad," and this
view was revived by J. D. Van Lennep in 1777.[1]
But the proverb is sometimes quoted without the
definite article, in which case it may simply mean,
" You do not know even three (verses) of Stêsi-
chorus ! " [2]

The Ode was usually sung in a hall or temple, or
in front of the victor's home, or during a festal
procession thereto. Three of the Odes, which have
no Epodes (*O.* xiv, *N.* ii, and *I.* viii), may be regarded
as processional poems.

With the possible exception of the eleventh
Olympian, it is not at all probable that any one of
the Odes was performed immediately after the
victory. The "chant of Archilochus, with its thrice
repeated refrain," [3] sufficed for the immediate
occasion, the performance of a new ode being
deferred to a victor's return to his home, or even
to some subsequent anniversary of the victory. The
chorus consisted of friends of the victor. The
number is unknown, and it probably varied. They
spoke in the person of the poet ; very rarely does the
Ode give dramatic expression to the point of view of

[1] *Phalaridis Epistolae,* No. xcvi, " Quo si inter alia referre
velis ἐπῳδοῦ inventionem, quae, ut ait Grammaticus περὶ τῶν
κώλων τῶν στροφῶν κτλ Pindaro praemissus, ἱσταμένοις
διεβιβάζετο εἰς εἰκόνα τῆς τῆς γῆς ἀκινησίας, non forte errabis."
[2] Crusius, *Comment. Ribbeck.* p. 1, quoted by H. W. Smyth,
Greek Melic Poets, 187.
[3] *O.* ix 1 f.

the chorus.[1] The singing was accompanied by the
lyre, or by the lyre and flute.[2]   Besides song and
music, there was a third element, that of the dance.
No two Odes of Pindar have the same metrical
form, except the two which appear in the MSS as
the third and fourth Isthmian, and the identity of
metre is one of the reasons for regarding them
as a single Ode.[3]

In the Odes of Pindar there are three kinds of
rhythm :—(1) the paeonic ; (2) the dactylo-epitritic ;
and (3) the logaoedic.

(1) *The paeonic rhythm* consists of the various
forms of the *paeon,* one long syllable combined with
three short ($- \cup \cup \cup$, or $\cup \cup \cup -$, or $\cup \cup - \cup$), and the
feet which (on the principle that one long syllable is
equal to two short) are its metrical equivalents,
namely the *cretic* ($- \cup -$), and the *bacchius* ($- - \cup$).
This rhythm is represented solely by the second
Olympian and the fifth Pythian.

(2) *The dactylo-epitritic rhythm* combines the *dactyl*
($- \cup \cup$) and its equivalents, with the *epitrite* ($- \cup - -$)
and its equivalents.   About half of the Odes are
in this rhythm :—*O.* iii, vi, vii, viii, xi, xii ; *P.* i, iii,
iv, ix, xii ; *N.* i, v, viii–xi ; *I.* i–vi.

(3) *The logaoedic rhythm,* from λόγος, " prose," and
ἀοιδή, " verse."   In this rhythm dactyls are combined
with trochees (and tribrachs).   This rhythm is used

---

[1] See note on *P.* v 75.
[2] *O.* iii 8 ; vii 12 ; x 93 ; *N.* ix 8.
[3] See Introduction to *I.* iii.

in the following Odes:—*O.* i, iv, v, ix, x, xiii, xiv;
P. ii, vi–viii, x, xi ; *N.* ii–iv, vi, vii ; *I.* vii, viii.

Pindar himself describes the *dactylo-epitritic* Ode,
O. iii, as *Dorian*,[1] and the *logaoedic* Ode, *O.* i, as
Aeolian.[2] We may assume that all the *dactylo-
epitritic* Odes are in the *Dorian* mode, and all the
logaoedic in the *Aeolian*. Lydian measures are also
mentioned in the logaoedic Odes, *O.* v 19, xiv 17,
and in *N.* iv 45. There was therefore some affinity
between the Aeolian and the Lydian measures.
Lydian measures are, however, also mentioned in
one dactylo-epitritic (or Dorian) Ode, *N.* viii 15.

The *Paeonic* rhythm was used in religious and
serious poems, namely, the second Olympian, which
includes a solemn description of the Islands of the
Blest, and the fifth Pythian, which dwells on the
Carneian festival and commemorates the departed
heroes of Cyrene. The *Dorian* rhythm of the
dactylo-epitritic Odes is grave and strong, steady
and impressive. The poet himself said in one
of his Paeans that "the Dorian strain is most
solemn." [3] Several of the Odes in this rhythm have
an epic tone and character. As examples we
have *O.* vi (the story of the birth of Iamus),
vii (the legend of the Sun-God and Rhodes); *P.* i
(the splendid Ode on the lyre, on the eruption

---

[1] iii 5, Δωρίῳ πεδίλῳ.
[2] i 102, Αἰοληίδι μολπᾷ, and similarly, in the logaoedic
N. iii 79, he refers to the "Aeolian breathings of the flutes."
[3] Δώριον μέλος σεμνότατον, quoted in Scholium on *O.* i 26.

of Etna, and on the legend of Philoctetes), iii (on
Hieron's illness), iv (the voyage of the Argonauts),
xii (Perseus and the Gorgon); *N*. i (the infant
Hercules), viii (Ajax and Odysseus). The *Aeolian*
rhythm was bright, full of movement, well suited for
a poem on the dashing horsemanship of a Castor.[1]
There is plenty of almost playful movement in the
second Pythian; for example, in the passage about
the ape, and the fox, and the wolf, and about the
poet floating like a cork above the net that is
plunged in the brine.[2] The Lydian measures some-
times associated with this rhythm were originally
accompanied by the flute, and were also sometimes
used in dirges.

V.—PINDAR'S DIALECT.

Pindar's dialect does not correspond to any
language that was actually spoken in any part of the
Hellenic world. It is a literary product resulting
from the combination of the epic language (which is
itself composite) with Doric and Aeolic elements.
The Doric dialect forms the groundwork. This arises
from the fact that the choral lyric poetry of Greece
was first cultivated by the Dorians, and principally
at Sparta, in the age of Alcman and Terpander.
Stêsichorus of Himera was also a Dorian, but his
poetry had close affinities with the Epic style. The
true Dorian tradition was maintained by Pindar,

[1] *P.* ii **69**, τὸ Καστόρειον ἐν Αἰολίδεσσι χορδαῖς.
[2] *P.* ii 72-80.

Simonides, and Bacchylides, all of whom are called
Dorian poets, though Pindar was an Aeolian of
Thebes, and Simonides and his nephew Ionians of
Ceôs.

While these dialects are blended together, there is
a general avoidance of the extreme forms character-
istic of each.[1] Thus Pindar has no Epic forms in -φι,
or infinitives in -εμεναι from verbs ending in -ω.
Similarly, while he uses ὦν for οὖν, he never uses the
Doric ω for ου in τῶ and τὼς and in Μῶσα. Nor, in
the inflexions of verbs, does he use -μες for -μεν.

Under the influence of the Lesbian poets, Alcaeus
and Sappho, certain Aeolic forms are introduced.
Thus we have οι for ου, in Μοῖσα, and in participles,
such as ἰδοῖσα and ἔοισα (for οὖσα). We also have -αις
for -ας in first aorist active participles, such as κλέψαις
and ὀλέσαις. Further, φαεννὸν and κλεεννὸν are used
for φαεινὸν and κλεινόν, and ὄνυμα, for ὄνομα, and
similarly ὀνυμάζω.

The Doric ᾱ is used for the Epic and Attic η in
words like ἀρχά, κράνα, Ἀχώ, Ἀώς. But, in forms
from βάλλω, πλήθω, χράω, η remains unchanged, e.g.
βεβλῆσθαι, πλήθοντος, χρησθέν. αο and αω are con-
tracted into ᾶ, e.g. πασᾶν (for πασάων, πασῶν), τᾶν,
Μοισᾶν. α is sometimes found instead of ε, as in
τάμνοισαι, τράφοισα, φρασίν.

Among changes of consonants may be noted,

---

[1] Eustathius, *Vita Pindari*, αἰολίζει δὲ τὰ πολλά, εἰ καὶ μὴ
ἀκριβῆ δίεισιν Αἰολίδα, καὶ κατὰ Δωριεῖς δὲ φράζει, εἰ καὶ τῆς
σκληρᾶς Δωρίδος ἀπέχεται.

γλέφαρον for βλέφαρον (*P.* iv 121), side by side with
ἑλικοβλεφάρου (*ib.* 172); ὄρνιχα for ὄρνιθα, αὖτις for
αὖθις, δέκονται for δέχονται, τεθμὸς for θεσμός, ἐσλὸς for
ἐσθλός, ξυνὸν for κοινόν, ὦτε for ὥστε.

The Epic tradition is followed in assuming the
survival of the *digamma* at the beginning of certain
words. Before these words vowels may stand, and
short vowels generally remain unelided. Among
these words are :—ἄναξ, ἀνάσσω, ἀνδάνω, ἀχώ, εἴδομαι,
εἶδος, εἰδώς, ἰδεῖν, ἴδρις, ἴσαντι, εἴκοσι, εἰπεῖν, ἐοικότα,
ἔπος, ἐλπίς, ἔργον, ἔρξας, ἑσπέρα, ἔτος, ἦθος, Ἰδαῖος, ἴδιος,
Ἰλιάδας, ἴσος, οἱ (*sibi*), ὃς (*suus*), οἶκος, οἰκίζω, and Ὤανις.

In nouns of the first declension, the genitive
singular (masculine) ends either in -ao or in -ᾱ; the
genitive plural (masculine or feminine), in ᾶν (not
άων), *e.g.* Αἰακιδᾶν, and ἀρετᾶν ἄπο πασᾶν. In the
second declension, the genitive singular ends in -ου
or (less often) in -οιο. The accusative plural has the
Doric ending in -ος in some old MSS in six passages :—
κακαγόρος (*O.* i. 53), ἐσλὸς (*N.* i. 24; iii 29), νᾶσος
(*O.* ii 71), ὑπέροχος (*N.* iii 24), ἥμενος (*N.* x 62).[1] In
the third declension, the dative plural in -εσσι is
preferred, *e.g.* ἐλαυνόντεσσιν (for ἐλαύνουσιν).

In personal pronouns we almost always find the
forms in μμ, as ἄμμες, ἄμμι (ἡμῖν), ἄμμε, ὔμμες, ὔμμι,
ὔμμε. For the second person singular we have nom.
τύ, gen. σέο, σεῦ, σέθεν, dat. τοί, τίν, (σοί ?). Among
possessive pronouns we have ἁμὸς for ἐμός, τεὸς for
σός.

[1] These forms in -ος are not accepted by Schröder.

In verbs, the third person plural never ends in -ουσι but either in the Doric -οντι or the Aeolic -οισιν. The infinitive oftener ends in the Doric -μεν than in the Attic -ειν, e.g. στᾶμεν, θέμεν, δόμεν, ἴμεν, θανέμεν, ἔμμεν (and ἔμμεναι). There is manuscript authority for -εν in γαρύεν (O. i 3), πορεύεν (O. iii 25), ἀγαγέν (P. iv 56), and τράφεν (P. iv 115). The feminine participle present and second aorist active ends in the Aeolic -οισα, and the first aorist active in -αις, -αισα.

Among the prepositions πεδὰ is used for μετά, ποτὶ is found as well as πρός, and the final vowel of ποτὶ and περὶ may be elided. ἐνς was the original form of εἰς and ἐς, and ἐν with the accusative is used for εἰς in P. ii 11, 86, and iv 258.

The language of the different odes has an Aeolic or a Doric colouring which varies with the rhythms in which they were composed.

VI.—MANUSCRIPTS

The 142 extant MSS of Pindar fall into two classes (1) the ancient MSS, and (2) the interpolated MSS. The ancient MSS belong to two recensions (a) the *Ambrosian*, best represented by a MS in the Ambrosian Library in Milan, and (b) the *Vatican*, at the head of which is the MS in the Vatican Library, in Rome. The following is a conspectus of the principal MSS belonging to these two recensions, with the portions of the Odes which they contain :—

INTRODUCTION

(1) (a) The Ambrosian Recension.

A (Milan) Ambr. C 222 inf.	} cent. xiii	{ *O.* i–xii, with Ambrosian scholia
C (Paris) Gr. 2774	} end of xiv	{ *O.* i–*P.* v 51, with Vatican scholia
M (Perugia) B 43 cent. xv		{ *O.* i–xii, *P.* i–iv, with scholia
N (Milan) Ambr. E 103 sup.	} ,, xiii–xiv	*O.* i–xiv, with scholia
O (Leyden) Q 4 end of xiii		{ *O.* i–xiii, with scholia on i–viii
V (Paris) Gr. 2403	} ,, xiii	{ *O.* i–*N.* iv 68, vi 38–44, with scholia

(1) (b) The Vatican Recension.

B (Rome) Vat. Gr. 1312	} cent. xii	{ *O.* i–*I.* viii, with scholia (om. *P.* i, and parts of *O.* i, v, *P.* ii, *I.* viii)
D (Florence) Laur. 32, 52	} ,, xiv	{ *O. P. N. I.* with scholia (*N.* i by another hand)
E (Florence) Laur. 32, 37	} ,, xiv	*O. P.* with scholia
G (Göttingen) Philol. 29	} ,, xiii	*O. P.* with scholia
I (Wolfenbüttel) Guelf. 48, 33	} ,, xv	*O.* (by second hand), *P.*
P (Heidelberg) Palat. 40	} ,, xiv	*O. P.*
Q (Florence) Laur. 32, 35	} ,, xiii	*O. P.* with scholia
U (Vienna) Hist. Gr. 130	} ,, xiii–xiv	*O. P. N.* i, ii with scholia

(2) *The interpolated mss* represent the editorial activity of three Byzantine scholars of century xiv :—Thomas Magister, Moschopulus, and Triclinius. Fifteen mss show the influence of the first of these scholars ; forty-two that of the second, and twenty-eight that of the third.

THE TEXT

The text of the present work is founded on Donaldson's revision of the second edition of Boeckh. But this has been further revised in many passages, after a careful consideration of the readings, or conjectures, preferred by more recent editors, namely Bergk, Tycho Mommsen, Christ and Schröder, as well as Fennell, Gildersleeve and Bury. The various readings of the MSS have been here recorded whenever they are really important, and in the case of Boeckh, and the last six of the above-mentioned editors, the text adopted by each has been cited, followed by the initial of the editor in question :—B for Boeckh (B² for his second edition); M for Tycho Mommsen (M² for his second edition); c for Christ's (edition of 1896); s for Schröder (s¹ for the edition of 1900, s³ for that of 1914); F for Fennell's second edition, G for Gildersleeve, and Bu for Bury.

In matters of orthography I have generally preferred to keep to the literary tradition represented by the MSS, instead of introducing changes suggested by inscriptional or other evidence. I have therefore retained the familiar form of the verbs τίσομεν and μῖξαι, and of the names of persons, such as Χείρων, Μιδυλίδαι, Κλυταιμνήστρα, Ὑπερμνήστρα, and of places, such as Κάμειρος, Σικυών, Ὀρχομενός, and Φλιοῦς, instead of following Schröder in printing τείσομεν, μεῖξαι, Χίρων, Μειδυλίδαι, Κλυταιμήστρα, Ὑπερμήστρα,

Κάμιρος, Σεκυών, Ἐρχομενός and Φλειοῦς. I have also
retained ἥρωες and other inflexions of ἥρως, and have
not thought it necessary (with Schröder) to change
ω into o, in cases where the long vowel is shortened.
The mss often vary between μιν and νιν, but, as it has
been shown by Tycho Mommsen that Pindar's usage
is really in favour of νιν, I have followed Schröder in
adopting that form throughout.

In accordance with the usual convention, an
asterisk is prefixed to the few emendations which
are here for the first time introduced into the text.
These are :—in *P*. x 69, ἀδελφεοὺς *ἔτ᾽, or, by a
further improvement due to Professor Housman,
*τ᾽ ἔτ᾽ (for ἀδελφεούς τ᾽ ἐπαινήσομεν, where one more
short syllable is needed between the two words); in
N. vi 51, νεῖκος Ἀχιλεὺς *ἔμβαλε (for ἔμπεσε); in
N. viii 46 τ᾽ *ἐλαφρὸν (for τε λάβρον) ὑπερεῖσαι λίθον;
in Paean iv 53, *ἁ δρῦς (for ἄδρυς); and in frag. 249[b],
Ἀχελωΐου—*εὐρεῖτα (for εὐρωπία). In Frag. 153 (125),
I have suggested δενδρέων δὲ γόνον (for νόμον or νομὸν)
Διόννσος—αὐξάνοι, and I have made several proposals
for filling the *lacunae* in some of the recently re-
covered fragments, *e.g.* in Frag. 104[a], 33, λιγυσφαρα-
γων [ἀν]τ[ί]να[κ]τα—φορμίγγων.

BIBLIOGRAPHY

EDITIONS

Editio princeps (Aldus Manutius, Venice, 1513). *Editio secunda* (Callierges, Rome, 1515). These editions were reprinted with slight changes by Ceporinus (Basel, 1526), Morel (Paris, 1558), and Henricus Stephanus (Geneva?, 1560 f). Many emendations were made by Erasmus Schmid (Wittenberg, 1616), whose text was reprinted by Johannes Benedictus (Saumur, 1620) ; both of these editors drew most of their explanations from the scholia.

Heyne's first edition (Göttingen, 1773) was followed by that of Beck (Leipzig, 1792–5). Heyne's second and third editions, of 1798 and 1817, included additional notes by Hermann.

A new epoch was begun by August Boeckh in his great edition (Leipzig, 1811–21). Of the three parts, the first (1811) contains the text, metres, and critical notes ; the second (1819), the scholia ; the third (1821), the Latin translation, explanatory notes, and an annotated edition of the Fragments. A second edition of the text appeared in 1825. Dissen, who had written the commentary on the Nemean and Isthmian Odes for Boeckh's edition, reprinted the text of 1825, and wrote an elaborate commentary on all the Odes (Gotha, 1830). Dissen's edition was revised by Schneidewin (1843 f.). Meanwhile, Donaldson's edition, with English notes, largely founded on Boeckh or Dissen, had appeared in 1841. The text of Boeckh was adopted by W. G. Cookesley, who added explanatory notes, in an edition published in three parts (Eton, 1842–49 ; second edition of *Olympians*, 1850, and *Pythians*, 1853).

Pindar formed an important part of the *Poetae Lyrici Graeci*, of which four editions were produced by Theodor Bergk (Leipzig, 1843, 1853, 1866, 1878). These editions were marked by not a few brilliant restorations of the text.

INTRODUCTION

J. A. Hartung's edition in two volumes, with notes and metrical German translation (Leipzig, 1855–56), abounds in suggestive remarks, but is unsuited for the ordinary student. For the readings of the various classes of MSS, the most important edition is that of Tycho Mommsen (Berlin, 1864 ; new edition of text with brief critical notes, 1866). The Teubner text by Wilhelm Christ of Munich (Leipzig, 1869, 1896), was followed by the same scholar's edition with Latin prolegomena, brief critical notes, and commentary (Leipzig, 1896). On the basis of Christ's text, a valuable commentary was published by Fr. Mezger (Leipzig, 1880). C. A. M. Fennell's Cambridge edition with explanatory English notes appeared in two volumes, *Olympian and Pythian Odes*, 1879, second edition 1893 ; *Nemean and Isthmian Odes, and Fragments*, 1883, second edition, 1899. The edition of the *Olympian and Pythian Odes* by Professor Gildersleeve of Baltimore was published in New York and London in 1885 ; and Professor Bury's *Nemeans* and *Isthmians* in London in 1890 and 1892 respectively. All the Odes were expounded and translated in Italian (after Tycho Mommsen's text) by Professor Fraccaroli of Messina (Verona, 1894). " Selected Odes " were edited with Introduction and Notes by Professor T. D. Seymour (Boston, 1882) ; and the Sicilian and the Epizephyrian Odes, by Ed. Boehmer (Bonn, 1891). Annotated selections from the Fragments were included in Professor H. W. Smyth's *Greek Melic Poets*, London, 1900.

A new and largely independent critical revision of Bergk's Pindar was produced by Otto Schröder (Leipzig, 1900), followed by Schröder's Teubner texts of 1908 and 1914. The latter includes the new Fragments, most of which were first published by Grenfell and Hunt in the *Oxyrhynchus Papyri*, vols. ii–v, 1899–1908.[1] The new Fragments are also printed and very briefly annotated by Ernst Diehl (Bonn, 1908 ; ed. 2, 1910) ; and translated by Fraccaroli (Milan, 1914).

The chief editions of the *Scholia* are those of Boeckh (Leipzig, 1819) ; Abel, on *Nemeans* and *Isthmians* (Berlin, 1883) ; Drachmann, on *Olympians* and *Pythians* (Leipzig, 1903 and 1910).

The principal English translations are those in prose by F. A. Paley (1868) ; and by Ernest Myers (1874) ; and in verse (including 31 Fragments) by T. C. Baring (London, 1875) ; and that published anonymously [by George Moberly,

---

[1] Further Fragments in vol. xiii, 1919.

BIBLIOGRAPHY

Bishop of Salisbury] (Winchester, 1876); the Olympian and Pythian Odes, by F. D. Morice (London, 1876); Olympians i–vi, by Reginald Heber (London, 1840 and 1870); and Pythians i–iv, ix, by W. R. Paton (Aberdeen, 1904). A dithyramb, a dirge, and the poem on the eclipse are translated on pp. 185–192 of Milman's *Agamemnon and Bacchanals* (London, 1865).

Among publications bearing on textual criticism or exegesis may be mentioned :—Hermann's papers reprinted in his *Opuscula*, 8 vols., especially those on Pindar's Dialect in i 245 ff. ; on *Nem.* vii, in iii 22 ff. ; on *Pythians* in vii 99–173; and on *Olympians* in viii 68–128. Von Wilamowitz, (1) *Textgeschichte der griechischen Lyriker* (Berlin, 1900); also, in Proceedings of Berlin Academy, (2) *Hieron und Pindaros,* 1901, pp. 1273 ff. ; (3) *Nem.* vii, 1908, pp. 328 ff. ; (4) *Nem.* v, xi, *Isth.* v, vi, viii, 1909, pp. 806–835. Sitzler in *Wochenschrift für Klassische Philologie,* 1911, on *Paean* ii, pp. 586–590; *Paean* iv, pp. 698–702; *Paean* v, pp. 1015–1018. Jurenka, on *Paean* ii, in *Philologus,* 1913, pp. 173–210.

The following will be found specially helpful to the Student :—R. C. Jebb, (1) *Pindar,* in *Journal of Hellenic Studies,* iii (1883), pp. 144–183, reprinted in *Essays and Addresses* (Cambridge, 1907), pp. 41–103 ; (2) *Lecture on Pindar* in " The Growth and Influence of Classical Greek Poetry " (London, 1893), pp. 143–177 ; F. D. Morice, *Pindar,* in " Ancient Classics for English Readers " (London, 1879) ; Alfred Croiset, *La Poésie de Pindare,* Paris, 1880 ; Rumpel, *Lexicon Pindaricum,* Leipzig, 1883 ; Gaspar, *Chronologie Pindarique,* Bruxelles, 1900 ; and E. Norman Gardiner, *Greek Athletic Sports and Festivals* (London, 1910).

We now have:—*Epinikia* ed. A. Turyn, New York, 1944; *Carmina cum Fragmentis* ed. A. Turyn, Oxford, 1952; *Carmina cum Fragmentis* ed. B. Snell, (1) Epinikia (2) Fragmenta, Leipzig, Teubner, ed. 3, 1959–1964, ed. 4, 1964; *Carmina cum Fragmentis* ed. C. M. Bowra, Oxford, 1935; Translation with Literary and Critical Commentaries, L. R. Farnell, 3 vols., London, 1930–1932; Translation by R. Lattimore, Chicago, 1947: *Les Scholies métriques de Pindare* ed. J. Irigoin, Paris, 1958; *Pindare au Banquet. Les Fragments des Scolies* ed. B. A. van Groningen, Leiden, 1960; *Untersuchungen zur Sprache Pindars,* B. Forssman, Wiesbaden, 1966.

THE OLYMPIAN ODES

OLYMPIAN I

FOR HIERON OF SYRACUSE

INTRODUCTION

GELON, Hieron, Thrasybûlus, and Polyzêlus were the four sons of Deinomenes of Gela in Sicily. In 491 B.C. Hippocrates, tyrant of Gela, was succeeded by Gelon, the eldest son of Deinomenes, the first of a new line of rulers. Gelon ruled over Gela from 491 to 485, when he subdued Syracuse. Thereupon, his younger brother Hieron, became ruler of Gela from 485 to 478. On the death of Gelon, Hieron became ruler of Syracuse from 478 to 466.

Gelon, as lord of Gela, had won the horse-race at Olympia in 488 (Pausanias vi 9, 2). His younger brother, Hieron, won the same race at the Pythian games of 482 and 478 (Schol. *Pyth.* iii), and, again, at the Olympian games of 476 and 472. Both of these victories are recorded in the list of Olympian victors preserved in the Oxyrhynchus papyrus, ii (1899) 88. It is the victory of **476** that is celebrated in the first Olympian ode. The steed with which this victory was won had already been victorious at the Pythian games of 482 and 478. At Olympia, Hieron's victories in the horse-race of 476 and 472 were followed by a victory in the chariot-race

2

INTRODUCTION

of 468, and all three were commemorated in an inscription set up at Olympia by Hieron's son, Deinomenes (Pausanias viii 42, 4).

The ode celebrates the glory of the Olympian games (1–7), the virtues of Hieron (8–17), and the victory won by Phereníhōus (17–23).

Hieron is famous in the land of Pelops, who was beloved of Poseidon (23–27). The poet denounces the popular story of the disappearance of Pelops, son of Tantalus, King of Lydia, as a lying myth inspired by envy, adding his own version. He also tells of the punishment of Tantalus and the return of Pelops from heaven to earth ; of his invocation of Poseidon, of his race with Oenomaus and of his thus winning as his wife that hero's daughter Hippodameia, and of his burial and his posthumous fame at Olympia (28–93)

The poet touches on the happiness and the renown of victors at Olympia (93–100), and expresses the hope that at some future festival Hieron will win the still higher honour of the Olympian victory in the four-horse-chariot-race. He concludes by praying for the continued prosperity of Hieron as a ruler, and for his own continued pre-eminence as a poet (100–116).

The present victory was also celebrated by Bacchylides (Ode 5). The hope that it would be followed by a victory with the four-horse-chariot was fulfilled in 468, but that victory was celebrated, not by Pindar, but by Bacchylides (Ode 3).

ΟΛΥΜΠΙΟΝΙΚΑΙ

I.—ΙΕΡΩΝΙ ΣΤΡΑΚΟΥΣΙΩ

ΚΕΛΗΤΙ

στρ. α΄

   Ἄριστον μὲν ὕδωρ, ὁ δὲ χρυσὸς αἰθόμενον πῦρ
  ἅτε διαπρέπει νυκτὶ μεγάνορος ἔξοχα πλούτου·
  εἰ δ᾽ ἄεθλα γαρύεν
  ἔλδεαι, φίλον ἦτορ,
5 μηκέθ᾽ ἁλίου σκόπει
  ἄλλο θαλπνότερον ἐν ἁμέρᾳ φαεννὸν ἄστρον ἐρή-
   μας δι᾽ αἰθέρος,   10
  μηδ᾽ Ὀλυμπίας ἀγῶνα φέρτερον αὐδάσομεν·
  ὅθεν ὁ πολύφατος ὕμνος ἀμφιβάλλεται
  σοφῶν μητίεσσι, κελαδεῖν
10 Κρόνου παῖδ᾽ ἐς ἀφνεὰν ἱκομένους
  μάκαιραν Ἱέρωνος ἑστίαν,

ἀντ. α΄

  θεμιστεῖον ὃς ἀμφέπει σκᾶπτον ἐν πολυμάλῳ
  Σικελίᾳ, δρέπων μὲν κορυφὰς ἀρετᾶν ἄπο
   πασᾶν,   20
  ἀγλαΐζεται δὲ καὶ
15 μουσικᾶς ἐν ἀώτῳ,
  οἷα παίζομεν φίλαν
  ἄνδρες ἀμφὶ θαμὰ τράπεζαν. ἀλλὰ Δωρίαν ἀπὸ
   φόρμιγγα πασσάλου

4

THE OLYMPIAN ODES

I.—FOR HIERON OF SYRACUSE

WINNER IN THE HORSE RACE, 476 B.C.

EVEN as water is most excellent, while gold, like fire flaming at night, gleameth more brightly than all other lordly wealth ; even so, fond heart, if thou art fain to tell of prizes won in the games, look not by day for any star in the lonely sky, that shineth with warmth more genial than the sun, nor let us think to praise a place of festival more glorious than Olympia.

Thence cometh the famous song of praise that enfoldeth the thoughts of poets wise, so that they loudly sing the son of Cronus, when they arrive at the rich and happy hearth of Hieron ; Hieron, who wieldeth the sceptre of law in fruitful Sicily, culling the prime of all virtues, while he rejoiceth in the full bloom of song, even in such merry strains as we men full often raise around the friendly board.

Now, take the Dorian lyre down from its resting-place, if in sooth the grateful thought of Pisa and of

λάμβαν’, εἴ τί τοι Πίσας τε καὶ Φερενίκου χάρις
νόον ὑπὸ γλυκυτάταις ἔθηκε φροντίσιν,   30
20 ὅτε παρ’ Ἀλφεῷ σύτο, δέμας
ἀκέντητον ἐν δρόμοισι παρέχων,
κράτει δὲ προσέμιξε δεσπόταν,

ἐπ. α’

Συρακόσιον ἱπποχάρμαν βασιλῆα. λάμπει δέ οἱ
    κλέος
ἐν εὐάνορι Λυδοῦ Πέλοπος ἀποικίᾳ·
25 τοῦ μεγασθενὴς ἐράσσατο γαιάοχος
Ποσειδᾶν, ἐπεί νιν καθαροῦ λέβητος ἔξελε
    Κλωθὼ   40
ἐλέφαντι φαίδιμον ὦμον κεκαδμένον.
ἦ θαυματὰ πολλά, καί πού τι καὶ βροτῶν φάτις
    ὑπὲρ τὸν ἀλαθῆ λόγον
δεδαιδαλμένοι ψεύδεσι ποικίλοις ἐξαπατῶντι
    μῦθοι.

στρ. β’

30 Χάρις δ’, ἅπερ ἅπαντα τεύχει τὰ μείλιχα θνατοῖς,
ἐπιφέροισα τιμὰν καὶ ἄπιστον ἐμήσατο πιστὸν   50
ἔμμεναι τὸ πολλάκις·
ἀμέραι δ’ ἐπίλοιποι
μάρτυρες σοφώτατοι.
35 ἔστι δ’ ἀνδρὶ φάμεν ἐοικὸς ἀμφὶ δαιμόνων καλά·
    μείων γὰρ αἰτία.
υἱὲ Ταντάλου, σὲ δ’, ἀντία προτέρων, φθέγξομαι,
ὁπότ’ ἐκάλεσε πατὴρ τὸν εὐνομώτατον   60
ἐς ἔρανον φίλαν τε Σίπυλον,
ἀμοιβαῖα θεοῖσι δεῖπνα παρέχων,
40 τότ’ Ἀγλαοτρίαιναν ἁρπάσαι

28 φάτις old mss (φρένας interpolated mss) : φάτιν B
(Donaldson).

6

Pherenîcus laid upon thy heart the spell of sweetest musings, what time, beside the Alpheüs, that steed rushed by, lending those limbs that in the race needed not the lash, and thus brought power unto his master, the lord of Syracuse, that warlike horseman for whom glory shineth in the new home of heroes erst founded by the Lydian Pelops ; Pelops, of whom Poseidon, the mighty shaker of the earth, was once enamoured, when Clôthô lifted him out of the purifying waters of the caldron with his shoulder gleaming with ivory.[1] Wonders are rife indeed ; and, as for the tale that is told among mortals, transgressing the language of truth, it may haply be that stories deftly decked with glittering lies lead them astray. But the Grace of song, that maketh for man all things that soothe him, by adding her spell, full often causeth even what is past belief to be indeed believed ; but the days that are still to come are the wisest witnesses.

In truth it is seemly for man to say of the gods nothing ignoble ; for so he giveth less cause for blame. Son of Tantalus ! I will tell of thee a tale far other than that of earlier bards :—what time thy father, in return for the banquets he had enjoyed, bade the gods come to his own dear Sipylus, and share his duly-ordered festal board, then it was that the god of the gleaming trident, with his heart

[1] Cp. Virgil, *Georgic* iii 3, "humeroque Pelops insignis eburno."

7

ἀντ. β΄

   δαμέντα φρένας ἱμέρῳ χρυσέαισί τ᾽ ἀν᾽ ἵπποις
   ὕπατον εὐρυτίμου ποτὶ δῶμα Διὸς μεταβᾶσαι,
   ἔνθα δευτέρῳ χρόνῳ
   ἦλθε καὶ Γανυμήδης   70
45 Ζηνὶ τωὔτ᾽ ἐπὶ χρέος.
   ὡς δ᾽ ἄφαντος ἔπελες, οὐδὲ ματρὶ πολλὰ μαιόμενοι
     φῶτες ἄγαγον,
   ἔννεπε κρυφᾷ τις αὐτίκα φθονερῶν γειτόνων,
   ὕδατος ὅτι σε πυρὶ ζέοισαν εἰς ἀκμὰν
   μαχαίρᾳ τάμον κάτα μέλη,
50 τραπέζαισί τ᾽, ἀμφὶ δεύτατα, κρεῶν   80
   σέθεν διεδάσαντο καὶ φάγον.

ἐπ. β΄

   ἐμοὶ δ᾽ ἄπορα γαστρίμαργον μακάρων τιν᾽
     εἰπεῖν. ἀφίσταμαι.
   ἀκέρδεια λέλογχεν θαμινὰ κακαγόρος.
   εἰ δὲ δή τιν᾽ ἄνδρα θνατὸν Ὀλύμπου σκοποὶ
55 ἐτίμασαν, ἦν Τάνταλος οὗτος· ἀλλὰ γὰρ κατα-
     πέψαι
   μέγαν ὄλβον οὐκ ἐδυνάσθη, κόρῳ δ᾽ ἕλεν
   ἄταν ὑπέροπλον, ἅν οἱ πατὴρ ὑπερκρέμασε καρ-
     τερὸν αὐτῷ λίθον,   90
   τὸν αἰεὶ μενοινῶν κεφαλᾶς βαλεῖν εὐφροσύνας
     ἀλᾶται.

στρ. γ΄

   ἔχει δ᾽ ἀπάλαμον βίον τοῦτον ἐμπεδόμοχθον,

41 χρυσέαισί τ᾽ Erasmus Schmid (s) : χρυσέαισιν mss.
48 εἰς scholia (MGCS) : ἐπ᾽ old mss ; ἀμφ᾽ interpolated mss (BF).
50 ἀμφὶ δεύτατα mss (GM²S) : ἄμφι δεύματα (BM¹F) ; ἀμφιδεύματα C.
53 κακαγόρος (Doric acc) AC² (BMGF) : —ους C¹D (CS).

8

enthralled with love, seized thee and carried thee
away on his golden chariot to the highest home of
Zeus, who is honoured far and wide,—that home to
which, in after-time, Ganymede was also brought
for the self-same service ; and when thou wast seen
no more, and, in spite of many a quest, men brought
thee not to thy mother, anon some envious neigh-
bours secretly devised the story that with a knife
they clave thy limbs asunder, and plunged them into
water which fire had caused to boil, and at the
tables, during the latest course, divided the morsels
of thy flesh and feasted.

Far be it from me to call any one of the blessed
gods a cannibal ! I stand aloof. Full oft hath little
gain fallen to the lot of evil-speakers. But, if
indeed there was any mortal man who was honoured
by the guardian-gods of Olympus, that man was
Tantalus ; but, alas ! he could not brook his great
prosperity, and, owing to his surfeit of good things,
he gat himself an overpowering curse, which the
Father hung over him in the semblance of a mon-
strous stone, which he is ever eager to thrust away
from his head, thus wandering from the ways of joy.
And thereby hath he a helpless life of never-ending

PINDAR

60 μετὰ τριῶν τέταρτον πόνον, ἀθανάτων ὅτι κλέψαις
   ἁλίκεσσι συμπόταις
      νέκταρ ἀμβροσίαν τε   100
   δῶκεν, οἷσιν ἄφθιτον
   θῆκαν. εἰ δὲ θεὸν ἀνήρ τις ἔλπεταί τι λαθέμεν
      ἔρδων, ἁμαρτάνει.
65 τοὔνεκα προῆκαν υἱὸν ἀθάνατοί οἱ πάλιν
   μετὰ τὸ ταχύποτμον αὗτις ἀνέρων ἔθνος.
   πρὸς εὐάνθεμον δ' ὅτε φυὰν
      λάχναι νιν μέλαν γένειον ἔρεφον,   110
   ἑτοῖμον ἀνεφρόντισεν γάμον

ἀντ. γ΄
70 Πισάτα παρὰ πατρὸς εὔδοξον Ἱπποδάμειαν
   σχεθέμεν. ἐγγὺς ἐλθὼν πολιᾶς ἁλὸς οἷος ἐν
      ὄρφνᾳ
   ἄπυεν βαρύκτυπον
   Εὐτρίαιναν· ὁ δ' αὐτῷ
   πὰρ ποδὶ σχεδὸν φάνη.
75 τῷ μὲν εἶπε· " Φίλια δῶρα Κυπρίας ἄγ' εἴ τι,
      Ποσείδαον, ἐς χάριν   120
   τέλλεται, πέδασον ἔγχος Οἰνομάου χάλκεον,
   ἐμὲ δ' ἐπὶ ταχυτάτων πόρευσον ἁρμάτων
   ἐς Ἆλιν, κράτει δὲ πέλασον.
   ἐπεὶ τρεῖς τε καὶ δέκ' ἄνδρας ὀλέσαις
80 ἐρῶντας ἀναβάλλεται γάμον

ἐπ. γ΄
   θυγατρός. ὁ μέγας δὲ κίνδυνος ἄναλκιν οὐ φῶτα
      λαμβάνει.   130
   θανεῖν δ' οἷσιν ἀνάγκα, τί κέ τις ἀνώνυμον

64 θῆκαν Rauchenstein (s): θέσαν αὐτὸν best mss, v.l.
ἔθεσαν (GF) or θέσσαν (BC); θέν νιν M.
   71 ἐγγὺς Bergk (MGFCS): ἐγγὺς δ' old mss; ἄγχι δ' inter-
polated mss (B).

10

labour, with three besides and his own toil the fourth,[1] because he stole from the gods the nectar and ambrosia, with which they had made him immortal, and gave them to the partners of his feast. But, if any man hopeth, in aught he doeth, to escape the eye of God, he is grievously wrong. Therefore it was that the immortals once more thrust forth the son of Tantalus amid the short-lived race of men. But when, about the time of youthful bloom, the down began to mantle his cheek with dusky hue, he turned his thoughts to a marriage that was a prize open to all, even to the winning of the glorious Hippodameia from the hand of her father, the lord of Pisa.

He drew near unto the foaming sea, and, alone in the darkness, called aloud on the loudly roaring god of the fair trident; who appeared to him, even close beside him, at his very feet; and to the god he said :—

"If the kindly gifts of Cypris count in any wise in one's favour, then stay thou, Poseidon, the brazen spear of Oenomaüs, and speed me in the swiftest of all chariots to Elis, and cause me to draw nigh unto power. Thirteen suitors hath he slain, thus deferring his daughter's marriage. But high emprise brooketh no coward wight. Yet, as all men must needs die, why should one, sitting idly in the darkness, nurse

[1] The three other punishments are those of Tityus, Sisyphus, and Ixion.

PINDAR

γῆρας ἐν σκότῳ καθήμενος ἕψοι μάταν,
ἀπάντων καλῶν ἄμμορος; ἀλλ᾽ ἐμοὶ μὲν οὗτος
    ἄεθλος
85 ὑποκείσεται· τὺ δὲ πρᾶξιν φίλαν δίδοι."
ὡς ἔννεπεν· οὐδ᾽ ἀκράντοις ἐφάψατ᾽ ὦν ἔπεσι.
τὸν μὲν ἀγάλλων θεὸς
ἔδωκεν δίφρον τε χρύσεον πτεροῖσίν τ᾽ ἀκάμαντας
    ἵππους.   140

στρ. δ'
ἕλεν δ᾽ Οἰνομάου βίαν παρθένον τε σύνευνον·
τέκε τε λαγέτας ἐξ ἀρεταῖσι μεμαλότας υἱούς.
90 νῦν δ᾽ ἐν αἱμακουρίαις
ἀγλααῖσι μέμικται,
Ἀλφεοῦ πόρῳ κλιθείς,
τύμβον ἀμφίπολον ἔχων πολυξενωτάτῳ παρὰ
    βωμῷ.   τὸ δὲ κλέος   150
τηλόθεν δέδορκε τᾶν Ὀλυμπιάδων ἐν δρόμοις
95 Πέλοπος, ἵνα ταχυτὰς ποδῶν ἐρίζεται
ἀκμαί τ᾽ ἰσχύος θρασύπονοι·
ὁ νικῶν δὲ λοιπὸν ἀμφὶ βίοτον
ἔχει μελιτόεσσαν εὐδίαν

ἀντ. δ'
ἀέθλων γ᾽ ἕνεκεν. τὸ δ᾽ αἰεὶ παράμερον ἐσλὸν   160
100 ὕπατον ἔρχεται παντὶ βροτῶν. ἐμὲ δὲ στεφανῶσαι
κεῖνον ἱππίῳ νόμῳ
Αἰοληΐδι μολπᾷ
χρή· πέποιθα δὲ ξένον
μή τιν᾽, ἀμφότερα καλῶν τε ἴδριν ἁμᾷ καὶ δύνα-
    μιν κυριώτερον,

100 βροτῶν good mss (MGS) : βροτῷ N (BFC).

104 ἁμᾷ καὶ Wilamowitz (S) : ἅμα καὶ old mss ; ἄλλον ἢ
Moschopulus (B) ; ἀλλὰ καὶ Hermann, Donaldson (FC) ; ἄμμε
καὶ (MG)

without aim an inglorious eld, reft of all share of blessings? As for me, on this contest shall I take my stand; and do thou grant a welcome consummation."

Even thus he spake, nor did he light upon language that came to naught. The god honoured him with the gift of a golden chariot and of steeds unwearied of wing; and he overcame the might of Oenomaüs, and won the maiden as his bride, and she bare him six sons, who were eager in deeds of valour. And now hath he a share in the splendid funeral-sacrifices, while he resteth beside the ford of the Alpheüs, having his oft-frequented tomb hard by the altar that is thronged by many a visitant; and the fame of the Olympic festivals shineth from afar amid the race-courses of Pelops, where strife is waged in swiftness of foot and in doughty deeds of strength; but he that overcometh hath, on either hand, for the rest of his life, the sweetest calm, so far as crowns in the games can give it. Yet for every one of all mortal men the brightest boon is the blessing that ever cometh day by day.

I must crown the victor with the horseman's song, even with the Aeolian strains, and I am persuaded that there is no host of the present time, whom I shall glorify with sounding bouts of song, as one

105 τῶν γε νῦν κλυταῖσι δαιδαλωσέμεν ὕμνων πτυ-
χαῖς.   170
   θεὸς ἐπίτροπος ἐὼν τεαῖσι μήδεται
   ἔχων τοῦτο κᾶδος, Ἱέρων,
   μερίμναισιν· εἰ δὲ μὴ ταχὺ λίποι,
   ἔτι γλυκυτέραν κεν ἔλπομαι
ἐπ. δ′
110 σὺν ἅρματι θοῷ κλεΐξειν, ἐπίκουρον εὑρὼν ὁδὸν
λόγων
   παρ’ εὐδείελον ἐλθὼν Κρόνιον. ἐμοὶ μὲν ὦν
   Μοῖσα καρτερώτατον βέλος ἀλκᾷ τρέφει·   180
   ἐπ’ ἄλλοισι δ’ ἄλλοι μεγάλοι. τὸ δ’ ἔσχατον
κορυφοῦται
   βασιλεῦσι. μηκέτι πάπταινε πόρσιον.
115 εἴη σέ τε τοῦτον ὑψοῦ χρόνον πατεῖν, ἐμέ τε τοσ-
σάδε νικαφόροις
   ὁμιλεῖν, πρόφαντον σοφίᾳ καθ’ Ἕλλανας ἐόντα
παντᾷ.

109 κεν Vatican mss : τε (s).
113 < ἐπ’ > BMGFC : < ἀμφ’ > s.

14

who is at once more familiar with things noble, or is more sovereign in power. A god who hath this care, watcheth and broodeth over thy desires; but, if he doth not desert thee too soon, I trust I shall celebrate a still sweeter victory, even with the swift chariot, having found a path that prompteth praises, when I have reached the sunny hill of Cronus.

Howsoever, for myself, the Muse is keeping a shaft most mighty in strength. Some men are great in one thing; others in another: but the crowning summit is for kings. Refrain from peering too far! Heaven grant that thou mayest plant thy feet on high, so long as thou livest, and that I may consort with victors for all my days, and be foremost in the lore of song among Hellenes in every land.

OLYMPIAN II

FOR THERON OF ACRAGAS

INTRODUCTION

UNDER Thêrôn and his brother Xenocratês, Acragas, a colony of Gela, was brought to the height of its glory. The brothers were descended from the Emmenidae, who were descended from Cadmus. They were allied to the rulers of Syracuse, Dâmareta, daughter of Thêrôn, having successively married Gelôn and his younger brother, Polyzêlus, while Thêrôn had already married a daughter of Polyzêlus, and Hierôn a daughter of Xenocrates.

Thêrôn became tyrant of Acragas about 488, and conquered Himera in 482. The tyrant of Himera appealed to his son-in-law Anaxilas, tyrant of Rhegium, who called in the aid of the Carthaginians, whom Thêrôn and his son-in-law, Gelôn of Syracuse, defeated at Himera in 480. In 476 Thêrôn won the chariot-race at Olympia, which is celebrated in the present ode. The date is recorded in the Oxyrhynchus papyrus, ii (1899) 88.

The God, the hero, and the man, we celebrate, shall be Zeus, the lord of Pisa, Heracles, the founder of

16

INTRODUCTION

the Olympic games, and the victor Thêrôn (1-6). Thêrôn's famous ancestors had settled and prospered in Sicily, and Zeus is prayed to continue their prosperity (6-15). But prosperity leads to forgetfulness of troubles, as is proved by the family of Cadmus, from which Thêrôn himself is descended (15-47). He and his brother have an hereditary claim to victory in the Greek games (48-51). Victory gives release from trouble (51 f.).

Glory may be won by wealth combined with virtue; while the unjust are punished, the just live in the Islands of the Blest, with Cadmus and Achilles (53-83).

The poet is like an eagle, while his detractors are like crows, but their cavil cannot prevail against the poet's praise (83-88). Thêrôn is the greatest benefactor that Acragas has had for a hundred years; though his fame is attacked by envy, his bounties are as countless as the sand of the sea (89-100).

II.—ΘΗΡΩΝΙ ΑΚΡΑΓΑΝΤΙΝΩ

ΑΡΜΑΤΙ

στρ. α΄
   Ἀναξιφόρμιγγες ὕμνοι,
   τίνα θεόν, τίν᾽ ἥρωα, τίνα δ᾽ ἄνδρα κελαδήσομεν;
   ἤτοι Πίσα μὲν Διός· Ὀλυμπιάδα δ᾽ ἔστασεν
   Ἡρακλέης
   ἀκρόθινα πολέμου·
5 Θήρωνα δὲ τετραορίας ἔνεκα νικαφόρου
   γεγωνητέον, ὅπι δίκαιον ξένων, ἔρεισμ᾽ Ἀκρά-
      γαντος,   10
   εὐωνύμων τε πατέρων ἄωτον ὀρθόπολιν·
ἀντ. α΄
   καμόντες οἳ πολλὰ θυμῷ
   ἱερὸν ἔσχον οἴκημα ποταμοῦ, Σικελίας τ᾽ ἔσαν
10 ὀφθαλμός, αἰὼν δ᾽ ἔφεπε μόρσιμος, πλοῦτόν τε
      καὶ χάριν ἄγων   20
   γνησίαις ἐπ᾽ ἀρεταῖς.
   ἀλλ᾽ ὦ Κρόνιε παῖ Ῥέας, ἕδος Ὀλύμπου νέμων
   ἀέθλων τε κορυφὰν πόρον τ᾽ Ἀλφεοῦ, ἰανθεὶς
      ἀοιδαῖς
   εὔφρων ἄρουραν ἔτι πατρίαν σφίσιν κόμισον
ἐπ. α΄
15 λοιπῷ γένει.   τῶν δὲ πεπραγμένων
   ἐν δίκᾳ τε καὶ παρὰ δίκαν, ἀποίητον οὐδ᾽ ἂν   30

---

6 ὅπι δίκαιον ξένων Hermann² (Β²S): ὁπὶ δ. ξένον mss ; ὅπι δ.
ξένον F ; ὅπιν δ. ξένων Hartung (MGC) ; ὅπιν δ. ξένον Hermann¹
(Β¹).

18

II.—FOR THERON OF ACRAGAS

WINNER IN THE CHARIOT RACE, 476 B.C.

YE hymns that rule the lyre! what god, what hero, aye, and what man shall we loudly praise? Verily Zeus is the lord of Pisa; and Heracles established the Olympic festival, from the spoils of war; while Thêrôn must be proclaimed by reason of his victorious chariot with its four horses, Thêrôn who is just in his regard for guests, and who is the bulwark of Acragas, the choicest flower of an auspicious line of sires, whose city towers on high,—those sires who, by much labour of mind, gat them a hallowed home beside the river, and were the eye of Sicily, while their allotted time drew on, bringing wealth and glory to crown their native merits. But, O thou son of Cronus and Rhea, that rulest over thine abode on Olympus, and over the foremost of festivals, and over the ford of the Alpheüs! soothed by our songs, do thou graciously preserve their ancestral soil for their future race. Even Time, the father of all, could not undo the accomplished end of things that

PINDAR

χρόνος ὁ πάντων πατὴρ δύναιτο θέμεν ἔργων τέλος·
λάθα δὲ πότμῳ σὺν εὐδαίμονι γένοιτ' ἄν.
ἐσλῶν γὰρ ὑπὸ χαρμάτων πῆμα θνάσκει
20 παλίγκοτον δαμασθέν,
στρ. β′
ὅταν θεοῦ Μοῖρα πέμπῃ
ἀνεκὰς ὄλβον ὑψηλόν. ἕπεται δὲ λόγος εὐθρόνοις
Κάδμοιο κούραις, ἔπαθον αἳ μεγάλα, πένθος δ'
ἐπίτνει βαρὺ   40
κρεσσόνων πρὸς ἀγαθῶν.
25 ζώει μὲν ἐν Ὀλυμπίοις ἀποθανοῖσα βρόμῳ
κεραυνοῦ τανυέθειρα Σεμέλα, φιλεῖ δέ νιν Παλλὰς
αἰεί,
καὶ Ζεὺς πατὴρ μάλα, φιλεῖ δὲ παῖς ὁ κισσο-
φόρος·   50
ἀντ. β′
λέγοντι δ' ἐν καὶ θαλάσσᾳ
μετὰ κόραισι Νηρῆος ἁλίαις βίοτον ἄφθιτον
30 Ἰνοῖ τετάχθαι τὸν ὅλον ἀμφὶ χρόνον. ἤτοι
βροτῶν γε κέκριται
πεῖρας οὔ τι θανάτου,
οὐδ' ἡσύχιμον ἁμέραν ὁπότε, παῖδ' ἁλίου,   59
ἀτειρεῖ σὺν ἀγαθῷ τελευτάσομεν· ῥοαὶ δ' ἄλλοτ'
ἄλλαι
εὐθυμιᾶν τε μετὰ καὶ πόνων ἐς ἄνδρας ἔβαν.
ἐπ. β′
35 οὕτω δὲ Μοῖρ', ἅ τε πατρώιον
τῶνδ' ἔχει τὸν εὔφρονα πότμον, θεόρτῳ σὺν ὄλβῳ
ἐπί τι καὶ πῆμ' ἄγει παλιντράπελον ἄλλῳ χρόνῳ·
ἐξ οὗπερ ἔκτεινε Λᾶον μόριμος υἱὸς   70
συναντόμενος, ἐν δὲ Πυθῶνι χρησθὲν
40 παλαίφατον τέλεσσεν.

have been finally completed, whether in right or in wrong; but, if fortune be favourable, that end may be forgotten. For, under the power of noble joys, a cruel trouble is quelled and dieth away, whenever good fortune is lifted on high by a god-sent fate.

This saying befitteth the fair-throned daughters of Cadmus, who sorely suffered, but their heavy sorrow was abated by the presence of greater blessings. Semelê of the streaming hair liveth amid the gods Olympian, when she had been slain by the thunderbolt,—Semelê, beloved for ever by Pallas and, in very deed, by father Zeus; beloved by her ivy-crowned son; while Ino, as the story telleth, hath allotted to her for all time a deathless life beneath the sea, amid the ocean-daughters of Nêreus. Verily, for mortal men at least, the time when their life will end in the bourne of death is not clearly marked; no, nor the time when we shall bring a calm day, the Sun's own child, to its close amid happiness that is unimpaired.

But diverse are the currents that at divers times come upon men, either with joys or with toils. Even thus Fate, which handeth a kindly fortune down from sire to son, bringeth at another time some sad reverse, together with the heaven-sent bliss, from the day when that fated son met and slew Laïus, and thus fulfilled the oracle spoken of old at Pytho. But the keen-eyed Fury saw

PINDAR

στρ. γ΄

  ἰδοῖσα δ᾽ ὀξεῖ᾽ Ἐρινὺς
  ἔπεφνέ οἱ σὺν ἀλλαλοφονίᾳ γένος ἀρήιον·
  λείφθη δὲ Θέρσανδρος ἐριπέντι Πολυνείκει, νέοις
    ἐν ἀέθλοις
  ἐν μάχαις τε πολέμου

45 τιμώμενος, Ἀδραστιδᾶν θάλος ἀρωγὸν δόμοις· 80
  ὅθεν σπέρματος ἔχοντα ῥίζαν, πρέπει τὸν Αἰνη-
    σιδάμου
  ἐγκωμίων τε μελέων λυρᾶν τε τυγχανέμεν.

ἀντ. γ΄

  Ὀλυμπίᾳ μὲν γὰρ αὐτὸς
  γέρας ἔδεκτο, Πυθῶνι δ᾽ ὁμόκλαρον ἐς ἀδελφεὸν
50 Ἰσθμοῖ τε κοιναὶ Χάριτες ἄνθεα τεθρίππων δυω-
    δεκαδρόμων
                              90
  ἄγαγον. τὸ δὲ τυχεῖν
  πειρώμενον ἀγωνίας παραλύει δυσφρονᾶν.
  ὁ μὰν πλοῦτος ἀρεταῖς δεδαιδαλμένος φέρει τῶν
    τε καὶ τῶν
  καιρόν, βαθεῖαν ὑπέχων μέριμναν ἀγροτέραν, 100

ἐπ. γ΄

55 ἀστὴρ ἀρίζηλος, ἐτήτυμον
  ἀνδρὶ φέγγος· εἰ δέ νιν ἔχων τις οἶδεν τὸ μέλλον,
  ὅτι θανόντων μὲν ἐνθάδ᾽ αὐτίκ᾽ ἀπάλαμνοι φρένες
  ποινὰς ἔτισαν,—τὰ δ᾽ ἐν τᾷδε Διὸς ἀρχᾷ
  ἀλιτρὰ κατὰ γᾶς δικάζει τις ἐχθρᾷ
60 λόγον φράσαις ἀνάγκᾳ·

46 ἔχοντα Erasmus Schmid (MGFCS) : ἔχοντι most mss (B).
    52 π. δυσφρονᾶν Dindorf (GFC) ; — δυσφρόνων Triclinius (B) ;
δυσφρονᾶν π. (S): δυσφροσυνᾶν π. C¹, —σύνας C², —σύναν ABD ;
ἀφροσυνᾶν π. Scholia (M).
    56 εἰ δέ (mss) νιν (MGFS) ; εἴ γε μιν (B), — νιν (C) ; εὖ δέ μιν
B in critical notes (Donaldson) ; εὐτέ νιν Hermann.

it, and caused his war-like sons to be slain by
one another's hands. Yet Polyneicês, when laid
low, left behind him a son, Thersander, who was
honoured amid youthful contests and amid the con-
flicts of war, a scion destined to succour the house
of the descendants of Adrastus; and it is fitting
that the son of Aristodêmus, who hath sprung from
that seed, should meet with songs of praise and with
notes of the lyre.   For at Olympia, he himself won
a prize, while, at Pytho and at the Isthmus, the
impartial Graces brought unto his brother, who shared
the same victorious lot, crowns that were won from
the teams of four horses that twelve times traverse
the course.   Now, to win the victory when essaying
the contest, giveth us release from hardships.

But, verily, wealth adorned with virtues bringeth
the fitting chance of divers boons, prompting the
heart of man to a keen and eager quest, wealth
which is that star conspicuous, that truest light of
man. But if, in very deed, when he hath that wealth,
he knoweth of the future, that immediately after
death, on earth, it is the lawless spirits that suffer
punishment,—and the sins committed in this realm
of Zeus are judged by One who passeth sentence
stern and inevitable; while the good, having the

PINDAR

στρ. δ΄

ἴσαις δὲ νύκτεσσιν αἰεί,
ἴσαις δ᾽ ἐν ἀμέραις ἅλιον ἔχοντες, ἀπονέστερον 110
ἐσλοὶ δέκονται βίοτον, οὐ χθόνα ταράσσοντες ἐν
χερὸς ἀκμᾷ
οὐδὲ πόντιον ὕδωρ
65 κεινὰν παρὰ δίαιταν· ἀλλὰ παρὰ μὲν τιμίοις
θεῶν, οἵτινες ἔχαιρον εὐορκίαις, ἄδακρυν νέ-
μονται
αἰῶνα· τοὶ δ᾽ ἀπροσόρατον ὀκχέοντι πόνον—   120

ἀντ. δ΄

ὅσοι δ᾽ ἐτόλμασαν ἐστρὶς
ἑκατέρωθι μείναντες ἀπὸ πάμπαν ἀδίκων ἔχειν
70 ψυχάν, ἔτειλαν Διὸς ὁδὸν παρὰ Κρόνου τύρσιν·
ἔνθα μακάρων
νᾶσος ὠκεανίδες
αὖραι περιπνέοισιν, ἄνθεμα δὲ χρυσοῦ φλέγει, 130
τὰ μὲν χερσόθεν ἀπ᾽ ἀγλαῶν δενδρέων, ὕδωρ δ᾽
ἄλλα φέρβει,
ὅρμοισι τῶν χέρας ἀναπλέκοντι καὶ στεφάνοις

ἐπ. δ΄

75 βουλαῖς ἐν ὀρθαῖσι Ῥαδαμάνθυος,
ὃν πατὴρ ἔχει <μέ>γας ἑτοῖμον αὐτῷ πάρεδρον,

---

61 f. ἴσαις δὲ .... ἴσαις δ᾽ best mss (MGFS): ἴσον δὲ ....
ἴσα δ᾽ ἐν Moschopulus, Triclinius (B); ἴσ᾽ ἐν δὲ ... ἴσα δ᾽
ἐν Schwickert (C).

65 κεινὰν interpolated mss (BGFC): κενεὰν old mss (MS).

71 νᾶσος (Doric acc.) G with note ἀντὶ νήσους Triclinius, and
paraphrase (BMGFC): νᾶσον old mss (S).

74 στεφάνοις C supra (GF); στεφάνους mss (MS); κεφαλὰς B,
κροτάφους Karsten (C).

76 γᾶς old mss ; <μέ>γας Pauw (CS): Κρόνος Triclinius
(BGF) ; χθονὸς (M¹), Διὸς M².

24

sun shining for evermore, for equal nights and equal days, receive the boon of a life of lightened toil, not vexing the soil with the strength of their hands, no, nor the water of the sea, to gain a scanty livelihood; but, in the presence of the honoured gods, all who were wont to rejoice in keeping their oaths, share a life that knoweth no tears, while the others endure labour that none can look upon — But, whosoever, while dwelling in either world, have thrice been courageous in keeping their souls pure from all deeds of wrong, pass by the highway of Zeus unto the tower of Cronus, where the ocean-breezes blow around the Islands of the Blest, and flowers of gold are blazing, some on the shore from radiant trees, while others the water fostereth; and with chaplets thereof they entwine their hands, and with crowns, according to the righteous councils of Rhadamanthys, who shareth for evermore the judgement-seat of the mighty Father, even the Lord of Rhea with her throne exalted beyond

πόσις ὁ πάντων Ῥέας ὑπέρτατον ἐχοίσας
θρόνον.   140
Πηλεύς τε καὶ Κάδμος ἐν τοῖσιν ἀλέγονται·
Ἀχιλλέα τ᾽ ἔνεικ᾽, ἐπεὶ Ζηνὸς ἦτορ
80 λιταῖς ἔπεισε, μάτηρ·
στρ. ε΄
ὃς Ἕκτορ᾽ ἔσφαλε, Τροίας
ἄμαχον ἀστραβῆ κίονα, Κύκνον τε θανάτῳ
πόρεν,
Ἀοῦς τε παῖδ᾽ Αἰθίοπα. πολλά μοι ὑπ᾽ ἀγκῶνος
ὠκέα βέλη   150
ἔνδον ἐντι φαρέτρας
85 φωνᾶντα συνετοῖσιν· ἐς δὲ τὸ πᾶν ἑρμηνέων
χατίζει. σοφὸς ὁ πολλὰ εἰδὼς φυᾷ· μαθόντες δὲ
λάβροι
παγγλωσσίᾳ, κόρακες ὣς, ἄκραντα γαρύετον
ἀντ. ε΄
Διὸς πρὸς ὄρνιχα θεῖον.
ἔπεχε νῦν σκοπῷ τόξον, ἄγε θυμέ, τίνα βάλ-
λομεν   160
90 ἐκ μαλθακᾶς αὖτε φρενὸς εὐκλέας ὀϊστοὺς ἱέντες;
ἐπί τοι
Ἀκράγαντι τανύσαις
αὐδάσομαι ἐνόρκιον λόγον ἀλαθεῖ νόῳ
τεκεῖν μή τιν᾽ ἑκατόν γε ἐτέων πόλιν φίλοις ἄνδρα
μᾶλλον   170
εὐεργέταν πραπίσιν ἀφθονέστερόν τε χέρα

85 τὸ πᾶν AC (MGFCS); τοπὰν B²: τὸ πᾶν BD.
87 γαρύετον mss and scholia (BGFC); γαρύεται M; γαρυέτων
Bergk (s).
91 τανύσαις· B.

26

all beside. And among them are numbered Pêleus and Cadmus, while Achilles was borne thither by his mother, when, by her prayers, she had entreated the heart of Zeus,—Achilles, who laid low Hector, that resistless, that unswerving tower of Troy, and who consigned to death Memnon, the son of Morning.

Full many a swift arrow have I beneath mine arm, within my quiver, many an arrow that is vocal to the wise; but for the crowd they need interpreters. The true poet.is he who knoweth much by gift of nature, but they that have only learnt the lore of song, and are turbulent and intemperate of tongue, like a pair of crows, chatter in vain against the god-like bird of Zeus.[1]

Now, bend thy bow toward the mark! tell me, my soul, whom are we essaying to hit, while we now shoot forth our shafts of fame from the quiver of a kindly heart? Lo! I would aim mine arrow at Acragas, and would loudly utter with true intent a saying sealed by a solemn oath, when I declare that, for these hundred years, no city hath given birth to a man more munificent in heart, more ungrudging in

---

[1] The dual, γαρύετον, is understood in some of the *scholia* as a reference to Pindar's rivals, the Cean poets, Simonides and his nephew, Bacchylides; and this is regarded as probable by Jebb (*Bacchylides*, pp. 17-19). It is far preferable to Freeman's suggestion that the pair are Capys and Hippocrates, kinsmen of Thêrôn, who unsuccessfully waged war against him (*Sicily*, ii 531), and Verrall's, that they are the Sicilian rhetoricians, Corax and Tisias (*Journal of Philology*, ix 130, 197). Wilamowitz, however, notices that in the spring of 476 (the date of this ode), Simonides was at Athens, and had not yet visited Sicily. He therefore prefers accepting, with Schröder, Bergk's proposal of the contemptuous imperative, γαρυέτων (for γαρυόντων, cp. Soph. *Ai.* 961, οἱ δ᾽ οὖν γελώντων), a rare form of the third person plural, like ἔστων and ἴτων (*Hieron und Pindaros*, 1302.)

27

PINDAR

ἐπ. ε

95 Θήρωνος. ἀλλ' αἶνον ἔβα κόρος
οὐ δίκᾳ συναντόμενος, ἀλλὰ μάργων ὑπ' ἀνδρῶν,
τὸ λαλαγῆσαι ἐθέλων κρύφον τε θέμεν ἐσλῶν
        καλοῖς
ἔργοις· ἐπεὶ ψάμμος ἀριθμὸν περιπέφευγεν,
καὶ κεῖνος ὅσα χάρματ' ἄλλοις ἔθηκεν   180
100 τίς ἂν φράσαι δύναιτο;

97 κρύφον τε θέμεν ἐσλῶν καλοῖς Aristarchus (BMFGS);
— τιθέμεν Hermann (C) — : κρύφιόν τε θέμεν ἐσ(θ)λῶν κακοῖς
old mss.

28

hand, than Thêrôn. But praise is attacked by envy,—
envy, not mated with justice, but prompted by
besotted minds, envy that is ever eager to babble,
and to blot the fair deeds of noble men; whereas
sand can never be numbered, and who could ever
count up all the joys that he hath given to
others?

OLYMPIAN III

FOR THERON OF ACRAGAS

INTRODUCTION

THE third Olympian celebrates the same victory as the second (that of 476), but, while the former Ode was probably sung in the palace of Thêrôn, the present was performed in the temple of the Dioscûri at Acragas, on the occasion of the festival of the Theoxenia, when the gods were deemed to be entertained by Castor and Polydeuces.

Acragas and Thêrôn are commended to the favour of the Twin Brethren and their sister Helen (1–4). The Muse has prompted the poet to invent a new type of Dorian song, to be sung to the accompaniment of the lyre and the flute (4–9). He was also summoned to sing by Pisa, whence odes of victory are sent to all whom the umpire crowns with the olive, which Heracles brought back from the Hyperboreans to the treeless Olympia (9–34).

Heracles is now attending the Theoxenia with the Twin Brethren, whom he caused to preside over the Olympic Games (34–38). Thêrôn's glory is a favour granted in return for his pious worship of the Twin Gods (38–41). Even as water and gold are supreme in their kind, so Thêrôn's exploits reach the Pillars of Heracles.

III.—ΘΗΡΩΝΙ ΑΚΡΑΓΑΝΤΙΝΩ

ΑΡΜΑΤΙ ΕΙΣ ΘΕΟΞΕΝΙΑ

στρ. α΄

  Τυνδαρίδαις τε φιλοξείνοις ἁδεῖν καλλιπλοκάμῳ
     θ᾽ Ἑλένᾳ
  κλεινὰν Ἀκράγαντα γεραίρων εὔχομαι,
  Θήρωνος Ὀλυμπιονίκαν ὕμνον ὀρθώσαις, ἀκα-
     μαντοπόδων
  ἵππων ἄωτον. Μοῖσα δ᾽ οὕτω ποι παρέστα μοι
     νεοσίγαλον εὑρόντι τρόπον
5 Δωρίῳ φωνὰν ἐναρμόξαι πεδίλῳ

ἀντ. α΄

  ἀγλαόκωμον. ἐπεὶ χαίταισι μὲν ζευχθέντες ἔπι
     στέφανοι   10
  πράσσοντί με τοῦτο θεόδματον χρέος,
  φόρμιγγά τε ποικιλόγαρυν καὶ βοὰν αὐλῶν ἐπέων
     τε θέσιν
  Αἰνησιδάμου παιδὶ συμμῖξαι πρεπόντως, ἅ τε
     Πίσα με γεγωνεῖν· τᾶς ἄπο
10 θεόμοροι νίσοντ᾽ ἐπ᾽ ἀνθρώπους ἀοιδαί,

ἐπ. α΄

  ᾧ τινι, κραίνων ἐφετμὰς Ἡρακλέος προτέρας, 20
  ἀτρεκὴς Ἑλλανοδίκας γλεφάρων Αἰτωλὸς ἀνὴρ
     ὑψόθεν

---

4 ποι παρέστα μοι *A B E* (M²s) ; τοι παρέστα μοι *D* (BF) ; μοι παρεστάκοι (M¹G) ; μοι παρεσταίη Naber (C).

10 θεόμοροι *MP*, Triclinius ; θεόμοιροι better mss. θεόμοροι νίσοντ᾽ (MGS), — νίσσοντ᾽ (*CD*) C ; θεύμοροι νίσοντ᾽ F, — νίσσοντ᾽ B.

3²

III.—FOR THERON OF ACRAGAS

WINNER IN THE CHARIOT RACE, 476 B.C.

I PRAY that I may find favour with the hospitable sons of Tyndareüs and with fair-haired Helen, while I honour the famous Acragas, by duly ordering my song in praise of Thêrôn's victory at Olympia, as the choicest guerdon for those steeds with unwearied feet. Even so, I ween, hath the Muse stood beside me, when I found out a fashion that is still bright and new, by fitting to the Dorian measure the voice of festive revellers. For the crowns that are about my hair prompt me to pay this sacred debt, that so, in honour of the son of Aenêsidâmus, I may duly blend the varied melody of the lyre, and the air played on the flutes, with the setting of the verses, while Pisa biddeth me raise my voice,—Pisa, whence heaven-sent strains of song are wafted over the world, in honour of any man, for whom the strict Aetolian umpire, in accordance with the olden ordinances of

ἀμφὶ κόμαισι βάλῃ γλαυκόχροα κόσμον ἐλαίας·
τάν ποτε
Ἴστρου ἀπὸ σκιαρᾶν παγᾶν ἔνεικεν Ἀμφι-
τρυωνιάδας,
15 μνᾶμα τῶν Οὐλυμπίᾳ κάλλιστον ἄθλων

στρ. β′

δᾶμον Ὑπερβορέων πείσαις Ἀπόλλωνος θερά-
ποντα λόγῳ.

πιστὰ φρονέων Διὸς αἴτει πανδόκῳ   30
ἄλσει σκιαρόν τε φύτευμα ξυνὸν ἀνθρώποις
στέφανόν τ' ἀρετᾶν.

ἤδη γὰρ αὐτῷ, πατρὶ μὲν βωμῶν ἁγισθέντων,
διχόμηνις ὅλον χρυσάρματος
20 ἑσπέρας ὀφθαλμὸν ἀντέφλεξε Μήνα,

ἀντ. β′

καὶ μεγάλων ἀέθλων ἁγνὰν κρίσιν καὶ πεντα-
ετηρίδ' ἁμᾶ
θῆκε ζαθέοις ἐπὶ κρημνοῖς Ἀλφεοῦ·
ἀλλ' οὐ καλὰ δένδρε' ἔθαλλεν χῶρος ἐν βάσσαις
Κρονίου Πέλοπος.   40
τούτων ἔδοξεν γυμνὸς αὐτῷ κᾶπος ὀξείαις ὑπα-
κουέμεν αὐγαῖς ἁλίου.
25 δὴ τότ' ἐς γαῖαν πορεύεν θυμὸς ὥρμα

ἐπ. β′

Ἰστρίαν νιν· ἔνθα Λατοῦς ἱπποσόα θυγάτηρ
δέξατ' ἐλθόντ' Ἀρκαδίας ἀπὸ δειρᾶν καὶ πολυ-
γνάμπτων μυχῶν,

25 πορεύεν . . . ὥρμα A alone (MS); πορεύειν . . ὥρμα (GF);
πόρευεν . . . ὁρμᾷ C; πορεύειν . . . ὥρμαιν' mss (B).

34

Heracles, flingeth o'er his brow and on his hair the
grey-hued adornment of the olive-spray; that olive-
spray, which, once upon a time, was brought by the
son of Amphitryon from the shady springs of Ister,
to be the fairest memorial of the Olympic contests,
after he had gotten it by persuading the servants of
Apollo, the people of the Hyperboreans.

With loyal heart was he entreating, for the hospit-
able precinct of Zeus, the gift of a tree, whose shade
should be for all men, and whose leaves should be a
crown of prowess. For already had the altars been
consecrated in his father's honour, and in the midst
of the month the Moon with her car of gold had at
eventide kindled before him the full orb of her light,
and he had ordained on the hallowed banks of
Alpheüs the impartial award of the great games,
together with the quadrennial festival. But that
plot of ground, sacred to Pelops, was not, as yet,
flourishing with trees in its valleys below the hill of
Cronus.

He deemed that his demesne, being bare of such
trees, lay beneath the power of the keen rays of the
sun. Then it was that his spirit prompted him to
journey to the land of the Ister, where he had
once been welcomed by Leda's daughter that driveth
the steed, on his coming from the ridges and from
the winding dells of Arcadia, what time, at the

εὖτέ νιν ἀγγελίαις Εὐρυσθέος ἔντυ᾽ ἀνάγκα
πατρόθεν 50
χρυσόκερων ἔλαφον θήλειαν ἄξονθ᾽, ἅν ποτε
Ταϋγέτα
30 ἀντιθεῖσ᾽ Ὀρθωσίᾳ ἔγραψεν ἱράν.

στρ. γ΄

τὰν μεθέπων ἴδε καὶ κείναν χθόνα πνοιᾶς ὄπιθεν
Βορέα
ψυχροῦ. τόθι δένδρεα θάμβαινε σταθείς.
τῶν νιν γλυκὺς ἵμερος ἔσχεν δωδεκάγναμπτον
περὶ τέρμα δρόμου
ἵππων φυτεῦσαι. καί νυν ἐς ταύταν ἑορτὰν
ἵλαος ἀντιθέοισιν νίσσεται 60
35 σὺν βαθυζώνου διδύμοις παισὶ Λήδας.

ἀντ. γ΄

τοῖς γὰρ ἐπέτραπεν Οὐλυμπόνδ᾽ ἰὼν θαητὸν
ἀγῶνα νέμειν
ἀνδρῶν τ᾽ ἀρετᾶς πέρι καὶ ῥιμφαρμάτος
διφρηλασίας. ἐμὲ δ᾽ ὦν πᾳ θυμὸς ὀτρύνει φάμεν
Ἐμμενίδαις
Θήρωνί τ᾽ ἐλθεῖν κῦδος, εὐΐππων διδόντων
Τυνδαριδᾶν, ὅτι πλείσταισι βροτῶν 70
40 ξεινίαις αὐτοὺς ἐποίχονται τραπέζαις,

ἐπ. γ΄

εὐσεβεῖ γνώμᾳ φυλάσσοντες μακάρων τελετάς.
εἰ δ᾽ ἀριστεύει μὲν ὕδωρ, κτεάνων δὲ χρυσὸς
αἰδοιέστατος,

32 θάμβαινε A (MGFCS) ; θαύμαινε most mss (B).
35 διδύμοις A (S), —μοισι other old mss ; διδύμνοις Hermann
(BMGFC).
38 πᾶ or πα mss : πᾳ MFS (καὶ ? S) ; πὰρ Moschopulus (BGC).

behest of Eurystheus, the fate that bound the sire
and son urged him on the quest of the doe with
the golden horns, which (the Pleiad) Taÿgetê had
inscribed with the name of Artemis, when she
devoted it to the goddess in her own stead.[1] On his
quest of that doe had he seen the far-off land
beyond the cold blast of Boreas; and there had he
stood and marvelled at the trees, and had been seized
with sweet desire for them, even to plant them along
the bounds of the race-ground with its courses
twelve.

And now he cometh to this our festival with the
twin sons divine of deep-zoned Leda. For Heracles,
when he passed unto Olympus, assigned to them the
ordering of the wondrous contest waged by men,
the contest in prowess and in the driving of swift
chariots. In any wise, my spirit strangely prompteth
me to say that it is by the gift of those noble horse-
men, the sons of Tyndareüs, that glory hath come
unto the Emmenidae and to Thêrôn, because that
house, beyond all mortal men, draweth near to them
with many more tables set for feasting, in pious
spirit keeping the rites that to the Blest are due.
But, even as water is most excellent, while gold is
the most adorable of possessions,[2] so now doth

---

[1] Taÿgetê was one of the daughters of Atlas, known
as the Pleiades. To escape the pursuit of Zeus, she was
changed by Artemis into a doe, and, on returning to her
human form, she consecrated a doe to the goddess. It was
in quest of this mythical "doe with the golden horns," that
Heracles went to the Hyperboreans. Dr. Ridgeway identifies
it with the reindeer of Northern Asia and Europe, the only
kind of deer, in which the female is armed with antlers
(*Proc. Camb. Philol. Soc.* 25 Oct. 1894).

[2] Cp. *O.* i 1 f.

PINDAR

νῦν δὲ πρὸς ἐσχατιὰν Θήρων ἀρεταῖσιν ἱκάνων
ἅπτεται
οἴκοθεν Ἡρακλέος σταλᾶν. τὸ πόρσω δ᾽ ἔστι
σοφοῖς ἄβατον ἄβατον
45 κἀσόφοις. οὔ νιν διώξω· κεινὸς εἴην.

43 νῦν δὲ *AD* (MGS): νῦν γε vulgo (BFC).
45 νιν *CN* (GCS): μιν *D* (BF); μὴν B, μὰν M. κεινὸς (BMGFCS[1]): κενὸς (κενεὸς?) S[3]; κενὸς <ἂν> Wackernagel.

Thêrôn by his deeds of prowess come unto the utmost verge, by his own true merit reaching even as far as the pillars of Heracles. All beyond that bourne cannot be approached either by the wise or by the unwise. I shall not pursue it ; else may I be deemed a fool.

OLYMPIAN IV

FOR PSAUMIS OF CAMARINA

INTRODUCTION

CAMARÎNA had been founded by Syracuse in 599 B.C. Destroyed by Syracuse after a revolt, it was rebuilt by Hippocratês, to be destroyed once more by Gelôn, and rebuilt in 461 by men of Gela, mainly with the aid of Psaumis.

The Ode was probably in honour of a victory in the chariot-race in 452, a victory not of a tyrant, but of a free citizen. Under the above date the List of Olympian victors in the Oxyrhynchus papyrus (ii, 1899, p. 90) places σαμιον καμ [αρινου τεθριππον], where σαμιον is possibly a mistake for Ψαυμιδος. The Ambrosian and the Paris MSS of Pindar (*A* and *C*) state that Psaumis won the chariot race in 452 B.C.

Zeus, the Thunderer, is invoked, Zeus whose daughters, the Seasons, had sent the poet to witness the Olympic games (1-3). Men of worth are gladdened by the prosperity of their friends (4, 5). May Zeus graciously welcome the chorus that celebrates the present triumph of Psaumis, and answer his further prayers (6-13). He is keen in the

40

INTRODUCTION

breeding of horses; and is hospitable and patriotic
(13–16). For mortal men, trial is the true test.
Even so, by trial, Ergînus, the Argonaut, was saved
from the reproach of the Lemnian women, when,
though his hair was grey, he won the race in
armour (17–28).

IV.—ΨΑΥΜΙΔΙ ΚΑΜΑΡΙΝΑΙῼ

ΑΡΜΑΤΙ

στρ.

Ἐλατὴρ ὑπέρτατε βροντᾶς ἀκαμαντόποδος Ζεῦ·
   τεαὶ γὰρ ὧραι
ὑπὸ ποικιλοφόρμιγγος ἀοιδᾶς ἑλισσόμεναί μ’
   ἔπεμψαν
ὑψηλοτάτων μάρτυρ’ ἀέθλων.
ξείνων δ’ εὖ πρασσόντων ἔσαναν αὐτίκ’ ἀγγελίαν
5 ποτὶ γλυκεῖαν ἐσλοί.
   ἀλλ’, ὦ Κρόνου παῖ, ὃς Αἴτναν ἔχεις,   10
   ἷπον ἀνεμόεσσαν ἑκατογκεφάλα Τυφῶνος ὀβρίμου,
   Οὐλυμπιονίκαν δέκευ
   Χαρίτων ἔκατι τόνδε κῶμον,

ἀντ.

10 χρονιώτατον φάος εὐρυσθενέων ἀρετᾶν. Ψαύμιος
   γὰρ ἵκει
ὀχέων, ὅς, ἐλαίᾳ στεφανωθεὶς Πισάτιδι, κῦδος
   ὄρσαι   20
σπεύδει Καμαρίνα. θεὸς εὔφρων
εἴη λοιπαῖς εὐχαῖς· ἐπεί νιν αἰνέω μάλα μὲν
τροφαῖς ἑτοῖμον ἵππων,
15 χαίροντά τε ξενίαις πανδόκοις
   καὶ πρὸς ἀσυχίαν φιλόπολιν καθαρᾷ γνώμᾳ
   τετραμμένον.

7 ὀβρίμου GFCS : ὀμβρίμου *CEV* (BM).
   9 Χαρίτων Triclinius (BM ²GC) ; — θ’ most old mss (FS¹) ;
— δ’ *V* (S³) ; — γ’ *A* (M¹).

42

IV.—FOR PSAUMIS OF CAMARINA

WINNER IN THE CHARIOT RACE, 452 B.C.

O ZEUS most high, whose chariot is the·tireless-footed thundercloud! on thee I call; for it is thine Hours that, in their circling dance to the varied notes of the lyre's minstrelsy, sent me to bear witness to the most exalted of all contests; and, when friends are victorious, forthwith the heart of the noble leapeth up with gladness at the sweet tidings.

But, Son of Cronus, that holdest Etna, that breeze-swept height which lieth heavily on the mighty Typhon! welcome the Olympian victor; welcome, for the Graces' sake, this minstrel band, this long-enduring light of widely potent prowess. 'Tis the minstrel-band that cometh in honour of the chariot of Psaumis,[1] who, crowned with the olive of Pisa, is eager to win high glory for Camarîna. May Heaven be gracious to his further prayers, for I praise one who is right ready in the rearing of coursers, one who rejoiceth in welcoming all his guests, and one who in pure heart devoteth himself to Peace that loveth the State. I shall utter a word untinged

---

[1] ὀχέων, gen. pl. of ὄχος, is also found in *P.* ix 11. It has been proposed to take it as the present participle of ὀχέω, in the intransitive sense of "ride," cp. *O.* vi 48, ἐλαύνων ἵκετο (W. A. Oldfather, in *Classical Review*, 1910, xxiv 82).

οὐ ψεύδεϊ τέγξω λόγον·
διάπειρά τοι βροτῶν ἔλεγχος·   30
ἐπ.
  ἄπερ Κλυμένοιο παῖδα
20 Λαμνιάδων γυναικῶν
  ἔλυσεν ἐξ ἀτιμίας.
  χαλκέοισι δ᾽ ἐν ἔντεσι νικῶν δρόμον
  ἔειπεν Ὑψιπυλείᾳ μετὰ στέφανον ἰών·
  "Οὗτος ἐγὼ ταχυτᾶτι·
25 χεῖρες δὲ καὶ ἦτορ ἴσαν.
  φύονται δὲ καὶ νέοις ἐν ἀνδράσιν   40
  πολιαὶ θαμὰ καὶ παρὰ τὸν ἁλικίας
  ἐοικότα χρόνον."

        27 θαμὰ καὶ most mss (BGFC); θαμάκι A (MS).

with falsehood. "Trial is the true test of mortal men."

This it was that caused the son of Clymenus [1] to cease to be mocked by the women of Lemnos. When, in armour of bronze, he won the foot-race, he spake on this wise to Hypsipylê, as he went to receive the crown : "Such am I in swiftness of foot, with hands and heart to match. Even young men full often find their hair growing grey, even before the fitting time of life."

[1] Ergînus.

OLYMPIAN V

FOR PSAUMIS OF CAMARINA

INTRODUCTION

THE race with the mule-car was introduced at Olympia in 500 B.C., and put down by proclamation in 444. The present Ode was probably composed for a victory won by Psaumis with the mule-car in 448. Such a car is implied by the term ἀπήνας in line 3.

Some suppose that *Ol.* 4 and *Ol.* 5 both refer to the same victory, namely a victory with the mule-car, which was possibly won in 456, four years before the victory with the horse-chariot of 452, recorded in MSS *A* and *C.* On this view, *Ol.* 4 was sung in the festal procession, and *Ol.* 5 at the banquet.

A scholium in the Ambrosian and five other MSS states that *Ol.* 5 was not in the original texts (ἐν τοῖς ἐδαφίοις), but was nevertheless assigned to Pindar in the annotations of the Alexandrian grammarian, Didymus.

The nymph of Camarîna is asked to accept the worship of Psaumis, who has done her honour by his victories (1–6). On his return from Olympia, he celebrates the holy grove of Pallas and the local lake, and the two rivers; and also, by swiftly building a forest of lofty houses, brings his people out of perplexity (9–14).

Toil and cost are involved, while the mere chance of victory is in view, but success makes even fellow-citizens give a victor credit for wisdom (15, 16).

May Zeus Sôtêr of Olympia bless Camarîna, and permit Psaumis to reach a hale old age, while he rejoices in victorious steeds. Let him be content with health, wealth, and renown (17–24).

V.—ΨΑΥΜΙΔΙ ΚΑΜΑΡΙΝΑΙΩ

ΑΠΗΝΗ

στρ. α΄

Ὑψηλᾶν ἀρετᾶν καὶ στεφάνων ἄωτον γλυκὺν
τῶν Οὐλυμπίᾳ, Ὠκεανοῦ θύγατερ, καρδίᾳ
γελανεῖ
ἀκαμαντόποδός τ᾽ ἀπήνας δέκευ Ψαύμιός τε δῶρα·

ἀντ. α΄

ὃς τὰν σὰν πόλιν αὔξων, Καμάρινα, λαοτρόφον
5 βωμοὺς ἓξ διδύμους ἐγέραιρεν ἑορταῖς θεῶν
μεγίσταις   10
ὑπὸ βουθυσίαις ἀέθλων τε πεμπαμέροις ἁμίλλαις,

ἐπ. α΄

ἵπποις ἡμιόνοις τε μοναμπυκίᾳ τε. τὶν δὲ κῦδος
ἁβρόν
νικάσαις ἀνέθηκε, καὶ ὃν πατέρ᾽ Ἄκρων᾽ ἐκάρυξε
καὶ τὰν νέοικον ἕδραν.

στρ. β΄

ἵκων δ᾽ Οἰνομάου καὶ Πέλοπος παρ᾽ εὐηράτων   20
10 σταθμῶν, ὦ πολιάοχε Παλλάς, ἀείδει μὲν ἄλσος
ἁγνὸν
τὸ τεόν, ποταμόν τε Ὤανιν, ἐγχωρίαν τε λίμναν,

ἀντ. β΄

καὶ σεμνοὺς ὀχετούς, Ἵππαρις οἷσιν ἄρδει στρατόν,

5 ἐγέραιρεν A alone (MGF); ἐγέραρεν (BCS); ἐγέραρε C
(γέραρε old mss).
6 πεμπ. Schneidewin (M²CS); πεμπτ. vulgo (BGF); πεντ. M¹.

48

V.—FOR PSAUMIS OF CAMARINA

WINNER IN THE MULE CHARIOT RACE, 448 (?) B.C.

DAUGHTER of Ocean! receive with happy heart
the choicest prize of deeds of prowess and of crowns
Olympian, the guerdon won by Psaumis and his tire-
less-footed team,—Psaumis who, exalting thy city,
Camarîna, that fostereth its people, at the greatest
festivals of the gods essayed to honour the twice six
altars with the slaughter of oxen, and also with
contests of games, lasting for five days, even with
horses and mules, and with the riding of the single
steed.   And, by his victory, he hath set up for thee
a bright renown, and hath caused to be proclaimed
by the herald his father Acron and his newly-
founded home.

Coming from the loved abodes of Oenomaüs and
of Pelops, he singeth of thy holy precinct, O Pallas,
thou guardian of the State, and the river Oânis,
and the lake of the land, and the sacred streams
with which Hipparis watereth the folk ; and he

49

κολλᾷ τε σταδίων θαλάμων ταχέως ὑψίγυιον
   ἄλσος,   30
ἀπ' ἀμαχανίας ἄγων ἐς φάος τόνδε δᾶμον ἀστῶν·
ἐπ. β'.
15 αἰεὶ δ' ἀμφ' ἀρεταῖσι πόνος δαπάνα τε μάρναται
   πρὸς ἔργον
κινδύνῳ κεκαλυμμένον· εὖ δ' ἔχοντες σοφοὶ καὶ
   πολίταις ἔδοξαν ἔμμεν.

στρ. γ'
Σωτὴρ ὑψινεφὲς Ζεῦ, Κρόνιόν τε ναίων λόφον   40
τιμῶν τ' Ἀλφεὸν εὐρὺ ῥέοντ' Ἰδαῖόν τε σεμνὸν
   ἄντρον,
ἱκέτας σέθεν ἔρχομαι Λυδίοις ἀπύων ἐν αὐλοῖς,
ἀντ. γ'
20 αἰτήσων πόλιν εὐανορίαισι τάνδε κλυταῖς
   δαιδάλλειν, σέ τ', Ὀλυμπιόνικε, Ποσειδανίαισιν
   ἵπποις   50
ἐπιτερπόμενον φέρειν γῆρας εὔθυμον ἐς τελευτάν,
ἐπ. γ'
υἱῶν, Ψαῦμι, παρισταμένων. ὑγίεντα δ' εἴ τις
   ὄλβον ἄρδει,
ἐξαρκέων κτεάτεσσι καὶ εὐλογίαν προστιθείς, μὴ
   ματεύσῃ θεὸς γενέσθαι.

16 εὖ δ' Hermann (BMGFC) : εὖ δὲ mss (ἐσλὰ δ' ? S).

swiftly weldeth together [1] a soaring forest of steadfast dwellings, bringing this people of citizens out of perplexity into the light of day.

But evermore, amid deeds of prowess, must toil and cost strive for the mastery with victory in view, veiled though it be in peril; and it is those that are prosperous who are deemed wise, even by their fellow-citizens.

O saviour Zeus, in the clouds on high! thou that dwellest on the hill of Cronus, and honourest the broad stream of Alpheüs, and the hallowed cave of Ida! as thy suppliant am I coming, while I call on thee amid the sound of Lydian flutes, praying thee to adorn this city with famous hosts of noble men, praying, too, that thou, the Olympian victor, mayest reach the end of life in a kindly eld, while rejoicing in the steeds of Poseidon, and with thy sons, O Psaumis, standing beside thee. But, if any one tendeth his wealth in wholesome wise by being bountiful with his possessions and by winning good report, let him not seek to become a god.

[1] The subject is Psaumis, according to Hermann (*Opusc.* viii 100), with whom Bergk agrees; the river Hipparis, according to Libanius, i 361, and the Scholiasts.

OLYMPIAN VI

FOR HAGESIAS OF SYRACUSE

INTRODUCTION

HĂGÊSIAS was a citizen of Syracuse, descended from an Iamid (associated with Archias in founding that city in 734). He was thus a descendant of Iamus, the son of Apollo. He was also a citizen of Stymphâlus in Arcadia. In Sicily he was a partisan of Hieron, and his success at Olympia was viewed with envy in Syracuse (74). The Ode was accordingly sung among the more generous citizens of his Arcadian home (7). It was sent by Pindar from Thebes to Stymphâlus by the hands of Aeneas, who trained the chorus for its performance in Arcadia, prior to the return of Hâgêsias to Syracuse.

The date may be as early as 476 or as late as 472, the earliest and the latest Olympic festivals, held during the rule of Hieron. Pindar's stay in Sicily is now assigned to 476 and 475 B.C., and 472 is consistent with the poet's presence in Thebes. 468 is proposed by Boeckh. " Aetnaean Zeus" in line 96 may imply a reference to the founding of Aetna in 476, and is consistent with either of the above dates.

INTRODUCTION

Our poem must have a splendid portal (1–4). Hâgêsias has many claims to distinction (4–9). There is no glory in achievements involving no risk (9–11). As seer and warrior, the victor resembles Amphiaraüs (12–18). Though the poet is not contentious, he is ready to swear to the truth of his praises of the victor (19–21). The charioteer is bidden to yoke mules to the car of song, that the poet may at once reach the story of the origin of the family (22–27).

The myth of Euadnê (28–34), and the myth of her son, Iamus (35–57). Iamus, when he comes of age, invokes Poseidon and Apollo (57–61), and Apollo summons him to Olympia, and grants the gift of divination to himself and his seed (64–70). The fame and the wealth of the Iamids (71–73).

The victory of Hâgêsias is due to Zeus and his ancestral god, Hermes Enagônius of Arcadia (77–78). Thebes and Arcadia are mythologically connected (82–87). The poet at Thebes addresses his messenger, Aeneas, the trainer of the chorus (87–91), sending a message to Syracuse, and praising Hieron (92–97) who, the poet hopes, will welcome the chorus, when it passes from Stymphâlus to Syracuse, from one of the victor's homes to the other (98–100). Two anchors are safest during a stormy voyage (101). May the citizens of both places be blest (101 f), and may Poseidon grant the victor a safe journey to Syracuse, and also prosper the poet's song.

VI.—ΑΓΗΣΙᾼ ΣΤΡΑΚΟΣΙῼ

ΑΠΗΝΗ

στρ. αʹ

Χρυσέας ὑποστάσαντες εὐτειχεῖ προθύρῳ θαλάμου
κίονας, ὡς ὅτε θαητὸν μέγαρον,
πάξομεν· ἀρχομένου δ᾽ ἔργου πρόσωπον
χρὴ θέμεν τηλαυγές. εἰ δ᾽ εἴη μὲν Ὀλυμπιονίκας,
5 βωμῷ τε μαντείῳ ταμίας Διὸς ἐν Πίσᾳ,
συνοικιστήρ τε τᾶν κλεινᾶν Συρακοσσᾶν· τίνα κεν
φύγοι ὕμνον
κεῖνος ἀνήρ, ἐπικύρσαις ἀφθόνων ἀστῶν ἐν ἱμερ-
ταῖς ἀοιδαῖς;   10

ἀντ. αʹ

ἴστω γὰρ ἐν τούτῳ πεδίλῳ δαιμόνιον πόδ᾽ ἔχων
Σωστράτου υἱός. ἀκίνδυνοι δ᾽ ἀρεταὶ
10 οὔτε παρ᾽ ἀνδράσιν οὔτ᾽ ἐν ναυσὶ κοίλαις
τίμιαι· πολλοὶ δὲ μέμνανται, καλὸν εἴ τι πονᾱθῇ.
Ἀγησία, τὶν δ᾽ αἶνος ἑτοῖμος, ὃν ἐν δίκᾳ
ἀπὸ γλώσσας Ἄδραστος μάντιν Οἰκλείδαν ποτ᾽
ἐς Ἀμφιάρηον   20
φθέγξατ᾽, ἐπεὶ κατὰ γαῖ᾽ αὐτόν τέ νιν καὶ φαιδί-
μας ἵππους ἔμαρψεν.

ἐπ. αʹ

15 ἑπτὰ δ᾽ ἔπειτα πυρᾶν νεκρῶν τελεσθεισᾶν Ταλαϊο-
νίδας

11 πονᾱθῇ most mss (BGF) : πονηθῇ C alone (MCS).
12, 77, 98 Ἀγησία s : Ἀγ. mss.
15 τελεσθεισᾶν Pauw, Hartung, Wilamowitz (s) : τελεσθέντων
mss (BMGFC).

54

VI.—FOR HAGESIAS OF SYRACUSE

WINNER IN THE MULE CHARIOT RACE, 472 (?) B.C.

On golden pillars raising the fair-walled porch of our abode, we shall build, as it were, a splendid hall ; even so, o'er our work's beginning we needs must set a front that shines afar. Now, if any one were a victor at Olympia, and were minister unto the prophetic altar of Zeus in Pisa, and were a fellow-founder of famous Syracuse, what strains of praise would such a man fail to win, by finding fellow-citizens who are ungrudging in delightful song ?

Let the son of Sôstratus [1] know that this sandal fitteth his foot, which is blessed of heaven. But deeds of prowess, apart from peril, win no honour either among men (on land) or on board the hollow ships, whereas if any fair fruit cometh of toil, there are many who remember it.

Even for thee, Hâgêsias, is the praise prepared, which in justice Adrastus of old spake freely forth of the seer Amphiaraüs, when the earth swallowed up that seer and his shining steeds. Nigh unto Thebes, when the seven funeral-pyres had been consumed,[2]

[1] Hâgêsias.
[2] Or (retaining $\tau\epsilon\lambda\epsilon\sigma\theta\acute{\epsilon}\nu\tau\omega\nu$) " when the full tale of the corpses of the seven pyres had been made up " (Gilbert Davies, in *Classical Review*, 1899, xiii 9).

εἶπεν ἐν Θήβαισι τοιοῦτόν τι ἔπος· "Ποθέω
στρατιᾶς ὀφθαλμὸν ἐμᾶς,
ἀμφότερον μάντιν τ' ἀγαθὸν καὶ δουρὶ μάρνασθαι."
τὸ καὶ
ἀνδρὶ κώμου δεσπότᾳ πάρεστι Συρακοσίῳ.　　30
οὔτε δύσηρις ἐὼν οὔτ' ὢν φιλόνικος ἄγαν,
20　καὶ μέγαν ὅρκον ὀμόσσαις τοῦτό γέ οἱ σαφέως
μαρτυρήσω· μελίφθογγοι δ' ἐπιτρέψοντι Μοῖσαι.

στρ. β'

Ὦ Φίντις, ἀλλὰ ζεῦξον ἤδη μοι σθένος ἡμιόνων,
ᾇ τάχος, ὄφρα κελεύθῳ τ' ἐν καθαρᾷ
βάσομεν ὄκχον, ἵκωμαί τε πρὸς ἀνδρῶν　　40
25　καὶ γένος· κεῖναι γὰρ ἐξ ἀλλᾶν ὁδὸν ἁγεμονεῦσαι
ταύταν ἐπίστανται, στεφάνους ἐν Ὀλυμπίᾳ
ἐπεὶ δέξαντο· χρὴ τοίνυν πύλας ὕμνων ἀναπιτνα-
μεν αὐταῖς·
πρός Πιτάναν δὲ παρ' Εὐρώτα πόρον δεῖ σάμερον
μ' ἐλθεῖν ἐν ὥρᾳ·

ἀντ. β'

ἅ τοι Ποσειδάωνι μιχθεῖσα Κρονίῳ λέγεται
30　παῖδα ἰόπλοκον Εὐάδναν τεκέμεν.　　50
κρύψε δὲ παρθενίαν ὠδῖνα κόλποις·
κυρίῳ δ' ἐν μηνὶ πέμποισ' ἀμφιπόλους ἐκέλευσεν
ἥρωι πορσαίνειν δόμεν Εἰλατίδᾳ βρέφος,
ὃς ἀνδρῶν Ἀρκάδων ἄνασσε Φαισάνᾳ λάχε τ'
Ἀλφεὸν οἰκεῖν·
35　ἔνθα τραφεῖσ' ὑπ' Ἀπόλλωνι γλυκείας πρῶτον
ἔψαυσ' Ἀφροδίτας.

19 φιλόνικος Bergk (s) : φιλόνεικος mss (BMGFC).

30 παῖδα Ϝιόπλοκον Bergk (MGCS), cp. I vii 23 : παῖδ'
ἰοπλόκαμον old mss ; παῖδ' ἰοβόστρυχον Byzantine mss (BF).

the son of Talaüs spake on this wise, " I have lost
the eye of my host,—one who was at once matchless
as a prophet, and as a warrior with the spear." And
this holdeth good no less of the man of Syracuse,
who is lord of this triumphant band. Though
neither prone to quarrel, no, nor over-fond of victory,
I would even swear a mighty oath, and herein at
least will I clearly bear witness for him ; and the
honey-toned Muses will grant me their consent.

But now it is high time, O Phintis, for thee to
yoke me the sturdy mules with all good speed, that
so we may mount the car in the clear and open path
of song, and that I may at last arrive at the theme
of the descent of our heroes ; for here those mules,
above all others, know how to lead the way, since
they have won crowns of victory at Olympia.

Therefore is it meet for us to ope for them the
portals of song, and on this very day, must we be-
times reach the presence of Pĭtănê, beside the ford
of Eurôtas,—the presence of that nymph, who, wedded
with Poseidon, son of Cronus, is said to have borne
Euadnê of the violet tresses. But she, with the
folds of her robe, concealed the fruit of her unwedded
love ; and, in the appointed month, she sent
messengers and bade them give the babe to the son
of Eilatus for him to tend it, even to Aepytus, who
ruled over the Arcadians at Phaesânê, and had his
allotted home on the Alpheüs, where it was that she
had first tasted the sweets of love in the arms of
Apollo ; and she did not escape the ken of

PINDAR

ἐπ. β΄

    οὐδ᾽ ἔλαθ᾽ Αἴπυτον ἐν παντὶ χρόνῳ κλέπτοισα
      θεοῖο γόνον·   60

    ἀλλ᾽ ὁ μὲν Πυθῶναδ᾽, ἐν θυμῷ πιέσαις χόλον οὐ
      φατὸν ὀξείᾳ μελέτᾳ,

    ᾤχετ᾽ ἰὼν μαντευσόμενος ταύτας περ᾽ ἀτλάτου
      πάθας.

    ἁ δὲ φοινικόκροκον ζώναν καταθηκαμένα

40 κάλπιδά τ᾽ ἀργυρέαν, λόχμας ὑπὸ κυανέας

    τίκτε θεόφρονα κοῦρον. τᾷ μὲν ὁ Χρυσοκόμας   70
    πραΰμητίν τ᾽ Ἐλείθυιαν παρέστασέν τε Μοίρας·

στρ. γ΄

    ἦλθεν δ᾽ ὑπὸ σπλάγχνων ὑπ᾽ ὠδῖνός τ᾽ ἐρατᾶς
      Ἴαμος

    ἐς φάος αὐτίκα. τὸν μὲν κνιζομένα

45 λεῖπε χαμαί· δύο δὲ γλαυκῶπες αὐτὸν

    δαιμόνων βουλαῖσιν ἐθρέψαντο δράκοντες ἀμεμφεῖ

    ἰῷ μελισσᾶν καδόμενοι. βασιλεὺς δ᾽ ἐπεὶ   80
    πετραέσσας ἐλαύνων ἵκετ᾽ ἐκ Πυθῶνος, ἅπαντας
      ἐν οἴκῳ

    εἴρετο παῖδα, τὸν Εὐάδνα τέκοι· Φοίβου γὰρ
      αὐτὸν φᾶ γεγάκειν

ἀντ. γ΄

50 πατρός, περὶ θνατῶν δ᾽ ἔσεσθαι μάντιν ἐπιχθονίοις
    ἔξοχον, οὐδέ ποτ᾽ ἐκλείψειν γενεάν.

    ὣς ἄρα μάννε. τοὶ δ᾽ οὔτ᾽ ὢν ἀκοῦσαι
    οὔτ᾽ ἰδεῖν εὔχοντο πεμπταῖον γεγενημένον. ἀλλ᾽ ἐν
    κέκρυπτο γὰρ σχοίνῳ βατιᾷ τ᾽ ἐν ἀπειράτῳ,   90

---

42 Ἐλείθυιαν παρέστασέν (MGFCS): Ἐλευθὼ συμπ. Byzantine
mss (B).

54 βατιᾷ Wilamowitz (S); βατείᾳ old mss (MGC); βατίᾳ (BF).
    ἀπειράτῳ (BMGFC), ἀπερά(ν)τῳ old mss; ἀπειρίτῳ Heyne,
W. Schulze (S).

58

Aepytus, while essaying to conceal her being with child by the god; but anon, he went to Delphi, with keen resolve quelling in his heart his wrath unutterable, to inquire of the oracle concerning this dire disaster. Meanwhile, she laid down her crimson zone and her silver pitcher, and 'neath the blue brake was about to bear a boy inspired of heaven; and the Lord of the golden hair sent to her aid the gentle goddess of birth, and the Fates; and from her womb, and amid sweet sorrow, forthwith came Iamus to the light of day. And she, though sore distressed, was fain to leave him there upon the ground; but, by the will of the gods, two grey-eyed serpents tended the babe with the bane, the harmless bane, of the honey-bees. Now, when the king had driven back from rocky Pytho, he inquired of all in the house, touching the child born to Euadnê; for he said that the babe was begotton of Phoebus, and was destined to be, for men on earth, a prophet far beyond all mortals, and his race would never fail.

Such then was his rede; but they averred that they had neither heard nor seen the babe, though it had been born five days before: and no marvel; for it had been hidden amid the rushes and in the

PINDAR

55 ἴων ξανθαῖσι καὶ παμπορφύροις ἀκτῖσι βεβρεγ
μένος ἁβρὸν
σῶμα· τὸ καὶ κατεφάμιξεν καλεῖσθαί νιν χρονῳ
σύμπαντι μάτηρ

ἐπ. γ΄
τοῦτ᾿ ὄνυμ᾿ ἀθάνατον. τερπνᾶς δ᾿ ἐπεὶ χρυσοστε
φάνοιο λάβεν
καρπὸν Ἥβας, Ἀλφεῷ μέσσῳ καταβὰς ἐκάλεσσε
Ποσειδᾶν᾿ εὐρυβίαν,
ὃν πρόγονον, καὶ τοξοφόρον Δάλου θεοδμάτας
σκοπόν,   100

60 αἰτέων λαοτρόφον τιμάν τιν᾿ ἑᾷ κεφαλᾷ,
νυκτὸς ὑπαίθριος. ἀντεφθέγξατο δ᾿ ἀρτιεπὴς
πατρία ὄσσα, μετάλλασέν τέ νιν· " Ὄρσο, τέκος,
δεῦρο πάγκοινον ἐς χώραν ἴμεν φάμας ὄπισθεν."

στρ. δ΄
ἴκοντο δ᾿ ὑψηλοῖο πέτραν ἀλίβατον Κρονίου·   110
65 ἔνθα οἱ ὤπασε θησαυρὸν δίδυμον
μαντοσύνας, τόκα μὲν φωνὰν ἀκούειν
ψευδέων ἄγνωστον, εὖτ᾿ ἂν δὲ θρασυμάχανος
ἐλθὼν
Ἡρακλέης, σεμνὸν θάλος Ἀλκαϊδᾶν, πατρὶ
ἑορτάν τε κτίσῃ πλειστόμβροτον τεθμόν τε μέ
γιστον ἀέθλων,
70 Ζηνὸς ἐπ᾿ ἀκροτάτῳ βωμῷ τότ᾿ αὖ χρηστήριον
θέσθαι κέλευσεν.

ἀντ. δ΄
ἐξ οὗ πολύκλειτον καθ᾿ Ἕλλανας γένος Ἰα
μιδᾶν.   120

62 τέκος in lemma of scholium of B (MGFS): τέκνον mss (BC).
67 ἄγνωστον CNO and Vatican mss (BGF and Bergk):
ἄγνωτον AM (MCS). Cp. I iv 30.

boundless brake, with its dainty form steeped in
the golden and the deep-purple light of pansies[1];
therefore it was that his mother declared that he
should be called for all time by the undying name
of Iamus.[2]

But, when he had attained the ripe bloom of Hêbê
of the golden crown, he stepped down into the
midst of the Alpheüs, and there invoked his grand-
sire Poseidon that ruleth afar, and the Archer that
watcheth over heaven-built Delos, praying that his
head might be crowned with honour, and with the
care of the people. There, in the night, he stood
beneath the open sky; and in accents clear his
father's voice replied to him, and sought him out:—
" Arise, my son, and follow thou my voice, and
hither come to a haunt that welcometh all ! " And so
they went to the steep rock of the lofty hill of Cronus,
where the god gave him a double boon of prophecy,
there and then to hear a voice that knoweth no
falsehood ; and, whensoever Heracles bold in might,
that honoured scion of the Alcîdae, came and
founded for his father's fame a festival frequented
of mortals, and the highest ordinance of games of
prowess, then did he command him to establish an
oracle on the crest of the altar of Zeus.

From that time forward, the race of the sons of
Iamus hath been famous throughout Hellas. Pros-

[1] The gold and purple of the context imply that the *viola
tricolor*, or pansy, is meant. The purple iris has been
suggested, but the Greeks had a separate name for that
plant, namely Ἶρις.

[2] Lit " this undying name," meaning Iamus, which was
assumed to be derived from the ἴα, or " pansies," among which
the babe was found.

PINDAR

ὄλβος ἅμ' ἕσπετο· τιμῶντες δ' ἀρετὰς
ἐς φανερὰν ὁδὸν ἔρχονται. τεκμαίρει
χρῆμ' ἕκαστον· μῶμος ἐξ ἄλλων κρέμαται φθο-
    νεόντων

75 τοῖς, οἷς ποτε πρώτοις περὶ δωδέκατον δρόμον
ἐλαυνόντεσσιν αἰδοία ποτιστάξῃ Χάρις εὐκλέα
    μορφάν.
εἰ δ' ἐτύμως ὑπὸ Κυλλάνας ὅροις, Ἀγησία,
    μάτρωες ἄνδρες   130
ἐπ. δ'

ναιετάοντες ἐδώρησαν θεῶν κάρυκα λιταῖς θυσίαις
πολλὰ δὴ πολλαῖσιν Ἑρμᾶν εὐσεβέως, ὃς ἀγῶνας
    ἔχει μοῖράν τ' ἀέθλων
80 Ἀρκαδίαν τ' εὐάνορα τιμᾷ· κεῖνος, ὦ παῖ
    Σωστράτου,
σὺν βαρυγδούπῳ πατρὶ κραίνει σέθεν εὐτυχίαν.
δόξαν ἔχω τιν' ἐπὶ γλώσσᾳ ἀκόνας λιγυρᾶς,   140
ἅ μ' ἐθέλοντα προσέρπει καλλιρόοισι πνοαῖς·
ματρομάτωρ ἐμὰ Στυμφαλίς, εὐανθὴς Μετώπα,
στρ. ε'

85 πλάξιππον ἃ Θήβαν ἔτικτεν, τᾶς ἐρατεινὸν ὕδωρ
πίομαι, ἀνδράσιν αἰχματαῖσι πλέκων
ποικίλον ὕμνον. ὄτρυνον νῦν ἑταίρους,
Αἰνέα, πρῶτον μὲν Ἥραν Παρθενίαν κελα-
    δῆσαι,   150

74 ἐξ (BMGCS); δ' ἐξ mss ; ἐκ δ' Erasmus Schmid (Donald-
son, F).
76 ποτιστάξῃ, twice in lemma of scholium in D, Bergk
(GCS) : —στάξει ABE (BMF).
77 ὅροις ABCE (BMFS) : ὕροις D, Moschopulus, Triclinius ;
ὕρους (CG), ὀρέων? S.
83 προσέρπει ABCE (BMGFS), —ἔρποι D : —ἕλκει para-
phrase 1, Donaldson (C).

62

perity followed in their train, and, by prizing deeds of
prowess, they pass along a road that is seen of all.
This is proved by all their acts. The cavil of others
that are envious hangeth over all,[1] whoever reach the
goal as victors in the race, as they round the twelfth
lap, while an adorable grace sheddeth over them a
noble beauty.

But if, in very deed, the men of thy mother's line,
Hâgêsias, who dwell beneath the bounds of Cyllênê,
full oft in piety presented sacrifices of supplication to
Hermes, herald of the gods, who ruleth over the
games and the duly ordered contests, and honoureth
the brave men of Arcadia ; he it is, O son of
Sôstratus, who with his father, the Lord of the loud
thunder, fulfilleth thy happy fortune.

Methinks I have upon my tongue a whetstone
shrill, that stealeth over me, nothing loth, with fair
streams of inspiration. A nymph of Stymphâlus
was my mother's mother, even the blooming Metôpê,
who bore Thêbê that driveth the steed, Thêbê,
whose sweet water I quaff, while I weave the varied
strains of song in honour of heroic spearmen.

Now bid thy comrades, Aenĕas, first to sound the
praises of Hêra, as the maiden goddess, and, next,

---

[1] W. G. Headlam preferred the rendering, "Cavil of the
envious hangs *beyond all others* over those," comparing line 25,
κεῖναι γὰρ ἐξ ἀλλᾶν κ.τ.λ. (*Journal of Philology*, xxx 297).

PINDAR

γνῶναί τ' ἔπειτ', ἀρχαῖον ὄνειδος ἀλαθέσιν
90 λόγοις εἰ φεύγομεν, Βοιωτίαν ὗν. ἐσσὶ γὰρ
  ἄγγελος ὀρθός,
  ἠΰκόμων σκυτάλα Μοισᾶν, γλυκὺς κρατὴρ ἀγα-
    φθέγκτων ἀοιδᾶν·

ἀντ. ε'

  εἶπον δὲ μεμνᾶσθαι Συρακοσσᾶν τε καὶ Ὀρτυγίας·
  τὰν Ἱέρων καθαρῷ σκάπτῳ διέπων,
  ἄρτια μηδόμενος, φοινικόπεζαν
95 ἀμφέπει Δάματρα, λευκίππου τε θυγατρὸς ἑορ-
    τάν,   160
  καὶ Ζηνὸς Αἰτναίου κράτος. ἀδύλογοι δέ νιν
  λύραι μολπαί τε γιγνώσκοντι. μὴ θράσσοι χρόνος
    ὄλβον ἐφέρπων.
  σὺν δὲ φιλοφροσύναις εὐηράτοις Ἀγησία δέξαιτο
    κῶμον

ἐπ. ε'

  οἴκοθεν οἴκαδ' ἀπὸ Στυμφαλίων τειχέων ποτινισ-
    σόμενον,
100 ματέρ' εὐμήλοιο λείποντ' Ἀρκαδίας. ἀγαθαὶ δὲ
    πέλοντ' ἐν χειμερίᾳ   170

97 θράσσοι Boeckh, Schneidewin (GCS) ; θραύσοι mss (M).
θραύσαι Hermann, Donaldson (F).
100 λείποντ' Byzantine mss (BMGYC) : λιποντ' old mss and
paraphrase (S).

64

to know whether in very truth we have escaped the
old reproach that telleth of "Boeotian swine."[1] For
thou art a faithful messenger, a very scroll-wand of
the fair-haired Muses, a sweet wassail-bowl of loudly-
sounding songs.[2]

Bid them remember Syracuse and Ortygia, which
Hieron ruleth with his unsullied sceptre, and with
befitting counsel, while he tendeth, not only the
worship of Dêmêtêr with the ruddy feet, and the
festival of her daughter with her white horses,[3] but
also the might of Zeus, the lord of Aetna.[4] Hieron
is a familiar theme to the sweetly sounding lyres and
to the strains of minstrelsy. Heaven grant that his
prosperity may not be impaired by any lapse of time :
but may he with kindly acts of courtesy welcome the
triumph-band of Hâgêsias, when it cometh from one
home to another, even from the walls of Stym-
phâlus, when it hath left the mother-city of that
land of flocks, Arcadia. In the stormy night it is

[1] The Scholiast quotes Pindar as saying in one of his
dithyrambs, "there was a time when they called the Boeotian
nation swine," Frag. 83 (51). Plutarch, *de esu carnium*, i 6,
says, "the men of Attica were in the habit of terming us
Boeotians dense and stupid and witless, mainly owing to
our enormous appetites ; they it was also who named us
pigs." Cp. W. Rhys Roberts, *The Ancient Boeotians*,
pp. 1-5.
[2] That is, "Around thee are enfolded the scrolls of the
fair-haired Muses ; in thee are blended the varied strains of
loudly-sounding songs." [3] Persephonê.
[4] The city founded by Hieron on the site of Catanê in 476.
Hieron is described as an "Aetnaean" in the superscription
of the first Pythian, and his minister, Chromius, in that
of the first Nemean, where "Zeus of Aetna" is mentioned in
line 6. Hieron was buried there in 467 (Cp. Freeman's
Sicily, ii 243 f, 302).

νυκτὶ θοᾶς ἐκ ναὸς ἀπεσκίμφθαι δύ' ἄγκυραι.
θεὸς
τῶν τε κείνων τε κλυτὰν αἶσαν παρέχοι φιλέων.
δέσποτα ποντόμεδων, εὐθὺν δὲ πλόον καμάτων
ἐκτὸς ἐόντα δίδοι, χρυσαλακάτοιο πόσις
105 Ἀμφιτρίτας, ἐμῶν δ' ὕμνων ἄεξ' εὐτερπὲς ἄνθος.

102 τῶν τε κείνων Heyne (B¹s) : τῶνδε κείνων (B²MGFC) ;
τῶνδ' ἐκείνων most mss, τῶν δ' ἐκ. A, τῶν τ' ἐκ. one ms.

103 ποντόμεδον mss (BMGFC) : —μέδων Boeckh in critical
notes (s).

well that anchors twain be let down from out the swift ship.

May God in his love grant that the fortunes of these and of those alike [1] may be famous. But do thou, O Master that rulest the main, thou Lord of Amphitrîtê with the golden distaff, grant a straight course without trouble o'er the sea, and give new growth to the gladsome flower of my songs.

[1] Stymphalians and Syracusans.

OLYMPIAN VII

FOR DIAGORAS OF RHODES

INTRODUCTION

THE island of Rhodes was regarded in Greek legend as deriving its name from a daughter of Aphrodîtê, who became the bride of the Sun. The Sun-god had been absent when the other gods had divided the earth among them, but he had seen an island rising from the depths of the sea, and was permitted to have this island as his special boon (54–76). The sons of Hêlios were afterwards bidden to raise an altar on a height, and there to sacrifice to Zeus and Athêna, but they had forgotten to bring fire, and thus the sacrifices which they offered were flameless; but the gods forgave them, and Zeus gave them gold, and Athêna skill in handicraft (39–53). Further, one of the sons of Heracles, who had slain the brother of Alcmêna, was sent by Apollo to Rhodes, where he became the founder of the Greek colony (27–34).

The Heracleidae occupied the three Rhodian cities of Lindus, Ialŷsus, and Cameirus. Ialŷsus in particular was settled by the Eratidae, and to this family belonged Diagoras. His father was probably the *prytanis* of Ialŷsus. Diagoras himself had been successful, not only in the local contests, but also in all the great games of Greece. At his first Pythian victory he had apparently been guilty of some inadvertent transgression ; possibly he had accidentally killed his opponent (cp. 10, 17, 24–30). He had now attained the crowning distinction of the prize

for the boxing-match at Olympia in 464 B.C. He
was the most famous of Greek boxers. His three
sons, and the two sons of his daughters, were also
distinguished at Olympia, where a statue was set up
in honour of Diagoras and his sons and grandsons
(Pausanias, vi 7, 1).

The ode is compared to a loving-cup (1–10), pre-
sented to the bridegroom by the father of the bride.
Even as the cup is the pledge of loving wedlock,
so is the poet's song an earnest of abiding fame, but
Charis, the gracious goddess of the epinician ode,
looks with favour, now on one, now on another
(10–12). The poet has come to Rhodes, to celebrate
the victor and his father (13–19).

The myth of Tlêpolemus, the Dorian founder of
Ialŷsus (20–53), and the myth of the gift of the
island of Rhodes to the Sun-god, one of whose sons
was the father of the three heroes, who gave their
names to Lindus, Ialŷsus, and Cameirus (54–76).

Tlêpolemus is commemorated by athletic games in
Rhodes, in which Diagoras has been victorious, as
elsewhere (77–87). Zeus is besought to grant his
blessing to the ode and to the victor (87–93). When
that victor's clan is prosperous, the State rejoices,
but Fortune is apt to be fickle (93–95).

According to one of the Scholiasts, Gorgon (the
historian of Rhodes) states that a copy of this ode,
in letters of gold, was preserved in the temple of
Athêna at Lindus. It has been suggested that,
possibly, the ode was transcribed in gold ink on a
scroll of parchment (Ch. Graux in *Revue de Philo-
logie*, April, 1881, and *Notices Bibliographiques*, 1884,
pp. 302–7).

VII.—ΔΙΑΓΟΡᾼ ΡΟΔΙῼ

ΠΥΚΤῌ

στρ. α΄

Φιάλαν ὡς εἴ τις ἀφνειᾶς ἀπὸ χειρὸς ἑλὼν
ἔνδον ἀμπέλου καχλάζοισαν δρόσῳ
δωρήσεται
νεανίᾳ γαμβρῷ προπίνων οἴκοθεν οἴκαδε, πάγ-
χρυσον κορυφὰν κτεάνων,
5 συμποσίου τε χάριν κᾶδός τε τιμάσαις ἑόν, ἐν δὲ
φίλων
παρεόντων θῆκέ νιν ζαλωτὸν ὁμόφρονος εὐνᾶς· 10

ἀντ. α΄

καὶ ἐγὼ νέκταρ χυτόν, Μοισᾶν δόσιν, ἀεθλοφόροις
ἀνδράσιν πέμπων, γλυκὺν καρπὸν φρενός,
ἱλάσκομαι,
10 Οὐλυμπίᾳ Πυθοῖ τε νικώντεσσιν· ὁ δ᾽ ὄλβιος, ὃν
φᾶμαι κατέχοντ᾽ ἀγαθαί.
ἄλλοτε δ᾽ ἄλλον ἐποπτεύει Χάρις ζωθάλμιος ἁδυ-
μελεῖ
20
θαμὰ μὲν φόρμιγγι παμφώνοισί τ᾽ ἐν ἔντεσιν
αὐλῶν.

ἐπ. α΄

καί νυν ὑπ᾽ ἀμφοτέρων σὺν Διαγόρᾳ κατέβαν
τὰν ποντίαν
ὑμνέων παῖδ᾽ Ἀφροδίτας Ἀελίοιό τε νύμφαν,
Ῥόδον,

1 ἀφνειᾶς most mss (BGFC): ἀφνεᾶς A and Athenaeus 504a
(MS).

70

VII.—FOR DIAGORAS OF RHODES

WINNER IN THE BOXING-MATCH, 464 B.C.

Even as when one taketh up in his wealthy hand
a golden bowl, the prime of his possessions, a bowl
that foameth with the dew of the vine, and giveth
it to the youth, whom, when betrothed unto his
daughter, with a friendly draught he welcometh from
one home to another, for the sake of them that sit
at meat with him, and in honour of his new alliance;
and thereby, in the presence of his friends, maketh
him envied for this union of true love.   Even so,
while I am sending to the men who win the prize
my liquid nectar, the Muses' gift, the sweet fruit of
my fancy, I pay homage to them, as victors at
Olympia and at Pytho.   Blessed is he who is ever
encompassed by good report; but the Grace that
giveth life its bloom looketh with favour, now on
one, now on another, not only with the sweetly-
sounding lyre, but also amid the varied notes of the
flute.[1]

And now, to the music of flute and lyre alike, have
I come to land, while singing of the daughter of the
sea, the child of Aphrodîtê, the bride of the Sun,
even Rhodes; that so I may honour, for his fairness

---

[1] The Greek "flute" (which had a mouth-piece like our
clarionet) consisted of two connected tubes.   It is probably
with reference to these two tubes that, here and in eight
other passages, Pindar prefers the plural, αὐλῶν, to the
singular, which he uses only twice.

15 εὐθυμάχαν ὄφρα πελώριον ἄνδρα παρ᾽ Ἀλφεῷ
    στεφανωσάμενον
  αἰνέσω πυγμᾶς ἄποινα   30
  καὶ παρὰ Κασταλίᾳ, πατέρα τε Δαμάγητον
    ἁδόντα Δίκᾳ,
  Ἀσίας εὐρυχόρου τρίπολιν νᾶσον πέλας
  ἐμβόλῳ ναίοντας Ἀργείᾳ σὺν αἰχμᾷ.
στρ. β᾽
20 ἐθελήσω τοῖσιν ἐξ ἀρχᾶς ἀπὸ Τλαπολέμου
  ξυνὸν ἀγγέλλων διορθῶσαι λόγον,
    Ἡρακλέος
  εὐρυσθενεῖ γέννᾳ. τὸ μὲν γὰρ πατρόθεν ἐκ Διὸς
    εὔχονται· τὸ δ᾽ Ἀμυντορίδαι   40
  ματρόθεν Ἀστυδαμείας. ἀμφὶ δ᾽ ἀνθρώπων φρασὶν
    ἀμπλακίαι
25 ἀναρίθμητοι κρέμανται· τοῦτο δ᾽ ἀμάχανον εὑρεῖν,
ἀντ. β᾽
  ὅ τι νῦν ἐν καὶ τελευτᾷ φέρτατον ἀνδρὶ τυχεῖν.
  καὶ γὰρ Ἀλκμήνας κασίγνητον νόθον   50
    σκάπτῳ θένων
  σκληρᾶς ἐλαίας ἔκταν᾽ ἐν Τίρυνθι Λικύμνιον
    ἐλθόντ᾽ ἐκ θαλάμων Μιδέας
30 τᾶσδέ ποτε χθονὸς οἰκιστὴρ χολωθείς. αἱ δὲ
    φρενῶν ταραχαὶ
  παρέπλαγξαν καὶ σοφόν. μαντεύσατο δ᾽ ἐς θεὸν
    ἐλθών.
ἐπ. β᾽
  τῷ μὲν ὁ Χρυσοκόμας εὐώδεος ἐξ ἀδύτου ναῶν
    πλόον
  εἶπε Λερναίας ἀπ᾽ ἀκτᾶς εὐθὺν ἐς ἀμφιθάλασσον
    νομόν,   60

in fight and his skill in boxing, that giant form which won the crown beside the Alpheüs and the stream of Castalia, and also his father Dâmâgêtus, in that he was well-pleasing unto Justice, while both of them are dwelling amid Argive spearmen in the isle of cities three, near the foreland of Asia.

Full fain shall I be to proclaim my message, and duly to tell my tale that toucheth all the common stock descended of old from Tlêpolemus, even the widely powerful race of Heracles. For, on the father's side, they boast descent from Zeus, while, on the mother's, they are sprung from Amyntor, through Astydameia, his daughter.[1] But countless are the snares that hang around the minds of men, and there is no means of finding what is best for a man to light on, not only now, but also in the end. For, on a day in Tiryns, Tlêpolemus, the founder of this land, struck with his staff of hard-grained olive-wood Licymnius, the bastard brother of Alcmênê, on his coming forth from the chamber of (his mother) Midea. Tumult of mind hath ere now caused even the wise man to go astray. Therefore Tlêpolemus went to the god of Delphi and asked of the oracle.

Then the Lord of the golden hair spake from the fragrant shrine of his temple, and bade him sail with his ships, straight from the shore of Lerna to the sea-washed pasture-land, where, in olden time, the great

[1] The genealogy is as follows :—

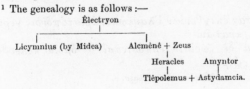

73

PINDAR

ἔνθα ποτὲ βρέχε θεῶν βασιλεὺς ὁ μέγας χρυσέαις
    νιφάδεσσι πόλιν,
35 ἁνίχ' Ἀφαίστου τέχναισιν
χαλκελάτῳ πελέκει πατέρος Ἀθαναία κορυφὰν
    κατ' ἄκραν
ἀνορούσαισ' ἀλάλαξεν ὑπερμάκει βοᾷ·
Οὐρανὸς δ' ἔφριξέ νιν καὶ Γαῖα μάτηρ.   70
στρ. γ΄
    τότε καὶ φαυσίμβροτος δαίμων Ὑπεριονίδας
40 μέλλον ἔντειλεν φυλάξασθαι χρέος
    παισὶν φίλοις,
ὡς ἂν θεᾷ πρῶτοι κτίσαιεν βωμὸν ἐναργέα, καὶ
    σεμνὰν θυσίαν θέμενοι
πατρί τε θυμὸν ἰάναιεν κόρᾳ τ' ἐγχειβρόμῳ. ἐν δ'
    ἀρετὰν
ἔβαλεν καὶ χάρματ' ἀνθρώποισι Προμαθέος
    Αἰδώς·   80
ἀντ. γ΄
45 ἐπὶ μὰν βαίνει τε καὶ λάθας ἀτέκμαρτα νέφος,
καὶ παρέλκει πραγμάτων ὀρθὰν ὁδὸν
    ἔξω φρενῶν.
καὶ τοὶ γὰρ αἰθοίσας ἔχοντες σπέρμ' ἀνέβαν
    φλογὸς οὔ· τεῦξαν δ' ἀπύροις ἱεροῖς
ἄλσος ἐν ἀκροπόλει· κείνοις ὁ μὲν ξανθὰν ἀγαγὼν
    νεφέλαν   90
50 πολὺν ὗσε χρυσόν· αὐτὰ δέ σφισιν ὤπασε τέχναν
ἐπ. γ΄
    πᾶσαν ἐπιχθονίων Γλαυκῶπις ἀριστοπόνοις χερσὶ
    κρατεῖν.
ἔργα δὲ ζωοῖσιν ἑρπόντεσσί θ' ὁμοῖα κέλευθοι
    φέρον·

39 φαυσ. mss: φαεσ. s.

74

King of the gods shed on a city a snow-shower of gold, what time, by the cunning craft of Hephaestus, at the stroke of the brazen hatchet, Athênê leapt forth from the crest of her father's head, and cried aloud with a mighty shout, while Heaven and Mother Earth trembled before her.

Then it was that the god that bringeth light unto men, even Hyperîon, enjoined his dear children to give heed to the rite that was soon to be due, how that they should be the first to build for the goddess an altar in sight of all men, and, by founding a holy sacrifice, gladden the heart of the Father,[1] and of the Daughter with the sounding spear.[2] Now it is Reverence, daughter of Forethought, that implanteth in men high merit and its attendant joys. Howbeit, a strange cloud of forgetfulness draweth near them in baffling wise, and causeth the path of duty to vanish from the mind. For, when they climbed to the height, the seed of blazing fire had been forgotten; and thus it was with fireless sacrifices that, on the citadel, they laid out the sacred precinct. He[1] caused a yellow cloud to draw nigh to them and rained on them abundant gold, while the grey-eyed goddess herself[2] bestowed upon them every art, so that they surpassed all mortal men by their deftness of hand, and along the roads rose works of art like unto beings that lived

[1] Zeus.   [2] Athênê.

PINDAR

ἦν δὲ κλέος βαθύ. δαέντι δὲ καὶ σοφία μείζων
    ἄδολος τελέθει.
φαντὶ δ' ἀνθρώπων παλαιαὶ   100
55 ῥήσιες, οὔπω, ὅτε χθόνα δατέοντο Ζεύς τε καὶ
    ἀθάνατοι,
φανερὰν ἐν πελάγει Ῥόδον ἔμμεν ποντίῳ,
ἁλμυροῖς δ' ἐν βένθεσιν νᾶσον κεκρύφθαι.

στρ. δ'
ἀπεόντος δ' οὔτις ἔνδειξεν λάχος Ἀελίου·
καί ῥά μιν χώρας ἀκλάρωτον λίπον,
60 ἁγνὸν θεόν.
μνασθέντι δὲ Ζεὺς ἄμπαλον μέλλεν θέμεν. ἀλλά
    νιν οὐκ εἴασεν· ἐπεὶ πολιᾶς   110
εἶπέ τιν' αὐτὸς ὁρᾶν ἔνδον θαλάσσας αὐξομέναν
    πεδόθεν
πολύβοσκον γαῖαν ἀνθρώποισι καὶ εὔφρονα
    μήλοις.

ἀντ. δ'
ἐκέλευσεν δ' αὐτίκα χρυσάμπυκα μὲν Λάχεσιν
65 χεῖρας ἀντεῖναι, θεῶν δ' ὅρκον μέγαν   120
    μὴ παρφάμεν,
ἀλλὰ Κρόνου σὺν παιδὶ νεῦσαι, φαεννὸν ἐς αἰθέρα
    νιν πεμφθεῖσαν ἑᾷ κεφαλᾷ
ἐξοπίσω γέρας ἔσσεσθαι. τελεύταθεν δὲ λόγων
    κορυφαὶ
ἐν ἀλαθείᾳ πετοῖσαι. βλάστε μὲν ἐξ ἁλὸς ὑγρᾶς

ἐπ. δ'
70 νᾶσος, ἔχει τέ νιν ὀξειᾶν ὁ γενέθλιος ἀκτίνων
    πατήρ,

61 ἄμπαλον all good mss (MGFS) : ἂμ πάλον Boeckh (C).
68 τελεύταθεν B (γράφεται) and scholium (MGFCS) : τελεύτα-
σαν mss (B).

76

and moved; and great was their fame. Yet, to the wise man, even surpassing art is no magic power.[1]

But the tale is told in ancient story that, when Zeus and the immortals were dividing the earth among them, the isle of Rhodes was not yet to be seen in the open main, but was hidden in the briny depths of the sea; and that, as the Sun-god was absent, no one put forth a lot on his behalf, and so they left him without any allotment of land, though the god himself was pure from blame. But when that god made mention of it, Zeus was about to order a new casting of the lot, but the Sun-god would not suffer it. For, as he said, he could see a plot of land rising from the bottom of the foaming main, a plot that was destined to prove rich in substance for men, and kindly for pasture; and he urged that Lachesis of the golden snood should forthwith lift up her hands and take, not in vain, the great oath of the gods, but consent with the Son of Cronus, that that island, when it had risen forth into the light of day, should for ever after be a boon granted to himself alone. And all these several words were fulfilled and fell out truly. From the waters of the sea arose an island, which is held by the Father of the piercing

---

[1] Probably an allusion to the mythical Telchînes, the wizards of Rhodes, who worked in brass and iron, and made images of the gods.

πῦρ πνεόντων ἀρχὸς ἵππων· ἔνθα Ῥόδῳ ποτὲ
μιχθεὶς τέκεν   130
ἑπτὰ σοφώτατα νοήματ' ἐπὶ προτέρων ἀνδρῶν
παραδεξαμένους
παῖδας, ὧν εἷς μὲν Κάμειρον
πρεσβύτατόν τε Ἰάλυσον ἔτεκεν Λίνδον τ'· ἀπά-
τερθε δ' ἔχον,
75 διὰ γαῖαν τρίχα δασσάμενοι πατρωίαν,
ἀστέων μοῖραν, κέκληνται δέ σφιν ἔδραι.   140

στρ. ε'

τόθι λύτρον συμφορᾶς οἰκτρᾶς γλυκὺ Τλαπολέμῳ
ἵσταται Τιρυνθίων ἀρχαγέτᾳ,
ὥσπερ θεῷ,
80 μήλων τε κνισσάεσσα πομπὰ καὶ κρίσις ἀμφ'
ἀέθλοις. τῶν ἄνθεσι Διαγόρας
ἐστεφανώσατο δίς, κλεινᾷ τ' ἐν Ἰσθμῷ τετράκις
εὐτυχέων,
Νεμέᾳ τ' ἄλλαν ἐπ' ἄλλᾳ, καὶ κρανααῖς ἐν
Ἀθάναις.   150

ἀντ. ε'

ὅ τ' ἐν Ἄργει χαλκὸς ἔγνω νιν, τά τ' ἐν Ἀρκαδίᾳ
ἔργα καὶ Θήβαις, ἀγῶνές τ' ἔννομοι
85 Βοιωτίων,
Πέλλανά τ' Αἴγινά τε νικῶνθ' ἑξάκις. ἐν Με-
γάροισίν τ' οὐχ ἕτερον λιθίνα
ψᾶφος ἔχει λόγον. ἀλλ', ὦ Ζεῦ πάτερ, νώτοισιν
Ἀταβυρίου
μεδέων, τίμα μὲν ὕμνου τεθμὸν Ὀλυμπιονίκαν,   160

76 μοῖραν mss (BMGFC) : μοίρας Meineke (S).

85 Βοιωτίων A (MGFCS) : Βοιωτῶν BDE ; Βοιώτιοι interpolated
mss (B).

86 Αἴγινα Πελλάνα τε Triclinius (C). Αἴγινά most mss :
Αἰγίνᾳ B (Boeckh).

78

beams of light, the ruler of the steeds whose breath
is fire. There it was that the Sun-god was wedded
of old with the nymph of the isle, and begat seven
sons, who inherited from him minds wiser than any
among the heroes of olden days ; and, of these, one
begat Cameirus, and Ialŷsus, the eldest born, and
Lindus ; and, with the land of their sire divided into
three shares, they had their several cities apart from
one another, and their dwelling-places were called
after their own names.

There it is that, in sweet requital for that sad
mischance, there is still established for Tlêpolemus,
the chief of the Tirynthians, even as for a god, a
reeking sacrifice of flocks that pass in procession, and
a contest of the games.

With flowers from that contest, twice hath Diagoras
crowned himself, and at the famous Isthmus four
times, in his good fortune ; and, again and again, at
Nemea and at rocky Athens; while he is not
unknown to the shield of bronze in Argos, and the
works of art given as prizes in Arcadia and at
Thebes, and to the duly ordered contests amid the
Boeotians, and to Pellana, and to Aegina, where he
was six times victor, while in Megara the reckoning
on the tablet of stone telleth no other tale.

But do thou, O father Zeus, that rulest over the
height of Atabyrium,[1] grant honour to the hymn
ordained in praise of an Olympian victor, and to the

---

[1] A mountain 4,070 feet high, above Cameirus, on the
western side of Rhodes. The name is also found in Sicily,
and is of Phoenician origin, being the same as Tabor, which
mountain is called Atabyrion by Greek writers (Tozer's
Islands of the Aegean, 221).

PINDAR

ἐπ. ε´

   ἄνδρα τε πὺξ ἀρετὰν εὑρόντα, δίδοι τέ οἱ αἰδοίαν
      χάριν
90 καὶ ποτ' ἀστῶν καὶ ποτὶ ξείνων. ἐπεὶ ὕβριος
      ἐχθρὰν ὁδὸν
   εὐθυπορεῖ, σάφα δαεὶς ἅ τέ οἱ πατέρων ὀρθαὶ
      φρένες ἐξ ἀγαθῶν
   ἔχρεον. μὴ κρύπτε κοινὸν   170
   σπέρμ' ἀπὸ Καλλιάνακτος· Ἐρατιδᾶν τοι σὺν
      χαρίτεσσιν ἔχει
   θαλίας καὶ πόλις· ἐν δὲ μιᾷ μοίρᾳ χρόνου
95 ἄλλοτ' ἀλλοῖαι διαιθύσσοισιν αὖραι.

92 ἔχρεον A, Ahrens (MGFS) ; ἔχραον most mss (BC).

hero who hath found fame for his prowess as a
boxer; and do thou give him grace and reverence
in the eyes of citizens and of strangers too. For he
goeth in a straight course along a path that hateth
insolence; he hath learnt full well all the lessons
prompted by the prudence which he inheriteth from
goodly ancestors. Suffer not the common glory of
the seed of Callianax to be buried in obscurity.
Whenever the Eratidae are victorious, the city also
holdeth festivities; but, in one single space of ap-
portioned time, the breezes swiftly change from day
to day.

OLYMPIAN VIII

FOR ALCIMEDON OF AEGINA

INTRODUCTION

AEGINA, originally known as Oenônê, was said to have derived its new name from a daughter of the river-god Asôpus, who was carried off to the island by Zeus and there bare him a son named Aeacus. The island was colonised first by Achaeans, and afterwards by Dorians from Epidaurus.

The victor, Alcimedon, was a Blepsiad of the stock of Aeacus (75). His grandfather was still living (70), but he had lost his father and his uncle (81 f). His brother had been a victor at Nemea (15), and his trainer was the famous Melêsias of Athens (53–66).

The ode was probably composed at short notice, and was sung at Olympia, immediately after the victory, during the procession to the great altar of Zeus in the Altis.

Olympia is invoked as the "queen of truth," by reason of the happy issue of the answer given to the competitor by the diviners at the altar of Zeus (1–11). Such happy issues do not come to all alike, (12–14); the victor's brother has been victorious at Nemea, and the victor himself at Olympia (15–18), thus bringing glory to Aegina, an island famed for its devotion to law and order and commerce, under Dorian rule, down from the days of Aeacus (19–30).

Myth of the building of the walls of Troy by Apollo, Poseidon, and Aeacus (31–52).

Praise of the trainer, Melêsias of Athens (53–66). The victor's triumph will rejoice the heart of his grandfather (67–73); six victories have already been won by the family (74–76). The message sending news of this victory will reach his father and his uncle in the other world (77–84). May Zeus grant to the family and to the island health and harmony and an untroubled life (84–88).

The victory belongs to **460** B.C. In the following year Aegina, the island of the boy-wrestler, Alcimedon, was defeated at sea ; and, in 456, disarmed, dismantled, and rendered tributary by Athens, the city of the boy's trainer, Melêsias.

VIII.—ΑΛΚΙΜΕΔΟΝΤΙ ΑΙΓΙΝΗΤΗ

στρ. α΄

Μᾶτερ ὦ χρυσοστεφάνων ἀέθλων, Οὐλυμπία,
δέσποιν᾽ ἀλαθείας· ἵνα μάντιες ἄνδρες
ἐμπύροις τεκμαιρόμενοι παραπειρῶνται Διὸς ἀργι-
κεραύνου,
εἴ τιν᾽ ἔχει λόγον ἀνθρώπων πέρι
5 μαιομένων μεγάλαν
ἀρετὰν θυμῷ λαβεῖν,
τῶν δὲ μόχθων ἀμπνοάν·

ἀντ. α΄

ἄνεται δὲ πρὸς χάριν εὐσεβίας ἀνδρῶν λιταῖς.   10
ἀλλ᾽ ὦ Πίσας εὔδενδρον ἐπ᾽ Ἀλφεῷ ἄλσος,
10 τόνδε κῶμον καὶ στεφαναφορίαν δέξαι. μέγα τοι
κλέος αἰεί,
ᾧτινι σὸν γέρας ἕσπητ᾽ ἀγλαόν·
ἄλλα δ᾽ ἐπ᾽ ἄλλον ἔβαν
ἀγαθῶν, πολλαὶ δ᾽ ὁδοὶ
σὺν θεοῖς εὐπραγίας.

ἐπ. α΄

15 Τιμόσθενες, ὔμμε δ᾽ ἐκλάρωσεν πότμος
Ζηνὶ γενεθλίῳ· ὃς σὲ μὲν Νεμέᾳ πρόφατον,   20
Ἀλκιμέδοντα δὲ πὰρ Κρόνου λόφῳ

11 ἕσπητ᾽ *GN* (BGFC) Bergk[3,4]: ἕσπετ᾽ *ABCE* (MS) Bergk[1,2].
16 ὃς σὲ μὲν Boeckh in notes p. 180 (GFS): ὃς σὲ μὲν ἐν
A²CDEG²; σὲ μὲν ἐν *AB*; ὃ σὲ μὲν ἐν *E¹* (M); ὅς σ᾽ ἐν
μὲν (BC).
πρόφᾱτον Triclinius (edd.): πρόφαντον *ABCD*.

84

VIII.—FOR ALCIMEDON OF AEGINA

WINNER IN THE BOYS' WRESTLING MATCH, 460 B.C.

O MOTHER of contests crowned with wreaths of gold, Olympia, queen of truth! where, by the test of sacrifices, diviners inquire the will of Zeus of the flashing thunderbolt, asking if he hath any message to give concerning men, who in their very heart are seeking to win great praise for prowess and a breathing-space from toils. For the prayers of men find in their fulfilment a recompense for reverent adoration.

O precinct of Pisa, with thy fair trees beside the Alpheüs! give welcome to this chorus of triumph, and this crowning of the victor. Great in sooth is his glory for ever, whoe'er is attended by this bright reward. Some blessings are wont to come to one man, some to another; and, with the favour of the gods, there are many paths of prosperity.

But fate hath allotted thee and thine, Timosthenês, to Zeus, as the god of thy race, Zeus who made thee the observed of all at Nemea, and made thy brother, Alcimedon, an Olympian victor beside the

θῆκεν Ὀλυμπιονίκαν.
ἦν δ' ἐσορᾶν καλός, ἔργῳ τ' οὐ κατὰ εἶδος ἐλέγχων
20 ἐξένεπε κρατέων πάλᾳ δολιχήρετμον Αἴγιναν
πάτραν·
ἔνθα σώτειρα Διὸς ξενίου
πάρεδρος ἀσκεῖται Θέμις

στρ. β'
ἔξοχ' ἀνθρώπων. ὅ τι γὰρ πολὺ καὶ πολλᾷ
   ῥέπῃ,
                         30
ὀρθᾷ διακρίνειν φρενὶ μὴ παρὰ καιρόν,
25 δυσπαλές· τεθμὸς δέ τις ἀθανάτων καὶ τάνδ'
ἁλιερκέα χώραν
παντοδαποῖσιν ὑπέστασε ξένοις
κίονα δαιμονίαν—
ὁ δ' ἐπαντέλλων χρόνος
τοῦτο πράσσων μὴ κάμοι—

ἀντ. β'
30 Δωριεῖ λαῷ ταμιευομέναν ἐξ Αἰακοῦ·   40
τὸν παῖς ὁ Λατοῦς εὐρυμέδων τε Ποσειδᾶν,
Ἰλίῳ μέλλοντες ἐπὶ στέφανον τεῦξαι, καλέσαντο
συνεργὸν
τείχεος, ἦν ὅτι νιν πεπρωμένον
ὀρνυμένων πολέμων
35 πτολιπόρθοις ἐν μάχαις
λάβρον ἀμπνεῦσαι καπνόν.

ἐπ. β'
γλαυκοὶ δὲ δράκοντες, ἐπεὶ κτίσθη νέον,
πύργον ἐσαλλόμενοι τρεῖς, οἱ δύο μὲν κάπετον, 50
αὖθι δ' ἀτυζομένω ψυχὰς βάλον·

23 ῥέπῃ Bergk (GCS) : ῥέποι all good mss (M) ; ῥέπει inferior mss (BF).
39 ἀτυζομένω D¹E supra, F supra (BMGFC) ; ἀτιζομένω CNV (Ambrosian mss) : ἀτυζόμενοι ABMO (S).

hill of Cronus. Comely was he to look upon, and verily he did not belie his beauty of form, when, by his victory in the wrestling-match, he caused Aegina with her long oars to be proclaimed as his fatherland, that land where the saving goddess, Themis, whose throne is beside the seat of Zeus, the god of hospitality, is honoured more than among all other men. For,[1] when there is a heavy weight in the balance, and it swayeth many ways, it is hard to wrestle with, so as to reach a decision with righteous mind in fitting wise. But it may be deemed an ordinance of the immortals that set up this sea-girt land to be as a pillar divine for visitants from every clime ; and may the time to come never weary of fulfilling this. 'Tis a land which obeyeth the rule of the Dorian folk from the time of Aeacus, whom the son of Lêto[2] and widely-ruling Poseidôn, when about to build a diadem of towers for Ilium, summoned to help them in building the wall. For[3] it was fated that, amid the onsets of wars, when cities are ruined by battles, those towers should breathe forth vast volumes of smoke. Scarce was the wall builded when grey-eyed serpents three essayed to leap into the tower, and two of them fell down, and anon in amazement gave up their lives, while the third leapt

[1] " For " introduces the reason why "Themis is honoured." It is because Aegina is a great commercial centre, where important issues are often at stake, that she is bound to reverence the rule of righteous dealing.   [2] Apollo.

[3] The help of Aeacus was asked by Apollo and Poseidon, because, "if a mortal did not join in the work, the city could never have been taken." Schol. quoted by Gildersleeve.

PINDAR

40 εἰς δ᾽ ἀνόρουσε βοάσαις.
  ἔννεπε δ᾽ ἀντίον ὁρμαίνων τέρας εὐθὺς Ἀπόλλων·
  " Πέργαμος ἀμφὶ τεαῖς, ἥρως, χερὸς ἐργασίαις
  ἁλίσκεται·
  ὡς ἐμοὶ φάσμα λέγει Κρονίδα
  πεμφθὲν βαρυγδούπου Διός·   58
στρ. γ
45 οὐκ ἄτερ παίδων σέθεν, ἀλλ᾽ ἅμα πρώτοις ἄρξεται
  καὶ τετράτοις." ὣς ἄρα θεὸς σάφα εἴπαις
  Ξάνθον ἤπειγεν καὶ Ἀμαζόνας εὐίππους καὶ ἐς
  Ἴστρον ἐλαύνων.
  Ὀρσοτρίαινα δ᾽ ἐπ᾽ Ἰσθμῷ ποντίᾳ
  ἅρμα θοὸν τανύεν,
50 ἀποπέμπων Αἰακὸν
  δεῦρ᾽ ἀν᾽ ἵπποις χρυσέαις,
ἀντ. γ
  καὶ Κορίνθου δειράδ᾽ ἐποψόμενος δαιτικλυτάν.
  τερπνὸν δ᾽ ἐν ἀνθρώποις ἴσον ἔσσεται οὐδέν.   70
  εἰ δ᾽ ἐγὼ Μελησίᾳ ἐξ ἀγενείων κῦδος ἀνέδραμον
  ὕμνῳ,
55 μὴ βαλέτω με λίθῳ τραχεῖ φθόνος·
  καὶ Νεμέᾳ γὰρ ὁμῶς
  ἐρέω ταύταν χάριν,
  τὰν δ᾽ ἔπειτ᾽ ἀνδρῶν μάχαν

  40 ἀνόρουσε B alone, with scholium on B (MS): ἐσύρουσε
vulgo (BGFC); ὄρουσε A, ἐπόρουσε O.
  46 τετράτοις mss (edd.) : τερτάτοις (Aeolic for τριτάτοις)
Ahrens, Bergk (S).
  52 δαιτικλυτάν Bergk (GFCS), cp. ναυσικλυτός ; δαιτακλυτάν
(M) : δαῖτα κλυτάν mss (B).
  54 Μελησίᾳ AB and scholium, Hermann (BMFC): Μελησίᾳ
(GS).
  58 μάχαν mss : μάχας S, μαχᾶν Wiskemann.

88

up with a cry; and Apollo, pondering on the adverse
omen, said straightway: "Pergamos is taken, O
hero, hard by the work of thy hands; so saith
a vision sent to me, a vision of Zeus, the loudly
thundering son of Cronus; not without thy sons;
but the capture will begin with the first generation,
and (will end) with the fourth."[1] Thus spake the
god full clearly, and hastened on his way to Xanthus,
and to the Amazons with their noble steeds, and to
the Ister.

And the wielder of the trident drove his swift
chariot toward the sea-washed Isthmus, to bring
Aeacus hither to his home in his golden car, and
to view the feast-famed ridge of Corinth.[2]

But nothing shall be equally pleasant among all
men; and, if I myself have, for Melêsias, rushed up
in song to the height of glory won by the training
of beardless youths, let not envy cast a rough stone
at me; for I could tell of his winning such another
victory himself (among boys) at Nemea, and of his
later contests among men, even in the pancratium.[3]

---

[1] (1) Telamon, son of Aeacus, aided Heracles in the first
capture of Troy. (2) Neoptolemus and Epeius, his great-
grandsons, joined the Atreidae in its second capture, being
(strictly speaking) in the *third* generation from Aeacus.
Cp. *I.* v 35 f.

[2] Famous for the Isthmian festival in its vicinity.

[3] A combination of boxing and wrestling.

ἐπ. γ΄

ἐκ παγκρατίου. τὸ διδάξασθαι δέ τοι

60 εἰδότι ῥᾴτερον· ἄγνωμον δὲ τὸ μὴ προμαθεῖν·
κουφότεραι γὰρ ἀπειράτων φρένες.　　　　　80
κεῖνα δὲ κεῖνος ἂν εἴποι
ἔργα περαίτερον ἄλλων, τίς τρόπος ἄνδρα προ-
　　βάσει
ἐξ ἱερῶν ἀέθλων μέλλοντα ποθεινοτάταν δόξαν
　　φέρειν.

65 νῦν μὲν αὐτῷ γέρας Ἀλκιμέδων
νίκαν τριακοστὰν ἑλών·

στρ. δ΄

ὃς τύχᾳ μὲν δαίμονος, ἀνορέας δ᾽ οὐκ ἀμπλακών
ἐν τέτρασιν παίδων ἀπεθήκατο γυίοις　　　90
νόστον ἔχθιστον καὶ ἀτιμοτέραν γλῶσσαν καὶ
　　ἐπίκρυφον οἶμον,

70 πατρὶ δὲ πατρὸς ἐνέπνευσεν μένος
γήραος ἀντίπαλον.
Ἀΐδα τοι λάθεται
ἄρμενα πράξαις ἀνήρ.

ἀντ. δ΄

ἀλλ᾽ ἐμὲ χρὴ μναμοσύναν ἀνεγείροντα φράσαι
75 χειρῶν ἄωτον Βλεψιάδαις ἐπίνικον,
ἕκτος οἷς ἤδη στέφανος περίκειται φυλλοφόρων
　　ἀπ᾽ ἀγώνων.　　　　　100
ἔστι δὲ καί τι θανόντεσσιν μέρος
κὰν νόμον ἐρδομένων·
κατακρύπτει δ᾽ οὐ κόνις
80 συγγόνων κεδνὰν χάριν.

ἐπ. δ΄

Ἑρμᾶ δὲ θυγατρὸς ἀκούσαις Ἰφίων

78 ἐρδομένων Erasmus Schmid (GCS) : ἐρδόμενον mss (BMF).

90

To teach, as ye know, is easier for him that himself
hath knowledge, while it is foolish not to learn
betimes. Flighty are the words of them that have
made no trial; but he,[1] beyond all others, could
speak of those brave deeds, telling what manner of
training will aid a man that is eager to win from
contests in the sacred games the fame that is most
yearned for. For himself it is a boon indeed that a
thirtieth victory hath been won for him by Alcime-
don, who, by heaven-sent good-fortune, but with no
slackness in his own prowess, thrust off from himself
on the bodies of four boys a most hateful return
amid jibes of contempt, while they slink to their
homes unseen; and hath inspired his father's sire
with strength that wrestles with old age. Ye know
that the grave is forgotten by him who hath won
befitting fame. But meet it is for me to awaken
Memory, and to tell of the fruit of the victorious
hands of the race of Blepsias, who have now been
wreathed with the sixth garland won from crownèd
contests. Even the dead have share in rites duly
paid in their honour, and the noble grace of their kins-
men on earth is not buried in the dust. But the
victor's father, Iphiôn, having listened to the Teller
of glad tidings, the daughter of Hermes, will haply

---

[1] The trainer, Melêsias.

Ἀγγελίας, ἐνέποι κεν Καλλιμάχῳ λιπαρὸν
κόσμον Ὀλυμπίᾳ, ὅν σφι Ζεὺς γένει
ὤπασεν. ἐσλὰ δ᾽ ἐπ᾽ ἐσλοῖς   110
85 ἔργ᾽ ἐθέλοι δόμεν, ὀξείας δὲ νόσους ἀπαλάλκοι.
εὔχομαι ἀμφὶ καλῶν μοίρᾳ Νέμεσιν διχόβουλον
    μὴ θέμεν·
ἀλλ᾽ ἀπήμαντον ἄγων βίοτοι
αὐτούς τ᾽ ἀέξοι καὶ πόλιν.

tell his own brother Callimachus of the bright glory
at Olympia, which Zeus hath given to their race.

May it be his pleasure to grant blessings heaped
upon blessings, and to keep afar all painful maladies.
I pray that, for the share of glory allotted them, he
may not cause Nemesis to be divided in counsel; but
may he grant a painless life, and thus give increase
to themselves and to their city.

OLYMPIAN IX

FOR EPHARMOSTUS OF OPUS

INTRODUCTION

EPHARMOSTUS the Opuntian, victor in the wrestling-ring in 468 B.C., was subsequently successful in the Pythian games, in a year stated by the Scholiast, in most of the MSS, to be the 30th Pythiad, which, as the Pythian era is ascertained to have begun in 582 B.C., corresponds to 466 B.c. The date of his present Olympic victory is **468**. This is determined by the Oxyrhynchus papyrus, ii (1899), p. 89, which names as victor in that year [Εφα]ρμοστος οπου[ντιος π]αλην.

The victor belongs to Opûs, a town of the Eastern Locrians, in the district North of Boeotia. He is a friend or kinsman of a *proxenus* of Thebes (84). Deucalion and Pyrrha were supposed to have dwelt in the neighbourhood of Opûs, and the town was said to have been founded by Opus, son of Locrus and Protogeneia. It was the native city of Patroclus, and was one of the Locrian towns subject to Ajax, son of Oileus (*Il.* ii 531).

The brief chant of Archilochus sufficed for the immediate welcome of the victor at Olympia; but now the Muses themselves must shoot their arrows at the hill of Cronus, with one more arrow aimed at Pytho (1-12). Not in vain is the praise of Opûs

and her son, whose home is renowned for Law and
Justice, and for Pythian and Olympian victories
(13–21). The poet will spread its fame far and
wide, for the Graces of song are bound to give
delight; but song, no less than strength, depends on
Heaven (21–29). Without the help of Heaven how
could Heracles have withstood the gods at Pylos?
(29–35). But it is folly to speak of the gods as
matched in war, and madness to boast of a poet's
song (35–39). Strife must not be named in the
same breath as the immortals (40 f).

Rather let me tell anew the tale of Opûs, the
city of Protogeneia, where Pyrrha and Deucalion
made men from stones (41–47). Praise wine that is
old, but lays that are new (48 f).

Then follows the story of the flood, and the myth
of the eponymous hero of Opûs, his friendship with
Menoetius, whose son, Patroclus, was the friend of
Achilles (41–79).

The poet prays that the Muses may inspire him
to sing the three victories already won by Ephar-
mostus and his friend at the Isthmus and at Nemea,
and by Epharmostus alone at Nemea and elsewhere
(80–99). That which comes by Nature and is the
gift of God is the best; men's pursuits are very
various, and all men have not the same training.
The heights of skill are steep; but in offering this
triumphal song, the poet loudly declares that, by the
gift of God, this victor in the wrestling is dexterous
and nimble, and has the glance of valour in his eyes,
and has, on this festal day, cast a new crown upon
the altar of Ajax, the son of Oïleus (100–112).

IX.—ΕΦΑΡΜΟΣΤΩ ΟΠΟΥΝΤΙΩ

ΠΑΛΑΙΣΤΗ

στρ. α΄

Τὸ μὲν Ἀρχιλόχου μέλος
φωνᾶεν Ὀλυμπίᾳ, καλλίνικος ὁ τριπλόος κε-
χλαδώς,
ἄρκεσε Κρόνιον παρ᾽ ὄχθον ἁγεμονεῦσαι
κωμάζοντι φίλοις Ἐφαρμόστῳ σὺν ἑταίροις·
5 ἀλλὰ νῦν ἑκαταβόλων Μοισᾶν ἀπὸ τόξων
Δία τε φοινικοστερόπαν σεμνόν τ᾽ ἐπίνειμαι   10
ἀκρωτήριον Ἄλιδος
τοιοῖσδε βέλεσσιν,
τὸ δή ποτε Λυδὸς ἥρως Πέλοψ
10 ἐξάρατο κάλλιστον ἕδνον Ἱπποδαμείας·

ἀντ. α΄

πτερόεντα δ᾽ ἵει γλυκὺν
Πυθῶναδ᾽ ὀϊστόν· οὔτοι χαμαιπετέων λόγων
ἐφάψεαι
ἀνδρὸς ἀμφὶ παλαίσμασιν φόρμιγγ᾽ ἐλελίζων   20
κλεινᾶς ἐξ Ὀπόεντος· αἰνήσαις ἑ καὶ υἱόν,
15 ἃν Θέμις θυγάτηρ τέ οἱ σώτειρα λέλογχεν
μεγαλόδοξος Εὐνομία, θάλλει δ᾽ ἀρεταῖσιν
σόν τε Καστάλια, πάρα

16 f. ἀρεταῖσιν σόν τε, Καστάλια, πάρα scholium to *A* [2], — παρά
τε τὸ σὸν, Bergk (GFCS) ; ἀρεταῖς ἷσόν τε Καστάλια(ια) παρὰ *BC*
vulgo ; ἀρεταῖσιν | ἔν τε Καστάλια παρὰ *A* alone (BM).

96

IX.—FOR EPHARMOSTUS OF OPUS

The chant of Archilochus that was vocal at Olympia, the song of victory swelling with its thrice repeated refrain,[1] sufficed to welcome Epharmostus when, with his dear comrades, he marched in triumph to the hill of Cronus. But now, from the bow of the far-darting Muses, do thou shoot a shower of such shafts of song as these, at Zeus, the Lord of the ruddy lightning, and at the hallowed crest of Elis, which, in olden time, the hero Pelops won as the fair dowry of Hippodameia; and speed thou to Pytho also a winged arrow sweet, for not unto the ground shall fall the words thou shalt essay, while trilling the lyre in honour of the wrestling of the hero from famous Opûs. Praise herself and her son; praise her whom Themis and her glorious daughter, the Saviour Eunomia, have received as their portion. She rejoiceth o'er the deeds of valour done beside thy

[1] Two lines of the famous hymn to Heracles, composed by Archilochus (*fl.* 650 B.C.), have been preserved by the Scholiast: ὦ καλλίνικε χαῖρ' ἄναξ Ἡράκλεες | αὐτός τε καὶ Ἰόλαος, αἰχμητὰ δύο, "Hail, Heracles! thou conquering king, | Thyself and Iolaüs, warriors twain!" In the absence of music, it was accompanied by the word τήνελλα, in imitation of the twanging of the strings of the lyre; probably τήνελλα καλλίνικε was thrice repeated as a refrain. The hymn was known as the καλλίνικος, and it was traditionally sung in honour of the "conquering hero," whenever no special ode was ready.

97

Ἀλφεοῦ τε ῥέεθρον·
ὅθεν στεφάνων ἄωτοι κλυτὰν 30
20 Λοκρῶν ἐπαείροντι ματέρ' ἀγλαόδενδρον.

ἐπ. α΄

ἐγὼ δέ τοι φίλαν πόλιν
μαλεραῖς ἐπιφλέγων ἀοιδαῖς,
καὶ ἀγάνορος ἵππου
θᾶσσον καὶ ναὸς ὑποπτέρου παντᾷ
25 ἀγγελίαν πέμψω ταύταν,
εἰ σύν τινι μοιριδίῳ παλάμᾳ
ἐξαίρετον Χαρίτων νέμομαι κᾶπον· 40
κεῖναι γὰρ ὤπασαν τὰ τέρπν'· ἀγαθοὶ δὲ καὶ σοφοὶ
κατὰ δαίμον' ἄνδρες

στρ. β΄

ἐγένοντ'· ἐπεὶ ἀντία
30 πῶς ἂν τριόδοντος Ἡρακλέης σκύταλον τίναξε
χερσίν,
ἁνίκ' ἀμφὶ Πύλον σταθεὶς ἤρειδε Ποσειδᾶν
ἤρειδεν δέ νιν ἀργυρέῳ τόξῳ πολεμίζων
Φοῖβος, οὐδ' Ἀίδας ἀκινήταν ἔχε ῥάβδον, 50
βρότεα σώμαθ' ᾇ κατάγει κοίλαν πρὸς ἀγυιὰν
35 θνασκόντων; ἀπό μοι λόγον
τοῦτον, στόμα, ῥῖψον·
ἐπεὶ τό γε λοιδορῆσαι θεοὺς
ἐχθρὰ σοφία, καὶ τὸ καυχᾶσθαι παρὰ καιρὸν

ἀντ. β΄

μανίαισιν ὑποκρέκει.
40 μὴ νῦν λαλάγει τὰ τοιαῦτ'· ἔα πόλεμον μάχαν τε
πᾶσαν 60

---

32 δέ νιν Hermann (GS) : τέ μιν mss (B) ; τέ νιν (MFC).
πολεμίζων mss (BGFC): πελεμίζων Thiersch, Bergk (MS),
but πελεμίζων requires τόξον, cp. *Od.* xxi 125.

stream, Castalia, and beside Alpheüs. Thence it is
that the choicest crowns do glorify the mother-city
of the Locrians amid her noble trees. Lo! I am
lighting up that city dear with dazzling songs of
praise, and I shall spread my message everywhere,
more swiftly than proud steed or wingèd ship, so
surely as I, by the ordering of destiny, am tilling
the choicest garden of the Graces, for 'tis they that
are givers of delight, but men become brave and
wise according unto fate divine.[1]

Else, how had Heracles wielded his club against
the trident? what time he was pressed hard by
Poseidon standing in defence of Pylos aye and
pressed hard by Phoebus, who was warring with his
silver bow, nor did Hades keep his wand unmoved,
the wand wherewith he leadeth mortal forms down
to the hollow way of the dead. Cast away this
word, O my lips! since to speak evil of the gods is
a skill that is hateful, and untimely boasting is in
unison with madness. Babble not, my Muse, of such
themes as these; let war and all battle remain far
from the immortals; but lend thy tongue to the city

[1] By "brave and wise" are meant "heroes and poets."
Pindar does not presume to dwell on the "poets," this would
have been "untimely boasting," l. 38; but he takes Heracles
as an example of the "heroes." But for the aid of a "fate
divine," Heracles could not have been a match for three
divinities when he fought against Poseidon in Messenian
Pylos, because the sea-god's son would not purge him of the
guilt of slaying Iphitus; against Phoebus, because he had
stolen a tripod from Delphi to avenge the refusal of an
oracle; and against Hades in Eleian Pylos, because he had
carried off Cerberus (Schol.). But the poet feels that in
telling of these differences between the gods, he is on
dangerous ground, and he soon turns to another topic.

χωρὶς ἀθανάτων· φέροις δὲ Πρωτογενείας
ἄστει γλῶσσαν, ἵν᾽ αἰολοβρόντα Διὸς αἴσᾳ
Πύρρα Δευκαλίων τε Παρνασοῦ καταβάντε
δόμον ἔθεντο πρῶτον, ἄτερ δ᾽ εὐνᾶς ὁμόδαμον
45 κτισσάσθαν λίθινον γόνον·   70
λαοὶ δ᾽ ὀνύμασθεν.
ἔγειρ᾽ ἐπέων σφιν οὖρον λιγύν,
αἴνει δὲ παλαιὸν μὲν οἶνον, ἄνθεα δ᾽ ὕμνων
ἐπ β′
νεωτέρων. λέγοντι μὰν
50 χθόνα μὲν κατακλύσαι μέλαιναν
ὕδατος σθένος, ἀλλὰ
Ζηνὸς τέχναις ἀνάπωτιν ἐξαίφνας
ἄντλον ἑλεῖν. κείνων ἔσαν
χαλκάσπιδες ὑμέτεροι πρόγονοι   80
55 ἀρχᾶθεν Ἰαπετιονίδος φύτλας
κοῦροι κορᾶν καὶ φερτάτων Κρονιδᾶν, ἐγχώριοι
βασιλῆες αἰεί,
στρ. γ′
πρὶν Ὀλύμπιος ἀγεμὼν
θύγατρ᾽ ἀπὸ γᾶς Ἐπειῶν Ὀπόεντος ἀναρπάσαις,
ἕκαλος
μίχθη Μαιναλίαισιν ἐν δειραῖς, καὶ ἔνεικεν
60 Λοκρῷ, μὴ καθέλοι μιν αἰὼν πότμον ἐφάψαις   90
ὀρφανὸν γενεᾶς. ἔχεν δὲ σπέρμα μέγιστον
ἄλοχος, εὐφράνθη τε ἰδὼν ἥρως θετὸν υἱόν,
μάτρωος δ᾽ ἐκάλεσέ νιν
ἰσώνυμον ἔμμεν,

45 κτισσάσθαν Mommsen, Bergk (GCS) : κτησσάσθαν (B) ;
κτισάσθαν, or κτησάσθαν mss (F).
46 ὀνύμασθεν (GCS) ; ὠνύμ. C ; ὀνομ. vulgo (BMF).
53 ἔσαν (S) ; δ᾽ ἔσαν all good mss ; δ᾽ ἔσσαν interpolated mss
(BMGFC).

of Protogeneia, where, by the ordinance of Zeus
with the gleaming thunderbolt, Pyrrha and Deucalion,
coming down from Parnassus, first fixed their home,
and, without wedlock, made the stone people to be
of one folk, and from the stones were the people
called.[1]

Raise in their honour a clearly sounding strain,
and, while thou praisest the wine that is old,
thou shalt also praise the flowers of songs that are
new. They tell, in sooth, how the mighty waters
drowned the dark earth, until, by the counsels of
Zeus, the ebbing tide suddenly drained off the flood.
From these were descended your ancestors with their
brazen shields, young men sprung of old from the
daughters of the race of Iapetus and from the mighty
sons of Cronus, being ever a native line of kings,
until the Lord of Olympus, having carried off the
daughter of Opûs from the land of the Epeians,[2] lay
by her side in a silent spot amid the Maenalian
mountains, and brought her to Locrus, that so Time
might not destroy him, laying upon him the doom of
childlessness. But his bride bare in her womb the
seed of the Mightiest, and the hero rejoiced at seeing
the son that had been given him, and called him by

---

[1] Lit. "they were called λαοί, people," from the λᾶες,
or stones, implied in the λίθινον γόνον, the "stone progeny,"
of the previous line. The legend that, after a deluge, a new
race of men was brought into being by Deucalion and Pyrrha
throwing stones behind them, is a fable founded on false
etymology. λαός has no connexion with λᾶας. Cp. Max
Müller's *Chips*, ii 12.

[2] The name for the original inhabitants of Elis. Cp. *Od.*
xiii 275, Ἤλιδα . . . ὅθι κρατέουσιν Ἐπειοί.

65 ὑπέρφατον ἄνδρα μορφᾷ τε καὶ
   ἔργοισι. πόλιν δ' ὤπασεν λαόν τε διαιτᾶν.   100
ἀντ. γ΄
   ἀφίκοντο δέ οἱ ξένοι,
   ἔκ τ' Ἄργεος ἔκ τε Θηβᾶν, οἱ δ' Ἀρκάδες, οἱ δὲ
     καὶ Πισᾶται·
   υἱὸν δ' Ἄκτορος ἐξόχως τίμασεν ἐποίκων
70 Αἰγίνας τε Μενοίτιον· τοῦ παῖς ἅμ' Ἀτρείδαις
   Τεύθραντος πεδίον μολὼν ἔστα σὺν Ἀχιλλεῖ
   μόνος, ὅτ' ἀλκᾶντας Δαναοὺς τρέψαις ἁλίαισιν   110
   πρύμναις Τήλεφος ἔμβαλεν·
   ὥστ' ἔμφρονι δεῖξαι
75 μαθεῖν Πατρόκλου βιατὰν νόον.
   ἐξ οὗ Θέτιος γόνος οὐλίῳ νιν ἐν Ἄρει
ἐπ. γ΄
   παραγορεῖτο μή ποτε
   σφετέρας ἄτερθε ταξιοῦσθαι
   δαμασιμβρότου αἰχμᾶς.
80 εἴην εὑρησιεπὴς ἀναγεῖσθαι   120
   πρόσφορος ἐν Μοισᾶν δίφρῳ·
   τόλμα δὲ καὶ ἀμφιλαφὴς δύναμις
   ἔσποιτο. προξενίᾳ δ' ἀρετᾷ τ' ἦλθον
   τιμάορος Ἰσθμίαισι Λαμπρομάχου μίτραις, ὅτ'
     ἀμφότεροι κράτησαν
στρ. δ΄
85 μίαν ἔργον ἀν' ἀμέραν.
   ἄλλαι δὲ δύ' ἐν Κορίνθου πύλαις ἐγένοντ' ἔπειτα
     χάρμαι,

76 γόνος οὐλίῳ mss (F²s), the metre normally requires
‒◡‒◡‒ : γ' οὐλίῳ γόνος Hermann (B); γονὸς οὐλίῳ Mingarelli
(M²C); Flννος — M¹, κοῦρος? F¹; γ' ἶνις—Heimer (G).
83 ἔσποιτο most mss (BGFC) : ἕποιτο MN (S); ἔσποιτ' αἰεὶ M.

the self-same name as his mother's sire.[1] Wondrous
he became in beauty of form and in the works of
his hands, and Locrus gave him a city and a people
to govern; and strangers gathered themselves to-
gether unto him from Argos and Thebes, from Arcadia
and Pisa; but, among the new settlers, he chiefly
honoured the son of Actor and Aegina, Menoetius.
It was the son of Menoetius[2] who went with Atreidae
to the plain of Teuthras, and stood alone beside
Achilles, when Têlephus turned to flight the valiant
Danai, and made onslaught on their ships beside the
sea; so that a man of understanding might clearly
discern the warrior spirit of Patroclus. From that
time forward the son of Thetis exhorted him never
in murderous war to post himself afar from his own
man-subduing spear.

Would I could find me words as I move onward as
a bearer of good gifts in the Muses' car; would I
might be attended by Daring and by all-embracing
Power! I have come at virtue's bidding, and in friend-
ship for the folk, to pay the further honour due to
the Isthmian wreath of Lampromachus, for that the
twain were victors in two events on the self-same
day; and, afterwards, there were two gladsome
victories at the portals of Corinth,[3] and others won

---

[1] Opus.   [2] Patroclus.   [3] *i.e.* in the Isthmian games.

ταὶ δὲ καὶ Νεμέας Ἐφαρμόστῳ κατὰ κόλπον· 130
Ἄργει τ' ἔσχεθε κῦδος ἀνδρῶν, παῖς δ' ἐν Ἀθά-
ναις,
οἷον δ' ἐν Μαραθῶνι συλαθεὶς ἀγενείων
90 μένεν ἀγῶνα πρεσβυτέρων ἀμφ' ἀργυρίδεσσιν·
φῶτας δ' ὀξυρεπεῖ δόλῳ
ἀπτῶτι δαμάσσαις
διήρχετο κύκλον ὅσσα βοᾷ, 140
ὡραῖος ἐὼν καὶ καλὸς κάλλιστά τε ῥέξαις.

ἀντ. δ

95 τὰ δὲ Παρρασίῳ στρατῷ
θαυμαστὸς ἐὼν φάνη Ζηνὸς ἀμφὶ πανάγυριν
Λυκαίου,
καὶ ψυχρᾶν ὁπότ' εὐδιανὸν φάρμακον αὐρᾶν
Πελλάνα φέρε· σύνδικος δ' αὐτῷ Ἰολάου
τύμβος εἰναλία τ' Ἐλευσὶς ἀγλαΐαισιν. 150
100 τὸ δὲ φυᾷ κράτιστον ἅπαν· πολλοὶ δὲ διδακταῖς
ἀνθρώπων ἀρεταῖς κλέος
ὤρουσαν ἀρέσθαι.
ἄνευ δὲ θεοῦ σεσιγαμένον
οὐ σκαιότερον χρῆμ' ἕκαστον. ἐντὶ γὰρ ἄλλαι

ἐπ. δ

105 ὁδῶν ὁδοὶ περαίτεραι,
μία δ' οὐχ ἅπαντας ἄμμε θρέψει 160
μελέτα· σοφίαι μὲν
αἰπειναί· τοῦτο δὲ προσφέρων ἄθλον,

102 ἀρέσθαι Bergk, afterwards found in A (MGFCS),
αἰρεῖσθαι Aristides : ἀνελέσθαι most old mss ; ἑλέσθαι inter-
polated mss (B).
103 ἄνευ δὲ A (MGFCS) : ἄνευθε δὲ BCD ; ἄνευθε (B).

by Epharmostus in the vale of Nemea, while at Argos he gained glory in a contest of men, and as a boy at Athens. And, when reft from the beardless company, what a glorious contest for the prize of silver cups did he maintain at Marathon, among the men! and, having vanquished those wights by the cunning skill that swiftly shifts its balance but never falls, amid what loud applause did he pass round the ring, a victor in life's prime, nobly fair, and one who had wrought most noble deeds! Then again he seemed marvellous to look upon, amid the Parrhasian people, at the festival of the Lycaean Zeus, and also on that day when, at Pellana, he carried off as his prize a warm remedy against the chilly blasts; and the tomb of Iolâus beareth witness to him, and the shore of Eleusis telleth of his glorious prowess.

That which cometh of Nature is ever best, but many men have striven to win their fame by means of merit that cometh from mere training; but anything whatsoever, in which God hath no part, is none the worse for being quelled in silence.[1] Yet some roads lead further than others, and it is not all of us that can prosper in a single path of work. Steep are the heights of skill; but, while offering this prize of song, with a ringing shout do I boldly

[1] The contrast between natural genius and imitative accomplishment is common in Pindar. Cp. *O.* ii 86 f, and *N.* iii 40–42. Natural genius is the gift of God, and is to be loudly proclaimed, while skill that is merely learnt is to be buried in silence.

PINDAR

ὄρθιον ὤρυσαι θαρσέων,
110 τόνδ' ἀνέρα δαιμονίᾳ γεγάμεν
εὔχειρα, δεξιόγυιον, ὁρῶντ' ἀλκάν,
Αἰάντειόν τ' ἐν δαιτὶ Ἰλιάδα νικῶν ἐπεστεφάνωσε
βωμόν.

112 Αἰάντειόν τ' ἐν δαιτὶ Ἰλιάδα old mss with slight variations (MGF): Αἰάντεόν τ' ἐν δαῖθ' ὃς Ἰλιάδα B; Αἶαν, τεόν τ' (Hermann) ἐν δαιτί, Ἰλιάδα (CS).

declare that our hero hath by the blessing of heaven been born with deftness of hand and litheness of limb, and with valour in his glance—our hero, who, at the banquet of the son of Oïleus, crowned by his victory the altar of Aias.

OLYMPIAN X

FOR HÂGÊSIDÂMUS OF LOCRI EPIZEPHYRII

INTRODUCTION

LOCRI EPIZEPHYRII, on the south-east coast of the Bruttian peninsula, was founded by one of the Greek tribes known as Locri, probably by the Locri Opuntii. It possessed a written code of law, which passed under the name of Zaleucus (600 B.C.). In 477 its independence was seriously threatened by Anaxilas, despot of Rhegium, but it was saved by the interposition of Hieron, ruler of Syracuse (*Pyth.* ii 35). The victory of the Epizephyrian Locrian, Hâgêsidâmus, in the boys' wrestling-match at Olympia, celebrated in the tenth and eleventh Olympians, was won in the very next year, 476, as is proved by the entry in the Oxyrhynchus papyrus, ii (1899), 88, [αγ]ησι[δα]μος λοκρος απ ιταλιας παιδ πυξ.

The eleventh Olympian was produced at Olympia immediately after the victory; it was followed by the tenth, celebrating the same victory at Locri some time after. It is probably because the later of the two Odes is longer and more elaborate than the other that it is placed before it in the MSS.

INTRODUCTION

The ode is a debt that has long been due, and must now be paid with interest (1-8). As the wave washes away the rolling shingle, so this new tide of song will wipe out the poet's growing debt (9-12).

The praise of the Western Locri, as the home of Justice, and of the heroic Muse, and the god of War (13-16). The praise of the victor's trainer (16-19), who, with the help of Heaven, can add a fine edge to native valour (20 f). The joy of the prize is seldom attained without toil (22 f).

Myth of the origin and the first celebration of the Olympic games (27-77).

In honour of an Olympian victory, the poet must now sing the thunderbolt of Zeus (78-83). The poet's song has come from Thebes at last, like the long expected heir granted to the old age of some wealthy sire (84-90). Without song, brave deeds are in vain, but our victor is sung by the Muses; and the poet himself, in his zeal, sings of the famous tribe of the Locrians, and the victor fair whom he has seen winning the boys' wrestling-match at Olympia (91-105).

X.—ΑΓΗΣΙΔΑΜΩ
ΛΟΚΡΩ ΕΠΙΖΕΦΥΡΙΩ

ΠΑΙΔΙ ΠΥΚΤῌ

στρ. α΄

  Τὸν Ὀλυμπιονίκαν ἀνάγνωτέ μοι
  Ἀρχεστράτου παῖδα, πόθι φρενὸς
  ἐμᾶς γέγραπται· γλυκὺ γὰρ αὐτῷ μέλος ὀφείλων
    ἐπιλέλαθ'· ὦ Μοῖσ', ἀλλὰ σὺ καὶ θυγάτηρ
  Ἀλάθεια Διός, ὀρθᾷ χερὶ
5 ἐρύκετον ψευδέων
  ἐνιπὰν ἀλιτόξενον.

ἀντ. α΄

  ἕκαθεν γὰρ ἐπελθὼν ὁ μέλλων χρόνος
  ἐμὸν καταίσχυνε βαθὺ χρέος.   10
  ὅμως δὲ λῦσαι δυνατὸς ὀξεῖαν ἐπιμομφὰν τόκος
    θνατῶν. νῦν ψᾶφον ἑλισσομέναν
10 ὅπα κῦμα κατακλύσσει ῥέον;
  ὅπα τε κοινὸν λόγον
  φίλαν τίσομεν ἐς χάριν;

ἐπ. α΄

  νέμει γὰρ Ἀτρέκεια πόλιν Λοκρῶν Ζεφυρίων,
  μέλει τέ σφισι Καλλιόπα
15 καὶ χάλκεος Ἄρης. τράπε δὲ Κύκνεια μάχα καὶ
    ὑπέρβιον   20

    9 τόκος θνατῶν old mss (s): ὁ τόκος ἀνδρῶν interpolated mss, γε τόκος ἀνδρῶν Kayser; τόκος ὀνάτωρ Hermann (B), — ὁπαδέων M, — ὁμαρτέων C; ὁρᾶτ' ἂν Schneidewin (GF).

    10 and 11 ὅπα mss (BGC): ὅπᾳ Hermann (M); ὁπᾷ Bergk (FS).

X.—FOR HÂGÊSIDÂMUS
OF LOCRI EPIZEPHYRII

WINNER IN THE BOYS' BOXING MATCH, 476 B.C.

READ me the name of the Olympian victor, the son of Archestratus ! Tell me where it is written in my heart ! For I have forgotten that I owed him a sweet song ; but do thou, O Muse, and also Truth, the daughter of Zeus, with a hand that setteth all things right, put an end to the blame for a broken promise, the blame for wronging a friend.

Lo, the lingering hours have come from afar, and have made me ashamed of my deep debt. Yet payment with usance hath power to do away with the bitter rebuke of mortal men. Now mark how the tide of song, as it floweth, is washing the rolling pebbles ashore ! Mark how we shall pay our debt as a welcome boon in our praise of the victor's home !

In that city of the Locrians in the West, dwelleth Justice [1] ; and dear to her is Calliopê, and Arês clad in bronze. Even the mighty Heracles yielded in his

---

[1] Lit. "strictness," "unswerving accuracy," probably an allusion to the severe code of the Locrian Zaleucus.

Ἡρακλέα. πύκτας δ' ἐν Ὀλυμπιάδι νικῶν
Ἴλᾳ φερέτω χάριν
Ἀγησίδαμος ὡς
Ἀχιλεῖ Πάτροκλος.
20 θήξαις δέ κε φύντ' ἀρετᾷ ποτὶ
πελώριον ὁρμάσαι κλέος ἀνὴρ θεοῦ σὺν παλάμᾳ·

στρ. β'

ἄπονον δ' ἔλαβον χάρμα παῦροί τινες,
ἔργων πρὸ πάντων βιότῳ φάος.
ἀγῶνα δ' ἐξαίρετον ἀεῖσαι θέμιτες ὦρσαν Διός,
ὃν ἀρχαίῳ σάματι πὰρ Πέλοπος   30
25 βωμῶν ἑξάριθμον ἐκτίσσατο,
ἐπεὶ Ποσειδάνιον
πέφνε Κτέατον ἀμύμονα,

ἀντ. β'

πέφνε δ' Εὔρυτον, ὡς Αὐγέαν λάτριον
ἀέκονθ' ἑκὼν μισθὸν ὑπέρβιον
30 πράσσοιτο, λόχμαισι δὲ δοκεύσαις ὑπὸ Κλεωνᾶν
δάμασε καὶ κείνους Ἡρακλέης ἐφ' ὁδῷ,
ὅτι πρόσθε ποτὲ Τιρύνθιον   40
ἔπερσαν αὐτῷ στρατὸν
μυχοῖς ἥμενον Ἄλιδος

ἐπ. β'

Μολίονες ὑπερφίαλοι. καὶ μὰν ξεναπάτας
35 Ἐπειῶν βασιλεὺς ὄπιθεν

18, 92 Ἀγησ. s : Ἀγησ. mss (BMGFC).
23 ἔργων πρὸ πάντων : ἐτέων προπάντων conjectured by
Bergk from Schol. in A, ἁπάντων τῶν ἐτῶν τοῦ βίου.
25 βωμῶν AE ἑξάριθμον (MGFC) ; βωμῷ — BDG (S) ; βωμὸν —
CNO ; μολὼν Headlam ; βίη Ἡρακλέος interpolated mss,
rightly regarded by B as corrupt.
33 ἥμενον most mss and old scholia (M²FS) : ἥμενοι Heyne
(BM¹GC).

112

battle with Cycnus; and Hâgêsidâmus, victorious as
a boxer at Olympia, may offer thanks to Ilas, even
as Patroclus did to Achilles. When anyone is
born for prowess, one may, as a man, with the help
of God, whet his keen spirit and prompt him to
great glory. Few indeed have won, without toil,
the joy that is a light of life above[1] all labours.

But the laws of Zeus prompt me to sing that
famous scene of contest, founded by Heracles with its
altars six in number, near the olden tomb of Pelops;
for Heracles slew Cteatus, the blameless son of
Poseidon, and slew Eurytus too, that he might
forthwith exact from the unwilling and over-weening
Augeas the wage for his menial service; and he,
even Heracles, lay in wait for them in the thicket
and overcame them below Cleônae by the roadside;
for aforetime the haughty Moliônes had destroyed
for him his Tirynthian host, when it was encamped in
the heart of Elis. And, verily, not long after, the
faithless king of the Epeians[2] saw his rich country,

---

[1] Or "before"; or "for," "in recompense for" (Christ),
but πρὸ (for ἀντὶ) can hardly be defended. Hence the force
of Bergk's conjecture ἐτέων προπάντων, "for all the years."

[2] The inhabitants of Elis. Cp. O. ix 58.

οὐ πολλὸν ἴδε πατρίδα πολυκτέανον ὑπὸ στερεῷ
    πυρὶ
πλαγαῖς τε σιδάρου βαθὺν εἰς ὀχετὸν ἄτας
ἵζοισαν ἑὰν πόλιν.
νεῖκος δὲ κρεσσόνων
40 ἀποθέσθ' ἄπορον.
καὶ κεῖνος ἀβουλίᾳ ὕστατος
ἁλώσιος ἀντάσαις θάνατον αἰπὺν οὐκ ἐξέφυγεν. 50
στρ. γ΄
  ὁ δ' ἄρ' ἐν Πίσᾳ ἔλσαις ὅλον τε στρατὸν
  λαίαν τε πᾶσαν Διὸς ἄλκιμος
45 υἱὸς σταθμᾶτο ζάθεον ἄλσος πατρὶ μεγίστῳ· περὶ
    δὲ πάξαις Ἄλτιν μὲν ὅγ' ἐν καθαρῷ
διέκρινε, τὸ δὲ κύκλῳ πέδον
ἔθηκε δόρπου λύσιν,
τιμάσαις πόρον Ἀλφεοῦ
ἀντ. γ΄
  μετὰ δώδεκ' ἀνάκτων θεῶν. καὶ πάγον
50 Κρόνου προσεφθέγξατο· πρόσθε γὰρ   60
  νώνυμνος, ἇς Οἰνόμαος ἄρχε, βρέχετο πολλᾷ
    νιφάδι. ταῦτα δ' ἐν πρωτογόνῳ τελετᾷ
παρέσταν μὲν ἄρα Μοῖραι σχεδὸν
ὅ τ' ἐξελέγχων μόνος
ἀλάθειαν ἐτήτυμον
ἐπ. γ΄
55 χρόνος. τὸ δὲ σαφανὲς ἰὼν πόρσω κατέφρασεν,
ὅπα τὰν πολέμοιο δόσιν
ἀκρόθινα διελὼν ἔθυε καὶ πενταετηρίδ' ὅπως ἄρα 70
ἔστασεν ἑορτὰν σὺν Ὀλυμπιάδι πρώτᾳ
νικαφορίαισί τε.

    44 λαίαν (BMGFC) ; λαῖαν old mss, λείαν interpolated mss ;
λᾷαν Ahrens (s).

aye, his own city, sinking into the deep gulf of ruin beneath the remorseless fire and the iron blows.[1] Hard it is to rid oneself of strife with them that are stronger than ourselves; so even he, by his ill counsel, last of all found himself captured, and could not escape falling into deep destruction.

Then did the brave son of Zeus gather all the host, with the whole of the spoil, in Pisa, and measured out a holy precinct for his sire supreme; and, fencing round the Altis, he marked it off in the open, and the soil around he set apart as a resting-place for the evening banquet, thus doing honour to the stream of the Alpheüs, among the twelve rulers divine. And he gave a name to the hill of Cronus, for aforetime it was nameless, while Oenomaüs was king, and it was besprent with many a shower of snow. But, in this rite primaeval, the Fates were standing near at hand, and Time, the sole declarer of the very truth. And Time, in passing onward, clearly told the plain story, how Heracles divided the spoils that were the gift of war, and offered sacrifice, and how he ordained the four years' festival along with the first Olympic games and with contests for victors.

[1] The Molîones, that is Cteatus and Eurytus, the twin sons of Poseidon (or of Actor), and the nephews of Augeas king of the Epeians, had attacked Heracles, and had slain in Elis the host he had brought from Tiryns. They had thus prevented his exacting the wage due for cleansing the stables of their uncle, Augeas. Accordingly, when the Molîones were on their way back from Elis to the Isthmus, Heracles lay in wait for them, and slew them near Cleônae. Thereupon, he marched against Augeas and put him to death. With the spoil thus acquired, he founded the Olympian games. Cp. *Iliad* xi 709, 750 and Pausanias, v 1, 7, and 2.

60 τίς δὴ ποταίνιον
ἔλαχε στέφανον
χείρεσσι ποσίν τε καὶ ἅρματι,
ἀγώνιον ἐν δόξᾳ θέμενος εὖχος, ἔργῳ καθελών;
στρ. δ'
σταδίου μὲν ἀρίστευσεν εὐθὺν τόνον
65 ποσσὶ τρέχων παῖς ὁ Λικυμνίου
Οἰωνός· ἵκεν δὲ Μιδέαθεν στρατὸν ἐλαύνων· ὁ δὲ
πάλᾳ κυδαίνων Ἔχεμος Τεγέαν·   80
Δόρυκλος δ' ἔφερε πυγμᾶς τέλος,
Τίρυνθα ναίων πόλιν·
ἀν' ἵπποισι δὲ τέτρασιν
ἀντ. δ'
70 ἀπὸ Μαντινέας Σᾶμος ὡλιροθίου·
ἄκοντι Φράστωρ ἔλασε σκοπόν·
μᾶκος δὲ Νικεὺς ἔδικε πέτρῳ χέρα κυκλώσαις
ὑπὲρ ἁπάντων, καὶ συμμαχία θόρυβον
παραίθυξε μέγαν· ἐν δ' ἕσπερον   90
ἔφλεξεν εὐώπιδος
75 σελάνας ἐρατὸν φάος.
ἐπ. δ'
ἀείδετο δὲ πᾶν τέμενος τερπναῖσι θαλίαις
τὸν ἐγκώμιον ἀμφὶ τρόπον.
ἀρχαῖς δὲ προτέραις ἑπόμενοι καί νυν ἐπωνυμίαν
χάριν
νίκας ἀγερώχου, κελαδησόμεθα βροντὰν
80 καὶ πυρπάλαμον βέλος
ὀρσικτύπου Διός,
ἐν ἅπαντι κράτει
αἴθωνα κεραυνὸν ἀραρότα.

72 δὲ Νικεὺς Meineke 1845, since found in A and scholium (MGFCS) : δ' Ἐνικεὺς most mss (B).

116

Tell me who it was that won the primal crown with hands or feet or chariot, when he had set before his mind the glory of the games and had attained that glory in very deed? In the *stadium* the bravest in running a straight course with his feet was Oeônus, son of Licymnius, who had come from Midea at the head of his host. And in *wrestling*, it was Echemus who gat glory for Tegea. And the prize in *boxing* was won by Doryclus, who dwelt in the city of Tiryns; and, in the *car of four horses*, the victor was Samos of Mantinea, the son of Halirhothius. Phrastor it was who hit the mark with the *javelin*, and Niceus, who, with a circling sweep of his hand, excelled all others in flinging afar the *weight* of stone; and all the friendly host raised a mighty cheer, while the lovely light of the fair-faced moon lit up the evening, and, in the joyous festival, all the precinct rang with song like banquet-music.

And even now, as we follow the first beginnings of the games, as a namesake song of the victory proud,[1] we shall loudly sing of the thunder, and the fire-flung bolt of Zeus, the lord of the levin, the gleaming thunder-bolt that is the fit emblem in every victory[2]; and there shall answer to the pipe

---

[1] χάριν ἐπωνυμίαν νίκας ἀγερώχου means ἀοιδὰν ἐπινίκιον or Ὀλυμπιόνικον.

[2] Thunder was a good omen (*P.* iv 197), and the thunder-bolt appears on coins of Elis, and on later coins of the Western Locrians.

χλιδῶσα δὲ μολπὰ πρὸς κάλαμον ἀντιάξει
    μελέων,   100
στρ. έ
85 τὰ παρ' εὐκλέϊ Δίρκα χρόνῳ μὲν φάνεν·
  ἀλλ' ὥτε παῖς ἐξ ἀλόχου πατρὶ
  ποθεινὸς ἵκοντι, νεότατος τὸ πάλιν ἤδη, μάλα δέ
    οἱ θερμαίνει φιλότατι νόον·
  ἐπεὶ πλοῦτος ὁ λαχὼν ποιμένα
  ἐπακτὸν ἀλλότριον,
90 θνᾴσκοντι στυγερώτατος·
ἀντ. έ
  καὶ ὅταν καλὰ ἔρξαις ἀοιδᾶς ἄτερ,
  'Αγησίδαμ', εἰς 'Αΐδα σταθμὸν   110
  ἀνὴρ ἵκηται, κενεὰ πνεύσαις ἔπορε μόχθῳ βραχύ
    τι τερπνόν. τὶν δ' ἀδυεπής τε λύρα
  γλυκύς τ' αὐλὸς ἀναπάσσει χάριν·
95 τρέφοντι δ' εὐρὺ κλέος
  κόραι Πιερίδες Διός.
ἐπ. έ
  ἐγὼ δὲ συνεφαπτόμενος σπουδᾷ, κλυτὸν ἔθνος
  Λοκρῶν ἀμφέπεσον μέλιτι
  εὐάνορα πόλιν καταβρέχων· παῖδ' ἐρατὸν <δ'>
    'Αρχεστράτου   120
100 αἴνησα, τὸν εἶδον κρατέοντα χερὸς ἀλκᾷ
  βωμὸν παρ' 'Ολύμπιον,
  κεῖνον κατὰ χρόνον
  ἰδέᾳ τε καλὸν
  ὥρᾳ τε κεκραμένον, ἅ ποτε
105 ἀναιδέα Γανυμήδει μόρον ἄλαλκε σὺν Κυπρογενεῖ.

87 οἱ Boeckh (GFCS): τοι most mss (BM); τι NO.
  99 <δ'> Moschopulus, Hermann (edd.).
  105 μόρον Mommsen (GC): πότμον (BFS[1]); θάνατον almost all mss (s[3]).
118

the swelling melody of songs, which at last have come to light beside the famous stream of Dircê.[1]

But, even as a son born of a wife is welcome to a father who hath already reached the reverse of youth, and maketh his heart to glow with happiness, since, for one who is dying, it is a hateful sight to see his wealth falling to the lot of a master who is a stranger from another home; even so, Hâgêsidâmus, whensoever a man, who hath done noble deeds, descendeth to the abode of Hâdês, without the meed of song, he hath spent his strength and his breath in vain, and winneth but a little pleasure by his toil; whereas thou hast glory shed upon thee by the soft-toned lyre and by the sweet flute, and thy fame waxeth widely by favour of the Pierid daughters of Zeus.

I, the while, who am eagerly lending a hand of help, have taken to my heart the famous tribe of the Locrians, while I besprinkle with honey a city of noble sons; and I have praised the beauteous son of Archestratus, whom, on that day, beside the Olympic altar, I saw winning victory with the might of his hands,—one who was fair to look upon, and was graced with that bloom which, in olden days, by the blessing of Aphrodîtê, warded from Ganymede a ruthless fate.

---

[1] The fountain of Pindar's Theban home, cp. *I.* vi 74.

OLYMPIAN XI

FOR HÂGÊSIDÂMUS OF LOCRI EPIZEPHYRII

INTRODUCTION

THE eleventh Olympian was produced at Olympia immediately after the victory won in 476 by Hâgêsidâmus of Locri Epizephyrii in the boys' boxing-match.

There is a time for all things, a time for winds, a a time for showers. The time for song is when victory is won as the reward of toil (1–6). Beyond the reach of envy is the praise that is thus stored up for Olympian victors (7 f). This glory the poet's tongue would fain increase, but God alone makes victor and poet alike to prosper and be wise (8–10). To the victor's olive-wreath the poet will add the adornment of his song, and will also praise the race of the Western Locrians (11–15). There, in the West, the Muses must join the revel, and the poet avers that the Muses will there find a hospitable, accomplished, and heroic race. Neither the fox nor the lion may change his nature (16–21).

XI.—ΑΓΗΣΙΔΑΜΩ
ΛΟΚΡΩ ΕΠΙΖΕΦΥΡΙΩ

ΠΑΙΔΙ ΠΥΚΤΗ

στρ.

Ἔστιν ἀνθρώποις ἀνέμων ὅτε πλεῖστα
χρῆσις, ἔστιν δ' οὐρανίων ὑδάτων,
ὀμβρίων παίδων νεφέλας.
εἰ δὲ σὺν πόνῳ τις εὖ πράσσοι, μελιγάρυες ὕμνοι
5 ὑστέρων ἀρχὰ λόγων
τέλλεται καὶ πιστὸν ὅρκιον μεγάλαις ἀρεταῖς.

ἀντ.

ἀφθόνητος δ' αἶνος 'Ολυμπιονίκαις
οὗτος ἄγκειται. τὰ μὲν ἁμετέρα
γλῶσσα ποιμαίνειν ἐθέλει·
10 ἐκ θεοῦ δ' ἀνὴρ σοφαῖς ἀνθεῖ πραπίδεσσιν
ὁμοίως.   10
ἴσθι νῦν, 'Αρχεστράτου
παῖ, τεᾶς, 'Αγησίδαμε, πυγμαχίας ἕνεκεν

ἐπ.

κόσμον ἐπὶ στεφάνῳ χρυσέας ἐλαίας
ἁδυμελῆ κελαδήσω,
15 Ζεφυρίων Λοκρῶν γενεὰν ἀλέγων.

2 f. ὑδάτων, ὀμβρίων παίδων νεφέλας Wilamowitz (s): ὑδάτων ὀμβίων, παίδων νεφέλας vulgo.
5 ἀρχὰ A (MGCS): ἀρχαὶ the other old mss (BF).
10 πραπίδεσσιν ὁμοίως from lemma in scholia to BC (GCS): πρ. ὁμῶς ὢν CNO (M); ἐσαεὶ πρ. Moschopulus (BF).
15 Ζεφυρίων Boehmer (S): τῶν 'Επιζ. mss (edd.).

122

XI.—FOR HÂGÊSIDÂMUS
OF LOCRI EPIZEPHYRII

WINNER IN THE BOYS' BOXING MATCH, 476 B.C.

THERE is a time when men welcome the winds, and a time when they welcome the waters of heaven, the rain-laden daughters of the cloud.[1] But, when anyone is victorious by aid of toil, then it is that honey-voiced odes are a foundation for future fame, even a faithful witness to noble exploits.

Far beyond envy is the praise that is thus stored up for victors at Olympia; and such praises my tongue would fain feed and foster; but by the gift of a god alone doth a man flourish for ever, as thou dost, with wisdom of heart.

For the present rest assured, Hâgêsidâmus, son of Archestratus, that, for the sake of thy victory in boxing, I shall loudly sing a sweet strain that shall lend a new grace to the crown of the golden olive, while I duly honour the folk of the Western

---

[1] Similarly the clouds are called the "rain-bearing maidens" in the *Clouds* of Aristophanes, 298.

PINDAR

ἔνθα συγκωμάξατ᾽· ἐγγυάσομαι
ὔμμιν, ὦ Μοῖσαι, φυγόξενον στρατὸν
μηδ᾽ ἀπείρατον καλῶν,
ἀκρόσοφον δὲ καὶ αἰχματὰν ἀφίξεσθαι. τὸ γὰρ
20 ἐμφυὲς οὔτ᾽ αἴθων ἀλώπηξ   20
οὔτ᾽ ἐρίβρομοι λέοντες διαλλάξαντο ἦθος.

17 ὔμμιν Jongh (GCS): μή μιν mss (BF), μή νιν (M).
19 δὲ EF (BGFC): τε ABCD (MS).
21 διαλλάξαντο, gnomic aorist, Lehrs (S): διαλλάξαιντο
(ἂν C supra) mss.

Locrians. There join, ye Muses, in the triumph-song ; for I shall pledge my word to you that we shall there find a race that doth not repel the stranger, or is unfamiliar with noble pursuits, but is wise beyond all others and warlike too ; for neither the tawny fox nor the roaring lion changes his inborn nature.

OLYMPIAN XII

FOR ERGOTELÊS OF HIMERA

INTRODUCTION

Ergotelês, when he was forced by political faction to leave his native city of Cnôssus in Crete, settled at Himera in Sicily. He reached Himera during the war waged from 478 to 476 between Hieron of Syracuse, and Thêrôn of Acragas (not between Hieron and Gelon, as wrongly stated by the Scholiast). The Ode assumes that Himera is now free, and the victor has there acquired the right of citizenship and that of holding land (Cp. Freeman's *Sicily*, ii 300).

Crete, his native island, was famous for its runners (Xen. *Anab.* iv 8, 27), and the Cretan exile, after winning races at the Pythian and Isthmian games, won the long-race at Olympia in 472, the event celebrated in the present Ode. He was again victorious in 468, and twice at Nemea (Pausanias, vi 4, 11).

The long-race is variously stated to be 7, 12, 20, or 24 furlongs (*i.e.* three miles). This last was probably the length adopted at Olympia.

The poet prays that Himera may be blessed by Fortune—Fortune who guides ships and wars and

INTRODUCTION

councils (1–5). Men's hopes are like ships tossed up and down at sea (5–9). The future is unseen; pleasure passes into pain; and a sea of troubles into peace profound (10–12). If the victor had not been driven from his home in Crete, he would merely have been cock of the walk at home, whereas now he has won prizes in the great games of Greece, and has exalted his new home of Himera, where he dwells amid broad acres of his own (13–19).

In l. 19 the victor's new home of Himera is described as "the hot baths of the Nymphs." This is an allusion to the hot springs, which, at the bidding of Athênê, the Nymphs of the land caused to burst forth for the refreshment of Heracles. It is from these hot baths, or *Thermae*, that Himera derives its modern name of *Termini*. Cp. Freeman's *Sicily*, i 59, 77, 417.

XII.—ΕΡΓΟΤΕΛΕΙ ΙΜΕΡΑΙΩ

ΔΟΛΙΧΟΔΡΟΜΩ

στρ.

Λίσσομαι, παῖ Ζηνὸς Ἐλευθερίου,
Ἱμέραν εὐρυσθενέ' ἀμφιπόλει, σώτειρα Τύχα.
τὶν γὰρ ἐν πόντῳ κυβερνῶνται θοαὶ
νᾶες, ἐν χέρσῳ τε λαιψηροὶ πόλεμοι
5 κἀγοραὶ βουλαφόροι. αἴ γε μὲν ἀνδρῶν
πόλλ' ἄνω, τὰ δ' αὖ κάτω ψεύδη μεταμώνια
τάμνοισαι κυλίνδοντ' ἐλπίδες·

ἀντ.

σύμβολον δ' οὔ πώ τις ἐπιχθονίων   10
πιστὸν ἀμφὶ πράξιος ἐσσομένας εὗρεν θεόθεν·
τῶν δὲ μελλόντων τετύφλωνται φραδαί.
10 πολλὰ δ' ἀνθρώποις παρὰ γνώμαν ἔπεσεν,
ἔμπαλιν μὲν τέρψιος, οἱ δ' ἀνιαραῖς
ἀντικύρσαντες ζάλαις ἐσλὸν βαθὺ πήματος ἐν
μικρῷ πεδάμειψαν χρόνῳ.

ἐπ.

υἱὲ Φιλάνορος, ἤτοι καὶ τεά κεν,
ἐνδομάχας ἅτ' ἀλέκτωρ, συγγόνῳ παρ' ἑστίᾳ   20
15 ἀκλεὴς τιμὰ κατεφυλλορόησε ποδῶν,
εἰ μὴ στάσις ἀντιάνειρα Κνωσίας ἄμερσε πάτρας.
νῦν δ' Ὀλυμπίᾳ στεφανωσάμενος
καὶ δὶς ἐκ Πυθῶνος Ἰσθμοῖ τ', Ἐργότελες,
θερμὰ Νυμφᾶν λουτρὰ βαστάζεις, ὁμιλέων παρ'
οἰκείαις ἀρούραις.

XII.—FOR ERGOTELÊS OF HIMERA

WINNER IN THE LONG FOOT-RACE, 470(?) B.C.

DAUGHTER of Zeus the Deliverer! thou saving goddess, Fortune! I pray thee to keep watch around mighty Himera; for, at thy bidding, swift ships are steered upon the sea, and speedy decisions of war and counsels of the people are guided on the land. Verily, the hopes of men are tossed, now high, now low, as they cleave the treacherous sea of fancies vain. But never yet hath any man on earth found a sure token sent from heaven to tell him how he shall fare in the future, but warnings of events to come are wrapped in gloom.

Full many things have befallen man, of which he little dreamed, bringing, to some, reversal of delight, while others, after battling with a sea of troubles, have, in a short space of time, exchanged their anguish for the deepest joy.

Son of Philânor! like some Chanticleer, who is courageous at home alone, the fame of thy swift feet would have shed its foliage ingloriously beside thy native hearth, had not hostile faction bereft thee of thy Cnossian fatherland. And now, Ergotelês! having won a wreath once at Olympia, and twice from Pytho, and at the Isthmus, thou art exalting the hot baths of the Nymphs, while dwelling near broad acres all thine own.

OLYMPIAN XIII

FOR XENOPHON OF CORINTH

INTRODUCTION

The father of Xenophon of Corinth won the foot-race at Olympia in 504 B.C. Xenophon himself is now lauded as having (in **464** B.C.) performed the unprecedented feat of winning the stadium and the pentathlon on the same day. The stadium was the short foot-race of about 200 yards; the length of the Olympic stadium was just under 630 feet. The pentathlon was a contest including five events, which Simonides enumerates as ἅλμα, ποδωκείην, δίσκον, ἄκοντα, πάλην. The actual order of the events was probably foot-race, long jump, discus, javelin, wrestling. Victory in three events was sufficient, but not necessary. If no competitor won three events, or if two won two events, the prize was probably decided by taking account of second or third places in the several results. (E. Norman Gardiner, *Greek Athletic Sports and Festivals*, 1910, p. 370).

The praise of the victor's family is bound up with the praise of Corinth (1–5), the dwelling-place of Law and Justice and Peace (6–10). A noble theme

INTRODUCTION

must be treated with truthful courage (11 f). Corinth is famed for athletic prowess and inventive spirit: it has invented the dithyramb, the bit, and the adornment of the pediment with the eagle. It is the home of the Muses and of the God of War (13–23). May Zeus preserve the people, and welcome the triumphal chorus in honour of Xenophon's victory in two events, which have never before been won on the same day (24–29). Victories previously won by Xenophon (29–34), and by his father (35–40), and his family (40–46). These victories are as countless as the sand of the sea, but it is now time to make an end of this theme (47 f); and thus the poet returns to the praise of Corinth, and of the famous Corinthians, Sisyphus, Medea, and Glaucus (49–62).

The myth of Bellerophon (63–92). But the poet must not hurl his javelins too often; he therefore checks himself (93–95), and returns to the successes won by the victor's house; ending with a prayer that it may continue to prosper (96–115).

XIII.—ΞΕΝΟΦΩΝΤΙ ΚΟΡΙΝΘΙΩ

ΣΤΑΔΙΟΔΡΟΜΩ ΚΑΙ ΠΕΝΤΑΘΛΩ

στρ. α΄

Τρισολυμπιονίκαν
ἐπαινέων οἶκον ἄμερον ἀστοῖς,
ξένοισι δὲ θεράποντα, γνώσομαι
τὰν ὀλβίαν Κόρινθον, Ἰσθμίου
5 πρόθυρον Ποτειδᾶνος, ἀγλαόκουρον.
ἐν τᾷ γὰρ Εὐνομία ναίει, κασίγνηταί τε, βάθρον
πολίων ἀσφαλές,
Δίκα καὶ ὁμότροφος Εἰρήνα, ταμίαι ἀνδράσι
πλούτου,   10
χρύσεαι παῖδες εὐβούλου Θέμιτος·

ἀντ. α΄

ἐθέλοντι δ᾽ ἀλέξειν
10 Ὕβριν, Κόρου ματέρα θρασύμυθον.
ἔχω καλά τε φράσαι, τόλμα τέ μοι
εὐθεῖα γλῶσσαν ὀρνύει λέγειν.
ἄμαχον δὲ κρύψαι τὸ συγγενὲς ἦθος.
ὔμμιν δέ, παῖδες Ἀλάτα, πολλὰ μὲν νικαφόρον
ἀγλαΐαν ὤπασαν
15 ἄκραις ἀρεταῖς ὑπερελθόντων ἱεροῖς ἐν ἀέθλοις, 20
πολλὰ δ᾽ ἐν καρδίαις ἀνδρῶν ἔβαλον

ἐπ. α΄

Ὧραι πολυάνθεμοι ἀρχαῖα σοφίσμαθ᾽. ἅπαν δ᾽
εὑρόντος ἔργον.

7 ὁμότροφος (Ambrosian recension) Εἰρήνα (MGCS): ὁπό-
τροπος (Vatican recension) Εἰράνα (BF).
    ταμίαι mss (BGFC): ταμί᾽ Ahrens (MS).

XIII.—FOR XENOPHON OF CORINTH

WINNER IN THE SHORT FOOT-RACE AND IN THE PENTATHLUM, 464 B.C.

WHILE I laud a house, thrice victor at Olympia, gentle to her own citizens, and kindly to strangers, I shall take knowledge of prosperous Corinth, portal of Isthmian Poseidon, glorious with her noble youths. Within her walls dwelleth Law, and her sisters, the firm-set foundation of cities, even Justice and Peace that is fostered beside her, those guardians of wealth for man, the golden daughters of Themis, who excelleth in counsel; and they are resolute in repelling Insolence, the bold-tongued mother of Surfeit. Fair is the tale I have to tell, and courage that maketh straight for the mark prompteth my tongue to speak; it is a hard struggle to quell one's inborn nature.

As for you, ye sons of Alêtês! full often have the Seasons rich in flowers endued you with the splendour of victory, while, by your highest merit, ye have excelled in the sacred games; full often too have those seasons put into the hearts of men the inventions of the olden time: but all the fame is due to the first finder.

ταὶ Διωνύσου πόθεν ἐξέφανεν
σὺν βοηλάτᾳ χάριτες διθυράμβῳ;
20 τίς γὰρ ἱππείοις ἐν ἔντεσσιν μέτρα,
ἢ θεῶν ναοῖσιν οἰωνῶν βασιλέα δίδυμον
ἐπέθηκ'; ἐν δὲ Μοῖσ' ἀδύπνοος,   30
ἐν δ' Ἄρης ἀνθεῖ νέων οὐλίαις αἰχμαῖσιν
        ἀνδρῶν.

στρ. β'
        ὕπατ' εὐρὺ ἀνάσσων
25 Ὀλυμπίας, ἀφθόνητος ἔπεσσιν
γένοιο χρόνον ἅπαντα, Ζεῦ πάτερ,
καὶ τόνδε λαὸν ἀβλαβῆ νέμων
Ξενοφῶντος εὔθυνε δαίμονος οὖρον·
δέξαι τέ οἱ στεφάνων ἐγκώμιον τεθμόν, τὸν ἄγει
        πεδίων ἐκ Πίσας,   40
30 πεντάθλῳ ἅμα σταδίου νικῶν δρόμον· ἀντεβόλη-
        σεν
τῶν ἀνὴρ θνατὸς οὔπω τις πρότερον.

ἀντ. β'
        δύο δ' αὐτὸν ἔρεψαν
πλόκοι σελίνων ἐν Ἰσθμιάδεσσιν
φανέντα· Νεμέα τ' οὐκ ἀντιξοεῖ.

---

29 τέ Ambrosian recension (ms): δέ Vatican recension
(bgfc).

Whence was it that the graces of Dionysus first came to light, with the ox-driving dithyramb?[1] Aye, and who was it that, amid the harness of horses, invented the restraining bridle,[2] or, on the temples of the gods, planted the twin king of birds?[3] And there the Muse with her sweet breath, there too the war-god flourisheth with the deadly spears of youthful heroes.

Lord supreme of Olympia! that reignest far and wide, O Father Zeus! never, for all time, be thou jealous of our language, but, ruling this people in all security, grant a straight course to the fair breeze of Xenophon's good fortune, and accept from him the duly ordered triumph-band in honour of his crowns, the band that he bringeth from the plains of Pisa, being victor in the five events, as well as in the foot-race. He hath thus attained what no mortal man ever yet attained before. And two wreaths of wild celery[4] crowned him, when he appeared at the Isthmian festival; and Nemea hath shown no unkindly

[1] In early times, an ox was the prize of the victor in the dithyramb. Simonides describes himself as the winner of "fifty-six bulls and tripods." Frag. 145 (202).

[2] In the rest of this ode, Pindar never directly names the "restraining bridle," or bit; but resorts to a series of happy periphrases :—"a bridle with a golden band" (65), "a charm for the steed" (68), "a wondrous thing" (73), "a golden tamer of the horse's temper" (78), and "the gentle spell" (85).

[3] *i.e.* placed the eagle, as a "finial," on the top of each of the two gables or pediments.

[4] The crown of σέλινον was given as a prize in the Isthmian games (cp. *N.* iv 88, and *I.* ii 16 and viii 64). σέλινον is best identified, not with "parsley," *Petroselinum sativum,* but with "wild celery," *Apium graveolens.* The river and the town Selinûs in Sicily derived their name from the wild celery which grew plentifully on the banks of the river (Head's *Historia Numorum,* p. 146, ed. 1887).

35 πατρὸς δὲ Θεσσαλοῦ ἐπ' Ἀλφεοῦ
ῥεέθροισιν αἴγλα ποδῶν ἀνάκειται,
Πυθοῖ τ' ἔχει σταδίου τιμὰν διαύλου θ' ἁλίῳ ἀμφ'
ἑνί, μηνός τέ οἱ   50
τωὐτοῦ κρανααῖς ἐν Ἀθάναισι τρία ἔργα ποδαρκὴς
ἀμέρα θῆκε κάλλιστ' ἀμφὶ κόμαις,
ἐπ. β΄
40 Ἑλλώτια δ' ἑπτάκις· ἐν δ' ἀμφιάλοισι Ποτειδᾶνος
τεθμοῖσιν
Πτοιοδώρῳ σὺν πατρὶ μακρότεραι
Τερψίᾳ θ' ἕψοντ' Ἐριτίμῳ τ' ἀοιδαί.   60
ὅσσα τ' ἐν Δελφοῖσιν ἀριστεύσατε
ἠδὲ χόρτοις ἐν λέοντος, δηρίομαι πολέσιν
45 περὶ πλήθει καλῶν, ὡς μὰν σαφὲς
οὐκ ἂν εἰδείην λέγειν ποντιᾶν ψάφων ἀριθμόν.
στρ. γ΄
ἕπεται δ' ἐν ἑκάστῳ
μέτρον· νοῆσαι δὲ καιρὸς ἄριστος.
ἐγὼ δὲ ἴδιος ἐν κοινῷ σταλεὶς
50 μῆτίν τε γαρύων παλαιγόνων   70
πόλεμόν τ' ἐν ἡρωΐαις ἀρεταῖσιν
οὐ ψεύσομ' ἀμφὶ Κορίνθῳ, Σίσυφον μὲν πυκνότατον
παλάμαις ὡς θεόν,
καὶ τὰν πατρὸς ἀντία Μήδειαν θεμέναν γάμον
αὐτᾷ,
ναῖ σώτειραν Ἀργοῖ καὶ προπόλοις.
ἀντ. γ΄
55 τὰ δὲ καί ποτ' ἐν ἀλκᾷ
πρὸ Δαρδάνου τειχέων ἐδόκησαν
ἐπ' ἀμφότερα μαχᾶν τάμνειν τέλος,   80

. 42 τερψίες θ' — ἐρίτιμοι τ' mss, corrected by Erasmus
Schmid.   ἕψοντ' mss (MGFCS): ἕσποντ' Bothe (B).

mood; and, at the stream of Alpheüs, is stored up
the glory won by the swift feet of his father, Thes-
salus. At Pytho, he hath the fame of the single
and the double foot-race, won within the circuit
of the self-same sun; and, in the same month, at
rocky Athens did one swift day fling o'er his hair
three fairest crowns of victory, and seven times was
he victorious at the festival of Athênâ Hellôtis.
In Poseidon's games betwixt the seas, too long
would be the songs which shall attain to all the
victories won by Terpsias and Eritîmus, with their
father Ptoeödôrus [1]; and, as for all your prowess at
Delphi, and in the Lion's haunts,[2] I am ready to
contend with many as to the number of your prizes;
for, in truth, I could not have the skill to tell the
number of the pebbles of the sea.

Yet measure due is meet in all things, and the
fitting moment is the best aim of knowledge; but I,
in the fleet of the common joy, setting forth on a course
of my own, and telling of the craft and the warrior-
worth of the men of yore, shall, in the tale of heroic
prowess, truly speak of Corinth. I shall tell of
Sisyphus, who, like a very god, was most wise in his
counsels; and of Mêdeia, who resolved on her own
marriage against her father's will, and thus saved the
ship Argo and her seamen. And, again, of old, in
the fight they [3] were deemed to decide the issue of
battles on either side, whether they were essaying,

---

[1] We might naturally suppose that Ptoeödôrus was the
father of Terpsias and Eritîmus; but the scholia make
Ptoeödôrus (son of Thessalus) a brother, and Eritîmus a son
or grandson, of Terpsias.
[2] Nemea.   [3] Corinthians, implied in the context.

τοὶ μὲν γένει φίλῳ σὺν Ἀτρέος
Ἑλέναν κομίζοντες, οἱ δ' ἀπὸ πάμπαν
60 εἴργοντες· ἐκ Λυκίας δὲ Γλαῦκον ἐλθόντα τρόμεον
Δαναοί. τοῖσι μὲν
ἐξεύχετ' ἐν ἄστεϊ Πειράνας σφετέρου πατρὸς ἀρχὰν
καὶ βαθὺν κλᾶρον ἔμμεν καὶ μέγαρον·

ἐπ. γ'
ὃς τᾶς ὀφιώδεος υἱόν ποτε Γοργόνος ἦ πόλλ' ἀμφὶ
κρουνοῖς   90
Πάγασον ζεῦξαι ποθέων ἔπαθεν,
65 πρίν γέ οἱ χρυσάμπυκα κούρα χαλινὸν
Παλλὰς ἤνεγκ'· ἐξ ὀνείρου δ' αὐτίκα
ἦν ὕπαρ· φώνασε δ'· "Εὕδεις, Αἰολίδα βασιλεῦ;
ἄγε φίλτρον τόδ' ἵππειον δέκευ,
καὶ Δαμαίῳ νιν θύων ταῦρον ἀργᾶντα πατρὶ
δεῖξον."

στρ. δ'
70 κυαναιγὶς ἐν ὄρφνα   100
κνώσσοντί οἱ παρθένος τόσα εἰπεῖν
ἔδοξεν· ἀνὰ δ' ἐπᾶλτ' ὀρθῷ ποδί.
παρκείμενον δὲ συλλαβὼν τέρας,
ἐπιχώριον μάντιν ἄσμενος εὗρεν,
75 δεῖξέν τε Κοιρανίδᾳ πᾶσαν τελευτὰν πράγματος,
ὥς τ' ἀνὰ βωμῷ θεᾶς
κοιτάξατο νύκτ' ἀπὸ κείνου χρήσιος. ὥς τέ οἱ
αὐτὰ
Ζηνὸς ἐγχεικεραύνου παῖς ἔπορεν   110

ἀντ. δ'
δαμασίφρονα χρυσόν.
ἐνυπνίῳ δ' ᾇ τάχιστα πιθέσθαι
80 κελήσατό μιν, ὅταν δ' εὐρυσθενεῖ

79 ᾇ E (MGFCS): ὡς Byzantine mss (B).

with the dear son of Atreus, to recover Helen, or were steadfastly opposing the attempt. And the Danai trembled before Glaucus, when hé came from Lycia, while he boasted before them that in the city of Peirênê lay the rule and the rich inheritance and the hall of his own ancestor; who verily suffered sorely when he was eager to bind beside the spring Pêgasus, the son of the snake-girt Gorgon, until at last the virgin Pallas brought a bridle with a golden band, and the dream became a vision of broad daylight, and she said :—" Sleepest thou, son of Aeolus? Come ! take this to charm thy steed; and, sacrificing a white bull, bring it into the presence of thy grandsire, the tamer of horses."[1] Such were the words which the queen of the dark aegis seemed to say to him as he slumbered in the darkness; and at once he leapt to his feet, and seizing the wondrous thing that lay beside him, he gladly went and found Polyîdus, the seer of that land, and told the son of Coeranus the whole story,—how that, at the bidding of the seer, he had laid him down to rest for the night on the altar of the goddess, and how the very daughter of Zeus who hurleth the thunderbolt had given him that golden tamer of the horse's temper. And the seer bade him with all speed do the bidding of the dream; and, when he sacrificed the strong-footed

[1] Bellerophon's father, Aeolus, was a reputed son of Poseidon.

καρταίποδ᾽ ἀναρύῃ Γεαόχῳ,
θέμεν Ἱππίᾳ βωμὸν εὐθὺς Ἀθάνᾳ.
τελεῖ δὲ θεῶν δύναμις καὶ τὰν παρ᾽ ὅρκον καὶ
    παρὰ ἐλπίδα κούφαν κτίσιν.
ἤτοι καὶ ὁ καρτερὸς ὁρμαίνων ἕλε Βελλερο-
    φόντας,   120
85 φάρμακον πραῢ τείνων ἀμφὶ γένυι,
ἐπ. δ´
ἵππον πτερόεντ᾽· ἀναβὰς δ᾽ εὐθὺς ἐνόπλια
    χαλκωθεὶς ἔπαιζεν.
σὺν δὲ κείνῳ καί ποτ᾽ Ἀμαζονίδων
αἰθέρος ψυχρᾶς ἀπὸ κόλπων ἐρήμων
τοξόταν βάλλων γυναικεῖον στρατόν,
90 καὶ Χίμαιραν πῦρ πνέοισαν καὶ Σολύμους
    ἔπεφνεν.
διασωπάσομαί οἱ μόρον ἐγώ·   130
τὸν δ᾽ ἐν Οὐλύμπῳ φάτναι Ζηνὸς ἀρχαῖαι
    δέκονται.
στρ. ε´
ἐμὲ δ᾽ εὐθὺν ἀκόντων
ἱέντα ῥόμβον παρὰ σκοπὸν οὐ χρὴ
95 τὰ πολλὰ βέλεα καρτύνειν χεροῖν.
Μοίσαις γὰρ ἀγλαοθρόνοις ἑκὼν
Ὀλιγαιθίδαισίν τ᾽ ἔβαν ἐπίκουρος.
Ἰσθμοῖ τά τ᾽ ἐν Νεμέᾳ παύρῳ ἔπει θήσω φανέρ᾽
    ἀθρό᾽, ἀλαθής τέ μοι   140

81 ἀναρύῃ old mss (MGFS³): αὐερύῃ lemma of scholium,
corrected by Drachmann (BCS¹).
83 τελεῖ δὲ most mss (MGFCS): τελεῖ D alone (B).
88 ψυχρᾶς mss (BMGFC), ψυχρῶν S.   ἐρήμων Hermann
(GC): ἐρήμου mss (BMFS).
97 ἐπίκουρος. Ἰσθμοῖ—Νεμέᾳ παύρῳ M in notes (GFCS)
ἐπίκουρος Ἰσθμοῖ—Νεμέᾳ. παύρῳ δ᾽ (B and M in text).

beast to the Lord of the earth, straightway to dedicate an altar to Athênê, the goddess of horses. Now the power of the gods maketh that which one would vow to be impossible and beyond all hope, a light achievement. Verily, even so the strong Bellerophon, after all his eager striving, caught the winged steed, solely by stretching athwart his jaws that gentle spell; and, mounting on his back, at once he played the weapon-play in his brazen armour; and, riding on that steed, he assailed from the lonely bosom of the chill air that army of womankind, the archer host of Amazons; and even slew the fire-breathing Chimaera, and the Solymi. I shall pass in silence over his doom; but Pegasus hath found his shelter in the olden stalls of Zeus in Olympus.

But I, while casting my javelins straight with a whirl must not miss the mark in plying my many darts with the might of my hands.[1] For gladly have I come, as a champion of the Muses enthroned in splendour, and also of the race of Oligaethus. As to their victories at the Isthmus and at Nemea, with a few words shall I make all of them manifest; and,

---

[1] παρὰ σκοπόν, "beside the mark," is taken with οὐ χρὴ by the scholia, and by Thiersch, Dissen, Mezger, and Gildersleeve. Any praise (like further details on the mythical glories of Corinth) that is not directly aimed at the victor, is a dart that goes beside the mark. παρὰ σκοπόν (rendered "by the mark") is, however, taken by Fennell with εὐθὺν ἀκόντων ἱέντα ῥόμβον. But παρὰ σκοπὸν is best placed in the second clause, where it is naturally contrasted with εὐθύν in the first.

PINDAR

ἔξορκος ἐπέσσεται ἑξηκοντάκι δὴ ἀμφοτέρωθεν
100 ἀδύγλωσσος βοὰ κάρυκος ἐσλοῦ.
ἀντ. ε΄
τὰ δ᾽ Ὀλυμπίᾳ αὐτῶν
ἔοικεν ἤδη πάροιθε λελέχθαι·
τά τ᾽ ἐσσόμενα τότ᾽ ἂν φαίην σαφές·
νῦν δ᾽ ἔλπομαι μέν, ἐν θεῷ γε μὰν
105 τέλος· εἰ δὲ δαίμων γενέθλιος ἕρποι,
Δὶ τοῦτ᾽ Ἐνναλίῳ τ᾽ ἐκδώσομεν πράσσειν. τὰ δ᾽
                ἐπ᾽ ὀφρύϊ Παρνασσίᾳ   150
ἔξ. Ἄργεϊ θ᾽ ὅσσα καὶ ἐν Θήβαις, ὅσα τ᾽ Ἀρκάσιν
                ἀνάσσων
μαρτυρήσει Λυκαίου βωμὸς ἄναξ,
ἐπ. ε΄
Πέλλανά τε καὶ Σικυὼν καὶ Μέγαρ᾽ Αἰακιδᾶν τ᾽
                εὐερκὲς ἄλσος,
110 ἅ τ᾽ Ἐλευσὶς καὶ λιπαρὰ Μαραθών,
ταί θ᾽ ὑπ᾽ Αἴτνας ὑψιλόφου καλλίπλουτοι
πόλιες, ἅ τ᾽ Εὔβοια· καὶ πᾶσαν κατὰ   160
Ἑλλάδ᾽ εὑρήσεις ἐρευνῶν μᾶσσον᾽ ἢ ὡς ἰδέμεν.
ἄνα, κούφοισιν ἐκνεῦσαι ποσίν·
115 Ζεῦ τέλει᾽, αἰδῶ δίδοι καὶ τύχαν τερπνῶν
                γλυκεῖαν.

99 δὴ ἀμφ. BMGFC ; δὴμφ. S ; δ᾽ ἀμφ. old mss.

103 τά τ᾽ Vatican recension (GFCS) : τὰ δ᾽ Ambrosian
recension (BM).

106 f. Παρνασσίᾳ ἔξ· BC and scholium ἑξάκις (GS) : Παρ-
νασίᾳ. ἐν NOB (BFC). Παρνασίᾳ, ἑξ ἄρατ᾽· ἐν Ἄργεϊ κἂν
Θήβαις M.

107 Ἀρκάσιν ἀνάσσων old mss (S³, Ἀρκάσι βάσσαις S¹):

as a true witness under solemn oath, the sweet-tongued voice of a goodly herald, heard full sixty times at both places, will ratify my words. As for the victories won by them at Olympia, they have, meseems, been already mentioned, and, of those in the future, I could tell clearly in the days to come. For the present I cherish hope, howbeit the issue is in God's hand; but, if the good fortune of the house have free course, we shall leave this to Zeus and Enyalius to accomplish. And the prizes won beneath the brow of Parnassus, six in number, and, all in Argos, and in Thebes, and all that shall be witnessed by the royal altar of the Lycaean mount that ruleth over the Arcadians, and by Pellâna, and Sicyon, and Megara, and the fair-walled precinct of the sons of Aeacus, and Eleusis, and fertile Marathon, and the cities beauteous in wealth beneath the lofty crest of Etna, and Euboea,—aye, even throughout all Hellas, you may search and find them too many for the eye to view. Get thee up and swim away with nimble feet! and do thou, O Zeus, the giver of perfection, grant reverence and the sweet good-fortune of a happy lot.

'Αρκάσ' ἀνάσσων interpolated mss; 'Αρκὰς ἀνάσσων Hermann (BG); 'Αρκάσιν ἆσσον ᴍ, — ἆσσων C, — ἀέθλων F.

114 ἄνα Pauw, and Kayser with old scholia (BGFCS¹) : ἀλλὰ mss (MS³).

114f. ποσίν· Ζεῦ τέλει', (MGFCS) : ποσίν, Ζεῦ τέλει·' (B).

OLYMPIAN XIV

FOR ASÔPICHUS OF ORCHOMENUS

INTRODUCTION

ORCHOMENUS in Boeotia was a most ancient city. It was the home of the primeval Minyae, and the Graces were there worshipped from the earliest times. The Ode is a brief processional hymn, mainly in honour of the Graces. The Scholiasts state that the victor won the short foot-race for boys at Olympia in *Ol.* 76 (476) or *Ol.* 77 (472), but these Olympiads, and also *Ol.* 75, 78, 79, are already assigned to other victors. *Ol.* 76 is probably a mistake for *Ol.* 73 (488 B.C.).

The Graces are invoked as the queens of Orchomenus, and as the givers of all blessings; they are enthroned beside the Pythian Apollo (1–11). Each of them is next invoked by name. The aid of Thalia has won the event, which has made the city of the Minyae victorious at Olympia (15–18). Echo is bidden to bear the glad tidings to the father of the victor in the world below (11–22).

XIV.—ΑΣΩΠΙΧΩ ΟΡΧΟΜΕΝΙΩ

ΣΤΑΔΙΕΙ (παιδὶ Κλεοδάμου)

στρ. α΄

Καφισίων ὑδάτων
λαχοῖσαι, αἵτε ναίετε καλλίπωλον ἕδραν,
ὦ λιπαρᾶς ἀοίδιμοι βασίλειαι
Χάριτες Ὀρχομενοῦ, παλαιγόνων Μινυᾶν ἐπί-
    σκοποι,
5 κλῦτ᾽, ἐπεὶ εὔχομαι. σὺν γὰρ ὕμμιν τὰ τερπνὰ
    καὶ
τὰ γλυκέ᾽ ἄνεται πάντα βροτοῖς,
εἰ σοφός, εἰ καλός, εἴ τις ἀγλαὸς ἀνήρ.   10
οὐδὲ γὰρ θεοὶ σεμνᾶν Χαρίτων ἄτερ
κοιρανέοισιν χοροὺς οὔτε δαῖτας· ἀλλὰ πάντων
    ταμίαι
10 ἔργων ἐν οὐρανῷ, χρυσότοξον θέμεναι παρὰ
Πύθιον Ἀπόλλωνα θρόνους,
ἀέναον σέβοντι πατρὸς Ὀλυμπίοιο τιμάν.

στρ. β΄

<ὦ> πότνι᾽ Ἀγλαΐα
φιλησίμολπέ τ᾽ Εὐφροσύνα, θεῶν κρατίστου   20
15 παῖδες, ἐπακοοῖτε νῦν, Θαλία τε
ἐρασίμολπε, ἰδοῖσα τόνδε κῶμον ἐπ᾽ εὐμενεῖ τύχᾳ

---

2 αἵτε mss (BMGFC) : ταί τε Bergk (S).
4 Ὀρχ. most mss (GFC) : Ἐρχ. two late mss (BMS).
6 γλυκέ᾽ ἄνεται Kayser (GCS) : γλυκέα γίνεται mss (BMF).
13 ὦ P (edd.). πότνιά τε Vatican recension.
15 ἐπακοοῖτε νῦν Bergk (M¹GFCS) ; ἐπάκοοι τὸ νῦν M² : ἐπάκοσι νῦν mss ; ἐπάκοος γενοῦ Hermann (B).

Yᴇ that have your portion beside the waters of
Cephîsus! Ye that dwell in a home of fair horses!
Ye Graces of fertile Orchomenus, ye queens of song
that keep watch over the ancient Minyae,[1] listen to
my prayer! For, by your aid, all things pleasant
and sweet are accomplished for mortals, if any man
be skilled in song, or be fair to look upon, or hath
won renown. Yea, not even the gods order the
dance or the banquet, without the aid of the holy
Graces. Nay, rather, they are the ministrants of all
things in heaven, where their thrones are set beside
the Lord of the golden bow, the Pythian Apollo,
and where they adore the ever-flowing honour of the
Olympian Father

O queen Aglaïa, and Euphrosynê, that lovest the
dance and song, ye daughters of the mightiest of
the gods! may ye listen now; and thou Thalîa, that
art enamoured of the song and dance, when thou hast
looked upon this triumphant chorus, as it lightly
steppeth along in honour of the victor's good

---

[1] The ancient inhabitants of Orchomenus.

κοῦφα βιβῶντα· Λυδῷ γὰρ ᾿Ασώπιχον τρόπῳ
ἔν τε μελέταις ἀείδων ἔμολον,
οὕνεκ᾿ ᾿Ολυμπιόνικος ἁ Μιννεία
20 σεῦ ἕκατι. μελανοτειχέα νῦν δόμον
Φερσεφόνας ἔλθ᾿, ᾿Αχοῖ, πατρὶ κλυτὰν φέροισ᾿
  ἀγγελίαν,   30
Κλεόδαμον ὄφρ᾿ ἰδοῖσ᾿, υἱὸν εἴπῃς ὅτι οἱ νέαν
κόλποις παρ᾿ εὐδόξοις Πίσας
ἐστεφάνωσε κυδίμων ἀέθλων πτεροῖσι χαίταν.

22 Κλεόδαμον (MGFCS) ; Κλεύδαμον Β : Κλεοδάμῳ Β alone.
23 εὐδόξοις Boeckh (FS) : εὐδόξοιο mss ; εὐδόξου (MGC).

fortune. For I have come to sing the praise of Asôpichus with Lydian tune and with meditated lays, because, thanks to thee, the house of the Minyae is victorious in Olympia.

Now! hie thee, Echo, to the dark-walled home of Persephonê, and bear the glorious tidings to the father, so that, when thou hast seen Cleodâmus, thou mayest tell him that, beside the famous vale of Pisa, his son hath crowned his youthful locks with garlands won from the ennobling games.

THE PYTHIAN ODES

PYTHIAN I

FOR HIERON OF AETNA

INTRODUCTION

In 476 B.C. Hieron, after transporting all the inhabitants of Catana to Leontîni, peopled it afresh with 5,000 settlers from the Peloponnêsus, and 5,000 from Syracuse, and gave this new city the name of Aetna. In 475 there was a great eruption of Mount Etna, described in the course of this Ode (21–28). In 474 the naval attack of the Etruscans on Cumae was repelled by the ships of Hieron (72); and, in the year 470, Hieron, as founder of the city of Aetna, caused himself to be proclaimed as " Aetnaean " (32) on the occasion of the Pythian victory celebrated in this Ode. This victory of Hieron's chariot was won in the 29th Pythiad, that is, in August, 470. The same victory is celebrated in the fourth Ode of Bacchylides.

The lyre or cithern is here invoked as the instrument of Apollo and the Muses; its music is obeyed by the dancer's step and by the singer's voice; even by the thunderbolt and the bird of Zeus, and by the son of Zeus, namely the god of War (1–12).

But Music is hated by all that Zeus loves not, as by Typhon, pinioned beneath Mount Etna, whence he flings up jets of unapproachable fire (13–28).

INTRODUCTION

The poet prays for the favour of the lord of Mount Etna, whose namesake city was glorified on the Pythian course by its famous founder, when the herald proclaimed him as the " Aetnaean " (29–33). This victory is a happy omen for the new city (33–38). Apollo is also prayed to make the land a land of noble men (39 f).

All the exploits of man are due to the gods (41 f). Then follow the praises of Hieron, and the prayer that, like Philoctêtês of old, he may be befriended by a god (43–57).

Let the victory be celebrated by the Muse at the palace of Hieron's son, Deinomenes, now King of Aetna (58–60), the city which Hieron has established according to the laws of the Dorian race (61–66). May this harmony between princes and people abide ; may peace be handed down from sire to son (67–70) ; and may Zeus keep the Carthaginian and the Etruscan in their own homes, now that they have seen the insolence of their ships quelled off Cumae (71–75). The victory of Himera is to Hieron and his brothers what Salamis is to Athens, what Plataea is to Sparta (75–80).

But brevity is best. Men hate to hear of the prosperity of others ; but it is better to be envied than pitied (81–85). Hieron is prompted to keep to the cause of justice and truth, and to continue to be generous and kindly (86–92). When men are dead, it is Fame that reveals their true lives to chroniclers and to poets. Neither the generous kindliness of Croesus, nor the cruelty of Phalaris is forgotten. Good fortune is first ; good fame is next ; and the winning of both is the highest crown (92–100).

ΠΥΘΙΟΝΙΚΑΙ

I.—ΙΕΡΩΝΙ ΑΙΤΝΑΙΩ

στρ. α´

Χρυσέα φόρμιγξ, Ἀπόλλωνος καὶ ἰοπλοκάμων
σύνδικον Μοισᾶν κτέανον· τᾶς ἀκούει μὲν βάσις,
ἀγλαΐας ἀρχά,
πείθονται δ᾽ ἀοιδοὶ σάμασιν,
ἀγησιχόρων ὁπόταν προοιμίων ἀμβολὰς τεύχῃς
ἐλελιζομένα.
5 καὶ τὸν αἰχματὰν κεραυνὸν σβεννύεις
ἀενάου πυρός. εὕδει δ᾽ ἀνὰ σκάπτῳ Διὸς αἰετός,
ὠκεῖαν πτέρυγ᾽ ἀμφοτέρωθεν χαλάξαις,   10

ἀντ. α´

ἀρχὸς οἰωνῶν, κελαινῶπιν δ᾽ ἐπί οἱ νεφέλαν
ἀγκύλῳ κρατί, γλεφάρων ἀδὺ κλαΐστρον, κατέ-
χευας· ὁ δὲ κνώσσων
ὑγρὸν νῶτον αἰωρεῖ, τεαῖς
10 ῥιπαῖσι κατασχόμενος. καὶ γὰρ βιατὰς Ἄρης,
τραχεῖαν ἄνευθε λιπὼν
ἐγχέων ἀκμάν, ἰαίνει καρδίαν   20
κώματι, κῆλα δὲ καὶ δαιμόνων θέλγει φρένας,
ἀμφί τε Λατοίδα σοφίᾳ βαθυκόλπων τε
Μοισᾶν.

ἐπ. α´

ὅσσα δὲ μὴ πεφίληκε Ζεύς, ἀτύζονται βοὰν

THE PYTHIAN ODES

I.—FOR HIERON OF AETNA

WINNER IN THE CHARIOT-RACE 470 B.C.

O GOLDEN lyre, that are owned alike by Apollo and by the violet-tressed Muses! thou lyre, which the footstep heareth, as it beginneth the gladsome dance; lyre, whose notes the singers obey, whenever, with thy quivering strings, thou preparest to strike up the prelude of the choir-leading overture!

Thou abatest even the warring thunderbolt of everlasting flame; and the eagle, king of birds, sleepeth on the sceptre of Zeus, while his swift pinions twain are drooping, and a darksome mist is shed over his bending head, sweetly sealing his eyelids; and the bird, as he slumbereth, heaveth his buxom back beneath the spell of thy throbbing tones. For even the stern god of war setteth aside his rude spears so keen, and warmeth his heart in deep repose; and thy shafts of music soothe even the minds of the deities, by grace of the skill of Lêto's son and the deep-zoned Muses.

But all the beings that Zeus hath not loved, are

Πιερίδων ἀΐοντα, γᾶν τε καὶ πόντον κατ᾽ ἀμαι-
        μάκετον,
15 ὅς τ᾽ ἐν αἰνᾷ Ταρτάρῳ κεῖται, θεῶν πολέμιος,   30
Τυφὼς ἑκατοντακάρανος· τόν ποτε
Κιλίκιον θρέψεν πολυώνυμον ἄντρον· νῦν γε μὰν
ταί θ᾽ ὑπὲρ Κύμας ἁλιερκέες ὄχθαι
Σικελία τ᾽ αὐτοῦ πιέζει στέρνα λαχνάεντα· κίων
        δ᾽ οὐρανία συνέχει,
20 νιφόεσσ᾽ Αἴτνα, πάνετες χιόνος ὀξείας τιθήνα·
στρ. β΄
τᾶς ἐρεύγονται μὲν ἀπλάτου πυρὸς ἁγνόταται   40
ἐκ μυχῶν παγαί· ποταμοὶ δ᾽ ἁμέραισιν μὲν προ-
        χέοντι ῥόον καπνοῦ
αἴθων᾽· ἀλλ᾽ ἐν ὄρφναισιν πέτρας
φοίνισσα κυλινδομένα φλὸξ ἐς βαθεῖαν φέρει πόν-
        του πλάκα σὺν πατάγῳ.
25 κεῖνο δ᾽ Ἀφαίστοιο κρουνοὺς ἑρπετὸν
δεινοτάτους ἀναπέμπει· τέρας μὲν θαυμάσιον
        προσιδέσθαι, θαῦμα δὲ καὶ παρεόντων
        ἀκοῦσαι,   50
ἀντ. β΄
οἷον Αἴτνας ἐν μελαμφύλλοις δέδεται κορυφαῖς
καὶ πέδῳ, στρωμνὰ δὲ χαράσσοισ᾽ ἅπαν νῶτον
        ποτικεκλιμένον κεντεῖ.
εἴη, Ζεῦ, τὶν εἴη ἀνδάνειν,
30 ὃς τοῦτ᾽ ἐφέπεις ὄρος, εὐκάρποιο γαίας μέτωπον,
        τοῦ μὲν ἐπωνυμίαν
κλεινὸς οἰκιστὴρ ἐκύδανεν πόλιν
γείτονα, Πυθιάδος δ᾽ ἐν δρόμῳ κάρυξ ἀνέειπέ νιν
        ἀγγέλλων Ἱέρωνος ὑπὲρ καλλινίκου   60

20 πανέτης S.
26 παρεόντων CM (MGCS) : παριόντων most mss (BF).

astonied, when they hear the voice of the Pierides, whether on the earth, or on the resistless sea; whereof is he who lieth in dread Tartarus, that foeman of the gods, Typhon with his hundred heads, who was nurtured of old by the famed Cilician cave, though now the steep shores above Cymê, and Sicily too, lieth heavy on his shaggy breast, and the column that soareth to heaven crusheth him, even snow-clad Etna, who nurseth her keen frost for the live-long year,—Etna, from whose inmost caves burst forth the purest founts of unapproachable fire, and, in the day-time, her rivers roll a lurid stream of smoke, while amid the gloom of night, the ruddy flame, as it sweepeth along, with crashing din whirleth rocks to the deep sea far below. And that monster flingeth aloft the most fearful founts of fire, a wondrous marvel to behold, a wonder even to hear, when men are hard by; such a being is he that lieth bound between those dark-leaved heights and the ground below, while all his out-stretched back is goaded by his craggy couch.

Grant, grant, we may find grace with thee, O Zeus, that hauntest that mount, that forefront of a fruitful land,—that mount, whose namesake city near at hand was glorified by its famous founder, when the herald proclaimed her in the Pythian course by telling of Hieron's noble victory with the chariot.[1] Even

---

[1] The city of Aetna, founded in 474 by Hieron.

ἐπ. βʹ

   ἅρμασι. ναυσιφορήτοις δ' ἀνδράσι πρῶτα χάρις
   ἐς πλόον ἀρχομένοις πομπαῖον ἐλθεῖν οὖρον·
     ἐοικότα γὰρ
35 καὶ τελευτᾷ φερτέρου νόστου τυχεῖν. ὁ δὲ λόγος
   ταύταις ἐπὶ συντυχίαις δόξαν φέρει   70
   λοιπὸν ἔσσεσθαι στεφάνοισί <νιν> ἵπποις τε
     κλυτὰν
   καὶ σὺν εὐφώνοις θαλίαις ὀνυμαστάν.
   Λύκιε καὶ Δάλου ἀνάσσων Φοῖβε, Παρνασσοῦ τε
     κράναν Κασταλίαν φιλέων,
40 ἐθελήσαις ταῦτα νόῳ τιθέμεν εὔανδρόν τε χώραν.

στρ. γʹ

   ἐκ θεῶν γὰρ μαχαναὶ πᾶσαι βροτέαις ἀρεταῖς,   80
   καὶ σοφοὶ καὶ χερσὶ βιαταὶ περίγλωσσοί τ' ἔφυν.
     ἄνδρα δ' ἐγὼ κεῖνον
   αἰνῆσαι μενοινῶν ἔλπομαι
   μὴ χαλκοπάραον ἄκονθ' ὡσείτ' ἀγῶνος βαλεῖν ἔξω
     παλάμᾳ δονέων,
45 μακρὰ δὲ ῥίψαις ἀμεύσασθ' ἀντίους·
   εἰ γὰρ ὁ πᾶς χρόνος ὄλβον μὲν οὕτω καὶ κτεάνων
     δόσιν εὐθύνοι, καμάτων δ' ἐπίλασιν παρά-
     σχοι.   90

ἀντ. γʹ

   ἦ κεν ἀμνάσειεν, οἵαις ἐν πολέμοισι μάχαις
   τλάμονι ψυχᾷ παρέμειν', ἁνίχ' εὑρίσκοντο θεῶν
     παλάμαις τιμάν,

35 καὶ τελευτᾷ φερτέρου C^1 and scholium (MGFCS): ἐν καὶ
τελευτᾷ DC^2; κὰν τελευτᾷ Moschopulus; καὶ τελευτὰν
φερτερὰν B.
37 στεφάνοισί <νιν> Heyne (BMGFCS): στεφάνοισιν old mss;
στεφάνοισί τε vulgo; στεφάνοισι σὺν Donaldson.
47 πολέμοισι mss (BMGFC): πολέμοιο Bergk (S).

as sea-faring men deem as their first blessing the
coming of a favouring breeze at the outset of their
voyage, for, haply, at the end also, they may win
them a more prosperous return to their home; even
so doth the thought inspired by his good fortune
prompt the hope that this city will from henceforth
be famous for victorious wreaths and coursers, and
that its name will be heard amid tuneful triumphs.
O Phoebus, lord of Lycia and of Delos, thou that
lovest the Castalian fount of Parnassus, mayest thou
be willing to make this purpose good, and this land
a land of noble men.

From the gods come all the means of mortal
exploits; thanks to the gods are men wise and brave
and eloquent. And, while I am eager to praise my
hero, I trust I may not fling, as it were, outside the
lists the bronze-tipped javelin which I brandish in
my hand, but may fling it afar, and thus surpass my
foes.[1] Oh that all time to come may, even as hereto-
fore, waft him in the straight course of prosperity and
of all the blessings of wealth, and also grant oblivion
of all pains. Then would he recall in what battles
amid wars he once held his ground with steadfast soul,
what time, from the hands of the gods, he and his won

[1] At the foundation of the Olympic games "Phrastor with
the javelin hit the mark" (*O.* x 71); but in the athletic
competitions of historic times, down to about 400 B.C.,
distance was the only object. See *N.* vii 71, *I.* ii 35, and cp.
E. Norman Gardiner's *Greek Athletic Sports and Festivals*,
pp. 339, 347, 353.

οἵαν οὔτις Ἑλλάνων δρέπει,
50 πλούτου στεφάνωμ' ἀγέρωχον. νῦν γε μὰν τὰν
    Φιλοκτήταο δίκαν ἐφέπων
ἐστρατεύθη· σὺν δ' ἀνάγκᾳ νιν φίλον
καί τις ἐὼν μεγαλάνωρ ἔσανεν. φαντὶ δὲ Λαμνόθεν
    ἕλκει τειρόμενον μεταβάσοντας ἐλθεῖν   100
ἐπ. γ'
    ἥρωας ἀντιθέους Ποίαντος υἱὸν τοξόταν·
ὃς Πριάμοιο πόλιν πέρσεν, τελεύτασέν τε πόνους
    Δαναοῖς,
55 ἀσθενεῖ μὲν χρωτὶ βαίνων, ἀλλὰ μοιρίδιον ἦν.
οὕτω δ' Ἱέρωνι θεὸς ὀρθωτὴρ πέλοι
    τὸν προσέρποντα χρόνον, ὧν ἔραται καιρὸν
    διδούς.   110
Μοῖσα, καὶ πὰρ Δεινομένει κελαδῆσαι
πίθεό μοι ποινὰν τεθρίππων. χάρμα δ' οὐκ ἀλ-
    λότριον νικαφορίᾳ πατέρος.
60 ἄγ' ἔπειτ' Αἴτνας βασιλεῖ φίλιον ἐξεύρωμεν ὕμνον·
στρ. δ'
    τῷ πόλιν κείναν θεοδμάτῳ σὺν ἐλευθερίᾳ
Ὑλλίδος στάθμας Ἱέρων ἐν νόμοις ἔκτισσ'. ἐθέ-
    λοντι δὲ Παμφύλου   120
καὶ μὰν Ἡρακλειδᾶν ἔκγονοι
ὄχθαις ὕπο Ταϋγέτου ναίοντες αἰεὶ μένειν τεθμοῖ-
    σιν ἐν Αἰγιμιοῦ

52 μεταβάσοντας anon. in Boeckh (M¹GS): μεταλ(λ)άσ(σ)οντας
mss ; μεταμείβοντας BF ; μετανάσσοντας Wakefield (M²C).
62 ἔκτισσ'. ἐθέλοντι MGC ; ἔκτισσε θέλοντι BFS : ἔκτισ(σ)ε(ν)
(ἐ)θέλοντι mss.

them honour, such as no other Greek hath gathered, even a lordly crown of wealth. But now he was following in the ways of Philoctêtês,[1] when he was prompted to take the field; for, under the stress of need, even the proud man fawned for his friendship.[2] Thus do they say that god-like heroes went to bring from Lemnos the bowman son of Poeas, who was wearied with his wound, but who yet sacked the city of Priam, and ended the toil of the Danai, though he went on his way with a frame that was weak; but thus was it ordered of Fate. Even so, for the time that is still to come, may God be the preserver of Hieron, giving him all he desireth in due season.

I would bid my Muse also stand beside Deinomenês,[3] while she loudly praiseth the guerdon won by the chariot of four steeds. The victory of the sire is a joy that also concerneth the son; therefore let us devise a friendly song in honour of Aetna's king, for whom Hieron founded that city with the aid of god-built freedom, according to the laws of the rule of Hyllus. And the sons of Pamphȳlus, aye, and verily of the Heracleidae also, though they dwell beneath the cliffs of Taȳgetus, are willing to abide for ever,

---

[1] Philoctêtês, son of Poeas, was wounded on his way to Troy, and was left in the island of Lemnos. He there remained until the tenth year of the Trojan war, when he was brought to Troy, as an oracle had declared that the city could not be taken without the arrows, which Heracles had bequeathed to Philoctêtês.

[2] " Kymê, hard pressed by the Etruscan enemy, prayed for help from the lord of Syracuse, whose intervention on behalf of Lokroi . . . may have gained him the reputation of the general defender of oppressed Italiot cities " (Freeman's *Sicily*, ii 250). Cp. Diodorus, xi 51 (474 B.C.), παραγενομένων πρὸς αὐτὸν πρεσβέων ἐκ Κύμης τῆς Ἰταλίας καὶ δεομένων βοηθῆσαι πολεμουμένοις ὑπὸ Τυρρηνῶν θαλαττοκρατούντων.

[3] Son of Hieron, and ruler of Aetna.

PINDAR

65 Δωριεῖς. ἔσχον δ' Ἀμύκλας ὄλβιοι,

Πινδόθεν ὀρνύμενοι, λευκοπώλων Τυνδαριδᾶν βα-
θύδοξοι γείτονες, ὧν κλέος ἄνθησεν αἰχμᾶς.

ἀντ. δ'

Ζεῦ τέλει', αἰεὶ δὲ τοιαύταν Ἀμένα παρ' ὕδωρ 130
αἶσαν ἀστοῖς καὶ βασιλεῦσιν διακρίνειν ἔτυμον
λόγον ἀνθρώπων,

σύν τοι τίν κεν ἀγητὴρ ἀνήρ,

70 υἱῷ τ' ἐπιτελλόμενος, δᾶμον γεραίρων τράποι
σύμφωνον ἐς ἀσυχίαν.

λίσσομαι νεῦσον, Κρονίων, ἄμερον

ὄφρα κατ' οἶκον ὁ Φοίνιξ ὁ Τυρσανῶν τ' ἀλαλατὸς
ἔχῃ, ναυσίστονον ὕβριν ἰδὼν τὰν πρὸ
Κύμας·
140

ἐπ. δ'

οἷα Συρακοσίων ἀρχῷ δαμασθέντες πάθον,
ὠκυπόρων ἀπὸ ναῶν ὅ σφιν ἐν πόντῳ βάλεθ'
ἁλικίαν,

75 Ἑλλάδ' ἐξέλκων βαρείας δουλίας. ἀρέομαι
πὰρ μὲν Σαλαμῖνος, Ἀθαναίων χάριν,
μισθόν, ἐν Σπάρτᾳ δ' ἐρέω τὰν πρὸ Κιθαιρῶνος
μάχαν,
150
ταῖσι Μήδειοι κάμον ἀγκυλότοξοι,

65 Δωριεῖς E, Bergk (MGF): Δωριῆς CD (C); Δωρίοις Her-
mann (B).
70 ἐς C with scholia (MGFCS); ἐφ' Moschopulus (B):
omitted in Vatican mss.
74 ὅς σφιν E with interpolated mss (B).
77 τὰν most mss (S²): omitted by EF alone (BMFGCS¹).

162

as Dorians, under the ordinances of Aegimius.[1] They gat them Amyclae [2] and prospered, sallying forth from Pindus, those glory-laden neighbours of the Tyndaridae with their white horses; and the fame of their spear burst into bloom.

O Zeus, that crownest all things, grant that the words of men may with truth assign no less good-fortune to citizens and kings alike, beside the waters of Amenas. With thy blessing may he who himself is the leader, and giveth his behests to his son, honour the people, and prompt them to concord and peace.

Grant, I beseech thee, O son of Cronus, that the battle-shout of the Carthaginians and Etruscans may abide at home in peace and quiet, now that they have seen that their over-weening insolence off Cumae hath brought lamentation on their ships[3]; such were the losses they suffered, when vanquished by the lord of the Syracusans,—a fate which flung their young warriors from their swift ships into the sea, delivering Hellas from grievous bondage. From Salamis shall I essay to win for my reward the favour of the Athenians,[4] but, at Sparta, I shall tell of the battle before Cithaeron,[5]—those battles twain in which the Medes with curved bows suffered sorely; but, by the well-watered bank of the river

[1] There were three Dorian tribes, the Hylleis, the Pamphýli, and the Dymânes. The Hylleis were descended from Hyllus, the son of Heracles; and the other two from Pamphýlus and Dymas, the sons of Aegimius.

[2] An old Achaean town in Laconia, 2½ miles S.E. of Sparta; finally taken by the Dorians with the aid of the Theban Aegeidae (cp. *I.* vii 14).

[3] The naval battle off Cumae, 474 B.C.

[4] The battle of Salamis, September, 480 B.C.

[5] The battle of Plataea, 479 B.C.

PINDAR

παρὰ δὲ τὰν εὔυδρον ἀκτὰν Ἱμέρα παίδεσσιν
   ὕμνον Δεινομένευς τελέσαις,
80 τὸν ἐδέξαντ' ἀμφ' ἀρετᾳ, πολεμίων ἀνδρῶν
   καμόντων.

στρ. ε'
   καιρὸν εἰ φθέγξαιο, πολλῶν πείρατα συντανύσαις
   ἐν βραχεῖ, μείων ἔπεται μῶμος ἀνθρώπων. ἀπὸ
      γὰρ κόρος ἀμβλύνει   160
   αἰανὴς ταχείας ἐλπίδας·
   ἀστῶν δ' ἀκοὰ κρύφιον θυμὸν βαρύνει μάλιστ'
      ἐσλοῖσιν ἐπ' ἀλλοτρίοις.
85 ἀλλ' ὅμως, κρέσσων γὰρ οἰκτιρμοῦ φθόνος,
   μὴ παρίει καλά. νώμα δικαίῳ πηδαλίῳ στρατόν·
      ἀψευδεῖ δὲ πρὸς ἄκμονι χάλκευε γλῶσσαν.

ἀντ. ε'
   εἴ τι καὶ φλαῦρον παραιθύσσει, μέγα τοι
      φέρεται   170
   πὰρ σέθεν. πολλῶν ταμίας ἐσσί· πολλοὶ μάρτυρες
      ἀμφοτέροις πιστοί.
   εὐανθεῖ δ' ἐν ὀργᾷ παρμένων,
90 εἴπερ τι φιλεῖς ἀκοὰν ἀδεῖαν αἰεὶ κλύειν, μὴ κάμνε
      λίαν δαπάναις·
   ἐξίει δ' ὥσπερ κυβερνάτας ἀνὴρ
   ἱστίον ἀνεμόεν. μὴ δολωθῇς, ὦ φίλος, κέρδεσιν
      εὐτράπλοις· ὀπιθόμβροτον αὔχημα δόξας   180

ἐπ. ε'
   οἷον ἀποιχομένων ἀνδρῶν δίαιταν μανύει

85 κρέσσων DV (BMGFC): κρείσσων E; κρέσσον lemma of
one Triclinian ms (s).
92 κέρδεσιν εὐτράπλοις Bücheler (s): κέρδεσιν εὐτραπέλοις
old mss : εὐτραπέλοις κέρδεσσ' Hermann (BMGFC); ὦ φίλε
κέρδεσιν ἐντραπέλοις C¹D¹.

Himeras, (I shall win reward) by paying my tribute of song to the sons of Deinomenês,—the song of praise, which they won by their valour, while their foemen were fore-spent.[1]

If thou shouldest speak in season due, blending the strands of many themes into a brief compass, less cavil followeth of men. For dull satiety blunteth all the eagerness of expectation; but that which is heard by fellow-citizens lieth heavy on their secret soul, and chiefly when it concerns the merits of others. Nevertheless, since envy is better than pity,[2] hold to thy noble course! Steer thy people with the helm of justice, and forge thy tongue on the anvil of truth! If any word, be it ever so light, falleth by chance, it is borne along as a word of weight, when it falleth from thee. Thou art the faithful steward of an ample store. Thou hast many trusty witnesses to thy deeds of either kind.[3] But do thou abide in a temper that bloometh in beauty, and, if indeed thou delightest in hearing evermore what is sweet to hear, wax not over-weary in thy spending. Rather, like a steersman, suffer thy sail to be set free to catch the breeze. Be not allured, my friend, by cunning gains! When men are dead and gone, it is only the loud acclaim of praise that surviveth mortals and revealeth their manner of

[1] At the battle of Himera, 480 B.C., Gelôn, the eldest of the sons of Deinomenês, held the supreme command (Freeman's *Sicily*, ii 189-207); but, in the lines of Simonides on the Delphian tripod, all the four sons, Gelôn, Hierôn, Polyzêlus, and Thrasybûlus, join in recording their share in the deliverance of Hellas (*ib.* note on p. 205).

[2] Cp. Herodotus, iii 52, "it is better to be envied than to be pitied."

[3] A polite euphemism for "good or evil deeds."

PINDAR

καὶ λογίοις καὶ ἀοιδοῖς· οὐ φθίνει Κροίσου
φιλόφρων ἀρετά·
95 τὸν δὲ ταύρῳ χαλκέῳ καυτῆρα νηλέα νόον
ἐχθρὰ Φάλαριν κατέχει παντᾷ φάτις,
οὐδέ νιν φόρμιγγες ὑπωρόφιαι κοινωνίαν
μαλθακὰν παίδων ὀάροισι δέκονται.   190
τὸ δὲ παθεῖν εὖ πρῶτον ἄθλων· εὖ δ᾽ ἀκούειν
δευτέρα μοῖρ᾽· ἀμφοτέροισι δ᾽ ἀνὴρ
100 ὃς ἂν ἐγκύρσῃ, καὶ ἕλῃ, στέφανον ὕψιστον
δέδεκται.

life to chroniclers and to bards alike. The kindly generosity of Croesus fadeth not away, while Phalaris,[1] ruthless in spirit, who burned his victims in his brazen bull, is whelmed for ever by a hateful infamy, and no lyres beneath the roof-tree welcome him as a theme to be softly blended with the warbled songs of boys. The first of prizes is good-fortune; the second falleth to fair fame; but, whosoever findeth and winneth both, hath received the highest crown.

[1] Tyrant of Acragas, 570–554 B.C.

PYTHIAN II

FOR HIERON OF SYRACUSE

INTRODUCTION

THIS Ode celebrates a victory, won by Hieron of
Syracuse, in a chariot-race, not at the Pythian
games, but (probably) at the Theban Iolaia. It
includes a reference to the deliverance of the
Western Locris (18 f) from the hostile designs of
Anaxilas of Rhegium in 477, and is therefore later
than that event. It was not until April or May, 476,
that Hieron took the title of βασιλεύς. This title
is not given him in the present Ode. Hence the
Ode is placed by Gaspar in 477–6 (probably late in
477). Schröder suggests 475, and Wilamowitz
474–0. The Ode was sung at Syracuse, whither it
was sent (apparently) with a promise of a hymn to
Castor at some future date (69 f). This hymn may
have been identical with that in which Hieron is
addressed as ζαθέων ἱερῶν ὁμώνυμε κτίστορ Αἴτνας, the
date of which must be later than the founding of
Aetna in 476 (Frag. 105).

To mighty Syracuse, rearer of men and of horses,
the poet brings from Thebes a lay in honour of
Hieron's victory. Hieron is aided by Artemis and
Hermes, when he yokes his horses, and prays to
Poseidon (1–12). Other lords have other praises,

and, even as Cinyras is praised by Cyprian voices, as beloved of Apollo, and as the minion of Aphroditê, so Hieron is praised by the grateful voice of the virgin of Western Locris, whose eye has won new courage from his aid (13–20). The awful doom of Ixion warns us to requite our benefactors (21–24).

The myth of Ixion (25–48).

God humbles the proud, and gives glory to the humble (49–52). The example of Archilochus warns us against calumny. Wealth and good fortune are the highest themes of song (53–56). Hieron deserves praise for his wealth and his honour ; he has never been rivalled in Greece ; he is famed for his exploits in war and in council, on horse and on foot. ' This song is sent as Tyrian cargo across the sea, and another song shall follow (57–71).

Be true to thyself ; the ape is pretty in the eyes of children only, and not in those of the blessed Rhadamanthys, whose soul has no delight in deceit (72–75). Slanderers are like foxes, that gain nothing by all their cunning. The deceitful citizen is always fawning, and never speaks with a straightforward courage (76–82). Such boldness the poet cannot share ; loyal to his friends, he will play the wolf against his foes. In every State straightforwardness is always best (83–88) ; man must not fight against God, who exalts divers persons at divers times. Even this diversity of good fortune does not satisfy the envious ; eager for more, they only over-reach themselves, and suffer hurt (89–92). It is best to bear God's yoke, and not to kick against the pricks (93–95). For himself, the poet would only wish to please, and to consort with, those who are noble (96).

II.—ΙΕΡΩΝΙ ΣΤΡΑΚΟΣΙΩ

ΑΡΜΑΤΙ

στρ. α΄

Μεγαλοπόλιες ὦ Συράκοσαι, βαθυπολέμου
τέμενος Ἄρεος, ἀνδρῶν ἵππων τε σιδαροχαρμᾶν
  δαιμόνιαι τροφοί,
ὕμμιν τόδε τᾶν λιπαρᾶν ἀπὸ Θηβᾶν φέρων
μέλος ἔρχομαι ἀγγελίαν τετραορίας ἐλελίχθονος,
5 εὐάρματος Ἱέρων ἐν ᾇ κρατέων
  τηλαυγέσιν ἀνέδησεν Ὀρτυγίαν στεφάνοις,   10
ποταμίας ἕδος Ἀρτέμιδος, ἆς οὐκ ἄτερ
κείνας ἀγαναῖσιν ἐν χερσὶ ποικιλανίους ἐδάμασσε
  πώλους.

ἀντ. α΄

ἐπὶ γὰρ ἰοχέαιρα παρθένος χερὶ διδύμᾳ
10 ὅ τ᾽ ἐναγώνιος Ἑρμᾶς αἰγλᾶντα τίθησι κόσμον,
  ξεστὸν ὅταν δίφρον   20
ἔν θ᾽ ἅρματα πεισιχάλινα καταζευγνύῃ
σθένος ἵππιον, ὀρσοτρίαιναν εὐρυβίαν καλέων
  θεόν.
ἄλλοις δέ τις ἐτέλεσσεν ἄλλος ἀνὴρ
εὐαχέα βασιλεῦσιν ὕμνον, ἄποιν᾽ ἀρετᾶς.
15 κελαδέοντι μὲν ἀμφὶ Κινύραν πολλάκις

8 κείνας mss : Νίκας Wilamowitz.

170

II.—FOR HIERON OF SYRACUSE

WINNER IN THE CHARIOT-RACE AT THE THEBAN IOLAIA
475(?) B.C.

MIGHTY city of Syracuse! holy ground of Ares,
that is ever plunged in war! thou nursing-place
divine of heroes and steeds that rejoice in steel!
Lo, I come from splendid Thebes, and I bring
a song that telleth of the race of the four-
horse chariot that shaketh the earth,—that race
in which Hieron was victorious with his glorious
team,[1] and thus crowned Ortygia with wreaths that
shine afar,—Ortygia, the haunt of the river-goddess
Artemis, not without whose aid he guided with his
gentle hands those steeds with broidered reins. For
that maiden-goddess of the chase, and Hermes, lord
of the wrestling-ring, with their twain hands present
him with those gleaming trappings, when he yokes
the strength of his steeds to his polished car, and to
the wheels that obey the bit, while he calleth on
the god who wieldeth the trident and ruleth far
and wide.

Other lords have other minstrels to pay them the
meed of melodious song, as the guerdon of victory.
Full oft do the praises of the men of Cyprus echo

---

[1] This victory is supposed by Boeckh to have been won by
Hieron at Thebes, either at the Heracleia, or at the Iolaia,
held in honour of Iolaüs, son of Iphicles, the half-brother of
Heracles. The stadium of Iolaüs was outside the N.E. gate
of Thebes (Pausanias ix 23, 11).

φᾶμαι Κυπρίων, τὸν ὁ χρυσοχαῖτα προφρόνως
ἐφίλασ᾽ Ἀπόλλων,　　　　　　　　　　30

ἐπ. α΄

ἱερέα κτίλον Ἀφροδίτας· ἄγει δὲ χάρις φίλων
ποίνιμος ἀντὶ ἔργων ὀπιζομένα·
σὲ δ᾽, ὦ Δεινομένειε παῖ, Ζεφυρία πρὸ δόμων
Λοκρὶς παρθένος ἀπύει, πολεμίων καμάτων ἐξ
ἀμαχάνων

20 διὰ τεὰν δύναμιν δρακεῖσ᾽ ἀσφαλές.
θεῶν δ᾽ ἐφετμαῖς Ἰξίονα φαντὶ ταῦτα βροτοῖς 40
λέγειν ἐν πτερόεντι τροχῷ
παντᾷ κυλινδόμενον·
τὸν εὐεργέταν ἀγαναῖς ἀμοιβαῖς ἐποιχομένους
τίνεσθαι.

στρ. β΄

25 ἔμαθε δὲ σαφές. εὐμενέσσι γὰρ παρὰ Κρονίδαις
γλυκὺν ἑλὼν βίοτον, μακρὸν οὐχ ὑπέμεινεν ὄλβον,
μαινομέναις φρασὶν
Ἥρας ὅτ᾽ ἐράσσατο, τὰν Διὸς εὐναὶ λάχον 50
πολυγαθέες· ἀλλά νιν ὕβρις εἰς ἀνάταν ὑπερά-
φανον
ὦρσεν· τάχα δὲ παθὼν ἐοικότ᾽ ἀνὴρ
30 ἐξαίρετον ἕλε μόχθον. αἱ δύο δ᾽ ἀμπλακίαι
φερέπονοι τελέθοντι· τὸ μὲν ἥρως ὅτι
ἐμφύλιον αἷμα πρώτιστος οὐκ ἄτερ τέχνας ἐπέμιξε
θνατοῖς,

ἀντ. β΄

ὅτι τε μεγαλοκευθέεσσιν ἔν ποτε θαλάμοις 60
Διὸς ἄκοιτιν ἐπειρᾶτο. χρὴ δὲ κατ᾽ αὐτὸν αἰεὶ
παντὸς ὁρᾶν μέτρον.

28 ἀνάταν mss (BM²); ἀυάταν Bergk (FC): ἀϜάταν (M¹G);
ἀάταν Beck (s); cp. iii 24.

the name of Cinyras, Aphrodîtê's priestly minion, who was gladly loved by golden-haired Apollo. For those praises are prompted by a gratitude which giveth reverential regard in requital for kindly deeds.

But, as for thee, O son of Deinomenês, the Locrian maiden in the West singeth thy praise before her door ; after bewildering troubles of war, thanks to thy power, her glance is now steadfast.

Men tell us that Ixion, as he whirleth round and round on his winged wheel, by the behests of the gods, teacheth the lesson that men should requite the benefactor with fresh tokens of warm gratitude. He learnt that lesson only too well ; for though he received the boon of a happy life among the gracious children of Cronus, he could not be content with his great prosperity, what time with madness of spirit he became enamoured of Hêra, the allotted partner of the wedded joys of Zeus. But his insolence drove him into overweening infatuation, and soon did the man, suffering what was fit, meet with a wondrous doom. For toil is the requital of both of his offences, firstly, in that the hero was the first who, not without guile, imbrued mortal men with kindred blood, and, again, in that, in the vast recesses of that bridal chamber, he tempted the honour of the spouse of Zeus. But it is ever right to mark the measure of all things by one's own station. For unlawful

35 εὐναὶ δὲ παράτροποι ἐς κακότατ᾽ ἀθρόαν
　　ἔβαλον· ποτὶ καὶ τὸν ἴκοντ᾽· ἐπεὶ νεφέλᾳ παρε-
　　　λέξατο,
　　ψεῦδος γλυκὺ μεθέπων, ἄιδρις ἀνήρ·
　　εἶδος γὰρ ὑπεροχωτάτᾳ πρέπεν οὐρανιᾶν　　　　70
　　θυγατέρι Κρόνου· ἄντε δόλον αὐτῷ θέσαν
40 Ζηνὸς παλάμαι, καλὸν πῆμα. τὸν δὲ τετράκνα-
　　μον ἔπραξε δεσμόν,

ἐπ. β´

　　ἑὸν ὄλεθρον ὅγ᾽· ἐν δ᾽ ἀφύκτοισι γυιοπέδαις πεσὼν
　　　τὰν πολύκοινον ἀνδέξατ᾽ ἀγγελίαν.
　　ἄνευ οἱ Χαρίτων τέκεν γόνον ὑπερφίαλον,
　　μόνα καὶ μόνον, οὔτ᾽ ἐν ἀνδράσι γερασφόρον οὔτ᾽
　　　ἐν θεῶν νόμοις·　　　　　　　　　　　　　　80
　　τὸν ὀνύμαξε τράφοισα Κένταυρον, ὃς
45 ἵπποισι Μαγνητίδεσσι ἐμίγνυτ᾽ ἐν Παλίου
　　σφυροῖς, ἐκ δ᾽ ἐγένοντο στρατὸς
　　θαυμαστός, ἀμφοτέροις
　　ὁμοῖοι τοκεῦσι, τὰ ματρόθεν μὲν κάτω, τὰ δ᾽
　　　ὕπερθε πατρός.

στρ. γ´

　　θεὸς ἅπαν ἐπὶ ἐλπίδεσσι τέκμαρ ἀνύεται,　　　90
50 θεός, ὃ καὶ πτερόεντ᾽ αἰετὸν κίχε, καὶ θαλασσαῖον
　　　παραμείβεται
　　δελφῖνα, καὶ ὑψιφρόνων τιν᾽ ἔκαμψε βροτῶν,

36 ποτὶ καὶ τὸν ἴκοντ᾽ most mss (M) : ποτὶ κοῖτον ἴκοντ᾽ Beck,
Hermann, — — ἰόντ᾽ (B¹C); ποτε καὶ τὸν ἔκοντ᾽ Bothe (B²);
ποτε καὶ τὸν ἴκοντ᾽ ("the suppliant," cp. Aesch. *Eum.* 441,
σεμνὸς προσίκτωρ ἐν τρόποις Ἰξίονος) Donaldson (F), — ἐλόντ᾽
Schneidewin (G).

38 οὐρανιᾶν *DE…*(BF) : Οὐρανιδᾶν Bergk (GC) cp. P. iv 194 ;
Οὐρανίδα scholium (MS).

41 ἀνδέξατ᾽ Moschopulus, Hermann² (BMGS), ἀνεδέξατ᾽ old
mss : ἀνεδείξατ᾽ Beck, ἀνδείξατ᾽ Mitscherlich, Hermann¹ (FC).

embraces have ere now flung men into the depth of
trouble ; such embraces came even on *him* ; since it
was a cloud that, all unwitting, he embraced in the
bliss of his delusive dream, for, in semblance, that
cloud was like unto the Queen of the Celestials, the
daughter of Cronus. It was the hands of Zeus that
had set that cloud as a snare for him, a beautiful
bane. And so he brought about his own binding to
the four spokes of the turning wheel, even his own
fell doom ; and, being thus entangled in bonds inex-
tricable, he received the message of warning for all
the world. Without the blessing of the Graces did
that mother bear him a monstrous offspring, there
was never such a mother, never such a son,[1]—an
offspring unhonoured either among men or amid the
ordinances of the gods. And she reared him up, and
called him by the name of Centaurus, who consorted
with the Magnesian mares by the spurs of Pêlion,
and thence there came into being a host wondrous
to look upon, resembling both their parents, the
dam's side down, the upper side the sire's.[2]

God fulfilleth every purpose, even as he desireth,
God that not only overtaketh the winged eagle, but
also surpasseth the dolphin on the sea, and bendeth

---

[1] Seymour's rendering.
[2] So rendered by Gildersleeve.

ἑτέροισι δὲ κῦδος ἀγήραον παρέδωκ'. ἐμὲ δὲ
χρεὼν
φεύγειν δάκος ἀδινὸν κακαγοριᾶν.
εἶδον γὰρ ἑκὰς ἐὼν τὰ πόλλ' ἐν ἀμαχανίᾳ
55 ψογερὸν Ἀρχίλοχον βαρυλόγοις ἔχθεσιν   100
πιαινόμενον· τὸ πλουτεῖν δὲ σὺν τύχᾳ πότμου
σοφίας ἄριστον.

ἀντ. γ΄

τὺ δὲ σάφα νιν ἔχεις, ἐλευθέρᾳ φρενὶ πεπαρεῖν,
πρύτανι κύριε πολλᾶν μὲν εὐστεφάνων ἀγυιᾶν καὶ
στρατοῦ. εἰ δέ τις
ἤδη κτεάτεσσί τε καὶ περὶ τιμᾷ λέγει   110
60 ἕτερόν τιν' ἀν' Ἑλλάδα τῶν πάροιθε γενέσθαι
ὑπέρτερον,
χαῦνα πραπίδι παλαιμονεῖ κενεά.
εὐανθέα δ' ἀναβάσομαι στόλον ἀμφ' ἀρετᾷ
κελαδέων. νεότατι μὲν ἀρήγει θράσος
δεινῶν πολέμων· ὅθεν φαμὶ καὶ σὲ τὰν ἀπείρονα
δόξαν εὑρεῖν,

ἐπ. γ΄

65 τὰ μὲν ἐν ἱπποσόαισιν ἄνδρεσσι μαρνάμενον, τὰ
δ' ἐν πεζομάχαισι· βουλαὶ δὲ πρεσβύτεραι   120
ἀκίνδυνον ἐμοὶ ἔπος <σὲ> ποτὶ πάντα λόγον
ἐπαινεῖν παρέχοντι. χαῖρε. τόδε μὲν κατὰ Φοί-
νισσαν ἐμπολάν
μέλος ὑπὲρ πολιᾶς ἁλὸς πέμπεται·
τὸ Καστόρειον δ' ἐν Αἰολίδεσσι χορδαῖς ἑκὼν
70 ἄθρησον χάριν ἑπτακτύπου
φόρμιγγος ἀντόμενος.   130

66 <σὲ> ποτὶ Bergk (MGFCS) : ποτὶ σὲ B ; ποτί ῥα Moscho-
pulus.

many a proud mortal beneath his sway, while to others he giveth glory that knoweth no eld.

But I must refrain from the violent bite of slanderous calumny; for, though far removed in time, I have seen the bitter-tongued Archilochus[1] full often in distress, because he battened on bitter abuse of his foes. But wealth, with wisdom allotted thereto, is the best gift of Fortune; and thou clearly hast this boon, so that thou canst show it forth with freedom of soul, thou prince and lord of many a battlemented street and of a host of men. But if, when wealth and honour are in question, any one saith that among the men of old any other king hath surpassed thee in Hellas, in his idle fancy he striveth in vain.

I shall ascend a prow that is crowned with flowers, while I sound the praise of valour.

Youth findeth its strength in courage amid dread wars; and thence do I declare that thou also hast won thy boundless fame by fighting, not only among warrior horsemen, but also among men on foot; and thy counsels, riper than thy years, prompt me to say what cannot be challenged, even to praise thee with the fullest praise. Now fare thee well.

This song of mine is being sped athwart the foaming sea, as Tyrian merchandise; but do thou look with favour on the strain in honour of Castor, the strain in mode Aeolian, greeting it in honour of the seven-toned cithern.

---

[1] Archilochus, the bitter satirist of Paros, flourished in 650 B.C., about 175 years before the time of the present poem.

PINDAR

γένοι᾽ οἷος ἐσσὶ μαθών· καλός τοι πίθων παρὰ
    παισίν, αἰεὶ

στρ. δ΄

καλός. ὁ δὲ Ῥαδάμανθυς εὖ πέπραγεν, ὅτι φρενῶν
ἔλαχε καρπὸν ἀμώμητον, οὐδ᾽ ἀπάταισι θυμὸν
    τέρπεται ἔνδοθεν·

75 οἷα ψιθύρων παλάμαις ἕπετ᾽ αἰεὶ βροτῷ.
ἄμαχον κακὸν ἀμφοτέροις διαβολιᾶν ὑποφάτιες, 140
ὀργαῖς ἀτενὲς ἀλωπέκων ἴκελοι.
κερδοῖ δὲ τί μάλα τοῦτο κερδαλέον τελέθει;
ἅτε γὰρ εἰνάλιον πόνον ἐχοίσας βαθὺν

80 σκευᾶς ἑτέρας, ἀβάπτιστός εἰμι, φελλὸς ὡς ὑπὲρ
    ἕρκος, ἅλμας.

ἀντ. δ΄

ἀδύνατα δ᾽ ἔπος ἐκβαλεῖν κραταιὸν ἐν ἀγαθοῖς
δόλιον ἀστόν· ὅμως μὰν σαίνων ποτὶ πάντας,
    ἀγὰν πάγχυ διαπλέκει. 150
οὔ οἱ μετέχω θράσεος· φίλον εἴη φιλεῖν·
ποτὶ δ᾽ ἐχθρὸν ἅτ᾽ ἐχθρὸς ἐὼν λύκοιο δίκαν
    ὑποθεύσομαι,

85 ἄλλ᾽ ἄλλοτε πατέων ὁδοῖς σκολιαῖς.
ἐν πάντα δὲ νόμον εὐθύγλωσσος ἀνὴρ προφέρει,
παρὰ τυραννίδι, χὠπόταν ὁ λάβρος στρατός, 160
χὠταν πόλιν οἱ σοφοὶ τηρέωντι. χρὴ δὲ πρὸς θεὸν
    οὐκ ἐρίζειν,

72 γένοι᾽, (S) : γένοι᾽ (BMGFC). γένοι᾽ οἷος ἐσσί· μαθὼν
("when he has been trained") Headlam.

75 βροτῷ Heindorf (BMFS) : βροτῶν mss (GC, preferred by
Bergk and Wilamowitz, *Hieron und Pindaros*, 1901, p. 1313).

76 ὑποφάτιες mss (MGCS) : ὑποφαύτιες Boeckh (F).

78 κερδοῖ Huschke (B²GFC) : κέρδει mss (B¹MS).

79 βαθὺν Bergk (S) : βαθὺ mss (BMGFC) ; βυθοῖ Wilamowitz.

82 ἀγὰν anon. (BMGFC) ; ἄγαν mss (†ἄγαν S¹) : ἄταν Heyne
(S³, Wilamowitz).

178

Be true to thyself, now that thou hast learnt what manner of man thou art. It is only in the eyes of children, as thou knowest, that the ape is "pretty," ever "pretty"; but Rhadamanthys is in bliss,[1] because he had for his allotted portion that fruit of thought which none can blame, nor is he gladdened in his inmost soul by cunning wiles, even such as always haunt a man by reason of the devices of whisperers. Stealthy purveyors of slander are a curse that baffles both sides alike; they are exceeding like unto foxes in temper. But what doth the cunning fox really gain by his cunning? For, while, when the rest of the tackle hath the fisherman's bait in the depth of the sea, I, like a cork above the net, float undipped in the brine; a deceitful citizen can never utter a word of force among noble men, yet he fawneth on all and thus weaveth on every side his tangled path. I cannot share his boldness; be it mine to befriend my friend, while, against my foe, as a foe indeed, will I play the wolf, by rushing stealthily upon him, pacing now here, now there, in diverse ways. But, under every mode of government, a man of straightforward speech cometh to the front, whether at the tyrant's court, or where the boisterous host, or where the wise, have care of the State.

But one must not fight against God, who, at one

[1] That is, "in the Islands of the Blest." Cp. *O.* ii 83. As a judge in the future life, Rhadamanthys (brother of Minos, and law-giver of Crete) owed his felicity to his love of justice.

PINDAR

ἐπ. δ´

   ὃς ἀνέχει τοτὲ μὲν τὰ κείνων, τότ᾽ αὖθ᾽ ἑτέροις
      ἔδωκεν μέγα κῦδος. ἀλλ᾽ οὐδὲ ταῦτα νόον
90 ἰαίνει φθονερῶν· στάθμας δέ τινος ἑλκόμενοι
   περισσᾶς ἐνέπαξαν ἕλκος ὀδυναρὸν ἑᾷ πρόσθε
      καρδίᾳ,
   πρὶν ὅσα φροντίδι μητίονται τυχεῖν.   170
   φέρειν δ᾽ ἐλαφρῶς ἐπαυχένιον λαβόντα ζυγὸν
   ἀρήγει· ποτὶ κέντρον δέ τοι
95 λακτιζέμεν τελέθει
   ὀλισθηρὸς οἶμος· ἀδόντα δ᾽ εἴη με τοῖς ἀγαθοῖς
      ὁμιλεῖν.

89 τοτὲ *BCE* (ms) : ποτὲ *D* (bgfc).

while, exalteth the power of yonder men, and, at another, granteth high honour to others. Yet not even this doth soothe the mind of the envious; but, stretching the measuring-line too tightly, they pierce their own heart with a galling wound,[1] ere they attain what they are devising with anxious thought. Yet is it best to bear lightly the yoke that resteth on one's neck, for, as ye know, it is a slippery course to kick against the goads. But may it be my lot to please them that are noble, and to consort with them.

[1] "The measuring-line has two sharp pegs. The measurer fastens one into the ground and pulls the cord tight, in order to stretch it over more space than it ought to cover (περισσᾶς). In so doing he runs the peg into his own heart" (Gildersleeve).

PYTHIAN III

FOR HIERON OF SYRACUSE

INTRODUCTION

THIS Ode celebrates the victory won on the Pythian racecourse by Hieron's horse, Pherenîcus. The Scholiast on this Ode states that Hieron was victorious at the Pythian games whose dates correspond to 482 and 478 B.C. Both of these victories are implied in this Ode by the use of the plural στεφάνοις in line 73. But the epithet Αἰτναῖος (69) shows that the composition of the Ode is later than 476, the year in which Hieron assumed the title. The composition of the Ode may therefore be assigned to the winter of 474, but the Ode commemorates the victories won by Pherenîcus in the Pythian festivals of 482 and 478. Pherenîcus is also the winning horse celebrated in the first Olympian, 476 B.C.

At the date of the present Ode, Hieron was in failing health; he was still suffering in 470 (*Pyth.* i 50–57), and he died in 467.

Would that Cheiron, the master of Asclêpius, were still alive (1–7), Apollo's son, Asclêpius, to whom his mother, Corônis, gave birth as she died on the funeral pyre (8–46). Many were the cures wrought by Asclêpius (47–53), who at last was slain by lightning for his presumption in raising a man from the dead (54–58). Mortal men must not presume; life immortal is beyond their reach (59–62).

Would that the poet might have prevailed on Cheiron to train another healer (63–67), and thus have crossed the sea to Sicily, bearing the double boon of health and song (68–76). But the poet must stay at Thebes, and, at his own door, pay vows to Rhea for the health of Hieron (77–79).

"The immortals give to mortals two ills for every blessing" (80–82). Ills are borne bravely by the noble, such as Hieron, who has prosperity for part of his lot (82–86). Unmixed prosperity was not allotted either to Pêleus or to Cadmus (86–103). We must enjoy what we can, while we may (103–106). The poet must be content, but he will pray for wealth, and will hope for fame (107–111). Fame rests on song; song has given fame to the long lives of Nestor and Sarpêdon. Song gives length of days to merit, but this is a lot attained by few (112–116).

III.—ΙΕΡΩΝΙ ΣΤΡΑΚΟΣΙΩ

ΚΕΛΗΤΙ

στρ. α΄

Ἤθελον Χείρωνά κε Φιλλυρίδαν,
  εἰ χρεὼν τοῦθ᾽ ἀμετέρας ἀπὸ γλώσσας κοινὸν
    εὔξασθαι ἔπος,
ζώειν τὸν ἀποιχόμενον,
Οὐρανίδα γόνον εὐρυμέδοντα Κρόνου, .βάσσαισί
    τ᾽ ἄρχειν Παλίου Φῆρ᾽ ἀγρότερον,
5 νοῦν ἔχοντ᾽ ἀνδρῶν φίλον· οἷος ἐὼν θρέψεν
    ποτὲ   10
τέκτονα νωδυνίας ἄμερον γυιαρκέος Ἀσκλήπιον,
ἥρωα παντοδαπᾶν ἀλκτῆρα νούσων.

ἀντ. α΄

τὸν μὲν εὐΐππου Φλεγύα θυγάτηρ
  πρὶν τελέσσαι ματροπόλῳ σὺν Ἐλειθυίᾳ, δαμεῖσα
    χρυσέοις
10 τόξοισιν ὑπ᾽ Ἀρτέμιδος,
εἰς Ἀΐδα δόμον ἐν θαλάμῳ κατέβα τέχναις
    Ἀπόλλωνος. χόλος δ᾽ οὐκ ἀλίθιος   20
γίνεται παίδων Διός. ἁ δ᾽ ἀποφλαυρίξαισά νιν
ἀμπλακίαισι φρενῶν, ἄλλον αἴνησεν γάμον κρύβ-
    δαν πατρός,
πρόσθεν ἀκειρεκόμᾳ μιχθεῖσα Φοίβῳ,

6 νωδυνίας — γυιαρκέος mss (Hermann³, MFGCS), —ος "must
be lengthened to save the metre": νωδυνιᾶν — γυιαρκέων
Hermann¹² (B).

14 ἀκειροκόμᾳ BCV (BMGFS¹): ἀκερσεκόμᾳ E with inferior
Vatican mss (S³), cp. I. i 7.

184

III.—FOR HIERON OF SYRACUSE

WINNER IN THE HORSE RACE, 482, 478; DATE OF ODE, 474 (?) B.C.

If the poet's tongue might breathe the prayer that is on the lips of all, I would pray that Cheiron, son of Philyra, who is dead and gone, were now alive again,—he who once ruled far and wide as the offspring of Cronus, who was the son of Heaven. Would that that rugged monster with spirit kindly unto men, were reigning still in Pêlion's glens, even such as when, in olden days, he reared Asclêpius, that gentle craftsman who drove pain from the limbs that he healed,—that hero who gave aid in all manner of maladies.

Or ever the daughter of Phlegyas [1] could bear him, in the fulness of time, with the aid of Eleithuia, the goddess of child-birth, she was stricken in her chamber by the golden arrows of Artemis, and thus descended to the home of Hades by the counsels of Apollo. Not in vain is the wrath of the sons of Zeus. For she, in the errors of her heart, had lightly regarded that wrath; and, although she had aforetime consorted with Phoebus of the unshorn hair,

[1] Corônis, l. 25.

185

PINDAR

ἐπ. α'

15 καὶ φέροισα σπέρμα θεοῦ καθαρόν.

οὐδ' ἔμειν' ἐλθεῖν τράπεζαν νυμφίαν

οὐδὲ παμφώνων ἰαχὰν ὑμεναίων, ἅλικες   30

οἷα παρθένοι φιλέοισιν ἑταῖραι

ἑσπερίαις ὑποκουρίζεσθ' ἀοιδαῖς· ἀλλά τοι

20 ἤρατο τῶν ἀπεόντων· οἷα καὶ πολλοὶ πάθον.

ἔστι δὲ φῦλον ἐν ἀνθρώποισι ματαιότατον,

ὅστις αἰσχύνων ἐπιχώρια παπταίνει τὰ πόρσω,

μεταμώνια θηρεύων ἀκράντοις ἐλπίσιν.   40

στρ. β'

ἔσχε τοιαύταν μεγάλαν ἀάταν

25 καλλιπέπλου λῆμα Κορωνίδος. ἐλθόντος γὰρ

εὐνάσθη ξένου

λέκτροισιν ἀπ' Ἀρκαδίας.

οὐδ' ἔλαθε σκοπόν· ἐν δ' ἄρα μηλοδόκῳ Πυθῶνι

τόσσαις ἄϊεν ναοῦ βασιλεὺς

Λοξίας, κοινᾶνι παρ' εὐθυτάτῳ γνώμαν πιθών,   50

πάντα ἴσαντι νόῳ· ψευδέων δ' οὐχ ἅπτεται·

κλέπτει τέ νιν

30 οὐ θεὸς οὐ βροτὸς ἔργοις οὔτε βουλαῖς.

ἀντ. β'

καὶ τότε γνοὺς Ἴσχυος Εἰλατίδα

ξεινίαν κοίταν ἄθεμίν τε δόλον, πέμψεν κασι-

γνήταν μένει

θύοισαν ἀμαιμακέτῳ

ἐς Λακέρειαν. ἐπεὶ παρὰ Βοιβιάδος κρημνοῖσιν

ᾤκει παρθένος. δαίμων δ' ἕτερος   60

24 ἀνάταν old mss (BMC), αὐάταν (F) : ἀάταν Moschopulus, Heyne (S) ; ἀϝάταν (M¹G) ; cp. ii 28.

28 γνώμαν BD (MGFCS) : γνώμᾳ C (B).

33 θύοισαν mss (BMGFC) : θυίοισαν Wilhelm Schulze (S).

and bare within her the pure seed of the god, yet
without her father's knowledge she consented to be
wedded to another. She waited not for the coming
of the marriage feast, nor for the music of the full-
voiced hymenaeal chorus, even the playful strains
that maiden-mates love to utter in evening songs.
No! she was enamoured of an absent love,—that
passion, which many, ere now, have felt. For, among
men, there is a foolish company of those, who, putting
shame on their home, cast their glances afar, and
pursue idle dreams in hopes that shall not be fulfilled.

Such was the strong infatuation that the spirit of
the fair-robed Corônis had caught. For she slept in
the couch of a stranger who came from Arcadia;
but she escaped not the ken of the watchful god;
for, although he was then at the sacrificial shrine of
Pytho, yet Loxias, the king of the temple, perceived
it in his mind that knoweth all things, with his
thought convinced by an unerring prompter. He
never deceiveth others; and he is not himself
deceived by god or man, in deed or counsel. Even
so, at that time, he knew of her consorting with the
stranger, Ischys, son of Elatus, and of her lawless
deceit. Thereupon did he send his sister, Artemis,
speeding with resistless might, even to Lacereia, for
the unwedded girl was dwelling by the banks of
the Boebian lake [1]; and a hateful doom perverted her

[1] In S.E. Thessaly. Corônis is one of Hesiod's heroines,
"who, dwelling in the Dôtian plain over against the vine-
clad Amyrus, as a maid unwedded washed her feet in the
Boebian lake." Cp. *Homeric Hymn* xvi, and Strabo,
pp. 442, 647.

35　ἐς κακὸν τρέψαις ἐδαμάσσατό νιν· καὶ γειτόνων
　　πολλοὶ ἐπαῦρον, ἁμᾷ δ᾽ ἔφθαρεν, πολλὰν δ᾽ ὄρει
　　　　πῦρ ἐξ ἑνὸς
　　σπέρματος ἐνθορὸν ἀίστωσεν ὕλαν.

ἐπ. β′
　　ἀλλ᾽ ἐπεὶ τείχει θέσαν ἐν ξυλίνῳ
　　σύγγονοι κούραν, σέλας δ᾽ ἀμφέδραμεν
40　λάβρον Ἀφαίστου, τότ᾽ ἔειπεν Ἀπόλλων· "Οὐ-
　　　　κέτι　　　　　　　　　　　　　　　　　　70
　　τλάσομαι ψυχᾷ γένος ἀμὸν ὀλέσσαι
　　οἰκτροτάτῳ θανάτῳ ματρὸς βαρείᾳ σὺν πάθᾳ."
　　ὣς φάτο· βάματι δ᾽ ἐν πρώτῳ κιχὼν παῖδ᾽ ἐκ
　　　　νεκροῦ
　　ἅρπασε· καιομένα δ᾽ αὐτῷ διέφαινε πυρά·
45　καί ῥά νιν Μάγνητι φέρων πόρε Κενταύρῳ
　　　　διδάξαι　　　　　　　　　　　　　　　　80
　　πολυπήμονας ἀνθρώποισιν ἰᾶσθαι νόσους.

στρ. γ′
　　τοὺς μὲν ὦν, ὅσσοι μόλον αὐτοφύτων
　　ἑλκέων ξυνάονες, ἢ πολιῷ χαλκῷ μέλη τετρωμένοι
　　ἢ χερμάδι τηλεβόλῳ,
50　ἢ θερινῷ πυρὶ περθόμενοι δέμας ἢ χειμῶνι, λύσαις
　　　　ἄλλον ἀλλοίων ἀχέων　　　　　　　　90
　　ἔξαγεν, τοὺς μὲν μαλακαῖς ἐπαοιδαῖς ἀμφέπων,
　　τοὺς δὲ προσανέα πίνοντας, ἢ γυίοις περάπτων
　　　　πάντοθεν
　　φάρμακα, τοὺς δὲ τομαῖς ἔστασεν ὀρθούς.

ἀντ. γ′
　　ἀλλὰ κέρδει καὶ σοφίᾳ δέδεται.

41 ἀμὸν BC² (ΒΜGFC) :· ἀμὸν C¹D (S), ἐμὸν E.
44 διέφαινε BC¹ (MGFS) : διέφανε DC² (B²C).

heart and laid her low, and many of her neighbours suffered for the same, and perished with her; even as, on a mountain, the fire that hath been sped by a single spark layeth low a mighty forest.

But, when the kinsmen had placed the girl in the midst of the wooden walls of the pyre, and the wild flame of the fire-god was playing around it, then spake Apollo:—" No longer can I endure in my heart to slay my own child by a death most piteous, at the self-same time as its mother's grievous doom." He stepped forward but once, and anon he found his child, and snatched it from the corse, while the kindled fire opened for him a path of light; and he bare the babe away, and gave it to the Magnesian Centaur to teach it how to heal mortal men of painful maladies.

And those whosoever came suffering from the sores of nature, or with their limbs wounded either by gray bronze or by far-hurled stone, or with bodies wasting away with summer's heat or winter's cold, he loosed and delivered divers of them from diverse pains, tending some of them with kindly incantations, giving to others a soothing potion, or, haply, swathing their limbs with simples or restoring others by the knife. But, alas! even the lore of leech-craft is

55 ἔτραπεν καὶ κεῖνον ἀγάνορι μισθῷ χρυσὸς ἐν χερ-
σὶν φανεὶς
ἄνδρ᾽ ἐκ θανάτου κομίσαι
ἤδη ἁλωκότα· χερσὶ δ᾽ ἄρα Κρονίων ῥίψαις δι᾽
ἀμφοῖν ἀμπνοὰν στέρνων καθέλεν   100
ὠκέως, αἴθων δὲ κεραυνὸς ἐνέσκιμψεν μόρον.
χρὴ τὰ ἐοικότα πὰρ δαιμόνων μαστευέμεν θναταῖς
φρασίν,
60 γνόντα τὸ πὰρ ποδός, οἵας εἰμὲν αἴσας.
ἐπ. γ΄
μή, φίλα ψυχά, βίον ἀθάνατον
σπεῦδε, τὰν δ᾽ ἔμπρακτον ἄντλει μαχανάν.   110
εἰ δὲ σώφρων ἄντρον ἔναι᾽ ἔτι Χείρων, καί τί οἱ
φίλτρον ἐν θυμῷ μελιγάρυες ὕμνοι
65 ἁμέτεροι τίθεν· ἰατρά τοί κέν νιν πίθον
καί νυν ἐσλοῖσι παρασχεῖν ἀνδράσιν θερμᾶν
νόσων
ἤ τινα Λατοΐδα κεκλημένον ἢ πατέρος.
καί κεν ἐν ναυσὶν μόλον Ἰονίαν τάμνων θάλασ-
σαν   120
Ἀρέθοισαν ἐπὶ κράναν παρ᾽ Αἰτναῖον ξένον,
στρ. δ΄
70 ὃς Συρακόσσαισι νέμει βασιλεὺς
πραῢς ἀστοῖς, οὐ φθονέων ἀγαθοῖς, ξείνοις δὲ θαυ-
μαστὸς πατήρ.
τῷ μὲν διδύμας χάριτας,
εἰ κατέβαν ὑγίειαν ἄγων χρυσέαν κῶμόν τ᾽ ἀέθλων
Πυθίων αἴγλαν στεφάνοις,   130
τοὺς ἀριστεύων Φερένικος ἕλ᾽ ἐν Κίρρᾳ ποτέ,
75 ἀστέρος οὐρανίου φαμὶ τηλαυγέστερον κείνῳ φάος
ἐξικόμαν κε βαθὺν πόντον περάσαις.

69 Ἀρέθοισαν Bergk ¹ (s) : Ἀρέθουσαν mss (BMGFC).

enthralled by the love of gain; even he was seduced, by a splendid fee of gold displayed upon his palm, to bring back from death one who was already its lawful prey. Therefore the son of Cronus with his hands hurled his shaft through both of them, and swiftly reft the breath from out their breasts, for they were stricken with sudden doom by the gleaming thunderbolt. We must seek from the gods for such boons as best befit a mortal mind, knowing what lieth before our feet, and knowing of what estate we are. Seek not, my soul, the life of the immortals; but enjoy to the full the resources that are within thy reach.

But, if only the sage Cheiron had still been dwelling in his cave, and if only our honey-sweet songs had cast a spell upon his soul, surely I had persuaded him to send some one to heal noble men from their fits of fever, some one called the son of Asclêpius or of Apollo.

Thus had I gone on shipboard, cleaving the Ionian main, on my voyage to the fount of Arethusa and to the presence of my friend, the lord of Aetna, who ruleth at Syracuse as a king who is gentle to his citizens, bearing no grudge against them that are noble, while he is adored as a father by his friends from afar. And, had I reached his shores with a double boon, bringing with me golden health, as well as the triumph-song that lendeth new lustre to those crowns from the Pythian contests, which Pherenîcus won in former years at Cirrha, I aver that, on crossing the deep sea, I had landed as a light which, in his eyes, would have shone afar more brightly than the orb of heaven itself. Yet, even

PINDAR

ἀντ. δ΄

ἀλλ᾽ ἐπεύξασθαι μὲν ἐγὼν ἐθέλω
Ματρί, τὰν κοῦραι παρ᾽ ἐμὸν πρόθυρον σὺν Πανὶ
    μέλπονται θαμὰ
σεμνὰν θεὸν ἐννύχιαι.   140

80 εἰ δὲ λόγων συνέμεν κορυφάν, Ἱέρων, ὀρθὰν ἐπί-
    στα, μανθάνων οἶσθα προτέρων·
  " ἓν παρ᾽ ἐσλὸν πήματα σύνδυο δαίονται βροτοῖς
ἀθάνατοι." τὰ μὲν ὦν οὐ δύνανται νήπιοι κόσμῳ
    φέρειν,
ἀλλ᾽ ἀγαθοί, τὰ καλὰ τρέψαντες ἔξω.

ἐπ. δ΄

τὶν δὲ μοῖρ᾽ εὐδαιμονίας ἕπεται.   150

85 λαγέταν γάρ τοι τύραννον δέρκεται,
  εἴ τιν᾽ ἀνθρώπων, ὁ μέγας πότμος. αἰὼν δ᾽ ἀσ-
    φαλὴς
  οὐκ ἔγεντ᾽ οὔτ᾽ Αἰακίδᾳ παρὰ Πηλεῖ
οὔτε παρ᾽ ἀντιθέῳ Κάδμῳ· λέγονται μὰν βροτῶν
ὄλβον ὑπέρτατον οἳ σχεῖν, οἵτε καὶ χρυσαμπύκων

90 μελπομενᾶν ἐν ὄρει Μοισᾶν καὶ ἐν ἑπταπύλοις 160
    ἄϊον Θήβαις, ὁπόθ᾽ Ἁρμονίαν γᾶμεν βοῶπιν,
    ὁ δὲ Νηρέος εὐβούλου Θέτιν παῖδα κλυτάν.

στρ. ε΄

  καὶ θεοὶ δαίσαντο παρ᾽ ἀμφοτέροις,
  καὶ Κρόνου παῖδας βασιλῆας ἴδον χρυσέαις ἐν
    ἕδραις, ἕδνα τε
95 δέξαντο· Διὸς δὲ χάριν
  ἐκ προτέρων μεταμειψάμενοι καμάτων ἔστασαν
    ὀρθὰν καρδίαν. ἐν δ᾽ αὖτε χρόνῳ   170
τὸν μὲν ὀξείαισι θύγατρες ἐρήμωσαν πάθαις
εὐφροσύνας μέρος αἱ τρεῖς· ἀτὰρ λευκωλένῳ γε
    Ζεὺς πατὴρ

192

so, 'tis my wish to offer a vow to the Mother-goddess, that adorable queen, whose praises, with those of Pan, are oft sung of maidens in the night beside my portal.

But since thou, Hieron, art skilled to learn the true lesson that is taught by the sayings of former time, the immortals, as thou knowest, apportion to man two trials for every boon they grant ; and these trials foolish men cannot bear with a good grace, but the noble can, by ever turning the fairer side to the front.

Yet thou art attended by a happy lot, for lo! the lord of his people, if any man, is viewed with favour by Fortune. But a life free from reverses was the fate neither of Pêleus, son of Aeacus, nor of god-like Cadmus. Yet we learn that they attained the highest happiness of all mortal men, in that they heard the Muses of the golden snood singing on mount Pêlion, and in seven-gated Thebes, what time Cadmus took to wife Harmonia, with those full-orbed eyes; and when Pêleus wedded Thetis, the famous daughter of wise Nêreus. And the gods banqueted with them, and they saw the royal sons of Cronus seated on their golden thrones, and received marriage-gifts from them ; and, by the favour of Zeus, they escaped from their former troubles, and lifted up their hearts again in gladness.

And yet, in time, Cadmus was reft of his portion of bliss by the bitter woes of three of his daughters,[1] although Father Zeus visited the bridal couch of

---

[1] Ino, Agauê, and Autonoê. Ino was wedded to Athamas, who in his madness slew one of his two sons, while Ino flung herself into the sea, with the other, Melicertes. Agauê and Autonoê in a fit of Bacchic frenzy killed Agauê's son, Pentheus.

ἤλυθεν ἐς λέχος ἱμερτὸν Θυώνᾳ.

ἀντ. ε΄

100 τοῦ δὲ παῖς, ὅνπερ μόνον ἀθανάτα
τίκτεν ἐν Φθίᾳ Θέτις, ἐν πολέμῳ τόξοις ἀπὸ
ψυχὰν λιπὼν   180
ὦρσεν πυρὶ καιόμενος
ἐκ Δαναῶν γόον. εἰ δὲ νόῳ τις ἔχει θνατῶν ἀλα-
θείας ὁδόν, χρὴ πρὸς μακάρων
τυγχάνοντ᾽ εὖ πασχέμεν. ἄλλοτε δ᾽ ἀλλοῖαι πνοαὶ
105 ὑψιπετᾶν ἀνέμων. ὄλβος οὐκ ἐς μακρὸν ἀνδρῶν
ἔρχεται
<σάος>, πολὺς εὖτ᾽ ἂν ἐπιβρίσαις ἕπηται.   190

ἐπ. ε΄

σμικρὸς ἐν σμικροῖς, μέγας ἐν μεγάλοις
ἔσσομαι· τὸν ἀμφέποντ᾽ αἰεὶ φρασὶν
δαίμον᾽ ἀσκήσω κατ᾽ ἐμὰν θεραπεύων μαχανάν.
110 εἰ δέ μοι πλοῦτον θεὸς ἁβρὸν ὀρέξαι,
ἐλπίδ᾽ ἔχω κλέος εὑρέσθαι κεν ὑψηλὸν πρόσω.
Νέστορα καὶ Λύκιον Σαρπηδόν᾽, ἀνθρώπων φάτις,
ἐξ ἐπέων κελαδεννῶν, τέκτονες οἷα σοφοὶ   200
ἅρμοσαν, γιγνώσκομεν. ἁ δ᾽ ἀρετὰ κλειναῖς ἀοιδαῖς
115 χρόνια τελέθει. παύροις δὲ πράξασθ᾽ εὐμαρές.

106 σῶς Emperius (c), σάος (s); ὃς mss. οὐ πολὺς B; ἄ-
πλετος Hermann (Donaldson, F); πάμπολυς Dissen (G); οἷς M.

194

their sister, the white-armed Semelê. Aye, and the son of Pêleus, the only son whom immortal Thetis bare in Phthia, reft of his life by the bow in battle, awakened the mourning of the Danai, while his body was burning on the pyre.

But, if any mortal hath in mind the course things take in very truth, right it is for one, who hath received favour from the blessed ones, to enjoy his lot. Yet changeful are the breezes of the winds that blow on high. The bliss of man doth not proceed unimpaired for long, whene'er it followeth them in its full weight and measure. Small shall I be, when small is my estate, and great, when it is great. The fortune that, ever and anon, attendeth me, I shall heartily honour, and shall do it service with all my might. But, if God were to give me the gladness of wealth, I hope, in future days, to find high fame. We know of Nestor, and of Lycian Sarpêdôn, whose names are on the lips of men, thanks to those lays of sounding song, such as wise builders framed for them. Virtue gaineth a long life by means of glorious strains; but they that find it easy to win those strains, are few.

PYTHIAN IV

FOR ARCESILAS OF CYRENE

INTRODUCTION

ARCESILAÜS IV, son of Battus IV, King of Cyrene, won the victory with his chariot in the Pythian games of 462 B.C. The fourth Pythian was apparently composed at the request of Dâmophilus, a noble who had been exiled for taking part in some aristocratic insurrection against the King of Cyrene, and had been staying at Thebes. The exile hopes to propitiate the king by the splendid offering of a' lyric encomium composed on an ample scale by Pindar. The Ode was sung at a banquet in the palace at Cyrene.

The Muse is bidden to celebrate the victory won by Arcesilaüs at Pytho (1–3), where his ancestor, Battus, had of old been bidden by the oracle to leave the island of Thêra and to found Cyrene (4–8), thus fulfilling the prophecy of Medea (9–12). Medea had told how, at the mouth of the Libyan Lake, Tritônis, the Argonaut Euphâmus had received from a deity in disguise, a marvellous clod, which was washed overboard and thus followed the Argonauts on their voyage to Thêra, whence the

descendants of Euphâmus were to go and possess
the land promised to their ancestor (13–58).

This prophecy was fulfilled by Battus, the founder
of Cyrene, to whose descendant in the eighth gener-
ation Apollo had given the glory of a victory in the
chariot-race at Pytho (59–67).

The voyage of the Argonauts (67–250). The
Argonauts, on their return, landed at Lemnos,
where they wedded the heroines of the island.
Such was the source of the race of Euphâmus,
which left Lemnos for Sparta and Thêra, and, at last
for Cyrene (251–262).

To lead up to the proposed reconciliation between
the exile and the King, the poet here introduces the
Allegory of the Lopped Oak (263–269). The king
is a healer; with heaven's help he can set Cyrene on
a firm foundation; let him remember that a fair
messenger brings fair tidings; the fair messenger is
the poet's Muse (270–287).

Dâmophilus is then named for the first time; and
his praises are blended with an appeal for forgive-
ness, such as Zeus granted to the Titans. Let the
exile see his home again; let him banquet beside
Apollo's fountain at Cyrene, making music on his
harp, and living a quiet and blameless life, and
telling of the fount of song he had found for the
king at Thebes (288–299).

IV.—ΑΡΚΕΣΙΛΑ ΚΥΡΗΝΑΙΩ

ΑΡΜΑΤΙ

στρ. α΄

Σάμερον μὲν χρή σε παρ᾽ ἀνδρὶ φίλῳ
στᾶμεν, εὐίππου βασιλῆι Κυράνας, ὄφρα κωμά-
ζοντι σὺν Ἀρκεσίλᾳ,
Μοῖσα, Λατοίδαισιν ὀφειλόμενον Πυθῶνί τ᾽ αὔξῃς
οὖρον ὕμνων,
ἔνθα ποτὲ χρυσέων Διὸς αἰητῶν πάρεδρος,
5 οὐκ ἀποδάμου Ἀπόλλωνος τυχόντος, ἱέρεα
χρῆσεν οἰκιστῆρα Βάττον καρποφόρου Λιβύας,
ἱερὰν   10
νᾶσον ὡς ἤδη λιπὼν κτίσσειεν εὐάρματον
πόλιν ἐν ἀργεννόεντι μαστῷ,

ἀντ. α΄

καὶ τὸ Μηδείας ἔπος ἀγκομίσαι
10 ἑβδόμᾳ καὶ σὺν δεκάτᾳ γενεᾷ Θήραιον, Αἰήτα τό
ποτε ζαμενὴς
παῖς ἀπέπνευσ᾽ ἀθανάτου στόματος, δέσποινα
Κόλχων. εἶπε δ᾽ οὕτως
ἡμιθέοισιν Ἰάσονος αἰχματᾶο ναύταις·   20
" Κέκλυτε, παῖδες ὑπερθύμων τε φωτῶν καὶ θεῶν·
φαμὶ γὰρ τᾶσδ᾽ ἐξ ἁλιπλάκτου ποτὲ γᾶς Ἐπάφοιο
κόραν

5 ἱέρεα old mss (MFCS); ἱερέα DZ, Hermann; ἱρέα B; ῾Ιρεα G.

8 ἀργεννόεντι S, ἀργενόεντι old mss, ἀργῖνόεντι Bergk (F), ἀργινόεντι (MGC): ἀργινέντι Triclinius, ἀργάεντι Hermann (B).

9 ἀγκομίσαι (MGCS): ἀγκομίσαιθ᾽ all old mss (BF).

IV.—FOR ARCESILAS OF CYRENE

WINNER IN THE CHARIOT-RACE, 462 B.C.

THOU must stand, my Muse! to-day in the presence
of a friend, even the king of Cyrênê with its noble
steeds, that so, beside Arcesilas, while he celebrateth
his triumph, thou mayest swell the gale of song
that is now due to the children of Lêtô, and to Pythô
also, where, in the olden time, on a day when Apollo
was not far away, the priestess throned beside the
golden eagles of Zeus gave for them an oracle,
naming Battus the coloniser of fruitful Libya, and
telling how he would at once leave the holy island,[1]
and build, on a gleaming hill,[2] a city of noble chariots,
and thus, in the seventeenth generation, fulfil the
word spoken at Thêra by Medea, which that brave
daughter of Aeêtês, that queen of the Colchians,
breathed forth from her immortal lips, when she
spake in this wise to the heroes who sailed with the
warrior Jason:—

"Listen, ye sons of high-spirited men, ye sons of
the gods! for I aver that, from this wave-washed land
of Thêra, the daughter of Epaphus,[3] will, in days

---

[1] Thêra.
[2] Literally "breast," "a white breast of the swelling
earth" (E. Myers). Scotland has its "Paps of Jura," and
France its "mamelon."   [3] Libya.

PINDAR

15 ἀστέων ῥίζαν φυτεύσεσθαι μελησίμβροτον
  Διὸς ἐν Ἄμμωνος θεμέθλοις.
ἐπ. α′
  ἀντὶ δελφίνων δ᾽ ἐλαχυπτερύγων ἵππους ἀμείψαν-
      τες θοάς, 30
  ἀνία τ᾽ ἀντ᾽ ἐρετμῶν δίφρους τε νωμάσοισιν ἀελ-
      λόποδας.
  κεῖνος ὄρνις ἐκτελευτάσει μεγαλᾶν πολίων
20 ματρόπολιν Θήραν γενέσθαι, τόν ποτε Τριτωνίδος
      ἐν προχοαῖς
  λίμνας θεῷ ἀνέρι εἰδομένῳ γαῖαν διδόντι
  ξείνια πρῴραθεν Εὔφαμος καταβὰς
  δέξατ᾽· αἴσιον δ᾽ ἐπί οἱ Κρονίων Ζεὺς πατὴρ
      ἔκλαγξε βροντάν· 40
στρ. β′
  ἀνίκ᾽ ἄγκυραν ποτὶ χαλκόγενυν
25 ναΐ κρημνάντων ἐπέτοσσε, θοᾶς Ἀργοῦς χαλινόν.
      δώδεκα δὲ πρότερον
  ἀμέρας ἐξ Ὠκεανοῦ φέρομεν νώτων ὕπερ γαίας
      ἐρήμων
  εἰνάλιον δόρυ, μήδεσιν ἀνσπάσσαντες ἀμοῖς.
  τουτάκι δ᾽ οἰοπόλος δαίμων ἐπῆλθεν, φαιδίμαν 50
  ἀνδρὸς αἰδοίου πρόσοψιν θηκάμενος· φιλίων δ᾽
      ἐπέων
30 ἄρχετο, ξείνοις ἅτ᾽ ἐλθόντεσσιν εὐεργέται
  δεῖπν᾽ ἐπαγγέλλοντι πρῶτον.
ἀντ. β′
  ἀλλὰ γὰρ νόστου πρόφασις γλυκεροῦ

    23 αἴσιον mss (BMGFC) : αἰσίαν (S).
    25 κρημνάντων most mss (BMGFC) : κριμνάντων B (S).
    30 ἄρχετο BFP.. (MGCS) : ἄρχεται CDEV and interpolated
  mss (BF).

200

to come, find planted in her a root of cities that
shall be fostered of men near the foundations of
Zeus Ammon.   Instead of the short-finned dolphins,
shall they take to themselves swift horses, and,
instead of oars, shall they ply the reins and the
chariots swift as the breeze.   That token shall bring
it to pass that Thêra shall become a mother of
mighty cities, the token which, on a day, beside
the out-flowing waters of lake Tritônis,[1] Euphêmus,[2]
descending from the prow of the Argo, did receive
from a god in the likeness of man, who offered him
earth as a hospitable gift.   And, thereupon, Father
Zeus, the son of Cronus, as a sign of favour, sounded
a peal of thunder, what time the stranger lighted
upon them as they slung beside the ship the brazen
anchor, the swift Argo's bridle.

And, ere that time, we had left the Ocean, and,
by my counsel, had dragged up our sea-faring ship,
and for twelve days had carried it across heavy ridges
of land.   Then was it that the lonely god (even the
Triton) drew near in the splendid semblance of a
venerable man, and began to utter friendly words,
such as kindly men are wont to use, when they first
offer welcome to strangers on their coming.   But
in very deed, the plea of our sweet return to home
forbade our lingering.   Now he averred that he

[1] After leaving Colchis, the Argonauts passed by the
Phasis to "Oceanus," and thence to the "Red Sea," carried
their ship overland twelve days, reached the Libyan lake
Tritônis, and found an outlet from the lake into the
Mediterranean Sea (Gildersleeve).

[2] A son of Poseidon, l. 45.

κώλυεν μεῖναι. φάτο δ᾽ Εὐρύπυλος Γαιαόχου παῖς
  ἀφθίτου Ἐννοσίδα
ἔμμεναι· γίγνωσκε δ᾽ ἐπειγομένους· ἂν δ᾽ εὐθὺς
  ἁρπάξαις ἀρούρας   60
35 δεξιτερᾷ προτυχὸν ξένιον μάστευσε δοῦναι.
  οὐδ᾽ ἀπίθησέ νιν, ἀλλ᾽ ἥρως ἐπ᾽ ἀκταῖσιν θορὼν
χειρί οἱ χεῖρ᾽ ἀντερείσαις δέξατο βώλακα δαιμο-
  νίαν.
πεύθομαι δ᾽ αὐτὰν κατακλυσθεῖσαν ἐκ δούρατος
  ἐναλίαν βᾶμεν σὺν ἅλμᾳ

ἐπ. β'

40 ἑσπέρας, ὑγρῷ πελάγει σπομέναν. ἦ μάν νιν
  ὤτρυνον θαμὰ   70
λυσιπόνοις θεραπόντεσσιν φυλάξαι· τῶν δ᾽ ἐλά-
  θοντο φρένες·
καί νυν ἐν τᾷδ᾽ ἄφθιτον νάσῳ κέχυται Λιβύας
εὐρυχόρου σπέρμα πρὶν ὥρας· εἰ γὰρ οἴκοι νιν
  βάλε πὰρ χθόνιον
Ἅιδα στόμα, Ταίναρον εἰς ἱερὰν Εὔφαμος ἐλθών,
45 υἱὸς ἱππάρχου Ποσειδάωνος ἄναξ,   80
τόν ποτ᾽ Εὐρώπα Τιτυοῦ θυγάτηρ τίκτε Καφισοῦ
  παρ᾽ ὄχθαις·

στρ. γ'

τετράτων παίδων κ᾽ ἐπιγινομένων
αἷμά οἱ κείναν λάβε σὺν Δαναοῖς εὐρεῖαν ἄπειρον.
τότε γὰρ μεγάλας
ἐξανίστανται Λακεδαίμονος Ἀργείου τε κόλπου
  καὶ Μυκηνᾶν.
50 νῦν γε μὲν ἀλλοδαπᾶν κριτὸν εὑρήσει γυναικῶν
ἐν λέχεσιν γένος, οἵ κεν τάνδε σὺν τιμᾷ θεῶν   90

36 νιν mss (BMGF) ; ἱν (= οἱ) Hermann (C), ἱν s.
50 μὲν (BMGFS¹C) : μὰν old mss (S³) ; γε μὲν = Attic γὲ μὴν.

was Eurypylus, the son of the immortal Shaker of the Earth which is Poseidon's portion; and when he began to know that we were hasting on our way, anon he seized some of the soil, and essayed to give to Euphêmus, as a friendly gift, whatever came to hand; nor did Euphêmus disobey him; nay, but the hero leaped down upon the beach, and, pressing his hand in the hand of the stranger, received from him that fateful clod of earth.

But they tell me that it was washed out of the ship and passed into the sea with the spray at eventide, following the waters of the main. Verily full often did I urge the several watches of seamen to guard it with all care, but their minds were forgetful, and now is the seed of broad Libya washed ashore on the island of Thêra before its full time. For, if Euphâmus, son of Poseidon, the ruler of horses, whom Eurôpa, daughter of Titys, erstwhile bare beside the banks of Cêphîsus, had only sped him to holy Taenarus, and there, in his home, cast the clod down beside that portal of the world below, the blood of the fourth generation descended from him would have taken possession of all the breadth of this vast continent. For, in that event, I see men departing thither from great Lacedaemon, and from the Argive Gulf, and from Mycênae.

But, as things be, Euphêmus shall find in the bridal beds of foreign dames a chosen race, which, by the blessing of the gods, shall come to this island

νᾶσον ἐλθόντες τέκωνται φῶτα κελαινεφέων
  πεδίων
δεσπόταν· τὸν μὲν πολυχρύσῳ ποτ' ἐν δώματι
Φοῖβος ἀμνάσει θέμισσιν

ἀντ. γ΄

55 Πύθιον ναὸν καταβάντα χρόνῳ
  ὑστέρῳ, νάεσσι πολεῖς ἀγαγὲν Νείλοιο πρὸς πῖον
  τέμενος Κρονίδα."
  ἦ ῥα Μηδείας ἐπέων στίχες. ἔπταξαν δ' ἀκίνητοι
  σιωπᾷ   100
  ἥρωες ἀντίθεοι πυκινὰν μῆτιν κλύοντες.
  ὦ μάκαρ υἱὲ Πολυμνάστου, σὲ δ' ἐν τούτῳ λόγῳ
60 χρησμὸς ὤρθωσεν μελίσσας Δελφίδος αὐτομάτῳ
  κελάδῳ·
  ἅ σε χαίρειν ἐς τρὶς αὐδάσαισα πεπρωμένον
  βασιλέ' ἄμφανεν Κυράνᾳ,   110

ἐπ. γ΄

δυσθρόου φωνᾶς ἀνακρινόμενον ποινὰ τίς ἔσται
  πρὸς θεῶν.
ἦ μάλα δὴ μετὰ καὶ νῦν, ὥστε φοινικανθέμου
  ἦρος ἀκμᾷ,
65 παισὶ τούτοις ὄγδοον θάλλει μέρος Ἀρκεσίλας·
  τῷ μὲν Ἀπόλλων ἅ τε Πυθὼ κῦδος ἐξ ἀμφικτιό-
  νων ἔπορεν

56 πολεῖς (mss) ἀγαγεῖν (C and scholium) (ΒΜ¹C), or ἄγαγε
BD, or ἀγαγὲν E (Μ²GF) : πόλις (Lehrs) ἀγαγὲν (S).
65 τούτοις mss (edd.) : τεοῖς? Wilamowitz (S¹).
66 ἀμφικτιόνων Boeckh here, and in P. x 8, N. vi 40, I. iii,
cp. περικτιόνων, N. ix 19, I. viii 64 (edd.) : Ἀμφικτυόνων mss.

204

of Thêra, and there beget a man who shall be the
lord of those plains which are mantled by the dark
cloud.[1]

The day shall come when Phoebus in his golden
home shall make mention of him in his oracles, when,
at a later time, he descendeth from the threshold
into the Pythian shrine, telling how he shall carry
many a man in his ships to the fertile precinct of
the son of Cronus beside the Nile."

Verily such were the lays that Medea sang ; and
the god-like heroes, while they listened to her deep
counsel, stirred not a whit, but bowed them down
in silence.

But, O thou happy son of Polymnêstus![2] 'twas
none other than thee that, in accord with this word
of prophecy, the oracle glorified by means of the
unprompted utterance of the Delphic Bee,[3] who
thrice, and that loudly, bade thee hail, and declared
thee the destined king of Cyrênê, when thou wast
asking the oracle what release the gods would grant
thee from thy stammering tongue.[4] In very deed,
even now, in the latter days, as in the prime of rosy
spring, eighth in the line of those descendants,
bloometh Arcesilas. 'Twas Apollo and Pytho that
granted him glory in the chariot-race among them

[1] "Cyrene had rain, the rest of Libya none" (Gilder-
sleeve). Cp. Herodotus, iv 158.   [2] Battus.

[3] The priestess of Apollo. The same title was given to
priestesses of Dêmêtêr, Persephonê, and the Great Mother.

[4] After Battus, who was born with a stammering tongue
in Thêra, had grown to man's estate, he journeyed to Delphi,
to consult the oracle about his voice, whereupon the priestess
replied :—

"Battus, thou camest to ask of thy voice ; but Phoebus Apollo
Bids thee establish a city in Libya, abounding in fleeces."
(Herodotus, iv 155.)

ἱπποδρομίας. ἀπὸ δ᾽ αὐτὸν ἐγὼ Μοίσαισι δώσω 120
καὶ τὸ πάγχρυσον νάκος κριοῦ· μετὰ γὰρ
κεῖνο πλευσάντων Μινυᾶν, θεόπομποί σφισιν
τιμαὶ φύτευθεν.

στρ. δ´
70 τίς γὰρ ἀρχὰ δέξατο ναυτιλίας;
τίς δὲ κίνδυνος κρατεροῖς ἀδάμαντος δῆσεν ἅλοις;
θέσφατον ἦν Πελίαν
ἐξ ἀγαυῶν Αἰολιδᾶν θανέμεν χείρεσσιν ἢ βουλαῖς
ἀκάμπτοις.
ἦλθε δέ οἱ κρυόεν πυκινῷ μάντευμα θυμῷ,   130
πὰρ μέσον ὀμφαλὸν εὐδένδροιο ῥηθὲν ματέρος·
75 τὸν μονοκρήπιδα πάντως ἐν φυλακᾷ σχεθέμεν
μεγάλᾳ,
εὖτ᾽ ἂν αἰπεινῶν ἀπὸ σταθμῶν ἐς εὐδείελον
χθόνα μόλῃ κλειτᾶς Ἰωλκοῦ,

ἀντ. δ´
ξεῖνος αἴτ᾽ ὢν ἀστός. ὁ δ᾽ ἄρα χρόνῳ
ἵκετ᾽ αἰχμαῖσιν διδύμαισιν ἀνὴρ ἔκπαγλος· ἐσθὰς
δ᾽ ἀμφοτέρα νιν ἔχεν·   140
80 ἅ τε Μαγνήτων ἐπιχώριος ἁρμόζοισα θαητοῖσι
γυίοις,
ἀμφὶ δὲ παρδαλέᾳ στέγετο φρίσσοντας ὄμβρους·
οὐδὲ κομᾶν πλόκαμοι κερθέντες ᾤχοντ᾽ ἀγλαοί,
ἀλλ᾽ ἅπαν νῶτον καταίθυσσον. τάχα δ᾽ εὐθὺς
ἰὼν σφετέρας
ἐστάθη γνώμας ἀταρμύκτοιο πειρώμενος   150
85 ἐν ἀγορᾷ πλήθοντος ὄχλου.

ἐπ. δ´
τὸν μὲν οὐ γίγνωσκον· ὀπιζομένων δ᾽ ἔμπας τις
εἶπεν καὶ τόδε·

79 ἀμφοτέρα EF (MCS) : ἀμφότερόν most mss (BFG).

that dwelt around[1] ; but I shall make himself, and the Golden Fleece, a theme for the Muses' song. For, when the Minyae sailed forth upon that quest, then were the heaven-sent honours planted for his race.

Tell me what was it that first befell them in their sea-faring? What was the peril that bound them with strong bolts of adamant? The oracle had said that Pelias would be slain by the proud Aeolidae,[2] either by their own hands or by their resistless counsels; for a response, which made his wary spirit shudder, came unto him in words spoken beside the central stone of tree-clad mother-earth, bidding him in any wise beware of one, shod with a single sandal, who, whether citizen or stranger, was to come down from the homesteads in the mountains to the sunny land of far-famed Iôlcus. And so, at last, he came, a hero terrible to look upon, as he brandished his twain spears; and he was clothed with a two-fold raiment, the garb of his Magnesian home closely fitting his comely limbs, while the skin of a pard protected him from shivering showers. Nor had his splendid locks of hair been shorn, but they rolled lustrous adown all his back. Then, to make trial of his dauntless spirit, he went anon and stood where all the crowd was thronging the market-place. Now they knew him not; howbeit one of the awed beholders spake and said :—

[1] "Around Delphi." There is no reference to the Am-phictyons.
[2] Jason was the great-grandson of Aeolus.

"Οὔτι που οὗτος Ἀπόλλων, οὐδὲ μὰν χαλκάρ-
    ματός ἐστι πόσις
Ἀφροδίτας· ἐν δὲ Νάξῳ φαντὶ θανεῖν λιπαρᾷ
Ἰφιμεδείας παῖδας, Ὦτον καὶ σέ, τολμάεις Ἐφι-
    άλτα ἄναξ.

90 καὶ μὰν Τιτυὸν βέλος Ἀρτέμιδος θήρευσε κραι-
    πνόν,   160
ἐξ ἀνικάτου φαρέτρας ὀρνύμενον,
ὄφρα τις τᾶν ἐν δυνατῷ φιλοτάτων ἐπιψαύειν
    ἔραται."

στρ. ε'
τοὶ μὲν ἀλλάλοισιν ἀμειβόμενοι
γάρυον τοιαῦτ'· ἀνὰ δ' ἡμιόνοις ξεστᾷ τ' ἀπήνᾳ
    προτροπάδαν Πελίας

95 ἵκετο σπεύδων· τάφε δ' αὐτίκα παπτάναις ἀρί-
    γνωτον πέδιλον
δεξιτερῷ μόνον ἀμφὶ ποδί. κλέπτων δὲ θυμῷ   170
δεῖμα προσέννεπε· "Ποίαν γαῖαν, ὦ ξεῖν', εὔχεαι
πατρίδ' ἔμμεν; καὶ τίς ἀνθρώπων σε χαμαιγενέων
    πολιᾶς
ἐξανῆκεν γαστρός; ἐχθίστοισι μὴ ψεύδεσιν

100 καταμιάναις εἰπὲ γένναν."

ἀντ. ε'
τὸν δὲ θαρσήσαις ἀγανοῖσι λόγοις
ὧδ' ἀμείφθη· "Φαμὶ διδασκαλίαν Χείρωνος οἴσειν.
    ἄντροθε γὰρ νέομαι   180
πὰρ Χαρικλοῦς καὶ Φιλύρας, ἵνα Κενταύρου με
    κοῦραι θρέψαν ἁγναί.
εἴκοσι δ' ἐκτελέσαις ἐνιαυτοὺς οὔτε ἔργον

105 οὔτ' ἔπος ἐντράπελον κείνοισιν εἰπὼν ἱκόμαν

105 ἐντράπελον most mss, scholium 2 (M²S): εὐτράπελον M
alone (BF); ἐκτράπελον scholium 1, Heyne (M¹GC).

" Surely this is not Apollo, nor verily is he Aphro-
dîtê's lord of the brazen chariot.[1] The sons, again,
of Iphimedeia, Ôtus, and thou, courageous king,
Ephialtês,[2] died, they say, in gleaming Naxos. And
Tityus, in sooth, was hunted down by the swift dart,
which Artemis sped from her unconquerable quiver,
warning men to aim only at loves within their
reach." [3]

Thus, in turn, spake they to one another. Mean-
while, driving his mules and his polished chariot with
head-long speed, came Pelias in hot haste, and, as he
gazed, he was astonied at the solitary sandal clearly
seen on the right foot alone of the stranger; but he
hid his fear in his heart, and said :—

" What country, O stranger, dost thou claim as
thy fatherland ? Which of the groundling wenches
was it that spawned thee forth from her aged womb ?
Tell me of thy birth, and befoul it not with most
hateful falsehoods."

Then the stranger bravely answered him with
gentle words in this wise :—

" I aver that I shall give proof of Cheiron's training ;
for from his cave am I come, from the presence of
Charîclo and Philyra,[4] where I was reared by the
pure daughters of the Centaur. And, having lived
for a score of years without having ever said to
them aught unseemly either in deed or in word, I

---

[1] Arês.

[2] The gigantic sons of Poseidon and Iphimedîa, commonly
called the Aloeidae, who put Arês into chains, and were
destroyed by Apollo.

[3] Tityus, a giant in Euboea, was slain by Artemis and
cast into Tartarus for attempting to offer violence to her, on
her way to Delphi.

[4] Charîclo was the wife, and Philyra the mother of
Cheiron.

οἴκαδ᾽, ἀρχαίαν κομίζων πατρὸς ἐμοῦ βασιλευο-
μέναν
οὐ κατ᾽ αἶσαν, τάν ποτε Ζεὺς ὤπασεν λαγέτᾳ   190
Αἰόλῳ καὶ παισί, τιμάν.
ἐπ. ε´
πεύθομαι γάρ νιν Πελίαν ἄθεμιν λευκαῖς πιθή-
σαντα φρασὶν
110 ἀμετέρων ἀποσυλᾶσαι βιαίως ἀρχεδικᾶν τοκέων·
τοί μ᾽, ἐπεὶ πάμπρωτον εἶδον φέγγος, ὑπερφιάλου
ἀγεμόνος δείσαντες ὕβριν, κᾶδος ὡσείτε φθιμένου
δνοφερὸν   200
ἐν δώμασι θηκάμενοι, μίγα κωκυτῷ γυναικῶν
κρύβδα πέμπον σπαργάνοις ἐν πορφυρέοις,
115 νυκτὶ κοινάσαντες ὁδόν, Κρονίδᾳ δὲ τράφεν Χεί-
ρωνι δῶκαν.
στρ. στ´
ἀλλὰ τούτων μὲν κεφάλαια λόγων
ἴστε. λευκίππων δὲ δόμους πατέρων, κεδνοὶ πολῖ-
ται, φράσσατέ μοι σαφέως·
Αἴσονος γὰρ παῖς ἐπιχώριος οὐ ξείναν ἱκοίμαν
γαῖαν ἄλλων.   210
Φὴρ δέ με θεῖος Ἰάσονα κικλήσκων προσηύδα.”
120 ὣς φάτο. τὸν μὲν ἐσελθόντ᾽ ἔγνον ὀφθαλμοὶ
πατρός.
ἐκ δ᾽ ἄρ᾽ αὐτοῦ πομφόλυξαν δάκρυα γηραλέων
γλεφάρων,
ἂν περὶ ψυχὰν ἐπεὶ γάθησεν ἐξαίρετον
γόνον ἰδὼν κάλλιστον ἀνδρῶν.
ἀντ. στ´
καὶ κασίγνητοί σφισιν ἀμφότεροι   220

120 ἔγνον Byzantine mss (BMGFCS), cp. P. ix 79 and I. ii 23:
ἔγνων old mss.

have come to my home to recover the ancient honour
of my father, now held in no rightful way, even that
honour which Zeus granted of old to Aeolus, the
leader of the people, and to his sons. For I hear
that lawless Pelias, yielding to his envious[1] passions,
violently reft it from my parents, who were lords by
primal right. As soon as ever I saw the light, fear-
ing the insolence of the overweening chieftain, then,
as though one had died, they made mourning in the
darkened home,[2] not without much wailing of
women, while, secretly, they sent me away en-
swathed in purple, with night alone as partner of
the path, and gave me to Cheiron the son of Cronus
to rear. The chief of all my story ye know
already ; and now, ye noble citizens, pray show me
clearly the palace of my fathers, who rode on white
steeds. For, being son of Aeson and having been
born in this land, fain would I hope that I have come
to my own country and not another's. The centaur
divine was wont to call me by the name of Jason."

Thus spake he, and, as he entered, his father's eyes
took note of him, and tears burst forth from those
aged eyelids ; for, with all his heart, he rejoiced when
he saw his son, the choicest and the fairest of men.
And both his father's brothers came, as soon as ever

---

[1] "Pale with envy"; or "frantic" (connected with λύσσα,
"madness") ; or "baneful," as in *Il.* ix 119, φρεσὶ λευγα-
λέῃσι πιθήσας.

[2] Literally, "made darksome mourning in the home."

125 ἤλυθον κείνου γε κατὰ κλέος· ἐγγὺς μὲν Φέρης
κράναν Ὑπερῇδα λιπών,
ἐκ δὲ Μεσσάνας Ἀμυθάν· ταχέως δ' Ἄδματος
ἵκεν καὶ Μέλαμπος,
εὐμενέοντες ἀνεψιόν. ἐν δαιτὸς δὲ μοίρᾳ
μειλιχίοισι λόγοις αὐτοὺς Ἰάσων δέγμενος,
ξείνι' ἁρμόζοντα τεύχων, πᾶσαν εὐφροσύναν
τάννυεν, 230
130 ἀθρόαις πέντε δραπὼν νύκτεσσιν ἔν θ' ἁμέραις
ἱερὸν εὐζωᾶς ἄωτον.

ἐπ. στ'
ἀλλ' ἐν ἕκτᾳ πάντα, λόγον θέμενος σπουδαῖον, ἐξ
ἀρχᾶς ἀνὴρ
συγγενέσιν παρεκοινᾶθ'· οἱ δ' ἐπέσποντ'. αἶψα
δ' ἀπὸ κλισιᾶν
ὦρτο σὺν κείνοισι. καί ῥ' ἦλθον Πελία μέγαρον·
135 ἐσσύμενοι δ' εἴσω κατέσταν. τῶν δ' ἀκούσαις
αὐτὸς ὑπαντίασεν 240
Τυροῦς ἐρασιπλοκάμου γενεά· πραῢν δ' Ἰάσων
μαλθακᾷ φωνᾷ ποτιστάζων ὄαρον
βάλλετο κρηπῖδα σοφῶν ἐπέων· "Παῖ Ποσειδᾶνος
Πετραίου,

στρ. ζ'
ἐντὶ μὲν θνατῶν φρένες ὠκύτεραι
140 κέρδος αἰνῆσαι πρὸ δίκας δόλιον, τραχεῖαν
ἑρπόντων πρὸς ἐπίβδαν ὅμως·
ἀλλ' ἐμὲ χρὴ καὶ σὲ θεμισσαμένους ὀργὰς ὑφαίνειν
λοιπὸν ὄλβον. 250
εἰδότι τοι ἐρέω· μία βοῦς Κρηθεῖ τε μάτηρ

129 εὐφρ. Bergk (MGCS), εὐφρ. B alone : εἰς C, ἐς other old
mss (F), ἐν Byzantine mss (B) εὐφρ.

212

they heard report of him. Hard by was Pherês, who came from the Hypereian fountain[1]; while Amythaon came from Messênê; and Admêtus also came in all speed, and Melampus, with kindly feeling for their cousin. And, while they joined in the banquet, Jason, welcoming them with gentle words and offering them befitting hospitality, gave them good cheer without stint, for five full nights and for as many days culling the sacred prime of festal life. But, on the sixth day, speaking in sober earnest, the hero told his kinsmen all the story from the beginning, and they followed his prompting; and at once he leapt with them from the tents, and so they came to the hall of Pelias, and hasted and stood within. And when Pelias heard them, he came forth himself to meet them, even the son of Tyro with the lovely locks; and Jason, with his soothing voice distilling gentle language, thus laid the foundation of wise words :—

"Son of Poseidon, the Cleaver of the Rock! the minds of mortals are only too swift to praise crafty gain rather than justice, even although they are moving toward a rude reckoning; but thou and I must rule our tempers by the law of right, and thus for the future weave the web of all our wealth. Thou knowest what I am soon to say.

[1] In the midst of the Thessalian city of Pherae; Strabo, p. 439.

καὶ θρασυμήδεϊ Σαλμωνεῖ· τρίταισιν δ' ἐν γοναῖς
ἄμμες αὖ κείνων φυτευθέντες σθένος ἀελίου
    χρύσεον
145 λεύσσομεν. Μοῖραι δ' ἀφίσταντ', εἴ τις ἔχθρα
    πέλει
ὁμογόνοις, αἰδῶ καλύψαι.   260

ἀντ. ζ′

οὐ πρέπει νῷν χαλκοτόροις ξίφεσιν
οὐδ ἀκόντεσσιν μεγάλαν προγόνων τιμὰν δά-
    σασθαι. μῆλά τε γάρ τοι ἐγὼ
καὶ βοῶν ξανθὰς ἀγέλας ἀφίημ' ἀγρούς τε πάντας,
    τοὺς ἀπούραις
150 ἁμετέρων τοκέων νέμεαι, πλοῦτον πιαίνων·
κοὔ με πονεῖ τεὸν οἶκον ταῦτα πορσύνοντ' ἄγαν·
ἀλλὰ καὶ σκᾶπτον μόναρχον καὶ θρόνος, ᾧ ποτε
    Κρηθεΐδας   270
ἐγκαθίζων ἱππόταις εὔθυνε λαοῖς δίκας,
τὰ μὲν ἄνευ ξυνᾶς ἀνίας

ἐπ. ζ′

155 λῦσον ἄμμιν, μή τι νεώτερον ἐξ αὐτῶν ἀνασταίη
    κακόν."

ὣς ἄρ' ἔειπεν. ἀκᾷ δ' ἀνταγόρευσεν καὶ Πελίας·
    "Ἔσομαι

τοῖος· ἀλλ' ἤδη με γηραιὸν μέρος ἁλικίας   280
ἀμφιπολεῖ· σὸν δ' ἄνθος ἥβας ἄρτι κυμαίνει·
    δύνασαι δ' ἀφελεῖν

155 ἀνασταίη Ahrens (MC), ἀναστάῃ S, ἀναστήῃ Hermann
(BGF): ἀναστήσῃ vulgo, v.l. ἀναστήσῃς.

It was one heifer that bare Crêtheus and Salmôneus [1]
bold in counsel; and we, in our day, who now look
upon the golden light of the sun, were sprung from
them in the third generation; but, if any feud
befall men of the same kin, the Fates withdraw
to hide their shame. It ill befitteth us twain to
appeal to brazen swords or spears in dividing the
great honours of our fathers. As for the flocks and
the tawny herds of cattle, and all the fields, which
thou hast taken from our parents and holdest for
thine own, while feeding fat thy wealth—all these
I leave thee, and it irketh me not that they give
provision to thy house beyond all measure. But, as
for the royal sceptre and the throne, in which Aeson
once sat, while he duly laid down the law for a
nation of horsemen, these do thou release to us
without vexation on either side, lest haply thou
shouldest cause fresh ill to spring up therefrom."

Thus spake he; and Pelias, on his part, gave a
soft answer :—

"I shall be even as thou wilt; but old age is
already coming over me, while thy bloom of youth
is even now swelling with fulness, and thou hast it
in thy power to remove the resentment of the gods

[1] The genealogy is as follows :—

μᾶνιν χθονίων.   κέλεται γὰρ ἑὰν ψυχὰν κομίξαι
160 Φρίξος ἐλθόντας πρὸς Αἰήτα θαλάμους,
    δέρμα τε κριοῦ βαθύμαλλον ἄγειν, τῷ ποτ' ἐκ
      πόντου σαώθη

στρ. η'

    ἔκ τε ματρυιᾶς ἀθέων βελέων.
    ταῦτά μοι θαυμαστὸς ὄνειρος ἰὼν φωνεῖ.   με
      μάντευμαι δ' ἐπὶ Κασταλίᾳ,   290
    εἰ μετάλλατόν τι.   καὶ ὡς τάχος ὀτρύνει με
      τεύχειν ναΐ πομπάν.
165 τοῦτον ἄεθλον ἑκὼν τέλεσον· καί τοι μοναρχεῖν
    καὶ βασιλευέμεν ὄμνυμι προήσειν.   καρτερὸς
    ὅρκος ἄμμιν μάρτυς ἔστω Ζεὺς ὁ γενέθλιος
      ἀμφοτέροις."
    σύνθεσιν ταύταν ἐπαινήσαντες οἱ μὲν κρίθεν·   300
    ἀτὰρ Ἰάσων αὐτὸς ἤδη

ἀντ. η'

170 ὤρνυεν κάρυκας ἐόντα πλόον
    φαινέμεν παντᾷ.   τάχα δὲ Κρονίδαο Ζηνὸς υἱοὶ
      τρεῖς ἀκαμαντομάχαι
    ἦλθον Ἀλκμήνας θ' ἑλικοβλεφάρου Λήδας τε,
      δοιοὶ δ' ὑψιχαῖται
    ἀνέρες, Ἐννοσίδα γένος, αἰδεσθέντες ἀλκάν,
    ἔκ τε Πύλου καὶ ἀπ' ἄκρας Ταινάρου· τῶν μὲν
      κλέος   310
175 ἐσλὸν Εὐφάμου τ' ἐκράνθη σόν τε, Περικλύμεν'
      εὐρυβία.
    ἐξ Ἀπόλλωνος δὲ φορμικτὰς ἀοιδᾶν πατὴρ
    ἔμολεν, εὐαίνητος Ὀρφεύς.

172 ἑλικοβλ. mss here (BMCGFC), and in frag. 123 (88):
ἑλικογλ. (s), cp. ἑανογλ. Alcman.
176 φορμικτὰς BDE (BMGFC): φορμιγκτὰς CMV (s).

below. For Phrixus biddeth us go to the halls of
Aeêtês, and bring his spirit home,[1] and recover the
fleecy fell of the ram, on which he was erstwhile
rescued from the sea, and from his step-dame's
impious weapons. Such is the message brought me
by a wondrous dream, and I have inquired of the
oracle at Castalia, whether there is need for further
quest, and the oracle bids me make ready with all
speed a ship to escort him home again. This is the
quest that I would have thee bring promptly to an
end; and, thereupon, I swear that I shall deliver
up to thee the sole sovereignty and kingdom. As
a mighty pledge, may Zeus, the father of our common
ancestor, be our witness!"

This agreement they approved, and then they
parted; and Jason forthwith sent messengers to tell
men everywhere that there would be a voyage
indeed. And soon there came the three sons
unwearied in war, whom the bright-eyed Alcmênê
and Lêda bare unto Zeus, the son of Cronus;[2] and
two heroes with their tresses waving on high, the
offspring of Poseidon, with a soul of honour inspired
by their lofty courage, from Pylos and from the
foreland at Taenarus; and goodly fame was won by
both of them, even by Euphêmus, and by thee,
Periclymenus, whose power extendeth far. And
Apollo's son came also, even that minstrel of the
lyre, that father of song, the famous Orpheus. And

[1] The Scholiast says that "they were wont to invoke the
souls of those who had died in foreign lands, as is clear from
the *Odyssey* (ix 65), where 'the ships did not leave the land,
until we had thrice called aloud for each of our comrades,
who had died in the plain.'"

[2] *i.e.* Heracles, and Castor and Polydeuces.

PINDAR

ἐπ. η΄

πέμπε δ' Ἑρμᾶς χρυσόραπις διδύμους υἱοὺς ἐπ'
    ἄτρυτον πόνον,
τὸν μὲν Ἐχίονα, κεχλάδοντας ἥβᾳ, τὸν δ' Ἔρυτον.
    ταχέες
180 ἀμφὶ Παγγαίου θεμέθλοις ναιετάοντες ἔβαν·   320
καὶ γὰρ ἑκὼν θυμῷ γελανεῖ θᾶσσον ἔντυνεν βα-
    σιλεὺς ἀνέμων
Ζήταν Κάλαΐν τε πατὴρ Βορέας, ἄνδρας πτεροῖσιν
νῶτα πεφρίκοντας ἄμφω πορφυρέοις.
τὸν δὲ παμπειθῆ γλυκὺν ἡμιθέοισιν πόθον ἔν-
    δαιεν Ἥρα

στρ. θ΄

185 ναὸς Ἀργοῦς, μή τινα λειπόμενον
τὰν ἀκίνδυνον παρὰ ματρὶ μένειν αἰῶνα πέσσοντ',
    ἀλλ' ἐπὶ καὶ θανάτῳ   330
φάρμακον κάλλιστον ἑᾶς ἀρετᾶς ἄλιξιν εὑρέσθαι
    σὺν ἄλλοις.
ἐς δ' Ἰαωλκὸν ἐπεὶ κατέβα ναυτᾶν ἄωτος,
λέξατο πάντας ἐπαινήσαις Ἰάσων. καί ῥά οἱ
190 μάντις ὀρνίχεσσι καὶ κλάροισι θεοπροπέων ἱεροῖς
Μόψος ἄμβασε στρατὸν πρόφρων. ἐπεὶ δ'
    ἐμβόλου   340
κρέμασαν ἀγκύρας ὕπερθεν,

ἀντ. θ΄

χρυσέαν χείρεσσι λαβὼν φιάλαν
ἀρχὸς ἐν πρύμνᾳ πατέρ' Οὐρανιδᾶν ἐγχεικέραυνον
Ζῆνα, καὶ ὠκυπόρους

179 ταχέες MGS, ταχέες δ' BCD (FC): ταχέως (B), ταχέως
δ' V.
184 ἔνδαιεν mss (MGFCS): πρόσδαιεν B, δαίεσκεν Hermann.
188 δ' Ἰαωλκὸν Erasmus Schmid (BF): δ' Ἰωλκὸν old mss,
δὲ Ἰωλκὸν Byzantine mss (C), δὲ Ϝιωλκὸν (MG), δ' Ἰαολκὸν (S).

Hermes of the golden wand sent two sons to take part in the unabating toil, even Echîon and Eurytus, exulting in their youth. Swiftly came they who dwell by the foot of the Pangaean mount, for with gladsome mind did their father, Boreas, lord of the winds, speedily equip Zêtês and Calais, with their purple pinions heaving adown their backs. And Hêra it was who enkindled in the demigods that all-persuasive sweet desire for the ship Argo, that none should be left behind, and stay by his mother's side, nursing a life that knoweth no peril; but should, even if death were to be the meed, win, with the aid of his comrades, a peerless elixir of prowess.[1]

But, when the flower of the seamen cáme down to the shore of Iôlcus, Jason numbered them and praised them, every one; and, to aid him, Mopsus, after inquiring the will of heaven by noting the flight of birds and by drawing lots, right gladly gave the host the signal to set forth. And, when they had slung the anchor over the vessel's prow, the leader took in his hands a golden goblet, and, standing at the stern, called on Zeus, the father of the sons of

---

[1] Keats, *Hyperion*, iii 119 f.
　　"As if some blithe wine,
Or bright elixir peerless I had drunk,
And so become immortal."

195 κυμάτων ῥιπὰς ἀνέμων τ᾽ ἐκάλει, νύκτας τε καὶ
　　　πόντου κελεύθους
　　ἅματά τ᾽ εὔφρονα καὶ φιλίαν νόστοιο μοῖραν·
　　ἐκ νεφέων δέ οἱ ἀντάϋσε βροντᾶς αἴσιον　　　350
　　φθέγμα· λαμπραὶ δ᾽ ἦλθον ἀκτῖνες στεροπᾶς
　　　ἀπορηγνύμεναι·
　　ἀμπνοὰν δ᾽ ἥρωες ἔστασαν θεοῦ σάμασιν
200 πιθόμενοι· κάρυξε δ᾽ αὐτοῖς
ἐπ. θ´
　　ἐμβαλεῖν κώπαισι τερασκόπος ἀδείας ἐνίπτων
　　　ἐλπίδας·
　　εἰρεσία δ᾽ ὑπεχώρησεν ταχειᾶν ἐκ παλαμᾶν
　　　ἄκορος.　　　360
　　σὺν Νότου δ᾽ αὔραις ἐπ᾽ Ἀξείνου στόμα πεμπό-
　　　μενοι
　　ἤλυθον· ἔνθ᾽ ἁγνὸν Ποσειδάωνος ἔσσαντ᾽ εἰναλίου
　　　τέμενος,
205 φοίνισσα δὲ Θρηϊκίων ἀγέλα ταύρων ὑπᾶρχεν
　　καὶ νεόκτιστον λίθων βωμοῖο θέναρ.
　　ἐς δὲ κίνδυνον βαθὺν ἱέμενοι δεσπόταν λίσσοντο
　　　νεῶν,
στρ. ι´
　　συνδρόμων κινηθμὸν ἀμαιμάκετον　　　370
　　ἐκφυγεῖν πετρᾶν. δίδυμαι γὰρ ἔσαν ζωαί, κυλιν-
　　　δέσκοντό τε κραιπνότεραι
210 ἢ βαρυγδούπων ἀνέμων στίχες· ἀλλ᾽ ἤδη τελευ-
　　　τὰν κεῖνος αὐταῖς
　　ἡμιθέων πλόος ἄγαγεν. ἐς Φᾶσιν δ᾽ ἔπειτεν
　　ἤλυθον· ἔνθα κελαινώπεσσι Κόλχοισιν βίαν
　　μῖξαν Αἰήτᾳ παρ᾽ αὐτῷ. πότνια δ᾽ ὀξυτάτων
　　　βελέων　　　380

195 ἀνέμων PQ (BMGFC): ἀνέμους other mss (8).

220

Heaven, whose lance is the lightning; called also on the swiftly rushing waves and winds, to speed them on their way; and on the night-watches and on the tracks across the main, praying that the days might be propitious, and that the fortune of their return to their home might be kindly. And from the clouds there answered an auspicious peal of thunder, and there came bright flashes of lightning bursting forth,[1] and the heroes took fresh courage at the bidding of the signals sent of heaven. And the seer inspired them with good hopes, while he loudly bade them lay their hands to the oars, and from under their swift palms the rowing sped on, and could not be sated. And so, sent on their way by the breezes of the South wind, they reached the mouth of the Inhospitable Sea, and there they marked out a plot of holy ground in honour of Poseidon; and withal there was a red herd of Thracian bulls, and a hollow of stone newly built on the summit of an altar.

And, as they sped on their way into deep peril, they besought the Lord of Ships, that they might escape the irresistible onset of the clashing rocks[2]; for twain were they, and alive withal, and they rolled onward more swiftly than the battle-lines of the loudly roaring winds; but that voyage of the demigods made them stand still in death. And then they went to Phâsis, where they mingled in battle with the swarthy Colchians in the realm of Aeêtês himself.

---

[1] Boeckh, however, regards it as more poetical to make στεροπᾶς the genitive after ἀπορηγνύμεναι, than to take it with ἀκτῖνες.   [2] The Symplêgades.

ποικίλαν ἴϋγγα τετράκναμον Οὐλυμπόθεν
215 ἐν ἀλύτῳ ζεύξαισα κύκλῳ

ἀντ. ί

μαινάδ᾽ ὄρνιν Κυπρογένεια φέρεν
πρῶτον ἀνθρώποισι, λιτάς τ᾽ ἐπαοιδὰς ἐκδιδά-
σκησεν σοφὸν Αἰσονίδαν·
ὄφρα Μηδείας τοκέων ἀφέλοιτ᾽ αἰδῶ, ποθεινὰ δ᾽
Ἑλλὰς αὐτὰν
ἐν φρασὶ καιομέναν δονέοι μάστιγι Πειθοῦς.   390
220 καὶ τάχα πείρατ᾽ ἀέθλων δείκνυεν πατρωΐων·
σὺν δ᾽ ἐλαίῳ φαρμακώσαισ᾽ ἀντίτομα στερεᾶν
ὀδυνᾶν
δῶκε χρίεσθαι. καταίνησάν τε κοινὸν γάμον
γλυκὺν ἐν ἀλλάλοισι μῖξαι.

ἐπ. ί

ἀλλ᾽ ὅτ᾽ Αἰήτας ἀδαμάντινον ἐν μέσσοις ἄροτρον
σκίμψατο
225 καὶ βόας, οἳ φλόγ᾽ ἀπὸ ξανθᾶν γενύων πνέον
καιομένοιο πυρός,   400
χαλκέαις δ᾽ ὁπλαῖς ἀράσσεσκον χθόν᾽ ἀμειβό-
μενοι,
τοὺς ἀγαγὼν ζεύγλᾳ πέλασσεν μοῦνος. ὀρθὰς δ᾽
αὔλακας ἐντανύσαις
ἤλαυν᾽, ἀνὰ βωλακίας δ᾽ ὀρόγυιαν σχίζε νῶτον
γᾶς. ἔειπεν δ᾽ ὧδε· "Τοῦτ᾽ ἔργον βασιλεύς,
230 ὅστις ἄρχει ναός, ἐμοὶ τελέσαις ἄφθιτον στρωμνὰν
ἀγέσθω,   410

228 ἀνὰ βωλακίας P... (ΒΜGFC): ἀναβωλακίας most mss (s),
ἀναβωλακίας δὲ τῆς ἐν τῇ τμήσει τὰς βώλους ἄνω πεμπούσης
schol.; ἀνὰ βωλακίας = ἀνὰ βώλακας Bergk; ἤλαυν᾽ ἀνὰ βώ-
λακας, ἐς δ᾽ ὀρόγυιαν Hartung ("egregie," Herwerden).

Then, for the first time, did the Queen of swiftest
darts, in Cyprus born, bind the dappled wryneck to
the four spokes of a wheel indissoluble, and brought
unto men that maddening bird;[1] and she taught the
son of Aeson the lore of suppliant incantations, that
so he might rob Medea of her reverence for her
parents, and that a longing for Hellas might lash her
with the whip of Suasion, while her heart was
all aflame.

And she quickly revealed the means of performing
the labours set by her father, and with oil she
mingled antidotes against sore pains, and gave them
to Jason, to anoint himself withal; and they vowed
sweet union in mutual wedlock. But when Aeêtês
had set steadfast in the midst the adamantine plough,
and the oxen, which from their tawny jaws were
breathing the flame of burning fire, and were ever
and anon pawing the ground with their brazen hoofs,
Jason led them along, and single-handed brought them
beneath the yoke, and straight stretched he the
furrows as he was driving, and clave a ridge of clods
a fathom deep.[2] Then Aeêtês spake on this wise:—

"Let the king, whosoever hath command of the
ship, complete this task for me, and then let him carry
off the coverlet imperishable, the fleece that gleameth

---

[1] The plumage of the wryneck, or "cuckoo's mate," is
"beautifully variegated with black, brown, buff and grey"
(Newton); hence the epithet ποικίλαν. The bird was used as
a love-charm. For this purpose it was tied by the legs and
wings to the four spokes of a wheel, which was made to
revolve continuously in one direction (Horace, *Epode*, xvii
7), while the words of incantation were repeated. Cp. *N* iv
35, and the refrain of the *Pharmaceutria* of Theocritus (ii):—
ἴυγξ, ἕλκε τὺ τῆνον ἐμὸν ποτὶ δῶμα τὸν ἄνδρα.

[2] ἀνὰ goes with σχίζε, and βωλακίας γᾶς is, literally, "the
clodded earth."

PINDAR

στρ. ια'

κῶας αἰγλᾶεν χρυσέῳ θυσάνῳ."
ὡς ἄρ' αὐδάσαντος ἀπὸ κροκόεν ῥίψαις Ἰάσων
εἷμα θεῷ πίσυνος
εἴχετ' ἔργου· πῦρ δέ νιν οὐκ ἐόλει παμφαρμάκου
ξείνας ἐφετμαῖς.
σπασσάμενος δ' ἄροτρον, βοέους δήσαις ἀνάγκας

235 ἔντεσιν αὐχένας ἐμβάλλων τ' ἐριπλεύρῳ φυᾷ
κέντρον αἰανὲς βιατὰς ἐξεπόνησ' ἐπιτακτὸν ἀνὴρ 420
μέτρον. ἴυξεν δ' ἀφωνήτῳ περ ἔμπας ἄχει
δύνασιν Αἰήτας ἀγασθείς.

ἀντ. ια'

πρὸς δ' ἑταῖροι καρτερὸν ἄνδρα φίλας

240 ὤρεγον χεῖρας, στεφάνοισί τέ νιν ποίας ἔρεπτον,
μειλιχίοις τε λόγοις
ἀγαπάζοντ'. αὐτίκα δ' Ἀελίου θαυμαστὸς υἱὸς
δέρμα λαμπρὸν
ἔννεπεν, ἔνθα νιν ἐκτάννυσαν Φρίξου μάχαιραι· 430
ἤλπετο δ' οὐκέτι οἱ κεῖνόν γε πράξεσθαι πόνον.
κεῖτο γὰρ λόχμᾳ, δράκοντος δ' εἴχετο λαβροτατᾶν
γενύων,

245 ὃς πάχει μάκει τε πεντηκόντορον ναῦν κράτει,
τέλεσαν ἂν πλαγαὶ σιδάρου.

ἐπ. ια'

μακρά μοι νεῖσθαι κατ ἀμαξιτόν· ὥρα γὰρ
συνάπτει· καί τινα 440
οἶμον ἴσαμι βραχύν· πολλοῖσι δ' ἄγημαι σοφίας
ἑτέροις.
κτεῖνε μὲν γλαυκῶπα τέχναις ποικιλόνωτον ὄφιν,

---

232 κροκόεν B alone (MGCS): κρόκεον most mss (BF).
234 βοέους—ἀνάγκας vulgo (BGFC) ; βοέοις ἀνάγκαις M ;
βοέους—ἀνάγκᾳ mentioned in scholium (s).

224

with its golden fringe." When thus he had spoken,
Jason flung off his saffron robe, and, putting his trust
in God, set his hand to the task; and, by grace of the
counsels of the magic maiden, he quailed not before
the fire; but seizing the plough, and binding the
necks of the oxen in the harness irresistible, and
ever thrusting the unwearied goad into their strong-
ribbed frame, the stalwart hero accomplished the
allotted measure of his task. And Aeêtês, though
he could find no voice for his anguish, shrilled forth
a cry, in amazement at the stranger's strength; and
his comrades stretched forth their hands towards the
sturdy hero, and crowned him with garlands of grass
and greeted him with gentle words; and at once the
wondrous offspring of the Sun-god spake of the
shining fleece, telling where it had been stretched
out by the falchion of Phrixus; and he hoped that
this further labour Jason would not be able to
accomplish. For the fleece lay in a dense thicket,
cleaving to the ravening jaws of a dragon, which, in
bulk and length, was vaster than a ship of fifty
oarsmen, built with many a hammer's blow.

'Tis too far for me to fare along the high-road: for
time is pressing; and I know a short path; to many
another am I a leader in the lore of song.[1] Thou
must know, Arcesilas, how Jason, by his cunning,
slew that serpent with its glaring eyes and spangled

---

[1] That is, "to many others am I a guide in the poetic art;
I can set them an example of conciseness of narrative."

PINDAR

250 ὦ 'ρκεσίλα, κλέψεν τε Μήδειαν σὺν αὐτᾷ, τὰν
  Πελίαο φόνον·
  ἔν τ' Ὠκεανοῦ πελάγεσσι μίγεν πόντῳ τ' ἐρυθρῷ
  Λαμνιᾶν τ' ἔθνει γυναικῶν ἀνδροφόνων·
  ἔνθα καὶ γυίων ἀέθλοις ἐπέδειξαν κρίσιν ἐσθᾶτος
    ἀμφίς,   450

στρ. ιβ′

  καὶ συνεύνασθεν. καὶ ἐν ἀλλοδαπαῖς
255 σπέρμ' ἀρούραις τουτάκις ὑμετέρας ἀκτῖνος ὄλβου
    δέξατο μοιρίδιον
  ἆμαρ ἢ νύκτες. τόθι γὰρ γένος Εὐφάμου φυτευθὲν
    λοιπὸν αἰεὶ
  τέλλετο· καὶ Λακεδαιμονίων μιχθέντες ἀνδρῶν
  ἤθεσι τάν ποτε Καλλίσταν ἀπῴκησαν χρόνῳ   460
  νᾶσον· ἔνθεν δ' ὔμμι Λατοΐδας ἔπορεν Λιβύας
    πεδίον
260 σὺν θεῶν τιμαῖς ὀφέλλειν, ἄστυ χρυσοθρόνου
  διανέμειν θεῖον Κυράνας
ἀντ. ιβ′

  ὀρθόβουλον μῆτιν ἐφευρομένοις.
  γνῶθι νῦν τὰν Οἰδιπόδα σοφίαν. εἰ γάρ τις ὄζους
    ὀξυτόμῳ πελέκει
  ἐξερείψειεν μεγάλας δρυός, αἰσχύνοι δέ οἱ θαητὸν
    εἶδος·   470
265 καὶ φθινόκαρπος ἐοῖσα διδοῖ ψᾶφον περ' αὐτᾶς,
  εἴ ποτε χειμέριον πῦρ ἐξίκηται λοίσθιον·
  ἢ σὺν ὀρθαῖς κιόνεσσιν δεσποσύναισιν ἐρειδομένα

253 ἐπέδειξαν κρίσιν Pauw (FS): ἐπεδείξαντο κρίσιν all mss
(M²); ἐπεδείξαντ' ἀγῶνα B; — κρῖμα Hermann (M¹) (— ἀν-
δρείαν scholium), — Fin' Kayser (GC).
  264 ἐξερείψειεν Thiersch (S): ἐξερείψαι κεν mss (BF), —ψη
κεν Bergk² (M), — ψῃ μὲν (GC).
  αἰσχύνοι Moschopulus (BF): αἰσχύνῃ Bergk (MGCS).

226

back, and stole away Medea, with her own aid, to be the death of Peleas. And they reached the streams of Ocean, and the Red Sea, and the race of the Lemnian wives who slew their lords. There it was that, in athletic contests, they proved their prowess, with raiment for their prize, and shared the marriage bed; and then it was that the fated day, or, haply, the night-watches, received in a foreign field the seed of your bright prosperity. There it was that the race of Ephêmus was planted, to increase for ever in the days to come; and, having mingled with the homes of the Lacedaemonians, in due time they went and dwelt in the isle once called Callistê. Thence was it that the son of Lêtô caused your race to bring prosperity to the plain of Libya by the honours granted of heaven, and to rule over the divine city of golden-throned Cyrene, having found for it counsel that ruleth in righteousness.

Now learn and know the lore of Oedipus :—If a man, with keen-edged axe, were to hew all the boughs of a mighty oak, and mar its comely form; even although its fruit may fail, it nevertheless giveth proof of itself, if ever it cometh at last to the wintry fire; or if, having left its own place desolate,

μόχθον ἄλλοις ἀμφέπει δύστανον ἐν τείχεσιν,
ἑὸν ἐρημώσαισα χῶρον.

ἐπ. ιβ

270 ἐσσὶ δ᾽ ἰατὴρ ἐπικαιρότατος, Παιάν τέ σοι τιμᾷ
φάος.   480
χρὴ μαλακὰν χέρα προσβάλλοντα τρῶμαν ἕλκεος
ἀμφιπολεῖν.
ῥάδιον μὲν γὰρ πόλιν σεῖσαι καὶ ἀφαυροτέροις·
ἀλλ᾽ ἐπὶ χώρας αὖτις ἕσσαι δυσπαλὲς δὴ γίγνεται,
ἐξαπίνας
εἰ μὴ θεὸς ἀγεμόνεσσι κυβερνατὴρ γένηται.

275 τὶν δὲ τούτων ἐξυφαίνονται χάριτες.   490
τλᾶθι τᾶς εὐδαίμονος ἀμφὶ Κυράνας θέμεν σπου-
δὰν ἅπασαν.

στρ. ιγ

τῶν δ᾽ Ὁμήρου καὶ τόδε συνθέμενος
ῥῆμα πόρσυν᾽· ἄγγελον ἐσλὸν ἔφα τιμὰν μεγίσταν
πράγματι παντὶ φέρειν·
αὔξεται καὶ Μοῖσα δι᾽ ἀγγελίας ὀρθᾶς. ἐπέγνω
μὲν Κυράνα

280 καὶ τὸ κλεεννότατον μέγαρον Βάττου δικαιᾶν
Δαμοφίλου πραπίδων. κεῖνος γὰρ ἐν παισὶν
νέος,   500
ἐν δὲ βουλαῖς πρέσβυς ἐγκύρσαις ἑκατονταετεῖ
βιοτᾷ,
ὀρφανίζει μὲν κακὰν γλῶσσαν φαεννᾶς ὀπός,
ἔμαθε δ᾽ ὑβρίζοντα μισεῖν,

ἀντ. ιγ

285 οὐκ ἐρίζων ἀντία τοῖς ἀγαθοῖς,
οὐδὲ μακύνων τέλος οὐδέν. ὁ γὰρ καιρὸς πρὸς
ἀνθρώπων βραχὺ μέτρον ἔχει.

270 σοι mss (BMGFC) : τοι Wilamowitz (s).

228

it resteth (as a beam) on the upright pillars of some palace, and doeth slavish service amid alien walls.

But thou, Arcesilas, art a most timely healer, and the God of Healing honoureth the light that cometh from thee. One must needs apply a gentle hand in tending a festering wound; for, even for the feeble, it is an easy task to shake a city to its foundation, but it is indeed a sore struggle to set it in its place again, unless God becometh a guide unto its rulers. But, for thee, the web of these fair fortunes is now being woven out toward its end. Deign to bestow all earnest heed on happy Cyrene; and, of the sayings of Homer, take to heart and cherish even this:—" A good messenger," said he, " bringeth honour to every business" [1]; even the Muse herself is exalted by a message rightly sped. Cyrene and the most glorious hall of Battus were familiar with the righteous heart of Dêmophilus; for he, as a youth among boys, and in counsels as an elder who hath attained a hundred years of life, robbeth calumny of her loud voice; he hath learnt to loathe insolence; he neither contendeth against the nobly born, nor delayeth any decisive deed. For, in the hands of men, the fitting moment hath but a brief limit of time. Well hath he taken note of it; it waiteth on him, as a willing servant,

---

[1] This is the only passage where Pindar quotes from Homer by name. The nearest approach to the quotation is in *Il.* xv 207, ἐσθλὸν καὶ τὸ τέτυκται, ὅτ' ἄγγελος αἴσιμα εἰδῇ, " how good a thing is a discreet messenger."

εὖ νιν ἔγνωκεν· θεράπων δέ οἱ, οὐ δράστας ὀπαδεῖ.
φαντὶ δ' ἔμμεν   510
τοῦτ' ἀνιαρότατον, καλὰ γιγνώσκοντ' ἀνάγκᾳ
ἐκτὸς ἔχειν πόδα. καὶ μὰν κεῖνος Ἄτλας οὐρανῷ
290 προσπαλαίει νῦν γε πατρῴας ἀπὸ γᾶς ἀπό τε
κτεάνων·
λῦσε δὲ Ζεὺς ἄφθιτος Τιτᾶνας. ἐν δὲ χρόνῳ
μεταβολαὶ λήξαντος οὔρου   520
ἐπ. ιγ'
ἱστίων. ἀλλ' εὔχεται οὐλομέναν νοῦσον διαντλή-
σαις ποτὲ
οἶκον ἰδεῖν, ἐπ' Ἀπόλλωνός τε κράνᾳ συμποσίας
ἐφέπων
295 θυμὸν ἐκδόσθαι πρὸς ἥβαν πολλάκις, ἔν τε σοφοῖς
δαιδαλέαν φόρμιγγα βαστάζων πολίταις ἡσυχίᾳ
θιγέμεν,
μήτ' ὦν τινι πῆμα πορών, ἀπαθὴς δ' αὐτὸς πρὸς
ἀστῶν.   530
καί κε μυθήσαιθ' ὁποίαν, Ἀρκεσίλα,
εὗρε παγὰν ἀμβροσίων ἐπέων, πρόσφατον Θήβᾳ
ξενωθείς.

298 Ἀρκεσίλα mss (BMGCS): Ἀρκεσίλᾳ Dissen, Donaldson (F).

not as a thrall. But they say the saddest lot of all is to know the good, and yet, perforce, to be debarred therefrom.

The famous Atlas indeed is still bearing up against heaven's weight, banished from his ancestral land and his possessions; but the Titans were set free by immortal Zeus; and, as time passeth on, there are shiftings of sails at the change of the breeze. But the exile avoweth that the day will come, when he shall have drained to the dregs the cup of baneful woe, and shall see his home again; and, near Apollo's fountain, shall betake himself to the joys of the banquet, and yield his soul, full oft, to youthful gladness, and, amid fellow-citizens skilled in song, shall hold in his hands his deftly carven cithern, and attain to peace, doing despite to no man, and being himself unscathed by his townsmen. And haply he will tell how fair a fountain of immortal song he found, Arcesilas, when lately welcomed by a friend at Thebes.

PYTHIAN V

FOR ARCESILAS OF CYRENE

INTRODUCTION

THE Fifth Pythian was written to celebrate the
same victory as the Fourth, the victory of Arcesilaüs
in the Pythian chariot-race of 462. It was sung at
Cyrene (84–87) on the return of the charioteer and
the horses (40 f), probably during the festival of the
Carneia (73–76). The charioteer was the brother of
the Queen of Cyrene.

Wealth wedded to Honour and blessed of Fortune
has wide sway (1–4). By Castor's aid, such wealth
has been won by Arcesilaüs, who keeps to the path of
Justice, is king of mighty cities, and has won the
chariot-race at Delphi (5–22). When he is hymned
in song, he must not forget to give God the glory,
and to praise the charioteer, who drove his chariot
safely, and dedicated it at Delphi (22–42). Such a
benefactor deserves an ungrudging welcome; he has
kept his chariot scatheless in a race, where forty
chariots were wrecked (43–54). He is attended by
the fortune—the varied fortune—of the house of
Battus, that founder of Cyrene, whose strange
tongue caused Libyan lions to flee in terror, at the

behest of Apollo, the god of healing and music, and
of those Delphic oracles, which prompted the
Heracleidae and the Dorians to settle in Sparta,
Argos, and Pylos (55–71). The chorus claims to be
descended from Aegeidae, who won fame at Sparta,
and went to Thêra, whither they brought the Carneian
festival, now celebrated at Cyrene (72–81). There
the descendants of the Trojan Antênôr are worshipped
as heroes by the followers of Battus, who made
Cyrene beautiful, and, on his death, was worshipped
as a hero (82–95), while, in their graves hard by, the
other ancestors of Arcesilaüs hear the news of his
victory, for which Apollo should be praised
(96–107).

Lastly, Arcesilaüs is lauded for his sense, his
eloquence, his courage, his skill in athletic contests,
and in music (108–116). May his prosperity con-
tinue, and may he be victorious at Olympia (117–124).

V.—ΑΡΚΕΣΙΛΑ ΚΥΡΗΝΑΙΩ

ΑΡΜΑΤΙ

στρ. α'

Ὁ πλοῦτος εὐρυσθενής,
ὅταν τις ἀρετᾷ κεκραμένον καθαρᾷ
βροτήσιος ἀνὴρ πότμου παραδόντος, αὐτὸν ἀνάγῃ
πολύφιλον ἑπέταν.

5 ὦ θεόμορ' Ἀρκεσίλα,
σύ τοί νιν κλυτᾶς
αἰῶνος ἀκρᾶν βαθμίδων ἄπο
σὺν εὐδοξίᾳ μετανίσεαι   10
ἔκατι χρυσαρμάτου Κάστορος·

10 εὐδίαν ὃς μετὰ χειμέριον ὄμβρον τεὰν
καταιθύσσει μάκαιραν ἑστίαν.

ἀντ. α'

σοφοὶ δέ τοι κάλλιον
φέροντι καὶ τὰν θεόσδοτον δύναμιν.
σὲ δ' ἐρχόμενον ἐν δίκᾳ πολὺς ὄλβος ἀμφινέμεται·

15 τὸ μέν, ὅτι βασιλεὺς
ἐσσὶ μεγαλᾶν πολίων,   20
ἔχει συγγενὴς
ὀφθαλμὸς αἰδοιότατον γέρας
τεᾷ τοῦτο μιγνύμενον φρενί·

20 μάκαρ δὲ καὶ νῦν, κλεεννᾶς ὅτι
εὖχος ἤδη παρὰ Πυθιάδος ἵπποις ἑλὼν

8 μετανίσεαι Vatican recension (MFGS) : μετανίσσεαι Ambrosian recension (BC).

18 αἰδοιότατον, on metrical grounds, Erasmus Schmid (BMGFCS[1]) : αἰδυιέστατον mss and scholia (S[3]).

V.—FOR ARCESILAS OF CYRENE

WINNER IN THE CHARIOT RACE, 462 B.C.

WIDE is the power of wealth, whene'er it is wedded with stainless honour, so that a mortal man receiveth it at the hands of Destiny, and taketh it to his home as a ministrant that bringeth him many friends.

O blest of Heaven! Arcesilas! From the first steps of thy famous life thou dost indeed seek for that wealth, and fair fame withal, by the help of Castor of the golden chariot, who, after the wintry storm, sheddeth beams of calm upon thy happy hearth.

They that are noble bear with a fairer grace even the power that is given of God; and thou, while thou walkest in the straight path, hast prosperity in abundance around thee. First, as thou art a king over mighty cities, the eye of thy ancestry looketh on this as a meed most fit for reverence, when wedded to a soul like thine; and even to-day art thou happy in that thou hast already, with thy coursers, won glory from the famous Pythian festival,

235

PINDAR

δέδεξαι τόνδε κῶμον ἀνέρων,
ἐπ. α΄

'Απολλώνιον ἄθυρμα. τῷ σε μὴ λαθέτω   30
Κυράνας γλυκὺν ἀμφὶ κᾶπον 'Αφροδίτας ἀειδό-
   μενον,
25 παντὶ μὲν θεὸν αἴτιον ὑπερτιθέμεν·
φιλεῖν δὲ Κάρρωτον ἔξοχ᾽ ἑταίρων·
ὃς οὐ τὰν 'Επιμαθέος ἄγων
ὀψινόου θυγατέρα Πρόφασιν, Βαττιδᾶν
ἀφίκετο δόμους θεμισκρεόντων·
30 ἀλλ᾽ ἀρισθάρματον
ὕδατι Κασταλίας ξενωθεὶς γέρας ἀμφέβαλε τεαῖ-
   σιν κόμαις,   40
στρ. β΄

ἀκηράτοις ἀνίαις
ποδαρκέων δωδεκάδρομον τέμενος.
κατέκλασε γὰρ ἐντέων σθένος οὐδέν· ἀλλὰ κρέ-
   μαται,
35 ὁπόσα χεριαρᾶν
τεκτόνων δαίδαλ᾽ ἄγων
Κρισαῖον λόφον
ἄμειψεν ἐν κοιλόπεδον νάπος   50
θεοῦ· τό σφ᾽ ἔχει κυπαρίσσινον
40 μέλαθρον ἀμφ᾽ ἀνδριάντι σχεδόν,
Κρῆτες ὃν τοξοφόροι τέγεϊ Παρνασσίῳ
κάθεσσαντο μονόδροπον φυτόν.

24 Κυράνας S : —να mss (Μ with ἀειδομένα) ; —νᾳ Erasmus
Schmid (BC) ; —ναν GF.
   26 φιλεῖν mss (MGFCS) : φίλει B
   33 δωδεκάδρομον recorded in V (S) : δωδεκαδρόμων E and
Ambrosian mss, Hermann[2] (Μ) ; δώδεκ᾽ ἂν δρόμων Thiersch
(B[2]FC) ; δυώδεκα δρόμων Vatican mss ; δώδεκα δρόμων Hermann[1]
(G).

236

and shalt soon give welcome to this triumph-band of men, in whom Apollo delighteth.

Therefore, when thou art hymned in song in Cyrene's garden of Aphrodite, do not forget to give God the glory; do not forget to love, above all thy comrades, Carrhôtus, who, on returning to the palace of them that reign by right, did not bring in his train Excuse, that daughter of After-thought, who is wise too late; but, when welcomed beside the waters of Castalia, flung over thy locks the guerdon of glory in the chariot-race with his reins unsevered in the sacred space of the twelve courses of swift feet. For he brake no part of his strong equipage; nay, he hath dedicated all the dainty handiwork of skilled craftsmen, with which he passed the hill of Crisa on his way to the god's own hollow glen. Wherefore are they all placed in the shrine of cypress-wood, hard by the statue cloven as a single block, that the Cretan bowmen dedicated beneath the roof Parnassian.[1]

---

[1] The Cretan offering was apparently a tree resembling a human figure, with some touches added by a rude form of art to complete the resemblance. The Cyrenian chariot was probably placed near the Cretan offering, because of the old connection between Crete and Cyrene (Müller's *Orchomenos*, p. 342). Pausanias tells us that, at Delphi, a chariot, with the image of Ammon in it, was dedicated by the Greeks of Cyrene; and that the Cyrenians also dedicated a statue of Battus in a chariot, this last being the work of a sculptor of Cnossos in Crete (x 13, 5 and 15, 6).

PINDAR

ἀντ. β΄

ἑκόντι τοίνυν πρέπει
νόῳ τὸν εὐεργέταν ὑπαντιάσαι.

45 Ἀλεξιβιάδα, σὲ δ᾽ ἠΰκομοι φλέγοντι Χάριτες. 60
μακάριος, ὃς ἔχεις
καὶ πεδὰ μέγαν κάματον
λόγων φερτάτων
μναμήϊ᾽· ἐν τεσσαράκοντα γὰρ
50 πετόντεσσιν ἀνιόχοις ὅλον
δίφρον κομίξαις ἀταρβεῖ φρενί,
ἦλθες ἤδη Λιβύας πεδίον ἐξ ἀγλαῶν
ἀέθλων καὶ πατρῳαν πόλιν. 70

ἐπ. β΄

πόνων δ᾽ οὔ τις ἀπόκλαρός ἐστιν οὔτ᾽ ἔσεται·
55 ὁ Βάττου δ᾽ ἕπεται παλαιὸς ὄλβος ἔμπαν τὰ καὶ
τὰ νέμων,
πύργος ἄστεος ὄμμα τε φαεννότατον
ξένοισι. κεῖνόν γε καὶ βαρύκομποι
λέοντες περὶ δείματι φύγον,
γλῶσσαν ἐπεί σφιν ἀπένεικεν ὑπερποντίαν·
60 ὁ δ᾽ ἀρχαγέτας ἔδωκ᾽ Ἀπόλλων 80
θῆρας αἰνῷ φόβῳ,
ὄφρα μὴ ταμίᾳ Κυράνας ἀτελὴς γένοιτο μαντεύ-
μασιν.

στρ. γ΄

ὃ καὶ βαρειᾶν νόσων
ἀκέσματ᾽ ἄνδρεσσι καὶ γυναιξὶ νέμει,
65 πόρεν τε κίθαριν, δίδωσί τε Μοῖσαν οἷς ἂν ἐθέλῃ,
ἀπόλεμον ἀγαγὼν
ἐς πραπίδας εὐνομίαν, 90

49 μναμήϊα D and scholium, μναμήϊ᾽ (BMCS³), μναμεῖα S¹:
μναμήϊον (μνημ. B) BC (F) ; μναμῆον (G).

238

Therefore is it fitting to requite with ready mind the doer of a good deed. Son of Alexibius! thy name is lit up by the fair-haired Graces. Thou art happy in that, after labour sore, thou hast the noblest praise to keep thy memory green. For, amid forty drivers who were laid low, thou, with thy fearless spirit, didst bring thy chariot through unscathed, and, from the glorious games, hast now returned to the plain of Libya, and to the city of thy sires. But no man is now, or ever shall be, without his share of trouble; yet, in spite of chequered fortune, there is present still the olden prosperity of Battus, that tower of the city of Cyrene, and that light most radiant to strangers from afar.

Even the loudly-roaring lions fled before Battus in terror when he unloosed on them his strange tongue,[1] and Apollo, the founder of the State, doomed the wild beasts to dread fear, that so his oracles might not be unfulfilled for the ruler of Cyrene. 'Tis Apollo that allotteth to men and to women remedies for sore diseases. 'Twas he that gave the cithern, and bestoweth the Muse on whomsoever he will, bringing into the heart the love of law that hateth strife.

---

[1] Battus was as much afraid of the lions as the lions were of Battus. "It is said that he was cured of his stammer in the following way. As he was traversing the district of Cyrene, he beheld in the utmost parts of it, which were still uninhabited, a lion, and terror at the sight forced from his lips a loud articulate cry." (Frazer's *Pausanias*, x 15, 7.)

μυχόν τ' ἀμφέπει
μαντήϊον· τῷ [καὶ] Λακεδαίμονι
70 ἐν Ἄργει τε καὶ ζαθέα Πύλῳ
ἔνασσεν ἀλκάεντας Ἡρακλέος
ἐκγόνους Αἰγιμιοῦ τε. τὸ δ' ἐμὸν γαρύειν
ἀπὸ Σπάρτας ἐπήρατον κλέος·

ἀντ. γ'
ὅθεν γεγεννναμένοι
75 ἵκοντο Θήρανδε φῶτες Αἰγεῖδαι,   100
ἐμοὶ πατέρες, οὐ θεῶν ἄτερ, ἀλλὰ μοῖρά τις ἄγεν·
πολύθυτον ἔρανον
ἔνθεν ἀναδεξάμενοι,
Ἄπολλον, τεᾷ,
80 Καρνήϊ', ἐν δαιτὶ σεβίζομεν
Κυράνας ἀγακτιμέναν πόλιν·
ἔχοντι τὰν χαλκοχάρμαι ξένοι
Τρῶες Ἀντανορίδαι. σὺν Ἑλένᾳ γὰρ μόλον,

69 μαντήϊον mss (MFCS³): μαντεῖον Hermann (BS¹), μαντῆον
(G).
72 γαρύειν C, γαρύεν Hermann, Bergk (G): γαρύετ' BDE
and scholium, γαρύέντ' PQR; γαρύοντ' B? Donaldson, F;
γαρύεται (M); γαρύει Wilamowitz (S).
76 f. ἄγεν πολ. ἔρανον GFCS: ἄγεν πολ. ἔρανον, B, — ἔρανον.
M¹, ἄγ' ἐν—Mingarelli (M²).
79 f. τεᾷ, Καρνήϊ' Boeckh (MGCS): τεὰ Καρνεῖα Moschopulus,
τεὰ Καρνήϊ' F.

[1] The first person singular elsewhere refers to the poet
himself (though examples are not wanting in which the Ode
is written from the point of view of the chorus, as in O. xiv
and P. viii). Hence it has been generally assumed that Pindar
here claims descent from the Aegeidae. These must have
been the *Theban* Aegeidae mentioned in *I.* vii 15. But we
find below that it was the *Spartan* Aegeidae, who colonised
Thêra. According to this view the subsequent context
implies that it was from Thêra that Thebes received the

'Tis he that ruleth the secret shrine of the oracles;
wherefore, even for sake of Lacedaemon, he planteth
the valiant descendants of Heracles and Aegimius in
Argos, and in hallowed Pytho.

But mine it is to sing of the dear glory that
cometh from Sparta, whence sprang the Aegeidae, my
own forefathers,[1] who, not without the gods, but led
by some providence divine, once went to Thêra,
whence it was that we have received the festal
sacrifice in which all have part, and, in thy banquet,
O Carneian Apollo,[2] we honour the nobly built city of
Cyrene; which is held by bronze-armed Trojans from
a foreign shore, even by the descendants of Antênôr.[3]
For they came with Helen, after they had seen their

Carneia, and in its local festivals paid honour to Cyrene as a
colony of Thêra.

But it seems out of place for the poet to make the chorus
say, at Cyrene, that "we Thebans do honour to Cyrene as a
colony of Thêra." It is more satisfactory to suppose that
it is the leader of the Cyrenaean chorus that here describes
the *Spartan* Aegeidae as his ancestors (see Studniczka,
Cyrene, pp. 73-85). It was from Sparta that the *Spartan*
Aegeidae carried to Thêra the festival of the Carneia, which
Thêra had since transferred to those who were now glorifying
their native city, Cyrene. The two interpretations are
summed up in the scholium ὁ λόγος ἀπὸ τοῦ χοροῦ τῶν Λιβύων
ἢ ἀπὸ τοῦ ποιητοῦ.

[2] The "Carneia" was an important national festival of the
Spartans, which was carried across the Aegean sea to Thêra.
The epitaph of a priest of the Carneian Apollo has been
found at Thêra, in which the priest claims descent from the
Spartan kings and also from Thessaly (Kaibel, *Epigr. Graeca*
Nos. 191, 192). Callimachus, the poet of Cyrene, traces
the Carneia from Sparta to Thêra, and from Thêra to
Cyrene (*Hymn*, ii 72 f).

[3] The local heroes of Cyrene prior to its colonisation by
Thêra.

καπνωθεῖσαν πάτραν ἐπεὶ ἴδον   110
ἐπ. γ'
85 ἐν Ἄρει. τὸ δ' ἐλάσιππον ἔθνος ἐνδυκέως
   δέκονται θυσίαισιν ἄνδρες οἰχνέοντές σφε δωρο-
       φόροι,
   τοὺς Ἀριστοτέλης ἄγαγε, ναυσὶ θοαῖς
   ἁλὸς βαθεῖαν κέλευθον ἀνοίγων.
   κτίσεν δ' ἄλσεα μείζονα θεῶν,   120
90 εὐθύτομόν τε κατέθηκεν Ἀπολλωνίαις
   ἀλεξιμβρότοις πεδιάδα πομπαῖς
   ἔμμεν ἱππόκροτον
   σκυρωτὰν ὁδόν, ἔνθα πρυμνοῖς ἀγορᾶς ἔπι δίχα
      κεῖται θανών.
στρ. δ'
   μάκαρ μὲν ἀνδρῶν μέτα
95 ἔναιεν, ἥρως δ' ἔπειτα λαοσεβής.
   ἄτερθε δὲ πρὸ δωμάτων ἕτεροι λαχόντες ἀΐδαν   130
   βασιλέες ἱεροὶ
   ἐντί, μεγάλαν δ' ἀρετὰν
   δρόσῳ μαλθακᾷ
100 ῥανθεῖσαν κώμων ὑπὸ χεύμασιν,
   ἀκούοντί που χθονίᾳ φρενί,
   σφὸν ὄλβον υἱῷ τε κοινὰν χάριν
   ἔνδικόν τ' Ἀρκεσίλᾳ. τὸν ἐν ἀοιδᾷ νέων
   πρέπει χρυσάορα Φοῖβον ἀπύειν,   140

98–100 μεγάλαν — ἀρετὰν — ῥανθεῖσαν MGFC ; μεγάλαν —
ἀρετᾶν — ῥανθεισᾶν BDE, both gen. and acc. are recognised
in scholia ; μεγαλᾶν — ἀρετᾶν — ῥανθεισᾶν S ; μεγάλα — ἀρετὰ —
ῥανθεῖσα B.

100 κώμων XZ, Moschopulus (BFS) : κώμων θ' BDE ; ὕμνων
Beck (MGC).   ὑπὸ χεύμασιν BE (edd.) : ὑποχεύμασιν DFG,
Moschopulus, Hermann, Donaldson.

101 που scholium, Hermann, Donaldson (C) : ποι mss
(MGFS) ; τοι B.

native city burnt in war, and that chariot-driving race was heartily welcomed with sacrifices by men who greeted them with gifts, men who were brought by Aristoteles,[1] when, with his swift steps, he opened a deep path across the sea. And he made the groves of the gods greater than aforetime, and ordained that, for the festivals of Apollo, which bring health unto mortals, there should be a straight and level road, paved with stone and trodden by the hoofs of horses,[2] where now, in death, he resteth apart, at the further end of the market-place.[3] Blessed was he, while he dwelt among men, and thereafter a hero worshipped by the people; and asunder, before the dwellings, are the other holy kings, whose portion is in Hades, and in their soul, in the world below, they haply hear of lofty prowess besprent with soft dew beneath the outpourings of revel-songs—a happy lot for themselves and a glory shared by their son, Arcesilas, and his rightful claim.

Meet it is that, amid the minstrelsy of youths, he should proclaim the praise of golden-lyred Apollo,

---

[1] The other name of the founder, Battus.

[2] The Scholiast states that Battus made τὴν λεγομένην Σκυρωτὴν πλατεῖαν, what was known as "the paved street." Della Cella, an Italian traveller who visited Cyrene in 1817, describes its principal street as "completely cut out of the living rock" (*Viaggio*, p. 139).

[3] At the west end, where tombs are marked in the maps of Cyrene. As at Mycenae and Megara and Sicyon, the tomb of the founder was in the market-place. The descendants of Battus were buried in a place apart from the founder's tomb.

ἀντ. δ´

105 ἔχοντα Πυθωνόθεν
τὸ καλλίνικον λυτήριον δαπανᾶν
μέλος χαρίεν. ἄνδρα κεῖνον ἐπαινέοντι συνετοί.
λεγόμενον ἐρέω·
κρέσσονα μὲν ἁλικίας

110 νόον φέρβεται
γλῶσσάν τε· θάρσος δὲ τανύπτερος
ἐν ὄρνιξιν αἰετὸς ἔπλετο·   150
ἀγωνίας δ᾽, ἕρκος οἷον, σθένος·
ἕν τε Μοίσαισι ποτανὸς ἀπὸ ματρὸς φίλας,

115 πέφανταί θ᾽ ἁρματηλάτας σοφός·
ἐπ. δ´

ὅσαι τ᾽ εἰσὶν ἐπιχωρίων καλῶν ἔσοδοι,
τετόλμακε. θεός τέ οἱ τὸ νῦν τε πρόφρων τελεῖ
            δύνασιν,
καὶ τὸ λοιπὸν <ὁμοῖα>, Κρονίδαι μάκαρες,
διδοῖτ᾽ ἐπ᾽ ἔργοισιν ἀμφί τε βουλαῖς   160

120 ἔχειν, μὴ φθινοπωρὶς ἀνέμων
χειμερία κατὰ πνοὰ δαμαλίζοι χρόνον.
Διός τοι νόος μέγας κυβερνᾷ
δαίμον᾽ ἀνδρῶν φίλων.
εὔχομαί νιν Ὀλυμπίᾳ τοῦτο

125 δόμεν γέρας ἔπι Βάττου γένει.

110 f. νόον φέρβεται γλῶσσάν τε· θάρσος δὲ Schneidewin
(M²GFCS): νόον φέρβεται· γλῶσσάν τε θάρσος τε BM¹.
    118 ὦ mss; <ὁμοῖα> Hartung (GCS): <ὕπισθε> Boeckh;
<ὁποῖα> or <ὅσ᾽ ἂν κε> M; <ὅσαν κε> F.
    121 κατὰ πνοὰ δαμαλίζοι Bergk (CGS), cp. καταδαμάζω:
καταπνοὰ δ. mss (BMF).

now that he receiveth from Pytho the gracious song
that is the victor's guerdon for all cost. That hero
is praised by the prudent. I shall only say what is
said by others. He cherisheth a mind and a tongue
that are beyond his years; in courage he is like a
broad-winged eagle among birds, while his might in
athlete-contests is a very tower of strength; and,
even from his mother's lap, he hath soared among
the Muses; and he hath proved himself a skilful
charioteer; and all the openings for noble exploits
around him, hath he boldly essayed. Even now
doth God readily bring his powers to perfect issue,
and, in the time to come, do ye blessed sons of
Cronus grant him a like boon, both in deeds and
counsels, lest haply some stormy blast of autumn
make havoc of his life. Lo! it is the mighty mind
of Zeus that guideth the fate of men that he
loveth. I beseech him to grant the race of Battus
this new guerdon at Olympia.

PYTHIAN VI

FOR XENOCRATES OF ACRAGAS

INTRODUCTION

THE Sixth Pythian purports to be in honour of the chariot-race won by Xenocrates of Acragas, the younger brother of Thêrôn, who, two years later, became ruler of Acragas. The date of the victory was 490 B.C., a few days before the battle of Marathon. In this Ode, as in the Second Isthmian, the subject is nominally Xenocrates, but really his son Thrasybûlus, who drove his father's chariot. Filial devotion is the main theme of the poem. It must be regarded as a personal tribute to the victor's son and not as the official Epinician Ode, which, on this occasion, was written by Simonides (Abel's *Scholia*, p. 371). Simonides was then 66 years of age, while Pindar was only 32, and this is one of his earliest Odes.

The poet's plough-share is once more turning up a field of Love or of the Graces, as he draws near to the Delphic temple, where a treasure-house of song has been built for Acragas and for the victor and his ancestors (1–9), a treasure-house, which will not be swept away by wintry rain or storm, but whose

fair frontal shall in clear light proclaim a victory
shared by the father of Thrasybûlus and his race
(10–18).

Thrasybûlus honours his father, and obeys the pre-
cept once given by Cheiron to Achilles, bidding him
reverence his parents, next to the gods (19–27). In
olden days Antilochus sacrificed his life for his
father, Nestor; and now Thrasybûlus has shown his
supreme devotion to his father, Xenocrates (28–
45).

He is as hospitable as his father's brother, Thêrôn;
he uses his wealth wisely; he is devoted to poetry;
he has a passionate love of horsemanship; and,
when he consorts with others, sweeter than honey is
the temper of his soul (46–54).

ΑΡΜΑΤΙ

στρ. α΄

Ἀκούσατ'· ἦ γὰρ ἑλικώπιδος Ἀφροδίτας
ἄρουραν ἢ Χαρίτων
ἀναπολίζομεν, ὀμφαλὸν ἐριβρόμου
χθονὸς ἐς νάϊον προσοιχόμενοι·
5 Πυθιόνικος ἔνθ' ὀλβίοισιν Ἐμμενίδαις
ποταμίᾳ τ' Ἀκράγαντι καὶ μὰν Ξενοκράτει
ἑτοῖμος ὕμνων
θησαυρὸς ἐν πολυχρύσῳ
Ἀπολλωνίᾳ τετείχισται νάπᾳ·

στρ. β΄

10 τὸν οὔτε χειμέριος ὄμβρος ἐπακτὸς ἐλθών,
ἐριβρόμου νεφέλας
στρατὸς ἀμείλιχος, οὔτ' ἄνεμος ἐς μυχοὺς
ἁλὸς ἄξοισι παμφόρῳ χεράδει
τυπτόμενον.   φάει δὲ πρόσωπον ἐν καθαρῷ
15 πατρὶ τεῷ, Θρασύβουλε, κοινάν τε γενεᾷ
λόγοισι θνατῶν
εὔδοξον ἄρματι νίκαν
Κρισαίαισιν ἐν πτυχαῖς ἀπαγγελεῖ.

1 ἦ old mss (MGFCS) : ἤ Moschopulus, Dissen (B).
4 ἐς νάϊον Hermann³ (MFCS); ἐς ναὸν mss: ἀέννναον Her-
mann¹² (B); ἐς λίθινον Bergk¹².
10 ὄμβρος, ἐπακτὸς ἐλθών S ; ἐπακτὸς C.
13 χεράδει grammarians (GS), cp. frag. 327 χεράδει σποδέων:
χεράδι mss (BMFC).

248

VI.—FOR XENOCRATES OF ACRAGAS

WINNER IN THE CHARIOT-RACE, 490 B.C.

Listen ! for, in very deed, are we once more ploughing the field of bright-eyed Aphrodîtê or of the Graces,[1] as we draw nigh unto the shrine that is the centre of the loudly echoing Earth ; where, for the prosperous Emmenidae and for Acragas between the rivers, and chiefly for Xenocrates, there hath been built and prepared in Apollo's golden glen a Pythian victor's treasure-house of song, which neither wintry rain with its invading onset, the pitiless host launched from deep-thundering clouds, nor the storm-wind with its swirl of shingle, shall buffet and sweep away into the recesses of the sea. But the porch, in its pure brightness, shall proclaim a famous victory with the chariot, celebrated by the lips of mortals, and shared by thy father, Thrasybûlus, and by his race, that was won in the dells of Crisa. 'Tis thou, then, that settest him

---

[1] The poet has elsewhere besought "the Graces and Aphrodite" at the beginning of the sixth Paean addressed "to Pytho by the Delphians" (Wilamowitz, *Hieron und Pindaros*, 1901, p. 1287.) But the date of that Paean is now known to be probably five years later than that of this Ode.

στρ. γ΄

σύ τοι σχεθών νιν ἐπιδέξια χειρός, ὀρθὰν
20 ἄγεις ἐφημοσύναν,
τά ποτ᾽ ἐν οὔρεσι φαντὶ μεγαλοσθενεῖ
Φιλύρας υἱὸν ὀρφανιζομένῳ
Πηλεΐδᾳ παραινεῖν· μάλιστα μὲν Κρονίδαν,
βαρυόπαν στεροπᾶν κεραυνῶν τε πρύτανιν,
25 θεῶν σέβεσθαι·
ταύτας δὲ μή ποτε τιμᾶς
ἀμείρειν γονέων βίον πεπρωμένον.

στρ. δ΄

ἔγεντο καὶ πρότερον Ἀντίλοχος βιατὰς
νόημα τοῦτο φέρων,
30 ὃς ὑπερέφθιτο πατρός, ἐναρίμβροτον
ἀναμείναις στράταρχον Αἰθιόπων
Μέμνονα. Νεστόρειον γὰρ ἵππος ἅρμ᾽ ἐπέδα
Πάριος ἐκ βελέων δαϊχθείς· ὁ δ᾽ ἔφεπεν
κραταιὸν ἔγχος·
35 Μεσσανίου δὲ γέροντος
δοναθεῖσα φρὴν βόασε παῖδα ὅν·

στρ. ε΄

χαμαιπετὲς δ᾽ ἄρ᾽ ἔπος οὐκ ἀπέριψεν· αὐτοῦ
μένων δ᾽ ὁ θεῖος ἀνὴρ
πρίατο μὲν θανάτοιο κομιδὰν πατρός,
40 ἐδόκησέν τε τῶν πάλαι γενεᾷ
ὁπλοτέροισιν, ἔργον πελώριον τελέσαις,
ὕπατος ἀμφὶ τοκεῦσιν ἔμμεν πρὸς ἀρετάν.
τὰ μὲν παρίκει·
τῶν νῦν δὲ καὶ Θρασύβουλος
45 πατρῴαν μάλιστα πρὸς στάθμαν ἔβα,

19 σχεθών Elmsley (s) : σχέθων mss (BMGFC).

ever at thy right hand, and upholdest the charge, even the precepts which, as the story telleth, the son of Philyra[1] erst enjoined on the stalwart son of Pêleus,[2] when parted from his parents:—First of all the gods to adore the son of Cronus, the loud-voiced lord of the lightnings and the thunders, and of such reverence never to deprive his parents during their allotted life.

Even aforetime was this spirit cherished by that man of might, Antilochus, who died for his father's sake, by awaiting the onslaught of Memnon, the leader of the Ethiopians.[3] For Nestor's chariot was entangled by his horse that had been stricken by the arrows of Paris, while Memnon was plying his sturdy spear, and the distracted soul of the aged hero of Messênê called aloud for his son; and his cry fell not to the ground, but, waiting there, the god-like son bought with his own life the rescue of his father, and, by doing this wondrous deed, was deemed by those of a younger generation to have proved himself, among men of old, supreme in filial devotion.

These things are of the past; but, in the present time, Thrasybûlus hath come nearest to the standard of duty to one's father, while he also vieth with his

---

[1] Cheiron.   [2] Achilles.
[3] This version of the story comes from the *Aethiopis*, an epic poem by Arctînus.   In the *Iliad* (viii 90–117) it is Diomêdês that comes to the rescue of Nestor; but the death of his son, Antimachus, is mentioned in the *Odyssey*, iv 187 f.

στρ. στ′

   πάτρῳ τ᾽ ἐπερχόμενος ἀγλαΐαν ἅπασαν.
   νόῳ δὲ πλοῦτον ἄγει,
   ἄδικον οὔθ᾽ ὑπέροπλον ἥβαν δρέπων,
   σοφίαν δ᾽ ἐν μυχοῖσι Πιερίδων·
50 τίν τ᾽, Ἐλέλιχθον, ἃς εὗρες ἱππίας ἐσόδους,
   μάλα ἁδόντι νόῳ, Ποσειδᾶν, προσέχεται.
   γλυκεῖα δὲ φρὴν
   καὶ συμπόταισιν ὁμιλεῖν
   μελισσᾶν ἀμείβεται τρητὸν πόνον.

46 τ᾽ mss : γ᾽ C¹ (G).   ἔδειξεν ἅπασαν old mss ; ἔδειξεν (BM ? F) ; ἅπασαν Bergk² (GCS).

50 ἃς εὗρες ἱππείας ἐσόδους Mommsen ; εὗρές θ᾽ ὃς ἱππέαν ἔσοδον Moschopulus ; ὃς θ᾽ εὗρες ἱππίαν ἔσοδον B in critical notes (Donaldson) : ὀργαῖς πάσαις ὃς ἱππείαν ἔσοδον old mss (S) ; ὀργαῖς ἐς ἱππίαν ἔσοδον B ; ὀργᾷς ὃς ἱππειᾶν ἐσόδων (CG) ; ὁρμᾷς ὃς ἱππίαν ἐς ὁδόν Rauchenstein, ὁρμᾷς ὃς πρὸς ἱππίαν ἔσοδον Bergk¹, – – ⏑ ἱππείαν ἔσοδον F. ὦ δέσποθ᾽ ἱππιᾶν ἐσόδων ? S.

father's brother[1] in all manner of splendour; but with wisdom tendeth he his wealth, not plucking the pleasures of youth with injustice or violence, but culling poesy in the quiet haunts of the Pierides; and with a spirit that hath found thy favour, O earth-shaking Poseidon, he clingeth to the chariot-contests first found by thee. Sweet also is his temper, and, as a boon companion, he outvieth the crannied work of the honey-bee.[2]

[1] Thêrôn, the future ruler of Acragas.
[2] That is, "he is sweeter than the honeycomb."

PYTHIAN VII

FOR MEGACLES OF ATHENS

INTRODUCTION

THE Seventh Pythian is in honour of Megacles of Athens, the son of Hippocrates, and the nephew and son-in-law of the Athenian legislator, Cleisthenes. He is the grandson of the Megacles who married Agaristê, daughter of Cleisthenes, tyrant of Sicyon (Hdt. vi 127 f), and the great-grandson of Alcmaeon, who won the chariot-race in the Olympic games. The present victory was won in **486** B.C. The seventh Nemean is the only other Ode in honour of an Athenian.

Athens is the fairest prelude to a song in honour of the Alcmaeonidae (1–8), a family which has made Apollo's temple at Delphi a marvel to behold, and has won two victories at the Isthmian, one at the Olympian, and two at the Pythian games (9–16). Their noble acts have been requited with envy and exile, but prosperity meets with varied fortune (17–22).

Megacles had been ostracised by Athens a few months before this victory.

ΤΕΘΡΙΠΠΩ

στρ.

Κάλλιστον αἱ μεγαλοπόλιες Ἀθᾶναι
προοίμιον Ἀλκμανιδᾶν εὐρυσθενεῖ γενεᾷ
κρηπῖδ᾽ ἀοιδᾶν
ἵπποισι βαλέσθαι.
5 ἐπεὶ τίνα πάτραν, τίνα οἶκον
ναίων ὀνυμάξεαι
ἐπιφανέστερον
Ἑλλάδι πυθέσθαι;

ἀντ.

πάσαισι γὰρ πολίεσι λόγος ὁμιλεῖ
10 Ἐρεχθέος ἀστῶν, Ἄπολλον, οἳ τεόν γε δόμον   10
Πυθῶνι δίᾳ
θαητὸν ἔτευξαν.
ἄγοντι δέ με πέντε μὲν Ἰσθμοῖ
νῖκαι, μία δ᾽ ἐκπρεπὴς
15 Διὸς Ὀλυμπιάς,
δύο δ᾽ ἀπὸ Κίρρας,

ἐπ.

ὦ Μεγάκλεες, ὑμαί τε καὶ προγόνων.
νέα δ᾽ εὐπραγίᾳ χαίρω τι· τὸ δ᾽ ἄχνυμαι,
φθόνον ἀμειβόμενον τὰ καλὰ ἔργα.
20 φαντί γε μὰν οὕτω κεν ἀνδρὶ παρμονίμαν   20
θάλλοισαν εὐδαιμονίαν
τὰ καὶ τὰ φέρεσθαι.

6 ναίων mss (FS): ναιόντ᾽ Erasmus Schmid (BG); αἰᾶν M:
αἰνέων Kayser (C).

ὀνυμάξεαι Boeckh (S), ὀνυμάξαι B, ὀνομάξαι D: ὀνυμάξομαι
Triclinius and scholia (MGFC).

VII. FOR MEGACLES OF ATHENS

WINNER IN THE FOUR-HORSE CHARIOT-RACE, 486 B.C.

The mighty city of Athens is the fairest prelude of song, which the widely powerful race of the Alcmaeonidae can lay as a foundation of odes in honour of their steeds.

What fatherland, what family, in which thou dwellest, shalt thou name as more illustrious of report in Greece? For all the cities are haunted by the story of those citizens of Erechtheus, who in divine Pytho made thy temple, O Apollo, a marvel to behold.

I am also prompted to song by five victories, one at the Isthmus, and one famous victory at the Olympian festival of Zeus, and two from Cirrha, won by yourselves, Megaclês, and by your ancestors. At this new good fortune I have no little joy; but it is very grievous that noble acts are requited by envy. Yet they say that prosperity which abideth in bloom bringeth evil as well as good in its train.

10 τεόν γε δόμον Moschopulus (BMGFC): τεόν τε δόμον Vatican recension; τεὸν πρόδομον? S.

257

PYTHIAN VIII

FOR ARISTOMENES OF AEGINA

INTRODUCTION

THE Eighth Pythian celebrates the victory in the boys' wrestling-match won by Aristomenes of Aegina. One of his uncles had been victorious in wrestling at Olympia, and another at the Isthmian games. He had himself been already successful at Megara, Marathon, and Aegina. Pindar had apparently been present at the Pythian contest (59). The Ode was sung at Aegina. The Scholiast refers it to the 35th Pythiad, that is, to 446 B.C. In 447 Athens had been defeated by Thebes at the battle of Coronea, and this defeat has been supposed to be indicated in the poet's reference to the overthrow of Porphyrion and Typhôeus (12–18). The " Thirty Years' Peace" between Athens and Sparta was signed towards the end of 446. Aegina obtained a relative degree of independence, so that the poet's prayer at the end of the Ode was partially answered (Gaspar's *Chronologie Pindarique*, 165–9).

The Ode begins with a tribute to the goddess of domestic tranquillity, who holds the keys of councils and of wars, but also has the strength to quell rebels

INTRODUCTION

such as Porphyrion and Typhôeus, who were over-
come by Apollo, who has welcomed the victor on his
return from the Pythian games (1–20). The praise
of Aegina for justice, athletic success, and valour
(21–28). The praise of the victor, who has followed
the example of his mother's brothers, and has thus
won the eulogy bestowed by Amphiaraüs on the
valour of his son and his son's comrades :—" The
courage of the sires is clearly seen in the sons "
(29–45). That eulogy of his son, Alcmaeon, is echoed
by the poet ; Alcmaeon is the poet's neighbour and
guardian of his goods, and speaks to him in oracles
(45–60).

The victor's successes have been given him by
Apollo (61–66), to whom the poet prays for a blessing
on his ode (67–72). Success is apt to be followed
by a reputation for wisdom, but success is uncertain
(73–78). The victor's successes are recounted, ending
with his victory at the Pythian games (78–87). Early
successes are welcome, but human happiness is
fleeting (88–92). May Aegina be brought safely
onwards in her course of freedom, under the blessing
of her heroes (98–100).

VIII.—ΑΡΙΣΤΟΜΕΝΕΙ ΑΙΓΙΝΗΤῌ

ΠΑΛΑΙΣΤῌ

στρ. α΄

    Φιλόφρον Ἡσυχία, Δίκας
    ὦ μεγιστόπολι θύγατερ,
    βουλᾶν τε καὶ πολέμων
    ἔχοισα κλαῗδας ὑπερτάτας,
5 Πυθιόνικον τιμὰν Ἀριστομένει δέκευ.
    τὺ γὰρ τὸ μαλθακὸν ἔρξαι τε καὶ παθεῖν ὁμῶς
    ἐπίστασαι καιρῷ σὺν ἀτρεκεῖ·

ἀντ. α΄

    τὺ δ᾽, ὁπόταν τις ἀμείλιχον   10
    καρδίᾳ κότον ἐνελάσῃ,
10 τραχεῖα δυσμενέων
    ὑπαντιάξαισα κράτει τιθεῖς
    Ὕβριν ἐν ἄντλῳ. τὰν οὐδὲ Πορφυρίων μάθεν
    παρ᾽ αἶσαν ἐξερεθίζων· κέρδος δὲ φίλτατον,
    ἑκόντος εἴ τις ἐκ δόμων φέροι.

ἐπ. α΄

15 βία δὲ καὶ μεγάλαυχον ἔσφαλεν ἐν χρόνῳ.   20
    Τυφὼς Κίλιξ ἑκατόγκρανος οὔ νιν ἄλυξεν,
    οὐδὲ μὰν βασιλεὺς Γιγάντων· δμᾶθεν δὲ κεραυνῷ
    τόξοισί τ᾽ Ἀπόλλωνος· ὃς εὐμενεῖ νόῳ
    Ξενάρκειον ἔδεκτο Κίρραθεν ἐστεφανωμένον
20 υἱὸν ποίᾳ Παρνασσίδι Δωριεῖ τε κώμῳ.

στρ. β΄

    ἔπεσε δ᾽ οὐ Χαρίτων ἑκὰς   30

     20 Παρνασσίδι s : Παρνασίῃ mss ; Παρνασίδι (BMGFC).

260

VIII.—FOR ARISTOMENES OF AEGINA

KINDLY Goddess of Peace, daughter of Justice, that makest cities great; thou that holdest the master-keys of councils and of wars, receive from Aristomenes the honour due for a Pythian victory; for thou knowest with perfect fitness the secret of gentleness, both in giving, and in taking.

And yet, whenever any man hurleth into his heart relentless wrath, rudely confronting the strength of thine enemies, thou plungest Insolence in the brine. Thy power Porphyrion [1] did not know, when he provoked thee beyond all measure, yet gain is best, whenever one getteth it from the home of a willing giver. But violence overthroweth the braggart at the last. The Cilician Typhôeus [2] with his hundred heads did not escape thy power; no, nor the king of the Giants. They were severally overcome by the thunderbolt of Zeus, and by the bow of Apollo, who with gracious mind welcomed the son of Xenarcês on his return from Cirrha, crowned with Parnassian verdure and with Dorian triumph-song.

Right near to the Graces hath fallen that isle

---

[1] The king of the giants (l. 17), who fought against the gods, and was slain by Zeus and Heracles.

[2] Son of Tartarus and Gaea; a monster with fearful eyes and terrible voices, who was ultimately subdued by the thunderbolt of Zeus. Cp. *O.* iv 8, *P.* i 15.

ἁ δικαιόπολις ἀρεταῖς
κλειναῖσιν Αἰακιδᾶν
θιγοῖσα νᾶσος· τελέαν δ' ἔχει
25 δόξαν ἀπ' ἀρχᾶς. πολλοῖσι μὲν γὰρ ἀείδεται
νικαφόροις ἐν ἀέθλοις θρέψαισα καὶ θοαῖς
ὑπερτάτους ἥρωας ἐν μάχαις·

ἀντ. β'

τὰ δὲ καὶ ἀνδράσιν ἐμπρέπει.
εἰμὶ δ' ἄσχολος ἀναθέμεν   40
30 πᾶσαν μακραγορίαν
λύρᾳ τε καὶ φθέγματι μαλθακῷ,
μὴ κόρος ἐλθὼν κνίσῃ. τὸ δ' ἐν ποσί μοι τράχον
ἴτω τεὸν χρέος, ὦ παῖ, νεώτατον καλῶν,
ἐμᾷ ποτανὸν ἀμφὶ μαχανᾷ.

ἐπ. β'

35 παλαισμάτεσσι γὰρ ἰχνεύων ματραδελφεοὺς
Ὀλυμπίᾳ τε Θέογνητον οὐ κατελέγχεις,   50
οὐδὲ Κλειτομάχοιο νίκαν Ἰσθμοῖ θρασύγυιον·
αὔξων δὲ πάτραν Μιδυλιδᾶν λόγον φέρεις,
τὸν ὅνπερ ποτ' Ὀϊκλέος παῖς ἐν ἑπταπύλοις ἰδὼν
40 υἱοὺς Θήβαις αἰνίξατο παρμένοντας αἰχμᾷ,

στρ. γ'

ὁπότ' ἀπ' Ἄργεος ἤλυθον
δευτέραν ὁδὸν Ἐπίγονοι.   60
ὣδ' εἶπε μαρναμένων·
" Φυᾷ τὸ γενναῖον ἐπιπρέπει
45 ἐκ πατέρων παισὶ λῆμα. θαέομαι σαφὲς
δράκοντα ποικίλον αἰθᾶς Ἀλκμᾶν' ἐπ' ἀσπίδος

24 θιγοῖσα Buttmann, Bergk (GCS); θίγοισα mss (BMF).
32 κνίσῃ mss (MGFC), cp. Bacchyl. xvii 8 κνίσεν : κνίσσῃ B ;
κνίξῃ S.
38 Μιδ. mss (BMGFC): Μειδ. Bergk (S).

where Justice reigneth; it knoweth the famous
merits of the sons of Aeacus, and hath perfect
glory from the beginning. It is famed in song
for having fostered heroes supreme in many a
victorious contest and in swift battles; and, again,
it is also conspicuous for its men; but time
would fail me to consign to the lyre and the gentle
voice of song all the long story of their fame, lest
haply envy should draw near and vex us; but let
that, which runneth before my feet, go forward,
even the debt that is due, my son, unto thee, the
latest of its glories, sped with wings of my skill.

For, in the contests of the ring, thou followest
hard on the track of thy mother's brothers, and
bringest no dishonour on Theognêtus, as victor at
Olympia, or on the conquest won by the sturdy
limbs of Cleitomachus at the Isthmus; and, by
exalting the clan of the Midylidae, thou earnest
the praise darkly prophesied of old by the son of
Oïclês,[1] when he saw those sons holding their
ground in battle before seven-gated Thebes, what
time the Epigoni came from Argos on that second
march. Thus spoke he, while they were fighting :—

"'Tis by the gift of Nature that there standeth forth
to view that noble spirit, which passeth from sires
to sons. I clearly see Alcmaeon,[2] the first to mount

---

[1] Amphiaraüs.   [2] Son of Amphiaraüs.

νωμῶντα πρῶτον ἐν Κάδμου πύλαις.
ἀντ. γ´
ὁ δὲ καμὼν προτέρᾳ πάθᾳ
νῦν ἀρείονος ἐνέχεται 70
50 ὄρνιχος ἀγγελίᾳ
Ἄδραστος ἥρως· τὸ δὲ οἴκοθεν
ἀντία πράξει. μοῦνος γὰρ ἐκ Δαναῶν στρατοῦ
θανόντος ὀστέα λέξαις υἱοῦ, τύχᾳ θεῶν
ἀφίξεται λαῷ σὺν ἀβλαβεῖ
ἐπ. γ´
55 "Ἄβαντος εὐρυχόρους ἀγυιάς." τοιαῦτα μὲν
ἐφθέγξατ' Ἀμφιάρηος. χαίρων δὲ καὶ αὐτὸς
Ἀλκμᾶνα στεφάνοισι βάλλω, ῥαίνω δὲ καὶ
ὕμνῳ, 80
γείτων ὅτι μοι καὶ κτεάνων φύλαξ ἐμῶν
ὑπάντασεν ἰόντι γᾶς ὀμφαλὸν παρ' ἀοίδιμον,
60 μαντευμάτων τ' ἐφάψατο συγγόνοισι τέχναις.
στρ. δ´
τὺ δ', ἑκαταβόλε, πάνδοκον
ναὸν εὐκλέα διανέμων 90
Πυθῶνος ἐν γυάλοις,
τὸ μὲν μέγιστον τόθι χαρμάτων
65 ὤπασας· οἴκοι δὲ πρόσθεν ἁρπαλέαν δόσιν
πενταθλίου σὺν ἑορταῖς ὑμαῖς ἐπάγαγες.
ἄναξ, ἑκόντι δ' εὔχομαι νόῳ
ἀντ. δ´
κατὰ τιν' ἁρμονίαν βλέπειν,
ἀμφ' ἕκαστον ὅσα νέομαι.

59 ὑπάντασέ τ' B.
67 ἄναξ EF (BMG) : ὦναξ most mss (FCS).
68 κατὰ τιν' MFCS³ : κατὰ τὶν BG ; κατ' ἐμὶν S¹.

upon the walls of Cadmus, wielding a glittering
dragon on his shining shield, while he that afore-
time suffered from disaster, even the hero Adrastus,[1]
is now compassed by tidings of a happier omen;
but, as for his own household, he shall fare far
otherwise. For he alone of the host of the Danai
shall gather the bones of his slain son, and by the
destiny sent by the gods, shall, with his folk un-
scathed, safely return to the spacious streets of
Abas.''[2]

Thus spake Amphiaraüs; and I too gladly fling
my garlands over Alcmaeon, and besprinkle him with
song, because he is my neighbour, and proffered
himself as guardian of my goods, when I was going
to the storied centre of the world, and himself had
a share in his ancestor's arts of prophecy.[3]

But thou, far-darting god, that rulest over the
famous temple that welcometh all in the dells of
Pytho, there hast thou granted the greatest of joys;
and, even aforetime, at home, with thine own and
thy sister's festival, thou didst bring him a welcome
boon in the prize for the five contests.[4]

I pray, O king, that, with willing mind, I may keep
due measure in view in every step of my path of song.

---

[1] An Argive hero, whose daughter was married to
Polyneices of Thebes, whom Adrastus endeavoured to restore
to that city, although Amphiaraüs had foretold that all who
took part in the expedition should perish, with the exception
of Adrastus. The expedition was known as that of the "Seven
against Thebes." Ten years later, their descendants, the
"Epigoni," marched against Thebes, and destroyed it.

[2] Twelfth King of Argos.

[3] Alcmaeon, as son of Amphiaraüs, was great-grandson of
the famous seer Melampus. The *scholia* make the first
person singular refer, not to Pindar, but to Aristomenês and
the Aeginetans.

[4] See Introduction to *O.* xiii 30 and note on *N.* vii 8.

PINDAR

70 κώμῳ μὲν ἁδυμελεῖ
Δίκα παρέστακε· θεῶν δ' ὄπιν 100
ἄφθονον αἰτέω, Ξείναρκες, ὑμετέραις τύχαις.
εἰ γάρ τις ἐσλὰ πέπαται μὴ σὺν μακρῷ πόνῳ,
πολλοῖς σοφὸς δοκεῖ πεδ' ἀφρόνων
ἐπ. δ

75 βίον κορυσσέμεν ὀρθοβούλοισι μαχαναῖς·
τὰ δ' οὐκ ἐπ' ἀνδράσι κεῖται· δαίμων δὲ παρίσχει,
ἄλλοτ' ἄλλον ὕπερθε βάλλων, ἄλλον δ' ὑπὸ
χειρῶν 110
μέτρῳ καταβαίνει. Μεγάροις δ' ἔχεις γέρας,
μυχῷ τ' ἐν Μαραθῶνος, Ἥρας τ' ἀγῶν' ἐπιχώριον
80 νίκαις τρισσαῖς, ὦ 'ριστόμενες, δάμασσας ἔργῳ·
στρ. ε

τέτρασι δ' ἔμπετες ὑψόθεν
σωμάτεσσι κακὰ φρονέων,
τοῖς οὔτε νόστος ὁμῶς
ἔπαλπνος ἐν Πυθιάδι κρίθη, 120
85 οὐδὲ μολόντων πὰρ ματέρ' ἀμφὶ γέλως γλυκὺς
ὦρσεν χάριν· κατὰ λαύρας δ' ἐχθρῶν ἀπάοροι
πτώσσοντι, συμφορᾷ δεδαγμένοι.
ἀντ. ε

ὁ δὲ καλόν τι νέον λαχὼν
ἁβρότατος ἔπι μεγάλας
90 ἐξ ἐλπίδος πέταται
ὑποπτέροις ἀνορέαις, ἔχων 130

72 ἄφθονον recorded in G (ἀνεπίφθονον in paraphrase) (MS) : ἄφθιτον mss (BGFC).
87 δεδαγμένοι noticed in scholium by Boeckh, Bergk (MGFCS) : δεδαϊγμένοι mss, δεδαιγμένοι Hermann (B).
89 f. ἁβρότατος ἔπι (or ἐπι) μεγάλας ἐξ ἐλπίδος (GFCS): ἁβρότατος ἔπι, μεγάλας ἐξ ἐλπίδος Hermann (B) ; ἁβρότατος ἄπο (ἀπὸ E, Moschopulus) μ. κτλ (M).

The sweet-voiced triumph-band hath Justice standing beside it; but I pray that the gods may regard with no envy the fortunes of thy home, Xenarcês. For, if anyone hath a glorious victory with no long toil, to many he seemeth to be wise among fools, and to be arming his life by powers of good counsel; yet victory doth not depend on men alone; but he that giveth is God, who, at one while, exalteth on high, and, at another, bringeth one below the level of his hands. In Megara, thou already hast a prize, and in the lonely plain of Marathon, and in Hêra's games at thine own home, hast thou, Aristomenês, been verily victor in three conflicts; and thou didst, with fell intent, fall heavily on the bodies of four youths, for whom fate had not ordained, at the Pythian festival, any gladsome home-coming, as for thee. Nor, indeed, as they returned to their mothers, did pleasant laughter awaken delight; but they slunk along the bye-ways, aloof from their foes, sorely wounded by their mischance. But he that hath won a fresh victory in his green youth, by reason of his high hopes, flieth lightly on the wings of his manly exploits, with his thought superior to the pursuit of wealth.

κρέσσονα πλούτου μέριμναν. ἐν δ' ὀλίγῳ βροτῶν
τὸ τερπνὸν αὔξεται· οὕτω δὲ καὶ πιτνεῖ χαμαί,
ἀποτρόπῳ γνώμᾳ σεσεισμένον.
ἐπ. ε

95 ἐπάμεροι· τί δέ τις; τί δ' οὔ τις; σκιᾶς ὄναρ
ἄνθρωπος. ἀλλ' ὅταν αἴγλα διόσδοτος ἔλθῃ,
λαμπρὸν φέγγος ἔπεστιν ἀνδρῶν καὶ μείλιχος
    αἰών·

Αἴγινα φίλα μᾶτερ, ἐλευθέρῳ στόλῳ   140
πόλιν τάνδε κόμιζε Δὶ καὶ κρέοντι σὺν Αἰακῷ
100 Πηλεῖ τε κἀγαθῷ Τελαμῶνι σύν τ' Ἀχιλλεῖ.

97 φέγγος ἔπεστιν Heyne (BMGFCS[1]): ἔπεστι φέγγος mss (S[3]).

Short is the space of time in which the happiness
of mortal men groweth up, and even so, doth it fall
to the ground, when stricken down by adverse doom.
Creatures of a day, what is any one? what is he not?
Man is but a dream of a shadow; but, when a gleam
of sunshine cometh as a gift of heaven, a radiant
light resteth on men, aye and a gentle life.

O mother dear, Aegina, do thou waft this city
onward in her voyage of freedom with the blessing
of Zeus and of king Aeacus, and of Pêleus and good
Telamon and Achilles.

PYTHIAN IX

FOR TELESICRATES OF CYRENE

INTRODUCTION

THE ninth Pythian celebrates the victory won by
Telesicrates of Cyrene in the race in full-armour
at the Pythian festival of 474. (After the date
of this Ode he also won a foot-race at Delphi in 466.)
The place where the Ode was performed is uncertain.
Thebes has been suggested, but Cyrene is more
probable. We cannot rely much on the view that
the future δέξεται in line 73 implies that, when the
Ode was sung, the victor had not yet been welcomed
at Cyrene.

Proclamation of the victory of Telesicrates of
Cyrene (1–4).

The myth of Cyrene, who was beloved by Apollo
(5–70).

Cyrene has received a new honour through this
victory (71–75).

The myth of Iolaüs, grandson of Amphitryon, to
whom and to Zeus Alcmênê bare Iphicles and
Heracles (76–88).

Heracles and Iphicles have fulfilled the poet's

prayer on behalf of the victor, who had already been successful at Aegina and Megara (88–92).

We must obey the precept of Nereus, and " praise even a foe, when his deeds are noble " (93–96). Hence let jealousy be silent, when the victor has brought credit to his country.

At the local games of Cyrene, the victor was much admired by the maidens and their mothers ; in the case of one of his ancestors, it was a foot-race that decided his suit for the hand of the daughter of Antaeus (97–125).

IX.—ΤΕΛΕΣΙΚΡΑΤΕΙ ΚΥΡΗΝΑΙΩ

ΟΠΛΙΤΟΔΡΟΜΩ

στρ. α΄

Ἐθέλω χαλκάσπιδα Πυθιονίκαν
σὺν βαθυζώνοισιν ἀγγέλλων
Τελεσικράτη Χαρίτεσσι γεγωνεῖν,
ὄλβιον ἄνδρα, διωξίππου στεφάνωμα Κυράνας·
5 τὰν ὁ χαιτάεις ἀνεμοσφαράγων ἐκ Παλίου κόλπων
      ποτὲ Λατοΐδας
ἅρπασ᾽, ἔνεικέ τε χρυσέῳ παρθένον ἀγροτέραν
      δίφρῳ, τόθι νιν πολυμήλου   10
καὶ πολυκαρποτάτας θῆκε δέσποιναν χθονὸς
ῥίζαν ἀπείρου τρίταν εὐήρατον θάλλοισαν οἰκεῖν.

ἀντ. α΄

ὑπέδεκτο δ᾽ ἀργυρόπεζ᾽ Ἀφροδίτα
10 Δάλιον ξεῖνον θεοδμάτων
ὀχέων, ἐφαπτομένα χερὶ κούφᾳ.
καί σφιν ἐπὶ γλυκεραῖς εὐναῖς ἐρατὰν βάλεν
      αἰδῶ,   20
ξυνὸν ἁρμόζοισα θεῷ τε γάμον μιχθέντα κούρᾳ θ᾽
      Ὑψέος εὐρυβία·
ὃς Λαπιθᾶν ὑπερόπλων τουτάκις ἦν βασιλεύς, ἐξ
      Ὠκεανοῦ γένος ἥρως
15 δεύτερος· ὅν ποτε Πίνδου κλεενναῖς ἐν πτυχαῖς
      Ναῒς εὐφρανθεῖσα Πηνειοῦ λέχει Κρείοισ᾽
      ἔτικτεν,   30

ἐπ. α΄

Γαίας θυγάτηρ. ὁ δὲ τὰν εὐώλενον

272

IX.—FOR TELESICRATES OF CYRENE

WINNER IN THE FOOT-RACE IN FULL ARMOUR, 474 B.C.

With the aid of the deep-zoned Graces, fain would I shout aloud, while I proclaim Telesicrates, the victor in the Pythian contest with the brazen shield, a happy man and the crowning glory of chariot-driving Cyrene; whom he of the flowing hair, even the son of Lêtô, erstwhile carried off from the wind-swept glens of Pêlion, and bore away, a huntress maiden, in his golden car to the place where he made her queen of a land rich in flocks and in fruits, that so she might find her home in the fair and flourishing foundation of a third continent.

And silver-footed Aphrodîtê welcomed the Delian guest, while, with light hand, she touched the car of workmanship divine, and shed a charming coyness on their union sweet, blending thus in bonds of mutual wedlock the god and the maiden-daughter of widely-ruling Hypseus. He was at that time king of the proud Lapithae, a hero second in descent from father Ocean, borne erstwhile by the daughter of Gaia, the Naiad Creüsa, who, in the famous glens of Pindus, had been the happy bride of the river-god Pêneius. And Hypseus cherished his fair-armed

273

θρέψατο παῖδα Κυράναν· ἁ μὲν οὔθ᾽ ἱστῶν
　　παλιμβάμους ἐφίλασεν ὁδούς,
οὔτε δείπνων οἰκοριᾶν μεθ᾽ ἑταιρᾶν τέρψιας,
20 ἀλλ᾽ ἀκόντεσσίν τε χαλκέοις
φασγάνῳ τε μαρναμένα κεράϊζεν ἀγρίους
θῆρας, ἦ πολλάν τε καὶ ἡσύχιον　　　　　40
βουσὶν εἰρήναν παρέχοισα πατρῴαις, τὸν δὲ
　　σύγκοιτον γλυκὺν
παῦρον ἐπὶ γλεφάροις
25 ὕπνον ἀναλίσκοισα ῥέποντα πρὸς ἀῶ.

στρ. β´

κίχε νιν λέοντί ποτ᾽ εὐρυφαρέτρας
ὀμβρίμῳ μούναν παλαίοισαν
ἄτερ ἐγχέων ἑκάεργος Ἀπόλλων.
αὐτίκα δ᾽ ἐκ μεγάρων Χείρωνα προσέννεπε φωνᾷ·
30 " Σεμνὸν ἄντρον, Φιλλυρίδα, προλιπὼν θυμὸν
　　γυναικὸς καὶ μεγάλαν δύνασιν　　　51
θαύμασον, οἷον ἀταρβεῖ νεῖκος ἄγει κεφαλᾷ,
　　μόχθου καθύπερθε νεᾶνις
ἦτορ ἔχοισα· φόβῳ δ᾽ οὐ κεχείμανται φρένες.
τίς νιν ἀνθρώπων τέκεν; ποίας δ᾽ ἀποσπασθεῖσα
　　φύτλας

ἀντ. β´

ὀρέων κευθμῶνας ἔχει σκιοέντων;　　　60
35 γεύεται δ᾽ ἀλκᾶς ἀπειράντου.
ὁσία κλυτὰν χέρα οἱ προσενεγκεῖν,
ἦ ῥα; καὶ ἐκ λεχέων κεῖραι μελιηδέα ποίαν; "

24 γλεφάροις V (ʙᴍɢꜰꜱᴄ): βλ. Vatican recension.
32 φρένες mss : φρένας Bergk⁴ (ɢ).
37 ἦ ῥα; B (ɢꜰ); ἦ ῥα, ᴍ (Bergk); ἦ ῥα ᴄ; ἤ ῥα
Hermann (ʙ).

daughter, Cyrene; she cared not for pacing to and fro before the loom, nor for merry banquets with stay-at-home maidens of her own age; but, contending with brazen darts and with the falchion, she would slay the fierce beasts of prey, thus in very deed assuring deep and perfect rest for her father's kine, while she spent on her eyelids but a scanty store of that slumber which is so sweet a bed-fellow when dawn draweth near. Once did Apollo, the far-darting god of the wide quiver, find her without spears, wrestling alone with a monstrous lion[1]; and forthwith he called Cheiron from out his halls and spake to him in this wise:—

"Son of Philyra, leave thy hallowed cave and look with wonder at a woman's spirit and mighty power. See what a contest she is waging with undaunted head,—this maiden with a heart which no toil can subdue, and a mind that no fear can overwhelm. From what mortal being was she born? From what race hath she been reft, that she should be dwelling in the hollows of the shadowy mountains? And she is putting to the test a strength that is inexhaustible. Is it right to lay an ennobling hand[2] upon her? aye, and, by consorting with her, to cull the honey-sweet flower of love?"

[1] Cyrene may be seen strangling a lion in a statuette (No. 1384) and a relief (No. 790) in the British Museum (reproduced in Studniczka's *Cyrene*, pp. 30, 31).
[2] Literally, "a renowned hand."

PINDAR

τὸν δὲ Κένταυρος ζαμενής, ἀγανᾷ χλαρὸν γελάσ-
σαις ὀφρύϊ, μῆτιν ἑὰν
εὐθὺς ἀμείβετο· "Κρυπταὶ κλαῗδες ἐντὶ σοφᾶς
Πειθοῦς ἱερᾶν φιλοτάτων,   70
40 Φοῖβε, καὶ ἔν τε θεοῖς τοῦτο κἀνθρώποις ὁμῶς
αἰδέοντ᾽, ἀμφανδὸν ἀδείας τυχεῖν τὸ πρῶτον εὐνᾶς.
ἐπ. β′

καὶ γὰρ σέ, τὸν οὐ θεμιτὸν ψεύδει θιγεῖν,
ἔτραπε μείλιχος ὀργὰ παρφάμεν τοῦτον λόγον.
κούρας δ᾽ ὁπόθεν γενεὰν
ἐξερωτᾷς, ὦ ἄνα; κύριον ὃς πάντων τέλος   80
45 οἶσθα καὶ πάσας κελεύθους·
ὅσσα τε χθὼν ἠρινὰ φύλλ᾽ ἀναπέμπει, χὠπόσαι
ἐν θαλάσσᾳ καὶ ποταμοῖς ψάμαθοι
κύμασιν ῥιπαῖς τ᾽ ἀνέμων κλονέονται, χὤ τι μέλ-
λει, χὠπόθεν
ἔσσεται, εὖ καθορᾷς.
50 εἰ δὲ χρὴ καὶ πὰρ σοφὸν ἀντιφερίξαι,
στρ. γ′

ἐρέω. ταύτᾳ πόσις ἵκεο βᾶσσαν
τάνδε, καὶ μέλλεις ὑπὲρ πόντον   90
Διὸς ἔξοχον ποτὶ κᾶπον ἐνεῖκαι·
ἔνθα νιν ἀρχέπολιν θήσεις, ἐπὶ λαὸν ἀγείραις
55 νασιώταν ὄχθον ἐς ἀμφίπεδον· νῦν δ᾽ εὐρυλείμων
πότνιά σοι Λιβύα
δέξεται εὐκλέα νύμφαν δώμασιν ἐν χρυσέοις πρό-
φρων· ἵνα οἱ χθονὸς αἶσαν
αὐτίκα συντελέθειν ἔννομον δωρήσεται,   100

38 χλαρὸν PQ (BMGFC); χλιαρὸν BDEV; χλοαρὸν s.
41 ἀμφανδὸν Erasmus Schmid (BGFC): ἀμφαδὸν mss (MS).
55 σοι mss (BMGFC): τοι s.

276

Then did the inspired Centaur, softly smiling with kindly brow, at once unfold his counsel in reply:—

"Secret, O Phoebus! are the keys of wise Persuasion, that unlock the shrine of love; and, among gods and men alike, do they shun to enter for the first time the sweet bridal-bed in the light of day. For thou, who canst not lawfully breathe a lie, hast been tempted by thy pleasant mood to dissemble in thy words. Dost thou ask, O king, of the maiden's birth? thou who knowest the end supreme of all things, and all the ways that lead thereto, the number of the leaves that the earth putteth forth in spring, the number of the sands that, in the sea and the rivers, are driven before the waves and the rushing winds, and that which is to be, and whence it is to come,—all this thou clearly seest. But, if I must measure myself against one that is wise, I needs must speak. Thou camest to this glade to be her wedded lord, and thou shalt bear her over the sea to the choicest garden of Zeus, where thou shalt make her queen of a city, when thou hast gathered the island-folk around the plain-encircled hill[1]; and soon shall queen Libya amid her broad meadows give in golden palaces a kindly welcome to thy glorious bride. There shall that queen grant her forthwith a portion of the land to be her lawful domain, a portion not

---

[1] Cp. "the white breast of the swelling earth," the site of Cyrene in *P.* iv 8.

οὔτε παγκάρπων φυτῶν νήποινον, οὔτ' ἀγνῶτα
   θηρῶν.
ἀντ. γ'
τόθι παῖδα τέξεται, ὃν κλυτὸς Ἑρμᾶς
60 εὐθρόνοις Ὥραισι καὶ Γαίᾳ
ἀνελὼν φίλας ὑπὸ ματέρος οἴσει.
ταὶ δ' ἐπιγουνίδιον κατθηκάμεναι βρέφος αὐταῖς,
νέκταρ ἐν χείλεσσι καὶ ἀμβροσίαν στάξοισι,
   θήσονταί τέ νιν ἀθάνατον   110
Ζῆνα καὶ ἁγνὸν Ἀπόλλων', ἀνδράσι χάρμα φίλοις
   ἄγχιστον, ὀπάονα μήλων,
65 Ἀγρέα καὶ Νόμιον, τοῖς δ' Ἀρισταῖον καλεῖν."
ὣς ἄρ' εἰπὼν ἔντυεν τερπνὰν γάμου κραίνειν
   τελευτάν.
ἐπ. γ'
ὠκεῖα δ' ἐπειγομένων ἤδη θεῶν
πρᾶξις ὁδοί τε βραχεῖαι. κεῖνο κεῖν' ἆμαρ διαί-
   τασεν· θαλάμῳ δὲ μίγεν   120
ἐν πολυχρύσῳ Λιβύας· ἵνα καλλίσταν πόλιν
70 ἀμφέπει κλεινάν τ' ἀέθλοις.
καί νυν ἐν Πυθῶνί νιν ἀγαθέᾳ Καρνειάδα
υἱὸς εὐθαλεῖ συνέμιξε τύχᾳ·
ἔνθα νικάσαις ἀνέφανε Κυράναν, ἅ νιν εὔφρων
   δέξεται,   130
καλλιγύναικι πάτρᾳ
75 δόξαν ἱμερτὰν ἀγαγόντ' ἀπὸ Δελφῶν.
στρ. δ'
ἀρεταὶ δ' αἰεὶ μεγάλαι πολύμυθοι·

---

62 <κατ>θηκάμενοι Moschopulus (B); θηκάμενοι DV,
θακάμενοι B; <προς>θηκάμενοι S: θησάμενοι EG..., θαησάμενοι
Bergk (MGFC), paraphrase " ἐπὶ τοῖς ἑαυτῶν γόνασι θεῖσαι τὸν
Ἀρ. καὶ θαυμάσασαι τὸ βρέφος."

without tribute of all manner of fruits, and not unfamiliar with the chase. There shall she bear a son, whom glorious Hermes shall take from his mother's womb and bear away to the enthroned Hours and to Mother-Earth; and they shall place the babe upon their laps, and drop nectar and ambrosia on his lips, and shall ordain that, as a delight to his friends among men, he shall be called immortal Zeus, and pure Apollo, and, as an ever-present guardian of flocks, Agreus and Nomius, while others shall name him Aristaeus."

So saying he prompted the god to accomplish the sweet fulfilment of wedlock. Swift is the achievement, short are the ways of gods, when bent on speed. That very day decided all, and they twain were made one in Libya's golden chamber, where she guardeth a city that is fair indeed, and is famous in athlete-contests.

And now hath the son of Carneiades crowned her with the flower of good fortune in hallowed Pytho, where, by his victory, he hath caused Cyrene to be proclaimed,—even her that shall give him a kindly welcome when he bringeth lovely fame from Delphi to his own land, the land of fair women.

Great deeds of prowess are ever rich in legends, but the deft fashioning of a few themes among

βαιὰ δ' ἐν μακροῖσι ποικίλλειν,
ἀκοὰ σοφοῖς· ὁ δὲ καιρὸς ὁμοίως
παντὸς ἔχει κορυφάν. ἔγνον ποτὲ καὶ Ἰόλαον

80 οὐκ ἀτιμάσαντά νιν ἑπτάπυλοι Θῆβαι· τόν,   140
   Εὐρυσθῆος ἐπεὶ κεφαλὰν
ἔπραθε φασγάνου ἀκμᾷ, κρύψαν ἔνερθ' ὑπὸ γᾶν
   διφρηλάτα Ἀμφιτρύωνος
σάματι, πατροπάτωρ ἔνθα οἱ Σπαρτῶν ξένος
κεῖτο, λευκίπποισι Καδμείων μετοικήσαις ἀγυιαῖς.

ἀντ. δ'
τέκε οἷ καὶ Ζηνὶ μιγεῖσα δαΐφρων
85 ἐν μόναις ὠδῖσιν Ἀλκμήνα
   διδύμων κρατησίμαχον σθένος υἱῶν.   150
κωφὸς ἀνήρ τις, ὃς Ἡρακλεῖ στόμα μὴ περι-
   βάλλει,
μηδὲ Διρκαίων ὑδάτων ἀὲ μέμναται, τά νιν θρέ-
   ψαντο καὶ Ἰφικλέα·
τοῖσι τέλειον ἐπ' εὐχᾷ κωμάσομαί τι παθὼν
   ἐσλόν, Χαρίτων κελαδεννᾶν
90 μή με λίποι καθαρὸν φέγγος. Αἰγίνᾳ τε γὰρ   160
   φαμὶ Νίσου τ' ἐν λόφῳ τρὶς δὴ πόλιν τάνδ'
   εὐκλεΐξαι,

ἐπ. δ'
σιγαλὸν ἀμαχανίαν ἔργῳ φυγών·
οὕνεκεν, εἰ φίλος ἀστῶν, εἴ τις ἀντάεις, τό γ' ἐν
   ξυνῷ πεπονᾱμένον εὖ
μὴ λόγον βλάπτων ἁλίοιο γέροντος κρυπτέτω.
95 κεῖνος αἰνεῖν καὶ τὸν ἐχθρὸν

79 ἔγνον Ahrens (MGFCS): ἔγνων mss (B), cp. P. iv 120.
88 ἀὲ Hermann (edd.): αἰεὶ (ἀεὶ) mss.
91 φαμὶ—εὐκλεΐξαι mss (BMGFC): φαμί,—εὐκλεΐξας Her-
mann (s).

many is what wise men love to hear.[1] And all things alike have for their crown the fitting season, which, as seven-gated Thebes knew of old, was not disregarded by Iolaüs,—that hero, who, when, with the edge of the sword, he had shorn off the head of Eurystheus, was buried beneath the earth beside the tomb of the charioteer Amphitryon, where rested his father's father,[2] the guest of the Sparti, having come to dwell in the streets of the Cadmeans, who ride on white horses. Wedded to Amphitryon and to Zeus, did the high-hearted Alcmêna bear at a single birth two children of victorious might. A dullard is he who doth not lend his tongue to sing of Heracles, and doth not remember for evermore the waters of Dircê that reared him and Iphicles, to both of whom, in fulfilment of a vow for the granting of their grace, I shall sing a triumph-song of praise. Let not the clear light of the voiceful Graces desert me! for I aver that I have already sung this city thrice at Aegina and by the hill of Nisus,[3] having thus escaped in very deed the doom of helpless dumbness.

Therefore, be a man friend or foe, let him not hide good work that is done for the common weal, and thus do wrong to the precept of the old man of

---

[1] σοφοῖς is often supposed to refer to the poets, but it seems best to understand it of the intelligent audience, cp. *O.* ii 92, φωνάεντα συνετοῖσιν. "Brevis ero, quum brevitas placeat intelligentibus" (Dissen).

[2] Amphitryon, father of Iphicles, and grandfather of Iolaüs, had been exiled from Tiryns and was welcomed by the Thebans, who were called Sparti because they claimed descent from the dragon's teeth sown by Cadmus.

[3] A mythical king of Megara.

281

παντὶ θυμῷ σύν γε δίκᾳ καλὰ ῥέζοντ᾽ ἔννεπεν. 170
πλεῖστα νικάσαντά σε καὶ τελεταῖς
ὡρίαις ἐν Παλλάδος εἶδον ἄφωνοί θ᾽ ὡς ἕκασται
    φίλτατον
παρθενικαὶ πόσιν ἢ
100 υἱὸν εὔχοντ᾽, ὦ Τελεσίκρατες, ἔμμεν,
στρ. ε´
  ἐν Ὀλυμπίοισί τε καὶ βαθυκόλπου
Γᾶς ἀέθλοις ἔν τε καὶ πᾶσιν
ἐπιχωρίοις. ἐμὲ δ᾽ ὦν τις ἀοιδὰν
δίψαν ἀκειόμενον πράσσει χρέος αὖτις ἐγεῖραι 180
105 καὶ παλαιὰν δόξαν ἑῶν προγόνων· οἷοι Λιβύσσας
    ἀμφὶ γυναικὸς ἔβαν
Ἴρασα πρὸς πόλιν, Ἀνταίου μετὰ καλλίκομον
    μναστῆρες ἀγακλέα κούραν·
τὰν μάλα πολλοὶ ἀριστῆες ἀνδρῶν αἴτεον
σύγγονοι, πολλοὶ δὲ καὶ ξείνων. ἐπεὶ θαητὸν
    εἶδος 190
ἀντ. ε´
  ἔπλετο· χρυσοστεφάνου δέ οἱ Ἥβας
110 καρπὸν ἀνθήσαντ᾽ ἀποδρέψαι
ἔθελον. πατὴρ δὲ θυγατρὶ φυτεύων
κλεινότερον γάμον, ἄκουσεν Δαναόν ποτ᾽ ἐν Ἄργει
οἷον εὗρεν τεσσαράκοντα καὶ ὀκτὼ παρθένοισι,
    πρὶν μέσον ἆμαρ ἑλεῖν,

98 ἕκασται B (MGCS): ἑκάστα UV (B); ἑκάστᾳ G (F).
103 ὦν τις ἀοιδὰν BDE (BGS); ὦν τις ἀοιδὰν διψάδ᾽ C: ὦν
τιν᾽ ἀοιδᾶς F: οὔ τις ἀοιδᾶν lemma of B (M).
105 παλαιὰν δόξαν ἑῶν Moschopulus (MS): παλαιὰ δόξα τεῶν
old mss (BF); τεῶν παλαιὰν δόξαν (G); τεῶν δόξαν παλαιὰν
Bergk (C); παλαιῶν δόξαν τεῶν BDE.
113 πρὶν μέσον ἆμαρ ἑλεῖν, (B¹GFC), — ἑλεῖν. M: πρὶν μέσον
ἆμαρ, ἑλεῖν Bergk (S).

the sea,[1] who bade us give praise that is hearty and fair, even to one's foe.

At the yearly rites of Pallas full often have the women seen thee after thy victory, and each, after their kind, have in silence prayed that they might have such a one as thee, Telesicrates, for their dear husband, or for their son; aye and also in the Olympian games, and in those of the deep-bosomed Earth, and in all other contests in thine own land.[2]

But, while I am quenching my thirst for song, there is one that exacteth an unpaid debt, and biddeth me once again awake the glory of thy fore-fathers of old, telling how, for the sake of a Libyan woman, they sped to Irasa[3] as suitors for the famous fair-haired daughter of Antaeus,—even for her, whom many a brave kinsman was wooing and many a stranger too, since her form was a marvel to look upon; and they were eager to pluck the blooming fruit of Hêbê of the golden crown. But her father, planning for her a nobler match, had heard how Danaüs in his day at Argos had found for his eight and forty daughters, ere noon came on them, a

[1] Nêreus.
[2] By the yearly rites of Pallas and the Olympian games and those of Mother Earth, are meant festivals held at Cyrene, as is proved by the conclusion of the paragraph, and by the presence of women. It was the armed Pallas that was worshipped at Cyrene.
[3] In Libya, near the lake Tritônis.

ὠκύτατον γάμον. ἔστασεν γὰρ ἄπαντα χορὸν ἐν
    τέρμασιν αὐτίκ᾽ ἀγῶνος·   200
115 σὺν δ᾽ ἀέθλοις ἐκέλευσεν διακρῖναι ποδῶν,
ἄντινα σχήσοι τις ἡρώων, ὅσοι γαμβροί σφιν
    ἦλθον.

ἐπ. ε´

οὕτω δ᾽ ἐδίδου Λίβυς ἁρμόζων κόρα
νυμφίον ἄνδρα· ποτὶ γραμμᾷ μὲν αὐτὰν στᾶσε
    κοσμήσαις τέλος ἔμμεν ἄκρον,   210
εἶπε δ᾽ ἐν μέσσοις ἀπάγεσθαι, ὃς ἂν πρῶτος θορὼν
120 ἀμφί οἱ ψαύσειε πέπλοις.
ἔνθ᾽ Ἀλεξίδαμος, ἐπεὶ φύγε λαιψηρὸν δρόμον,
παρθένον κεδνὰν χερὶ χειρὸς ἑλὼν
ἆγεν ἱππευτᾶν Νομάδων δι᾽ ὅμιλον. πολλὰ μὲν
    κεῖνοι δίκον
φύλλ᾽ ἔπι καὶ στεφάνους·
125 πολλὰ δὲ πρόσθεν πτερὰ δέξατο νικᾶν.   220

114 ἐν mss (BMGFC): πρὸς Boeckh de metris (s), but cp.
ποτὶ in 118.

speedy bridal; for, at once, he ranged the whole band of suitors at the limits of the lists, and bade them run a race to decide which of his daughters was to be won by the heroes who would fain be wedded to them. Such offer did the Libyan also make in wedding his daughter to a husband. He placed her at the goal, when he had arrayed her as the crowning prize, and in their midst he proclaimed that whoever was the first to leap forward and touch her robes in the race, should lead her to his home. There it was that Alexidâmus, when he had out-stripped the rest, took the noble maiden's hand in his own, and led her through the host of Nomad horsemen. Many leaves did they fling upon him, and many a wreath, and many plumes of victory had he received before.

PYTHIAN X

FOR HIPPOCLEAS OF THESSALY

INTRODUCTION

THIS Ode celebrates the victory of the Thessalian Hippocleas of Pelinna in the boys' double stadium-race at Delphi. The length of that race is about 400 yards; the date of the victory is the 22nd Pythiad, or **498** B.C. This is the earliest of Pindar's extant epinician Odes.

The father of the victor had been successful twice at Olympia and once at Delphi, and he was himself subsequently victorious at the Olympic festivals of 492 and 488. The commission for the Ode was given, not by the family of Hippocleas, but by the Aleuadae, the aristocratic rulers of Larissa.

The Heracleidae hold sway in Thessaly, as well as in Lacedaemon, and it is the Thessalian Heracleidae, the Aleuadae of Larissa, who summon me to celebrate the Pythian victory of Hippocleas (1–9). The victory is due to Apollo, and to the victor's emulation of his father's virtues (10–16). May the prosperity of the family continue (17–21). The victor's father is to be congratulated on his good fortune; he has

286

gone as far in bliss as man may go, though you cannot reach the Hyperboreans (21–30).

But, by Athêna's aid, Perseus visited the Hyperboreans, and slew the Gorgon, and brought back the head of Medusa, with which he turned the Seriphians into stone (31–48), for, when the gods lend their aid, nothing is incredible (48–50). Thus far for this digression (51–54).

The poet hopes to compose future triumph-songs for the same victor (58–59). Men's desires vary; their attainment brings eager delight; but the future is unforeseen (59–63). Thorax has generously provided the chorus (64–66); his rectitude has been tried like gold (67f). His noble brothers bear up the State; the best government depends on the continuance of the rule of good men (69–72).

X.—ΙΠΠΟΚΛΕΙ ΘΕΣΣΑΛΩ

ΠΑΙΔΙ ΔΙΑΥΛΟΔΡΟΜΩ

στρ. α΄

Ὀλβία Λακεδαίμων,
μάκαιρα Θεσσαλία· πατρὸς δ᾽ ἀμφοτέραις ἐξ ἑνὸς
ἀριστομάχου γένος Ἡρακλεῦς βασιλεύει.
τί κομπέω παρὰ καιρόν; ἀλλά με Πυθώ τε καὶ τὸ
    Πελινναῖον ἀπύει

5 Ἀλεύα τε παῖδες, Ἱπποκλέᾳ ἐθέλοντες
ἀγαγεῖν ἐπικωμίαν ἀνδρῶν κλυτὰν ὄπα.   10

ἀντ. α΄

γεύεται γὰρ ἀέθλων·
στρατῷ τ᾽ ἀμφικτιόνων ὁ Παρνάσιος αὐτὸν μυχὸς
διαυλοδρομᾶν ὕπατον παίδων ἀνέειπεν.

10 Ἄπολλον, γλυκὺ δ᾽ ἀνθρώπων τέλος ἀρχά τε
    .δαίμονος ὀρνύντος αὔξεται·
ὁ μέν που τεοῖς γε μήδεσι τοῦτ᾽ ἔπραξεν·
τὸ δὲ συγγενὲς ἐμβέβακεν ἴχνεσιν πατρὸς   20

ἐπ. α΄

Ὀλυμπιονίκα δὶς ἐν πολεμαδόκοις
Ἄρεος ὅπλοις·

15 ἔθηκε καὶ βαθυλείμων ὑπὸ Κίρρας ἀγὼν

11 τεοῖς γε Moschopulus (BMGFC): τεοῖσί τε old mss, τεοῖς
τε Triclinius, Kayser (S), τεοῖσι Calliergus (approved in M[1]
note).
15 βαθυλείμων D (GCS): βαθυλείμωιτα most mss (BMF).
    ὑπὸ Κίρρας ἀγὼν Triclinius (BMGFCS): ἀγὼν ὑπὸ Κίρρας old
mss ; ὑπὸ Κίρρας πέτρας ἀγὼν Hartung.

X.—FOR HIPPOCLEAS OF THESSALY

WINNER IN THE DOUBLE-STADIUM BOYS' FOOT-RACE, 498 B.C.

HAPPY is Lacedaemon; blessed is Thessaly; and both of them are under the royal sway of a race descended from Heracles, prince of warriors. Why this untimely boast? Nay, but I am summoned by Pytho and Pelinna and the sons of Aleuas, who desire to bring to Hippocleas the ringing voices of a triumphant band of men. For he is making trial of contests, and the gorge of Parnassus hath proclaimed him to the host of them that dwell around as foremost of the boys in the double course.

Sweet, O Apollo, becometh the end and the beginning of man's work, when it is sped of Heaven; and, haply, it was even by thy counsels that he hath attained this prize. And his inborn valour hath trodden in the foot-prints of his father, who was twice victor at Olympia in the armour of Arês that bears the brunt of war; and the contest in the deep meadow stretching beneath the rock of Cirrha made

πέτραν κρατησίποδα Φρικίαν.
ἔσποιτο μοῖρα καὶ ὑστέραισιν
ἐν ἀμέραις ἀγάνορα πλοῦτον ἀνθεῖν σφίσιν·

στρ. β′

τῶν δ᾽ ἐν Ἑλλάδι τερπνῶν
20 λαχόντες οὐκ ὀλίγαν δόσιν, μὴ φθονεραῖς ἐκ
      θεῶν   30
μετατροπίαις ἐπικύρσαιεν. θεὸς εἴη
ἀπήμων κέαρ· εὐδαίμων δὲ καὶ ὑμνητὸς οὗτος
      ἀνὴρ γίγνεται σοφοῖς,
ὃς ἂν χερσὶν ἢ ποδῶν ἀρετᾷ κρατήσαις
τὰ μέγιστ᾽ ἀέθλων ἕλῃ τόλμᾳ τε καὶ σθένει,

ἀντ. β′

25 καὶ ζώων ἔτι νεαρὸν
κατ᾽ αἶσαν υἱὸν ἴδῃ τυχόντα στεφάνων Πυθίων. 40
ὁ χάλκεος οὐρανὸς οὔ ποτ᾽ ἀμβατὸς αὐτῷ.
ὅσαις δὲ βροτὸν ἔθνος ἀγλαΐαις ἁπτόμεσθα,
      περαίνει πρὸς ἔσχατον
πλόον. ναυσὶ δ᾽ οὔτε πεζὸς ἰών <κεν> εὕροις
30 ἐς Ὑπερβορέων ἀγῶνα θαυματὰν ὁδόν.

ἐπ. β′

παρ᾽ οἷς ποτε Περσεὺς ἐδαίσατο λαγέτας,   50
δώματ᾽ ἐσελθών,
κλειτὰς ὄνων ἑκατόμβας ἐπιτόσσαις θεῷ
ῥέζοντας· ὧν θαλίαις ἔμπεδον
35 εὐφαμίαις τε μάλιστ᾽ Ἀπόλλων
χαίρει, γελᾷ θ᾽ ὁρῶν ὕβριν ὀρθίαν κνωδάλων.

16 πέτραν — Φρικίαν mss (BMGFC): πάτραν — Φρικία (S);
πάτρων Jurenka.
28 βροτὸν Erasmus Schmid (GFCS): βρότεον mss (B²M).
29 ἰών <κεν> εὕροις Hermann (GS): ἰὼν εὕρης DG,
— εὕροις other old mss, — ἂν εὕροις Moschopulus (BMC).

Phricias[1] victorious in the race. Even in the days to come may good fortune attend them, so that their noble wealth may flourish; may they win no small share of the pleasant things of Hellas, and suffer no envious reversal at the hands of the gods. He that is free from pain of heart may well be divine; but by poets wise that man is held happy, and is a theme for their song, whosoever, by being victorious with his hands or with the prowess of his feet, gaineth the greatest prizes by courage or by strength, and who, while still living, seeth his youthful son win more than one Pythian crown. The brazen heaven he cannot climb; but, as for all the bright achievements which we mortals attain, he reacheth the utmost limit of that voyage. Neither by ships nor by land canst thou find the wondrous road to the trysting-place of the Hyperboreans.[2]

Yet among them, in olden days, Perseus, the leader of the people, shared the banquet on entering their homes and finding them sacrificing famous hecatombs of asses in honour of the god. In the banquets and praises of that people Apollo chiefly rejoiceth, and he laugheth as he looketh on the brute beasts in their rampant lewdness.

[1] Probably the name of the horse, called "Bristler" from his long outstanding mane (L. and S.). Cp. Eustathius, *Pref.* p. 56, ὡς ὅτε λέγει (Πίνδαρος) ἵππον κρατησίποδα τὸν δρόμῳ νικήσαντα (Hermann, *Opusc.* vii 166 n.). One of the scholia, however, makes Phricias the father of Hippocleas. Hence Schröder conjecturers ἔθηκε ... πάτραν κρατησίποδα Φρικίου, "made the father-land of Phricias victorious in the foot-race." The father had already won the foot-race in armour twice at Olympia.

[2] The northern limit of the world; here mentioned in preference to the other limits, such as the "pillars of Heracles" to the west, and the "Phasis," and "Nile," to the east (*I.* ii 41), because it supplies a convenient transition to the legend of Perseus.

PINDAR

στρ. γ΄

Μοῖσα δ' οὐκ ἀποδαμεῖ
τρόποις ἐπὶ σφετέροισι· παντᾷ δὲ χοροὶ παρθένων
λυρᾶν τε βοαὶ καναχαί τ' αὐλῶν δονέονται·   60
40 δάφνᾳ τε χρυσέᾳ κόμας ἀναδήσαντες εἰλαπινάζοι-
σιν εὐφρόνως.
νόσοι δ' οὔτε γῆρας οὐλόμενον κέκραται
ἱερᾷ γενεᾷ· πόνων δὲ καὶ μαχᾶν ἄτερ

ἀντ. γ΄

οἰκέοισι φυγόντες
ὑπέρδικον Νέμεσιν. θρασείᾳ δὲ πνέων καρδίᾳ
45 μόλεν Δανάας ποτὲ παῖς, ἁγεῖτο δ' Ἀθάνα,   70
ἐς ἀνδρῶν μακάρων ὅμιλον· ἔπεφνέν τε Γοργόνα,
καὶ ποικίλον κάρα
δρακόντων φόβαισιν ἤλυθε νασιώταις
λίθινον θάνατον φέρων. ἐμοὶ δὲ θαυμάσαι

ἐπ. γ΄

θεῶν τελεσάντων οὐδέν ποτε φαίνεται
50 ἔμμεν ἄπιστον.
κώπαν σχάσον, ταχὺ δ' ἄγκυραν ἔρεισον χθονὶ   80
πρῴραθε, χοιράδος ἄλκαρ πέτρας.
ἐγκωμίων γὰρ ἄωτος ὕμνων
ἐπ' ἄλλοτ' ἄλλον ὧτε μέλισσα θύνει λόγον.

στρ. δ΄

55 ἔλπομαι δ' Ἐφυραίων
ὄπ' ἀμφὶ Πηνεῖὸν γλυκεῖαν προχεόντων ἐμὰν
τὸν Ἱπποκλέαν ἔτι καὶ μᾶλλον σὺν ἀοιδαῖς
ἕκατι στεφάνων θαητὸν ἐν ἅλικι θησέμεν ἐν καὶ
παλαιτέροις,   90
νέαισίν τε παρθένοισι μέλημα. καὶ γὰρ

Yet, such are their ways that the Muse is not banished, but, on every side, the dances of maidens and the sounds of the lyre and the notes of the flute are ever circling; and, with their hair crowned with golden bay-leaves, they hold glad revelry; and neither sickness nor baneful eld mingleth among that chosen people; but, aloof from toil and conflict, they dwell afar from the wrath of Nemesis. To that host of happy men, went of old the son of Danaë, breathing boldness of spirit, with Athêna for his guide. And he slew the Gorgon, and came back with her head that glittered with serpent-locks, to slay the islanders[1] by turning them into stone. But, as for me, in the handiwork of the gods, nothing ever seemeth too incredible for wonder.

Now, stay thine oar, and swiftly let the anchor slip from the prow to grapple with the ground, and guard thy ship against the rocky reef. For the blossom of these hymns of praise flitteth, like a bee, from theme to theme.

But I trust that, while the Ephyreans[2] pour forth my sweet strain beside the Pêneius, I may, with my strains of minstrelsy, cause Hippocleas to be admired still more among his fellows and his elders, and to be looked upon with a sweet care by the young maidens; for the heart is thrilled with

---

[1] The inhabitants of Serîphus. Cp. *P.* xii 12.

[2] Inhabitants of Ephyra, afterwards called Crannon, on a tributary of the Pêneius.

60 ἑτέροις ἑτέρων ἔρως ὑπέκνισε φρένας·
ἀντ. δ'

  τῶν δ' ἕκαστος ὀρούει,
  τυχών κεν ἁρπαλέαν σχέθοι φροντίδα τὰν πὰρ
      ποδός·
  τὰ δ' εἰς ἐνιαυτὸν ἀτέκμαρτον προνοῆσαι.
  πέποιθα ξενίᾳ προσανέϊ Θώρακος, ὅσπερ ἐμὰν
      ποιπνύων χάριν   100
65 τόδ' ἔζευξεν ἅρμα Πιερίδων τετράορον,
  φιλέων φιλέοντ', ἄγων ἄγοντα προφρόνως.
ἐπ. δ'

  πειρῶντι δὲ καὶ χρυσὸς ἐν βασάνῳ πρέπει
  καὶ νόος ὀρθός.
  ἀδελφεοὺς *ἔτ' ἐπαινήσομεν ἐσλούς, ὅτι
70 ὑψοῦ φέροντι νόμον Θεσσαλῶν
  αὔξοντες· ἐν δ' ἀγαθοῖσι κεῖνται   110
  πατρώϊαι κεδναὶ πολίων κυβερνάσιες.

60 ὑπέκνισε (BMGF); ὑπέκνιξε Hermann (C): ἔκνιξε old mss (S).
φρένας: ἐλπίδας? S.
69 ἔτ' Sandys, cp. N. iv 80, μάτρῳ μ' ἔτι . . . κελεύεις
στάλαν θέμεν; τ' old mss; μὲν ἐπ. (BG); ἐπί τ' αἰν. Bergk;
τε ποταιν. (M); τε μέγ' αἰν. (C); νυν ἐπ. (F); καὶ (S); — οἷσί τ'
ἐπαιν. ἐσλοῖς Wilamowitz.
71 κεῖνται most mss (GCS): κεῖται DG (BMF).

love for objects varied as men are varied ; but what-
ever each man striveth for, if he win it, he must
hold it as his near and dear delight; but that
which is a year hence hath no sure sign for our
foreseeing.

I trust in the kindly hospitality of Thorax [1] who,
busying himself for my sake, hath yoked this my
four-horsed chariot of the Muses, loving one who
loveth him in return, and readily offering hand to
hand. But, even as gold showeth its nature, when
tried by the touchstone, so is it with an upright
mind. We shall further praise his noble brethren,
in that they increase and exalt the State of
Thessaly ; and it is in the hands of high-born men
that there resteth the good piloting of cities, while
they pass from sire to son.

[1] The eldest of the Aleuadae, Herodotus, ix 1, 58.

295

PYTHIAN XI

FOR THRASYDAEUS OF THEBES

INTRODUCTION

THRASYDAEUS of Thebes won the boys' foot-race in
474 B.C. He belonged to a wealthy and illustrious
house; his father had won a Pythian victory (43),
and another member of the family had won the
chariot-race at Olympia (47). The Ode is sung at
Thebes during a procession to the temple of the
Ismenian Apollo.

The Scholiast states that Thrasydaeus also won
the double-stadium-race twenty years later, in 454,
and, as there is no mention of any trainer, Gilder-
sleeve prefers to regard the present Ode as
celebrating the later victory.

The poet calls on the Theban heroines to come to
the temple of the Ismenian Apollo, there to sing
of the Pythian games, in which Thrasydaeus has won
a third victory in the land of Pylades, the host of
Orestes (1–16).

The myth of Orestes (17–37). The poet admits
that he has wandered from his path, and brings the
digression to a close (38–40).

His Muse is bound, by the fee she has accepted, to
praise Thrasydaeus and his father for their victories

INTRODUCTION

in the games (41–50). The middle estate is to be preferred to the lot of tyrants (50–54). A victorious athlete, who lives a quiet life, baffles envy, dies happy, and leaves a good name behind him (54–58). Hence the fame of Iolaüs, and of Castor and Pollux (59–64).

XI.—ΘΡΑΣΥΔΑΙΩ ΘΗΒΑΙΩ

ΠΑΙΔΙ ΣΤΑΔΙΕΙ

στρ. α΄

Κάδμου κόραι, Σεμέλα μὲν Ὀλυμπιάδων
  ἀγυιᾶτις,
Ἰνώ τε Λευκοθέα ποντιᾶν ὁμοθάλαμε Νηρηΐδων,
ἴτε σὺν Ἡρακλέος ἀριστογόνῳ
ματρὶ πὰρ Μελίαν χρυσέων ἐς ἄδυτον τριπόδων
5 θησαυρόν, ὃν περίαλλ᾽ ἐτίμασε Λοξίας,

ἀντ. α΄

Ἰσμήνιον δ᾽ ὀνύμαξεν, ἀλαθέα μαντίων θῶκον,   10
ὦ παῖδες Ἁρμονίας, ἔνθα καί νυν ἐπίνομον
  ἡρωΐδων
στρατὸν ὁμαγερέα καλεῖ συνίμεν,
ὄφρα Θέμιν ἱερὰν Πυθῶνά τε καὶ ὀρθοδίκαν
10 γᾶς ὀμφαλὸν κελαδήσετ᾽ ἄκρᾳ σὺν ἑσπέρᾳ,

ἐπ. α΄

ἑπταπύλοισι Θήβαις
χάριν ἀγῶνί τε Κίρρας,   20
ἐν τῷ Θρασυδαῖος ἔμνασεν ἑστίαν
τρίτον ἐπὶ στέφανον πατρῴαν βαλών,
15 ἐν ἀφνεαῖς ἀρούραισι Πυλάδα
νικῶν ξένου Λάκωνος Ὀρέστα.

στρ. β΄

τὸν δὴ φονευομένου πατρὸς Ἀρσινόα Κλυταιμνή-
  στρας

8 ὁμαγερέα (Μ¹S), ὁμηγερέα BE (Μ²): ὁμαγυρέα (BGFC),
ὁμηγυρέα DG...   17 Κλυταιμήστρας S.

XI.—FOR THRASYDAEUS OF THEBES

WINNER IN THE BOYS' SHORT FOOT-RACE, 474 B.C.

YE daughters of Cadmus, Semelê that dwellest beside the Olympian gods, and Ino Leucothea, that sharest the chamber of the Nereid sea-nymphs, come with the nobly born mother of Heracles to the presence of Melia.[1] Come to the inmost treasure-house of the golden tripods, the treasure-house which Loxias honoured supremely and named the Ismenian shrine, the seat of truthful oracles. Come, ye children of Harmonia, where Loxias biddeth the host of heroines assemble to visit the shrine, that so at nightfall ye may sing the praises of holy Themis and Pytho and the centre of the world that judgeth rightly, in honour of seven-gated Thebes and the contest at Cirrha, in which Thrasydaeus caused his ancestral home to be remembered by flinging over it a third wreath, as victor in the rich fields of Pylades, the friend of Laconian Orestes.

Orestes, in sooth, at the slaying of his father, was received by his nurse Arsinoë from the strong hands of Clytaemnêstra and from her direful treachery,

---

[1] A daughter of Oceanus, who bore to Apollo at Thebes two sons Ismênius and Tênerus, and was therefore honoured in the Theban temple of Apollo Ismênius, south of the Cadmeia, near the river Ismênus, to which the other heroines are invited. Cp. Frag. 29 (5).

χειρῶν ὕπο κρατερᾶν ἐκ δόλου τροφὸς ἄνελε
 δυσπενθέος,
ὁπότε Δαρδανίδα κόραν Πριάμου
20 Κασσάνδραν πολιῷ χαλκῷ σὺν Ἀγαμεμνονίᾳ 30
ψυχᾷ πόρευσ' Ἀχέροντος ἀκτὰν παρ' εὔσκιον
ἀντ. β'
 νηλὴς γυνά. πότερόν νιν ἄρ' Ἰφιγένει' ἐπ' Εὐρίπῳ
σφαχθεῖσα τῆλε πάτρας ἔκνισεν βαρυπάλαμον
 ὄρσαι χόλον;
ἢ ἑτέρῳ λέχεϊ δαμαζομέναν
25 ἔννυχοι πάραγον κοῖται; τὸ δὲ νέαις ἀλόχοις 40
ἔχθιστον ἀμπλάκιον καλύψαι τ' ἀμάχανον
ἐπ. β'
 ἀλλοτρίαισι γλώσσαις·
κακολόγοι δὲ πολῖται.
ἴσχει τε γὰρ ὄλβος οὐ μείονα φθόνον·
30 ὁ δὲ χαμηλὰ πνέων ἄφαντον βρέμει.
θάνεν μὲν αὐτὸς ἥρως Ἀτρείδας
ἵκων χρόνῳ κλυταῖς ἐν Ἀμύκλαις,
στρ. γ'
 μάντιν τ' ὄλεσσε κόραν, ἐπεὶ ἀμφ' Ἑλένᾳ
πυρωθέντων 50
Τρώων ἔλυσε δόμους ἁβρότατος. ὁ δ' ἄρα
 γέροντα ξένον
35 Στρόφιον ἐξίκετο, νέα κεφαλά,
Παρνασοῦ πόδα ναίοντ'· ἀλλὰ χρονίῳ σὺν Ἄρει
πέφνεν τε ματέρα θῆκέ τ' Αἴγισθον ἐν φοναῖς.
ἀντ. γ'
 ἦ ῥ', ὦ φίλοι, κατ' ἀμευσιπόρους τριόδους
 ἐδινήθην,

21 πόρευσ' Vatican mss (BMGFC) : πόρευ' V (s).
23 ἔκνισεν Byzantine mss (BMGFC), ἔκνισε old mss: ἔκνιξεν S.

what time that ruthless woman with gray blade of
bronze, sped Cassandra, the Dardan daughter of
Priam, together with the soul of Agamemnon, to the
shadowy shore of Acheron. Was it haply the
slaughter of Iphigeneia at the Eurîpus, far from her
fatherland, that goaded her to the arousal of heavy-
handed wrath? or was it that nightly couchings led
her astray, when seduced by her union to another
lord?—a sin for newly wedded wives, most hate-
ful and impossible to dissemble by reason of alien
tongues; and even fellow-townsmen are apt to speak
evil. For prosperity is envied to its full heigth,
while the man of humble aspirations murmureth
unobserved.

The heroic son of Atreus, on his return after long
absence, was himself slain in famous Amyclae,[1] and
he caused the destruction of the prophetic maiden,
when he bereft of luxury the halls of the Trojans,
who were visited by fire for the sake of Helen;
while Orestes, the young child, safely reached
Strophius, the aged friend of the house, who dwelt
at the foot of Parnassus—Orestes, who, with the
tardy help of Ares, slew his mother, and laid
Aegisthus low in gore.

Verily, my friends, have I been in a whirl of con-
fusion at the point where one road changeth into two,

---

[1] Pindar, who in l. 16 describes Orestes as a Laconian,
here agrees with Stêsichorus in placing Agamemnon's palace
at Amyclae, near Sparta, where the traveller, Pausanias, saw
the monument of Agamemnon and the statue of Cassandra
(iii 19, 5). Homer and Aeschylus placed the palace at
Mycênae.

ὀρθὰν κέλευθον ἰὼν τὸ πρίν· ἦ μέ τις ἄνεμος ἔξω
    πλόου   60
40 ἔβαλεν, ὡς ὅτ᾽ ἄκατον εἰναλίαν;
    Μοῖσα, τὸ δὲ τεόν, εἰ μισθοῖο συνέθευ παρέχειν
    φωνὰν ὑπάργυρον, ἄλλοτ᾽ ἄλλᾳ ταρασσέμεν

ἐπ. γ′

    ἢ πατρὶ Πυθονίκῳ
    τό γέ νυν ἢ Θρασυδαίῳ·
45 τῶν εὐφροσύνα τε καὶ δόξ᾽ ἐπιφλέγει.   70
    τὰ μὲν <ἐν> ἅρμασι καλλίνικοι πάλαι,
    Ὀλυμπίᾳ ἀγώνων πολυφάτων
    ἔσχον θοὰν ἀκτῖνα σὺν ἵπποις·

στρ. δ′

    Πυθοῖ τε γυμνὸν ἐπὶ στάδιον καταβάντες ἤλεγξαν
50 Ἑλλανίδα στρατιὰν ὠκύτατι. θεόθεν ἐραίμαν
        καλῶν,
    δυνατὰ μαιόμενος ἐν ἁλικίᾳ.
    τῶν γὰρ ἂμ πόλιν εὑρίσκων τὰ μέσα μακροτέρῳ
    ὄλβῳ τεθαλότα, μέμφομ᾽ αἶσαν τυραννίδων·   80

ἀντ. δ′

    ξυναῖσι δ᾽ ἀμφ᾽ ἀρεταῖς τέταμαι. φθονεροὶ
        δ᾽ ἀμύνονται
55 ἆται, εἴ τις ἄκρον ἑλὼν ἀσυχᾷ τε νεμόμενος αἰνὰν
    ὕβριν

41 τὸ δὲ τεόν Moschopulus (BGFCS): τὸ δ᾽ ἐτεόν old mss
(M, Wilamowitz).   μισθοῖο (Christ) συνέθευ (GFCS),
παρέχειν: μισθῷ συνέθευ παρέχειν old mss; μισθῷ συνετίθεν
παρέχειν B; μισθῷ παρεχέμεν συνέθευ M.
46 <ἐν> Triclinius (edd.).
47 Ὀλυμπίᾳ Pauw (M¹FCS): Ὀλυμπίᾳ τ᾽ mss (M²); Ὀλυμπίαν
(BG); Ὀλυμπίας Erasmus Schmid.
52 ἄμ Hermann (BGC), ἂν Moschopulus: ἀνὰ BDE (MFS).
54 ξυναῖσι δ᾽ Vatican mss (BMGFC): ξυναῖσι Ambrosian mss,
—σιν Moschopulus (s).

although, aforetime, I was keeping to the right track ; or, haply, some breeze hath cast me out of my course, as though it had caught a skiff upon the sea. But, as thou, my Muse, didst bind thyself to lend thy tongue for fee of silver, thou must needs suffer it to flit, now one way, now another,—now to the father, who was victor at Pytho, now to his son, Thrasydaeus. For their glory and their good cheer shineth as one, with lustre new. Some prizes did they win of old, as famous victors in the chariot-race, when, from the noble contests at Olympia, they gat them glory for speed with their horses ; and again, at Pytho, when they went down into the lists of the stripped runners, they put to shame the Hellenic host by reason of their swiftness of foot. May the gods inspire my love for things fair, while, in the bloom of my life, I am eager only for that which is within my power. For of all the orders in the State, I find that the middle rank flourisheth with a more enduring prosperity, and I condemn the lot of tyrannies. I am eager for those virtues that serve the folk, but envious mischief-makers are warded off, if anyone, who hath won the highest place and

---

54 f. ἀμύνονται ἆται, εἴ τις Hermann (GC): ἀμύνονται ἆτα, εἴ τις mss ; —ἄτᾳ (scholium), εἴ τις (M) ; — ἆτα· τίς (S) ;—τᾶν εἴ τις Thiersch (B), — τᾶνδ' εἴ τις Maur. Schmidt.

ἀπέφυγεν· μέλανος ἂν ἐσχατιὰν
καλλίονα θανάτου <στείχοι>, γλυκυτάτᾳ γενεᾷ
εὐώνυμον κτεάνων κρατίσταν χάριν πορών.   90
ἐπ. δ'
      ἅ τε τὸν Ἰφικλείδαν
60 διαφέρει Ἰόλαον
      ὑμνητὸν ἐόντα, καὶ Κάστορος βίαν,
      σέ τε, ἄναξ Πολύδευκες, υἱοὶ θεῶν,
      τὸ μὲν παρ᾽ ἆμαρ ἕδραισι Θεράπνας,
      τὸ δ᾽ οἰκέοντας ἔνδον Ὀλύμπου.

56 f. μέλανος ἂν ἐσχατίαν — θανάτου <στείχοι> Wilamowitz
(s): μέλανος δ᾽ ἂν... mss; μέλανος ἂν Erasmus Schmid;
μέλανα δ᾽ (Hermann) ἀν᾽ ἐσχ. — θανάτον σχήσει B, — ἔσχεν F;
μέλανος ἂν ἐσχ. — θάνατον τοῦτον M¹; μέλανος ἀν᾽ ἐσχ. — θανάτου
ταύταν M²; μέλανος ὃ δ᾽ ἐσχ. — θανάτου τέτμεν G; μέλανα δ᾽ ἀν᾽
ἐσχ. κάλλιπεν θανατοῖ αἶσαν C.

dwelleth in peace, avoideth fell insolence. Such a man would march to the utmost verge of dark death, —death that is all the fairer because he hath left to his dearest offspring the grace of a good name, the best of all treasures.

Such is the grace that spreadeth abroad the fame of Iolaüs, son of Iphiclês, who is hymned in story, aye and of the mighty Castor, and of thee, king Polydeucês, ye sons of the gods—ye that dwell, for one day, in the homes of Therapnê, and, for the other, within the halls of Olympus.

PYTHIAN XII

FOR MIDAS OF ACRAGAS

INTRODUCTION

MIDAS of Acragas won the prize for flute-playing in the 24th and 25th Pythiads, that is, in 490 and 486 B.C. It is probably the earlier success (that of 490) which is here celebrated; otherwise, that earlier success would naturally have been mentioned in any commemoration of the later victory. Xenocrates of Acragas was successful in the chariot-race at the same Pythian festival (*Pyth.* vi). Midas was the master of the Athenian Lamprocles, who, in his turn, instructed Sophocles and Damon.

The αὐλὸς resembled a modern clarionet, and was played with a metal mouth-piece. The Scholiast states that Midas had the misfortune to break his mouth-piece, but continued playing, to the delight of the audience, and won the prize. Possibly this is the point of the reference to " unexpected success " in the last sentence of the Ode.

Acragas is summoned to welcome Midas on his return from a victory in the art invented by Athêna

INTRODUCTION

to imitate the wail of the Gorgons on the occasion
when Medusa was slain by Perseus (1–11).

The rest of the myth of Perseus (12–27).

There is no happiness without toil, but a god can
bring toil to an end, and either grant an unexpected
success, or withhold it (28–32).

XII.—ΜΙΔΑ ΑΚΡΑΓΑΝΤΙΝΩ

ΑΥΛΗΤΗ

στρ. α΄

Αἰτέω σε, φιλάγλαε, καλλίστα βροτεᾶν πολίων,
Φερσεφόνας ἕδος, ἅ τ᾽ ὄχθαις ἔπι μηλοβότου
ναίεις Ἀκράγαντος ἐΰδματον κολώναν, ὦ ἄνα,
ἵλαος ἀθανάτων ἀνδρῶν τε σὺν εὐμενίᾳ

5 δέξαι στεφάνωμα τόδ᾽ ἐκ Πυθῶνος εὐδόξῳ Μίδᾳ,   10
αὐτόν τέ νιν Ἑλλάδα νικάσαντα τέχνᾳ, τάν ποτε
Παλλὰς ἐφεῦρε θρασειᾶν Γοργόνων
οὔλιον θρῆνον διαπλέξαισ᾽ Ἀθάνα·

στρ. β΄

τὸν παρθενίοις ὑπό τ᾽ ἀπλάτοις ὀφίων κεφαλαῖς
10 ἄϊε λειβόμενον δυσπενθέϊ σὺν καμάτῳ,
Περσεὺς ὁπότε τρίτον ἄννυσεν κασιγνητᾶν
        μέρος,   20
εἰναλίᾳ τε Σερίφῳ λαοῖσί τε μοῖραν ἄγων.
ἦτοι τό τε θεσπέσιον Φόρκοιο μαύρωσεν γένος,
λυγρόν τ᾽ ἔρανον Πολυδέκτᾳ θῆκε ματρός τ᾽
        ἔμπεδον

---

12 τε Σερίφῳ λαοῖσί τε ΒΜ² ; τε Σερίφῳ τοῖσί τε Hermann¹²
(G) ; ἐ Σερίφῳ λαοῖσί τε : Σερίφῳ λαοῖσί τε mss (F? CS).

XII.—FOR MIDAS OF ACRAGAS

WINNER IN THE FLUTE-PLAYING MATCH, 490 B.C.

Lover of splendour, fairest of mortal cities, home of Persephonê! thou that inhabitest the hill of noble dwellings above the banks, where feed the sheep beside the stream of Acragas! I beseech thee, O queen, along with the kindly favour of gods and men, graciously to welcome, at the hands of renowned Midas, this coronal from Pytho. I beseech thee also to welcome himself, as champion over all Hellas in that art, which Pallas Athênê invented when she wove into music the dismal death-dirge of the Gorgons bold,—the dirge, that Perseus heard, while it was poured forth, amid direful woe, from beneath those maidens' awful serpent-heads, what time he did to death the third of those sisters three,[1] on the day when he brought doom on sea-girt Serîphus and its people. Verily, he reft of eye-sight the wondrous brood of Phorcus,[2] and made Polydectês bitterly rue his levying of gifts,[3] and the mother's[4]

---

[1] *i.e.* the Gorgons.

[2] The three Phorcides, who guarded the Gorgons, had only one eye among them. This eye was stolen by Perseus.

[3] "Polydectês, pretending that he was about to marry Hippodameia, called together the chiefs of his island (Serîphus) in order to receive from them the marriage gifts, ἕδνα, here called ἔρανος. Perseus offered him any gift he chose, even the head of Medusa, and Polydectês eagerly accepted his offer. Consequently, the head of Medusa which turned Polydectês into stone is here called a λυγρὸς ἔρανος" (Donaldson).   [4] Danaë's.

15 δουλοσύναν τό τ᾽ ἀναγκαῖον λέχος,
    εὐπαράου κρᾶτα συλάσαις Μεδοίσας
στρ. γ΄
    υἱὸς Δανάας· τὸν ἀπὸ χρυσοῦ φαμεν αὐτορύτου 30
    ἔμμεναι. ἀλλ᾽ ἐπεὶ ἐκ τούτων φίλον ἄνδρα
        πόνων
    ἐρρύσατο, παρθένος αὐλῶν τεῦχε πάμφωνον
        μέλος,
20 ὄφρα τὸν Εὐρυάλας ἐκ καρπαλιμᾶν γενύων
    χριμφθέντα σὺν ἔντεσι μιμήσαιτ᾽ ἐρικλάγκταν
        γόον.
    εὗρεν θεός· ἀλλά νιν εὑροῖσ᾽ ἀνδράσι θνατοῖς
        ἔχειν, 40
    ὠνόμασεν κεφαλᾶν πολλᾶν νόμον,
    εὐκλεᾶ λαοσσόων μναστῆρ᾽ ἀγώνων,
στρ. δ΄
25 λεπτοῦ διανισσόμενον χαλκοῦ θαμὰ καὶ δονάκων,
    τοὶ παρὰ καλλιχόρῳ ναίοισι πόλει Χαρίτων.
    Καφισίδος ἐν τεμένει, πιστοὶ χορευτᾶν μάρτυρες.
    εἰ δέ τις ὄλβος ἐν ἀνθρώποισιν, ἄνευ καμάτου 50
    οὐ φαίνεται· ἐκ δὲ τελευτάσει νιν ἤτοι σάμερον
30 δαίμων—τὸ δὲ μόρσιμον οὐ παρφυκτόν,—ἀλλ᾽
        ἔσται χρόνος
    οὗτος, ὃ καί τιν᾽ ἀελπτίᾳ βαλὼν
    ἔμπαλιν γνώμας τὸ μὲν δώσει, τὸ δ᾽ οὔπω.

26 πόλει V (BMGF); πόλῑ Bergk (S) : πόλιν BD (C).
30 τὸ δὲ Triclinius and scholium, Hermann (MCS): τό γε
mss (BGF).
31 ἀελπτίᾳ (BGFC), ἀελπτία DV : ἀελπία BPQ, ἀελπίᾳ (M),
ἀελπείᾳ conjectured by M (S).

long slavery and enforced wedlock, when the head
of the fair-faced Medusa was carried off by that son
of Danaë, by him who, we aver, was begotten of a
shower of gold. But, when the maiden goddess had
released her liegeman from these labours, she essayed
to invent the many-voiced music of flutes, that so,
by aid of music, she might imitate the cry exceeding
shrill that burst from the ravening jaws of Euryalê.[1]

'Twas the goddess that found it : but, when she
had found it for the use of mortal men, she called it
the "many-headed tune,"[2] that glorious incentive to
contests, where the folk foregather,—that tune,
which swelleth forth from the thin plate of brass,
and from the reeds which grow beside the fair city
of the Graces, in the holy ground of the nymph of
Cêphîsus, to be the true witnesses to the dancers.

But, if there be any bliss among mortal men, it
doth not reveal itself without toil ; yet a god may
bring that bliss to an end, verily, even to-day. That
which is fated cannot be fled ; but a time shall come
which, smiting with a stroke that is unforeseen, shall
grant one boon beyond all hope, but shall withhold
another.

---

[1] The name of one of the Gorgons.

[2] So called because it imitates the hisses of the many
serpents entwined in the Gorgons' hair. Plutarch, *De musica*,
c. 7, ascribes this tune either to the Phrygian Olympus, or
to his pupil Cratês. Schröder suggests that, though this
tune may refer to the serpent-headed Gorgons, it probably
characterised the variety of rhythm and content of the
"tune of Athênê," which was a counterpart of the famous
Pythian tune (*Hermes*, xxxix).

THE NEMEAN ODES

NEMEAN I

FOR CHROMIUS OF AETNA

INTRODUCTION

CHROMIUS, who claimed to be one of the Heracleidae, was originally a citizen of Gela. He distinguished himself under three Sicilian princes. Under Hippocrates, tyrant of Gela (488–491), he fought bravely in the battle on the Helôrus in 492 (*Nemean* ix 40), when Gela defeated Syracuse. Under Hippocrates' successor, Gelon (491–478), he married Gelon's sister, and, on Gelon's death in 478, become guardian of that ruler's son. Under Gelon's brother, Hieron, in 477 he was sent from Syracuse to save Locri from the hostile designs of Anaxilas of Rhegium, and, in 476, he was appointed governor of the newly founded city of Aetna and guardian to Hieron's son, Deinomenes, king of the new city. Of the four principal MSS, in which this Ode is preserved, two (*B* and *D*) have no superscription; the other two (*U* and *V*) have the superscription Χρομίῳ Αἰτναίῳ.

The date of the victory of Chromius in the chariot-race in the Nemean games is uncertain. It has been ascribed to the following years in which Nemean games were held :— 481 (Gaspar), 477 (L. Schmidt),

INTRODUCTION

476 (Schröder), 473 (Boeckh, Christ, Fennell, and Bury), and 471 (Bergk). If the victory was won in the Nemean games of 477, the celebration of the victory may have been deferred to 476, when Pindar was in Sicily. The most natural interpretations of lines 19–22, ἔσταν δ' ἐπ' αὐλείαις θύραις ἀνδρὸς φιλοξείνου κτλ, is that Pindar was present. The date of the Ode is therefore probably 476.

The Ode starts forth from Ortygia in Syracuse to laud Zeus the lord of Aetna, and to celebrate the victory won at Nemea by the chariot of Chromius (1–7). The foundation of the Ode is thus laid in heaven, and in the merits of the victor, and the Muse rejoices in celebrating victories won in the Greek games (8–12).

The praises of Sicily; its fertility, its famous cities, its glory in war, its success in the Olympic games (13–18). The hospitality of Chromius, whose merits must be set against the calumnies of his enemies (19–25). His gifts of strength and wisdom (25–30). Wealth must not be hoarded, but used for one's own enjoyment and for the benefit of friends (31f). Life is short and full of trouble (32f).

The myth of the infant Heracles, with the prophecy of his future labours, and of his final happiness (35–72).

NEMEONIKAI

I.—ΧΡΟΜΙΩ ΑΙΤΝΑΙΩ

ΙΠΠΟΙΣ

στρ. α΄

Ἄμπνευμα σεμνὸν Ἀλφεοῦ,
κλεινᾶν Συρακοσσᾶν θάλος Ὀρτυγία,
δέμνιον Ἀρτέμιδος,
Δάλου κασιγνήτα, σέθεν ἁδυεπὴς
5 ὕμνος ὁρμᾶται θέμεν
αἶνον ἀελλοπόδων μέγαν ἵππων, Ζηνὸς Αἰτναίου
χάριν·
ἅρμα δ᾽ ὀτρύνει Χρομίου Νεμέα θ᾽ ἔργμασιν
νικαφόροις ἐγκώμιον ζεῦξαι μέλος.   10

ἀντ. α΄

ἀρχαὶ δὲ βέβληνται θεῶν
κείνου σὺν ἀνδρὸς δαιμονίαις ἀρεταῖς.
10 ἔστι δ᾽ ἐν εὐτυχίᾳ
πανδοξίας ἄκρον· μεγάλων δ᾽ ἀέθλων
Μοῖσα μεμνᾶσθαι φιλεῖ.
σπεῖρέ νυν ἀγλαΐαν τινὰ νάσῳ, τὰν Ὀλύμπου
δεσπότας

7 θ᾽ ἔργμασιν mss (BMFCBu) : τ᾽ ἔργμασιν S.

316

THE NEMEAN ODES

I.—FOR CHROMIUS OF AETNA

WINNER IN THE CHARIOT RACE, 476 (?) B.C.

Hallowed spot, where Alpheüs breathed again,[1] Ortygia, scion of famous Syracuse,[2] resting-place of Artemis, sister of Delos[3]! From thee the sweet-voiced song speedeth forth to sound the mighty praise of storm-footed steeds, by grace of Zeus, the lord of Aetna. 'Tis the chariot of Chromius and Nemea that impel me to harness a song of praise for deeds of victory.

The foundations of our song have now been laid in the names of the gods, and in our hero's god-like merits; but in success is the crown of perfect glory; and mighty contests the Muse delighteth to remember.

Sow then some seed of fame athwart the isle, that

[1] The Arcadian river Alpheüs was said to have been enamoured of the nymph Arethusa, and to have followed her beneath the sea from Arcadia to Sicily, where she reappeared in the form of a fountain in Syracuse. Cp. Virgil, *Aen.* iii 695 f, and Milton's *Arcades*, 30 f.

[2] The island of Ortygia (with its fountain of Arethusa) was an important part of Syracuse. It was the site of the first settlement, and a bridge connected it with the later settlement on the mainland.

[3] Artemis was worshipped in Ortygia, because Arethusa was one of her nymphs. Ortygia, as well as Dêlos, was a haunt of Artemis; hence Ortygia is here called a "Sister of Delos."

PINDAR

Ζεὺς ἔδωκεν Φερσεφόνᾳ, κατένευσέν τέ οἱ χαίταις,
    ἀριστεύοισαν εὐκάρπου χθονὸς   20

ἐπ. α´

15 Σικελίαν πίειραν ὀρθώσειν κορυφαῖς πολίων
    ἀφνεαῖς.

    ὤπασε δὲ Κρονίων πολέμου μναστῆρά οἱ χαλκεν-
      τέος

    λαὸν ἵππαιχμον θαμὰ δὴ καὶ Ὀλυμπιάδων φύλ-
      λοις ἐλαιᾶν χρυσέοις

    μιχθέντα. πολλῶν ἐπέβαν καιρὸν οὐ ψεύδει
      βαλών.

στρ. β´

    ἔσταν δ᾽ ἐπ᾽ αὐλείαις θύραις

20 ἀνδρὸς φιλοξείνου καλὰ μελπόμενος,   30
    ἔνθα μοι ἁρμόδιον

    δεῖπνον κεκόσμηται, θαμὰ δ᾽ ἀλλοδαπῶν
    οὐκ ἀπείρατοι δόμοι

    ἐντί· λέλογχε δὲ μεμφομένοις ἐσλοὺς ὕδωρ καπνῷ
      φέρειν

25 ἀντίον. τέχναι δ᾽ ἑτέρων ἕτεραι· χρὴ δ᾽ ἐν εὐθείαις
    ὁδοῖς στείχοντα μάρνασθαι φυᾷ.

ἀντ. β´

    πράσσει γὰρ ἔργῳ μὲν σθένος,

    βουλαῖσι δὲ φρήν, ἐσσόμενον προϊδεῖν   40
    συγγενὲς οἷς ἕπεται.

    Ἀγησιδάμου παῖ, σέο δ᾽ ἀμφὶ τρόπῳ

30 τῶν τε καὶ τῶν χρήσιες.

    οὐκ ἔραμαι πολὺν ἐν μεγάρῳ πλοῦτον κατακρύ-
      ψαις ἔχειν,

24 λέλογχε mss (edd.): λέλογχα Gildersleeve, *A.J.P.* xxx
(1909) 233.

318

Zeus, the lord of Olympus, gave to Persephonê, and shook his locks in token unto her that, as queen of the teeming earth, the fertile land of Sicily would be raised to renown by the wealth of her glorious cities; and the son of Cronus granted that the host of armed horsemen, that awaketh the memory of bronze-clad war, would full oft be wedded with the golden leaves of Olympia's olive.

Lo! I have lighted on a varied theme, without flinging one false word. Sweet are the strains that I sing as I stand at the portals of the court of a hospitable hero, where a befitting banquet hath been prepared for me, and where the halls are oft familiar with strangers from afar. His lot it is to have true friends to ply against his slanderers, like water against smoke. Various men excel, indeed, in various ways; but it is meet that a man should walk in straight paths, and strive according to his powers of Nature; for might of limb maketh itself manifest by action, and might of mind by counsel, for those who are attended by the inborn skill of foreseeing the future. But, within the compass of thy character, O son of Agesidâmus, thou hast the use of both these boons alike.

I love not to keep much wealth buried in my hall, but of my abundance to do good to myself

ἀλλ' ἐόντων εὖ τε παθεῖν καὶ ἀκοῦσαι φίλοις
ἐξαρκέων. κοιναὶ γὰρ ἔρχοντ' ἐλπίδες
ἐπ. β'
πολυπόνων ἀνδρῶν. ἐγὼ δ' Ἡρακλέος ἀντέχομαι
προφρόνως,   50
ἐν κορυφαῖς ἀρετᾶν μεγάλαις ἀρχαῖον ὀτρύνων
λόγον,
35 ὡς, ἐπεὶ σπλάγχνων ὕπο ματέρος αὐτίκα θαητὰν
ἐς αὔγλαν παῖς Διὸς
ὠδῖνα φεύγων διδύμῳ σὺν κασιγνήτῳ μόλεν,
στρ. γ'
ὡς οὐ λαθὼν χρυσόθρονον
Ἥραν κροκωτὸν σπάργανον ἐγκατέβα·
ἀλλὰ θεῶν βασίλεα
40 σπερχθεῖσα θυμῷ πέμπε δράκοντας ἄφαρ.   60
τοὶ μὲν οἰχθεισᾶν πυλᾶν
ἐς θαλάμου μυχὸν εὐρὺν ἔβαν, τέκνοισιν ὠκείας
γνάθους
ἀμφελίξασθαι μεμαῶτες· ὁ δ' ὀρθὸν μὲν ἄντεινεν
κάρα, πειρᾶτο δὲ πρῶτον μάχας,
ἀντ. γ'
δισσαῖσι δοιοὺς αὐχένων
45 μάρψαις ἀφύκτοις χερσὶν ἑαῖς ὄφιας·
ἀγχομένοις δὲ χρόνος
ψυχὰς ἀπέπνευσεν μελέων ἀφάτων.   70
ἐκ δ' ἄρ' ἄτλατον βέλος
πλᾶξε γυναῖκας, ὅσαι τύχον Ἀλκμήνας ἀρήγοι-
σαι λέχει·
50 καὶ γὰρ αὐτά, ποσσὶν ἄπεπλος ὀρούσαισ' ἀπὸ
στρωμνᾶς, ὅμως ἄμυνεν ὕβριν κνωδάλων.

39 βασίλεα Heyne, Bergk (cBus): βασίλεια mss; βασιλέα
(BMF).

320

and to win a good name by bestowing it on my friends; for the hopes and fears of toiling men come unto all alike.

But, as for me, my heart cleaveth fast unto the theme of Heracles, while, amid the greatest and loftiest deeds of prowess, I wake the memory of that olden story, which telleth how, at the time when the son of Zeus, with his twin-brother, suddenly came from his mother's birth-pangs with the light of day;—how, I say, when he was laid in his saffron swathing-bands, he escaped not the ken of Hêra on her golden throne. Stung with wrath, that queen of the gods sent anon two serpents.

Soon as the doors were opened, they crept on to the spacious inner-chamber, yearning to coil their darting jaws around the babes. Yet he lifted up his head, and made his first essay of battle, by seizing the twain serpents by their necks in his twain irresistible hands, and, while they were being strangled, the lapse of time breathed forth their souls from out their monstrous limbs. Meanwhile, a pang intolerable pierced the hearts of the women, who at the time were rendering help by the bedside of Alcmena; for even she herself leapt with all speed to her feet, and, unrobed as she was, she yet essayed to stay the rude onslaught of the monsters.

ἐπ. γ΄

   ταχὺ δὲ Καδμείων ἀγοὶ χαλκέοις ἀθρόοι σὺν
     ὅπλοις ἔδραμον·
   ἐν χερὶ δ᾿ Ἀμφιτρύων κολεοῦ γυμνὸν τινάσσων
     <φάσγανον>   80
   ἵκετ᾿, ὀξείαις ἀνίαισι τυπείς. τὸ γὰρ οἰκεῖον πιέζει
     πάνθ᾿ ὁμῶς·
   εὐθὺς δ᾿ ἀπήμων κραδία κᾶδος ἀμφ᾿ ἀλλότριον.

στρ. δ΄

55 ἔστα δὲ θάμβει δυσφόρῳ
   τερπνῷ τε μιχθείς. εἶδε γὰρ ἐκνόμιον
   λῆμά τε καὶ δύναμιν
   υἱοῦ· παλίγγλωσσον δέ οἱ ἀθάνατοι
   ἀγγέλων ῥῆσιν θέσαν.
60 γείτονα δ᾿ ἐκκάλεσεν Διὸς ὑψίστου προφάταν
     ἔξοχον,   90
   ὀρθόμαντιν Τειρεσίαν· ὁ δέ οἱ φράζε καὶ παντὶ
     στρατῷ, ποίαις ὁμιλήσει τύχαις,

ἀντ. δ΄

   ὅσσους μὲν ἐν χέρσῳ κτανών,
   ὅσσους δὲ πόντῳ θῆρας ἀϊδροδίκας·
   καί τινα σὺν πλαγίῳ
65 ἀνδρῶν κόρῳ στείχοντα τὸν ἐχθρότατον
   φᾶσέ νιν δώσειν μόρῳ.
   καὶ γὰρ ὅταν θεοὶ ἐν πεδίῳ Φλέγρας Γιγάντεσσιν
     μάχαν   100
   ἀντιάζωσιν, βελέων ὑπὸ ῥιπαῖσι κείνου φαιδίμαν
     γαίᾳ πεφύρσεσθαι κόμαν

52 <φάσγανον> Moschopulus (edd.).

66 μόρῳ B²F; τῷ ἐχθροτάτῳ—μόρῳ C; φᾶσ᾿ αἰστώσειν
μόρῳ S¹ : μόρον mss (MS³); φᾶσέ νιν πώσειν μόρον Bury.

322

Then swiftly the chiefs of the Cadmeans hastened
in a throng with their brazen armour; and Amphi-
tryon, brandishing in his hand a sword bared from the
scabbard, came smitten with keen throes of anguish.
For each alike is distressed by his own trouble,
whereas, for a stranger's sorrow, the heart is at once
consoled.   And there he stood, possessed with
rapture overpowering and delightful; for he saw the
strange spirit and power of his son, since the immor-
tals had turned to falsehood for him the story of the
messengers. And he called forth one that dwelt nigh
to him, even that chosen prophet of Zeus supreme,
the truthful seer, Teiresias.   And the prophet told
him and all the host, what fortunes the boy was
destined to encounter,—how many lawless monsters
he would slay on the dry land and how many upon
the sea; and he said that there was one most hateful,
one who walked in the crooked path of envy, whom
he would do to death.[1]   He said, moreover, that
when the gods shall meet the giants[2] in battle on
the plain of Phlegra, their foes shall soon find their
bright tresses befouled with dust beneath that

[1] The giant Antaeus. Cp. *I.* iii 70.
[2] Alcyoneus, and the other giants, slain by Heracles in the
Phlegraean plain, in Campania. Cp. *I.* vi 32.

PINDAR

ἐπ. δ´

ἔνεπεν· αὐτὸν μὰν ἐν εἰράνᾳ καμάτων μεγάλων
    ‹ἐν› σχερῷ
70 ἀσυχίαν τὸν ἅπαντα χρόνον ποινὰν λαχόντ᾽ ἐξαί-
    ρετον
ὀλβίοις ἐν δώμασι, δεξάμενον θαλερὰν ῞Ηβαν
    ἄκοιτιν καὶ γάμον
δαίσαντα, πὰρ Δὶ Κρονίδᾳ σεμνὸν αἰνήσειν
    δόμον.   110

69 ‹ἐν› Hermann (edd.).
72 δόμον Vatican recension (B), σεμνὸς mainly an epithet of
holy persons and *places*: γάμον Ambrosian recension; νόμον
scholium (MCS); λέχος F; σταθμόν Bury.

hero's rushing arrows, but he himself, at rest from mighty labours, shall have allotted to him, as his choicest prize, peace that would endure for ever in the homes of bliss, where, on receiving Hêbê as his blushing bride, and celebrating the marriage feast, he shall glorify his hallowed home in the presence of Zeus the son of Cronus.

NEMEAN II

FOR TÎMODÊMUS OF ACHARNAE

INTRODUCTION

TÎMODÊMUS, son of Tîmonoüs, belonged to the deme
Acharnae (16) and the family of the Tîmodêmidae.
He was probably brought up in Salamis (13). He
was victorious in the pancratium (a combination of
boxing and wrestling, first introduced in the 33rd
Olympiad, 648 B.C.)

As Salamis is mentioned in this Ode only in
connexion with Ajax, and without any mention of
the naval battle of 480, it may be assumed that the
Ode is earlier than the date of that battle. It may
possibly belong to the Nemean year **485** (suggested
by Schröder) or 487 (preferred by Gaspar). In the
latter case the victor's hopes of future successes may
have been fulfilled at the Isthmian games of April,
and the Pythian of August 486, and the Olympian of
August 484. These dates are not already filled up
with the names of any other pancratiasts.

As the rhapsodes begin by invoking Zeus, so
Tîmodêmus has begun his career with a victory in the
Nemean grove of Zeus (1–5). He may hope to con-
tinue to follow the example of his family by victories

at the Isthmian and Pythian games (6–10). It is meet that the constellation of Orion should rise not far from that of the Pleiades [1] (10–12). Salamis can rear fighting men, whether it be the warrior Ajax, or the pancratiast, Tîmodêmus (13–15). Acharnae is famous of old, and the victor's family has been successful in the Pythian, Isthmian, and Nemean games, and in the Athenian festival of the Olympian Zeus (16–24). Let the citizens, in their triumphal chorus, worship the god, and honour the victor (24 f).

---

[1] Explained by Bury as a reference to the *seven* Nemean victories of his family. See also note on l. 11.

II.—ΤΙΜΟΔΗΜΩ ΑΧΑΡΝΕΙ

ΠΑΓΚΡΑΤΙΑΣΤῌ

στρ. α΄

Ὅθεν περ καὶ Ὁμηρίδαι
ῥαπτῶν ἐπέων τὰ πόλλ᾽ ἀοιδοὶ
ἄρχονται, Διὸς ἐκ προοιμίου· καὶ ὅδ᾽ ἀνὴρ
καταβολὰν ἱερῶν ἀγώνων νικαφορίας δέδεκται
    πρῶτον Νεμεαίου
5 ἐν πολυυμνήτῳ Διὸς ἄλσει.

στρ. β΄

ὀφείλει δ᾽ ἔτι, πατρίαν
εἴπερ καθ᾽ ὁδόν νιν εὐθυπομπὸς   10
αἰὼν ταῖς μεγάλαις δέδωκε κόσμον Ἀθάναις,
θαμὰ μὲν Ἰσθμιάδων δρέπεσθαι κάλλιστον ἄωτον,
    ἐν Πυθίοισί τε νικᾶν
10 Τιμονόου παῖδ᾽· ἔστι δ᾽ ἐοικὸς

στρ. γ΄

ὀρειᾶν γε Πελειάδων
μὴ τηλόθεν Ὠαρίωνα νεῖσθαι.
καὶ μὰν ἁ Σαλαμίς γε θρέψαι φῶτα μαχατὰν   20
δυνατός. ἐν Τρωΐᾳ μὲν Ἕκτωρ Αἴαντος ἄκουσεν·
    ὦ Τιμόδημε, σὲ δ᾽ ἀλκὰ
15 παγκρατίου τλάθυμος ἀέξει.

---

4 πρῶτον mss and scholia : πρώταν? Heyne (B).
12 Ὠαρίωνα mss (BMFCBu) : Ὀαρίωνα Athenaeus 490 f (S).
  νεῖσθαι TUV (BMFCS) : ἀνεῖσθαι BD (Bury).
14 ἄκουσεν mss (BMFBuS²) : ἄεισεν W. Schulze (S¹F) ; ἐπάϊσ᾽
Bergk (C).

328

II.—FOR TIMODÊMUS OF ACHARNAE

WINNER IN THE PANCRATIUM, 485 (?) B.C.

Even as the sons of Homer, those singers of deftly woven lays, begin most often with Zeus for their prelude; even so hath our hero laid a first foundation for a tale of achievements in the sacred games by receiving a crown in the storied grove of Nemean Zeus. But if fate, which guideth him aright in his ancestral path, hath indeed given him as a glory to great Athens, it needs must be that the son of Tîmonoüs should full often, in the days to come, cull the flower most fair of the Isthmian games and be victorious in the Pythian contests. And meet it is that Orion should not move far behind the (seven) mountain Pleiads.[1] And, verily, Salamis might well be able to rear a warrior:—in Troy did Hector hear of [2] Aias, while thou, O Tîmodêmus, art exalted by thy enduring courage in the pancratium. But Acharnae

---

[1] In mythology, the hunter Orion pursued the Pleiades for five years through the woods of Boeotia; and, when they were placed among the stars, the constellation of Orion was immediately to the south of that of Taurus, which included the seven Pleiades. The Pleiades rise about the middle of May, and Orion, a week later. Pindar implies that the seven Nemean victories of the sons of Tîmonoüs will soon be succeeded by a great Pythian victory on the part of Tîmodêmus.

[2] (1) "learned by experience" the might of Aias, or, more probably, (2) "heard from" Aias the renown of Salamis (cp. *Il.* vii 198), *Class. Rev.* vi 3.

στρ. δ

Ἀχάρναι δὲ παλαίφατοι
εὐάνορες· ὅσσα δ' ἀμφ' ἀέθλοις,
Τιμοδημίδαι ἐξοχώτατοι προλέγονται.
παρὰ μὲν ὑψιμέδοντι Παρνασῷ τέσσαρας ἐξ
ἀέθλων νίκας ἐκόμιξαν·   30
20 ἀλλὰ Κορινθίων ὑπὸ φωτῶν

στρ. ε

ἐν ἐσλοῦ Πέλοπος πτυχαῖς
ὀκτὼ στεφάνοις ἔμιχθεν ἤδη·
ἑπτὰ δ' ἐν Νεμέᾳ—τὰ δ' οἴκοι μάσσον' ἀριθμοῦ—
Διὸς ἀγῶνι. τόν, ὦ πολῖται, κωμάξατε Τιμοδήμῳ
σὺν εὐκλέϊ νόστῳ·
25 ἀδυμελεῖ δ' ἐξάρχετε φωνᾷ.   40

even of old is famous for heroes; and, for all that
toucheth contests, the sons of Tîmodêmus are pro-
claimed preëminent.   By the lofty throne of
Parnassus, they bore away four victories from the
games, while by the Corinthians they have ere now
been wedded with eight garlands in the glades of
mighty Pelops,[1] and with seven at Nemea in the con-
test of Zeus; while the prizes they have won at home
are beyond all counting.   Praise him, O ye citizens,
with the song of triumph, at the bidding of
Tîmodêmus, when he cometh home again with glory,
and begin the song with sweetly-sounding strains.

[1] At the Isthmian games.

NEMEAN III

FOR ARISTOCLEIDES OF AEGINA

INTRODUCTION

THE third Nemean celebrates a victory in the pancratium won by Aristocleides of Aegina, where he appears to have belonged to a guild of festal envoys sent from time to time from Aegina to Delphi. Some years had passed since the victory had been won, and the victor was now, apparently, advanced in age (73–76). The close resemblance between the passages on the "Pillars of Heracles" (21) and on the "Eagle and the daws," (80–82), and those in the Third Olympian (43 f) and the Second (54 f) respectively, have led to the present poem being ascribed to the same general time as the Olympian odes of 476, and, in particular, to the Nemean year of 475. Aegina was then enjoying the tranquillity which followed the battles of Salamis and Plataea. The Ode was sung in the Hall [1] of the festal envoys (70), on an anniversary of the victory (2).

---

[1] The Alexandrian critic, Aristarchus, supposed that it was sung on the site of the Nemean victory, and that the Asôpus of l. 4 was "near Phlius and Nemea"; but Nemea is separated from the valley of the Asôpus, which flows from Phlius to Sicyon (N. ix 9), by a mountain 3000 feet high. Another Alexandrian critic, Didymus, suggested that there may have been a stream of that name in Aegina, but the largest stream in that island is dry for the greater part of the year, and it falls into the sea on a side of the island far distant from the town of Aegina. See further in note on l. 4.

INTRODUCTION

The Muse is bidden to come to Aegina, because the chorus is waiting beside the Asopian water [1] to rehearse the Ode which is the victor's highest ambition (1–8).

She is also bidden to sing of the Nemean Zeus, and of Aegina, the island of the Myrmidons (9–14), on which no discredit has been brought by the victor (14–18), who, by his surpassing valour in the pancratium, has reached the Pillars of Heracles (19–26).

From this digression the poet returns to tell of the race of Aeacus (28) and the myth of Peleus (31–39), and illustrates the doctrine of the importance of innate merit by the legend of the youth of Achilles (40–64).

Thereupon he invokes Zeus, whose Nemean festival is the theme of the Ode (15 f). The victor has added glory to Aegina and to the guild of the festal envoys (87–90), Trial gives proof of merit in all the four stages of life, and the victor has all the virtues appropriate to each (70–76).

The poet, in sending his Ode, adds that, late though it be, the eagle can swoop from afar on his enemy (80–82). By the blessing of Clio, Aristocleides has won glory from Nemea and Epidaurus and Megara (83 f).

[1] The best course is to assume that the "Asopian water" is the famous river Asôpus, which flows across southern Boeotia, south of the poet's native town of Thebes. On beginning to compose this Ode in his own home, Pindar calls on the Muse to "come" to Aegina, i.e. the theme of Aegina. As a reason he adds that the young men of his chorus are waiting at Thebes for her inspiration. Clearly the composition of the Ode has been long delayed (cp. l. 80). By "this isle" (l. 68) the poet means "the isle which is my theme," but, to the ultimate audience, it becomes the isle which is the scene of the final performance of the Ode.

III.—ΑΡΙΣΤΟΚΛΕΙΔῌ ΑΙΓΙΝΗΤῌ

ΠΑΓΚΡΑΤΙΑΣΤῌ

στρ. α΄

Ὦ πότνια Μοῖσα, μᾶτερ ἁμετέρα, λίσσομαι,
τὰν πολυξέναν ἐν ἱερομηνίᾳ Νεμεάδι
ἵκεο Δωρίδα νᾶσον Αἴγιναν· ὕδατι γὰρ
μένοντ᾽ ἐπ᾽ Ἀσωπίῳ μελιγαρύων τέκτονες
5 κώμων νεανίαι, σέθεν ὄπα μαιόμενοι.
διψῇ δὲ πρᾶγος ἄλλο μὲν ἄλλου· 10
ἀεθλονικία δὲ μάλιστ᾽ ἀοιδὰν φιλεῖ,
στεφάνων ἀρετᾶν τε δεξιωτάταν ὀπαδόν·

ἀντ. α΄

τᾶς ἀφθονίαν ὄπαζε μήτιος ἀμᾶς ἄπο·
10 ἄρχε δ᾽ οὐρανοῦ πολυνεφέλα κρέοντι, θύγατερ,
δόκιμον ὕμνον· ἐγὼ δὲ κείνων τέ νιν ὀάροις
λύρᾳ τε κοινάσομαι. χαρίεντα δ᾽ ἕξει πόνον 20
χώρας ἄγαλμα, Μυρμιδόνες ἵνα πρότεροι
ᾤκησαν, ὧν παλαίφατον ἀγορὰν
15 οὐκ ἐλεγχέεσσιν Ἀριστοκλείδας τεὰν
ἐμίανε κατ᾽ αἶσαν ἐν περισθενεῖ μαλαχθεὶς

ἐπ. α΄

παγκρατίου στόλῳ· καματωδέων δὲ πλαγᾶν

9 ἁμᾶς V (BMFBu) : ἁμᾶς B (CS).

10 οὐρανοῦ (BFCBuS) οὐρανῷ mss (M). πολυνεφέλα mss
(BFCBu) : —λα Aldus (MS). οὐρανοῦ πολυνεφέλᾳ (BFCBu), οὐ-
ρανοῦ πολυνεφέλᾳ (S), οὐρανῷ πολυνεφέλᾳ (M).

334

III.—FOR ARISTOCLEIDES OF AEGINA

WINNER IN THE PANCRATIUM, 475 (?) B.C.

O QUEENLY Muse, our mother! come, I beseech thee, on the festal day of Nemea, to the hospitable isle of the Dorian Aegina. For, lo! beside the Asôpian water,[1] youthful craftsmen of honey-sweet triumph-songs are waiting, longing for thy voice. Various deeds thirst for various rewards; but victory in the games loveth beyond all things the meed of song, the fittest accompaniment of crowns and of valiant exploits. Grant thou thereof no grudging share, the fruit of mine own fancy; and, in honour of the ruler of the cloud-wrapt heaven, do thou, his daughter, begin a hymn approved of all, while I shall blend it with the lays of those singers, and with the lyre. It will be a gladsome toil to glorify the land, where dwelt the Myrmidons of old, the ancient fame of whose meeting for the games Aristocleides, thanks to thy favour, did not sully with dishonour by proving himself too weak amid the host that strove in the pancratium; but, in the deep

[1] Among the daughters of the Boeotian river-god Asôpus, were the Asôpides, Thêbê and Aegina (*I.* viii 19). The latter was wedded to Zeus in the island, which derived from her its new name of Aegina. Asôpis, the synonym for the nymph, might easily be used as a name for the island. "Asôpian water" may therefore mean "the water of Aegina," *i.e.* the water of the sea off the town of Aegina, where the youths were waiting to sing this Ode. Miss Hutchinson, in the *Ridgeway Essays*, p. 222, similarly makes it "the sea around Aegina." See also p. 332 *supra.*

ἄκος ὑγιηρὸν ἐν βαθυπεδίῳ Νεμέᾳ τὸ καλλί-
   νικον φέρει.   30
   εἰ δ' ἐὼν καλὸς ἔρδων τ' ἐοικότα μορφᾷ
20 ἀνορέαις ὑπερτάταις ἐπέβα παῖς Ἀριστοφάνεος·
      οὐκέτι πρόσω
   ἀβάταν ἅλα κιόνων ὑπὲρ Ἡρακλέος περᾶν εὐ-
      μαρές,
στρ. β´

   ἥρως θεὸς ἃς ἔθηκε ναυτιλίας ἐσχάτας
   μάρτυρας κλυτάς· δάμασε δὲ θῆρας ἐν πελά-
      γεσιν   40
   ὑπερόχοις, διά τ' ἐξερεύνασε τεναγέων
25 ῥοάς, ὅπα πόμπιμον κατέβαινε νόστου τέλος,
   καὶ γᾶν φράδασσε. θυμέ, τίνα πρὸς ἀλλοδαπὰν
   ἄκραν ἐμὸν πλόον παραμείβεαι;
   Αἰακῷ σε φαμὶ γένει τε Μοῖσαν φέρειν,
   ἕπεται δὲ λόγῳ δίκας ἄωτος, "ἐσλὸς αἰνεῖν·"   50
ἀντ. β´

30 οὐδ' ἀλλοτρίων ἔρωτες ἀνδρὶ φέρειν κρέσσονες·
   οἴκοθεν μάτευε. ποτίφορον δὲ κόσμον ἔλαβες
   γλυκύ τι γαρυέμεν. παλαιαῖσι δ' ἐν ἀρεταῖς
   γέγαθε Πηλεὺς ἄναξ ὑπέραλλον αἰχμὰν ταμών·
   ὃς καὶ Ἰωλκὸν εἷλε μόνος ἄνευ στρατιᾶς,
35 καὶ ποντίαν Θέτιν κατέμαρψεν   60

18 ἐν βαθυπεδίῳ *BD* (MFCBuS) : ἐν βαθυπέδῳ *XZ*¹, ἔν γε
βαθυπέδῳ Moschopulus, Hermann, B, Bergk.
20 Ἀριστοφάνεος (MFS) : —φάνευς *V* (BCBu) ; —φάνους
Vatican recension.   22 ἥρῳ θεὸς Postgate.
24 ὑπερόχοις (Doric acc.) old mss (BF) : —χους Moschopulus
(MCBuS).
29 ἐσλὸς (Doric acc.) *D* (BMFCBu) : ἐσλὸν *B* (S).
31 ἔλαβες mss (BMFCBu) : ἔλαχες scholium, Bergk (S).
32 γαρυέμεν παλαιαῖσιν ἐν ἀρεταῖς. Donaldson.
34 καὶ Ἰωλκὸν mss (BMF) : καὶ Φιωλκὸν (CBu) ; κίαολκὸν (S).

plain of Nemea, he carrieth off his victory as a
healing remedy for all those weary blows. But, if
the son of Aristophanes, being fair to look upon, and
doing deeds that befit the fairness of his form, em-
barked on the highest achievements of manly
prowess, no further is it easy for him to sail across
the trackless sea beyond the pillars of Heracles,
which that hero and god set up as far-famed wit-
nesses of the furthest limit of voyaging. He quelled
the monstrous beasts amid the seas, and tracked to
the very end the streams of the shallows, there where
he reached the bourne that sped him home again ;
and he made known the limits of the land.

To what foreign foreland, O my fancy, art thou
turning aside the course of thy voyage ? I bid thee
summon the Muse in honour of Aeacus, but the
flower of justice still attendeth the precept, " praise
the noble." Nor should any man prefer to foster pas-
sionate longings for what belongeth to others. Search
at home, and thou hast won a fitting theme for
praise, to prompt sweet melody. For, among older
examples of valour is king Pêleus, who rejoiced in
having cloven a matchless spear,[1]—who, alone,
without a host, overcame Iolcus, and after many a
struggle seized as a captive the sea-nymph Thetis.[2]

[1] Cut by Pêleus on Mount Pêlion, *Il.* xvi 143.
[2] Cp. note on *N.* iv 65.

ἐγκονητί. Λαομέδοντα δ' εὐρυσθενὴς
Τελαμὼν Ἰόλᾳ παραστάτας ἐὼν ἔπερσεν·

ἐπ. β´

καί ποτε χαλκότοξον Ἀμαζόνων μετ' ἀλκὰν
ἕπετό οἱ· οὐδέ νίν ποτε φόβος ἀνδροδάμας ἔπαυ-
σεν ἀκμὰν φρενῶν.

40 συγγενεῖ δέ τις εὐδοξίᾳ μέγα βρίθει·   70
ὃς δὲ διδάκτ' ἔχει, ψεφηνὸς ἀνὴρ ἄλλοτ' ἄλλα
πνέων οὔ ποτ' ἀτρεκεῖ
κατέβα ποδί, μυριᾶν δ' ἀρετᾶν ἀτελεῖ νόῳ γεύεται.

στρ. γ´

ξανθὸς δ' Ἀχιλεὺς τὰ μὲν μένων Φιλύρας ἐν
δόμοις
παῖς ἐὼν ἄθυρε μεγάλα ἔργα, χερσὶ θαμινὰ
45 βραχυσίδαρον ἄκοντα πάλλων, ἴσα τ' ἀνέμοις   80
μάχᾳ λεόντεσσιν ἀγροτέροις ἔπρασσεν φόνον,
κάπρους τ' ἔναιρε, σώματα δὲ παρὰ Κρονίδαν
Κένταυρον ἀσθμαίνοντα κόμιζεν,
ἑξέτης τὸ πρῶτον, ὅλον δ' ἔπειτ' ἂν χρόνον·
50 τὸν ἐθάμβεον Ἄρτεμίς τε καὶ θρασεῖ Ἀθάνα,

ἀντ. γ´

κτείνοντ' ἐλάφους ἄνευ κυνῶν δολίων θ' ἑρκέων·
ποσσὶ γὰρ κράτεσκε. λεγόμενον δὲ τοῦτο προ-
τέρων   90
ἔπος ἔχω· βαθυμῆτα Χείρων τράφε λιθίνῳ
Ἰάσον' ἔνδον τέγει, καὶ ἔπειτεν Ἀσκληπιον,
55 τὸν φαρμάκων δίδαξε μαλακόχειρα νόμον·

41 ψεφηνὸς mss, and lemma of scholia in *BV* (BMFBu).
ψεφεννὸς (CS).
50 ἐθάμβεον Moschopulus (MFCBuS): ἐθάμβευν *BV*; ἐθάμβεεν
Triclinius (B).   53 Χίρων S.

And Laomedon was laid low by Telamon, whose might is famed afar as comrade of Iolaüs, whom erst he followed, to fight the mighty Amazons with their brazen bows ; nor did fear, that quelleth men, ever subdue that heroic soul. 'Tis by means of inborn valour that a man hath mighty power, but he who hath learnt all his lore, dwelleth in darkness, breathing changeful purposes, never entering the lists with a firm step, but essaying countless forms of prowess with ineffectual spirit. Whereas Achilles of the golden hair, while lingering in the home of Philyra,[1] and while yet a child, disported himself in mighty deeds, full often brandishing in his hands a javelin with its tiny blade ; and fleet as the wind, he was wont to deal slaughter in fight with savage lions, and he would slay wild boars and carry their panting bodies to the Centaur, son of Cronus, at six years of age at first, but afterwards for all his time : while Artemis and bold Athênê gazed at him with wonder, as he slew stags without help of hounds or of crafty nets, for he excelled in fleetness of foot. Oft told by men of yore is the tale I have to tell :— The sage Cheiron, dwelling under a rocky roof, nurtured the youth of Jason, and after him that of Asclêpius, whom he taught the gentle-handed lore of simples. In due time he won in wedlock for

---

[1] The mother of the Centaur Cheiron.

PINDAR

νυμφευσε δ᾽ αὖτις ἀγλαόκαρπον
Νηρέος θύγατρα, γόνον τέ οἱ φέρτατον
ἀτίταλλεν, <ἐν> ἁρμένοισι πᾶσι θυμὸν αὔξων· 100

ἐπ. γ´

ὄφρα θαλασσίαις ἀνέμων ῥιπαῖσι πεμφθεὶς
60 ὑπὸ Τρωΐαν, δορίκτυπον ἀλαλὰν Λυκίων τε προσ-
μένοι καὶ Φρυγῶν
Δαρδάνων τε, καὶ ἐγχεσφόροις ἐπιμίξαις
Αἰθιόπεσσι χεῖρας, ἐν φρασὶ πάξαιθ᾽, ὅπως σφίσι
μὴ κοίρανος ὀπίσω
πάλιν οἴκαδ᾽ ἀνεψιὸς ζαμενὴς Ἑλένοιο Μέμνων
μόλοι. 110

στρ. δ´

τηλαυγὲς ἄραρε φέγγος Αἰακιδᾶν αὐτόθεν·
65 Ζεῦ, τεὸν γὰρ αἷμα, σέο δ᾽ ἀγών, τὸν ὕμνος
ἔβαλεν
ὀπὶ νέων ἐπιχώριον χάρμα κελαδέων.
βοᾷ δὲ νικαφόρῳ σὺν Ἀριστοκλείδᾳ πρέπει,
ὃς τάνδε νᾶσον εὐκλέϊ προσέθηκε λόγῳ 120
καὶ σεμνὸν ἀγλααῖσι μερίμναις
70 Πυθίου Θεάριον. ἐν δὲ πείρᾳ τέλος
διαφαίνεται, ὧν τις ἐξοχώτερος γένηται,

ἀντ. δ´

ἐν παισὶ νέοισι παῖς, ἐν ἀνδράσιν ἀνήρ, τρίτον
ἐν παλαιτέροισι, μέρος ἕκαστον οἷον ἔχομεν
βρότεον ἔθνος. ἐλᾷ δὲ καὶ τέσσαρας ἀρετὰς 130

56 ἀγλαόκολπον Vatican recension (CS): ἀγλαόκαρπον Ambrosian recension (B²M); v.l. ἀγλαόκρανον (B¹FBu).
58 <ἐν> Erasmus Schmid (edd.). πᾶσι Mingarelli (S), cp. Theognis 275, 695; Hesiod, *Scutum Herculis* 84, *Theogonia*, 639 : πάντα mss (BMFCBu).
73 ἐν παλαιτέροισι, μέρος (CBuS): ἐν παλ. μέρος Erasmus Schmid, Hermann (BMF).

Pêleus the bright-bosomed daughter of Nêreus, and
fondly fostered for her their matchless offspring,[1]
bracing his spirit with all things fitting, that so, when
sped on his way to the walls of Troy by the blasts
that breathe athwart the sea, he might withstand the
clashing onset and the war-shout of the Lycians, and
the Phrygians and Dardanians, and, after closing in
conflict with the Ethiopians that wield the spear,
might set it in his soul that their Prince should
not return to his home, even Memnon the inspired
kinsman of Helenus.   Hence it was that the
far-shining splendour of the Aeacidae hath been
made immortal; for they are thy blood, O Zeus,
and thine is the contest on which my song hath
lighted, a song that chanteth with the voice of
youths the glory of the land.

That burst of song doth well beseem the triumph
of Aristocleides, who linked this isle with glorious
praise, and the holy Theoric temple[2] of the Pythian
god with bright ambitions.   For it is trial that
maketh manifest the prime of those virtues, in
which any one shall have proved himself preëminent,
whether as a boy among boys, a man among men, or,
thirdly, as an elder among elders, according to the
several portions of life which we, the race of men,
possess.[3]   But mortal life will bring as many as four

[1] Achilles.
[2] The Hall of the Guild of the Theori, or sacred envoys
sent from time to time from Aegina to the festivals at Delphi.
[3] "Each division [of the games] answering to a division of
man's life" is the suggestion made by Dr. Rouse, in *Proc.
Camb. Philol. Soc.* 30 April, 1891.

75 <ὁ> θνατὸς αἰών, φρονεῖν δ' ἐνέπει τὸ παρκεί-
    μενον.
τῶν οὐκ ἄπεστι. χαῖρε, φίλος. ἐγὼ τόδε τοι
πέμπω μεμιγμένον μέλι λευκῷ
σὺν γάλακτι, κιρναμένα δ' ἔερσ' ἀμφέπει,
πόμ' ἀοίδιμον Αἰολῆσιν ἐν πνοαῖσιν αὐλῶν,
ἐπ. δ

80 ὀψέ περ. ἔστι δ' αἰετὸς ὠκὺς ἐν ποτανοῖς,   140
ὃς ἔλαβεν αἶψα, τηλόθε μεταμαιόμενος, δαφοινὸν
    ἄγραν ποσίν·
κραγέται δὲ κολοιοὶ ταπεινὰ νέμονται.
τίν γε μέν, εὐθρόνου Κλεοῦς ἐθελοίσας, ἀεθλο-
    φόρου λήματος ἕνεκεν
Νεμέας Ἐπιδαυρόθεν τ' ἄπο καὶ Μεγάρων δέ-
    δορκεν φάος.

75 <ὁ> Triclinius (edd.) θνατὸς B, Aristarchus (MFBuS) :
μακρὸς DV (BC).
76 ἄπεστι mss (BMFBu) : ἄπεσσι Bergk (CS).

virtues, and it prompteth us to be prudent as regards the present; and of these virtues thou hast a goodly share.

Farewell, my friend! Lo! I am sending thee this honey-sweet strain, mingled with white milk and the foam of its mingling mantleth around it,—a draught of minstrelsy accompanied by the breathing of Aeolian flutes, late though it be. Swift among birds is the eagle, who, swooping down from afar, suddenly seizeth with his talons his blood-stained quarry; meanwhile the chattering daws have a low range of flight.[1] Verily on thyself, by grace of Clio on her beauteous throne, and in virtue of thy athlete-spirit, from Nemea and Epidaurus and Megara light hath looked forth.

[1] Cp. *O.* ii 96 f.

NEMEAN IV

FOR TÎMASARCHUS OF AEGINA

INTRODUCTION

THE fourth Nemean celebrates the victory of
Tîmasarchus of Aegina in the boys' wrestling-match.
The victor's father, now no longer living, was a
skilful musician (13 f); his maternal grandfather
was a poet (89); and his maternal uncle, Callicles,
had been a victor in the Isthmian games (80, 88).
The victor himself had been trained by Melêsias of
Athens (also mentioned in *O*. 8 and *N*. 6), and had
already been successful at Athens and Thebes.
Pindar describes the victor's Athenian successes as
won λ ι π α ρ ῶ ν . . ἀπ' 'Αθανᾶν, an epithet connecting
this Ode with the dithyramb of March 474, in which
Athens is invoked as ὦ ταὶ λ ι π α ρ α ὶ . . . 'Αθᾶναι
(Frag. 76). The present poem is assigned to **473**.

Feasting and song are the best remedies for toil
(1–8). Such is the prelude of an Ode in honour of
the Nemean Zeus, and the merits of the victor, and
of his native island, Aegina (9–13). Had his father
been living, he would have celebrated with music his
son's victories at Nemea, and at Athens and Thebes
(13–24).

344

INTRODUCTION

Exploits of the Aeginetan hero, Telamon, as comrade of the Theban hero, Heracles (25-30). Exploits great as these involve suffering (30-32). The poet pauses and bids the victor strive boldly against calumny (33-43).

Praise of the race of Aeacus (44-68). The poet pauses again (69-72).

Praise of the victor and his family, and of his trainer, Melêsias (73-96).

IV.—ΤΙΜΑΣΑΡΧΩ ΑΙΓΙΝΗΤῌ

ΠΑΙΔΙ ΠΑΛΑΙΣΤῌ

στρ. α´

Ἄριστος εὐφροσύνα πόνων κεκριμένων
ἰατρός· αἱ δὲ σοφαὶ
Μοισᾶν θύγατρες ἀοιδαὶ θέλξαν νιν ἁπτόμεναι.
οὐδὲ θερμὸν ὕδωρ τόσον γε μαλθακὰ τέγγει
5 γυῖα, τόσσον εὐλογία φόρμιγγι συνάορος.
ῥῆμα δ᾽ ἐργμάτων χρονιώτερον βιοτεύει,   10
ὅ τι κε σὺν Χαρίτων τύχᾳ
γλῶσσα φρενὸς ἐξέλοι βαθείας.

στρ. β´

τό μοι θέμεν Κρονίδᾳ τε Δὶ καὶ Νεμέᾳ
10 Τιμασάρχου τε πάλᾳ
ὕμνου προκώμιον εἴη· δέξαιτο δ᾽ Αἰακιδᾶν
ἠΰπυργον ἕδος, δίκᾳ ξεναρκέϊ κοινὸν   20
φέγγος. εἰ δ᾽ ἔτι ζαμενεῖ Τιμόκριτος ἁλίῳ
σὸς πατὴρ ἐθάλπετο, ποικίλον κιθαρίζων
15 θαμά κε, τῷδε μέλει κλιθείς,
υἱὸν κελάδησε καλλίνικον

στρ. γ´

Κλεωναίου τ᾽ ἀπ᾽ ἀγῶνος ὅρμον στεφάνων
πέμψαντα καὶ λιπαρᾶν
εὐωνύμων ἀπ᾽ Ἀθανᾶν, Θήβαις τ᾽ ἐν ἑπτα-
πύλοις,   30

6, 84 ἐργμάτων *B V* (ʙᴍꜰʙu) : ἐργ. (ᴄꜱ).
16 υἱὸν Bergk ²(ʙuꜱ); γόνον ꜰ : ὕμνον mss and scholia (ʙᴍᴄ).

346

WINNER IN THE BOYS' WRESTLING-MATCH, 473 (?) B.C.

WHEN toilsome contests have been decided, the best of healers is good cheer ; and songs, that are the sage daughters of the Muses, are wont to soothe the victor [1] by their touch. Nor doth warm water soothe the limbs in such welcome wise as praise that is linked with the lyre. Longer than deeds liveth the word, whatsoever it be that the tongue, by the favour of the Graces, draweth forth from the depth of the mind.

Such a word may it be mine to set forth, in honour of Zeus, the son of Cronus, in honour also of Nemea and the wrestling-match of Tîmasarchus, as a triumphant prelude to my song. And may it be welcomed by the seat of the Aeacidae with its goodly towers, that beacon-light which shineth for all, that bulwark of justice to the stranger. But if thy father, Tîmocritus, had been basking to-day in the light of the sun, full oft would he have touched the cithern's varied strings, and, bending the while over this strain, would have celebrated his triumphant son, in that he had brought home a wreath of crowns from the games of Cleônae,[2] and from the gleaming city of far-famed Athens, and also because, at

---

[1] Bury prefers : "can charm her forth" (making νιν refer to εὐφροσύναν). Headlam, *Class. Rev.* xix 148, makes νιν refer to πόνους.   [2] See note on *N.* x 42.

20 οὕνεκ' Ἀμφιτρύωνος ἀγλαὸν παρὰ τύμβον
   Καδμεῖοί νιν οὐκ ἀέκοντες ἄνθεσι μίγνυον,
   Αἰγίνας ἕκατι. φίλοισι γὰρ φίλος ἐλθὼν
   ξένιον ἄστυ κατέδραμεν
   Ἡρακλέος ὀλβίαν πρὸς αὐλάν.

στρ. δ´

25 σὺν ᾧ ποτε Τρωΐαν κραταιὸς Τελαμὼν   40
   πόρθησε καὶ Μέροπας
   καὶ τὸν μέγαν πολεμιστὰν ἔκπαγλον Ἀλκυονῆ,
   οὐ τετραορίας γε πρὶν δυώδεκα πέτρῳ
   ἥρωάς τ' ἐπεμβεβαῶτας ἱπποδάμους ἕλεν
30 δὶς τόσους. ἀπειρομάχας ἐών κε φανείη   50
   λόγον ὁ μὴ συνιείς· ἐπεὶ
   " ῥέζοντά τι καὶ παθεῖν ἔοικεν."

στρ. ε´

   τὰ μακρὰ δ' ἐξενέπειν ἐρύκει με τεθμὸς
   ὧραί τ' ἐπειγόμεναι·
35 ἴυγγι δ' ἕλκομαι ἦτορ νουμηνίᾳ θιγέμεν.
   ἔμπα, καίπερ ἔχει βαθεῖα ποντιὰς ἅλμα
   μέσσον, ἀντίτειν' ἐπιβουλίᾳ· σφόδρα δόξομεν   60
   δαΐων ὑπέρτεροι ἐν φάει καταβαίνειν·
   φθονερὰ δ' ἄλλος ἀνὴρ βλέπων
40 γνώμαν κενεὰν σκότῳ κυλίνδει

στρ. στ´

   χαμαὶ πετοῖσαν· ἐμοὶ δ' ὁποίαν ἀρετὰν
   ἔδωκε πότμος ἄναξ,
   εὖ οἶδ' ὅτι χρόνος ἕρπων πεπρωμέναν τελέσει.   70
   ἐξύφαινε, γλυκεῖα, καὶ τόδ' αὐτίκα, φόρμιγξ,
45 Λυδίᾳ σὺν ἁρμονίᾳ μέλος πεφιλημένον

   23 κατέδραμεν Triclinius (BFC); κατέδρακεν BD and scholium
   (MBuS).
   41 χαμαὶ πετοῖσαν D² (CBuS): χαμαιπετοῖσαν BV (BMF).

seven-gated Thebes, beside Amphitryon's glorious
tomb, the Cadmeans gladly crowned him with flowers,
for the love of Aegina. For, coming as a friend to
friends, he found his haven in a hospitable town,
at the wealthy hall of Heracles, with whom in olden
times the stalwart Telamon destroyed Troy and the
Meropes and the great and terrible warrior,
Alcyoneus, though not before that giant had, by the
hurling of a rock, subdued twelve chariots and
twice twelve heroic horsemen, who rode therein.
Unversed in battles would he plainly be who
knoweth not the proverb that in truth 'tis fitting
that whoso doeth aught should suffer also.[1] But from
telling all the story, I am stayed by the law of my
song and by the onward pressing hours, for I am
drawn by a magic spell that resteth on my heart,[2]
prompting me to touch on the new-moon's festival.
What though the deep brine of the sea holdeth thee
round the waist, yet stand thou thy ground against
the dark design. We shall yet be seen to come
forth in the light of day far stronger than our foes,
while another, with envious glance, broodeth in
darkness over some fruitless purpose that falleth to
the ground. But, whatsoever excellence Lord
Destiny assigned me, well I know that the lapse of
time will bring it to its appointed perfection.

Weave out, weave out forthwith, sweet lyre, the
web of lovely song with Lydian harmony, in honour

[1] A primitive principle of justice, ascribed to Rhada-
manthys in Aristotle's *Ethics*, v 5, 3, τὸ ʽΡαδαμάνθυος δίκαιον·
εἴ κε πάθοι τά κ' ἔρεξε, δίκη κ' ἰθεῖα γένοιτο. Cp. Aesch. *Choëph.*
314, δράσαντι παθεῖν, τριγέρων μῦθος τάδε φωνεῖ.

[2] See note on *P.* iv 214.

349

PINDAR

Οἰνώνᾳ τε καὶ Κύπρῳ, ἔνθα Τεῦκρος ἀπάρχει
ὁ Τελαμωνιάδας· ἀτὰρ
Αἴας Σαλαμῖν' ἔχει πατρῴαν·

στρ. ζ'

  ἐν δ' Εὐξείνῳ πελάγει φαεννὰν Ἀχιλεὺς   80
50 νᾶσον· Θέτις δὲ κρατεῖ
Φθίᾳ· Νεοπτόλεμος δ' Ἀπείρῳ διαπρυσίᾳ,
βουβόται τόθι πρῶνες ἔξοχοι κατάκεινται
Δωδώναθεν ἀρχόμενοι πρὸς Ἰόνιον 'πόρον.
Παλίου δὲ πὰρ ποδὶ λατρείαν Ἰαωλκὸν
55 πολεμίᾳ χερὶ προστραπὼν   90
Πηλεὺς παρέδωκεν Αἱμόνεσσιν.

στρ. η'

δάμαρτος Ἱππολύτας Ἄκαστος δολίαις
τέχναισι χρησάμενος
τᾷ Δαιδάλου τε μαχαίρᾳ φύτευέ οἱ θάνατον
60 ἐκ λόχου, Πελίαο παῖς· ἄλαλκε δὲ Χείρων,
καὶ τὸ μόρσιμον Διόθεν πεπρωμένον ἔκφερεν· 100
πῦρ δὲ παγκρατὲς θρασυμαχάνων τε λεόντων
ὄνυχας ὀξυτάτους ἀκμὰν
τε δεινοτάτω· σχάσαις ὀδόντων

στρ. θ'

65 ἔγαμεν ὑψιθρόνων μίαν Νηρεΐδων,

---

54 λατρείαν mss (BMFC) : λατρίαν Erasmus Schmid, Heyne (BuS).

Ἰαωλκὸν Vatican recension (BMFBu) : Ἰαολκὸν V (CS).

55 προστραπὼν mss (BMFCBu) : προτραπὼν Heyne, Bergk (S).

56 Αἱμόνεσσιν. S : Αἱμόνεσσι, B ; —ιν, MFCBu.

57 Ἄκαστος S : Ἀκάστου mss (BMFCBu).

58 χρησάμενος S : χρησάμενος. BMFCBu.

59 Δαιδάλου τε S : Δαιδάλου δὲ mss (CBu) ; δαιδάλῳ δὲ Didymus Hermann (BMF).

64 τε mss (BMFCBu) : καὶ Ahlwardt (s) ; τ' ἢ Bergk⁴ ; τ' ἀλγεινοτάτων Boehmer.

350

of Oenônê[1] and of Cyprus, where Teucer, son of Telamon, reigneth afar, while Aias still holdeth the Salamis of his fathers, and Achilles dwelleth in that gleaming isle in the Euxine sea,[2] and Thetis ruleth in Phthia, and Neoptolemus over the broad spaces of Epîrus, where oxen feed on jutting forelands that slope gently down from Dodona to the Ionian sea. But, beside the foot of Pêlion, having turned Iolcus to subjection with hostile hand, Pêleus gave it over to the Haemones. Acastus, the son of Pelias, with the aid of the treacherous wiles of Hippolytê, and with the sword of Daedalus, was craftily plotting the death of Pêleus, but Cheiron rescued him and carried out the destiny which had been fated by Zeus.[3] So Pêleus, having escaped the violence of fire, and the keen claws of bold lions, and the edge of their terrible teeth, wedded one of the enthronèd Nereids,[4] and beheld the circle of fair seats, whereon

[1] Aegina.

[2] Leucê, or White Island, at the mouth of the Ister.

[3] During the funeral games held by Acastus at Iolcus in memory of his father Pelias, Hippolytê, the wife of Acastus, fell in love with Pêleus. When Pêleus refused to listen to her, she accused him to her husband. Soon afterwards, while Acastus and Pêleus were hunting on mount Pêlion, Acastus plotted the death of Pêleus by stealing the sword forged for him by Daedalus, and suborning the Centaurs to lie in wait for the hero, while he was searching for his sword. Pêleus, however, was protected by Cheiron, and, on his return to Iolcus, slew Acastus and Hippolytê.

[4] "Thetis changed herself into various forms to escape from the embraces of Pêleus, but the counsels of Cheiron enabled the hero to overcome the fire, the lion, the dragon and other shapes which she assumed" (Bury). This subject was represented, by primitive art, on the Chest of Cypselus (Pausanias, v 18, 5); also on a vase in the Berlin Museum (reproduced in Miss Harrison's *Greek Vase Paintings*, No. xxiii).

PINDAR

εἶδεν δ' εὔκυκλον ἕδραν,
τᾶς οὐρανοῦ βασιλῆες πόντου τ' ἐφεζόμενοι
δῶρα καὶ κράτος ἐξέφαναν ἐγγενὲς αὐτῷ.   110
Γαδείρων τὸ πρὸς ζόφον οὐ περατόν· ἀπότρεπε
70 αὖτις Εὐρώπαν ποτὶ χέρσον ἔντεα ναός·
ἄπορα γὰρ λόγον Αἰακοῦ
παίδων τὸν ἅπαντά μοι διελθεῖν.

στρ. ι'

Θεανδρίδαισι δ' ἀεξιγυίων ἀέθλων
κάρυξ ἑτοῖμος ἔβαν   120
75 Οὐλυμπίᾳ τε καὶ Ἰσθμοῖ Νεμέᾳ τε συνθέμενος,
ἔνθα πεῖραν ἔχοντες οἴκαδε κλυτοκάρπων
οὐ νέοντ' ἄνευ στεφάνων, πάτραν ἵν' ἀκούομεν,
Τιμάσαρχε, τεὰν ἐπινικίοισιν ἀοιδαῖς
πρόπολον ἔμμεναι. εἰ δέ τοι
80 μάτρῳ μ' ἔτι Καλλικλεῖ κελεύεις   130

στρ. ια'

στάλαν θέμεν Παρίου λίθου λευκοτέραν·
ὁ χρυσὸς ἑψόμενος
αὐγὰς ἔδειξεν ἁπάσας, ὕμνος δὲ τῶν ἀγαθῶν
ἐργμάτων βασιλεῦσιν ἰσοδαίμονα τεύχει
85 φῶτα· κεῖνος ἀμφ' Ἀχέροντι ναιετάων ἐμὰν
γλῶσσαν εὑρέτω κελαδῆτιν, Ὀρσοτριαίνα   140
ἵν' ἐν ἀγῶνι βαρυκτύπου
θάλησε Κορινθίοις σελίνοις·

στρ. ιβ'

τὸν Εὐφάνης ἐθέλων γεραιὸς προπάτωρ
90 σὸς ἄεισέν ποτε, παῖ.

68 ἐγγενὲς scholia, Ritterhausen (CBuS): ἐς γένος Ursinus
(bMF); ἐς γενεὰς mss.

90 σὸς ἄεισέν ποτε Hermann (BS), — τότε (C): ὁ σὸς ἀείσεται
mss; ἀείσεται, παῖ, ὁ σὸς M; ὁ σὸς <διδάσκετο> παῖ F; ἀείσεται
φθιμένοις? Bury.

352

the lords of heaven and sea were seated, when they declared gifts of sovereignty for himself and his children after him. Beyond Gadeira toward the gloom we must not pass; turn back the sails of thy ship once more to the mainland of Europe, for it were impossible for me to tell in all its fulness the story of the sons of Aeacus.

'Tis in honour of the Theandridae that I have come, in obedience to my plighted word, as a ready herald of their stalwart contests at Olympia, and at the Isthmus and at Nemea, where, whenever they make trial of their skill, it is not without the fruit of glorious garlands that they return to that home, where we hear, Tîmasarchus, that thy clan is a minister unto songs of victory. But if, in sooth, thou wouldest have me also build, in honour of Callicles, thine eme,[1] a monument whiter than the Parian stone,—for even as gold, when refined, is made to show all radiance, so doth song in honour of brave deeds make a man the peer of kings—may he, who now dwelleth beside the stream of Acheron, find an ear for my voice that ringeth loudly here on earth, where, in the contest of the loudly roaring wielder of the trident, he burst into bloom with the Corinthian (*i.e.* Isthmian) crown of wild celery. He, in his day, was gladly sung by Euphanes, the aged grandsire of thee, victorious boy! Each victor hath

---

[1] Used for "uncle" by Chaucer and Spenser (*Faery Queene*, ii 10, 47), and long retained in this sense in Staffordshire. It corresponds to the German *Oheim*.

PINDAR

ἄλλοισι δ' ἄλικες ἄλλοι· τὰ δ' αὐτὸς ἄν τις ἴδῃ,
ἔλπεταί τις ἕκαστος ἐξοχώτατα φάσθαι.   150
οἷον αἰνέων κε Μελησίαν ἔριδα στρέφοι,
ῥήματα πλέκων, ἀπάλαιστος ἐν λόγῳ ἕλκειν,
95 μαλακὰ μὲν φρονέων ἐσλοῖς,
τραχὺς δὲ παλιγκότοις ἔφεδρος.

91 ἄν τις ἴδῃ, supported by schol. ἅπερ αὐτὸς εἶδε, and
ἅπερ ἄν τις τύχῃ θεώμενος, (BMC): ἄν τις τύχῃ mss ; <ὧν κε>
τύχῃ F ; ἄν τις ἴσῃ Bury ; ἀντιτύχῃ Mingarelli (s).

his poet in his day, but every bard aspireth to sing
best of all, whatever his own eyes have seen. Thus,
were he to sound the praises of Melêsias, he would
grapple indeed in the strife, bending the words be-
neath his grasp, not budging an inch as he wrestleth
in speech,—a gentle antagonist towards a noble
adversary, but stern indeed when he waiteth to fight
a froward foe.[1]

[1] The language, in which Euphanes is described as praising
the trainer, is borrowed from the wrestling-school.

NEMEAN V

FOR PYTHEAS OF AEGINA

INTRODUCTION

PYTHEAS, the son of Lampon, of Aegina, was victor in the boys' pancratium at the Nemean games.

He was trained by Menander, and the poet adds that a trainer of athletes was bound to come from Athens (48 f). This complimentary reference to Athens makes it probable that the Ode was composed before open hostilities had broken out between Aegina and Athens in 488. The victory of Pytheas has accordingly been assigned to the Nemean games of July 489 (so Gaspar, and Schröder), or of 485 or 483 (Wilamowitz). The same victory was celebrated in the 13th Ode of Bacchylides. Phylacidas, the younger brother of Lampon, afterwards obtained two victories in the pancratium, probably in April 484 and 480. The former is commemorated in the sixth Isthmian, and the latter in the fifth.

The poet bids his song set sail in every craft from Aegina, to spread the news of the victory of Pytheas (1–6), which had done honour to the Aeacidae and to Aegina (7 f), the island for whose future glory the sons of Aeacus (Telamon and Pêleus, and their

half-brother Phôcus) prayed not in vain to Zeus
(9–13). Telamon and Pêleus left Aegina for a
reason which the poet declines to tell; silence is
often the best policy (14–18).

Praises of the Aeacidae (19–21), for whom the
Muses sang at the marriage of Pêleus and Thetis
(19–37).

The Isthmian victory of Euthymenês (37–42), the
maternal uncle of Pytheas, who has followed in his
steps (43). Praise of the trainer, Melêsias of Athens
(48 f). Prizes for boxing and for the pancratium,
won at Epidaurus by the victor's maternal grand-
father, Themistius (50–54).

V.—ΠΥΘΕΑ ΑΙΓΙΝΗΤΗ

ΑΓΕΝΕΙΩ ΠΑΓΚΡΑΤΙΑΣΤΗ

στρ. α'

Οὐκ ἀνδριαντοποιός εἰμ', ὥστ' ἐλινύσοντα ἐργάζε-
σθαι ἀγάλματ' ἐπ' αὐτᾶς βαθμίδος
ἑσταότ'· ἀλλ' ἐπὶ πάσας ὁλκάδος ἔν τ' ἀκάτῳ,
γλυκεῖ' ἀοιδά,
στεῖχ' ἀπ' Αἰγίνας, διαγγέλλοισ', ὅτι
Λάμπωνος υἱὸς Πυθέας εὐρυσθενὴς
5 νίκη Νεμείοις παγκρατίου στέφανον,
οὔπω γένυσι φαίνων τέρειναν ματέρ' οἰνάνθας
ὀπώραν,   10

ἀντ. α'

ἐκ δὲ Κρόνου καὶ Ζηνὸς ἥρωας αἰχματὰς φυτευ-
θέντας καὶ ἀπὸ χρυσεᾶν Νηρηίδων
Αἰακίδας ἐγέραιρεν ματρόπολίν τε, φίλαν ξένων
ἄρουραν·
τάν ποτ' εὔανδρόν τε καὶ ναυσικλυτὰν
10 θέσσαντο πὰρ βωμὸν πατέρος Ἑλλανίου
στάντες, πίτναν τ' εἰς αἰθέρα χεῖρας ἁμᾶ   20
Ἐνδαΐδος ἀρίγνωτες υἱοὶ καὶ βία Φώκου κρέοντος,

ἐπ. α'

ὁ τᾶς θεοῦ, ὃν Ψαμάθεια τίκτ' ἐπὶ ῥηγμῖνι πόντου.
αἰδέομαι μέγα εἰπεῖν ἐν δίκᾳ τε μὴ κεκινδυνευ-
μένον,

1 ἐλινύσοντα mss (MFCBuS): ἐλινύσοντά μ' Brubach 1542 (B).
8 ἐγέραιρεν mss and scholia (MFS): ἐγέραρεν Calliergus
(LCBu).

358

V.—FOR PYTHEAS OF AEGINA

WINNER IN THE BOYS' PANCRATIUM, 485 (?) B.C.

No sculptor am I, that I should carve statues doomed to linger only on the pedestal where they stand. No! I would bid my sweet song speed from Aegina, in every argosy, and in every skiff, spreading abroad the tidings that the stalwart Pytheas, son of Lampon, hath won the crown for the pancratium at the Nemean games, or ever he showed on his cheeks the hue of summer, the soft harbinger of youthful bloom. And he hath brought honour to the Aeacidae, those heroic spearmen descended from Cronus and Zeus, and from the golden Nereids; honour also to the mother city, the friendly home of strangers, which the famous sons of Endais,[1] and the mighty prince Phôcus,[2] son of the goddess Psamatheia, whom she bare by the beach of the sea, prayed might some day be rich in heroes and famed for ships, as they stood beside the altar of Father Zeus Hellênius,[3] and together stretched their hands toward the sky. Reverence restraineth me from telling of a mighty deed, a

[1] Daughter of Cheiron, wife of Aeacus, and mother of Telamon and Pêleus.

[2] The son of Aeacus, by the Nereid Psamatheia, who was murdered by his half-brothers, Telamon and Pêleus.

[3] The ancestral divinity of the Myrmidons, who, on migrating to Aegina, built a temple in his honour on the highest point of the island.

15 πῶς δὴ λίπον εὐκλέα νᾶσον, καὶ τίς ἄνδρας
    ἀλκίμους
  δαίμων ἀπ' Οἰνώνας ἔλασεν. στάσομαι· οὔ τοι
    ἅπασα κερδίων   30
  φαίνοισα πρόσωπον ἀλάθει' ἀτρεκής·
  καὶ τὸ σιγᾶν πολλάκις ἐστὶ σοφώτατον ἀνθρώπῳ
    νοῆσαι.

στρ. β′

  εἰ δ' ὄλβον ἢ χειρῶν βίαν ἢ σιδαρίταν ἐπαινῆσαι
    πόλεμον δεδόκηται, μακρά μοι
20 αὐτόθεν ἅλμαθ' ὑποσκάπτοι τις· ἔχω γονάτων
    ἐλαφρὸν ὁρμάν·
  καὶ πέραν πόντοιο πάλλοντ' αἰετοί.   40
  πρόφρων δὲ καὶ κείνοις ἄειδ' ἐν Παλίῳ
  Μοισᾶν ὁ κάλλιστος χορός, ἐν δὲ μέσαις
  φόρμιγγ' Ἀπόλλων ἑπτάγλωσσον χρυσέῳ πλά-
    κτρῳ διώκων

ἀντ. β′

25 ἁγεῖτο παντοίων νόμων· αἱ δὲ πρώτιστον μὲν
    ὕμνησαν Διὸς ἀρχόμεναι σεμνὰν Θέτιν
  Πηλέα θ', ὥς τέ νιν ἁβρὰ Κρηθεῒς Ἱππολύτα
    δόλῳ πεδᾶσαι
  ἤθελε ξυνᾶνα Μαγνήτων σκοπὸν   50
  πείσαισ' ἀκοίταν ποικίλοις βουλεύμασιν,
  ψεύσταν δὲ ποιητὸν συνέπαξε λόγον,
30 ὡς ἄρα νυμφείας ἐπείρα κεῖνος ἐν λέκτροις
    Ἀκάστου

ἐπ. β′

  εὐνᾶς. τὸ δ' ἐναντίον ἔσκεν· πολλὰ γάρ νιν παντὶ
    θυμῷ

19 μακρά μοι mss (MFCBuS) : μακρὰ δὴ Thiersch, B².

360

deed hazarded in no righteous wise,[1]—how at last
they left the famous island, and what was the doom
that drave the bold heroes from Oenônê. I will halt:
it is not every truth that is the better for showing its
face undisguised; and full oft is silence the wisest
thing for a man to heed. But, if any one be resolved
on praising riches, or might of hands, or mail-clad
war, I would that some one might delve me the
ground for long leaps from this point.[2] I have a light
some spring in my knees; the eagle swoopeth e'en
beyond the sea.

Yea, for the sons of Aeacus themselves, the glad-
some song was sung on Pêlion by the fairest choir
of the Muses, while, in their midst, Apollo, sweep-
ing with golden quill the seven-fold notes of the
lyre, led the varied strains. And the Muses, after
a prelude to Zeus, first of all sang of holy Thetis and
of Pêleus, telling how Hippolytê, the dainty daughter
of Crêtheus, would fain have caught Pêleus by guile,
having by crafty counsels persuaded her husband, the
lord of the Magnêtes, to be partner in her plot. And
so she forged a lying tale of her own invention,
pretending he had attempted her honour in the bed
of Acastus, when the very contrary was the truth
indeed; for many a time had she with all her heart

[1] The murder of their half-brother.
[2] "The Greeks jumped into a pit (σκάμμα), the ground of
which had been carefully dug up and levelled." . . . The
ground was thus made soft, " so as to take the impress of the
jumper's feet " (E. Norman Gardiner, *Greek Athletic Sports
and Festivals*, p. 297, and *Journal of Hellenic Studies*, xxiv
(1904) 70 f).

παρφαμένα λιτάνευεν· τοῦ δὲ ὀργὰν κνίζον
αἰπεινοὶ λόγοι·
εὐθὺς δ' ἀπανάνατο νύμφαν, ξεινίου πατρὸς
χόλον   60
δείσαις· ὁ δ' ἐφράσθη κατένευσέν τέ οἱ ὀρσινεφὴς
ἐξ οὐρανοῦ
35 Ζεὺς ἀθανάτων βασιλεύς, ὥστ' ἐν τάχει
ποντίαν χρυσαλακάτων τινὰ Νηρεΐδων πράξειν
ἄκοιτιν,
στρ. γ'
γαμβρὸν Ποσειδάωνα πείσαις, ὃς Αἰγᾶθεν ποτὶ
κλειτὰν θαμὰ νίσσεται Ἰσθμὸν Δωρίαν·
ἔνθα μιν εὔφρονες ἶλαι σὺν καλάμοιο βοᾷ θεὸν
δέκονται,   70
καὶ σθένει γυίων ἐρίζοντι θρασεῖ.
40 πότμος δὲ κρίνει συγγενὴς ἔργων πέρι
πάντων. τὺ δ' Αἰγίναθε δίς, Εὐθύμενες,
Νίκας ἐν ἀγκώνεσσι πίτνων ποικίλων ἔψαυσας
ὕμνων.
ἀντ. γ'
ἤτοι μεταΐξαντα καὶ νῦν τεὸς μάτρως ἀγάλλει
κείνου ὁμόσπορον ἔθνος, Πυθέα.   80
ἁ Νεμέα μὲν ἄραρεν μείς τ' ἐπιχώριος, ὃν φίλασ'
Ἀπόλλων·
45 ἅλικας δ' ἐλθόντας οἴκοι τ' ἐκράτεις
Νίσου τ' ἐν εὐαγκεῖ λόφῳ. χαίρω δ', ὅτι
ἐσλοῖσι μάρναται πέρι πᾶσα πόλις.

32 τοῦ δὲ BD (MBuS): τοῦ μὲν (B); τοῖο δ' Hermann; τοῦ
δ' ἄρ' Rauchenstein (FC).
41 Αἰγίναθε δίς Ed. Schwartz, Wilamowitz (S³): Αἰγίνα θεᾶς
mss; Αἰγίνα θεοῦ Erasmus Schmid (BMF); Αἰγίναθεν ἅπ' (C);
Αἰγᾶθεν ποτί Bury.
43-5 Πυθέα. — τ' ἐκράτεις Kayser (s): Πυθέας. — τε κρατεῖ or

362

besought him with beguiling words.[1] But her bold
language stung him to wrath, and at once he spurned
her embraces in reverent awe of the anger of Father
Zeus, who defendeth the rights of hospitality; and
Zeus, the king of the immortals, who marshalleth
the clouds of heaven, marked the deed, and decreed
that ere long he should win for his wife a sea-nymph
from among the Nereids with their golden distaffs,
after gaining the consent of their kinsman, Poseidon,
who oft cometh from Aegina to the famous Dorian
Isthmus, where the joyous bands welcome the god
with the music of the flute, and wrestle with all the
hardy prowess of their limbs.

It is the natal star that ruleth over every deed;
and thou, Euthymenes from Aegina, twice falling in
the lap of victory, didst win thee a varied strain of
song. Verily even now, O Pytheas, thine eme
doth glorify that hero's kindred clan, by following in
his steps. Nemea is linked with thee,[2] and Aegina's
festal month beloved of Apollo, and thou wast
victorious over thy comrades who entered the lists,
both at home and in the fair dells of the hill of
Nîsus.[3] I rejoice that all the State striveth for glory.

---

[1] Cp. *N.* iv 57-65.
[2] ἄρᾱρεν, perfect of ἀραρίσκω, "ever clave to him" (Tyrrell
in *Proc. Camb. Philol. Soc.* 25 Feb. 1886).   [3] Megara.

κράτει mss ; μετ' ἀίξαντα — Πυθέας — ἐκράτει M.   Πυθέα, — τ'
ἐκράτει B ; μάτρω σ' — ἔρνος, Πυθέα. — ἐκράτει F ; μάτρως σ'
— καί σου ὁμόσπορον ἔθνος, Πυθέα. — ἐκράτεις C ; Ἰσθμοῖ τ' ἀίξας
ἄντα. καὶ νῦν τεὸς μάτρως ἀγάλλει — Πυθέα. — ἐκράτει Bury ;
μεταίξας τε (= σε, Euthymenes) — Πυθέας. — ἐκρατει Wilamo-
witz.

ἴσθι, γλυκεῖάν τοι Μενάνδρου σὺν τύχᾳ μόχθων
    ἀμοιβὰν

ἐπ.´γ´

ἐπαύρεο· χρὴ δ᾽ ἀπ᾽ Ἀθανᾶν τέκτον᾽ ἀθληταῖσιν
    ἔμμεν.   90

50 εἰ δὲ Θεμίστιον ἵκεις, ὥστ᾽ ἀείδειν, μηκέτι ῥίγει·
    δίδοι

φωνάν, ἀνὰ δ᾽ ἱστία τεῖνον πρὸς ζυγὸν καρχασίου,

πύκταν τέ νιν καὶ παγκρατίῳ φθέγξαι ἑλεῖν
    Ἐπιδαύρῳ διπλόαν

νικῶντ᾽ ἀρετάν, προθύροισιν δ᾽ Αἰακοῦ

ἀνθέων ποιάεντα φέρε στεφανώματα σὺν ξανθαῖς
    Χάρισσιν.

52 παγκρατίῳ B (MCBuS) : παγκρατίου D, Triclinius (BF).
54 ἀνθέων Hermann (edd.) : ἄνθεα mss.   ποιᾶντα B.
    φέρε Wilamowitz (S³) : φέρειν mss (BMFCBu).

Bear in mind that, by the good fortune of Menander,
thou didst win a sweet requital for thy toils. Meet
it is that a fashioner of athletes should come from
Athens; but, if thou art come to sing the praises of
Themistius, away with cold reserve. Lift up thy voice,
and hoist the sails to the top-most yard; proclaim
him as a boxer, and tell that he hath won a double
victory in the pancratium by his conquest in
Epidaurus; and bring to the portals of Aeacus grassy
garlands of flowers in the company of the fair-haired
Graces.

NEMEAN VI

FOR ALCIMIDAS OF AEGINA

INTRODUCTION

THE sixth Nemean celebrates the victory of
Alcimidas of Aegina in the boys' wrestling-match.
The victor belongs to the clan of the Bassidae,
which traces its descent from the Heracleidae. In
athletic contests the victor's family had been
successful in alternate generations. His father
Theon, had won no athletic distinctions, while his
grandfather, Praxidamas (17 f), besides winning
several prizes in the Nemean and Isthmian games,
was the first Aeginetan to have been victorious at
Olympia (in 544 B.C., his statue in cypress-wood having
been, according to Pausanias, vi 18, 5, the oldest
Olympian statue of any victorious athlete). Again,
his great-grandfather, Sôcleidês, had been undistin-
guished (24), but the three younger brothers of
Sôcleidês had, by their successes, brought fame to
their father, Hâgêsimachus (25 f). Pythian, Nemean,
and Isthmian victories had been won by earlier
members of the clan (39 ff, 44 ff); at Olympia,
Alcimidas, and another member of the family, had
been disappointed, owing to the accident of the lot
(67-73). The trainer, Melêsias of Athens, was the

same as in *N.* 4 (473) and *O.* 8 (460). An intervening date (463) is accordingly assigned by Schröder, while Gaspar places it as late as 447, after the Boeotian victory over the Athenians at Coronea. It contains one or two passages recalling Odes that are distinctly late :—that on the fields which lie fallow in alternate years (8–11, cp. *N.* xi 37–43), and that on the feebleness and transitoriness of man contrasted with the power and the eternity of God (1–4, cp. *P.* viii 95–97, and *N.* xi 15 f).

Men and gods have a common origin, but diverse powers ; yet men are partly like to the gods, although they cannot foresee the future (1–7). This is exemplified by the victor's family, who have been successful in alternate generations (8–11). Prizes won by the victor and his ancestors, who have been eminent in boxing (11–27). The poet's praise shall hit the mark, and the Muse shall glorify the victor (27–30). Men of past ages have won fame in song and story, and of such fame this clan has had no lack (30–46).

Praise of the Aeacidae, and of Achilles in particular (47–56).

The present, however, has its peculiar interest (57–59), and the poet gladly bears the double burden of praising the clan and the victor for having won the twenty-fifth victory for the clan (59–63). At Olympia, the lot deprived them of two victories (63–65). Praise of the trainer, Melêsias (66–69).

VI.—ΑΛΚΙΜΙΔῌ ΑΙΓΙΝΗΤῌ

ΠΑΙΔΙ ΠΑΛΑΙΣΤῌ

στρ. α΄

Ἐν ἀνδρῶν, ἐν θεῶν γένος· ἐϛ μιᾶς δὲ πνέομεν
ματρὸς ἀμφότεροι· διείργει δὲ πᾶσα κεκριμένα
δύναμις, ὡς τὸ μὲν οὐδέν, ὁ δὲ χάλκεος ἀσφαλὲς
αἰὲν ἕδος
μένει οὐρανός. ἀλλά τι προσφέρομεν ἔμπαν ἢ
μέγαν
5 νόον ἤτοι φύσιν ἀθανάτοις,
καίπερ ἐφαμερίαν οὐκ εἰδότες οὐδὲ μετὰ νύκτας
ἄμμε πότμος   10
οἵαν τιν' ἔγραψε δραμεῖν ποτὶ στάθμαν.

ἀντ. α΄

τεκμαίρει καί νυν Ἀλκιμίδας τὸ συγγενὲς ἰδεῖν
ἄγχι καρποφόροις ἀρούραισιν, αἵτ' ἀμειβόμεναι
10 τόκα μὲν ὦν βίον ἀνδράσιν ἐπηετανὸν πεδίων
ἔδοσαν,
τόκα δ' αὖτ' ἀναπαυσάμεναι σθένος ἔμαρψαν.
ἦλθέ τοι   20
Νεμέας ἐξ ἐρατῶν ἀέθλων
παῖς ἐναγώνιος, ὃς ταύταν μεθέπων Διόθεν αἶσαν
νῦν πέφανται
οὐκ ἄμμορος ἀμφὶ πάλᾳ κυναγέτας,

---

6 νύκτας mss (BMFCBu) : νύκτα Hartung, Wilamowitz (S).

7 οἵαν τιν' Hermann (BMFC): ἄν τιν' mss, ἄντιν' Triclinius (S);
ἄναξ τίν' Bury.   δραμέμεν S[1].

368

VI.—FOR ALCIMIDAS OF AEGINA

WINNER IN THE BOYS' WRESTLING-MATCH, 463(?) B.C.

ONE is the race of men, one is the race of gods,
and from one mother[1] do we both derive our breath ;
yet a power that is wholly sundered parteth us, in
that the one is naught, while for the other the
brazen heaven endureth as an abode unshaken for
evermore. Albeit, we mortals have some likeness,
either in might of mind or at least in our nature, to
the immortals, although we know not by what course,
whether by day, no nor yet in the night watches,
fate hath ordained that we should run.

Even now doth Alcimidas prove to all eyes that the
inborn valour of his race resembleth the corn-bearing
fields, which in changing seasons, at one while, give to
man abundant sustenance from the plains, and, at
another while, gather strength by repose. Lo! from
the lovely games of Nemea hath now returned that
athlete boy, who, following this heaven-sent destiny,
hath now shone forth no luckless hunter in the
wrestling ring, by planting his step in the foot-prints

---

[1] Gaia, or Earth, who, by her son Uranus, became the
mother of Cronos, father of Zeus, father of Hephaestus, who
made Pandôra, by whose union with Prometheus, son of
Iâpetus, son of Gaia, the human race came into being.

ἐπ. α΄

15 ἴχνεσιν ἐν Πραξιδάμαντος ἑὸν πόδα νέμων
πατροπάτορος ὁμαιμίου.
κεῖνος γὰρ Ὀλυμπιόνικος ἐὼν Αἰακίδαις   30
ἔρνεα πρῶτος <ἔνεικεν> ἀπ᾽ Ἀλφεοῦ,
καὶ πεντάκις Ἰσθμοῖ στεφανωσάμενος,
20 Νεμέᾳ δὲ τρίς,
ἔπαυσε λάθαν
Σωκλείδᾳ, ὃς ὑπέρτατος
Ἀγησιμάχῳ υἱέων γένετο.

στρ. β΄

ἐπεὶ οἱ τρεῖς ἀεθλοφόροι πρὸς ἄκρον ἀρετᾶς
25 ἦλθον, οἵτε πόνων ἐγεύσαντο. σὺν θεοῦ δὲ τύχᾳ 40
ἕτερον οὔ τινα οἶκον ἀπεφάνατο πυγμαχία
<πλεόνων>
ταμίαν στεφάνων μυχῷ Ἑλλάδος ἁπάσας.
ἔλπομαι
μέγα εἰπὼν σκοποῦ ἄντα τυχεῖν
ὥτ᾽ ἀπὸ τόξου ἱείς· εὔθυν᾽ ἐπὶ τοῦτον, ἄγε, Μοῖσα,
οὖρον ἐπέων
30 εὐκλέα. παροιχομένων γὰρ ἀνέρων   50

ἀντ. β΄

ἀοιδαὶ καὶ λόγοι τὰ καλά σφιν ἔργ᾽ ἐκόμισαν,
Βασσίδαισιν ἅ τ᾽ οὐ σπανίζει· παλαίφατος γενεά,
ἴδια ναυστολέοντες ἐπικώμια, Πιερίδων ἀρόταις

16 ὁμαιμίοις s.
18 <ἔνεικεν> Bergk (cs); <ἐλαίας> B; <ἐπεὶ δράπεν> M;
<ἐπάρκεσ᾽> F; <ἔτοσσεν> Bury.
20 τρίς mss (BFCBu): τρεῖς Hermann (MS), sc. νίκας cp. O.
vii 82.
22 Σωκλείδα old mss (BMFC), —δ͵ Triclinius (Bu): Σαοκλείδα᾽
s¹, Σωῒκλείδα᾽ Wackernagel (s²).
23 υἱέων Triclinius (BMFCBu): υἱῶν old mss; ὑέων
W. Schulze (s).

of his own true grandsire, Praxidamas.   For he, as
an Olympian victor, was the first to bring sprays from
the Alpheüs to the sons of Aeacus and by winning
the garland five times at Isthmus, and thrice at
Nemea, put an end to the obscurity of Socleides, who
was the eldest born of the sons of Hâgêsimachus ;
since, to his joy, the very crown of prowess was
attained by those athletes who made trial of the toil ;
and, by favour of heaven, no other house hath the
contest in wrestling proclaimed the possessor of
more garlands in the very heart of all Hellas.

Now that I have uttered this mighty vaunt, I trust
I have hit the mark, as though I were shooting with
the bow.   Come, O my Muse, waft to this victor a
glorious breeze of song.   For, when heroes have
passed away, lays and legends treasure for them their
noble deeds, and in these the house of Bassus is
not wanting.   A clan of ancient fame, laden with a
goodly cargo of their own renown, they are well

26 <πλεόνων> scholia, Erasmus Schmid (edd.).

28 σκοποῦ ἄντα τυχεῖν Mingarelli (edd.): ἄντα σκοποῦ
τυχεῖν D (τετυχεῖν B) ; v.l. in scholium ἂν τετυχεῖν or ἄντα
τυχεῖν.

29 ἄγε, Μοῖσα, οὖρον ἐπέων εὐκλέα mss (BuS³), — εὐκλεῖα (F) :
ἐπέων, ὦ Μοῖσ', ἄγ', οὖρον εὐκλεῖα (BMC).   εὐκλέα παροιχ. mss :
εὔκλέ'· ἀποιχ. Erasmus Schmid, Schneidewin (S¹).

31 ἀοιδαὶ καὶ λόγοι Pauw (CBuS) : ἀοιδοὶ καὶ λόγιοι mss and
scholia (M¹), — λόγοι (BM²) ; ἀοιδαὶ καὶ λόγιοι (F).

δυνατοὶ παρέχειν πολὺν ὕμνον ἀγερώχων ἐργμά-
των

35 ἕνεκεν.   καὶ γὰρ ἐν ἀγαθέᾳ
χεῖρας ἱμάντι δεθεὶς Πυθῶνι κράτησεν ἀπὸ ταύτας
αἷμα πάτρας   60
χρυσαλακάτου ποτὲ Καλλίας ἁδὼν
ἐπ. β'
ἔρνεσι Λατοῦς, παρὰ Κασταλίᾳ τε Χαρίτων
ἑσπέριος ὁμάδῳ φλέγεν·

40 πόντου τε γέφυρ' ἀκάμαντος ἐν ἀμφικτιόνων
ταυροφόνῳ τριετηρίδι Κρεοντίδαν
τίμασε Ποσειδάνιον ἂν τέμενος·   70
βοτάνα τέ νιν
πόθ' ἁ λέοντος

45 νικάσαντ' ἤρεφε δασκίοις
Φλιοῦντος ὑπ' ὠγυγίοις ὄρεσιν.
στρ. γ'
πλατεῖαι πάντοθεν λογίοισιν ἐντὶ πρόσοδοι
νᾶσον εὐκλέα τάνδε κοσμεῖν· ἐπεί σφιν Αἰακίδαι
ἔπορον ἔξοχον αἶσαν ἀρετὰς ἀποδεικνύμενοι με-
γάλας·   80

50 πέταται δ' ἐπί τε χθόνα καὶ διὰ θαλάσσας
τηλόθεν
ὄνυμ' αὐτῶν· καὶ ἐς Αἰθίοπας
Μέμνονος οὐκ ἀπονοστάσαντος ἐπᾶλτο· βαρὺ δέ
σφιν νεῖκος Ἀχιλεὺς
*ἔμβαλε χαμαὶ καταβὰς ἀφ' ἁρμάτων,

34 ἔργμ. most mss (BMFBu) : ἐργμ. *V* (CS).
38 Κασταλίᾳ paraphrase (BMFCBu), —λίᾳ Vatican recension :
—λίαν *V* (S).
45 ἤρεφε δασκίοις Hermann (CBuS), ἔρεψε δασκίοις old mss,
ἔχε δ. (M): ἔρεψ' ἀσκίοις Triclinius, ἐρεφ' ἀσκίοις Erasmus
Schmid (BF).

fitted by their gallant deeds to provide a rich theme
of song to those who till the Muses' field. For, like-
wise in hallowed Pytho, a scion of this clan, with his
hands bound with the cestus, was victorious, even
Callias, who erstwhile found favour with the children
of Lêtô with the golden distaff; and, beside Castalia
he was glorified at eventide by the loud chorus of the
Graces; and the unwearied bridge of the sea [1] paid
honour to Creontidas in the biennial festivals, when
bulls are slain in the sacred precinct of Poseidon;
and the lion's herb of Nemea [2] crowned him once on a
time, when he was victor beneath the shady primeval
mountains of Phlius.

To those who are skilled in ancient story, broad on
every side are the avenues that lie open for glori-
fying this famous island, since the race of Aeacus
bestowed on them that dwell therein a distinguished
destiny, by setting forth an ensample of great virtues;
and their name hath winged its way afar, over the
land and across the sea. Even to the Ethiopians
hath it sped its flight when Memnon returned not to
his home [3]; for Achilles flung on them a heavy

---

[1] The Isthmus of Corinth, with the Isthmian games.

[2] The wild celery from the haunts of the Nemean lion.

[3] Memnon, son of Tithônus and Eôs, king of the Ethiopians,
came to the aid of Priam, but was slain by Achilles. Cp.
P. vi 32, *N.* iii 63, *I.* v 41, viii 58.

---

53 ἔμβαλε Sandys: ἔμπεσε mss (s³). …καββὰς D, κἀμβὰς B.
βαρὺ δέ σφι <δεῖξε> νεῖκος χαμαὶ καταβὰς Ἀχ. Dissen (b²);
— νεῖκος ἔμπας καββὰς Ἀχ. <ἐπέδειξ'> M; — ν. Ἀχ. ἔμπαιε
χ. καταβὰς F; — ν. ἔπλεν Ἀχ. χ. κ. s¹; — ν. Ἀχ. φᾶνε χαμᾶζε
καβὰς Bury; βαρὺ δ' ἔμπεσέ σφι νεῖκος χ. ν. Ἀχ. Kayser (c).

PINDAR

ἀντ. γ΄

φαεννᾶς υἱὸν εὖτ᾽ ἐνάριξεν Ἀόος ἀκμᾷ
55 ἔγχεος ζακότοιο. καὶ ταύταν μὲν παλαιότεροι 90
ὁδὸν ἁμαξιτὸν εὗρον· ἕπομαι δὲ καὶ αὐτὸς ἔχων
    μελέταν·
τὸ δὲ πὰρ ποδὶ ναὸς ἑλισσόμενον αἰεὶ κυμάτων
λέγεται παντὶ μάλιστα δονεῖν
θυμόν. ἑκόντι δ᾽ ἐγὼ νώτῳ μεθέπων δίδυμον
    ἄχθος ἄγγελος ἔβαν,
60 πέμπτον ἐπὶ εἴκοσι τοῦτο γαρύων 100
ἐπ. γ΄

εὖχος ἀγώνων ἄπο, τοὺς ἐνέποισιν ἱερούς,
Ἀλκιμίδα, τέ γ᾽ ἐπαρκέσαι
κλειτᾷ γενεᾷ· δύο μὲν Κρονίου πὰρ τεμένει,
παῖ, σέ τ᾽ ἐνόσφισε καὶ Πουλυτιμίδαν
65 κλᾶρος προπετὴς ἄνθε᾽ Ὀλυμπιάδος.
δελφῖνί κεν
τάχος δι᾽ ἅλμας
ἴσον εὔποιμι Μελησίαν, 110
χειρῶν τε καὶ ἰσχύος ἀνίοχον.

55 ταύταν mss and scholia (BMFBu) : ταῦτα Pauw, Hermann (CS).
59 ἔβαν mss (FBuS³) : βᾶν Hermann (BMCS¹).
60 πέμπτον mss (FBuS³) ; — γ᾽ Hermann (BMC) ; — τ᾽ (S¹).
62 Ἀλκιμίδᾶ, τέ (= σέ) γ᾽ ἐπαρκέσαι P. Maas (S³) : Ἀλκιμίδας τό γ᾽ εἴπρκεσε mss (C, —ν Bu) ; Ἀλκιμίδα τό γ᾽ ἐπάρκεσεν (M) ; Ἀλκιμίδ, ὅ τοι ἐπάρκεσεν (F) ; Ἀλκιμίδαν ἐπαρκέσαι (S¹) : Ἀλκιμίδα ὅ γ᾽ ἐπάρκεσεν κλειτὰ γενεὰ Erasmus Schmid (B).
66 κεν Triclinius (BMFCBu) ; κε old mss : καί s.

374

conflict, when he stepped down to the ground from his chariot, what time he slew the son of the gleaming Dawn with the edge of his wrathful sword.

This was the theme, which the bards of old found for their beaten path, and I myself am following in their steps, while I meditate my theme; yet it is ever the wave that is rolling nearest to the vessel,[1] which causeth most concern to the mind of every mariner. But I, who am bearing on my willing shoulders a double burden, have come as a messenger to proclaim that thou, Alcimidas, hast won for thy famous family this five and twentieth triumph, from the games which men call holy. Two crowns indeed of the Olympic contest beside the sacred precinct of the hill of Cronus were robbed from thee, the youthful victor, and from Polytimidas, by a lot at random drawn.[2] Of Melêsias, as a trainer deft in strength of hands, I would say that in speed he is a match for the dolphin that darteth through the brine.

[1] τὸ πὰρ ποδός, in P. iii 60 and x 62, and τὸ πρὸ ποδός, in I. viii 13, mean "that which is before one's foot," "that which is present" or "near"; cp. N. ix 38 παρποδίου, "imminent." (Similarly, Mezger, and Dr. Rouse and Dr. Postgate, in Proc. Camb. Philol. Soc. 30 April, 1891). The scholiast, however, makes πούς the rudder, and this is approved by Bury, cp. Od. x 32, αἰεὶ γὰρ πόδα νηὸς ἐνώμων. Servius, followed by Fennell and others, makes it the "main sheet"; and Dissen, "the keel of the vessel."

[2] Or "a lot prematurely drawn," implying that they presented themselves to draw lots when they were too young.

NEMEAN VII

FOR SÔGENÊS OF AEGINA

INTRODUCTION

THE seventh Nemean celebrates the victory of
Sôgenês of Aegina in the boy's pentathlum. The
Scholiast states, in one MS (*B*), that the victory was
won in the 14th Nemead (*ιδ'*), and, in the other (*D*),
in the 24th (*κδ'*), corresponding respectively to 547
and 527 B.C., both of which dates are earlier than
that of Pindar's birth (522 or 518). The Ode has
been placed by Gaspar in 493, by Wilamowitz and
Schröder in 485, and by Hermann in 461.

The Scholium on line 64 (94) states that, in
this Ode, the poet wished to apologize to the
Aeginetans for the way in which he had referred
to the death of Neoptolemus, as the Aeginetans had
found fault with Pindar for stating, in a paean written
for the Delphians, that Neoptolemus had died, while
disputing with the attendant for certain sacrificial
dues, ἀμφιπόλοισι μαρνάμενον μυρίαν περὶ τιμάν (cor-
rected by Boeckh into μοιρᾶν περὶ τιμᾶν). This view
of the object of part of the Ode was adopted by
Boeckh, and also by Rauchenstein, Dissen, and
Hartung, but not by Hermann (*Opusc.* iii 22 f).
However, the statement of the Scholiast was proved
to be correct, when part of Pindar's Delphic paean

was discovered in Egypt, and published in 1908, including the words ἀμφιπόλοις δὲ [μ]<οι>ρ[ιᾶν] περὶ τιμᾶν [δηρι]αζόμενον, or, more probably, κυριᾶν περὶ τιμᾶν. Grenfell and Hunt, *Oxyrhynchus papyri* (1900), pp. 47, 98. See *Paean* vi 118.

The poet invokes the goddess of birth, who destines man to divers careers, and has given strength in the pentathlum to Sôgenês (1–8), who dwells in the city of the Aeacidae (9 f).

Victory is a welcome theme to poets, who (like men who are weather-wise) know that a wind is coming on the third day (*i.e.* know that the truth will be duly honoured in the future [1]), and do not suffer loss, owing to eagerness for gain (17 f). Rich and poor alike go to the grave (19 f). Homer, by the magic of his song, has given Odysseus more credit than he deserved; most men are blind, for, had they seen the truth, Odysseus would not have won the prize of valour, and Ajax would not have slain himself (20–30). Death comes upon all; but honour, fostered of Heaven, survives for the heroes who have passed to their graves at Delphi (30–32). Among them was Neoptolemus, who was slain in a contest for the flesh of sacrifice, but, by his death, fulfilled the doom that, for the future, one of the Aeacidae should preside over the sacred rites at Delphi. It is enough to say that infallible is the witness, who thus presides over the Pythian games (35–49).

Aegina has many glories, but the poet must not dwell on them unduly (50–53). All men are not perfectly happy, but the victor's father has a fair

[1] Wilamowitz, *Berlin Akad.* 1908, 334.

share of happiness, in that he has courage and good sense (54–60). The poet repels the charge of having calumniated Neoptolemus (61–69).

Praise of the victor (70–79). Honour due to Zeus (80–84), the father of Aeacus, who was the comrade of Heracles (84–86). A good neighbour is a great blessing, and the victor has a temple of Heracles on either side of his home (87–94). The poet prays to Heracles on behalf of the victor and his father (94–101), and says, for the second time, that he has not calumniated Neoptolemus (102–4). To say the same thing, for the third or fourth time, is folly (105–6).

VII.—ΣΩΓΕΝΕΙ ΑΙΓΙΝΗΤῌ

ΠΑΙΔΙ ΠΕΝΤΑΘΛῼ

στρ. α′

Ἐλείθυια, πάρεδρε Μοιρᾶν βαθυφρόνων,
παῖ μεγαλοσθενέος, ἄκουσον, Ἥρας, γενέτειρα
   τέκνων· ἄνευ σέθεν
οὐ φάος, οὐ μέλαιναν δρακέντες εὐφρόναν
τεὰν ἀδελφεὰν ἐλάχομεν ἀγλαόγυιον Ἥβαν.

5 ἀναπνέομεν δ᾽ οὐχ ἅπαντες ἐπὶ ἶσα·
εἴργει δὲ πότμῳ ζυγένθ᾽ ἕτερον ἕτερα. σὺν δὲ τὶν
   καὶ παῖς ὁ Θεαρίωνος ἀρετᾷ κριθεὶς   10
εὔδοξος ἀείδεται Σωγένης μετὰ πενταέθλοις.

ἀντ. α′

πόλιν γὰρ φιλόμολπον οἰκεῖ δορικτύπων
10 Αἰακιδᾶν·   μάλα δ᾽ ἐθέλοντι σύμπειρον ἀγωνίᾳ
   θυμὸν ἀμφέπειν.
εἰ δὲ τύχῃ τις ἔρδων, μελίφρον᾽ αἰτίαν
ῥοαῖσι Μοισᾶν ἐνέβαλε· ταὶ μεγάλαι γὰρ ἀλκαὶ
σκότον πολὺν ὕμνων ἔχοντι δεόμεναι·
ἔργοις δὲ καλοῖς ἔσοπτρον ἴσαμεν ἑνὶ σὺν τρόπῳ, 20
15 εἰ Μναμοσύνας ἕκατι λιπαράμπυκος
εὕρηται ἄποινα μόχθων κλυταῖς ἐπέων ἀοιδαῖς.

---

9 δορικτύπων Ambrosian recension (MFCBuS): δορύκτυπον D,
δορυκτύπων (B).

12 ἐνέβαλε· ταὶ Hermann (FCBuS¹): ἔβαλε. ταὶ old mss
(ἐνέβαλε scholia); ἐνέβαλεν· αἱ (BM); ἐνέβαλε· καὶ Wilamowitz
(S³).

16 εὕρηται Hermann (edd.), — τις mss.

GODDESS of birth, that art enthroned beside the brooding Destinies! Listen, thou daughter of mighty Hêra, thou that createst offspring. Without thine aid we see not the light, no nor the dark gloom, ere we attain unto thy sister, Hêbê with the glowing limbs. Yet it is not for equal aims that all of us draw our breath, for various indeed are the fates that severally fetter mortals in the chain of destiny.

But it is by thy favour alone that Sôgenês, the son of Thearion, is sung to-day as one who, for his prowess, is deemed glorious among pentathletes.[1] For he dwelleth in a city that loveth music, a city of the race of Aeacus with their clashing spears; and verily eager are they to cherish a spirit familiar with contests. But, if a man prospereth in his doings, he supplieth a sweet source for the Muses' rills; for mighty deeds of prowess are wrapt in darkness deep, if destitute of song; but for noble deeds, we can hold up a mirror, in one way only— if, by grace of Memory with the gleaming crown, one findeth a meed in sounding streams of song. But mariners

---

[1] On the *pentathlum*, cp. Introduction to *O*. xiii.

381

PINDAR

ἐπ. αʹ

σοφοὶ δὲ μέλλοντα τριταῖον ἄνεμον
ἔμαθον, οὐδ᾽ ὑπὸ κέρδει βλάβεν·
ἀφνεὸς πενιχρός τε θανάτου πέρας
20 ἅμα νέονται. ἐγὼ δὲ πλέον᾽ ἔλπομαι
λόγον Ὀδυσσέος ἢ πάθαν διὰ τὸν ἁδυεπῆ γενέσθ᾽
        Ὅμηρον·   30

στρ. βʹ

ἐπεὶ ψεύδεσί οἱ ποτανᾷ <τε> μαχανᾷ
σεμνὸν ἔπεστί τι· σοφία δὲ κλέπτει παράγοισα
μύθοις· τυφλὸν δ᾽ ἔχει
ἦτορ ὅμιλος ἀνδρῶν ὁ πλεῖστος. εἰ γὰρ ἦν
25 ἓ τὰν ἀλάθειαν ἰδέμεν, οὔ κεν ὅπλων χολωθεὶς
ὁ καρτερὸς Αἴας ἔπαξε διὰ φρενῶν
λευρὸν ξίφος· ὃν κράτιστον Ἀχιλέος ἄτερ μάχᾳ 40
ξανθῷ Μενέλᾳ δάμαρτα κομίσαι θοαῖς
ἐν ναυσὶ πόρευσαν εὐθυπνόου Ζεφύροιο πομπαὶ

ἀντ. βʹ

30 πρὸς Ἴλου πόλιν. ἀλλὰ κοινὸν γὰρ ἔρχεται
κῦμ᾽ Ἀΐδα, πέσε δ᾽ ἀδόκητον ἐν καὶ δοκέοντα·
τιμὰ δὲ γίνεται
ὧν θεὸς ἁβρὸν αὔξει λόγον τεθνακότων
βοαθόων, τοὶ παρὰ μέγαν ὀμφαλὸν εὐρυκόλπου

18 ὑπὸ κέρδει βλάβεν Boeckh (edd.): — βάλον mss; ἀπὸ κέρδει βάλον Donaldson.
19 f. θανάτου πέρας ἅμα Wieseler (MFCS): θανάτου παρὰ σᾶμα mss (retained by Wilamowitz); θάνατον πάρα θαμὰ Hermann (B²); θανάτου πάρος ἅμα Bury.
21 πάθαν BD (MFBuS): πάθεν Triclinius (BC).
22 <τε> Hermann (BMFCS): <ʼμφὶ> Bury.
25 ἓ τὰν Boeckh (MFCS): ἐὰν (ἐὰν) mss; ἐτὰν Bergk (Bu), cp. I. ii 10.
32 αὔξῃ scholium (Wilamowitz).
33 βοαθόων BD (MFBuS): βοαθόον Hermann (B); βίᾳ θάνεν τοι — μολὼν C.

382

wise knew well of a blast that is bound to blow on the third day after, nor do they suffer loss through greed of gain. The rich man and the poor alike wend their way together to the bourn of death.

But I deem that Odysseus hath won fame far beyond all his sufferings, thanks to the sweet lays of Homer. For on Homer's fictions and on his winged skill, there resteth a solemn spell; and the poet's lore beguileth us, leading us astray with legends; but the mass of mortal men have a heart that is blind indeed.[1] For, had they only been able to see the truth, never would stalwart Aias, in wrath for the armour, have planted the smooth sword-blade in his breast;—Aias, the bravest, save Achilles, in the battle; Aias, whom the breath of the unswerving Zephyr wafted in swift ships to the city of Ilus, to bring back his wife for the golden-haired Menelaus.

But the billow of Hades rolleth over all alike; that billow breaketh on the dimly known and on the famous; but honour groweth for those, whose fame a god causeth to wax fairer, even the departed champions, who came to the mighty centre of

---

[1] The story of Odysseus is cited as a proof of the power of poetry. Homer had deceived his readers by making Odysseus more famous than he really deserved. Had the Greeks before Troy known his true character, they would never have awarded him the prize for valour, and thus led to the suicide of Ajax.

μόλον χθονός· ἐν Πυθίοισι δὲ δαπέδοις   50
35 κεῖται, Πριάμου πόλιν Νεοπτόλεμος ἐπεὶ πράθεν,
τᾷ καὶ Δαναοὶ πόνησαν· ὁ δ' ἀποπλέων
Σκύρου μὲν ἅμαρτε, πλαγχθέντες δ' εἰς Ἐφύραν
  ἵκοντο·

ἐπ. β'

Μολοσσίᾳ δ' ἐμβασίλευεν ὀλίγον
χρόνον· ἀτὰρ γένος αἰεὶ φέρεν
40 τοῦτό οἱ γέρας. ᾤχετο δὲ πρὸς θεόν,
κτέαν' ἄγων Τρωΐαθεν ἀκροθινίων·   60
ἵνα κρεῶν νιν ὑπὲρ μάχας ἔλασεν ἀντιτυχόντ'
  ἀνὴρ μαχαίρᾳ.

στρ. γ'

βάρυνθεν δὲ περισσὰ Δελφοὶ ξεναγέται.
ἀλλὰ τὸ μόρσιμον ἀπέδωκεν· ἐχρῆν δέ τιν' ἔνδον
  ἄλσει παλαιτάτῳ
45 Αἰακιδᾶν κρεόντων τὸ λοιπὸν ἔμμεναι
θεοῦ παρ' εὐτειχέα δόμον, ἡρωΐαις δὲ πομπαῖς
θεμίσκοπον οἰκεῖν ἐόντα πολυθύτοις
εὐώνυμον ἐς δίκαν. τρία ἔπεα διαρκέσει·   70
οὐ ψεῦδις ὁ μάρτυς ἔργμασιν ἐπιστατεῖ.
50 Αἴγινα, τεῶν Διός ·τ' ἐκγόνων θρασύ μοι τόδ'
  εἰπεῖν

ἀντ. γ'

φαενναῖς ἀρεταῖς ὁδὸν κυρίαν λόγων
οἴκοθεν· ἀλλὰ γὰρ ἀνάπαυσις ἐν παντὶ γλυκεῖα
ἔργῳ· κόρον δ' ἔχει
καὶ μέλι καὶ τὰ τέρπν' ἄνθε' Ἀφροδίσια.

41 κτέαν' ἄγων B (BMFCBu): κτέατ' ἀνάγων D; κτέατ' ἄγων S.
47 πολυθύτοις. B (MS).
48 δίκαν. D, Hermann (BFCBu).
49 μάρτυς· Mezger, Bury.   ἔργῳ. D (BMFBu): ἔργ. B (CS).
49 f. ἐπιστατεῖ, — ἐκγόνων. Hermann (Mezger, S).

Earth's broad bosom. So in the Pythian soil low
lieth the hero Neoptolemus, who erstwhile sacked
the city of Priam, where the Danai themselves were
sore distressed. But while he was returning over the
sea, he failed of Scyros, and, after wandering from
their course, they came to Ephyra.[1] And, for a brief
while, he ruled in Molossia, and, in his honour, this
dignity was borne by his race for ever. Now the
hero himself had gone to consult the God, bearing
with him precious things from the choicest of the
spoil of Troy; and there, while entangled in strife con-
cerning the flesh of his victim, a man smote him with
the sword; and grieved, beyond measure, were the
hospitable men of Delphi. But he only fulfilled his
fate, for it was doomed that one of the royal race of
Aeacus should, for all time to come, dwell in the
heart of that primeval grove, beside the fair walls of
the God's own temple, and, dwelling there, should pre-
side over the processions of heroes, which are honoured
by many sacrifices, for enforcement of auspicious
guest-right.[2] Three words will suffice; no false loon
is the witness that presideth over doughty deeds.

Aegina, I have this bold speech to utter con-
cerning the race that sprang from thyself and Zeus,
that, by their brilliant deeds of prowess, they have
won from their home a path of glory that is all
their own. But enough, for in every manner of
work, sweet is repose; even honey may cloy, and
the gladsome flowers of Aphroditê's garden. By

[1] The capital of Thesprôtia (the old Molossia) in Epîrus,
afterwards called Cichyrus.

[2] Neoptolemus was to preside at the festival, and enforce
the laws of hospitality. So Bury, following Hermann.

PINDAR

φυᾷ δ' ἕκαστος διαφέρομεν βιοτὰν λαχόντες,　80
55 ὁ μὲν τά, τὰ δ' ἄλλοι· τυχεῖν δ' ἕν' ἀδύνατον
εὐδαιμονίαν ἅπασαν ἀνελόμενον· οὐκ ἔχω
εἰπεῖν, τίνι τοῦτο Μοῖρα τέλος ἔμπεδον
ὤρεξε. Θεαρίων, τὶν δ' ἐοικότα καιρὸν ὄλβου

ἐπ. γ΄
δίδωσι, τόλμαν τε καλῶν ἀρομένῳ
60 σύνεσιν οὐκ ἀποβλάπτει φρενῶν.
ξεῖνός εἰμι· σκοτεινὸν ἀπέχων ψόγον,　90
ὕδατος ὥτε ῥοὰς φίλον ἐς ἄνδρ' ἄγων
κλέος ἐτήτυμον αἰνέσω· ποτίφορος δ' ἀγαθοῖσι
μισθὸς οὗτος.

στρ. δ΄
ἐὼν δ' ἐγγὺς Ἀχαιὸς οὐ μέμψεταί μ' ἀνὴρ
65 Ἰονίας ὑπὲρ ἁλὸς οἰκέων· προξενίᾳ πέποιθ'· ἔν τε
δαμόταις
ὄμματι δέρκομαι λαμπρόν, οὐχ ὑπερβαλών,
βίαια πάντ' ἐκ ποδὸς ἐρύσαις, ὁ δὲ λοιπὸς εὔφρων
ποτὶ χρόνος ἕρποι. μαθὼν δέ τις ἀνερεῖ,　100
εἰ πὰρ μέλος ἔρχομαι ψόγιον ὄαρον ἐννέπων.
70 Εὐξενίδα πάτραθε Σώγενες, ἀπομνύω
μὴ τέρμα προβὰς ἄκονθ' ὥτε χαλκοπάρᾳον ὄρσαι
ἀντ. δ΄
θοὰν γλῶσσαν, ὃς ἐξέπεμψεν παλαισμάτων

---

59 f. ἀρομένῳ σύνεσιν Hermann (BMFBuS): ἀραμένῳ σύνεσις BD;
ἀρομένῳ σύνεσις (C).
68 ἀνερεῖ Gildersleeve (BuS²): ἂν ἐρεῖ mss (BMFCS¹).

---

[1] Ephyra, the capital of Thesprôtia, stood upon a cliff, a
short distance inland; but Pindar may be referring to the
mountainous region stretching down from Dodona to the sea,
described, in N. iv 51–53, as the kingdom of Neoptolemus.
"Achaean" here means "Molossian"; the Achaeans of

386

our several natures do we differ, for we have received
for our allotted life boons that vary from each other;
but for any one man to win the prize of happiness
complete is impossible. I cannot say to whom Fate
hath proffered this crowning boon as a sure
possession. But to thee, Thearion, she giveth a
fitting season of success, and, whereas thou didst
aforetime show a daring spirit for noble deeds, she
now suffereth not the wisdom of thy mind to be
impaired. Guest-friend am I; averting the dark
shadow of blame, and bringing true glory, like
streams of water, to the hero that I love, I shall
sing his praise; and meet for the good is this reward.
But if, of the Achaeans, any one be near, who
dwelleth above the Ionian sea,[1] he will not blame
me. I rely on my being their representative[2]; and,
among my fellow-townsmen too, bright is the glance
of mine eye, for I have not overshot the mark, but
have thrust all violence away from my steps; and
may the rest of my life draw nigh with kindly
purpose. But whoso truly knoweth me will pro-
claim, whether I go on my way breathing the
whisper of blame, that jars on the music of life.
Sôgenês, of Euxenid clan, I swear that I over-
stepped not the line, when I shot forth my swift
tongue, like that bronze-tipped spear, which releaseth
the neck and thews from the sweat of the wrestling-

Thessaly, who served under Neoptolemus, followed him to
Molossia, on his return from Troy.

[2] Pindar appears to have represented the Epeirotes at
Thebes, as their *proxenus* or Theban consul. He appeals to
this as proof of his standing well with the descendants
of Neoptolemus, whose memory he has been accused of
traducing.

αὐχένα καὶ σθένος ἀδίαντον, αἴθωνι πρὶν ἁλίῳ
  γυῖον ἐμπεσεῖν.
εἰ πόνος ἦν, τὸ τερπνὸν πλέον πεδέρχεται.
75 ἔα με· νικῶντί γε χάριν, εἴ τι πέραν ἀερθεὶς   110
ἀνέκραγον, οὐ τραχύς εἰμι καταθέμεν.
εὔρειν στεφάνους ἐλαφρόν· ἀναβάλεο· Μοῖσά τοι
κολλᾷ χρυσὸν ἔν τε λευκὸν ἐλέφανθ' ἁμᾷ
καὶ λείριον ἄνθεμον ποντίας ὑφελοῖσ' ἐέρσας.
ἐπ. δ´
80 Διὸς δὲ μεμναμένος ἀμφὶ Νεμέᾳ
πολύφατον θρόον ὕμνων δόνει
ἡσυχᾷ. βασιλῆα δὲ θεῶν πρέπει   120
δάπεδον ἂν τόδε γαρυέμεν ἁμέρᾳ
ὀπί· λέγοντι γὰρ Αἰακόν νιν ὑπὸ ματροδόκοις
  γοναῖς φυτεῦσαι,
στρ. ε´
85 ἑᾷ μὲν πολίαρχον εὐωνύμῳ πάτρᾳ,
Ἡράκλεες, σέο δὲ προπρεῶν' ἔμεν ξεῖνον ἀδελφεόν
τ'. εἰ δὲ γεύεται
ἀνδρὸς ἀνήρ τι, φαῖμέν κε γείτον' ἔμμεναι
νόῳ φιλάσαντ' ἀτενέϊ γείτονι χάρμα πάντων   130

74 πεδέρχομαι Wilamowitz.
  83 ἁμέρᾳ Hermann (BMFCBuS[1]): θαμερᾶ B; θεμερᾶ D,
Wilamowitz (S[3]), cp. Aesch. P.V. 134 θεμέρωπις Αἰδώς.
  85 ἑᾷ Hermann (BCS): ἐμᾷ mss (MF), Wilamowitz; τεᾷ
Pauw; ἐτᾷ Bury.
  86 προπρεῶνα (mss) ἔμεν Jurenka: προπρεῶνα μὲν mss
(BMFCBu); προπράον' ἔμεν (S).

---

[1] ἀδίαντον, " unwet," from διαίνω. Wilamowitz, however,
makes it " unbuffeted," " unbruised," from αἴνειν· κατα-
κόπτοντα πτίσσειν.
  [2] These words prove that Sôgenês actually went through
the toil of competing in the wrestling, which was the last
event in the pentathlum.

match,[1] ere the limb falleth under the burning sun.
If toil there was, greater is the delight that followeth.[2]
Forgive me ; even if, in undue elation, I uttered a loud
scream, yet, to please the victor, I am not too rude
to retract it.[3]

The weaving of wreaths is an easy task. Strike
up the prelude![4] Lo! the Muse is welding gold and
ivory white in one, with the lily[5] she hath stolen from
beneath the ocean's dew.

But, in remembrance of Zeus, swell, softly swell,
for Nemea a far-famed strain of song. For, on this
spot, it is meet indeed to chant with gentle voice the
king of the gods, for they tell that here by a mortal
mother he begat Aeacus to be a ruler of cities for
his own illustrious land, and to be a kindly friend
and brother to thee, O Heracles. But, if a man
hath any fruition of his fellow, we should say that
a neighbour is to his neighbour a priceless joy, if he

---

[3] Here, as often, Pindar uses metaphors suggested by the
particular athletic contest which he is commemorating. The
general sense is : "I have not overstepped the line, in darting
out my remark about Neoptolemus. I have not broken the
rules of the game, and thus forfeited admission to further
competition. Like yourself, Sôgenês, I have borne all the
burden and pain of the final contest. You and I have had
to fight and to endure ; but now, after success, the pleasure
that follows is greater than the pain. If I used language
that was too strong, then, to please the victor, I would gladly
withdraw it." The poet is ready to retract any remark about
Neoptolemus that had given offence to the Aeginetans.
(Wilamowitz, Pindar's *siebentes nemeisches Gedicht*, Berlin
Academy, 1908, esp. p. 339 f, summarised by Gildersleeve in
A.J.P. xxxi 150). For other views see Fennell's and Bury's
notes.
[4] Here the poet appears to make a fresh start, by calling
for a new prelude. The Scholiast has ἀνακρούου. The phrase
is also interpreted " wait a while. " [5] Coral.

ἐπάξιον· εἰ δ' αὐτὸ καὶ θεὸς ἀνέχοι,
90 ἐν τίν κ' ἐθέλοι, Γίγαντας ὃς ἐδάμασας, εὐτυχῶς
ναίειν πατρὶ Σωγένης ἀταλὸν ἀμφέπων
θυμὸν προγόνων εὐκτήμονα ζαθέαν ἀγυιάν·
ἀντ. έ
ἐπεὶ τετραόροισιν ὥθ' ἁρμάτων ζυγοῖς
ἐν τεμένεσσι δόμον ἔχει τεοῖς, ἀμφοτέρας ἰὼν
χειρός. ὦ μάκαρ,
95 τὶν δ' ἐπέοικεν Ἥρας πόσιν τε πειθέμεν   140
κόραν τε γλαυκώπιδα· δύνασαι δὲ βροτοῖσιν
ἀλκὰν
ἀμαχανιᾶν δυσβάτων θαμὰ διδόμεν.
εἰ γάρ σφισιν ἐμπεδοσθενέα βίοτον ἁρμόσαις
ἥβᾳ λιπαρῷ τε γήραϊ διαπλέκοις
100 εὐδαίμον' ἐόντα, παίδων δὲ παῖδες ἔχοιεν αἰεὶ
ἐπ. έ
γέρας τό περ νῦν καὶ ἄρειον ὄπιθεν.
τὸ δ' ἐμὸν οὔ ποτε φάσει κέαρ   150
ἀτρόποισι Νεοπτόλεμον ἑλκύσαι
ἔπεσι· ταὐτὰ δὲ τρὶς τετράκι τ' ἀμπολεῖν
105 ἀπορία τελέθει, τέκνοισιν ἅτε μαψυλάκας, "Διὸς
Κόρινθος."

loved him with steadfast heart[1]; but if a god also should uphold this truth, 'tis by thy favour, O thou who didst quell the Giants[2] that, Sôgenês, fostering a spirit of devotion to his sire, would fain dwell happily beside the rich and hallowed road, where once his fathers dwelt; for he hath his house in the precincts of thy temples, which face him, like the yoke-arms of a four-horsed chariot, on either hand as he goeth forth. And thee, O blessed Heracles, it beseemeth to persuade the consort of Hêra and the grey-eyed maiden[3]; for full often canst thou grant to mortals relief from distress inexplicable. Oh that, having harnessed their youth and happy eld to a life of steadfast strength, thou mightest weave it to its close in happiness, and that children's children may have for ever the boon that is now present, and a nobler boon hereafter. But my heart will not confess that I have, with words offensive, dragged in the dirt the name of Neoptolemus. Howsoever, to traverse the same ground thrice and four times is poverty of thought, like that of one who vainly babbles to babes of "Corinth, the city of Zeus."[4]

[1] Bury.   [2] Heracles.   [3] Athênê.

[4] The Scholiast states that, when the Megarians revolted from Corinth, the Corinthians sent envoys to Megara protesting that "Corinth, the city of Zeus" (ὁ Διὸς Κόρινθος) would not tolerate this presumption (and probably harped upon this phrase). In a subsequent engagement the Megarians made a battle-cry of not sparing "Corinth, the city of Zeus" (τὸν Διὸς Κόρινθον). μαψυλάκας is best taken as a genitive singular feminine, "like that of a vain babbler."

NEMEAN VIII

FOR DEINIAS OF AEGINA

INTRODUCTION

THE eighth Nemean celebrates a victory in the foot-race (the double stadium of more than 400 yards), won by the youthful athlete, Deinias, son of Megas, of Aegina. His father, who had been similarly successful in the Nemean games, was no longer living. The Ode has been assigned by Mezger and Gaspar to 451 B.C. The myth of the quarrel between Ajax and Odysseus for the armour of Achilles has been regarded by Mezger (followed by Bury and Gaspar) as a reference to the fact that, when, in 491, the envoys of Darius demanded earth and water in token of submission, Aegina had consented, and had therefore been accused by Athens of treachery to the cause of Hellenic freedom (Herodotus vi, 49, 50). Hence it has been supposed that Aegina and Athens are referred to, under the guise of Ajax and Odysseus respectively. But Ajax was a favourite hero at Athens, and the mention of the myth of Ajax and Odysseus, without any reference to unfair voting (as in *N.* vii 23 f), has suggested to Dr. Fennell that the date (463?) was shortly before that of *N.* vii (461?).

INTRODUCTION

The date **459** has been suggested or approved by Schröder and others.

The goddess of Youth is sometimes kind, sometimes cruel (1–3). We must be content to aim only at noble desires (4 f). Such desires were fulfilled by the union between Zeus and Aegina, which led to the birth of Aeacus, who was courted by the heroes of Athens and Sparta (6–12).

The poet dedicates to Zeus and Aegina an ode in honour of the victories won in the Nemean stadium by Deinis and his father, Megas (13–16). Prosperity granted by the aid of a god is apt to be more abiding (17); such was the prosperity of Cinyras of Cyprus (18).

The poet pauses, like a runner on the point of starting. Anything novel is perilous; the noble are attacked by envy, as Ajax was attacked in his claim to the armour of Achilles (19–32). Calumny and cunning detraction have existed of old (32–34). Such a temper is disowned by the poet, who hopes that, to the end of his days, he may be praised by his fellow-citizens for being plain and straightforward, whether in praise or in blame (35–39). Success is enhanced by song (40–42). The poet cannot restore to life the victor's father, but he can raise a monument of song in honour of the victories won by the father and the son, and thus assuage pain (44–50). The antidote of song is even older than the strife between Adrastus and Thebes (50)—that is, older even than the foundation of the Nemean games.

VIII.—ΔΕΙΝΙΑ ΑΙΓΙΝΗΤΗ

ΔΙΑΥΛΟΔΡΟΜΩ

στρ. α΄

Ὥρα πότνια, κάρυξ Ἀφροδίτας ἀμβροσιᾶν φιλο-
τάτων,

ἅτε παρθενηΐοις παίδων τ' ἐφίζοισα γλεφάροις,

τὸν μὲν ἀμέροις ἀνάγκας χερσὶ βαστάζεις, ἕτερον
δ' ἑτέραις.

ἀγαπατὰ δὲ καιροῦ μὴ πλαναθέντα πρὸς ἔργον
ἕκαστον

5 τῶν ἀρειόνων ἐρώτων ἐπικρατεῖν δύνασθαι.

ἀντ. α΄

οἷοι καὶ Διὸς Αἰγίνας τε λέκτρον ποιμένες ἀμφε-
πόλησαν   10

Κυπρίας δώρων· ἔβλαστεν δ' υἱὸς Οἰνώνας βασι-
λεύς

χειρὶ καὶ βουλαῖς ἄριστος. πολλά νιν πολλοὶ
λιτάνευον ἰδεῖν.

ἀβοατὶ γὰρ ἡρώων ἄωτοι περιναιεταόντων

10 ἤθελον κείνου γε πείθεσθ' ἀναξίαις ἑκόντες,

ἐπ. α΄

οἵ τε κρανααῖς ἐν Ἀθάναισιν ἅρμοζον στρατόν,   20

οἵ τ' ἀνὰ Σπάρταν Πελοπηϊάδαι.

ἱκέτας Αἰακοῦ σεμνῶν γονάτων πόλιός θ' ὑπὲρ
φίλας

ἀστῶν θ' ὑπὲρ τῶνδ' ἅπτομαι φέρων

2 γλεφάροις edd. : βλ. mss.

394

VIII.—FOR DEINIAS OF AEGINA

WINNER IN THE DOUBLE FOOT-RACE, 459 (?) B.C.

QUEEN of youthful prime, harbinger of the divine desires of Aphrodîtê, thou that, resting on the eyes of maidens and of boys, bearest one in the hands of gentle destiny, but handlest another far otherwise. 'Tis sweet for one who hath not swerved from due measure in aught that he doeth, to be able to win the nobler prizes of love.

Such loves were the ministers of Cypria's boons, who hovered round the couch of Zeus and of Aegina, when there sprang from that union a son, who, as Oenônê's king, was foremost in might and in counsel. Many a time did many a man pray they might behold him ; for the flower of the heroes that dwelt around him longed with gladness to submit to his rule of their own free will, both those who marshalled the host in craggy Athens, and the descendants of Pelops in Sparta.

Even as a suppliant, do I stretch my hands to the hallowed knees of Aeacus, offering him on behalf of

15 Λυδίαν μίτραν καναχηδὰ πεποικιλμέναν,
  Δείνιος δισσῶν σταδίων καὶ πατρὸς Μέγα Νε-
    μεαῖον ἄγαλμα.
  σὺν θεῷ γάρ τοι φυτευθεὶς ὄλβος ἀνθρώποισι
    παρμονώτερος·

στρ. β΄

  ὅσπερ καὶ Κινύραν ἔβρισε πλούτῳ ποντίᾳ ἔν ποτε
    Κύπρῳ.   30
  ἵσταμαι δὴ ποσσὶ κούφοις, ἀμπνέων τε πρίν τι
    φάμεν.
20 πολλὰ γὰρ πολλᾷ λέλεκται· νεαρὰ δ' ἐξευρόντα
    δόμεν βασάνῳ
  ἐς ἔλεγχον, ἅπας κίνδυνος· ὄψον δὲ λόγοι φθονε-
    ροῖσιν·
  ἅπτεται δ' ἐσλῶν ἀεί, χειρόνεσσι δ' οὐκ ἐρίζει.

ἀντ. β΄

  κεῖνος καὶ Τελαμῶνος δάψεν υἱὸν φασγάνῳ ἀμ-
    φικυλίσαις.   40
  ἦ τιν' ἄγλωσσον μέν, ἦτορ δ' ἄλκιμον, λάθα
    κατέχει
25 ἐν λυγρῷ νείκει· μέγιστον δ' αἰόλῳ ψεύδει γέρας
    ἀντέταται.
  κρυφίαισι γὰρ ἐν ψάφοις Ὀδυσσῆ Δαναοὶ θερά-
    πευσαν·
  χρυσέων δ' Αἴας στερηθεὶς ὅπλων φόνῳ πάλαισεν.

ἐπ. β΄

  ἦ μὰν ἀνόμοιά γε δάοισιν ἐν θερμῷ χροῒ
  ἕλκεα ῥῆξαν πελεμιζόμενοι   50
30 ὑπ' ἀλεξιμβρότῳ λόγχᾳ, τὰ μὲν ἀμφ' Ἀχιλεῖ
    νεοκτόνῳ,

16 Δείνιος, ἤτοι τοῦ Δεινίου Schol.
25 ψεύδῖ Wilamowitz.
29 πελεμιζόμενοι Wakefield (MFCBuS): πολ. mss (B).

396

his dear city and of these his citizens a Lydian fillet
decked with song, a thing of grace from Nemea,
in honour of the double victory won in the foot-race
by Deinias and his father Megas.   For, as ye know,
prosperity is all the more abiding if it be planted
with the blessing of a god, even such prosperity as
in olden days loaded Cinyras with wealth in sea-girt
Cyprus.[1]

Lo! I am standing on feet lightly poised, taking
breath before I speak.   For many a tale hath been
told in many a way; but for any one to coin new
fancies, and submit them to the touchstone for
assay, is perilous indeed. Tales are a dainty morsel to
the envious, and envy ever fasteneth on the noble
and striveth not with the mean.   Envy it was that
devoured the son of Telamon when his flesh closed
upon his sword.   Verily, in him, one without gift
of speech, though bold of heart, is overwhelmed in
oblivion amid grievous strife, while the greatest prize
hath been held forth to cunning falsehood.   For
the Danai, by their secret votes, unfairly favoured
Odysseus; and Aias, reft of the golden armour,
wrestled with death. In very sooth unequal were the
wounds which they tore in the warm flesh of the
foe with their succouring spears, when sorely prest,
at one time over the corse of Achilles newly slain,

---

[1] Cinyras, son of Apollo, and king of Cyprus, was priest
of the Paphian Aphroditê.   Cp. *P.* ii 15.

ἄλλων τε μόχθων ἐν πολυφθόροις
ἀμέραις. ἐχθρὰ δ' ἄρα πάρφασις ἦν καὶ πάλαι,
αἱμύλων μύθων ὁμόφοιτος, δολοφραδής, κακοποιὸν
   ὄνειδος·
ἃ τὸ μὲν λαμπρὸν βιᾶται, τῶν δ' ἀφάντων κῦδος
   ἀντείνει σαθρόν.

στρ. γ´

35 εἴη μή ποτέ μοι τοιοῦτον ἦθος, Ζεῦ πάτερ, ἀλλὰ
      κελεύθοις   60
ἁπλόαις ζωᾶς ἐφαπτοίμαν, θανὼν ὡς παισὶ κλέος
μὴ τὸ δύσφαμον προσάψω. χρυσὸν εὔχονται,
      πεδίον δ' ἕτεροι
ἀπέραντον· ἐγὼ δ' ἀστοῖς ἁδὼν καὶ χθονὶ γυῖα
      καλύψαιμ',
αἰνέων αἰνητά, μομφὰν δ' ἐπισπείρων ἀλιτροῖς.

ἀντ. γ´

40 αὔξεται δ' ἀρετά, χλωραῖς ἐέρσαις ὡς ὅτε δένδρεον
      ᾄσσει,
<ἐν> σοφοῖς ἀνδρῶν ἀερθεῖσ' ἐν δικαίοις τε πρὸς
      ὑγρὸν   70
αἰθέρα. χρεῖαι δὲ παντοῖαι φίλων ἀνδρῶν· τὰ μὲν
      ἀμφὶ πόνοις
ὑπερώτατα· μαστεύει δὲ καὶ τέρψις ἐν ὄμμασι
      θέσθαι
πιστόν. ὦ Μέγα, τὸ δ' αὖτις τεὰν ψυχὰν κομίξαι

ἐπ. γ´

45 οὔ μοι δυνατόν· κενεᾶν δ' ἐλπίδων χαῦνον τέλος·

38 καλύψαιμ' mss (BM¹FCBu); καλύψαιν Bergk² (M²);
καλύψαι Wackernagel (s).
   41 <ἐν> Boeckh (edd.).
   44 πιστόν paraphrase (MCS): πιστά B (F), πιστά Ϝοι (ᾦ mss)
Bury; πίσταν D, πίστιν Triclinius (B).

and also on days of carnage spent on other toils.
Thus, even in days of old, there was malignant
misrepresentation, walking in the ways of crafty
language, imagining deceit, mischief-making calumny.
She doeth violence to the illustrious, and for the
obscure raiseth on high a glory that is rottenness.
O father Zeus, may I never have such a spirit as
this. May I tread the straightest path of life, that,
when I die, I may leave my children a name that
hath no ill-repute. Gold men pray for, or for
illimitable land; but I only pray that I may find
favour with my people, while I ever praise that
which merits praise, and cast blame on the doers of
wrong, until at last my limbs are covered by the sod.
The fame of glorious deeds doth grow, even as when
a tree shooteth forth beneath refreshing dews; even
so is fame borne aloft to the liquid air among men
who love the song and who love the right. Varied
indeed are the uses of friends; the help that is
given in the time of distress standeth highest, yet
joy is also eager to set before men's eyes a pledge
of friendship.

To call thy soul, O Megas, to life again is, for
me, impossible; of futile hopes the end is vain; but

PINDAR

σεῦ δὲ πάτρα Χαριάδαις τ᾽ * ἐλαφρὸν
ὑπερεῖσαι λίθον Μοισαῖον ἕκατι ποδῶν εὐωνύ-
μων   80
δὶς δὴ δυοῖν. χαίρω δὲ πρόσφορον
ἐν μὲν ἔργῳ κόμπον ἱείς, ἐπαοιδαῖς δ᾽ ἀνὴρ
50 νώδυνον καί τις κάματον θῆκεν. ἦν γε μὰν ἐπι-
κώμιος ὕμνος
δὴ πάλαι καὶ πρὶν γενέσθαι τὰν ᾽Αδράστου ταν τε
Καδμείων ἔριν.

46 τ᾽ ἐλαφρόν conjectured by Bergk, Cookesley, and present
editor, cp. N. vii 77, εὑρεῖν στεφάνους ἐλαφρόν: τε λαῦρον B;
τελαβρον D, τε λάβρον (BMGFCS), cp. Schol. λάβρον δὲ τὸν
λίθον τῶν Μουσῶν ἀλληγορικῶς τὴν ἀπὸ τῶν λόγων εὔτονον
στήλην φησί. Elsewhere, the penultimate of ἐλαφρός, and
also of λάβρος, is long in Pindar; but the former is short in
Aesch. P. V. 125, and the latter in Eur. Or. 697, H. F. 861.

it is easy to uprear a Muses' monument of song
for thy clan and for the Chariadae, in honour of
those twice twain feet of happy omen. I rejoice
in sounding forth the exultant praise that befitteth
such an exploit; and ere now hath one made toil
painless by the spell of song. Verily, there was
indeed a song of triumph, even in the olden time,
even before the strife between Adrastus and the race
of Cadmus.

NEMEAN IX

FOR CHROMIUS OF AETNA

INTRODUCTION

THE last three of the " Nemean " Odes have no connection with the Nemean festival. The Nemean Odes were placed by the Alexandrian critics at the end of the epinician Odes, and at the end of the Nemean Odes were added (by way of Appendix) the ninth, tenth, and eleventh Odes, which are connected, not with Nemea, but with Sicyon, Argos, and Tenedos.

This ninth Ode celebrates a victory won in the chariot-race, at Sicyon, by Chromius, the brother-in-law of Hieron. The prize consists of silver cups (51). The Ode was performed at the city of Aetna, founded in 476 by Hieron, who placed it under the rule of Chromius, whose victory at Nemea itself had already been celebrated by Pindar in the first Nemean, assigned to 476. The present Ode has been assigned by Gaspar to 476, shortly after the first and second Olympic Odes, all three Odes belonging to the time of Pindar's stay in Sicily. It has also been conjecturally assigned by Schröder and others to a slightly later date, **474.**

The Muses are summoned from Sicyon to the newly-founded city of Aetna, there to celebrate the

INTRODUCTION

victory won by Chromius in games sacred to the Pythian Apollo (1-5). This deed of prowess must not be buried in oblivion (6 f). With lyre and flute, we must celebrate the chariot-race founded of old by Adrastus in honour of Apollo (8 f).

The myth of the Seven against Thebes (9-27).

The poet prays Zeus to grant to the Aetnaeans peace, and civil order, and success in the games (28-32). They are fond of horses, and are generous in their expenditure (32-34). Praise of the heroism of Chromius, who, beside the river Helôrus, and elsewhere by land and sea, was as brave as Hector beside the Scamander (34-43). He is already blessed with riches and honour, and he deserves a peaceful old age (44-47). Peace loves the banquet, and the flowing bowl gives new courage to the voice. Let the silver bowls won as prizes at Sicyon be filled with wine (48-53).

The poet concludes by calling Zeus to witness that, in his hymns of victory, he shoots not far from the mark (53-55).

IX.—ΧΡΟΜΙΩ ΑΙΤΝΑΙΩ

ΑΡΜΑΤΙ

στρ. α΄

Κωμάσομεν παρ᾽ Ἀπόλλωνος Σικυώνοθε, Μοῖσαι,
τὰν νεόκτισταν ἐς Αἴτναν, ἔνθ᾽ ἀναπεπταμέναι
ξείνων νενίκανται θύραι,
ὄλβιον ἐς Χρομίου δῶμ᾽. ἀλλ᾽ ἐπέων γλυκὺν
ὕμνον πράσσετε.
τὸ κρατήσιππον γὰρ ἐς ἅρμ᾽ ἀναβαίνων ματέρι
καὶ διδύμοις παίδεσσιν αὐδὰν μανύει   10
5 Πυθῶνος αἰπεινᾶς ὁμοκλάροις ἐπόπταις.

στρ. β΄

ἔστι δέ τις λόγος ἀνθρώπων, τετελεσμένον ἐσλὸν
μὴ χαμαὶ σιγᾷ καλύψαι· θεσπεσία δ᾽ ἐπέων καύ-
χαις ἀοιδὰ πρόσφορος.
ἀλλ᾽ ἀνὰ μὲν βρομίαν φόρμιγγ᾽, ἀνὰ δ᾽ αὐλὸν ἐπ᾽
αὐτὰν ὄρσομεν
ἱππίων ἄθλων κορυφάν, ἅτε Φοίβῳ θῆκεν Ἄδρα-
στος ἐπ᾽ Ἀσωποῦ ῥεέθροις· ὧν ἐγὼ   20
10 μνασθεὶς ἐπασκήσω κλυταῖς ἥρωα τιμαῖς,

στρ. γ΄

ὃς τότε μὲν βασιλεύων κεῖθι νέαισί θ᾽ ἑορταῖς
ἰσχύος τ᾽ ἀνδρῶν ἁμίλλαις ἅρμασί τε γλαφυροῖς
ἄμφαινε κυδαίνων πόλιν.

---

3 πράσσετε B (BMCS): πράσσεται D in erasure (FB).

7 καύχαις Benedictus (BFBu): καύχας mss (MS); καυχᾶσσ-
Schneidewin (C).

IX.—FOR CHROMIUS OF AETNA

Ye Muses, we shall revel forth from Apollo's
fane at Sicyon unto the newly-founded Aetna,
where doors flung open wide are too narrow for
all the guests, even unto the rich palace of
Chromius; but do ye make a sweet strain of verse.[1]
For, mounting his chariot of victorious steeds, he
proclaimeth a song in honour of the Mother (Lêtô)
and of her twin offspring (Apollo and Artemis),
who hold united sway over lofty Pytho.

Now there is a saying among men, that it is
not meet that a deed nobly done should be buried
silently in the ground, and a lay divine of verse is
well fitted for loud acclaim. But we shall wake
the pealing lyre, shall wake the flute, in honour of
the most exalted of all contests with the steed,—
contests which Adrastus at the streams of Asôpus[2]
founded in honour of Phoebus; and when I make
mention thereof, I shall deck with loudly-sounding
words of praise the hero who, erst, when he was
monarch there, exalted and glorified his city with fresh
festivals and contests that prove men's strength,
and with chariots of cunning work. For, of old

---

[1] πράσσεται, written in an erasure in *D*, is preferred by
Fennell and Bury :—" but he (Chromius) exacts the debt of
a sweet strain of verse."

[2] A river rising near Phliûs, and flowing past Sicyon.

405

PINDAR

φεῦγε γὰρ Ἀμφιαρῆ ποτε θρασυμήδεα καὶ δεινὰν
  στάσιν   30
πατρῴων οἴκων ἀπό τ᾽ Ἄργεος· ἀρχοὶ δ᾽ οὐκ ἔτ᾽
  ἔσαν Ταλαοῦ παῖδες, βιασθέντες λύᾳ.
15 κρέσσων δὲ καππαύει δίκαν τὰν πρόσθεν ἀνήρ.

στρ. δ´

ἀνδροδάμαντ᾽ Ἐριφύλαν, ὅρκιον ὡς ὅτε πιστόν,
δόντες Οἰκλείδᾳ γυναῖκα, ξανθοκομᾶν Δαναῶν
  ἔσσαν μέγιστοι καί ποτε   40
ἐσ<λὸν ἐς> ἑπταπύλους Θήβας ἄγαγον στρατὸν
  ἀνδρῶν αἰσιᾶν
οὐ κατ᾽ ὀρνίχων ὁδόν· οὐδὲ Κρονίων ἀστεροπὰν
  ἐλελίξαις οἴκοθεν μαργουμένους
20 στείχειν ἐπώτρυν᾽, ἀλλὰ φείσασθαι κελεύθου.

στρ. ε´

φαινομέναν δ᾽ ἄρ᾽ ἐς ἄταν σπεῦδεν ὅμιλος ἱκέ-
  σθαι   50
χαλκέοις ὅπλοισιν ἱππείοις τε σὺν ἔντεσιν· Ἰσμη-
  νοῦ δ᾽ ἐπ᾽ ὄχθαισι γλυκὺν
νόστον ἐρεισάμενοι λευκανθέα σώματ᾽ ἐπίαναν
  καπνόν·
ἑπτὰ γὰρ δαίσαντο πυραὶ νεογυίους φῶτας· ὁ δ᾽
  Ἀμφιάρῃ σχίσσεν κεραυνῷ παμβίᾳ
25 Ζεὺς τὰν βαθύστερνον χθόνα, κρύψεν δ᾽ ἅμ᾽
  ἵπποις,   60

14 πατρῴων old mss, πατρῴων (edd.) ; πατέρων Triclinius ;
πατρίων Erasmus Schmid (s).
17 f. καί ποτε | ἐσ<λὸν ἐς> Boehmer, approved in Bury's
Isthmians (1892) p. xiii : <δὴ τόθεν> | Boeckh (MF), <λα-
γέται> | (C) ; _ ⌣ _ (s) | καί ποτ᾽ ἐς.
23 ἐρεισάμενοι *B* (MFBₙS), ἀμερσαμενοι? s ; ἐρυσάμενοι *D* and
Triclinius ; ἐρυσσάμενοι Hermann (BC).
σώματ᾽ ἐπίαναν Hermann (BFBₙ) : σώμασιν ἐπίαναν *BD* ;
σώμασ᾽ ἐπίαναν Triclinius ; σώμασι πίαναν Bergk (MCS).

time, Adrastus had fled from his ancestral home,
even from Argos, before the bold-hearted Amphiaraüs
and the dread sedition. Thus the sons of Talaüs were
no longer rulers, as they had been over-powered by
civil strife, but, when a stronger man cometh, he
doeth away with existing right.[1]

The man-quelling Eriphŷlê had been given as
wife to Amphiaraüs, the son of Oicles, as a sure
pledge, by the sons of Talaüs, and they then be-
came the most mighty among the golden-haired
Danaï; and, once on a day, they led to seven-gated
Thebes a brave host of men on a march attended
by no happy omens; for the son of Cronus, by
whirling his levin-bolt, urged them in their
frenzy not to go forth from their home, but to
abstain from the journey. And so that company
was hastening to plunge into manifest doom, and, on
the banks of Ismênus, when they had laid down
their longings for a happy return to their home, as
blanched corpses they fed fat the smoke[1]; for seven
funeral piles feasted on the limbs of the young
men; but, for the sake of Amphiaraüs, Zeus, with
his all-powerful thunder-bolt, clave asunder the
broad breast of earth, and buried him with his
steeds, before his warrior-soul could be dishonoured

---

[1] Bury.

24 Ἀμφιάρηϊ BD, Ἀμφιάρῃ ʙᴍғᴄʙᴜ : Ἀμφιαρεῖ ѕ.
σχίσε B², σχίσεν D²; σχίσσεν (ʙᴍғᴄѕ): σχίσσαις B¹ (ʙᴜ,
with κρύψ' ἄνδρ' ἅμ' in next line).

PINDAR

στρ. στ'

δουρὶ Περικλυμένου πρὶν νῶτα τυπέντα μαχατὰν
θυμὸν αἰσχυνθῆμεν. ἐν γὰρ δαιμονίοισι φόβοις
    φεύγοντι καὶ παῖδες θεῶν.
εἰ δυνατόν, Κρονίων, πεῖραν μὲν ἀγάνορα φοινι-
        κοστόλων
ἐγχέων ταύταν θανάτου πέρι καὶ ζωᾶς ἀναβάλ-
    λομαι ὡς πόρσιστα, μοῖραν δ' εὔνομον   70
30 αἰτέω σε παισὶν δαρὸν Αἰτναίων ὀπάζειν,
στρ. ζ'

Ζεῦ πάτερ, ἀγλαΐαισιν δ' ἀστυνόμοις ἐπιμῖξαι
λαόν. ἐντί τοι φίλιπποί τ' αὐτόθι καὶ κτεάνων
    ψυχὰς ἔχοντες κρέσσονας
ἄνδρες. ἄπιστον ἔειπ'· αἰδὼς γὰρ ὑπὸ κρύφα
    κέρδει κλέπτεται,
ἃ φέρει δόξαν. Χρομίῳ κεν ὑπασπίζων παρὰ
    πεζοβόαις ἵπποις τε ναῶν τ' ἐν μάχαις   80
35 ἔκρινας ἂν κίνδυνον ὀξείας ἀϋτᾶς,
στρ. η'

οὔνεκεν ἐν πολέμῳ κείνα θεὸς ἔντυεν αὐτοῦ
θυμὸν αἰχματὰν ἀμύνειν λοιγὸν Ἐννυαλίου. παῦροι
    δὲ βουλεῦσαι φόνου
παρποδίου νεφέλαν τρέψαι ποτὶ δυσμενέων ἀν-
        δρῶν στίχας   90
χερσὶ καὶ ψυχᾷ δυνατοί· λέγεται μὰν Ἕκτορι
    μὲν κλέος ἀνθῆσαι Σκαμάνδρου χεύμασιν
40 ἀγχοῦ, βαθυκρήμνοισι δ' ἀμφ' ἀκταῖς Ἑλώρου,
στρ. θ'

ἔνθα Ῥέας πόρον ἄνθρωποι καλέοισι, δέδορκεν

28 φοινικοστόλων Mezger, Bury : Φοιν. BMFCS.
35 ἀν' (= ἀνὰ) Heyne, Bergk.
41 ἔνθα Ῥέας Boeckh n.c. (CBuS): ἔνθ' Ἀρείας mss (MF) ;
ἔνθ' Ἀρέας B¹.

408

by his being stricken in the back by the spear of Periclymenus. For, amid panics sent from heaven, even the offspring of gods betake themselves to flight.

If it be possible, O son of Cronus, I would fain defer, as long as may be, this fierce arbitrament of empurpled spears,[1] this contest for life and death, but I pray thee, O father Zeus, long to bestow on the men of Aetna the blessing of righteous laws, and to gladden the people by splendid celebrations in their city. There, as thou knowest, there are lovers of horsemanship, and heroes who have souls superior to wealth. My words are hard to believe ; for honour is secretly beguiled by greed, honour that bringeth renown. Hadst thou been shield-bearer to Chromius, amid footmen or horses, or in conflicts of ships,[2] thou wouldest have marked the peril of keen conflict, because, in war, it was that honour divine[3] who harnessed his warrior-soul to repel the onslaught of the god of battle. But few have the power of conspiring with hand and soul to turn back upon the ranks of the foe the rolling cloud of carnage at their feet ; verily, for Hector did glory bloom beside the streams of Scamander, and, about the banks of the Helôrus with their craggy cliffs, at the place which men

---

[1] φοινικοστόλων is an adjective (like λινόστολος, φοινικοείμων), not a proper name, as supposed by the scholiast. But the adjective, while referring primarily to such a sanguinary enterprise as that of the Seven against Thebes above-mentioned, also alludes to the Phoenicians of Carthage, who were continually threatening Sicily (so Mezger and Bury).

[2] At the battle off Cumae, 474 B.C. Cp. *P.* i 71–75.

[3] Αἰδώς is here personified as a goddess.

παιδὶ τοῦθ᾽ Ἀγησιδάμου φέγγος ἐν ἁλικίᾳ πρώτᾳ·
τὰ δ᾽ ἄλλαις ἀμέραις   100
πολλὰ μὲν ἐν κονίᾳ χέρσῳ, τὰ δὲ γείτονι πόντῳ
φάσομαι.
ἐκ πόνων δ᾽, οἳ σὺν νεότατι γένωνται σύν τε δίκᾳ,
τελέθει πρὸς γῆρας αἰὼν ἀμέρα.
45 ἴστω λαχὼν πρὸς δαιμόνων θαυμαστὸν ὄλβον.

στρ. ί

εἰ γὰρ ἅμα κτεάνοις πολλοῖς ἐπίδοξον ἄρηται   110
κῦδος, οὐκ ἔστι πρόσωθεν θνατὸν ἔτι σκοπιᾶς
ἄλλας ἐφάψασθαι ποδοῖν.
ἡσυχία δὲ φιλεῖ μὲν συμπόσιον· νεοθαλὴς δ᾽
αὔξεται
μαλθακὰ νικαφορία σὺν ἀοιδᾷ· θαρσαλέα δὲ παρὰ
κρητῆρα φωνὰ γίνεται.
50 ἐγκιρνάτω τίς νιν, γλυκὺν κώμου προφάταν,   120

στρ. ία

ἀργυρέαισι δὲ νωμάτω φιάλαισι βιατὰν
ἀμπέλου παῖδ᾽, ἅς ποθ᾽ ἵπποι κτησάμεναι Χρομίῳ
πέμψαν θεμιπλέκτοις ἁμᾷ
Λατοΐδα στεφάνοις ἐκ τᾶς ἱερᾶς Σικυῶνος. Ζεῦ
πάτερ,
εὔχομαι ταύταν ἀρετὰν κελαδῆσαι σὺν Χαρίτεσ-
σιν, ὑπὲρ πολλῶν τε τιμαλφεῖν λόγοις   130
55 νίκαν, ἀκοντίζων σκοποῖ᾽ ἄγχιστα Μοισᾶν.

47 οὐκ ἔστι πρόσωθεν Boehmer (s): οὐκέτι πόρσω B, οὐκ ἔστι
πρόσω D; οὐκέτ᾽ ἐστὶ πόρσω Triclinius (BM); οὐκ ἔνεστι πόρσω
Pauw (FC); οὐ πόρσω πόρος τις Bury.
48 ἡσυχία old mss (MBuS); ἀσυχία F: ἡσυχίαν Triclinius (BC).
52 ἁμᾷ S; ἅμα scholia, Erasmus Schmid (edd.): ἀμφὶ mss.
55 σκοποῖ᾽ Ahrens (MFCBuS): σκοποῦ mss (B).

¹ "At whose mouth is that which men call the Ford (or
Passage) of Rhea," *i.e.* the Ionian Sea. Cp. *N.* iv 53, ᾽Ιόνιον
πόρον, and Aeschylus, *P.V.* 826, μέγαν κόλπον ᾽Ρέας. The

call "the Passage of Rhea,"[1] this light hath dawned upon the son of Hâgêsidâmus, in his earliest manhood; and I shall tell of the honours he won at other times, many amidst the dust of dry land, and many on the neighbouring sea.[2] But, out of labours undertaken with the aid of youth and right, there cometh a gentle life at the approach of eld. Let him know full well that he hath had wondrous bliss allotted him by the gods. For, if any man winneth famous glory, as well as goodly store of wealth, further than this it is no longer possible for a mortal to plant his feet on any higher eminence.

But peace loveth the banquet, and a victor's fame flourisheth anew by help of gentle song, and the voice waxeth brave beside the goblet. Let some one mix the wassail-bowl,—that sweet prompter of the triumph-song, and let him hand around the potent produce of the vine in those silver cups which the steeds erst won for Chromius, and sent to him, together with the duly twined garlands of Latona's son, from holy Sicyon. O father Zeus, I pray that I may sound the praises of this deed of prowess by the favour of the Graces, and that I may excel many a bard in honouring victory by my verses, shooting my dart of song nearest of all to the mark of the Muses.

alternatives 'Ρείας and 'Αρείας, mentioned in one of the scholia, imply that 'Ρέας must have been written 'Ρείας, and ἔνθα 'Ρείας wrongly divided as ἔνθ' 'Αρείας. To make the latter intelligible, we have awkwardly to understand κρήνης or πηγῆς, "the place which men call the Ford of Ares' fountain." The change, which introduces the "Ionian Sea," and "the mouth of the Helôrus," is opposed, however, by Freeman, on the ground that the battle "must have been fought a good way inland" (*Sicily*, ii 492). In the battle of the Helôrus, 492 B.C., Chromius fought on the side of Hippocrates, tyrant of Gela, and defeated the Syracusans.   [2] At the battle off Cumae.

NEMEAN X

FOR THEAEUS OF ARGOS

INTRODUCTION

THIS poem commemorates the victory in the wrestling match, which had been twice won by Theaeus of Argos in the festival of Hêra known as the Hecatomboea. The victor had already been successful in wrestling-matches at the Panathenaic festival at Athens, and also in the Pythian, Isthmian, and Nemean games; and he was now preparing to compete at Olympia.

From the fact that Amphitryon is called an Argive and not a Mycenean, it has been inferred that the Ode is later than 468, the date of the overthrow of Mycenae by Argos. Again, since the Argives, as allies of Athens, fought against Thebes, the city of Pindar, in 458, it is argued that the Ode is earlier than that year. The victor was preparing to compete at the Olympic games of 464 or 460; thus the date of the Ode may be either 465, or 463, or 461. **463** is accepted as the approximate date by Schröder. Gaspar, however, assigns it to 500 B.C., thus placing it among Pindar's earliest Odes.

The Graces are summoned to celebrate Argos, the city of Hêra (1–3), a city famous for its legendary glories (4–18).

412

INTRODUCTION

Pausing in his recital of those glories, the poet sings of wrestling in connection with the festival of Hêra (19-23), at which the victor has been twice triumphant; he has also won prizes at the Pythian, Isthmian, and Nemean games, and may Zeus grant his prayer for a victory at Olympia, for which his Panathenaic prize is a happy omen (24-36). His victory is due to his inherited merits, and to the blessing of the Graces, and of Castor and Polydeuces. Victories of his maternal ancestors, some of whom hospitably entertained those heroes (37-54).

The death of Castor and the devotion of Polydeuces (54-90).

X.—ΘΕΑΙΩ ΑΡΓΕΙΩ

ΠΑΛΑΙΣΤῌ

στρ. α΄

　Δαναοῦ πόλιν ἀγλαοθρόνων τε πεντήκοντα κορᾶν,
　　Χάριτες,
　Ἄργος Ἥρας δῶμα θεοπρεπὲς ὑμνεῖτε· φλέγεται
　　δ᾽ ἀρεταῖς
　μυρίαις ἔργων θρασέων ἕνεκεν.
　μακρὰ μὲν τὰ Περσέος ἀμφὶ Μεδοίσας Γοργόνος·

5 πολλὰ δ᾽ Αἰγύπτῳ καταοίκισθεν ἄστη ταῖς Ἐπά-
　　φου παλάμαις·
　οὐδ᾽ Ὑπερμνήστρα παρεπλάγχθη, μονόψαφον ἐν
　　κολεῷ κατασχοῖσα ξίφος.　　　　　　　　　10

ἀντ. α΄

　Διομήδεα δ᾽ ἄμβροτον ξανθά ποτε Γλαυκῶπις
　　ἔθηκε θεόν·
　γαῖα δ᾽ ἐν Θήβαις ὑπέδεκτο κεραυνωθεῖσα Διὸς
　　βέλεσιν
　μάντιν Οἰκλείδαν, πολέμοιο νέφος·
10 καὶ γυναιξὶν καλλικόμοισιν ἀριστεύει πάλαι·
　Ζεὺς ἐπ᾽ Ἀλκμήναν Δανάαν τε μολὼν τοῦτον
　　κατέφανε λόγον·　　　　　　　　　　　20

---

5 καταοίκισθεν s ; κατῴκισθεν vulgo ; τὰ κατῴκισεν (BF) ; τὰ
κατέκτιθεν (MC) ; κατενάσσατο Hardie C.R. iv 318, κτίσεν
Ἰναχὶς Bury, ib. vii 347.

6 Ὑπερμνήστρα D, Triclinius (BFBu) : —μήστρα B (MCS).

414

X.—FOR THEAEUS OF ARGOS

WINNER IN THE WRESTLING-MATCH, 463(?) B.C.

CHANT, ye Graces, the city of Danaüs and his fifty daughters on their gorgeous thrones, even Argos, the home of Hêra, home meet for a goddess; for it is lit up with countless distinctions by reason of deeds of prowess. Long indeed is the legend of Perseus and the Gorgon Medûsa,[1] and many are the cities which were founded in Egypt by the hands of Epaphus[2]; nor did Hypermnêstra wander from the path of honour, when she restrained in her scabbard her sword of solitary purpose.[3] And of old did the grey-eyed goddess of the golden hair make Diomêdês an immortal god[4]; and, near unto Thebes, the earth, thunder-stricken by the bolts of Zeus, swallowed up the seer Amphiaraüs,[5] that storm-cloud of the fray; and of old is Argos famous for its fair-haired dames. Zeus, by his visit to Alcmênê and to Danaë, made this saying true beyond dispute.

[1] The head of Medûsa, who was slain by the Argive hero Perseus, was buried under a mound near the market-place of Argos (Pausanias, ii 21, 6).

[2] Son of Zeus and Io; king of Egypt, father of Libya, and builder of Memphis.

[3] When the fifty sons of Aegyptus were murdered by the fifty daughters of his twin-brother, Danaüs, king of Argos. Lynceus alone was spared by his wife, Hypermnêstra (cp, Horace, *Carm.* iii 11, 33).

[4] The Argive hero, Diomêdês, received from Athênê the gift of immortality which she had intended to confer on his father Tydeus.   [5] The great prophet and hero of Argos.

πατρὶ δ' Ἀδράστοιο Λυγκεῖ τε φρενῶν καρπὸν
   εὐθείᾳ συνάρμοξεν δίκᾳ·

ἐπ. α'

θρέψε δ' αἰχμὰν Ἀμφιτρύωνος. ὁ δ' ὄλβῳ φέρ-
   τατος
ἵκετ' ἐς κείνου γενεάν, ἐπεὶ ἐν χαλκέοις ὅπλοις
15 Τηλεβόας ἔναρεν· τῷ ὄψιν ἐειδόμενος
ἀθανάτων βασιλεὺς αὐλὰν ἐσῆλθεν
σπέρμ' ἀδείμαντον φέρων Ἡρακλέος· οὗ κατ'
   Ὄλυμπον   30
ἄλοχος Ἥβα τελείᾳ παρὰ ματέρι βαίνοισ' ἔστι,
   καλλίστα θεῶν.

στρ. β'

βραχύ μοι στόμα πάντ' ἀναγήσασθ', ὅσων Ἀρ-
   γεῖον ἔχει τέμενος
20 μοῖραν ἐσλῶν· ἔστι δὲ καὶ κόρος ἀνθρώπων βαρὺς
   ἀντιάσαι·
ἀλλ' ὅμως εὔχορδον ἔγειρε λύραν,
καὶ παλαισμάτων λάβε φροντίδ'· ἀγών τοι χάλ-
   κεος   40
δᾶμον ὀτρύνει ποτὶ βουθυσίαν Ἥρας ἀέθλων τε
   κρίσιν·
Οὐλία παῖς ἔνθα νικάσαις δὶς ἔσχεν Θεαῖος εὐφό-
   ρων λάθαν πόνων.

ἀντ. β'

25 ἐκράτησε δὲ καί ποθ' Ἕλλανα στρατὸν Πυθῶνι,
   τύχᾳ τε μολὼν

---

12 πατρὶ δ' in lemma to scholium in *D* (CBuS): πατρὶ τ' *BD*
(BMF).

15 ἔναρεν· τῷ Mingarelli (s), — τῷ <δ'> C: ἔναρε or -εν
τί οἱ mss; -εν καί οἱ B; ἐναρόντος M; ἔναρ', ἔν θ' οἱ F; ἐνα-
ρόντι οἱ Bury.

She hath also united the fruit of discretion with even-handed justice in the father of Adrastus [1] and in Lynceus [2]; and, again, she nourished the warrior Amphitryon, who, when, clad in brazen armour, he had slain the Têleboae, had the surpassing fortune to enter into kinship with Zeus. In semblance of Amphitryon, Zeus, the king of the immortals, entered the hall of that hero, bearing the dauntless seed of Heracles, whose bride Hêbê, fairest of goddesses, walketh for ever in Olympus beside her mother Hêra, who maketh marriage perfect. My mouth is of small measure to tell all the story, to wit all the fair things, of which the holy precinct of Argos hath a share. There is, moreover, the envy of man, which is grievous to encounter; natheless, awake the well-strung lyre, and muse upon those feats of wrestling.

Lo! the contest for the shield of bronze calleth the people to the sacrifice of oxen in honour of Hêra, and to the award of the prizes. There it was that the son of Ulias, Theaeus, was twice victorious, and thus gat him oblivion of toils that were bravely borne; and, once upon a time, he was also victor over the Hellenic host at Pytho, and, coming with better

[1] Talaüs, king of Argos.
[2] Successor of Danaüs as king of Argos.

καὶ τὸν Ἰσθμοῖ καὶ Νεμέᾳ στέφανον, Μοίσαισί τ᾿
   ἔδωκ᾿ ἀρόσαι,
τρὶς μὲν ἐν πόντοιο πύλαισι λαχών,   50
τρὶς δὲ καὶ σεμνοῖς δαπέδοις ἐν Ἀδραστείῳ νόμῳ.
Ζεῦ πάτερ, τῶν μὰν ἔραται φρενί, σιγᾷ οἱ στόμα·
   πᾶν δὲ τέλος
30 ἐν τὶν ἔργων· οὐδ᾿, ἀμόχθῳ καρδίᾳ προσφέρων
   τόλμαν, παραιτεῖται χάριν·

ἐπ. β´

γνώτ᾿ ἀείδω οἵ τε καὶ ὅστις ἁμιλλᾶται περὶ
ἐσχάτων ἄθλων κορυφαῖς· ὕπατον δ᾿ ἔσχεν
   Πίσα   60
Ἡρακλέος τεθμόν· ἀδεῖαί γε μὲν ἀμβολάδαν
ἐν τελεταῖς δὶς Ἀθαναίων νιν ὀμφαὶ
35 κώμασαν· γαίᾳ δὲ καυθείσᾳ πυρὶ καρπὸς ἐλαίας
   ἔμολεν Ἥρας τὸν εὐάνορα λαὸν ἐν ἀγγέων ἔρκεσιν
   παμποικίλοις.

στρ. γ´

ἕπεται δέ, Θεαῖε, ματρώων πολύγνωτον γένος
   ὑμετέρων   70
εὐάγων τιμὰ Χαρίτεσσί τε καὶ <σὺν> Τυνδαρίδαις
   θαμάκις.

ἀξιωθείην κεν, ἐὼν Θρασύκλου
40 Ἀντία τε ξύγγονος, Ἄργει μὴ κρύπτειν φάος
ὀμμάτων. νικαφορίαις γὰρ ὅσαις Προίτοιο τόδ᾿
   ἱπποτρόφον

31 ἀείδω οἵ τε Kayser (CS): ἀείδω θεῷ τε mss (BMFBu), Θεαίῳ
τε Hermann, Dissen.
   38 <σὺν> Erasmus Schmid (edd.).
   41 f. ὅσαις Προίτοιο τόδ᾿ ἱπποτρόφον | ἄστυ θάλησεν BM and F
(who proposes Προίτου θέσαν ἱππ. | ἄστυ θαλῆσαι); ἔταις Προίτοιο
κτλ. Bury; — καθ᾿ (Rauchenstein) ἱππ. | ἄστυ θάλλησαν C;
ὅσαις ἱππ. ἄστυ τὸ Προί|τοιο θάλησεν mss (S); ὅσαις Προίτοιό τ᾿
ἀν᾿ ἱπποτρόφον | ἄστυ θάλησαν Bergk⁴.

fortune, he won the crown at the Isthmus and at Nemea, and gave the Muses a field for their tilling, for he had thrice won the crown at the portals of the sea, and thrice also on the hallowed ground, according to the ordinance of Adrastus. O father Zeus, his mouth is dumb of his heart's desire, but the end of all labours resteth in thine hands alone ; nor doth he, with a heart that shrinketh from toil, pray amiss for thy grace, for he bringeth a spirit of daring. The burden of my song is familiar to himself, and to all who strive for the chief crown in the foremost of the games. Highest indeed is the ordinance of Heracles, which was granted to Pisa. Yet, amid the sacred rites of the Athenians, twice did voices sweet exalt him in the prelude of a triumphal ode, and in earth baked by the fire came the olive oil in richly painted vases to the manly people of Hêra.[1] But full often, Theaeus, doth the glory of successful contests attend on the famous race of the maternal ancestors of your house, by the favour of the Graces and the twin sons of Tyndareüs. Were I a kinsman of Thrasyclus and of Antias, I should deem it meet in no wise to veil the light of mine eyes. For with how many victories hath the city of Proetus[2] flourished, this

---

[1] Vases filled with the olive oil of Attica were given as prizes at the Panathenaic festivals of Athens. These prizes had been won by the Argive hero of this ode.

[2] Proetus and his twin-brother, Acrisius, contended for the kingdom of Argos, which they ultimately agreed to divide between them.

ἄστυ θάλησεν Κορίνθου τ' ἐν μυχοῖς καὶ Κλεω-
    ναίων πρὸς ἀνδρῶν τετράκις·
ἀντ. γ΄
Σικυωνόθε δ' ἀργυρωθέντες σὺν οἰνηραῖς φιάλαις
    ἐπέβαν,   80
ἐκ δὲ Πελλάνας ἐπιεσσάμενοι νῶτον μαλακαῖσι
    κρόκαις·
45 ἀλλὰ χαλκὸν μυρίον οὐ δυνατὸν
ἐξελέγχειν· μακροτέρας γὰρ ἀριθμῆσαι σχολᾶς·
ὅντε Κλείτωρ καὶ Τεγέα καὶ Ἀχαιῶν ὑψίβατοι
    πόλιες
καὶ Λύκαιον πὰρ Διὸς θῆκε δρόμῳ, σὺν ποδῶν
    χειρῶν τε νικᾶσαι σθένει.   90
ἐπ. γ΄
Κάστορος δ' ἐλθόντος ἐπὶ ξενίαν πὰρ Παμφάη
50 καὶ κασιγνήτου Πολυδεύκεος, οὐ θαῦμα σφίσιν
ἐγγενὲς ἔμμεν ἀεθληταῖς ἀγαθοῖσιν· ἐπεὶ
εὐρυχόρου ταμίαι Σπάρτας ἀγώνων
μοῖραν Ἑρμᾷ καὶ σὺν Ἡρακλεῖ διέποντι θάλειαν,
μάλα μὲν ἀνδρῶν δικαίων περικαδόμενοι. καὶ μὰν
    θεῶν πιστὸν γένος.   100
στρ. δ΄
55 μεταμειβόμενοι δ' ἐναλλὰξ ἀμέραν τὰν μὲν παρὰ
    πατρὶ φίλῳ
Δὶ νέμονται, τὰν δ' ὑπὸ κεύθεσι γαίας ἐν γυάλοις
    Θεράπνας,
πότμον ἀμπιπλάντες ὁμοῖον· ἐπεὶ
τοῦτον, ἢ πάμπαν θεὸς ἔμμεναι οἰκεῖν τ' οὐρανῷ,
εἵλετ' αἰῶνα φθιμένου Πολυδεύκης Κάστορος ἐν
    πολέμῳ.   110

48 δόμῳ Abel, Bury (retracted *Isth.* p. xiii).

city that breedeth horses! and four times in the glens of Corinth, and at the hand of the men of Cleônae.[1] But from Sicyon, they returned with silver wine-cups, and from Pellana with their shoulders clad with softest woofs,[2] while the countless prizes of bronze it is impossible to reckon,—for it were a work of longer leisure to number them,—the bronze, which Cleitôr and Tegea[3] and the high-throned cities of the Achaeans[4] and the Lycaean mount set by the race-course of Zeus as prizes for man to win by strength of feet and hands.

But, since Castor and his brother Polydeuces came to Pamphaës, in quest of friendly entertainment, it is no marvel that it should be a mark of their race to be good athletes, seeing that, along with Hermês and Heraclês, the guardians of Sparta's spacious dancing-floor cause their ordinance of the games to prosper, caring in very deed for men who strive lawfully. Verily faithful is the race of the gods.

In alternate changes the twin brethren spend the one day beside their dear father Zeus and, the other, down in the hollow earth in the depths of Therapnê, thus fulfilling an equal lot, since, when Castor was slain in war, Polydeuces preferred this life to being wholly a god and dwelling in heaven. For,

---

[1] The site of the Nemean games lay between Phliûs and Cleônae, and the management of the games was at this time in the hands of the Cleônaeans. Cp. *N.* iv 17.

[2] The prize at Pellana was a woollen cloak. Cp. *O.* ix 97.

[3] The games at Cleitôr were in honour of Persephonê and Dêmêtêr ; and those at Tegea, in honour of Athênê Aleaea (Pausanias viii 21, 2, and 47, 3).

[4] Some of the loftily situated cities of Achaia are named in *Il.* ii 573 f.

60 τὸν γὰρ Ἴδας ἀμφὶ βουσίν πως χολωθεὶς ἔτρωσεν
   χαλκέας λόγχας ἀκμᾷ.

ἀντ. δ'

ἀπὸ Ταϋγέτου πεδαυγάζων ἴδεν Λυγκεὺς δρυὸς ἐν
   στελέχει
ἥμενος. κείνου γὰρ ἐπιχθονίων πάντων γένετ'
   ὀξύτατον
ὄμμα. λαιψηροῖς δὲ πόδεσσιν ἄφαρ
ἐξίκεσθαν, καὶ μέγα ἔργον ἐμήσαντ' ὠκέως.   120

65 καὶ πάθον δεινὸν παλάμαις Ἀφαρητίδαι Διός.
   αὐτίκα γὰρ
ἦλθε Λήδας παῖς διώκων· τοὶ δ' ἔναντα στάθεν
   τύμβῳ σχεδὸν πατρωΐῳ·

ἐπ. δ'

ἔνθεν ἁρπάξαντες ἄγαλμ' Ἀΐδα, ξεστὸν πέτρον,
ἔμβαλον στέρνῳ Πολυδεύκεος· ἀλλ' οὔ νιν φλάσαν,
οὐδ' ἀνέχασσαν· ἐφορμαθεὶς δ' ἄρ' ἄκοντι θοῷ 130
70 ἤλασε Λυγκέος ἐν πλευραῖσι χαλκόν.
   Ζεὺς δ' ἐπ' Ἴδᾳ πυρφόρον πλᾶξε ψολόεντα κε-
      ραυνόν·
ἅμα δ' ἐκαίοντ' ἔρημοι. χαλεπὰ δ' ἔρις ἀνθρώποις
   ὁμιλεῖν κρεσσόνων.

στρ. ε'

ταχέως δ' ἐπ' ἀδελφεοῦ βίαν πάλιν χώρησεν ὁ
   Τυνδαρίδας,
καί νιν οὔπω τεθναότ', ἄσθματι δὲ φρίσσοντα
   πνοὰς ἔκιχεν.   140
75 θερμὰ δὴ τέγγων δάκρυα στοναχαῖς
   ὄρθιον φώνασε· "Πάτερ Κρονίων, τίς δὴ λύσις

60 ἀκμᾷ Pauw (BMFCS): αἰχμᾷ mss; ἀκᾷ 'point' Bury.
62 ἥμενος (Doric acc.) scholia on BD (Bury); ἥμενος BD;
ἡμένως Triclinius; ἡμένους (BF); ἥμενον Aristarchus (MCS).

422

Idas being in some sort angered about his oxen,
stabbed Castor with the point of his brazen spear.
Keenly gazing from Taÿgetus, Lynceus saw them
seated in the hollow of an oak; for, of all that live on
earth, he had the keenest sight; and Lynceus and
Idas, those sons of Aphareus, at once with swift feet
reached the spot, and quickly contrived a great
deed, and themselves suffered dread punishment by
the hands of Zeus, for immediately the son of Leda
(Polydeuces) came in pursuit. But they were
stationed hard by the tomb of their father, Aphareus;
thence did they seize the carven stone that adorned
the grave, and flung it against the breast of
Polydeuces, but they crushed him not, nor drave him
backward; but, rushing forward with his swift javelin,
he thrust its brazen point into the ribs of Lynceus.
And Zeus hurled against Idas a smouldering thunder-
bolt of fire; and in that lonely place they were
consumed together; for men find it hard indeed to
strive with those who are stronger. Then did the
son of Tyndareüs (Polydeuces) swiftly return to his
mighty brother, and found him not yet dead, but
drawing his breath in convulsive gasps. Then it
was that, shedding hot tears, amid moanings, he
said aloud:

"O father, son of Cronus! when, O when will

PINDAR

ἔσσεται πενθέων; καὶ ἐμοὶ θάνατον σὺν τῷδ'
    ἐπίτειλον, ἄναξ.
οἴχεται τιμὰ φίλων τατωμένῳ φωτί· παῦροι δ' ἐν
    πόνῳ πιστοὶ βροτῶν

ἀντ. ε΄
    καμάτου μεταλαμβάνειν." ὣς ἔννεπε· Ζεὺς δ'
        ἀντίος ἤλυθέ οἱ
80 καὶ τόδ' ἐξαύδασ' ἔπος· " Ἐσσί μοι υἱός· τόνδε
        δ' ἔπειτα πόσις   150
    σπέρμα θνατὸν ματρὶ τεᾷ πελάσαις
    στάξεν ἥρως. ἀλλ' ἄγε τῶνδέ τοι ἔμπαν αἵρεσιν
    παρδίδωμ'· εἰ μὲν θάνατόν τε φυγὼν καὶ γῆρας
        ἀπεχθόμενον
    αὐτὸς Οὔλυμπον θέλεις <ναίειν ἐμοὶ> σύν τ'
        Ἀθαναίᾳ κελαινεγχεῖ τ' Ἄρει,

ἐπ. ε΄
85 ἔστι τοι τούτων λάχος· εἰ δὲ κασιγνήτου πέρι   160
    μάρνασαι, πάντων δὲ νοεῖς ἀποδάσσασθαι ἴσον,
    ἥμισυ μέν κε πνέοις γαίας ὑπένερθεν ἐών,
    ἥμισυ δ' οὐρανοῦ ἐν χρυσέοις δόμοισιν."
    ὣς ἄρ' αὐδάσαντος οὐ γνώμᾳ διπλόαν θέτο βουλάν.
90 ἀνὰ δ' ἔλυσεν μὲν ὀφθαλμόν, ἔπειτα δὲ φωνὰν
        χαλκομίτρα Κάστορος.   170

84 ἐθέλεις BD <ναίειν ἐμοὶ> Boeckh (s) ; οἰκεῖν σὺν ἐμοὶ
scholium, <οἰκεῖν ἐμοὶ> Benedictus ; θέλεις Triclinius <οἰκεῖν
ἐμοὶ> C ; νοεῖς <οἰκεῖν ἐμοὶ> Kayser ; <νέμειν μέλλεις ἐμοὶ>
M ; οἰκεῖν αἶτος Οὐλύμπου θέλεις Bury.
    85 τοι τούτων S ; σοὶ τούτων mss (MFCBu): σοὶ μὲν τῶν
Boeckh.

there be a release from sorrows? Bid me also die,
O king, with this my brother. Honour hath perished,
when a man is bereft of his friends; and, among
mortals, few can be trusted in time of trouble to be
partners in one's pain."

He ceased, and before him came Zeus, and spake
in this wise :—

"Thou art my son, whereas Castor was begotten by
thy mother's husband, of mortal seed, after thine own
conception. But lo! I grant thee thy full choice in
this; if thou desirest to escape death and grievous eld,
and to dwell thyself in Olympus with me, and with
Athênê, and with Arês of the darksome spear, thou
canst have this lot appointed thee. But, if thou
contendest for thy brother, and art minded to have
an equal share with him in all things, then mayest
thou breathe for half thy time beneath the earth, and
for half thy time in the golden homes of heaven."

When thus the god had spoken, the hero had no
double purpose in his heart; and Zeus opened once
more the eye, and then released the voice of the
bronze-clad warrior, Castor.[1]

---

[1] *i.e.* Zeus restored Castor to life.

NEMEAN XI

FOR ARISTAGORAS OF TENEDOS

INTRODUCTION

This is an "installation ode" sung in honour of
Aristagoras on his entering on office as President of
the Council of the island of Tenedos. He is
described as a person of local athletic distinction in
the wrestling-ring and the pancratium, and it is
suggested that, but for the timidity of his parents,
he might have competed with success at the Pythian
and Olympic games. According to one of the MSS,
he is the son not of Arcesilas, but of Agesilas, or
Agesilaüs. If so, he may have been an elder brother
of Theoxenus of Tenedos, a son of Agesilas, and a
favourite of Pindar, who wrote a poem in praise of
Theoxenus (fragment 123), and died in his arms
at Argos.[1] The Ode has been conjecturally assigned
to 446 B.C.; in any case, it is among the poet's latest
works.

After invoking Hestia, the goddess of the hearth
of the State (1-10), the poet praises Aristagoras
(11 f), and reminds him that, for all his wealth and
strength, he is mortal (13-16); he recounts his

[1] Wilamowitz, *Berlin Akad.* 1909, 829-835.

athletic victories in local contests (17–21), and suggests that it was only the timidity of his parents that had debarred him from being victorious at Olympia (22–29). Timidity is no less harmful than rashness (29–32). His noble descent (33–37), the athletic distinctions of his family (37–43). We embark on heroic schemes, although we cannot foresee the future (43–46). To our love of gain we must set a limit. Too keen are the pangs that arise from indulging in unattainable desires (47 f.)

XI.—ΑΡΙΣΤΑΓΟΡΑ ΤΕΝΕΔΙΩ

ΠΡΥΤΑΝΕΙ

στρ. α΄

Παῖ Ῥέας, ἅ τε πρυτανεῖα λέλογχας, Ἑστία,
Ζηνὸς ὑψίστου κασιγνήτα καὶ ὁμοθρόνου Ἥρας,
εὖ μὲν Ἀρισταγόραν δέξαι τεὸν ἐς θάλαμον,
εὖ δ᾽ ἑταίρους ἀγλαῷ σκάπτῳ πέλας,
5 οἵ σε γεραίροντες ὀρθὰν φυλάσσοισιν Τένεδον,

ἀντ. α΄

πολλὰ μὲν λοιβαῖσιν ἀγαζόμενοι πρώταν θεῶν,
πολλὰ δὲ κνίσσᾳ· λύρα δέ σφι βρέμεται καὶ
    ἀοιδά·
καὶ ξενίου Διὸς ἀσκεῖται Θέμις ἀενάοις
ἐν τραπέζαις. ἀλλὰ σὺν δόξᾳ τέλος   10
10 δωδεκάμηνον περᾶσαι σὺν ἀτρώτῳ κραδίᾳ,

ἐπ. α΄

ἄνδρα δ᾽ ἐγὼ μακαρίζω μὲν πατέρ᾽ Ἀγησίλαν,
καὶ τὸ θαητὸν δέμας ἀτρεμίαν τε ξύγγονον.
εἰ δέ τις ὄλβον ἔχων μορφᾷ παραμεύσεται ἄλλους,
ἔν τ᾽ ἀέθλοισιν ἀριστεύων ἐπέδειξεν βίαν,

8 αἰενάοις S.

10 περᾶσαι σὺν? Boeckh (FBu); περάσαι σὺν mss (C): περᾶσαί νιν Dissen (MS).

11 Ἀγησίλαν Wilamowitz (1909), p. 833, cp. frag. 123 (88) 9, on Theoxenus of Tenedos, υἱὸν — Ἀγησίλα. (S); ἀγησίλαν B; Ἀγεσίλαν P. Maas: Ἀρκεσίλαν D (BMFCBu).

13 μορφᾷ mss — ἄλλους Hartung (CS); μορφᾷ — ἄλλων mss (F); μορφὰν Boeckh — ἄλλων mss (BM); μορφᾷ περαμεύσεται ἄλλων Bury.

XI.—FOR ARISTAGORAS OF TENEDOS

ON HIS ELECTION AS PRESIDENT OF THE COUNCIL, 446 (?) B.C.

Daughter of Rhea, who hast the hearths of States allotted to thy care, Hestia, thou sister of Zeus supreme and of Hêra, the consort of his throne! welcome Aristagoras to thy hall, welcome also, to a place beside thy gleaming sceptre, those comrades who, while paying due honour unto thee, are upholding Tenedos, oft with libations adoring thee, as first of the goddesses, and oft with savour of sacrifice. At their bidding peal the lyre and the lay; and Themis is venerated ever at the perpetual feasts ruled by the god of hospitality.

Heaven grant that he may pass with glory through his time of twelve moons with heart unscathed As for our hero, I deem his father Hâgêsilas blessed, and I praise his own goodly frame, and his inborn constancy of soul. But, if any man who hath riches, excelleth others in beauty of form, and is wont to display prowess by his courage in the games, let him

429

15 θνατὰ μεμνάσθω περιστέλλων μέλη,   20
 καὶ τελευτὰν ἁπάντων γᾶν ἐπιεσσόμενος.

στρ. β′

 ἐν λόγοις δ᾽ ἀστῶν ἀγαθοῖσί νιν αἰνεῖσθαι χρεών,
 καὶ μελιγδούποισι δαιδαλθέντα μελιζέμεν ἀοιδαῖς.
 ἐκ δὲ περικτιόνων ἑκκαίδεκ᾽ Ἀρισταγόραν
20 ἀγλααὶ νῖκαι πάτραν τ᾽ εὐώνυμον
 ἐστεφάνωσαν πάλᾳ καὶ μεγαυχεῖ παγκρατίῳ.

ἀντ. β′

 ἐλπίδες δ᾽ ὀκνηρότεραι γονέων παιδὸς βίαν
 ἔσχον ἐν Πυθῶνι πειρᾶσθαι καὶ Ὀλυμπίᾳ ἄθλων.
 ναὶ μὰ γὰρ ὅρκον, ἐμὰν δόξαν παρὰ Κασταλίᾳ   30
25 καὶ παρ᾽ εὐδένδρῳ μολὼν ὄχθῳ Κρόνου
 κάλλιον ἂν δηριώντων ἐνόστησ᾽ ἀντιπάλων,

ἐπ. β′

 πενταετηρίδ᾽ ἑορτὰν Ἡρακλέος τέθμιον
 κωμάσαις ἀνδησάμενός τε κόμαν ἐν πορφυρέοις
 ἔρνεσιν. ἀλλὰ βροτῶν τὸν μὲν κενεόφρονες αὖχαι
30 ἐξ ἀγαθῶν ἔβαλον· τὸν δ᾽ αὖ καταμεμφθέντ᾽ ἄγαν   41
 ἰσχὺν οἰκείων παρέσφαλεν καλῶν
 χειρὸς ἕλκων ὀπίσσω θυμὸς ἄτολμος ἐών.

στρ. γ′

 συμβαλεῖν μὰν εὐμαρὲς ἦν τό τε Πεισάνδρου
  πάλαι
 αἷμ᾽ ἀπὸ Σπάρτας· Ἀμύκλαθεν γὰρ ἔβα σὺν
  Ὀρέστᾳ,
35 Αἰολέων στρατιὰν χαλκεντέα δεῦρ᾽ ἀνάγων·
 καὶ παρ᾽ Ἰσμηνοῦ ῥοὰν κεκραμένον
 ἐκ Μελανίπποιο μάτρωος. ἀρχαῖαι δ᾽ ἀρεταί

17 ἀγαθοῖσί Triclinius νιν αἰνεῖσθαι (MF), — μιν — (BC): ἀγα-
θοῖς μὲν αἰνεῖσθαι old mss; — ἐπαινεῖσθαι Bury; ἀγαθοῖσιν
ἐπαιν. S.

remember that the limbs he is robing are mortal, and
that, in the end of all, he will be clad in a vesture of
clay.   Yet right it is that he should be praised with
friendly words by his fellow citizens ; right it is that
we should celebrate him by adorning his fame with
honey-sweet strains.   For, by those who dwell around
him, Aristagoras and his famous clan were crowned
by sixteen glorious victories in the wrestling-match
and in the proud pancratium.   But the halting hopes
of his parents restrained his strength, as a boy, from
competing for the prizes at Pytho and Olympia.
Else, I solemnly aver that, in my judgment, had he
entered the lists, he would have returned with
greater glory than his rivals, whether they strove
beside Castalia, or beside the tree-clad hill of Cronus,
after celebrating the quadrennial festival ordained by
Heracles, and after binding his hair with gleaming
garlands.   But, among mortals, *one* is cast down
from his blessings by empty-headed conceit, whereas
another, underrating his strength too far, hath been
thwarted from winning the honours within his reach,
by an uncourageous spirit that draggeth him back
by the hand.

It was easy indeed to infer his Spartan descent
from Peisander of old, who came from Amyclae with
Orestes, bringing hither an armed host of Aetolians,
and also the blending of his blood with that of his
mother's ancestor Melanippus, beside the stream of

PINDAR

ἀντ. γ´

  ἀμφέροντ᾽ ἀλλασσόμεναι γενεαῖς ἀνδρῶν σθένος·
  ἐν σχερῷ δ᾽ οὔτ᾽ ὦν μέλαιναι καρπὸν ἔδωκαν
    ἄρουραι,   50
40 δένδρεά τ᾽ οὐκ ἐθέλει πάσαις ἐτέων περόδοις
  ἄνθος εὐῶδες φέρειν πλούτῳ ἴσον,
  ἀλλ᾽ ἐν ἀμείβοντι. καὶ θνατὸν οὕτως ἔθνος ἄγει

ἐπ. γ´

  μοῖρα. τὸ δ᾽ ἐκ Διὸς ἀνθρώποις σαφὲς οὐχ ἕπεται
  τέκμαρ· ἀλλ᾽ ἔμπαν μεγαλανορίαις ἐμβαίνομεν,
45 ἔργα τε πολλὰ μενοινῶντες· δέδεται γὰρ ἀναιδεῖ
  ἐλπίδι γυῖα· προμαθείας.δ᾽ ἀπόκεινται ῥοαί.   60
  κερδέων δὲ χρὴ μέτρον θηρευέμεν·
  ἀπροσίκτων δ᾽ ἐρώτων ὀξύτεραι μανίαι.

42 οὕτως ἔθνος Heyne (edd.) : οὕτω σθένος mss.

Ismênus.   But the virtues of olden time yield strong
men, as their progeny, in alternate generations; for
neither do the dark fields give us of their harvest for
evermore, nor are the fruit-trees wont, in all the
circling years, to bear a fragrant blossom equal in
wealth of produce, but in alternation only.   Even so
is the race of mortal men driven by the breeze of
destiny.   As for that which cometh from Zeus, there
is no clear sign in heaven that waiteth on man ; but
yet we embark upon bold endeavours, yearning after
many exploits; for our limbs are fettered by unfor-
tunate hope, while the tides of foreknowledge lie far
away from our sight.   In our quest of gain, it is right
to pursue the due measure; but far too keen are
the pangs of madness that come from unattainable
longings.

THE ISTHMIAN ODES

ISTHMIAN I

FOR HERODOTUS OF THEBES

INTRODUCTION

The first Isthmian Ode celebrates the victory of Herodotus of Thebes in the chariot-race at the Isthmian games. His father, Asôpodôrus, is described as having in some sense, whether literally or metaphorically, suffered shipwreck, and as having come ashore at Orchomenus. The grammarian Didymus states that Asôpodôrus had been exiled from Thebes, and had taken refuge in Orchomenus, the city of his fathers. He may be safely identified with a person of that name not unknown in Greek History. Herodotus, in his account of the battle of Plataea, describes Asôpodôrus, son of Timander, as captain of a squadron of Theban cavalry, that charged certain Megarians and Phliasians with such effect that 600 were left dead on the field (Herodotus, ix 69). On the capture of the city, the leaders of the medizing party were given up to Pausanias, the Spartan commander, who afterwards caused them to be put to death (ix 86–88). Asôpodôrus, who had been so prominent an officer on the side of the Medes, may well have been, at the same time, sent into exile. In this Ode, the Thebans and Spartans are represented as allied in the persons of Iolaüs and Castor (17, 28–31). In 458, the year before the battle of Tanagra, in which the Lacedaemonians and Thebans defeated Athens, the alliance between Sparta and

INTRODUCTION

Thebes was on the point of being accomplished. This Ode may, accordingly, be assigned to April 458, a few months before the Pythian games, for which (as well as for the Olympian games) Herodotus was training his horses.

Early in the Ode, the poet apologises to Dêlos for laying aside a poem, which he was writing in honour of Apollo on behalf of the island of Ceôs, to compose an Ode in praise of a Theban fellow-citizen, who was victor at the Isthmian games. The poem afterwards written on behalf of Ceôs was a paean in honour of Dêlos and Apollo, a large part of which has been discovered in Egypt, and published in the *Oxyrhynchus papyri*, v (1908) No. 841, pp. 18, 35 f, 88 f. See below, *Paean* iv.

The poet invokes the goddess of his native city, Thebes, while he begs Dêlos to excuse his delay in writing, on behalf of Ceôs, a paean to the Delian Apollo (1–10).

Six prizes have been lately won by Thebes (10–12), the birth-place of Heracles (12 f). In honour of the victor, the poet is prepared to compose a poem, in praise of Castor or Iolaüs (14–16), whose athletic prowess he sets forth (17–31).

The victor's family, his father's exile and restoration to good fortune (32–40).

Cost and toil spent on athletic pursuits deserve the poet's praise (40–52). The victories of Herodotus cannot be enumerated within the limits of a brief ode (53–63). The poet hopes that he may also be victorious in the Pythian and Olympian games (64–67). Hoarding one's wealth and jeering at those who spend it, can only end in an inglorious death (67 f).

ΙΣΘΜΙΟΝΙΚΑΙ

I.—ΗΡΟΔΟΤΩ ΘΗΒΑΙΩ

ΑΡΜΑΤΙ

στρ. α΄

Μᾶτερ ἐμά, τὸ τεόν, χρύσασπι Θήβα,
πρᾶγμα καὶ ἀσχολίας ὑπέρτερον
θήσομαι. μή μοι κραναὰ νεμεσάσαι
Δᾶλος, ἐν ᾇ κέχυμαι.

5 τί φίλτερον κεδνῶν τοκέων ἀγαθοῖς;
εἶξον, ὠπολλωνιάς· ἀμφοτερᾶν τοι χαρίτων σὺν
θεοῖς ζεύξω τέλος,

ἀντ. α΄

καὶ τὸν ἀκειρεκόμαν Φοῖβον χορεύων
ἐν Κέῳ ἀμφιρύτᾳ σὺν ποντίοις
ἀνδράσιν, καὶ τὰν ἁλιερκέα Ἰσθμοῦ   10

10 δειράδ᾽· ἐπεὶ στεφάνους
ἓξ ὤπασεν Κάδμου στρατῷ ἐξ ἀέθλων,
καλλίνικον πατρίδι κῦδος. ἐν ᾇ καὶ τὸν ἀδεί-
μαντον Ἀλκμήνα τέκεν

ἐπ. α΄

παῖδα, θρασεῖαι τόν ποτε Γηρυόνα φρίξαν κύνες.
ἀλλ᾽ ἐγὼ Ἡροδότῳ τεύχων τὸ μὲν ἅρματι τεθρίπ-
πῳ γέρας,

15 ἀνία τ᾽ ἀλλοτρίαις οὐ χερσὶ νωμάσαντ᾽ ἐθέλω   20

---

7 ἀκειροκόμαν mss (edd.): ἀκερσεκόμαν s³, cp. P. iii 14, and
Paean, iv 1.

THE ISTHMIAN ODES

I.—FOR HERODOTUS OF THEBES

WINNER IN THE CHARIOT-RACE, 458 (?) B.C.

O MOTHER mine, O Thêbê of the golden shield,
I shall deem thy behest enough to outweigh all
lack of leisure. Let not rocky Delos be indig-
nant at me, for in her praise have I been fully
spent. What is dearer to the good than noble
parents? Give place, Apollo's isle; for, in very
deed, by help of heaven shall I bring to an
end both hymns of praise alike, by honouring in the
dance, not only the unshorn Phoebus in wave-
washed Ceôs with its mariners, but also the Isthmian
reef that severeth seas asunder; since to the host of
Cadmus that Isthmus gave from her games six
garlands, to grace with glorious triumph my father-
land, the very land in which Alcmênê bare her
dauntless son, before whom trembled erst the
savage hounds of Gêryon.[1]

But I, while framing for Herodotus an honour for
his chariot of four horses, and for his having plied
the reins in his own hands and not another's, would

[1] The cattle of Gêryon, who lived in an island of the
ocean near Gadeira, were guarded by a two-headed hound
named Orthros. Heracles slew the hound, and carried off
the cattle.

ἢ Καστορείῳ ἢ Ἰολάου ἐναρμόξαι νιν ὕμνῳ.
κεῖνοι γὰρ ἡρώων διφρηλάται Λακεδαίμονι καὶ
    Θήβαις ἐτέκνωθεν κράτιστοι·

στρ. β΄

ἔν τ᾽ ἀέθλοισι θίγον πλείστων ἀγώνων,
καὶ τριπόδεσσιν ἐκόσμησαν δόμον
20 καὶ λεβήτεσσιν φιάλαισί τε χρυσοῦ,
    γευόμενοι στεφάνων
νικαφόρων· λάμπει δὲ σαφὴς ἀρετά ·   30
ἔν τε γυμνοῖσι σταδίοις σφίσιν ἔν τ᾽ ἀσπιδοδού-
    ποισιν ὁπλίταις δρόμοις,

ἀντ. β΄

οἷά τε χερσὶν ἀκοντίζοντες αἰχμαῖς,
25 καὶ λιθίνοις ὁπότ᾽ ἐν δίσκοις ἵεν.
οὐ γὰρ ἦν πεντάθλιον, ἀλλ᾽ ἐφ᾽ ἑκάστῳ
ἔργματι κεῖτο τέλος.
τῶν ἀθρόοις ἀνδησάμενοι θαμάκις
ἔρνεσιν χαίτας ῥεέθροισί τε Δίρκας ἔφανεν καὶ
    παρ᾽ Εὐρώτᾳ πέλας,

ἐπ. β΄

30 Ἰφικλέος μὲν παῖς ὁμόδαμος ἐὼν Σπαρτῶν
    γένει,   40
Τυνδαρίδας δ᾽ ἐν Ἀχαιοῖς ὑψίπεδον Θεράπνας
    οἰκέων ἕδος.
χαίρετ᾽. ἐγὼ δὲ Ποσειδάωνι Ἰσθμῷ τε ζαθέα
Ὀγχηστίαισίν τ᾽ ἀϊόνεσσιν περιστέλλων ἀοιδὰν
γαρύσομαι τοῦδ᾽ ἀνδρὸς ἐν τιμαῖσιν ἀγακλέα τὰν
    Ἀσωποδώρου πατρὸς αἶσαν   50

στρ. γ΄

35 Ὀρχομενοῖό τε πατρῴαν ἄρουραν,
ἅ νιν ἐρειδόμενον ναυαγίαις

27 ἔργματι B (BM²FBu), ἔρματι D, Γέργματι (M¹) : ἔργματι CS.

wed him to the strain of Castor or of Iolaüs, for,
of all the heroes, they were the bravest charioteers,
the one in Sparta born, in Thebes the other. And,
in the games, they essayed the greatest number
of contests, and decked their homes with tripods
and cauldrons and with bowls of gold, by tasting of
crowns victorious. Clear shineth their prowess,
both in the courses of stript runners, and amid the
warrior-races with the sounding shield; and in all
the deeds of their hands, in flinging the spear, and
whensoe'er they hurled the discs of stone. For, as
yet, there was no pentathlum, but for each several
feat a separate prize was set up. Full oft, with
their hair enwreathed with coronals from these
contests, did they appear beside the streams of
Dircê, or hard by the Eurôtas, (by the first) the son
of Iphiclês, clansman of the dragon's brood,[1] (by the
other) the son of Tyndareüs, dwelling amid the
Achaeans in his highland home of Therapnê.

Now fare ye well, while I, arraying with song
Poseidon and the hallowed Isthmus and the shores
of Onchêstus, shall, amid the honours of this hero,
tell aloud of the fortune, the famous fortune of
his sire Asôpodôrus, and of the ancestral glebe of
Orchomenus, which welcomed him, when, hard
pressed by shipwreck, he came in chilly plight from

[1] Cadmus slew the dragon, which guarded the fountain of
Arês, and, on the advice of Athênê, sowed the dragon's
teeth, out of which armed men grew up. The five survivors
of these became the ancestors of the Thebans.

ἐξ ἀμετρήτας ἁλὸς ἐν κρυοέσσᾳ
δέξατο συντυχίᾳ·
νῦν δ' αὖτις ἀρχαίας ἐπέβασε πότμος
40 συγγενὴς εὐαμερίας. ὁ πονήσαις δὲ νόῳ καὶ
    προμάθειαν φέρει·

ἀντ. γ´

εἰ δ' ἀρετᾷ κατάκειται πᾶσαν ὀργάν,
ἀμφότερον δαπάναις τε καὶ πόνοις,
χρή νιν εὑρόντεσσιν ἀγάνορα κόμπον   60
μὴ φθονεραῖσι φέρειν
45 γνώμαις. ἐπεὶ κούφα δόσις ἀνδρὶ σοφῷ
    ἀντὶ μόχθων παντοδαπῶν ἔπος εἰπόντ' ἀγαθὸν
    ξυνὸν ὀρθῶσαι καλόν.

ἐπ. γ´

μισθὸς γὰρ ἄλλοις ἄλλος ἐφ' ἔργμασιν ἀνθρώποις
    γλυκύς,
μηλοβότᾳ τ' ἀρότᾳ τ' ὀρνιχολόχῳ τε καὶ ὃν
    πόντος τρέφει·
γαστρὶ δὲ πᾶς τις ἀμύνων λιμὸν αἰανῆ τέταται· 70
50 ὃς δ' ἀμφ' ἀέθλοις ἢ πολεμίζων ἄρηται κῦδος
    ἁβρόν,
εὐαγορηθεὶς κέρδος ὕψιστον δέκεται, πολιατᾶν
    καὶ ξένων γλώσσας ἄωτον.

στρ. δ´

ἄμμι δ' ἔοικε Κρόνου σεισίχθον' υἱὸν
γείτον' ἀμειβομένοις εὐεργέταν
ἁρμάτων ἱπποδρόμιον κελαδῆσαι,
55 καὶ σέθεν, 'Αμφιτρύω:,
    παῖδας προσειπεῖν, τὸν Μινύα τε μυχὸν   80

41 κατάκειται mss : 'ντέταταί τις Christ.
47 ἐφ' ἔργμασιν B (BMFCBu), — ἅρμασιν D : ἐπ' ἔργμασιν S.

out the boundless main. But now, once more, hath the fortune of his home embarked him on the fair weather of the olden days. Yet he, who hath suffered troubles, winneth forethought also in his heart; and, whensoever a man, with all his spirit, throweth himself into pursuit of prowess, sparing neither cost nor pains, 'tis meet that, when the prize is won, we should, with thoughts ungrudging, give him ennobling praise. For the wise poet finds it an easy boon, in requital for manifold toil, to say his good word, and thus, besides, to set on high the fame of the State. Aye! even as divers meeds for divers works are sweet to men, to the shepherd and to the ploughman, to the fowler and to him whom the sea doth nourish, while every man straineth his strength in defending his belly from weary famine; even so, whosoever winneth bright renown, either in the games or in war, receiveth the highest gain in the choicest praises of citizens and of strangers.

'Tis meet for us, in strains of grateful song, to sound aloud the praises of our neighbour, the earth-shaking son of Cronus, for blessing our chariots as the god of racing steeds.[1] 'Tis meet, again, to invoke thy sons,[2] Amphitryon, and the secluded valley of Minyas,[3] and Eleusis, the famous precinct

---

[1] Poseidon, of Onchêstus, is here described as the neighbour of Thebes.

[2] Heracles and Iolaüs, in whose honour the Heraclea and the Iolaïa were held at Thebes.   [3] At Orchomenus.

καὶ τὸ Δάματρος κλυτὸν ἄλσος Ἐλευσῖνα καὶ
  Εὔβοιαν ἐν γναμπτοῖς δρόμοις·
ἀντ. δ΄
Πρωτεσίλα, τὸ τεὸν δ΄ ἀνδρῶν Ἀχαιῶν
ἐν Φυλάκᾳ τέμενος συμβάλλομαι.
60 πάντα δ΄ ἐξειπεῖν, ὅσ΄ ἀγώνιος Ἑρμᾶς
Ἡροδότῳ ἔπορεν
ἵπποις, ἀφαιρεῖται βραχὺ μέτρον ἔχων
ὕμνος. ἦ μὰν πολλάκι καὶ τὸ σεσωπαμένον
  εὐθυμίαν μείζω φέρει.
ἐπ. δ΄
εἴη νιν εὐφώνων πτερύγεσσιν ἀερθέντ᾽ ἀγλααῖς 90
65 Πιερίδων ἔτι καὶ Πυθῶθεν Ὀλυμπιάδων τ᾽
  ἐξαιρέτοις
Ἀλφεοῦ ἔρνεσι φράξαι χεῖρα τιμὰν ἑπταπύλοις
Θήβαισι τεύχοντ᾽. εἰ δέ τις ἔνδον νέμει πλοῦτον
  κρυφαῖον,
ἄλλοισι δ᾽ ἐμπίπτων γελᾷ, ψυχὰν Ἀΐδᾳ τελέων
  οὐ φράζεται δόξας ἄνευθεν. 100

of Demêter, and Euboea too, among the circling
race-courses. And I add, beside, thy sacred ground,
Prôtesilas, in Phylacê,[1] the home of Achaean heroes.
But to tell of all the victories that Hermes, lord
of games, granted to Herodotus and his steeds, is
reft from me by the brief limits of my song. Yea,
full oft doth even that which is hushed in silence
bring the greater joy. Heaven grant that, wafted
on the beaming pinions of the voiceful Pierides,
he yet may fill his hand with wreaths from Pytho,
with choicest wreaths from the Alpheüs and the
Olympian games, thus winning glory for seven-
gated Thebes. But, if any one broodeth at home
over hoarded wealth, and rejoiceth in oppressing
others, he little thinketh that he is giving up his
soul to death—death without glory.

[1] In Thessaly, on the Pagasaean gulf.

ISTHMIAN II

FOR XENOCRATES OF ACRAGAS

INTRODUCTION

The second Isthmian commemorates a victory in
the chariot-race won in 477 (?) by Xenocrates of
Acragas. The victory in question falls between the
Sixth Pythian of 490, in honour of Xenocrates (and
his son, Thrasybulus) and the Second and Third
Olympian Odes of 476, in honour of his brother
Thêrôn. The Second Olympian (54 f) mentions the
Isthmian, as well as the Pythian, victory of Xeno-
crates. The date of the Isthmian victory is probably
477, but the present Ode is of later date; it was
composed, certainly after the death of Xenocrates,
and probably after the death of his brother Thêrôn
(472). The official Odes in celebration of the
Pythian victory of 490 and the Isthmian of 477 were
written by Simonides. Here, as in the Sixth
Pythian, Pindar is voluntarily paying a personal
compliment to the victor's son, Thrasybûlus, who is
also addressed in Frag. 124.

Poets of old freely sang of their favourites (1-5),
for, in those days, the Muse was not yet a hireling
(6-8); whereas now she bids us obey the maxim of

the Argive, Aristodêmus: " Money maketh man "
(9–11).

The Pythian and the Isthmian victories of Xenocrates are well known. They were won by his charioteer Nicomachus (12–22), whom the heralds of the Olympian truce had already met, when they recognised and welcomed him at Olympia (23–28), where Thêrôn and Xenocrates attained immortal honours (20 f). These honours are familiar with songs of triumph, for men of renown are ˙readily praised in song (30–34). Xenocrates was a man of charming manners, and was fond of horsemanship, and his hospitality knew no bounds (35–42).

The poet bids the bearer of the Ode, Nicasippus, tell Thrasybûlus not to allow the envy of others to make him bury in silence his father's merits and these lays of praise, for they were not wrought to remain idle (43–48).

II.—ΞΕΝΟΚΡΑΤΕΙ ΑΚΡΑΓΑΝΤΙΝΩ

ΑΡΜΑΤΙ

στρ. α΄

Οἱ μὲν πάλαι, ὦ Θρασύβουλε, φῶτες, οἳ χρυσαμ-
πύκων
ἐς δίφρον Μοισᾶν ἔβαινον κλυτᾷ φόρμιγγι συναν-
τόμενοι,
ῥίμφα παιδείους ἐτόξευον μελιγάρυας ὕμνους,
ὅστις ἐὼν καλὸς εἶχεν Ἀφροδίτας
5 εὐθρόνου μνάστειραν ἁδίσταν ὀπώραν.

ἀντ. α΄

ἁ Μοῖσα γὰρ οὐ φιλοκερδής πω τότ᾽ ἦν οὐδ᾽
ἐργάτις·   10
οὐδ᾽ ἐπέρναντο γλυκεῖαι μελιφθόγγου ποτὶ Τερ-
ψιχόρας
ἀργυρωθεῖσαι πρόσωπα μαλθακόφωνοι ἀοιδαί.
νῦν δ᾽ ἐφίητι <τὸ> τὠργείου φυλάξαι
10 ῥῆμ᾽ ἀλαθείας <ἑτᾶς> ἄγχιστα βαῖνον,

ἐπ. α΄

" χρήματα, χρήματ᾽ ἀνήρ," ὃς φᾶ κτεάνων θ᾽ ἅμα
λειφθεὶς καὶ φίλων.
ἐσσὶ γὰρ ὦν σοφός, οὐκ ἄγνωτ᾽ ἀείδω
Ἰσθμίαν ἵπποισι νίκαν,   20
τὰν Ξενοκράτει Ποσειδάων ὀπάσαις,

9 <τὸ> Heyne (edd.).
10 <ἑτᾶς> Bergk (BuS) : <ὁδῶν> Hermann (BMFC), cp.
P. iii 103.
11 θ᾽ ἅμα mss and scholia (CBuS) : θαμὰ (BMF), θάμα Bergk.

448

II.—FOR XENOCRATES OF ACRAGAS

WINNER IN THE CHARIOT-RACE, 472 (?) B.C.

THE men of old, O Thrasybûlus, who mounted the
car of the golden-wreathed Muses, taking up the
sounding lyre, lightly shot forth their honey-sweet
songs in honour of their loves, whensoever one fair
in form had that precious bloom which turneth the
thoughts to[1] Aphrodîtê on her beauteous throne.
For, in those days, the Muse was not yet fond of
gain, no, nor yet a hireling; nor did sweet warbling
songs pass for sale, with their silvered faces,[2] from out
the hands of honey-voiced Terpsichorê. But now
doth she bid us heed the Argive's word that
cometh nearest to the very truth. "Money, money
maketh man," quoth he, when reft of wealth and
friends alike.[3]

But enough, for thou art wise! I sing the famous
Isthmian victory with the steeds, by granting which
to Xenocratês, Poseidon sent him to entwine about

[1] Or "which wooeth."

[2] Probably, "the personified songs, like Eastern dancers,
plastered their faces with silver coins." Cp. W. R. Paton, in
Classical Review, ii (1888) 180; and J. G. Frazer, *ib.* 261;
also *A.J.P.* xxx 358.

[3] The Argive was Aristodêmus, who, according to Alcaeus
(49), as quoted in the scholia, said these words in Sparta:—

> ὡς γὰρ δή ποτε φασιν Ἀριστόδημον
> ἐν Σπάρτῃ λόγον οὐκ ἀπάλαμνον εἰπεῖν·
> χρήματ' ἀνήρ· πενιχρὸς δὲ οὐδεὶς
> πέλετ' ἐσλὸς οὐδὲ τίμιος.

15 Δωρίων αὐτῷ στεφάνωμα κόμᾳ
    πέμπεν ἀναδεῖσθαι σελίνων,
στρ. β'
    εὐάρματον ἄνδρα γεραίρων, Ἀκραγαντίνων φάος.
    ἐν Κρίσᾳ δ' εὐρυσθενὴς εἶδ' Ἀπόλλων νιν πόρε τ'
        ἀγλαΐαν
    καὶ τόθι· κλειναῖς <δ'> Ἐρεχθειδᾶν χαρίτεσσιν
        ἀραρὼς
20 ταῖς λιπαραῖς ἐν Ἀθάναις, οὐκ ἐμέμφθη   30
    ῥυσίδιφρον χεῖρα πλαξίπποιο φωτός,
ἀντ. β'
    τὰν Νικόμαχος κατὰ καιρὸν νεῖμ' ἁπάσαις ἀνίαις·
    ὅντε καὶ κάρυκες ὡρᾶν ἀνέγνον, σπονδοφόροι
        Κρονίδα
    Ζηνὸς Ἀλεῖοι, παθόντες πού τι φιλόξενον ἔργον·
25 ἁδυπνόῳ τέ νιν ἀσπάζοντο φωνᾷ
    χρυσέας ἐν γούνασιν πιτνόντα Νίκας
ἐπ. β'
    γαῖαν ἀνὰ σφετέραν, τὰν δὴ καλέοισιν Ὀλυμπίου
        Διὸς   40
    ἄλσος· ἵν' ἀθανάτοις Αἰνησιδάμου
    παῖδες ἐν τιμαῖς ἔμιχθεν.
30 καὶ γὰρ οὐκ ἀγνῶτες ὑμῖν ἐντὶ δόμοι
    οὔτε κώμων, ὦ Θρασύβουλ', ἐρατῶν,
    οὔτε μελικόμπων ἀοιδᾶν.

18 f. ἀγλαΐαν | καὶ τόθι· BC ; ἀγλαΐαν καὶ τόθι κτλ Bu ;
ἀγλαΐαν· | καὶ τόθι MFS.

19 κλειναῖς mss (MFS): — <δ'> Heyne (BC), — <τ'>
Bergk, Bury.

22 νεῖμ' ἁπάσαις Hermann (edd.): νώμα πάσαις mss.

23 ἀνέγνον (MCS): ἀνέγνων mss (BFC); cp. ἔγνον P. iv 120,
ix 79.

his hair a wreath of the wild Dorian celery, thus honouring the hero of the goodly chariot, the light of the people of Acragas. And in Crisa also did the mighty Apollo look graciously upon him, and gave him glory even there.

And in gleaming Athens, when he attained those famous, those gracious victories, among the sons of Erechtheus, he had no fault to find with the deftly driving hand of the man that lashed the steeds, the hand wherewith Nicomachus gave the horses full rein at the fittest moment—that very driver whom the heralds of the Olympian seasons, the Elean truce-bearers of Zeus, son of Cronus, knew once again,[1] since they had won, I ween, some friendly favour from him.[2] And with sweetly breathing voice they greeted him, when he fell upon the lap of golden Victory in their own land, which men call the precinct of Olympian Zeus; where the sons of Aenêsidâmus[3] were linked with deathless honours. For the homes of your clan, O Thrasybûlus, are not unfamiliar with gladsome triumph-songs, nor with sweet-voiced minstrelsy. For 'tis no hill, no, nor

---

[1] Recognised, at Olympia.   [2] At Athens.
[3] Thêrôn, and Xenocratês, the father of Thrasybûlus.

PINDAR

στρ. γ´

   οὐ γὰρ πάγος, οὐδὲ προσάντης ἁ κέλευθος γίνεται,
   εἴ τις εὐδόξων ἐς ἀνδρῶν ἄγοι τιμὰς Ἑλικων-
      ιάδων.   50

35 μακρὰ δισκήσαις ἀκοντίσσαιμι τοσοῦθ᾽, ὅσον
      ὀργὰν

   Ξεινοκράτης ὑπὲρ ἀνθρώπων γλυκεῖαν
   ἔσχεν. αἰδοῖος μὲν ἦν ἀστοῖς ὁμιλεῖν,

ἀντ. γ´

   ἱπποτροφίας τε νομίζων ἐν Πανελλάνων νόμῳ·
   καὶ θεῶν δαῖτας προσέπτυκτο πάσας· οὐδέ ποτε
      ξενίαν

40 οὖρος ἐμπνεύσαις ὑπέστειλ᾽ ἱστίον ἀμφὶ τρά-
      πεζαν·   60

   ἀλλ᾽ ἐπέρα ποτὶ μὲν Φᾶσιν θερείαις,
   ἐν δὲ χειμῶνι πλέων Νείλου πρὸς ἀκτάς.

ἐπ. γ´

   μή νυν, ὅτι φθονεραὶ θνατῶν φρένας ἀμφικρέμαν-
      ται ἐλπίδες,

   μήτ᾽ ἀρετάν ποτε σιγάτω πατρῴαν,

45 μηδὲ τούσδ᾽ ὕμνους· ἐπεί τοι
   οὐκ ἐλινύσοντας αὐτοὺς εἰργασάμαν.
   ταῦτα, Νικάσιππ᾽, ἀπόνειμον, ὅταν
   ξεῖνον ἐμὸν ἠθαῖον ἔλθῃς.

is the path steep, if one bringeth the praises of the maids of Helicon to the homes of famous men. By a long throw may I fling my dart as far beyond all others,[1] as Xenocratês surpassed all men in sweetness of temper. Right gracious was he in his townsmen's company, and he upheld the breeding of horses after the ordinance of all the Greeks. He welcomed too each banquet of the gods ; and never did the breeze, that blew around his hospitable board, cause him to furl his sail ; but, in the summer seasons, he passed as far as Phâsis, and in his winter voyage, unto the banks of the Nile.[2] What though the broodings of envy beset the minds of mortals ? Let him never hush in silence, either his father's prowess, no, nor yet these hymns of praise; for not to stand idle did I devise them. Give this message, Nîcâsippus, when thou comest unto my trusty friend.

[1] Cp. note on *P.* i 45.

[2] The fame of his hospitality extended to the eastern limits of the known world, reaching as far as Phâsis, the distant river of the Euxine, in the summer, and as far as the Nile in the winter. The Euxine was open to navigation in the summer alone, and it was only to Egypt that the Greeks sailed-in the winter.

ISTHMIAN III

FOR MELISSUS OF THEBES

INTRODUCTION

MELISSUS of Thebes obtained two victories,—a victory in the pancratium at the Isthmus (iv 44) and a victory in the chariot-race at Nemea (iii 13). The Ode celebrating the Isthmian pancratium is commonly called the fourth Isthmian, but it was apparently composed before the third. Melissus afterwards won the chariot-race at the Nemean games, and accordingly a short poem, commonly called the third Isthmian, was composed in the same metre as the fourth, and prefixed to it. Thus both poems could be sung to the same music, by the same chorus, and, probably, at a smaller expense. This is in agreement with the view of Mr. Bury, who regards the first metrical system, the eighteen lines of Strophê, Antistrophê, and Epode, as a new proeme to an earlier ode.

The evidence of the MSS is divided. The two poems are separated in the Vatican MS and in the Scholia,[1] but they are united in the Florentine MS. They are regarded as one ode by Boeckh, Dissen, Hermann, and Schröder, and by Fennell, who marks

[1] Schol. iii 24, ἐν τῇ ἑξῆς ᾠδῇ.

a lacuna, consisting of one metrical system, between
the two parts of the composition. Bergk and Christ
regard them as separate poems.

The Isthmian victory in the pancratium (iv) is
assigned by Gaspar to April 476 and the Nemean
victory (iii) in the chariot-race to July 475. The
battle in which four of the Cleônymidae fell would
in that case be the battle of Plataea (479). Schröder
suggests as the date of the Odes 478–7 ; Fraccaroli,
476 ; Bornemann, April 494 and July 493.
Schröder's date for the two Isthmian Odes (478–7)
is supported by the fact that Bacchylides (v 31), in
an Ode on Hieron's Olympic victory of 476, imitates
Isth. iv 1, in the words τὼς νῦν καὶ ἐμοὶ μυρία παντᾷ
κέλευθος.

Praise is due to him who, either in the glory
of the games, or in the power of wealth, enjoys good
fortune, without becoming insolent (1–3). Zeus
grants to the devout a longer enjoyment of their
wealth (4–6). Praise is due to the man of prowess,
for Melissus has been victorious at the Isthmus, as
well as at Nemea, where he won the chariot-race and
thus brought glory to Thebes (7–13). His merits
are inherited from his ancestor Cleônymus ; his clan
had long made efforts to win the chariot-race, but
they have had varying fortunes ; for only the sons of
the gods are never hurt (13–18).

III.—ΜΕΛΙΣΣΩ ΘΗΒΑΙΩ

ΙΠΠΟΙΣ

στρ. α΄

Εἴ τις ἀνδρῶν εὐτυχήσαις ἢ σὺν εὐδόξοις ἀέθλοις
ἢ σθένει πλούτου κατέχει φρασὶν αἰανῆ κόρον,
ἄξιος εὐλογίαις ἀστῶν μεμίχθαι.
Ζεῦ, μεγάλαι δ᾽ ἀρεταὶ θνατοῖς ἕπονται
5 ἐκ σέθεν· ζώει δὲ μάσσων ὄλβος ὀπιζομένων,
πλαγίαις δὲ φρένεσσιν
οὐχ ὁμῶς πάντα χρόνον θάλλων ὁμιλεῖ.   10

ἀντ. α΄

εὐκλέων δ᾽ ἔργων ἄποινα χρὴ μὲν ὑμνῆσαι τὸν
    ἐσλόν,
χρὴ δὲ κωμάζοντ᾽ ἀγαναῖς χαρίτεσσιν βαστάσαι.
ἔστι δὲ καὶ διδύμων ἀέθλων Μελίσσῳ
10 μοῖρα πρὸς εὐφροσύναν τρέψαι γλυκεῖαν
ἦτορ, ἐν βάσσαισιν Ἰσθμοῦ δεξαμένῳ στεφάνους,
τὰ δὲ κοίλα λέοντος
ἐν βαθυστέρνου νάπᾳ κάρυξε Θήβαν   20

ἐπ. α΄

ἱπποδρομίᾳ κρατέων. ἀνδρῶν δ᾽ ἀρετὰν
σύμφυτον οὐ κατελέγχει.
15 ἴστε μὰν Κλεωνύμου
δόξαν παλαιὰν ἅρμασιν·
καὶ ματρόθε Λαβδακίδαισιν σύννομοι πλούτου
διέστειχον τετραοριᾶν πόνοις.
αἰὼν δὲ κυλινδομέναις ἁμέραις ἄλλ᾽ ἄλλοτ᾽ ἐξάλ-
    λαξεν· ἄτρωτοί γε μὰν παῖδες θεῶν.   30

III.—FOR MELISSUS OF THEBES

WINNER IN THE CHARIOT RACE AT NEMEA, 477 (?) B.C.

IF any one among men hath had good fortune, by the winning of glorious prizes, or by might of wealth, yet in his heart restraineth insatiate insolence, such a man is worthy to be blended with his townsmen's praises. For, from thee, O Zeus, do mighty merits attend upon mortals; and, when they reverence thee, their good fortune hath a longer life, but with froward hearts it liveth not in prosperity for all time alike.

But, as a guerdon for glorious exploits, it is meet for us to celebrate the hero, and, amid triumph-songs, exalt him with kindly hymns of praise. Even in two contests hath good fortune been shared by Melissus, to turn his heart to sweet good-cheer. For, in the vales of the Isthmus, hath he won garlands, and again, in the hollow dell of the deep-chested lion,[1] did he cause Thêbê to be proclaimed by his victory in the chariot-race. And he bringeth no disgrace on the manliness inherited from his fathers. Ye know, I ween, the olden glory of Cleônymus in the chariot-races: and, being on their mother's side akin to the Labdacidae, they walked in the ways of wealth with toilsome training of their teams of four horses. But time with its rolling days bringeth manifold changes; scatheless indeed are none but the sons of the gods.

[1] The Nemean lion.

ISTHMIAN IV

FOR MELISSUS OF THEBES

INTRODUCTION

This Ode relates to an Isthmian victory in the pancratium, won by Melissus of Thebes, probably in 478 B.C., the year preceding the Nemean victory in the chariot-race, celebrated in the third Isthmian.

Thanks to the gods, the Isthmian victory of Melissus has given the poet a boundless opening for the praise of his famous family, which, in spite of the fitful breath of fortune, ever flourishes in deeds of prowess (19–24). They have been honoured in Thebes, and have been renowned in war (25–33): yet, in one day, four of them fell in battle (34 f), but their winter of gloom has been followed by the flowers of spring (36 f). Poseidon (the god of the Isthmus) has given their race this hymn of praise, and has thus revived their ancient fame, which had proclaimed their victories at Athens and Sicyon, while they also strove for victory in the Panhellenic chariot-races (37–48). But the issues of athletic contests are uncertain; and the craft of inferior persons may get the advantage over their betters (49–53), as in the legend of Ajax, who was forced to

slay himself; but Homer has done him honour and
has made him a theme for heroic song (53–57).
Praise passes over land and sea, as a light that shines
for ever (58–60). May we light such a beacon-flame
of song for Melissus, in honour of his victory in the
pancratium (61–63). Brave as a lion, and crafty as
a fox, he is small in stature, even as Heracles, in
comparison with Antaeus,—Heracles, who, after all
his labours, lives in Olympus (63–78), and is honoured
at Thebes with annual festivals, at which Melissus
was thrice victorious, thanks to his trainer, Orseas
(79–90).

IV.—ΜΕΛΙΣΣΩ ΘΗΒΑΙΩ

ΠΑΓΚΡΑΤΙΩ

στρ. α΄

Ἔστι μοι θεῶν ἕκατι μυρία παντᾷ κέλευθος·
ὦ Μέλισσ᾽, εὐμαχανίαν γὰρ ἔφανας Ἰσθμίοις
ὑμετέρας ἀρετὰς ὕμνῳ διώκειν·
αἶσι Κλεωνυμίδαι θάλλοντες αἰεὶ
5 σὺν θεῷ θνατὸν διέρχονται βιότου τέλος.   ἄλλοτε
δ᾽ ἀλλοῖος οὖρος
πάντας ἀνθρώπους ἐπαΐσσων ἐλαύνει.   10

ἀντ. α΄

τοὶ μὲν ὦν Θήβαισι τιμάεντες ἀρχᾶθεν λέγονται
πρόξενοί τ᾽ ἀμφικτιόνων κελαδεννᾶς τ᾽ ὀρφανοὶ
ὕβριος· ὅσσα δ᾽ ἐπ᾽ ἀνθρώπους ἄηται
10 μαρτύρια φθιμένων ζωῶν τε φωτῶν
ἀπλέτου δόξας, ἐπέψαυσαν κατὰ πᾶν τέλος·   ἀνο-
ρέαις δ᾽ ἐσχάταισιν
οἴκοθεν στάλαισιν ἅπτονθ᾽ Ἡρακλείαις·   20

ἐπ. α΄

καὶ μηκέτι μακροτέραν σπεύδειν ἀρετάν.
ἱπποτρόφοι τ᾽ ἐγένοντο,
15 χαλκέῳ τ᾽ Ἄρει ἄδον.
ἀλλ᾽ ἀμέρᾳ γὰρ ἐν μιᾷ
τραχεῖα νιφὰς πολέμοιο τεσσάρων
17ᵇ ἀνδρῶν ἐρήμωσεν μάκαιραν ἑστίαν·

5 βιότου Donaldson, Schneidewin (CMCBuS); βίου mss (B); βίου ἐς F.

460

IV.—FOR MELISSUS OF THEBES

WINNER IN THE PANCRATIUM AT THE ISTHMUS, 478 (?) B.C.

THANKS to the gods, I have countless paths open-
ing on every side, for thou, Melissus, at the Isthmian
games, hast shown me a ready resource to celebrate
in song the valour of thy race;—the valour with which
the sons of Cleônymus flourish evermore, as they
pass with heaven's blessing to the term of mortal
life. But changeful are the gales that at changeful
times rush down upon all men and speed them on.
These men verily are spoken of as honoured of old in
Thebes, as patrons of the neighbour-towns, and as
untainted by [1] boisterous insolence ; and, as for the
memorials of men now dead or of men that live,
the memorials of boundless fame that fly through
all the world—all of these did they attain in all
their fulness. And by far-reaching deeds of native
valour,[2] did they touch the pillars of Heracles ; and
let none pursue prowess that passeth beyond that
bound ! Aye, and they became breeders of horses,
and were the joy of the mail-clad Arês. But alas !
for, on a single day,[3] the rude hail-storm of war bereft
a happy hearth of four of its heroes ; but now, once

---

[1] Lit. "reft of."

[2] οἴκοθεν· διὰ τῶν οἰκείων ἀρετῶν, scholium on the parallel
passage, *O.* iii 44.   [3] The battle of Plataea, 479 B.C.

461

νῦν δ᾽ αὖ μετὰ χειμέριον ποικίλων μηνῶν ζόφον
18ᵇ χθὼν ὦτε φοινικέοισιν ἄνθησεν ῥόδοις   30
στρ. β′

    δαιμόνων βουλαῖς. ὁ κινητὴρ δὲ γᾶς Ὀγχηστὸν
      οἰκέων
20 καὶ γέφυραν ποντιάδα πρὸ Κορίνθου τειχέων,
    τόνδε πορὼν γενεᾷ θαυμαστὸν ὕμνον
    ἐκ λεχέων ἀνάγει φάμαν παλαιὰν
    εὐκλέων ἔργων· ἐν ὕπνῳ γὰρ πέσεν· ἀλλ᾽ ἀνεγει-
      ρομένα χρῶτα λάμπει,   40
    Ἀωσφόρος θαητὸς ὡς ἄστροις ἐν ἄλλοις·
ἀντ. β′
25 ἅ τε κἂν γουνοῖς Ἀθανᾶν ἅρμα καρύξαισα νικᾶν
    ἔν τ᾽ Ἀδραστείοις ἀέθλοις Σικυῶνος ὥπασεν
    τοιάδε τῶν τότ᾽ ἐόντων φύλλ᾽ ἀοιδᾶν.
    οὐδὲ παναγυρίων ξυνᾶν ἀπεῖχον
    καμπύλον δίφρον, Πανελλάνεσσι δ᾽ ἐριζόμενοι
      δαπάνᾳ χαῖρον ἵππων.   50
30 τῶν ἀπειράτων γὰρ ἄγνωστοι σιωπαί,
ἐπ. β′
    ἔστιν δ᾽ ἀφάνεια τύχας καὶ μαρναμένων,
    πρὶν τέλος ἄκρον ἱκέσθαι·
    τῶν τε γὰρ καὶ τῶν διδοῖ·
    καὶ κρέσσον᾽ ἀνδρῶν χειρόνων
35 ἔσφαλε τέχνα καταμάρψαισ᾽. ἴστε μὰν Αἴαντος
    ἀλκὰν φοίνιον, τὰν ὀψίᾳ   59

    18 χειμέριον ποικίλων mss (BMFBu): χειμερίων ποικίλα
Hartung (c), χειμέριον ποικίλα (s).
    27 ἀοιδᾶν Triclinius (BFBuS): ἀοιδῶν B (MC); ἀοιδὰν D.
    30 ἄγνωστοι mss (BBu): ἄγνωτοι MFCS, cp. O. vi 67.
    35 f. ἀλκάν, φοίνιον τὰν — ταμὼν "feriendo cruentavit"
Madvig (s).

more, after the wintry gloom of the many-hued months, hath the ground, as it were, blossomed anew with ruddy roses[1] by the will of heaven.   And the shaker of the earth, who dwelleth at Onchêstus, and on the wave-washed reef before the walls of Corinth, by granting that house this wondrous ode of victory, raiseth from her resting-place the olden fame of noble deeds; for she was fallen on sleep; but now she is roused again with beaming form, like the star of morning, a sight to see amid the other stars—that olden fame which, even in the fertile fields of Athens, proclaimed their chariot as victorious, and also in Sicyon at the games of Adrastus; and thus gave them from the bards of old leaves of minstrelsy that are like unto mine.[2]   Nor from the general games did they keep aloof their curvèd chariot, but striving with all the Hellenic hosts, they rejoiced in spending their wealth upon steeds.   For those who make no trial have an inglorious obscurity; and, even when men strive indeed, fortune doth not show herself until they reach the final goal.   For she giveth of this, and of that; and ere now hath the skill of weaker men overtaken and overturned a stronger than they.

Verily ye know of the valorous form of the blood-dyed Aias, which at the dead of night he pierced by

---

[1] Probably scarlet anemones, among the most prominent flowers of spring-time in Greece.

[2] Probably "an allusion to the shower of leaves flung over victors, a practice known as φυλλοβολία" (Fennell and Bury). Cp. *P.* ix 124.

PINDAR

ἐν νυκτὶ ταμὼν περὶ ᾧ φασγάνῳ, μομφὰν ἔχει
    παίδεσσιν Ἑλλάνων ὅσοι Τρῴανδ᾽ ἔβαν.

στρ. γ΄

ἀλλ᾽ Ὅμηρός τοι τετίμακεν δι᾽ ἀνθρώπων, ὃς
    αὐτοῦ
πᾶσαν ὀρθώσαις ἀρετὰν κατὰ ῥάβδον ἔφρασεν
θεσπεσίων ἐπέων λοιποῖς ἀθύρειν.

40 τοῦτο γὰρ ἀθάνατον φωνᾶεν ἔρπει,
    εἴ τις εὖ εἴπῃ τι· καὶ πάγκαρπον ἐπὶ χθόνα καὶ
        διὰ πόντον βέβακεν   70
ἐργμάτων ἀκτὶς καλῶν ἄσβεστος αἰεί.

ἀντ. γ΄

προφρόνων Μοισᾶν τύχοιμεν, κεῖνον ἅψαι πυρσὸν
    ὕμνων
καὶ Μελίσσῳ, παγκρατίου στεφάνωμ᾽ ἐπάξιον,

45 ἔρνεϊ Τελεσιάδα. τόλμα γὰρ εἰκὼς
θυμὸν ἐριβρεμετᾶν θηρῶν λεόντων
ἐν πόνῳ, μῆτιν δ᾽ ἀλώπηξ, αἰετοῦ ἅ τ᾽ ἀναπιτνα-
    μένα ῥόμβον ἴσχει.   80
χρὴ δὲ πᾶν ἔρδοντα μαυρῶσαι τὸν ἐχθρόν.

ἐπ. γ΄

οὐ γὰρ φύσιν Ὠαριωνείαν ἔλαχεν·
50 ἀλλ᾽ ὀνοτὸς μὲν ἰδέσθαι,
συμπεσεῖν δ᾽ ἀκμᾷ βαρύς.

---

46 θηρῶν Heyne (MFCS) : θηρᾶν mss ; θηρᾷ scholium, Thiersch,
Hermann (BBu).
51 ἀκμᾷ Pauw (BMFCS) : αἰχμᾷ mss (Bu).

464

falling on his own sword, thus bringing blame on all
the sons of the Greeks, as many as went to Troy.[1]
But lo! he is honoured throughout all the world
by Homer, who, having set forth all his prowess,
told it after the rule of his epic divine for other bards
to toy with. For whatsoever one hath well said goeth
forth with a voice that never dieth; and thus, o'er
the fruitful earth and athwart the sea, hath passed
the light of noble deeds unquenchable for ever. O
may we win the favour of the Muses, that, for Me-
lissus also, we may kindle that torch of song, as a
well-won prize from the pancratium, even for this
scion of the race of Telesias. For, in toil of conflict,
he resembleth the spirit of loudly-roaring lions in
boldness, while, in craft, he is like the fox, which
lieth on her back and so stayeth the swoop of the
eagle.[2] But right it is to leave naught undone in
throwing one's adversary into the shade. For fate
had not allotted him the stature of an Orion, but he
was mean to look upon, though heavy to grapple
with in his strength.

[1] Cf. Headlam in *Classical Rev.* xvii (1903), 208 f.

[2] In the wrestling, which is an important part of the
pancratium, Melissus had been as bold as a lion, and as
cunning as a fox. The fox, when attacked by the eagle,
throws itself on its back, probably with a view to defending
itself with its feet. It may also be suggested that, as the
fur on its belly is lighter than that on its back, the eagle
might be baulked by the sudden change of colour. In the
pentathlum, and in wrestling competitions proper, "upright
wrestling" alone was permitted. "Ground wrestling"
only existed as part of the pancratium, in which hitting and
kicking were also allowed (E. Norman Gardiner, *Greek
Athletic Sports*, p. 376). As a pancratiast, Melissus had
probably resorted to some kind of wrestling trick, like that
called the τρόπος χαμαί, or ὑπτιασμός. Antaeus, who is
mentioned below, is said to have excelled in the former.

καίτοι πότ' Ἀνταίου δόμους
Θήβαν ἀπὸ Καδμεῖαν μορφὰν βραχύς, ψυχὰν δ'
    ἄκαμπτος, προσπαλαίσων ἦλθ' ἀνὴρ   90
τὰν πυροφόρον Λιβύαν, κρανίοις ὄφρα ξένων ναὸν
    Ποσειδάωνος ἐρέφοντα σχέθοι,

στρ. δ'

55 υἱὸς Ἀλκμήνας· ὃς Οὐλυμπόνδ' ἔβα, γαίας τε
    πάσας
καὶ βαθύκρημνον πολιᾶς ἁλὸς ἐξευρὼν θέναρ,
ναυτιλίαισί τε πορθμὸν ἀμερῶσαις.
νῦν δὲ παρ' Αἰγιόχῳ κάλλιστον ὄλβον
ἀμφέπων ναίει, τετίματαί τε πρὸς ἀθανάτων
    φίλος, Ἥβαν τ' ὀπυίει,   100
60 χρυσέων οἴκων ἄναξ καὶ γαμβρὸς Ἥρας.

ἀντ. δ'

τῷ μὲν Ἀλεκτρᾶν ὕπερθεν δαῖτα πορσύνοντες
    ἀστοὶ
καὶ νεόδματα στεφανώματα βωμῶν αὔξομεν
ἔμπυρα χαλκοαρᾶν ὀκτὼ θανόντων,
τοὺς Μεγάρα τέκε οἱ Κρειοντὶς υἱούς·
65 τοῖσιν ἐν δυθμαῖσιν αὐγᾶν φλὸξ ἀνατελλομένα
    συνεχὲς παννυχίζει   110
αἰθέρα κνισάεντι λακτίζοισα καπνῷ,

ἐπ. δ'

καὶ δεύτερον ἆμαρ ἐτείων τέρμ' ἀέθλων
γίνεται, ἰσχύος ἔργον.
ἔνθα λευκωθεὶς κάρα

56 βαθύκρημνον Heyne (s) : βαθυκρήμνου mss (BMFCBu).
65 δυθμαῖσιν BD and scholia (MFCBuS) : δυσμαῖσιν Triclinius
(B).
66 κνισαέντι (MFCBuS) : κνισάντι mss ; κνισσᾶντι Hermann
(B).

Yet, once on a time, from Thebes, the city of Cadmus, there went a hero, short in stature, but in soul unflinching, even unto the home of Antaeus, in corn-bearing Libya, to stay him from roofing Poseidon's temple with the skulls of strangers, even Alcmênê's son; who to Olympus passed, after he had tracked out all the lands and even the cliff-girt level of the foaming sea, and had tamed the wild straits for the seamen. And now he dwelleth beside the aegis-bearer,[1] lord of a happiness supreme, by the immortals honoured as a friend; and is wedded to Hêbê, is king of a golden home, and husband of Hêra's daughter. For him, above the Electran gates, we Thebans, busily preparing the banquet, and setting the circle of our newly built altars, kill many a victim in honour of those eight slain warriors,[2] the sons whom Megara, Creon's daughter, bare him—the sons for whom the flame ariseth in the gloaming, and blazeth for the livelong night, lashing with fragrant reek the height of heaven. And, on the second day, is that struggle of strength, the crowning event of the annual games. And there it was that our hero, with head enwreathed with myrtle white, showed

[1] Zeus.
[2] Literally, "those eight mail-clad men, now dead."

70 μύρτοις ὅδ᾽ ἀνὴρ διπλόαν
  νίκαν ἀνεφάνατο παίδων <τε> τρίταν πρόσθεν
    κυβερνατῆρος οἰακοστρόφου   120
  γνώμᾳ πεπιθὼν πολυβούλῳ. σὺν Ὀρσέᾳ δέ νιν
    κωμάξομαι, τερπνὰν ἐπιστάζων χάριν.

71 παίδων <τε> BS : <καὶ> παίδων MFCBu.
72 κωμάξομαι D (MFCBuS) : κωμάζομαι B (B).

forth a double victory, after another won erstwhile
among the boys by heeding the wise counsels of his
helmsman and trainer, Orseas.   Linking his own
name with that of Orseas, I shall honour him in the
triumph-song, shedding on both my glad tribute of
praise.

ISTHMIAN V

FOR PHYLACIDAS OF AEGINA

INTRODUCTION

WHILE the fifth Nemean celebrates the victory of Pytheas, the elder son of Lampon of Aegina, the fifth and sixth Isthmian Odes celebrate those of his younger son, Phylacidas. But of these Isthmian Odes, the sixth is earlier than the fifth. The sixth recalls one Nemean and one Isthmian victory won by Pytheas and Phylacidas respectively (vi 1–7); in the fifth, a second Isthmian victory won by Phylacidas is added to the Nemean victory of his elder brother (v 16–19). The date of the fifth Isthmian is determined by the references to the glorious part played by the seamen of Aegina in the battle of Salamis. If the victory of Phylacidas was won in April 480, it must have been celebrated after the battle of September 480. Gaspar places the fifth Nemean in July 489, the sixth Isthmian in April 484, and the fifth Isthmian after September 480. Schröder's dates are similar, while Bornemann prefers 483, 482, and 478 respectively. Wilamowitz places the fifth Nemean in 485 or 483, the sixth Isthmian in 480, and the fifth Isthmian as latè as **476**, but before Pindar's departure for Sicily.

INTRODUCTION

The poet invokes Theia, as the mother of the Sun-god, and the giver of gold and of victory (1–10); for it is thanks to the deities that distinction is gained by deeds of prowess (11). The two things which make a wealthy man happy are well-being and good report (12 f); with such blessings be content; mortal aims befit mortal men (14–16).

In the pancratium Phylacidas has been for a second time victor at the Isthmus, while Pytheas has previously been victorious at Nemea (17–19).

Coming to the island of Aegina, the poet's soul cannot taste of song without singing the race of Aeacus (19–22); and, as Aegina is devoted to noble deeds, he must not grudge to mingle a draught of wine in recompense for toil (22–25).

The fame of the Aeacidae (26–44).

Aegina has long been conspicuous for lofty virtues (44 f). It was sailors of Aegina that won the battle of Salamis (46–50), but we must be silent, for heaven sends evil as well as good (51–53).

An athlete's victories delight in being celebrated in song (54). The house of Cleonîcus has spared neither toil nor cost (54–58). Pytheas has made a clear course for his younger brother's victories as a pancratiast (59–61). Give the victor a wreath and a new ode of victories (62 f).

ΠΑΓΚΡΑΤΙῼ

στρ. α΄

Μᾶτερ Ἀλίου πολυώνυμε Θεία,
σέο ἕκατι καὶ μεγασθενῆ νόμισαν
χρυσὸν ἄνθρωποι περιώσιον ἄλλων·
καὶ γὰρ ἐριζόμεναι
5 νᾶες ἐν πόντῳ καὶ <ὑφ'> ἅρμασιν ἵπποι
διὰ τεάν, ὤνασσα, τιμὰν ὠκυδινάτοις ἐν ἁμίλλαισι
    θαυμασταὶ πέλονται·

ἀντ. α΄

ἔν τ' ἀγωνίοις ἀέθλοισι ποθεινὸν
κλέος ἔπραξεν, ὅντιν' ἀθρόοι στέφανοι
χερσὶ νικάσαντ' ἀνέδησαν ἔθειραν   10
10 ἢ ταχυτᾶτι ποδῶν.
κρίνεται δ' ἀλκὰ διὰ δαίμονας ἀνδρῶν.
δύο δέ τοι ζωᾶς ἄωτον μοῦνα ποιμαίνοντι τὸν
    ἄλπνιστον εὐανθεῖ σὺν ὄλβῳ,

ἐπ. α΄

εἴ τις εὖ πάσχων λόγον ἐσλὸν ἀκούῃ.
μὴ μάτευε Ζεὺς γενέσθαι· πάντ' ἔχεις,
15 εἴ σε τούτων μοῖρ' ἐφίκοιτο καλῶν.
θνατὰ θνατοῖσι πρέπει.   20
τὶν δ' ἐν Ἰσθμῷ διπλόα θάλλοισ' ἀρετά,

2 σέο scholium, Bergk (MFCBuS) : σέο γ' mss (B).
5 <ὑφ'> scholium, Bergk (MFCBuS) : ἐν B, Triclinius (B) ;
om. D.
13 ἀκούῃ B (MCS) : ἀκούσῃ D, Triclinius (BFBu).

V.—FOR PHYLACIDAS OF AEGINA

O MOTHER of the Sun-god, Theia of many names!
for thy sake men even set a stamp upon gold, as
mighty beyond all beside[1]; because, for the sake of
thy worth, O queen, not only ships racing on the
sea, but also mares yoked to chariots in the swiftly-
whirling struggles of battle, win wonder.[2] And, in the
contests of the games, he it is that reapeth the fame
for which he yearneth, whose hair is wreathed with
many a garland, when he hath been victorious with
his hands, or with swiftness of feet. But it is owing to
the gods that the prowess of men is approved; and two
things alone there are which, amid the fair flowers of
wealth, cherish the sweetest bloom of life, if a man
have good hap and win fair praise. Strive not
to be a Zeus; all things are thine, should a share
of these fair boons fall to thy lot. Mortal aims befit
mortal men. But for thee, Phylacidas, there is stored
up at the Isthmus a two-fold meed of fame unfading,

[1] Theia, "the goddess divine," is mentioned in Hesiod's
Theogony, 371, as the mother of the Sun, the Moon, and the
Dawn. She is thus the principle of Light, which gives
brightness to all her offspring. She appears in many forms,
and it is only for this reason that she is here said to have
"many names." It is this Light that gives gold its bright-
ness, and prompts men to stamp it as current coin. Cf.
Wilamowitz, *Berlin Akad.* 1909, p. 826 f.

[2] "Wars are undertaken by land and sea, for treasure;
and are thus due to the influence of Theia." (Bury.)

Φυλακίδα, κεῖται, Νεμέᾳ δὲ καὶ ἀμφοῖν,
Πυθέᾳ τε παγκρατίου. τὸ δ' ἐμὸν
20 οὐκ ἄτερ Αἰακιδᾶν κέαρ ὕμνων γεύεται·
σὺν Χάρισιν δ' ἔμολον Λάμπωνος υἱοῖς

στρ. β'

τάνδ' ἐς εὔνομον πόλιν. εἰ δὲ τέτραπται
θεοδότων ἔργων κέλευθον ἂν καθαράν,
μὴ φθόνει κόμπον τὸν ἐοικότ' ἀοιδᾷ   30
25 κιρνάμεν ἀντὶ πόνων.
καὶ γὰρ ἡρώων ἀγαθοὶ πολεμισταὶ
λόγον ἐκέρδαναν, κλέονται δ' ἔν τε φορμίγγεσσιν
      ἐν αὐλῶν τε παμφώνοις ὁμοκλαῖς

ἀντ. β'

μυρίον χρόνον· μελέταν δὲ σοφισταῖς
Διὸς ἕκατι πρόσβαλον σεβιζόμενοι
30 ἐν μὲν Αἰτωλῶν θυσίαισι φαενναῖς
Οἰνεΐδαι κρατεροί,
ἐν δὲ Θήβαις ἱπποσόας Ἰόλαος   40
γέρας ἔχει, Περσεὺς δ' ἐν Ἄργει, Κάστορος δ'
      αἰχμὰ Πολυδεύκεος τ' ἐπ' Εὐρώτα ῥεέθροις.

ἐπ. β'

ἀλλ' ἐν Οἰνώνᾳ μεγαλήτορες ὀργαὶ
35 Αἰακοῦ παίδων τε· τοὶ καὶ σὺν μάχαις
δὶς πόλιν Τρώων πράθον ἑσπόμενοι
Ἡρακλῆϊ πρότερον,
καὶ σὺν Ἀτρείδαις. ἔλα νῦν μοι πεδόθεν·
λέγε, τίνες Κύκνον, τίνες Ἕκτορα πέφνον,
40 καὶ στράταρχον Αἰθιόπων ἄφοβον   50
Μέμνονα χαλκοάραν· τίς ἄρ' ἐσλὸν Τήλεφον

36 πράθον ἑσπόμενοι B (BMFCBu), Wilamowitz: ἔπραθον,
σπόμενοι Bergk¹ (8).
37 Ἡρακλῆϊ Triclinius (MFCBuS¹):—κλεῖ old mss ;— κλέϊ S³.

bibliotheca SelfCheck System

Items that you checked out

Title: Forbidden colors
ID: 33477489439811
Due: Tuesday, December 26, 2023

Title: Pow!
ID: 33477480312306
Due: Tuesday, December 26, 2023

Title: The odes of Pindar : including the
principal fragments
ID: R0161714688
Due: Tuesday, December 26, 2023

Total items: 3
Account balance: $0.00
Checked out: 7
Overdue: 0
Hold requests: 0
Ready for pickup: 0
12/4/2023 10:19 AM

Thank you for using the bibliotheca SelfCheck
System.

and at Nemea for you both, even for Pytheas with thee, the prize of the pancratium.

But my heart cannot taste of songs without telling of the race of Aeacus. At the call of Lampon's sons have I come, with the Graces, to this city of good laws ; and, if she hath entered the clear high-road of heavenly deeds, then grudge not to mix for her in song the fitting meed in recompense for toil. For, even in the heroic time, brave warriors of (Aegina) were wont to win fame, and they are praised on the lyre and on the manifold music of the flute for uncounted time ; and, by grace of Zeus, they have given a new theme to poets wise. And so the brave sons of Oeneus[1] are adored in the gleaming sacrifices of the Aetolians, and in Thebes the bold horseman Iolaüs hath his reward, and Perseus in Argos, and the spear of Castor and Polydeuces by the streams of Eurôtas ; but in Oenônê[2] the high-hearted spirits of Aeacus and his sons, who, by battles,[3] twice joined in sacking the Trojans' town, first when they followed Heracles, and again with the sons of Atreus. Drive now, my Muse, away from earth ; tell me who they were that slew Cycnus,[4] and who Hector, and the dauntless leader of the Aethiop hosts, the armed warrior, Memnon ? Who, again, was he who, by the

[1] Tydeus and Meleager.
[2] The old name of Aegina. Cp. N. v 15, viii 7.
[3] Or, reading συμμάχοις, " for their allies," Bury.
[4] Cp. O. ii 82, a son of Poseidon, slain by Achilles, and changed into a swan.

τρῶσεν ἐῷ δορὶ Καΐκου παρ' ὄχθαις;

στρ. γ´

  τοῖσιν Αἴγιναν προφέρει στόμα πάτραν
  διαπρεπέα νᾶσον· τετείχισται δὲ πάλαι
45 πύργος ὑψηλαῖς ἀρεταῖς ἀναβαίνειν.
  πολλὰ μὲν ἀρτιεπὴς
  γλῶσσά μοι τοξεύματ' ἔχει περὶ κείνων
  κελαδέσαι· καὶ νῦν ἐν Ἄρει μαρτυρῆσαι κεν πόλις
      Αἴαντος ὀρθωθεῖσα ναύταις   60

ἀντ. γ´

  ἐν πολυφθόρῳ Σαλαμὶς Διὸς ὄμβρῳ
50 ἀναρίθμων ἀνδρῶν χαλαζάεντι φόνῳ.
  ἀλλ' ὅμως καύχημα κατάβρεχε σιγᾷ·
  Ζεὺς τά τε καὶ τὰ νέμει,
  Ζεὺς ὁ πάντων κύριος. ἐν δ' ἐρατεινῷ
  μέλιτι καὶ τοιαίδε τιμαὶ καλλίνικον χάρμ' ἀγαπά-
      ζοντι. μαρνάσθω τις ἔρδων   70

ἐπ. γ´

55 ἀμφ' ἀέθλοισιν γενεὰν Κλεονίκου
  ἐκμαθών· οὔτοι τετύφλωται μακρὸς
  μόχθος ἀνδρῶν· οὐδ' ὁπόσαι δαπάναι
  ἐλπίδων ἔκνισ' ὄπιν.
  αἰνέω καὶ Πυθέαν ἐν γυιοδάμαις
60 Φυλακίδα πλαγᾶν δρόμον εὐθυπορῆσαι
  χερσὶ δεξιόν, νόῳ ἀντίπαλον.
  λάμβανέ οἱ στέφανον, φέρε δ' εὔμαλλον μίτραν,
  καὶ πτερόεντα νέον σύμπεμψον ὕμνον.   80

48 κελαδέσαι Bruno Keil (S³): κελαδῆσαι mss; κελαδέειν (BMFBu); κελαδέμεν Erasmus Schmid (S¹); κελαρύσαι Bergk (C).

58 ἐλπίδων ἔκνισ' ὄπιν (MFCBu): ἐλπίδων ἔκνιξ' ὄπιν B (S¹), — ἔκνιζ' — D; ἐλπίδων, ἔκνισ' ὄπιν (B); ἐλπίδ' ἔκνισαν (ὄπιν = ἐξοπίσω) Wilamowitz (S³).

61 χερσὶ δεξιόν, MCS: χερσί, δεξιὸν B; χερσὶ δεξιὸν FBu.

banks of Caîcus,[1] wounded Têlephus with his spear?
Men for whom the lips tell of Aegina as their father-
land, Aegina, glorious isle, builded of old as a tower
for men to climb by lofty deeds.[2] Full many an arrow
hath my deftly speaking tongue to ring out in praise
of those heroes; and even now could the land of
Aias attest in war that she was saved from falling by
her sailors, yes, Salamis, in the ruinous, heaven-sent
storm, when slaughter thick as hail fell on un-
numbered warriors. Yet, do thou drown thy boast
in silence. Zeus giveth *this*, and giveth *that*,—Zeus,
who is lord of all.

But, in lovely song that is sweet as honey, such
honours also as these welcome a gladsome strain of
victory. Let a man strive and contend in the games
(if he dare), when he hath fully heard of the clan
of Cleonîcus. The long toil of the brave is not
quenched in darkness, nor hath counting the cost
fretted away the zeal of their hopes.[3] I praise
Pytheas also among pancratiasts, who, in guiding
aright the course of Phylacidas' blows, was skilful
with hands, and a match in mind. Take for him a
crown and carry him a fillet of fine wool, and speed
him on his way with this new-winged song.

[1] A river of Mysia, *Mysusque Caïcus* (Virgil, *Georg.* iv
370).

[2] ἀρεταῖς is here taken with ἀναβαίνειν. Cp. Frag. 213 (233),
πότερον δίκᾳ τεῖχος ὕψιον | ἢ σκολιαῖς ἀπάταις ἀναβαίνει | ἐπι-
χθόνιον γένος ἀνδρῶν. *Aeginetis iam dudum turris exstructa est,
quam excelsis virtutibus escendant* (Boeckh). But Dissen takes
ἀρεταῖς with τετείχισται, and ὑψηλαῖς with ἀναβαίνειν, *structa
stat iam diu turris sublimibus* (sc. *arduis adscensu*) *virtutibus*
(and so Fennell and Bury).

[3] Or "nor did the expenses prompted by their hopes,
check their interest (in the games)"; similarly Fennell. Wil-
amowitz prefers ἐλπίδ᾽ ἔκνισαν ὄπιν, regarding ὄπιν as
equivalent to ἐξοπίσω, "wear away their zeal for the future."

ISTHMIAN VI

FOR PHYLACIDAS OF AEGINA

INTRODUCTION

THE sixth Isthmian celebrates a victory in the pancratium won by Phylacidas, son of Lampon, of Aegina. This Ode mentions only one Isthmian victory gained by Phylacidas (vi 5), and is therefore earlier than the fifth Isthmian, which mentions two (v 16–19). The date is probably either 484 (Gaspar and Schröder) or 480 (Wilamowitz).

As when a banquet is at its height, the first libation has been poured out for the elder son of Lampon, and a second is now being poured out for his younger son, to Poseidon, lord of the Isthmus; may a third libation to Zeus Sôtêr be poured out to the Olympian god, for a third victory of the son of Lampon (1–9). When a man spares neither pains nor cost in striving for athletic fame, and heaven blesses his efforts, he has reached the utmost bounds of prosperity (10–13). Lampon prays that he may have this experience before he grows old and dies (14–16). May the Fates favour his prayer (16–18).

The poet cannot approach Aegina without praising the Aeacidae, whose fame has spread over all the world. Time would fail him to tell of all their merits (19–56).

But he must briefly tell of the victories won by the two brothers and their maternal uncle (55–66). Praise of Lampon for hospitality, moderation, candour, and keen encouragement of athletes (66–73).

The poet offers the family a draught of song from the fountain of Dirce, which Memory has caused to spring up beside the gates of Thebes (74 f.).

VI.—ΦΥΛΑΚΙΔΑ ΑΙΓΙΝΗΤΗ

ΠΑΓΚΡΑΤΙΩ

στρ. α΄

Θάλλοντος ἀνδρῶν ὡς ὅτε συμποσίου
δεύτερον κρητῆρα Μοισαίων μελέων
κίρναμεν Λάμπωνος εὐάθλου γενεᾶς ὕπερ, ἐν Νε-
μέᾳ μὲν πρῶτον, ὦ Ζεῦ,
τίν γ᾽ ἄωτον δεξάμενοι στεφάνων,

5 νῦν αὖτε Ἰσθμοῦ δεσπότᾳ
Νηρεΐδεσσί τε πεντήκοντα, παίδων ὁπλοτάτου
Φυλακίδα νικῶντος. εἴη δὲ τρίτον   10
σωτῆρι πορσαίνοντας Ὀλυμπίῳ Αἴγιναν κάτα
σπένδειν μελιφθόγγοις ἀοιδαῖς.

ἀντ. α΄

10 εἰ γάρ τις ἀνθρώπων δαπάνᾳ τε χαρεὶς
καὶ πόνῳ πράσσει θεοδμάτους ἀρετάς,
σύν τέ οἱ δαίμων φυτεύει δόξαν ἐπήρατον, ἐσχα-
τιαῖς ἤδη πρὸς ὄλβου
βάλλετ᾽ ἄγκυραν θεότιμος ἐών.
τοίαισιν ὀργαῖς εὔχεται   20

15 ἀντιάσαις ἀίδαν γῆράς τε δέξασθαι πολιὸν
ὁ Κλεονίκου παῖς· ἐγὼ δ᾽ ὑψίθρονον
Κλωθὼ κασιγνήτας τε προσεννέπω ἑσπέσθαι
κλυταῖς
ἀνδρὸς φίλου Μοίρας ἐφετμαῖς.

5 αὖτε Hermann (M¹FBuS³), αὖτεν (S¹); αὖτ᾽ ἐν mss (M²):
αὖτις B.
12 ἐσχατιαῖς B (MFCS): —ὰς D (BBu).
17 ἑσπέσθαι mss (BFCBu), Wilamowitz; ἔσπεσθαι M; σπέσθαι
Pauw (S).

480

VI.—FOR PHYLACIDAS OF AEGINA

WINNER IN THE PANCRATIUM, 484 (?) OR 480 (?) B.C.

EVEN as when men are holding high festival, so mingle we a second bowl of the Muses' songs in honour of the athlete-house of Lampon. At Nemea was the *first*, when at thy hands, O Zeus, we won the flower of crowns, and now, a *second* time, at the hands of the lord of the Isthmus and the fifty Nereids, on the victory of the youngest son, Phylacidas. Heaven grant that we may make ready a *third* bowl for Zeus Sôtêr of Olympia, and thus pour over Aegina a libation of honied strains of song.[1] For, if a man, rejoicing in expense and in toil, achieveth distinctions on a divine foundation, and if heaven help by sowing for him the seed of fair fame, honoured of God he casteth his anchor at fortune's farthest shore. The son of Cleonîcus prayeth that he may light on feelings such as these, ere he meeteth death or grey old age. And I myself implore Clôthô enthroned on high, to listen, with her sister Fates, to the loud entreaties of the man I love.

---

[1] The scholiast states that the banquet was usually succeeded by three libations, (1) to the Olympian Zeus, (2) to Earth and the heroes, and (3) to Zeus Sôtêr. In the present passage the second libation is offered, not to " Earth and the heroes," but to the " Earth-shaker and the Nereids."

PINDAR

ἐπ. αʹ

　ὔμμε τ᾽, ὦ χρυσάρματοι Αἰακίδαι,
20 τέθμιόν μοι φαμὶ σαφέστατον ἔμμεν
　τάνδ᾽ ἐπιστείχοντα νᾶσον ῥαινέμεν εὐλογίαις.　30
　μυρίαι δ᾽ ἔργων καλῶν τέτμηνθ᾽ ἑκατόμπεδοι ἐν
　　σχερῷ κέλευθοι,
　καὶ πέραν Νείλοιο παγᾶν καὶ δι᾽ Ὑπερβορέους·
　οὐδ᾽ ἔστιν οὕτω βάρβαρος οὔτε παλίγγλωσσος
　　πόλις,
25 ἅτις οὐ Πηλέος ἀίει κλέος ἥρωος, εὐδαίμονος
　　γαμβροῦ θεῶν,

στρ. βʹ

　οὐδ᾽ ἅτις Αἴαντος Τελαμωνιάδα
　καὶ πατρός· τὸν χαλκοχάρμαν ἐς πόλεμον
　ἆγε σὺν Τιρυνθίοισι πρόφρονα σύμμαχον ἐς
　　Τρωΐαν, ἥρωσι μόχθον,　40
　Λαομεδοντίαν ὑπὲρ ἀμπλακίαν
30 ἐν ναυσὶν Ἀλκμήνας τέκος.
　εἷλε δὲ Περγαμίαν, πέφνεν δὲ σὺν κείνῳ Μερόπων
　ἔθνεα καὶ τὸν βουβόταν οὔρεϊ ἶσον
　Φλέγραισιν εὑρὼν Ἀλκυονῆ, σφετέρας δ᾽ οὐ φεί-
　　σατο
　χερσὶν βαρυφθόγγοιο νευρᾶς　50

ἀντ. βʹ

35 Ἡρακλέης. ἀλλ᾽ Αἰακίδαν καλέων
　ἐς πλόον <κεῖνον> κύρσε δαινυμένων.
　τὸν μὲν ἐν ῥινῷ λέοντος στάντα κελήσατο νεκτα-
　　ρέαις σπονδαῖσιν ἄρξαι
　καρτεραίχμαν Ἀμφιτρυωνιάδαν,

---

20 ἔμμεν Boeckh (M²CBᵤS) : εἶναι mss (M¹F).

36 <κεῖνον?> κύρησεν ꜱ : <τοῦτον> D (MF), <ξυνὸν> C,
<τετμὼν> Tyrrell, Bᵤ ; κύρησε <πάντων> B.

482

And, as for you, ye sons of Aeacus with your golden chariots, I deem it my clearest law, to shower praises on you, whene'er I set foot on this isle. For countless roads are cleft for your noble deeds, roads with their hundred feet of continuous breadth, extending even beyond the springs of the Nile, and through the land beyond the North wind. Nor is there any city so rude in speech, so strange in tongue, that it knoweth not the fame of the hero Pêleus, that happy husband of a deity, nor of Aias, nor of Telamon, his sire. Him the son of Alcmênê, because of Laomedon's wrong,[1] led in ships unto war that rejoiceth in armour, even unto Troy, that weary quest of heroes,[2] as an eager ally along with the men of Tiryns. And he took Pergamos, and with help of Telamon, slew the tribes of Meropes, and that herdsman, huge as a mountain, Alcyoneus, whom he found at Phlegrae, when the loudly twanging bow-string was not left untouched by the hands of Heracles. But, when he came to call the son of Aeacus to that famous voyage, he found them feasting, and, as in lion's skin he stood, Amphitryon's

[1] When Hêsionê, daughter of Làomedon, king of Troy, was about to be sacrificed to a marine monster sent by Poseidôn, Heracles slew the monster, but Lâomedôn refused the promised reward. Thereupon Heracles sailed with Telamon against Troy, slew Lâomedôn and all his sons, except Priam, and gave Hêsionê to Telamon.   [2] Bury.

ἄνδωκε δ' αὐτῷ φέρτατος
40 οἰνοδόκον φιάλαν χρυσῷ πεφρικυῖαν Τελαμών,
ὁ δ' ἀνατείναις οὐρανῷ χεῖρας ἀμάχους   60
αὔδασε τοιοῦτον ἔπος· "Εἴ ποτ' ἐμάν, ὦ Ζεῦ πάτερ,
θυμῷ ἐθέλων ἀρὰν ἄκουσας,

ἐπ. β'

νῦν σε, νῦν εὐχαῖς ὑπὸ θεσπεσίαις
45 λίσσομαι παῖδα θρασὺν ἐξ Ἐριβοίας
ἀνδρὶ τῷδε, ξεῖνον ἀμὸν μοιρίδιον τελέσαι,
τὸν μὲν ἄρρηκτον φυάν, ὥσπερ τόδε δέρμα με νῦν
    περιπλανᾶται
θηρός, ὃν πάμπρωτον ἄθλων κτεῖνά ποτ' ἐν
    Νεμέᾳ·   70
θυμὸς δ' ἐπέσθω." ταῦτ' ἄρα οἱ φαμένῳ πέμψεν
    θεὸς
50 ἀρχὸν οἰωνῶν μέγαν αἰετόν· ἀδεῖα δ' ἔνδον νιν
    ἔκνιξεν χάρις,

στρ. γ'

εἶπέν τε φωνήσαις ἅτε μάντις ἀνήρ·
"Ἔσσεταί τοι παῖς, ὃν αἰτεῖς, ὦ Τελαμών·
καί νιν ὄρνιχος φανέντος κέκλε' ἐπώνυμον εὐρυ-
    βίαν Αἴαντα, λαῶν
ἐν πόνοις ἔκπαγλον Ἐνναλίου."   80
55 ὡς ἄρα εἰπὼν αὐτίκα
ἕζετ'. ἐμοὶ δὲ μακρὸν πάσας <ἀν>αγήσασθ'
    ἀρετάς·

42 τοιοῦτον Ϝέπος Heyne (MFCBuS) : τοιοῦτόν τι old mss ;
τοιοῦτόν γ' Pauw (B).

46 τῷδε, ξεῖνον ἀμὸν S, τῶδε ξεῖνον ἀμὸν corr. B ; τόνδε κεῖνον
ἀμὸν D ; τῷδε ξεῖνον ἀμὸν (BM) ; τῷδε Ξεῖνι', ἅμαρ F ; τῷδε
ξεῖνίόν μου C ; τῷδε ξυνόδαμον Bury.

53 κέκλε' Bergk (C), cp. Hesychius κέκλεο· κάλεσον ; κέκλευ
Melanchthon (Bus) : κέκλετ' BD (BMF).

56 <ἀν> — ἀρετάς Mingarelli (edd.), — ἀρετᾶς mss.

warrior-son was summoned to pour out the first
libation of nectar,—summoned by good Telamon,
who lifted up to him the wine-bowl rough with
gold; and he, the while, outstretching unto heaven
his hands invincible, spake out on this wise:—

"If ever, O father Zeus, thou hast heard my
prayer with willing heart, now, even now, with
strong entreaty, I pray thee to bring to perfection
for Telamon a brave son, to be my fated guest-friend.
I pray thee to make him as hardy in frame as this
hide that is wrapped around me, hide of the beast
whom, as the very first of my labours, I slew that
day in Nemea; and may he have courage to
match."

He ceased, and, thereupon, the god sent him a
mighty eagle, king of birds, and sweet delight
thrilled his heart, and prophet-like he spake and
said:—

"Lo! Thou shalt have the son, for whom thou
askest, Telamon; and, after the name of the bird
that hath appeared, thou shalt call him the mighty
Aias,[1] dread foeman in the war-toils of the people."

Thus having said, forthwith he sate him down.
But, as for me, it would take too long to tell of all
their deeds of prowess; for, O my Muse, it is for

---

[1] The name of Αἴας is here derived from αἰετός.

Φυλακίδα γὰρ ἦλθον, ὦ Μοῖσα, ταμίας
Πυθέᾳ τε κώμων Εὐθυμένει τε. τὸν Ἀργείων
 τρόπον
εἰρήσεταί που κἂν βραχίστοις.

ἀντ. γ́

60 ἄραντο γὰρ νίκας ἀπὸ παγκρατίου
τρεῖς ἀπ' Ἰσθμοῦ, τὰς δ' ἀπ' εὐφύλλου Νεμέας,
ἀγλαοὶ παῖδές τε καὶ μάτρως· ἀνὰ δ' ἄγαγον ἐς
 φάος οἵαν μοῖραν ὕμνων·   90
τὰν Ψαλυχιδᾶν δὲ πάτραν Χαρίτων
ἄρδοντι καλλίστᾳ δρόσῳ,
65 τόν τε Θεμιστίου ὀρθώσαντες οἶκον τάνδε πόλιν
θεοφιλῆ ναίοισι. Λάμπων δὲ μελέταν
ἔργοις ὀπάζων Ἡσιόδου μάλα τιμᾷ τοῦτ' ἔπος,
υἱοῖσί τε φράζων παραινεῖ,   100

ἐπ. γ́

ξυνὸν ἄστει κόσμον ἑῷ προσάγων,
70 καὶ ξένων εὐεργεσίαις ἀγαπᾶται,
μέτρα μὲν γνώμᾳ διώκων, μέτρα δὲ καὶ κατέχων·
γλῶσσα δ' οὐκ ἔξω φρενῶν· φαίης κέ νιν ἀνδράσιν
 ἀθληταῖσιν ἔμμεν
Ναξίαν πέτραις ἐν ἄλλαις χαλκοδάμαντ' ἀκόναν.
πίσω σφε Δίρκας ἁγνὸν ὕδωρ, τὸ βαθύζωνοι κόραι
75 χρυσοπέπλου Μναμοσύνας ἀνέτειλαν παρ' εὐτει-
 χέσιν Κάδμου πύλαις.   110

59 που κἂν Heyne ; που κὲν B, πα κ' ἐν D (B); πᾳ κ' ἐν
Triclinius (F) ; πᾳ δ' ἐν (M); ποι κἂν Wilamowitz ; πάντ' ἐν
Schneidewin (C), πολλ' ἐν (S), βαῖ ἐν Bury.
72 νιν ἀνδράσιν ἀθλ. Heyne, Hermann (B), — ἀεθλ. (FC) : νιν
ἀνδρ' ἐν ἀθλ. mss, — ἀεθλ. S ; Μένανδρον ἐν ἀεθλ. Mommsen
(Nezger, Bury).

---

[1] The Argive brevity of speech was proverbial. Aeschylus
Supplices, 196, says of Argos, "the city doth not love a
lengthy speech."

Phylacidas and Pytheas and Euthymenês, that I
have come to marshall the triumph-march. In
Argive fashion, shall the tale be told, I ween, even in
briefest words.[1] Three victories in the pancratium
from the Isthmus, and others again from leafy Nemea,
were carried off by those glorious boys and by their
eme. And oh! the goodly boon of praises which
they raised to the light! Aye! and with brightest
dew of song they refresh the clan of the Psalychidae;
they have firmly founded the house of Themistius,
and they dwell here in a city which is loved of
heaven. And Lampon himself, "spending pains on all
his work," holdeth in honour that saying of Hesiod,[2]
quoting and commending it to his sons besides, and
thus bringing a general fame to his own city, while he
is loved for his good deeds to strangers also, in heart
pursuing the true mean, and holding to that mean in
act beside; and his tongue departeth not from his
thoughts. You might say that, amid the athletes,
he was a very stone of Naxos among all others,
the metal-mastering whetstone.[3] I shall give him to
drink of the pure water of Dircê, which the deep-
zoned daughters of golden-robed Memory made to
gush forth beside the noble gates of the walls of
Cadmus.

[2] *Works and Days*, 412, μελέτη δέ τε ἔργον ὀφέλλει,
"taking pains doth help the work."

[3] "Emery has been worked from a remote period in the
isle of Naxos, whence the stone was called *Naxium* by Pliny
and other Roman writers" (*Enc. Brit.* ed. 1910). Cp. Pliny,
36, § 164; 37, § 109. Whetstones of similar formation in
Cyprus were called "Naxian" (36, § 54); and ",Cretan" as
well as "Naxian" whetstones are mentioned as famous in
36, § 164. The statement of the Scholiast that the whet-
stone in the text came from "Naxos in Crete" is probably
due to some confusion between Naxian and Cretan whet-
stones.

ISTHMIAN VII

FOR STREPSIADES OF THEBES

INTRODUCTION

THE seventh Isthmian celebrates the victory in the pancratium won by Strepsiades of Thebes. The victor's uncle, of the same name, had died in battle. The Scholiast says that he had fallen "in the Peloponnesian war." Heyne, Thiersch, Bergk, and Gaspar connect this battle with the invasion of Attica by the Peloponnesian forces, in 506, under the command of Cleomenes, who was allied with the Boeotians and Chalcidians. They accordingly assume that Strepsiades the elder fell in one of the battles between the Boeotians and Athenians, and that the Isthmian victory of Strepsiades the younger was in April 502, a few months before the Pythian games of August, for which Strepsiades was preparing.

Mezger, followed by Bury, holds that the battle in which Strepsiades the elder fell was that of Tanagra, fought in Nov. 457, in which the Peloponnesians and the Thebans defeated the Athenians. Two months later, early in 456, the Thebans were defeated by the Athenians at Oenophyta. Boeckh and Dissen, Fennell, Schröder and Wilamowitz, hold that this was the battle in which Strepsiades fell. Those who, like Gaspar, place the Ode in 502, imply that this was one of Pindar's earliest poems, but the approach of old age is implied in l. 41, which is in favour of the date conjecturally adopted by Schröder, **456.**

The poet asks the guardian-goddess of Thebes which of her legendary glories has given her the greatest delight (1–15). Men are apt to forget any event which has not been commemorated in song (16–19). Therefore we must sing of the victory in the pancratium won by Strepsiades (20–23).

His wreath has a common interest to his uncle of the same name, who bravely died in battle for his dear country, while the bravest of our warriors endured intolerable woe (24–36). But now Poseidon, lord of the Isthmus, has given the poet calm after storm by wreathing his hair with garlands for an Isthmian victory (37–39).

The poet hopes that the envy of the immortals may not mar whatever happiness he pursues, while he is awaiting old age and death (39–42). We all die, but our fortune is unequal, and, however far anyone may gaze, he is too short to reach the heavens. Stolen sweets have a bitter ending (42–48).

May Apollo grant the victor a crown at the next Pythian games (49–51).

VII.—ΣΤΡΕΨΙΑΔΗ ΘΗΒΑΙΩ

ΠΑΓΚΡΑΤΙΩ

στρ. α΄

Τίνι τῶν πάρος, ὦ μάκαιρα Θήβα,
καλῶν ἐπιχωρίων μάλιστα θυμὸν τεὸν
εὔφρανας; ἦ ῥα χαλκοκρότου πάρεδρον
Δαμάτερος ἁνίκ' εὐρυχαίταν
5 ἄντειλας Διόνυσον; ἦ χρυσῷ μεσονύκτιον νίφοντα
    δεξαμένα τὸν φέρτατον θεῶν,

ἀντ. α΄

ὁπότ' Ἀμφιτρύωνος ἐν θυρέτροις
σταθεὶς ἄλοχον μετῆλθεν Ἡρακλείοις γοναῖς; 10
ἦ ὅτ' ἀμφὶ πυκναῖς Τειρεσίαο βουλαῖς;
ἦ ὅτ' ἀμφ' Ἰόλαον ἱππόμητιν;
10 ἦ Σπαρτῶν ἀκαμαντολογχᾶν; ἦ ὅτε καρτερᾶς
    Ἄδραστον ἐξ ἀλαλᾶς ἄμπεμψας ὀρφανὸν

ἐπ. α΄

μυρίων ἑτάρων ἐς Ἄργος ἵππιον;
ἦ Δωρίδ' ἀποικίαν οὕνεκεν ὀρθῷ
ἔστασας ἐπὶ σφυρῷ
Λακεδαιμονίων, ἕλον δ' Ἀμύκλας 20
15 Αἰγεῖδαι σέθεν ἔκγονοι, μαντεύμασι Πυθίοις;

6 ὁπότ' mss (edd.) : ἦ ὅτ' Tyrrell.
8 f. ἦ ὅτ' (BF) : ἦ [ὅτ'] Erasmus Schmid (MCS); ἦτ'...ἦτ
Bury.
12 οὕνεκεν Thiersch (MFCBuS) : οὕνεκ' mss ; ἁνίκ' ἆρ' Heyne
(B).

---

[1] This implies the transference to the legend of Alcmêna
(at Thebes) of the leading feature of the legend of Danaë
(at Argos). [2] Cp. note on *I.* i 30.

VII.—FOR STREPSIADES OF THEBES

WINNER IN THE PANCRATIUM, 456 (?) B.C.

O HAPPY Thêbê, tell me over which of the olden
glories of thy land thou hast chiefly gladdened thy
heart? Was it haply, when thou didst bring into
being Dionysus of the flowing locks, who is enthroned
beside Dêmêtêr of the clashing cymbals? or when
thou gavest welcome to the greatest of the gods
amid a snow-shower of gold at dead of night,[1] what
time he stood at Amphitryon's portal and drew near
Amphitryon's wife for the begetting of Heracles?
or was it when thou rejoicedst over the wise
counsels of Teiresias? or when over the deft horse-
man Iolaüs, or over the dragon-brood [2] and their
unwearied spears? or when from the rude battle
thou didst send Adrastus back to Argos, home of
horses, reft of countless comrades? or again, because
thou madest the Dorian colony of the men of
Lacedaemon to stand upright on its feet, when
thy descendants, the Aegeidae, captured Amyclae
according to the Pythian oracles? [3]

---

[3] Amyclae was a few miles south of Sparta, which was
not firmly established until it had captured Amyclae. The
scholia quote Aristotle as saying (in his treatise on the
Spartan constitution) that when the Lacedaemonians were
at war with Amyclae, they consulted the oracle, and were
told to seek the alliance of the Aegeidae. For this purpose
they went first to Athens, and next to Thebes, where they
found the Aegeidae holding a feast, and obtained their
alliance. The leader of these Aegeidae was Timomachus,
who was the first to organise the forces of the Lacedae-
monians, and was highly honoured by them.

ἀλλὰ παλαιὰ γὰρ
εὕδει χάρις, ἀμνάμονες δὲ βροτοί,
στρ. βʹ
ὅ τι μὴ σοφίας ἄωτον ἄκρον
κλυταῖς ἐπέων ῥοαῖσιν ἐξίκηται ζυγέν.
20 κώμαζʼ ἔπειτεν ἁδυμελεῖ σὺν ὕμνῳ
καὶ Στρεψιάδᾳ· φέρει γὰρ Ἰσθμοῖ
νίκαν παγκρατίου· σθένει τʼ ἔκπαγλος ἰδεῖν τε μορ-
φάεις· ἄγει τʼ ἀρετὰν οὐκ αἴσχιον φυᾶς.   30
ἀντ. βʹ
φλέγεται δὲ ἰοπλόκοισι Μοίσαις,
μάτρωΐ θʼ ὁμωνύμῳ δέδωκε κοινὸν θάλος,
25 χάλκασπις ᾧ πότμον μὲν Ἄρης ἔμιξεν,
τιμὰ δʼ ἀγαθοῖσιν ἀντίκειται.
ἴστω γὰρ σαφὲς ὅστις ἐν ταύτᾳ νεφέλᾳ χάλαζαν
αἵματος πρὸ φίλας πάτρας ἀμύνεται,   40
ἐπ. βʹ
λοιγὸν ἄντα φέρων ἐναντίῳ στρατῷ,
ἀστῶν γενεᾷ μέγιστον κλέος αὔξων
30 ζώων τʼ ἀπὸ καὶ θανών.
τὺ δέ, Διοδότοιο παῖ, μαχατὰν
αἰνέων Μελέαγρον, αἰνέων δὲ καὶ Ἕκτορα
Ἀμφιάρηόν τε,
εὐανθέʼ ἀπέπνευσας ἁλικίαν
στρ. γʹ
35 προμάχων ἀνʼ ὅμιλον, ἔνθʼ ἄριστοι

23 δὲ Ϝιοπλοκοισι Bergk (MFCBuS), cp. O. vi 30 : δʼ ἰοπλοκά-
μοισι mss ; δʼ ἰοβοστρύχοισι Boeckh.

28 ἄντα φέρων Thiersch (BC), ἐναντίον φέρων scholium :
ἀμύνων mss (†FS) ; ἀμπεπαλὼν (M) ; ἀντιφέρων Bury.

33 ἀμφʼ Ἀμφιάρειον Bergk (Bu).

But ah! for the olden glory sleepeth, and mortals are unmindful, save of that which winneth its way to the perfect bloom of poesy by being blended with the sounding streams of song.

Therefore with melodious strain begin the festal triumph-song, even for Strepsiades; for at the Isthmus he is winner of the victory in the pancratium; wondrous in strength is he, and yet comely to look upon, and he hath also courage no whit inferior to his frame. And he is lit up with glory by the violet-tressed Muses; and to his eme of the self-same name hath he given a share in the crown, even to him for whom Ares of the brazen shield mingled the draught of death; and yet honour is laid up in recompense for the brave. For whoso, in this cloud of war, defendeth his dear father-land against the hailstorm of blood, by dealing death to the host of the foemen, let him know assuredly that he is causing the greatest glory to grow for the race of his fellow-townsmen,—both while he liveth and when he is dead.

But thou, O son of Diodotus, vying with the warrior Meleager, vying also with Hector and Amphiaraüs, didst breathe forth the fair bloom of thy youth amid the host of warriors in the van,

PINDAR

ἔσχον πολέμοιο νεῖκος ἐσχάταις ἐλπίσιν.   50
ἔτλαν δὲ πένθος οὐ φατόν· ἀλλὰ νῦν μοι
Γαιάοχος εὐδίαν ὄπασσεν
ἐκ χειμῶνος. ἀείσομαι χαίταν στεφάνοισιν ἁρμό-
    σαις. ὁ δ' ἀθανάτων μὴ θρασσέτω φθόνος,

ἀντ. γ´

40 ὅ τι τερπνὸν ἐφάμερον διώκων
ἔκαλος ἔπειμι γῆρας ἔς τε τὸν μόρσιμον
αἰῶνα. θνάσκομεν γὰρ ὁμῶς ἅπαντες·
δαίμων δ' ἄϊσος· τὰ μακρὰ δ' εἴ τις   60
παπταίνει, βραχὺς ἐξικέσθαι χαλκόπεδον θεῶν
    ἕδραν· ὅτι πτερόεις ἔρριψε Πάγασος

ἐπ. γ´

45 δεσπόταν ἐθέλοντ' ἐς οὐρανοῦ σταθμοὺς
ἐλθεῖν μεθ' ὁμάγυριν Βελλεροφόνταν
Ζηνός· τὸ δὲ πὰρ δίκαν
γλυκὺ πικροτάτα μένει τελευτά.
ἄμμι δ', ὦ χρυσέα κόμα θάλλων, πόρε, Λοξία,   70
50 τεαῖσιν ἁμίλλαισιν
εὐανθέα καὶ Πυθόϊ στέφανον.

36 ἐσχάταις (-οισιν D) ἐπ' ἐλπ. BD : ἐπ' omitted by Callier-
gus (edd.).
39 φθόνος, BD, scholia, Erasmus Schmid (BF) : φθόνος.
(MCBuS).

494

where the bravest sustained the strife of war in hope forlorn. And they suffered sorrow beyond all telling; but now hath the Upholder of the Earth given me fair weather after storm.[1] I shall sing with my hair entwined with garlands, while I only pray that the envy of the immortals may not mar whatever pleasure I pursue, sufficient for my day, as I calmly pass onward to old age and to the destined bourne of life. For we die all alike, albeit our doom is diverse. But, if any man lifteth up his eyes to things afar, he is too short to attain unto the brass-paved floor of heaven; for the winged Pêgasus threw Bellerophon, his rider, who would fain have gone to the homes of heaven and the goodly company of Zeus.[2] Stolen sweets are awaited by an end most bitter. But grant to us, O Loxias, that art glorious with thy golden hair, a crown of fairest flowers even from thine own contests at Pytho.

[1] Poseidon, the Lord of the Isthmus, is here the giver of calm, because he has granted a victory in the Isthmian games.   [2] Cp. *O.* xiii 64.

ISTHMIAN VIII

FOR CLEANDROS OF AEGINA

INTRODUCTION

THE eighth and last Isthmian celebrates the
victory won in the boys' pancratium by Cleander of
Aegina. He had already been successful in the
Nemean games, presumably, of July 479, and he
has now been victorious in the Isthmian games of,
presumably, April 478. Phylacidas has been
victorious in the two preceding Isthmian festivals,
that of 484 (*Isth.* vi.) and that of 480 (*Isth.* v.).

The liberties of Greece had been saved by the
victories of Salamis and Plataea ; Sparta and Athens
were exultant, but Thebes (which had capitulated in
the autumn of 479) was in mourning. Almost alone
of all the Hellenic States, she had made common
cause with the Medes. The Ode reflects the poet's
mingled feelings of sorrow for the part played by
Thebes, and of joy at the liberation of Hellas from
the intolerable burden which had been hanging
over her head.

The poet rouses himself from grief, mingled with
joy at the removal of an intolerable burden that had
been oppressing Hellas ; he calls upon the chorus

to celebrate the Isthmian victory of Cleander (1-13).
When our path is beset with treachery, we must
walk warily, but the ills of mortals can be cured,
provided they have liberty (14-16). It is manly to
cherish good hopes for the future, and it is the duty
of a Theban to sing the praises of Aegina, for
Aegina and Thêbê were sisters, both of them
beloved by Zeus, who made one of them queen of
Thebes, and the other the mother of Aeacus
(17-23).

The myth of the Aeacidae (23-60).

Even as Achilles was honoured of all, so must
we haste to raise the Muses' memorial in honour of
the victor's cousin, Nicocles, and of his Isthmian
victory in the boxing match (61-65). The praise
of Cleander, and of his victories at Megara and
Epidaurus (65-70).

VIII.—ΚΛΕΑΝΔΡΩ ΑΙΓΙΝΗΤΗ

ΠΑΓΚΡΑΤΙΩ

στρ. α΄

Κλεάνδρῳ τις ἁλικίᾳ τε λύτρον
εὔδοξον, ὦ νέοι, καμάτων
πατρὸς ἀγλαὸν Τελεσάρχου παρὰ πρόθυρον ἰὼν
ἀνεγειρέτω
κῶμον, Ἰσθμιάδος τε νίκας ἄποινα, καὶ Νεμέᾳ
5 ἀέθλων ὅτι κράτος ἐξεῦρε. τῷ καὶ ἐγώ, καίπερ
ἀχνύμενος
θυμόν, αἰτέομαι χρυσέαν καλέσαι   10
Μοῖσαν. ἐκ μεγάλων δὲ πενθέων λυθέντες
μήτ᾽ ἐν ὀρφανίᾳ πέσωμεν στεφάνων,
μήτε κάδεα θεράπευε· παυσάμενοι δ᾽ ἀπρήκτων
κακῶν
γλυκύ τι δαμωσόμεθα καὶ μετὰ πόνον·
ἐπειδὴ τὸν ὑπὲρ κεφαλᾶς   20
10 τὸν Ταντάλου λίθον παρά τις ἔτρεψεν ἄμμι θεός,
στρ. β΄

ἀτόλματον Ἑλλάδι μόχθον. ἀλλά
μοι δεῖμα μὲν παροιχόμενον
καρτερὰν ἔπαυσε μέριμναν· τὸ δὲ πρὸ ποδὸς
ἄρειον ἀεὶ <σκοπεῖν>.

10 τὸν Heimsoeth (FS): mss have τε, or γε (BC); καὶ (M);
ἅτε Bury.
12 δεῖμα mss (edd.) : χάρμα M.   παροιχόμενον mss (BFCS¹):
—ομένων Benedictus (MBᵘˢ²).
13 <σκοπεῖν> Thiersch (BMFCS): <θέμεν> Bury.

498

VIII.—FOR CLEANDROS OF AEGINA

WINNER IN THE PANCRATIUM, 478 (?) B.C.

Ho youths! go one of you to the gleaming portal of Telesarchus, and awake the festal triumph-song in honour of Cleandros and his comrades, in reward for his victory at the Isthmus, no less than for his winning the prize in the contests at Nemea. Therefore, I also, though stricken sorely at heart, am bidden[1] to invoke the golden Muse. Yet, now that we are set free from mighty woes, let us not fall into any lack of festal garlands, nor do thou brood over sorrows; but ceasing to dwell on unavailing ills, we shall delight the people with some strain of sweetness, even after toil; inasmuch as the trouble that Hellas could not brook, the stone of Tantalus above our head, hath now been turned aside for us by one of the gods; but, as for me, the passing away of terror hath caused stern care to cease;[2] yet is it better to look evermore at that which lieth before one's foot, for man is entangled in a

---

[1] Understood as Middle by Wilamowitz, "darum bitte auch ich . . . dass man die goldne Muse rufe," i.e. "I also bid them invoke the Muse."

[2] Wilamowitz, retaining παροιχομένων, understands the sentence to mean "fear for perils now past hath hampered the power of my poetry."

χρῆμα πᾶν. δόλιος γὰρ αἰὼν ἐπ' ἀνδράσι κρέ-
    μαται,
15 ἐλίσσων βίου πόρον· ἰατὰ δ' ἔστι βροτοῖς σύν γ'
    ἐλευθερίᾳ   30
καὶ τά. χρὴ δ' ἀγαθὰν ἐλπίδ' ἀνδρὶ μέλειν·
χρὴ δ' ἐν ἑπταπύλοισι Θήβαις τραφέντα
Αἰγίνᾳ Χαρίτων ἄωτον προνέμειν,
πατρὸς οὕνεκα δίδυμαι γένοντο θύγατρες Ἀσω-
    πίδων
ὁπλόταται, Ζηνί τε ἅδον βασιλέι.   40
ὁ τὰν μὲν παρὰ καλλιρόῳ
20 Δίρκᾳ φιλαρμάτου πόλιος ᾤκισσεν ἀγεμόνα·
στρ. γ'
σὲ δ' ἐς νᾶσον Οἰνοπίαν ἐνεγκὼν
κοιμᾶτο, δῖον ἔνθα τέκες
Αἰακὸν βαρυσφαράγῳ πατρὶ κεδνότατον ἐπι-
    χθονίων· ὃ καὶ
δαιμόνεσσι δίκας ἐπείραινε· τοῦ μὲν ἀντίθεοι   50
25 ἀρίστευον υἱέες υἱέων τ' ἀρηΐφιλοι παῖδες ἀνορέα
χάλκεον στονόεντ' ἀμφέπειν ὅμαδον·
σώφρονές τ' ἐγένοντο πινυτοί τε θυμόν.
ταῦτα καὶ μακάρων ἐμέμναντ' ἀγοραί,
Ζεὺς ὅτ' ἀμφὶ Θέτιος ἀγλαός τ' ἔρισαν Ποσειδᾶν
    γάμῳ,   60
ἄλοχον εὐειδέ' ἐθέλων ἑκάτερος
ἑὰν ἔμμεν· ἔρως γὰρ ἔχεν.
30 ἀλλ' οὔ σφιν ἄμβροτοι τέλεσαν εὐνὰν θεῶν
    πραπίδες,
στρ. δ'
ἐπεὶ θεσφάτων ἐπάκουσαν· εἶπε δ'

31 ἐπάκουσαν Triclinius, Hermann¹ (MFCS): ἤκουσαν *D* (Bu):
ὕπ' ἄκουσαν Hermann².

treacherous time that maketh crooked the path of
life. Yet even this may be healed for mortals, if
only they have freedom. Howsoever, it is meet for
man to take to heart good hope; aye, meet it is
for one who was reared at Thebes, the city of
seven gates, to give Aegina the brightest flower of
graceful song.

For to one father, Asôpus, were twin daughters
born, the youngest of his children, and they found
favour with Zeus the king. Wherefore he caused
one of them to dwell beside fair Dircê's stream, as
queen of a city rejoicing in chariots; while thee,
the other, he carried unto the isle Oenopia[1] and
made his bride,—that isle where, to the sire who
loudly thundereth, thou barest Aeacus divine, most
virtuous of all the race of earth. Therefore it was
that even for the gods he became arbiter of strife.
His god-like sons and their warlike children were
ever bravest in courage, and they were pure in life,
and wise in heart.

All this was remembered even by the assembly of
the blessed gods, when Zeus and glorious Poseidon
strove for the hand of Thetis, both of them desiring her
to be his beauteous bride, for love enthralled them.
Yet the immortal counsels of the gods did not bring
that marriage to pass, when they had heard a certain

---

[1] One of the old names of Aegina; also called Oenônê in
N. iv 46, v 15, viii 7, *I.* v 35.

PINDAR

εὔβουλος ἐν μέσοισι Θέμις,
οὕνεκεν πεπρωμένον ἦν φέρτερον γόνον ἄνακτα
   πατρὸς τεκεῖν   70
ποντίαν θεόν, ὃς κεραυνοῦ τε κρέσσον ἄλλο βέλος
35 διώξει χερὶ τριόδοντός τ' ἀμαιμακέτου, Δί τε
   μισγομέναν
ἢ Διὸς παρ' ἀδελφεοῖσιν.—" ἀλλὰ τὰ μὲν
   παύσατε· βροτέων δὲ λεχέων τυχοῖσα
υἱὸν εἰσιδέτω θανόντ' ἐν πολέμῳ,   80
χεῖρας "Αρεΐ <τ'> ἐναλίγκιον στεροπαῖσί τ' ἀκμὰν
   ποδῶν.
τὸ μὲν ἐμὸν Πηλέϊ γάμου θεόμορον
ὀπάσσαι γέρας Αἰακίδᾳ,
40 ὄντ' εὐσεβέστατον φάτις 'Ιωλκοῦ τράφειν πεδίον·
στρ. ε'
ἰόντων δ' ἐς ἄφθιτον ἄντρον εὐθὺς
Χείρωνος αὐτίκ' ἀγγελίαι·   90
μηδὲ Νηρέος θυγάτηρ νεικέων πέταλα δὶς ἐγ-
   γυαλιζέτω
ἄμμιν· ἐν διχομηνίδεσσιν δὲ ἑσπέραις ἐρατὸν
45 λύοι κεν χαλινὸν ὑφ' ἥρωϊ παρθενίας." ὣς φάτο
   Κρονίδαις
   ἐννέποισα θεά· τοὶ δ' ἐπὶ γλεφάροις

33 οὕνεκεν Donaldson (BuS), cp. N. ix 36 : εἵνεκεν D,
Triclinius, (BMFC).
   γόνον ἄνακτα (i.e. Fάνακτα) πατρὸς τεκεῖν mss (FBu) : γόνον
<οἱ> ἄνακτα π.τ. Boeckh ; γόνον <ἂν> ἄνακτα π.τ. Bergk
(C) ; πατέρος ἄνακτα γόνον τεκεῖν Ahlwardt (S) ; τεκέμεν ἄνακτα
πατρὸς γόνον M.
   35 Δὶ δαμαζομέναν Bergk⁴ (Bu).
   37 χεῖρας "Αρεΐ <τ'> Boeckh (MFCS¹) ; χεῖρας "Αρεΐ Her-
mann¸(S³) ; "Αρεΐ χεῖρας D (χέρας Triclinius) ; ἄνδρ' "Αρει χέρας
Bury.
   38 f. γάμου θεόμορον ὀπάσσαι γέρας Αἰακίδᾳ Hermann (I)

oracle. For Themis, wise in counsel, spake in their
midst, saying how that it was fated that the sea-
queen should bear a princely son, who would be
stronger than his father, and who in his hand
would wield another weapon, mightier than the
thunder-bolt or the stubborn trident, if she were
wedded either to Zeus or to his brethren.[1]

" Nay, cease from this," she added, " rather let her
win a mortal marriage and see her son fall in war,
after vying with Arês in the might of his hands, and
with the lightnings in the speed of his feet. My
counsel is to grant this marriage-boon divine to the
son of Aeacus, even to Pêleus, who is famed to be
the holiest man that liveth in the plain of Iolcus.
At once let the message be sent with all speed to
Cheiron's cave divine ; and let not the daughter of
Nêreus ever again place in our hands the leaves of
strife[2] ; but, in the evenings of full-moon, let her
unloose her maiden-girdle in love for that hero."

So said the goddess, speaking unto the sons of
Cronus, and they gave assent with their brows

---

[1] Poseidon. For the plural cp. Frag. 53 (45), 10 f.
[2] In Syracuse and Athens olive-leaves were sometimes used
for inscribing votes of banishment. In the former city this
procedure was called πεταλισμός ; in the latter ἐκφυλλοφορεῖν.

Donaldson (MFC): θεάμοιρον ὀπάσαι γάμου Αἰακίδα γέρας D,
θεόμορον — Αἰακίδα τὸ γέρας B ; γέρας θεόμορον ὀπάσσαι γάμου
Αἰακίδα Hermann (2) (S), — γάμον Αἰακίδα Bury.

40 φάτις Ἰωλκοῦ Bothe (BMFC), — Ἰαολκοῦ (S) : φασὶν Ἰαωλ-
κοῦ D ; φάσ' Ἰαωλκοῦ Triclinius ; φρασὶν Ἰωλκοῦ Bergk⁴, φρασὶ,
Ϝιωλκοῦ τράφει Bury.

νεῦσαν ἀθανάτοισιν· ἐπέων δὲ καρπὸς   100
οὐ κατέφθινε. φαντὶ γὰρ ξύν' ἀλέγειν
καὶ γάμον Θέτιος ἄνακτα. καὶ νεαρὰν ἔδειξαν
   σοφῶν
στόματ' ἀπείροισιν ἀρετὰν Ἀχιλέος·
ὃ καὶ Μύσιον ἀμπελόεν
50 αἵμαξε Τηλέφου μέλανι ῥαίνων φόνῳ πεδίον,   110
στρ. στ'
γεφύρωσέ τ' Ἀτρεΐδαισι νόστον,
Ἑλέναν τ' ἐλύσατο, Τρωΐας
ἶνας ἐκταμὼν δορί, ταί νιν ῥύοντό ποτε μάχας
   ἐναριμβρότου
ἔργον ἐν πεδίῳ κορύσσοντα, Μέμνονός τε βίαν
55 ὑπέρθυμον Ἕκτορά τ' ἄλλους τ' ἀριστέας· οἷς
   δῶμα Φερσεφόνας   120
μανύων Ἀχιλεύς, οὖρος Αἰακιδᾶν,
Αἴγιναν σφετέραν τε ῥίζαν πρόφαινεν.
τὸν μὲν οὐδὲ θανόντ' ἀοιδαὶ ἔλιπον,
ἀλλά οἱ παρά τε πυρὰν τάφον θ' Ἑλικώνιαι
   παρθένοι
στάν, ἐπὶ θρῆνόν τε πολύφαμον ἔχεαν.
ἔδοξ' ἄρα τόδ' ἀθανάτοις,   130
60 ἐσλόν γε φῶτα καὶ φθίμενον ὕμνοις θεᾶν διδόμεν.
στρ. ζ'
τὸ καὶ νῦν φέρει λόγον, ἔσσυταί τε
Μοισαῖον ἅρμα Νικοκλέος
μνᾶμα πυγμάχου κελαδῆσαι. γεραίρετέ νιν, ὃς
   Ἴσθμιον ἂν νάπος
Δωρίων ἔλαχεν σελίνων· ἐπεὶ περικτίονας

47 ἄνακτα old mss (BMFBu): ἄνακτε Triclinius (cs).
56 οὐδὲ Dissen (edd.): οὔτε mss. ἀοιδαί τι λίπον? S.
60 ἐσλόν γε Calliergus (edd.): ἐς λόγον γε mss.

immortal; and the fruit of her words did not wither
away, for they tell how that Zeus joined in favouring
even the marriage of Thetis. And the lips of poets
wise made known the youthful prowess of Achilles to
those who had heard it not before;—Achilles who
stained and besprent the vine-clad plain of Mysia
with the dark blood of Têlephus, and enabled the
Atreidae to return by a safe path across the sea.
'Twas Achilles who rescued Helen, when with the
sword he hewed asunder the sinews of Troy, that
aforetime stayed him in plying on the plain the work
of murderous war,—hewed asunder the over-weening
might of Memnon, and Hector, and other brave
heroes, to whom Achilles, champion of the house of
Aeacus, pointed the road to the house of Persephonê,
and thus brought fame to Aegina and to his race.
And even when dead, he was not forsaken of song,
but, beside his funeral pyre and tomb, there stood
the maids of Helicon, and poured over him the
dirge of many voices.[1] Thus was it proved to be
the will of the immortals to make a brave man,
even when dead, a theme for the hymns of goddesses;
and even now this law holdeth good, and therefore
doth the Muses' car start forth to sound aloud the glory
of the boxer, Nîcoclês. O praise ye him, who won the
crown of wild Dorian celery in the Isthmian glade,

---

[1] πολύφαμος means "many-voiced" in the *Odyssey* (ii 150)
and in Alcman (Frag. 34); and the dirge mentioned in the
text is described in the *Odyssey* (xxiv 60) as sung by all the
nine Muses in turn, ἀμειβόμεναι ὀπὶ καλῇ. This is better
than making the epithet synonymous with πολύφατος, "very
famous."

65 ἐνίκασε δή ποτε καὶ κεῖνος ἄνδρας ἀφύκτῳ χερὶ
    κλονέων.   140
   τὸν μὲν οὐ κατελέγχει κριτοῦ γενεὰ
   πατραδελφεοῦ· ἁλίκων τῷ τις ἁβρὸν
  ἀμφὶ παγκρατίου Κλεάνδρῳ πλεκέτω
  μυρσίνας στέφανον, ἐπεί νιν Ἀλκαθόου τ' ἀγὼν
    σὺν τύχᾳ
  ἐν Ἐπιδαύρῳ τε νεότας δέκετο πρίν·   150
  τὸν αἰνεῖν ἀγαθῷ παρέχει·
70 ἥβαν γὰρ οὐκ ἄπειρον ὑπὸ χειᾷ καλῶν δάμασεν.

since he too,[1] in his day, was victorious over all that dwelt around him, smiting them with his resistless hands. He is not dishonoured by the offspring of his father's noble brother.[2] Therefore let a bright crown of myrtle, in honour of the pancratium, be entwined for Cleandros by one of his comrades, since the contest of Alcathoüs, and the young men of Epidaurus gave him welcome aforetime. 'Tis fitting for the good to praise him, for he hid not the spirit of his youth in a hole unknown to fame.

[1] Like Achilles.   [2] His cousin, Cleandros.

FRAGMENTS

FRAGMENTS

INTRODUCTION TO THE FRAGMENTS

THE life of Pindar in the Ambrosian MS in Milan states that the poet was the author of seventeen works :—(1) Hymns, (2) Paeans, (3) and (4) two books of Dithyrambs, (5) and (6) two books of Processional Songs (Προσόδια), (7) and (8) two books of Maidens' Songs (Παρθένεια or Παρθένια), (9) a separate book of the same, (10) and (11) two books of Dance-songs (Ὑπορχήματα), (12) Eulogies (Ἐγκώμια), (13) Dirges (Θρῆνοι), and, lastly, (14), (15), (16), (17), four books of Epinician Odes (Ἐπινίκια). In the order adopted by the first editor, Aristophanes of Byzantium, these Odes were arranged as follows :— *Olympia, Pythia, Isthmia, Nemea*, in the sequence of the foundation of the four festivals (776, 582, 581, 573), with three other Odes (*Nem.* ix, x, xi) connected with Sicyon, Argos, and Tenedos, added at the end.

In the above order of the poet's works, the first place is assigned to poems celebrating the gods, and the last to those in commemoration of men ; and, in the Epinician Odes, the order is, first the Odes on horse-races or chariot-races, next those on boxing or wrestling, and, lastly, those on foot-races.

The order in which Horace (*Carm.* iv 2), alludes to the Odes of Pindar is (1) Dithyrambs, (2) other Odes

INTRODUCTION

relating to the gods, (3) Eulogies of kings, (4) Epinician Odes, and (5) Dirges.

The *Oxyrhynchus Papyri* have helped to determine the dates of several of the Epinician Odes, and have added much to our knowledge of the *Paeans* and the *Partheneia* and the *Dithyrambs*. The first and second of these works are represented in vols. iv, v (1904–8); the third in vol. xiii (1919). This last (besides new readings in *O.* ii 39, πατρωιαν, and vi 77, ορος) includes fragments from three *Dithyrambs*, the second of which, written for the Thebans, enables us to combine in a consecutive form three passages previously known as fragments 79a, 79b, and 208 (see p. 558 ff).

The following selection includes all the principal Fragments, old and new.

ΙΣΘΜΙΟΝΙΚΑΙ

ΑΙΓΙΝΗΤΗ

1 Bergk (4 Boeckh)

Κλεινὸς Αἰακοῦ λόγος, κλεινὰ δὲ καὶ ναυσικλυτὸς
Αἴγινα· σὺν θεῶν δέ νιν αἴσᾳ
Ὕλλου τε καὶ Αἰγιμιοῦ
Δωριεὺς ἐλθὼν στρατὸς ἐκτίσσατο·
5 τῶν μὲν ὑπὸ στάθμᾳ νέμονται
οὐ θέμιν οὐδὲ δίκαν ξείνων ὑπερβαίνοντες· οἷοι δ᾽
   ἀρετὰν
δελφῖνες ἐν πόντῳ, ταμίαι τε σοφοὶ
Μοισᾶν ἀγωνίων τ᾽ ἀέθλων.

Appended to I viii in Laur. ms *D*.

2 θεῶν B : θεῶ *D*.
4 f. ἐκτίσσατο· τῶν Hermann : ἐκτήσατο· τὰ *D*.

ΥΜΝΟΙ

ΘΗΒΑΙΟΙΣ

29–30 Bergk (5–6 Boeckh)

Ἰσμηνὸν ἢ χρυσαλάκατον Μελίαν,
ἢ Κάδμον, ἢ σπαρτῶν ἱερὸν γένος ἀνδρῶν,
ἢ τὰν κυανάμπυκα Θήβαν,
ἢ τὸ πάντολμον σθένος Ἡρακλέος,

FROM AN ISTHMIAN ODE

FOR AN ISTHMIAN VICTORY OF AN AEGINETAN

FAMOUS is the story of Aeacus; famous too is Aegina, renowned for her navy. It was under heaven's blessing that she was founded by the coming of the Dorian host of Hyllus and Aegimius,[1] beneath whose rule they dwell. They never transgress right, nor yet the justice due to strangers; on the sea they are a match for dolphins in prowess, and they are wise ministrants of the Muses and of athletic contests.

[1] Cp. *P.* i 61–65.

HYMNS

FOR THE THEBANS

SHALL we sing of Ismênus, or of Melia[2] with her golden distaff, or of Cadmus, or of the holy race of the Sparti,[3] or Thêbê with her purple snood, or the all-daring might of Heracles, or the gladsome honour

[2] See note on *P.* xi 4.   [3] See note on *P.* ix 82.

PINDAR

(29)5 ἢ τὰν Διωνύσου πολυγαθέα τιμάν,
ἢ γάμον λευκωλένου Ἁρμονίας ὑμνήσομεν; –◡◡––

*　　　*　　　*　　　*

(30)　πρῶτον μὲν εὔβουλον Θέμιν οὐρανίαν
χρυσέαισιν ἵπποις Ὠκεανοῦ παρὰ παγᾶν
Μοῖραι ποτὶ κλίμακα σεμνὰν
ἆγον Οὐλύμπου λιπαρὰν καθ' ὁδὸν
5　σωτῆρος ἀρχαίαν ἄλοχον Διὸς ἔμμεν·
ἁ δὲ τὰς χρυσάμπυκας ἀγλαοκάρπους τίκτεν
ἀλαθέας Ὥρας.

The first part is derived from [Lucian], *Demosth. Encom.*
c. 19, and Plutarch, *de glor. Athen.* c. 4. The second part is
found in Clemens Alexandrinus, *Strom.* vi 731.

(30) 6 ἀλαθέας Ὥρας в (from Hesychius): ἀγαθὰ σωτῆρας
Clemens.

42 (171)

. . . ἀλλοτρίοισιν μὴ προφαίνειν τίς φέρεται
μόχθος ἄμμιν· τοῦτό γέ τοι ἐρέω.
καλῶν μὲν ὦν μοῖράν τε τερπνῶν ἐς μέσον χρὴ
παντὶ λαῷ
δεικνύναι· εἰ δέ τις ἀνθρώποισι θεόσδοτος ἀταρὰ
κακότας
5　προστύχῃ, ταύταν σκότει κρύπτειν ἔοικεν.

Stobaeus, *Flor.* cix 1. This Fragment and the next two
belong to a poem setting forth the good counsel given by
Amphiaraüs to his son Amphilochus on his departure for
Thebes.

180 (172)

μὴ πρὸς ἅπαντας ἀναρρῆξαι τὸν ἀχρεῖον λόγον·
ἔσθ' ὅτε πιστοτάτα σιγᾶς ὁδός·
κέντρον δὲ μάχας ὁ κρατιστεύων λόγος.

Clemens Alexandrinus, *Strom.* i 345.

due to Dionysus, or the bridal of white-armed Harmonia ? [1]

First did the Fates in their golden chariot bring heavenly Themis, wise in counsel, by a gleaming pathway from the springs of Ocean to the sacred stair of Olympus, there to be the primal bride of the Saviour Zeus. And she bare him the Hours with golden fillet and with gleaming fruit,—the Hours that are ever true.

[1] The above passage was one of the poet's earliest compositions. It was so full of mythological allusions that the poetess Corinna, who had suggested his turning his attention to mythology, told him " to sow with the hand, not with the whole sack " (Plutarch, *de glor. Athen.* c. 4).

COUNSELS GIVEN BY AMPHIARAÜS TO HIS SON AMPHILOCHUS

Disclose not to strangers our burden of care; this at least shall I advise thee. Therefore is it fitting to show openly to all the folk the fair and pleasant things allotted us; but, if any baneful misfortune sent of heaven befalleth man, it is seemly to shroud this in darkness.

4 ἀταρὰ (ἀτηρὰ Wilamowitz) κακότας : ἀτλητηκότας or ἄτη mss ; ἀτλάτα (ἄτλατος Dindorf) κακότας (BS).

Blurt not out unto all the word that is needless. There are times when the path of silence is the safest, while the word that is overbearing is a spur unto strife.

1 ἀχρεῖον BS : ἀρχαῖον mss.

PINDAR

43 (173)

ὦ τέκνον,
ποντίου θηρὸς πετραίου χρωτὶ μάλιστα νόον
προσφέρων πάσαις πολίεσσιν ὁμίλει·
τῷ παρεόντι δ᾽ ἐπαινήσαις ἑκὼν
ἄλλοτ᾽ ἀλλοῖα φρόνει.

Athenaeus, xii 513ᶜ, and vii 317ᵃ.

πουλύποδός μοι, τέκνον, ἔχων νόον, 'Αμφίλοχ᾽ ἥρως,
τοῖσιν ἐφαρμόζου, τῶν κεν καὶ δῆμον ἵκηαι.

ΕΙΣ ΑΠΟΛΛΩΝΑ ΠΤΩΟΝ

51 Schröder (70)

οἱ δὲ ποιηταὶ κοσμοῦσιν ἄλση καλοῦντες τὰ ἱερὰ
πάντα, κἂν ᾖ ψιλά· τοιοῦτόν ἐστι τὸ τοῦ Πινδά-
ρου περὶ τοῦ Ἀπόλλωνος λεγόμενον·
...... <δι>νηθεὶς ἐπῆεν
γᾶν τε καὶ <πᾶσαν> θάλασσαν
καὶ σκοπιαῖσιν <ἐπ᾽ αἰπειναῖ>ς ὀρέων ὕπερ ἔστα
καὶ μυχοὺς διζάσατο βαλλόμενος κρηπῖδας ἄλ-
σεων ...
5 καί ποτε τὸν τρικάρανον
Πτωΐου κευθμῶνα κατέσχεθε κούρα ...
καὶ τὸν Τήνερον καλεῖ
ναοπόλον μάντιν δαπέδοισιν ὁμοκλέα.

Strabo, ix 412 f. ll. 1, 2, 4 restored by Meineke ; l. 3 by s.
From a poem in honour of Apollo, the father of Tênerus
and Ismênius by Melia, referring to the foundation of an
oracle and temple of Apollo at the foot of mount Ptôon, near
Acraephia on the Lake Côpâis.

My son, in all the cities wherewith thou consortest, make thy mind like unto the (changing) skin of the polypus, that clingeth to the rocks of the sea.[1] Aye, and, by readily praising him that is present, change thy thought with the changing time.

[1] Aristotle, quoted in Athenaeus, 318^b, describes one of two kinds of polypus as "colour-changing," τρεψίχρως. In the *Historia Animalium*, ix 37, 9, he says that the polypus, in preying on fishes, changes its colour to that of any stones which it approaches. This polypus is identical with the octopus, which, like certain other *Cephalopoda*, has the power of changing its colour.

TO APOLLO

On the foundation of his temple at the foot of mount Ptôon on the lake Copaïs in Boeotia.

But the poets use adornment, when they call all temples "groves," although they are bare of trees. Such is the language of Pindar concerning Apollo :—

"Whirling around, he passed over the land and over all the sea, and stood on the lofty watch-towers of the mountains, and explored the caverns, while he laid for himself the foundations of his groves . . ."

"And erst the maiden [1] dwelt in the cavern of the triple peak of Ptôon."

And the poet calls Tênerus, "the temple-haunting prophet, who giveth his name to the plain."

[1] Zeuxippe, daughter of Athamas, king of Orchomenus.

517

PINDAR

ΠΑΙΑΝΕΣ

THE paean was one of the earliest forms of Greek
lyrical poetry. It was primarily connected with the
worship of Apollo, as the giver of joy, and the averter
of calamity. It derived its name from the cries
addressed, in the burden of the poem, to Apollo as
the god of healing, ἰὴ Παιάν. It was also used in

1. ΘΗΒΑΙΟΙΣ

<ἰήϊε Παιάν>
πρὶν ὀδυναρὰ γήραος σ[χεδὸν μ]ολεῖν,
πρίν τις εὐθυμία σκιαζέτω
νόημ' ἄκοτον ἐπὶ μέτρ', ἰδὼν
5 δύναμιν οἰκόθετον.
ἰὴ ἰή, νῦν ὁ παντελὴς ἐνιαυτὸς
Ὧραί τε Θεμίγονοι
πλάξ]ιππον ἄστυ Θήβας ἐπῆλθον,
Ἀπόλλωνι δαῖτα φιλησιστέφανον ἄγοντες·
10 τὰν δὲ λαῶν γενεὰν δαρὸν ἐρέπτοι
σώφρονος ἄνθεσιν εὐνομίας.

Grenfell and Hunt, *Oxyrhynchus Papyri*, V (1908) 11 f.;
text, 25 f.; trans. 80 f. Cp. A. E. Housman, *Class. Rev.*
(1908), 8 f.

2. ΑΒΔΗΡΙΤΑΙΣ

στρ. α΄
Ναΐδος Θρονίας Ἄβδηρε χαλκοθώραξ
Ποσειδᾶνός τε παῖ,
σέθεν Ἰάονι τόνδε λαῷ

1 Θρονίας, the eponymous nymph of the Opuntian Thronium.

518

PAEANS

the worship of Apollo's sister, Artemis. At Delphi a
paean was chanted early in the spring of every year.
The choruses, which were usually composed of men,
were accompanied by the lyre or the flute, or by
both. (For further details, see H. W. Smyth's *Greek
Melic Poets*, xxxvi–xlii.)

1. FOR THE THEBANS

Oʜ! Paean, to whom we cry!

Ere the pains of eld draw near, let a man clothe
his ungrudging mind with gladness, and be content
in measure due, when he hath seen the wealth that
is stored in his home.[1]

Oh joy! Oh joy! Now hath the year in its full
circle, and the Hours, the daughters of Themis, come
unto Thêbê's city that driveth the steed, bringing to
Apollo the banquet that loveth the garland. Long
may he crown the progeny of her peoples with the
flowers of sober love of law.

---

[1] "*i.e.* the more a man has, the greater should be his
thankfulness." ɢ-ʜ. Cf. *P.* v 12–14.

---

1 < ἰήϊε Παιάν > s.
2 ὀδυνηρα pap. : ὀδυναρὰ s, cp. *P.* ii 91.   σ[χεδὸν μ]ολεῖν
cp. *Pæan* ii 73.   4 ἄκοτον· ἀόργητον Hesychius.
8 πλάξ]ιππον Housman, *O.* vi 85 (s) : φίλ]ιππον ɢ-ʜ, Diehl.

2. FOR THE ABDERITANS

Abdêrus, with breast-plate of bronze, thou son of the
Naiad Thronia and of Poseidon! beginning with thee
shall I pursue this paean for the Ionian folk, now

PINDAR

παιᾶνα διώξω,
5 Δήρηνον Ἀπόλλωνα πάρ τ' Ἀφροδίταν [μολών].

(blank of 18 lines.)

ἐπ. α΄

24 ‿ατινα [τάνδε] ναίω
25 Θρηϊκίαν γαῖαν ἀμπελόεσσάν τε καὶ
εὔκαρπον· μή μοι μέγας ἕρπων
κάμοι ἐξοπίσω χρόνος ἔμπεδος.
νεόπολίς εἰμι· ματρὸς
δὲ ματέρ' ἐμᾶς ἔ‹πιδ›ον ἔμπαν
30 πολεμίῳ πυρὶ πλαγεῖ-
σαν. εἰ δέ τις ἀρκέων φίλοις
ἐχθροῖσι τραχὺς ὑπαντιάζει,
μόχθος ἡσυχίαν φέρει
καιρῷ καταβαίνων.
35 f. ἰήϊε Παιάν, ἰήϊε· Παιὰν [δὲ μήποτε λείπ]οι.

στρ. β΄

− ‿ − ‿ ‿ − ἀλκᾷ δὲ τεῖχος ἀνδρῶν
[ὕψιστον ἵστατ]αι

5 [Δή]ρηνον, scholium on Lycophron *Alex.* 440 ,Δήραινος· τόπος οὕτω καλούμενος ἐν Ἀβδήροις, ἔνθα Δηραίνου Ἀπόλλωνος ἱερόν ἐστιν, οὗ μνημονεύει καὶ Πίνδαρος ἐν Παιᾶσιν. 5 μολών Jurenka.
24 [κείναν δὲ λιπών, νῦν θρ]α[συάν|ορ]α τινα [τάνδε] ναίω Jurenka in *Philologus* 17 (1912) 173–210.
25 θ(ρ)ᾱϊκιαν ms.
26 f. Cp. *O.* viii 29, *N.* vii 68.
29 ἔπιδον G–H (S, Diehl): ἔτεκον ms, supported by Verrall and Jurenka.
37–50 ‹ὕβρις ἅστε· ὄλεσσ'›, ἀλκαὶ δὲ τεῖχος ἀνδρῶν [ὕψιστον ἵστατ]αι. ‹νόῳ ἔχειν πά›ρα· μάρναμαι μὰν ‹ἵππων ἔπι› [δαῖο]ις· ‹ἀρκεῖ δὲ› Ποσειδάνιον γένος ἵππων ‹ἐμοί·› τῶν γὰρ ἀντομένων ‹ὁμαλὸν ἵντα› φέρεσθαι ‹νίκας ἔπορεν› σέλας, . . . ‹δεινὸν ἂν› ποτικύρσῃ· ‹δαίμων δὲ κακῶ›ι μανίει· τὸ φύγοιμι πάμπαν.› ‹μήποθ' ὕβρις ἀναιδὴς› [τόνδε λ]αδὸν ἀστῶν ‹ἀλκᾶς λελασμένον στάσιν ἄγοισα λάβ›οι· Jurenka.

520

PAEAN II

that I have come to the shrine of Aphrodîtê and of
Dêrênian [1] Apollo . . .

[But, having left that island of Teôs,] [2] I [now]
dwell in this [brave] Thracian land, a land rich in vines
and fertile in fruits.   May mighty Time, as it draweth
on, never weary of a settled course for me.   Young
is my city, yet I lived to see my mother's mother [3]
stricken by the foeman's fire; but, if any man, in
aiding his friends, fiercely resisteth his foes, such toil
bringeth peace, when it entereth the lists in due
time.

Oh Paean! to whom we cry, we cry!   May Paean
never leave us!

[Insolence is the ruin of cities, but brave men
stand as their loftiest bulwark; this may we keep

---

[1] So called from Dêrênus, or Deraenus, in the territory of
Abdêra, where there was a temple of Apollo (Pausanias, vi
5, 3).

[2] The words enclosed in brackets are renderings of the
conjectural restoration printed in the Note on l. 24.

[3] ματρὸς ματέρ' ἐμᾶς, Athens, which colonised Teôs, the
mother-city of Abdêra.   Anacreon, the poet of Teôs, was
among those who colonised Abdêra in 523.   In 480 Abdêra
was one of the cities which had the expensive honour of
entertaining Xerxes on his march into Greece, and men of
Abdêra may have subsequently seen the havoc wrought
by Xerxes at Athens.

For another restoration, see Sitzler in *Woch. f. Kl. Phil.* 1911,
p. 58 ff.

37 ἀλκᾷ G–H: the scholium compares Frag. 213; cp. also
I. v 44 f.

40 ‿‿‿–‿ ρᾰ· μάρναμαι μὰν ––‿‿ δαΐο]ις
  ––‿ Ποσ]ειδάνιον γένος [ἵππων] ‿–
  τῶν γὰρ ἀντομένων
  ‿‿‿–‿ φέρεσθαι
  ––‿‿ σέλας
45 –‿–πο]τικύρσῃ
  ––‿‿ι μανίει
  ‿‿–‿–

ἀντ. β′
  –‿ λαὸν ἀστῶν
  ⏖–⏖–‿–

50f. ‿‿‿–‿‿ οι· τὸ δ' εὐβουλίᾳ τε καὶ αἰδοῖ
  ἐγκείμενον αἰεὶ θάλλει μαλακαῖς ε[ὐ]δίαι[ς·]
  καὶ τὸ μὲν διδότω
  θεός· [ὁ δ'] ἐχθρὰ νοήσας
55 ἤδη φθόνος οἴχεται
  τῶν πάλαι προθανόντων·
  χρὴ δ' ἄνδρα καὶ τοκεῦσι<ν> φέρειν
  βαθύδοξον αἶσαν.

ἐπ. β′
  τοὶ σὺν πολέμῳ κτησάμενοι
60 χθόνα πολύδωρον, ὄλβον
  ἐγκατέθηκαν πέραν Ἀ[θόῳ] Παιόνων
  αἰχματᾶν [λαοὺς ἐλάσαντε]ς,
  ζαθέας τροφοῦ· ἀλλὰ [δυσώνυμος]
  ἐπέπεσε μοῖρα· τλάντων
65 δ' ἔπειτα θεοὶ συνετέλεσσαι,
  ὁ δὲ καλόν τι πονήσαις εὐαγορίαισιν φλέγει·

61 f. Ἀ[θόω] . . . [λαοὺς ἐλάσαντε]ς Arnim (s), schol.
ὑ]π[ὲ]ρ [τὸ]ν Ἄθω ἐκβληθέντες κτλ : ἀ[γρίων] . . . [τε Στρυμονίας
γᾶ]ς G–H (Diehl).
  63 ἄλλα [δὲ μωμένα] Wilamowitz (s); ἄλλα [δ' ἄγοισα τοι]

in mind. I am fighting against mounted foemen,
but I myself have a goodly supply of Poseidon's
coursers, for contending against the enemy with
forces a match for his own bringeth the light of
victory ; . . . if anything terrible befall us. But
heaven is wroth with a coward, and may I flee afar
from that reproach. Never may shameless Insolence
bring faction in her train and seize this company of
citizens, when they have forgotten their courage.] [1]

By courage of men is a tower raised up most
high . . . but I fight against the foe [2] . . .

Whatsoever is planted in wise counsel and in
reverent regard, bloometh for aye in a gentle calm.
May this boon be granted us of God. But malicious
envy of those who died long ago hath now passed
away; and a man must offer his fathers their lawful
meed of ample praise.

They won by war a land with dower of wealth,
and planted prosperity firm, when they had pursued
the tribes of the Paeonian warriors beyond mount
Athos, their nurse divine; but an adverse fate befell
them. Yet they endured, and the gods joined at
last in fulfilling their desire. For he that hath done

---

[1] A rendering of the restoration printed in the Note on
lines 37-50.

[2] A rendering of lines 37-40, as printed in the text on
page 520.

G-H; ἀλλὰ [δυνώνυμος] Housman (Diehl); ἀλλὰ [βαρεῖα τοῖς]
Jurenka.

66 φλέγει, cp. N. vi 39, and φλέγεται, N. x 2, I. vii 23.

PINDAR

κείνοις δ' ὑπέρτατον ἦλθε φέγγος
70 ἄντα δυσμενέων Μελαμφύλλου προπάροιθεν.
ἰήϊε Παιάν, ἰήϊε· Παιὰν δὲ μήποτε λείποι.

στρ. γ΄
ἀλλά νιν ποταμῷ σχεδὸν μολόντα φύρσει
βαιὸς σὺν ἔντεσιν
75 ποτὶ πολὺν στρατὸν δὲ μηνὸς
πρῶτον τύχεν ἇμαρ·
ἄγγελλε δὲ φοινικόπεζα λόγον παρθένος
εὐμενὴς Ἑκάτα
τὸν ἐθέλοντα γενέσθαι·
80 ν]ῦν δ' αὖ γλυκυμαχάνων
(blank of 14 lines.)

ἐπ. γ΄
95 – – ◡◡ – – ◡◡ –
◡ ε καλέοντι μολπαὶ
ναὸ]ν ἀν' εὔοδμον, ἀμφί τε Παρνασσίαις
πέτραις ὑψηλαῖς θαμὰ Δελφῶν
ἑλικώπιδες ἱστάμεναι χορὸν
100 ταχύποδα παρθένοι χαλ-
κέα κελαδ[έο]ντι γλυκὺν αὐδᾷ
νόμ]ον· ἐμο[ὶ δὲ ἑκὼ]ν ἐσλῶν εὐκλέα [κραίνω]ν
χάριν,

73-5 ἀλλὰ νιν—φύρσει—στρατόν regarded as the quotation
of an oracle by Blass (s).

73 φύρσει ὁ ἡμέτερος στρατὸς τῶν γονέων schol. ; φύρσεν
φέγγος Arnim, ἇμαρ Fraccaroli, Jurenka.

74 βαιὸς Wilamowitz, cp. Soph. O.T. 750, ἐχώρει βαιὸς :
βαιοῖς G–H.

75 ἐν δὲ G–H, ἐν δὲ schol.

80 ν]ῦν Arnim (s) : σ]ὺν G–H (Diehl).

95 f [ὦ Λατογενὲς παῖ σὲ δ' ἑκάβολ]ε Jurenka.

97 ναὸ]ν Arnim, cp. O. vii 32 εὐώδεος ἐξ ἀδύτου, Callimach.
Ep. 53, 4 εὐώδης νηός ; οἶκο]ν Kampas ; Δᾶλο]ν Housman (s) ;
Πίνδο]ν G–H (Diehl) ; Πτῷο]ν Sitzler.

524

a noble deed is illumined with praises ; but upon those (our fathers) fell the light supreme, when they faced the foe, in front of Melamphyllon.[1]

Oh joy ! Paean, Oh joy ! May Paean never leave us !

Yet, when he hath drawn near unto the river,[2] a small armed force shall confound the foe, though it faceth a mighty host.

It was the first of the month when this befell, and the gracious Hecatê,[3] the maid of the ruddy feet, was thereby sending us a message that was longing for fulfilment . . .

[But, O thou far-darting son of Lêto,][4] songs are invoking thee in thy fragrant temple ; and, on both of the lofty rocks of Parnassus, the bright-eyed maidens of Delphi full often set the fleet-footed dance, and ring out a sweet strain with resonant voice. But, as for me, mayest thou,

---

[1] Mentioned in Pliny, *N.H.*, iv 50, as one of the mountains of Thrace.

[2] The river Nestus is to the West of Abdêra, in the general direction of Mount Athos and the land of the Paeonians

[3] Hecatê was a moon-goddess, and offerings were made to her on the morning of the new moon. She was identified with the moon-goddess Artemis, to whom Sôphrôn of Syracuse gave the name of Ἄγγελος, and she is here described as sending a message which was an omen of victory.

[4] A rendering of the restoration in the Note on l. 95.

---

102 ἐκὼ]ν G–H (S) : ἐπέω]ν Drechsel, τυχὼ]ν Jurenka.
103 [κραίνω]ν G–H (S) : πρᾶξον Arnim ; τεῖσον Jurenka.

PINDAR

Ἄβδηρε, καὶ στρατὸν ἱπποχάρμαν
105 σᾷ β]ίᾳ πολέμῳ τελευταίῳ προβιβάζοις.
ἰήϊε Παιάν, ἰήϊε· Παιὰν δὲ μήποτε λείποι.

Grenfell and Hunt, *Oxyrhynchus Papyri*, v 27 f, 82 f.
Verrall, *Classical Review*, 1908, pp. 110 ff. ; Arnim, *Wiener Eranos*, 1909 ; Sitzler, *Woch. f. Klassische Philologie*, 1911, 586–590 ; Jurenka, *Philologus*, 1912, 173–210 ; Wilamowitz-Moellendorff, *Sappho und Simonides*, 1913, 246–256.

3

Of this paean even the title is unknown. It originally consisted of 102 lines, but only small portions of 24 have been preserved (*Oxyrhynchus Papyri*, v 18, 33, 87). It began with an appeal to the Graces, of which too little is left for any satisfactory restoration. The words in the second line are suggested by the present editor.

4. ΚΕΙΟΙΣ ΕΙΣ ΔΗΛΟΝ

This is the paean to which Pindar alludes in lines 3–10 of the first Isthmian. He there apologises for delaying the completion of a paean to the Delian Apollo (to be sung in Ceôs), in order that he might

στρ. αʹ
1 [Τὸν ἀκειροκόμαν τε καὶ] Ἄρτεμιν
[ὦ Δᾶλε, Λατώ τε χορε]ύσομαι ...
ος αὐδὰν

1 f. [τὸν ἀκειροκόμαν τε καὶ] Ἄρτεμιν, [ὦ Δᾶλε, Λατώ τε χορε]ύσομαι Blass in G–H (Diehl, and with ἀκερσοκόμαν, S, as in *P.* iii 14, *I.* i 7).
3–10 [εὐαχέα φθεγγόμεν]ος αὐδάν· [τὸ κλέος ὦνπερ ποτὶ

526

Abdêrus, readily fulfil the famous favour of good things, and, by thy might, even lead forward our host of fighting horsemen for a final war.

Oh joy! Paean, Oh joy! May Paean never leave us!

105 [—]ία G–H (Diehl); σᾷ β]ία Bury (s); οὐρ]ία Blass; εὐδ]ία Fraccaroli.

3

[. . . . .] . ν ἀγλαο[. . . . .]ναι Χάριτε[ς]
[χαίρετε, Μοισ]ᾶν ἀγλαο[θρόνων σεμ]ναὶ Χάριτε[ς
  ξυνάονες] ?

"Hail, holy Graces! companions of the Muses, enthroned in splendour" . . .

O. xiii 96, Μοίσαις ἀγλαοθρόνοις. Frag. 95 (63), 2, σεμνᾶν
Χαρίτων. *P.* iii 48, ξυνάονες.

4. FOR THE CEANS TO DELOS

first celebrate the Isthmian victory won by his countryman, Herodotus.

Cp. J. Sitzler, in *Woch. f. Klass. Philol.* 1911, 698–702.

I shall dance, O Delos, in honour of the un-shorn god and Artemis, and in honour of Lêtô . . . [uttering a tuneful sound. Their praise will be

γυν]αικῶν ἐδνώσεται [καὶ αἰὲν ἀνδρῶν· κόσμον] δ' ἐπέων δυνατώ-
τερον [εὕροιτ' ἂν μελέτ]α κατὰ πᾶσαν ὁδὸν [σοφίας σφίν; οἵγ'
ἡ]συχίαν Κέῳ [νόῳ σὺν εὐμενεῖ ὄλ]βον τε παρέσχον πολυγαθέα,
τῷ μέγα δᾶμος ἀγ]άλλεται Sitzler.

PINDAR

γυν]αικῶν ἑδνώσεται
δ᾽ ἐπέων δυνατώτερον
α κατὰ πᾶσαν ὁδὸν
ἡ]συχίαν Κέῳ

ἀ]γάλλεται.

ἀντ. α´

11 ∪∪–∪∪–ν χρόνον ὀρνύει
––∪– Δᾶλον ἀγακλέα
––∪– σὺν Χάρισι· Κάρθαι-
[α μὲν ἀλαθέως ἐλα]χύνωτον στέρνον χθονός,
15 [ὅμως γε μὰν οὗτοι] νιν Βαβυλῶνος ἀμείψομαι·
20 ends with ἰχθύσιν·

ἐπ. α´

ἤτοι καὶ ἐγὼ σ[κόπ]ελον ναίων * διά[σαμον,
γινώσκομαι μὲν ἀρεταῖς ἀέθλων
Ἑλλανίσιν· γινώσκομαι δὲ καὶ
μοῖσαν παρέχων ἅλις·
25 ἢ καί τι Διω[νύσ]ου ἄρο[υρ]α φέρει
βιόδωρον ἀμαχανίας ἄκος.
ἄνιππός εἰμι καὶ βουνομίας ἀδαέστερος·
ἀλλ᾽ ὅ γε Μέλαμπος οὐκ ἤθελεν
λιπὼν πατρίδα μοναρχεῖν Ἄργει,
30 θέμενος οἰωνοπόλον γέρας.
ἰὴ ἰή, ὦ ἰεπαιάν.

στρ. β´

τὸ δὲ οἴκοθεν ἄστυ κα[ὶ ἄλικες
καὶ συγγενεῖ ἀνδρὶ φ[ίλ᾽ ὥστε καὶ

11 f. [ἐμὲ δ᾽ εἰς ζάθεο]ν χρόνον ὀρνύει [Μοῖσ᾽ ἱγμένον] Δᾶλον ἀγακλέα [αἰνεῖν πάτραν σὺν] Χάρισιν Sitzler.

14 ἐλα]χύνωτον G–H (S) : βρα[χύνωτον Diehl, Sitzler.

21 διά[σαμον? Housman (or διαπρεπέα, as in I. v 44, if ἄδρυα is preferred in l. 52); δια-γιγνώσκομαι G–H (Diehl) ; διαγινώσκομαι S.

528

furnished forth by women, and evermore by men.
Could our meditation, in any way of wisdom, win
a more potent grace of language for them, who
with bounteous mind have provided for Ceôs peace
and gladsome prosperity, in which the people
greatly rejoiceth?][1]

[But the Muse prompteth me, on coming to famous
Delos for a holy time, to praise my fatherland
with the Graces' aid.][2]

Carthaia indeed is but a narrow ridge of land,[3] but
yet I shall not exchange it for Babylon.

Verily, even I, who dwell on a famous rock, am
known for prowess in Hellenic contests, known also
for providing poesy in plenty[4]; verily too my land
produceth Dionysus' life-giving medicine for all
trouble.

No horses have I, and I know but little of the
tending of oxen. But Melampus was unwilling to
leave his native country, and lay aside his gift of
divination to be king in Argos.[5]

Oh joy! Oh joy! O Paean!

Dear to a man is his own home-city and comrades
and kinsmen, so that he is well content. But to

[1] A rendering of the restoration in the Note on lines 3–10.
[2] A rendering of the restoration in the Note on lines
11 f.
[3] Bent, *Cyclades*, 466 (of Carthaia), "a long spur runs down
a valley . . . the town and the acropolis are on the spur."
[4] A reference to Simonides of Ceôs, and his nephew
Bacchylides.   [5] Cp. Herodotus, ix 43.

στέρξαι· ματαίων δ' ἔ[πλετ' ἔρως τῶν
35 ἑκὰς ἐόντων· λόγον ἄνακτος Εὐξαντίου
ἐπαίνεσα, [Κρητ]ῶν μαιομένων ὃς ἀνα[ίνετο
αὐταρχεῖν, πολίων δ' ἑκατὸν πεδέχειν
μέρος ἕβδομον Πασιφάας <σὺν> υἱ[οῖ]-
σι· τέρας δ' ἑὸν εἶ-
40 πέν σφι· "Τρέω τοι πόλεμον
Διὸς Ἐννοσίδαν τε βαρύκτυπον.

ἀντ. β′

χθόνα τοί ποτε καὶ στρατὸν ἀθρόον
πέμψαι κεραυνῷ τριόδοντί τε
ἐς τὸν βαθὺν Τάρταρον, ἐμὰν μα-
45 τέρα λιπόντες καὶ ὅλον οἶκον εὐερκέα·
ἔπειτα πλούτου πειρῶν μακάρων τ' ἐπιχώριον
τεθμὸν πάμπαν ἐρῆμον ἀπωσάμενος,
μέγαν ἄλλοθι κλᾶρον ἔχω; λίαν
μοι [δέο]ς ἔμπεδον εἴ-
50 η κεν. ἔα, φρήν, κυπάρισ-
σον, ἔα δὲ νομὸν Περιδάϊον.

ἐπ. β′

ἐμοὶ δ' ὀλίγον δέδοται μὲν γᾶς, ὅθεν * ἁ δρῦς,
οὐ πενθέων δ' ἔλαχον, οὐ στασίων."

Grenfell and Hunt, *Oxyrhynchus Papyri*, v 35 f, 88 f.

34 ματαίων δ' ἔ[πλετ' ἔρως τῶν] Housman ; ματαίων δέ [γ′ ἔραται νόος] Sitzler ; ματ[αί]ων δὲ [μάκαρ ἀνδρῶν] G–H (Diehl, S).
36 ἐπαίνεσα, [Κρητ]ῶν Housman : ἐπαίνεσ', ἁ[λίκ]ων G–H (S).
38 σὺν υἱοῖσι Housman (Diehl) : υἱοῖσιν G–H : ὑέσσιν S.
49 [δέο]s Housman (Diehl) : [πῶ]s G–H (S).
50 ff. ἔα, φρήν, —cp. the corrupt quotation in Plutarch, *de exilio*, c. 9, ἐλαφρὰν κυπάρισσον φιλέειν ἐᾶν δὲ νομὸν Κρήτας περιδαίων· ἐμοὶ δ' ὀλίγον μὲν γᾶς δέδοται, ὅθεν ἄδρυς, οὐκ ἔλαχον οὐδὲ στασέων. Plato's *Laws*, 625a, κυπαρίττων ἐν τοῖς ἄλσεσιν ὕψη καὶ κάλλη θαυμάσια, (of Crete).
51 νομὸν Περιδάϊον : Περιδάϊον νομόν "metri gratia" Sitzler.
52 δέδοται μὲν γᾶς Housman : μὲν γᾶς δέδοται Plutarch :

foolish men belongeth a love for things afar. I com-
mend the story told of King Euxantius, who, although
the men of Crete so desired, would not consent to
rule, or to take a seventh share of her hundred cities
along with the sons of Pasiphaë ; but he declared to
them the marvel that had once befallen him :—

"Know ye that I fear war with Zeus, I fear the
loudly thundering Shaker of the earth. They, on a
day, with thunderbolt and trident, sent the land and
a countless host into the depths of Tartarus, while
they left alone my mother,[1] and her well-walled home.
And, after this, am I to covet wealth? Am I to
thrust aside that which the blessed gods have de-
creed for my own country, and receive a vast allotment
on another shore ? Let alone, my heart, the cypress-
tree ; let alone the pasture of Ida. To myself
hath been given but little land, the home of the oak-
tree ; but I have had no lot in sorrow or in strife."

---

[1] Euxantius was son of Minos by Dexithea of Ceôs.
Bacchylides calls Ceôs Εὐξαντίδα νᾶσον (ii 8).

δέδοται s. 52 f. In the papyrus nothing is preserved except
marginalia restored as δέ]δοται θά[μνος (and λάχον, part of
ἔλαχον in next line) ; hence θά[μνος δρυός] G–H (Diehl, s).
I should prefer extracting from Plutarch's ὅθεν ἄδρυς, either
ὅθεν ἀ δρῦς, or ὅθεν ἄδρυα. Boeckh observed (in 1821):—" Nisi
cum Reiskio . . . amplectaris coniecturam sane incommodam
ὅθεν ἀ δρῦς, nihil melius invenies, quam quod et Heynio ipsi
et mihi in mentem venit ἄδρυα . . . poma, et maxime pruna."
But ἄδρυα is a synonym for ἀκρόδρυα, which properly means
" hard-shelled " fruits (Geop. 10, 74), and may well have been
applied to "acorns." Oaks and acorns are now the principal
product of Ceos. It " boasts of about a million and a half
oak trees." . . . "The acorns are huge things." . . . " Many
of the oaks are centuries old" (Bent's Cyclades, p. 450), cp.
Ross, Reisen auf den griechischen Inseln, i 128 f. The oak of
Ceos is the Quercus Aegilops, which produces the " valonia "
of commerce, one of the richest of tanning materials.

PINDAR

5. ΑΘΗΝΑΙΟΙΣ ΕΙΣ ΔΗΛΟΝ

στρ. α΄, β΄, γ΄, δ΄, ε΄, ϛ΄, blank of six strophae, each
                    beginning with the line—
    ἰήϊε Δ[άλι᾽ ᾽Απόλλον
       (blank of three lines of seventh strophê.)
35 –◡◡–◡◡ Εὔ-
    βοιαν ἕλον καὶ ἔνασσαν·
στρ. ζ΄
    ἰήϊε Δάλι᾽ ᾽Απόλλον·
    καὶ σποράδας φερεμήλους
    ἔκτισαν νάσους ἐρικυδέα τ᾽ ἔσχον
40 Δᾶλον, ἐπεί σφιν ᾽Απόλλων
    δῶκεν ὁ χρυσοκόμας
    ᾽Αστερίας δέμας οἰκεῖν·
στρ. η΄
    ἰήϊε Δάλι᾽ ᾽Απόλλον·
    Λάτοος ἔνθα με παῖδες·
45 εὐμενεῖ δέξασθε νόῳ θεράποντα
    ὑμέτερον κελαδεννᾷ
    σὺν μελιγάρυϊ παι-
    ᾶνος ἀγακλέος ὀμφᾷ.

      Grenfell and Hunt, *Oxyrhynchus Papyri*, v 39 f, 93.

   1 Cp. Soph. *O.T.* 154, ἰήϊε Δάλιε Παιάν.
   36 ἔνασσαν (*sc.* οἱ ἀπ᾽ ᾽Αθανᾶν ᾽Ιωνες), cp. *P.* v 71, ἔνασσεν.
   38 φερεμήλους, schol. πολυμάλους (-μήλους).

6. ΔΕΛΦΟΙΣ ΕΙΣ ΠΥΘΩ

    This Paean was written for performance at the
Delphic Theoxenia (l. 61), an ancient festival at
which the gods were regarded as the guests of their
worshippers. In historical times Apollo and his mother,
Lêtô, were specially honoured at the Delphic festival.

5. FOR THE ATHENIANS TO DELOS

Oh joy! O Delian Apollo!

(The Ionians from Athens) took Euboea, and
dwelt there.

Oh joy! O Delian Apollo!
And they made homes in the scattered islands
rich in flocks, and held far-famed Dêlos since Apollo
of the golden locks gave them the body of Asteria [1]
to inhabit.

Oh joy! O Delian Apollo!
There may ye, O children of Lêtô, graciously
welcome me as your ministrant, to the clear-voiced
honied strain of a glorious paean.

[1] Asteria, sister of Lêtô, was changed into the island after-
wards called Dêlos.

39 ἐρικυδέα — Δᾶλον, cp. ἄστυ ἐρικυδὲς quoted by Herodotus,
vii 220.
42 *sc.* Delos; Asteria, sister of Leto, was transformed into
the island of Delos.   45 Cp. *P.* viii 18.

6. FOR THE DELPHIANS TO PYTHO

The sketch of the fall of Troy and the subsequent for-
tunes of Neoptolemus (74–120) includes the account of
the hero's death, which, as we learn from the seventh
Nemean (461 B.C.), gave offence to the Aeginetans.
Cp. Sitzler, *Woch. f. Kl. Phil.* 1911, 1015–8.

PINDAR

στρ. α΄

Πρὸς Ὀλυμπίου Διός σε, χρυσέα
κλυτόμαντι Πυθοῖ,
λίσσομαι Χαρίτεσ-
σί\<ν\> τε καὶ σὺν Ἀφροδίτᾳ,
5 ἐν ζαθέῳ με δέξαι χρόνῳ
ἀοιδίμων Πιερίδων προφάταν.
ὕδατι γὰρ ἐπὶ χαλκοπύλῳ
ψόφον ἀΐων Κασταλίας
ὀρφανὸν ἀνδρῶν χορεύσιος, ἦλθον
10 ἔταις ἀμαχανίαν ἀ[λ]έξων
τεοῖσιν ἐμαῖς τε τιμαῖς.
ἤτορι δὲ φίλῳ παῖς ἅτε ματέρι κεδνᾷ
πειθόμενος κατέβαν στεφάνων
καὶ θαλιᾶν τροφὸν ἄλσος Ἀ-
15 πόλλωνος, τόθι Λατοΐδαν
θαμινὰ Δελφῶν κόραι χθονὸς ὀμφαλὸν
παρὰ σκιάεντα μελπόμεναι
ποδὶ κροτέο[ντι γᾶν θοῷ].

(lines 19 to 49 lost)

ἐπ. α΄

50 καὶ πόθεν ἀθαν[άτων ἔρις ἄ]ρξατο,
ταῦτα θεοῖς μὲν
πιθεῖν σοφοὺς δυνατόν,
βροτοισὶν δ' ἀμάχανον εὑρέμεν·

1-6 quoted by Aristides, ii 160 Bruno Keil. Cp. *P.*
vi 1-3.

2 κλυτόμαντι, not found elsewhere.

6 αοιδιμ.ῠ̈.ν : ἀοίδιμον Aristides (Diehl, s) ; —μων G–H.

7 χαλκοπύλῳ, Schol. ''the Cephisus (?) flows into it (the
Castalian fountain) through the mouths of brazen lions.'

10 ἀ[λ]έξων, superscribed [ρ]η, for ἀρήξων, with ἀέξων in the
margin. With the first reading cp. *O.* xiii 9, ἀλέξειν ὕβριν.

534

PAEAN VI

O golden Pytho, that art famed for thine oracles !
I beseech thee, by the Olympian Zeus, with the
Graces and Aphroditê, to welcome me at this
sacred season as a prophet of the tuneful Piërides.
For, beside the water of Castalia, with its outlet of
brass, I have no sooner heard a sound of dancing
reft of men,[1] than I have come to relieve the need of
the townsmen, and of mine own honour. I have
obeyed my dear heart, even as a son obeyeth his
kind mother, and have come down to Apollo's
grove, the home of garlands and of banquets,
where, beside the shadowy centre of the earth,
the maidens of Delphi full often beat the ground
with nimble step, while they sing the son of
Lêtô.

And, whence the strife of the immortals arose,
of this the gods are able to prompt sage poets ;
while, for mortal men, it is impossible to find it.

---

[1] " A dancing in which men are unrepresented," *i.e.* the
maidens dance alone. Grenfell and Hunt quote this as
preferred by Bury to their own rendering :—" I hear that
there are wanting men to dance to the music of the Castalian
fount."

---

13 κατέβαν . . . ἄλσος ᾿Απόλλωνος, cp. *P.* iv 55, Πύθιον ναὸν
καταβάντα.
17 σκιάεντα Housman (s) : σκιόεντα.
50 ἔρις Bury (Diehl), cp. 87 f, ἔριξε κτλ.

ἀλλὰ παρθένοι γὰρ ἴστε <γε> Μοῖσαι
55 πάντα, κελαινεφεῖ σὺν
πατρὶ Μναμοσύνα τε
τοῦτον ἔσχετ[ε τεθ]μόν,
κλῦτέ νυν· ἔραται δέ μοι,
γλῶσσα μέλιτος ἄωτον γλυκὺν [καταλείβειν],
60 ἀγῶνα Λοξία καταβάντ' εὐρὺν
ἐν θεῶν ξενία.

στρ. β΄

θύεται γὰρ ἀγλαᾶς ὑπὲρ πανελ-
λάδος ἄντε Δελφῶν
ἔθνος εὔξατο λι-
65 μοῦ σ ∪ – – ∪ – ∪ – –
εκδ ∪ ∪ – ∪ – – – ∪ –
φιλε̄ ∪ – – ∪ ∪ – ∪ – ◡
Κρόν ∪ ∪ ∪ ∪ – ∪ ∪ –
πρύτα[νι ∪ – – ∪ ∪ –
70 τοὶ πᾰ ∪ – – ∪ – ∪ ∪ ∪ ◡
χρηστηρι – ∪ ∪ –
∪ – – Πυθωνόθεν – ∪ – –
καί ποτε ∪ ∪ – – ∪ ∪ – ∪ ∪ – –
Πάνθοο[ς – ∪ ∪ – ∪ ∪ –

---

59 καταλείβειν Wilamowitz (s) : προχέειν εἰς (or κελαδῆσαι)
G–H (Diehl).

60 Λοξία G–H (Diehl) : Λοξία Oxyrh. pap. (s).

64–72 λιμοῦ σ[φαγὰν ἀποτρόπαιον·] εὖ δ' [ἐπέτειλ' Ἀπόλλων
σφίσιν] φίλ' ἐ[ννέπων ἐξ ἀδύτοιο, τῷ παῖς] Κρόν[ιος ἔπορ' ἐπιχθο-
νίοις] πρύτα[νιν ἀκούειν θεμίτων·] τοὶ πα[ρὰ γᾶς ὀμφαλὸν θάμ'
ἱκνέονται] χρηστη[ριαζόμενοι μεριμνᾶν] Πυθωνόθ[εν ἄλκαρ εὑρεῖν·]
Sitzler.

66 f. εκδ and φιλει Hermupolis papyrus: ευδ and φιλε
Oxyrh. papyrus.

68 Κρόν[ιε βαρυόπα στεροπᾶν] Tosi, *Atena e Roma*, 1908,
p. 201 (s).

PAEAN VI

But, since ye Muses know all things, (ye have had this ordinance allotted to yourselves along with the cloud-wrapt Father, and with Mnemosyne,) [1] listen now! for my tongue loveth to pour forth the choicest and sweetest meed of song, when, at the festival of the gods, I have entered the broad lists of Loxias.

The sacrifice is being offered on behalf of the splendid panhellenic (feast), which the people of Delphi vowed, [even a sacrifice to avert] [2] the famine. [And right well did Apollo prompt them by uttering friendly oracles from his shrine, Apollo to whom the son of Cronus assigned the right to be known as the lord of oracular decrees for all mortal men, who full often come to the centre of the earth to consult the oracle and thus to find from Pytho a safeguard from their cares.] [2]

[And, on a day, Priam besought the god, and he, having sent his priest, Panthoüs, warded off misfortune from Troy, so far as was lawful, and he brought a remedy, what time the savage son of Pêleus wrought his dread deeds of woe.] [2]

---

[1] i.e. the Muses, together with their mother, Mnemosyne, and their father, Zeus, are able to inspire the poet.

[2] A rendering of the restoration suggested by Sitzler.

73–77 καί ποτε [Πρίαμος θεὸν ἱκέτευσ', ὁ δ' ὀπάσσαις] Πάνθοο[ν ἱρε' ἄλεξεν ἀα]δὲς Τροΐα[ς, ὅσον ἦν θέμις·] ἤνεγκέ[ν τ' ἄκος, αἶν' ὅτε κά]δεα πᾶϊς [Πηλέος τέλεσ' ὠμόφρων·] Sitzler.

74 Πάνθοο[ν — Δαναῶν ὅτε παῖ]δες Τρωΐα[ν πόλιν ἔπραθον] ἤνεγκε[ν . . .] Diehl, or (better) [τ ὸ ν Δαναῶν π ο τ ε παῖ]δες.

75 δες Τροία· [χαλεπώτατα δ'] ή-
νεγκεν [◡◡–θρασυμή-
δεα πάϊς [Ζηνὸς Αἰακίδαν] ◡––◡–
ὃν ἐμβα[λὼν ἰὸν ἔσχε μάχας]
Πάριος ἑ[κάβολος βροτη-]
80 σίῳ δέμαϊ θεός·
Ἰλίου δὲ θῆκεν ἄφαρ
ὀψιτέραν ἅλωσιν,

ἀντ. β'

κυανοπλόκοιο παῖδα ποντίας
Θέτιος βιατάν,
85 πιστὸν ἕρκος Ἀχαι-
ῶν, θρασεῖ φόνῳ πεδάσαις·
ὅσσα τ' ἔριξε λευκωλένῳ
ἄκναμπτον Ἥρᾳ μένος ἀντερείδων
ὅσα τε Πολιάδι· πρὸ πόνων
90 δέ κε μεγάλων Δαρδανίαν
ἔπραθον, εἰ μὴ φύλασσεν Ἀπόλλων·
νέφεσσι δὲ χρυσεοῖς Ὀλύμποι-
ο καὶ κορυφαῖσιν ἵζων
μόρσιμ' ἀναλύεν Ζεὺς ὁ θεῶν σκοπὸς οὐ τόλ-
95 μα· περὶ δ' ὑψικόμῳ Ἑλένᾳ
χρῆν ἄρα Πέργαμον εὐρὺ [δὶ]α-
στῶσαι σέλας αἰθομένου
πυρός· ἐπεὶ δ' ἄλκιμον νέκυν ἐν τάφῳ
πολυστόνῳ θέντο Πηλεΐδα,
100 ἁλὸς ἐπὶ κῦμα βάντες ἦλ-
θον ἄγγελοι ὀπίσω
Σκυρόθεν Νεοπτόλεμον

75 [χαλεπώτατα δ'] ἤνεγκεν Sandys.
76 [θρασυμή]δεα πάϊς [Ζηνὸς Αἰακίδαν] Housman (Diehl):
[Διομή]δεα πάϊς [Ζηνὸς ◡◡◡] G–H (S).

The son of Zeus (Apollo) was sorely vexed with
the valiant son of Aeacus, whom, by shooting an
arrow, the far-darting god, in the mortal form of
Paris, stayed from the battle, and thus at once
delayed the fall of Ilium, by quelling with a bold
deed of blood the doughty son of the dark-haired
Nereid Thetis, the trusty bulwark of the Achaeans.

What a strife Apollo waged with white-armed
Hera, in matching against her his unflinching spirit!
And what a strife with Athênê, guardian of the city!
Even before the (final) toils of war they would have
razed the Dardan city, had it not been protected by
Apollo. But Zeus, the warder of the gods, seated
above the golden clouds and crests of Olympus,
dared not relax the decrees of destiny.

Yet, for high-coifed Helen's sake, it was fated, in the
end, that the flame of blazing fire should destroy the
spacious city of Troy; but, when they had laid in the
sore-lamented tomb the brave body of the son of
Pêleus, messengers went over the sea-wave and
returned again, bringing with them from Scyros

91 ἔπραθον Bury (edd.): ἔπραθεν.
95 ὑψικόμῳ, P. iv 172, ὑψιχαῖται.
96 εὐρὺν διαστῶσαι G–H: εὐρὺν ἀιστῶσαι S.
97 αἰθόμενος papyrus.

εὐρυβίαν ἄγοντες,

ἐπ. β΄

ὃς διέπερσεν Ἰλίου πόλιν·

105 ἀλλ᾽ οὔτε ματέρ᾽ ἔπειτα κεδνὰν
εἶδεν οὔτε πατρω-
ίαις ἐν ἀρούραις
ἵππους, Μυρμιδόνων
χαλοκορυστὰν
ὅμιλον ἐγείρων.

110 σχεδὸν δ[ὲ Το]μάρου Μολοσσίδα γαῖαν
ἐξίκετ᾽, οὐδ᾽ ἀνέμους ἔλαθεν
οὐδὲ τὸν εὐρυφαρέτραν ἑκάβολον·
ὤμοσε γὰρ θεός,
γεραιὸν ὃς Πρίαμον
πρὸς ἔρκειον ἤναρε βωμὸν ἑ-

115 πενθορόντα, μή μιν εὔφρον᾽ ἐς οἶ[κ]ον
μήτ᾽ ἐπὶ γῆρας ἵξε-
μεν βίου· ἀμφιπόλοις δὲ
[κ]υρ[ίαν] περὶ τιμᾶν
[δηρι]αζόμενον κτάνεν

120 [<ἐν>] τεμέ]νεῖ φίλῳ γᾶς
παρ᾽ ὀμφαλὸν εὐρύν.
[ἰὴ ἰήτε], νῦν μέτρα παιηό-
νων, ἴητε, νέοι.

109 [ἐγείρ]ων Hermupolis papyrus (s): εγε[. . . .] Oxyrh.
pap., ἔγειρε G–H (Diehl).

115 εὔφρον᾽ ἐς οἶκον Housman (Diehl, s), cp. 105 f. *Il.* v 686,
οὐκ ἄρ᾽ ἔμελλον ἐγώ γε | νοστήσας οἰκόνδε φίλην ἐς πατρίδα
γαῖαν | εὐφρανέειν ἄλοχόν τε φίλην καὶ νήπιον υἱόν, and Lucr.
iii 894, iam iam non *domus* accipiet te *laeta*.

117–119 = Pindar Frag. 52 Bergk[4] in schol. *N.* vii 94,
ἀμφιπόλοισι μαρνάμενον μυριᾶν περὶ τιμᾶν ἀπολωλέναι (μοιριᾶν
suggested to Boeckh by paraphr. τῶν νομιζομένων τιμῶν).

the mighty Neoptolemus,[1] who sacked the city of
Ilium.

But, thereafter, he lived not to see his kind mother,
nor his horses in the fields of his father, while he
marshalled the bronze-armed host of the Myrmidons.
Nigh indeed to mount Tomarus,[2] he reached the
Molossian land, but he escaped not the ken of the
winds, nor of the Far-darter with his spacious
quiver ; for the god had sworn that he who slew the
aged Priam, when he sprang upon the altar of the
court, should never be welcomed by his home, nor
attain to life's old age. But while he was contending
with the attendants over the customary dues, the god
slew him in his own precinct beside the broad
centre of the earth.

Cry now! Oh cry! Now for the full measure of
your paeans! Cry, O ye youths!

[1] Neoptolemus, son of Achilles and Deidamia, daughter of
Lycomêdes, king of Scyros, was brought up in Scyros, and
was brought from that island by Odysseus, because it had
been prophesied that Troy could not be taken without his
aid. At the capture of the city he slew Priam, who had
fled for refuge to the sacred hearth of Zeus. Cp. Virgil,
Aeneid, ii 550.

[2] A mountain of Molossia (*i.e.* Thesprotia), at the foot of
which was Dodona, with the oracular sanctuary of Zeus.

---

118 [κ]υρ[ιᾱν] Housman (Diehl): [μ]υρ[ιᾱν] ? pap., μοιριᾱν
Boeckh, G–H (S) ; Πυθιᾱν Zenodotus. Cp. p. 377.

PINDAR

στρ. γ′
  ὀνομακλύτα γ′ ἔνεσσι Δωριεῖ
  μεδέοισα πόντῳ
125 νᾶσος, ὦ Διὸς Ἑλ-
  λανίου φαεννὸν ἄστρον.
  οὕνεκεν οὔ σε παιηόνων
  ἄδορπον εὐνάξομεν, ἀλλ᾽ ἀοιδᾶν
  ῥόθια δεκομένα κατερεῖς
130 πόθεν ἔλαβες ναυπρύτανιν
  δαίμονα καὶ τὰν θεμίξενον ἀρετάν.
  ὁ πάντα τοι τά τε καὶ τὰ τεύχων
  σὸν ἐγγυάλιξεν ὄλβον
  εὐρύοπα Κρόνου παῖς, ὑδάτ<εσσ>ι γὰρ ἐπ᾽ Ἀσω-
135 ποῦ π[οτ᾽ ἀ]πὸ προθύρων βαθύκολ-
  πον ἀ[να]ρέψατο παρθένον
  Αἴγιναν· τότε χρύσεαι ἀ-
  έρος ἔκρυψαν κόμαι ἐπιχώριον
  κατάσκιον νῶτον ὑμέτερον,
140 ἵνα λεχέων ἐπ᾽ ἀμβρότων

  *   *   *

176 – ◡ – ◡ – ◡ ἀπ]είρονας ἀρετὰς

Grenfell and Hunt, *Oxyrhynchus Papyri*, v (1908), pp. 20, 41 f, 93 ; Sitzler, in *Woch. f. Klass. Philol.* 1911, 1015–18.

123 ὀνομακλύτα, this feminine is quoted by Schol. T on *Il.* 20, 51 ; cp. ναυσικλύτα *N.* v 9, and Bergk's δαιτικλυτάν *O.* viii 52.

125 f. Schol. ἱερὸν Διὸς Ἑλληνίου ἐν Αἰγίνῃ, ὅπου συνελθόντες εὔξαντο περὶ τοῦ αὐχμοῦ, cp. *N.* v 10 and schol.

129 ῥόθια, Arist. *Eq.* 546 αἴρεσθ᾽ αὐτῷ πολὺ τὸ ῥόθιον.

PAEAN VI

An isle of glorious name, thou reignest in the
Dorian sea, O brightly beaming star of Hellenic
Zeus! For we shall lay thee to rest, Aegina, not
without banquet of paeans; but thou shalt receive
our surging songs, and shalt tell whence thou didst
receive the god that ruleth thy ships, and thy care
for the right of the stranger.

Verily he that bringeth all things to pass, whether
this or that, even the far-seeing son of Cronus,
placed thy happiness in thy hand, and, beside the
waters of the Asôpus, he once carried off from the
portal the deep-breasted maiden, Aegina. Then
did the golden tresses of the mist hide the over-
shadowed ridge of your land, that so, on the couch
immortal . . .

. . . boundless merits . . .

129 δεκ. Hermup. (s): δεχ. Oxyrh. (G–H, Diehl).
130 f. ναυπρύτανιν, and θεμίξενον (cp. *O.* viii 20 f., *N.* iv 11 f.
v 8, and Frag. 1, 3–4) are not found elsewhere.
132 Cp. Frag. 141 (105), θεὸς ὁ πάντα τεύχων, and, for τά τε
καὶ τά, *P.* v 55, vii 22, *I.* v 52.
134 'Ασώπου, father of Aegina, *I.* viii 17 f.
136 ἀναρέψατο, cp. Bekker's *Anecdota*, p. 401, ἀνερεψάμενοι,
from ἀναρέπτομαι, a variant of the ordinary form ἀνερείπομαι,
whence the Homeric ἀνηρείψαντο.

PINDAR

7 (*a*) ΘΗΒΑΙΟΙΣ Ε[ΙΣ ΠΥΘΩ?]

Fragments of 18 lines are printed in the *Oxy-rhynchus Papyri*, v (1908) 51, and the first 13 lines are less imperfectly preserved in the Hermupolis

7 (*b*)

Frag. 16, 10

[ἐπεύχομαι] δ' Οὐρανοῦ τ' εὐπέπλῳ θυγατρὶ
Μναμοσύνᾳ κόραισί τ' εὐμαχανίαν δίδομεν.
τυφλαὶ γὰρ ἀνδρῶν φρένες
ὅστις ἄνευθ' Ἑλικωνιάδων
15 βαθεῖαν ἐλθ[όν]των ἐρευνᾷ σοφίαις ὁδόν·
ἀντ. or ἐπ.
ἐμοὶ τοῦτον διέδωκαν ἀθάνατον πόνον

Oxyrhynchus Papyri, v (1908) 52 f.

15 βαθεῖαν — ὁδόν, "seeks the steep path of them who walked it by their wisdom." G–H. The second word may begin with ἐλθ- or ἐλε- or ἐλο·, and end with των or γων

8. ΘΗΒΑΙΟΙΣ

Frag. 82, Col. ii, 20

20 σπεύδοντ', ἔκλαγξε θ' ἱερώτατον
δαιμόνιον κέαρ ὀλοαῖσι στοναχαῖς ἄφαρ,
καὶ τοιᾷδε κορυφᾷ σάμαινεν λόγων·
25 ὦ πανάπ[ειρον εὐ]ρύοπα Κρονίων,
τελεῖς σ[ὺ νῦν τὰν πάλαι
πεπρωμέναν πάθαν,
ἁνίκα Δαρδανίδαις Ἑκάβ[α φράσεν ὄψιν]
[ἄν] ποτ' εἶδεν ὑπὸ σπλάγχνοις
φέροισα τόνδ' ἀνέρ', ἔδοξ[ε δὲ

Oxyrhynchus Papyri, v (1908) 64 f.

20 σπεύδοντα sc. Πάριν, ἔκλαγξε sc. Κασσάνδρα.

544

7 (a)

papyrus (Florence, 1913). The *strophe* of 12 lines begins with μαντευμάτων τε θεσπεσίων δοτῆρα, and the *antistrophe* with ἥρωα Τήνερον λέγομεν ‿ − −

7 (b)

But I pray to Mnemosyne, the fair-robed child of Uranus, and to her daughters, to grant me a ready resource ; for the minds of men are blind, whosoever, without the maids of Helicon, seeketh the steep path of them that walked it by their wisdom.

To me have they handed on this immortal task.

(G-H) ; ἰλι[γγ]ιῶν ?   σοφίαις ὁδόν G-H (S), σοφίας ὁδόν in *Paean* ix 4.

16 πόνον written above πόρον.

8. FOR THE THEBANS

(Seeing Paris) hasting forth, at once Cassandra's most holy inspired heart cried aloud with grievous moanings and made utterance on this wise :—

" O infinite, O far-seeing son of Cronus, surely now shalt thou fulfil the doom that was destined long ago, when Hecuba told the Trojans the vision which she saw, when she carried this man [1] in her womb. She

[1] Paris ; Eur. *Troades*, 921 f. ; Virgil, *Aen.* vii 320 f.

545

PINDAR

30 τεκεῖν πυρφόρον Ἐρινὺν
   ἑκατόγχειρα, σκληρᾷ [δὲ βίᾳ
   Ἴλιον πᾶσάν νιν ἐπὶ π[έδον
   καταρεῖψαι· ἔειπε δὲ . . . .
   . . . ᾳ τέρας ὑπνα[λέον.
35 ἔσφαλε ?] προμάθεια

9. ΘΗΒΑΙΟΙΣ

The subject of the first part of this poem is an
eclipse of the sun. This may be identified with the
total eclipse of 30 April, 463 B.C. (when, at 2 P.M.,
eleven twelfths of the sun were obscured to spectators
at Thebes), rather than with the annular eclipse of
17 Feb., 478. It has been suggested, however, that,
if the poem was written in 463, Pindar would pro-
bably have referred to the eclipse of 478, and the
mention of snow and frost has been quoted in favour
of the eclipse of 17 Feb. The rest of the poem is on

στρ. αʹ
   Ἀκτὶς ἀελίου, τί πολύσκοπε μήσεαι,
   ὦ μᾶτερ ὀμμάτων, ἄστρον ὑπέρτατον
   ἐν ἁμέρᾳ
      κλεπτόμενον; [τί δ᾽] ἔθηκας ἀμάχανον
      ἰσχύν τ᾽ ἀνδράσιν
   καὶ σοφίας ὁδόν,
5 ἐπίσκοτον ἀτραπὸν ἐσσυμένα;

1 ἀκτὶς ἀελίου Soph. *Ant.* 100.
1-2 τί πολύσκοπε μήσεαι, ὦ μᾶτερ Boissonade, ὀμμάτων Blass
(G–H, Diehl, S), cp. *Od.* xi 474, τίπτ᾽ ἔτι μεῖζον ἐνὶ φρεσὶ
μήσεαι ἔργον, and Philostr. *Epp.* 52 (72), κἀκεῖνό που κατὰ
Πίνδαρον, τὸ τὴν ἀκτῖνα τὴν ἀπὸ σοῦ πηδῶσαν εἶναι τῶν ἐμῶν
ὀφθαλμῶν μητέρα· τί πολύσκοπ᾽ ἐμησθεῶ μ᾽ ἄτερ ὀμμάτων
Dionys. ; τί πολύσκοπ᾽ ἐμήσαο (ἐμήσω Bamberger) θοῶν μᾶτερ

PAEANS VIII, IX

deemed that she bare a fiery hundred-handed
Fury, who with his stern strength hurled all Ilium
to the ground; and she told the marvel of her
slumber. But her forethought was unavailing.

9. FOR THE THEBANS

the mythological history of Thebes, and it may be
suspected that this ordinary mythological matter
was written first, and the passage on the eclipse
prefixed by the poet at the last moment, in his
desire to take note of the extraordinary event which
had just happened. It is difficult to imagine Pindar
beginning by writing the impressive passage on the
eclipse, and then going on with the commonplace
mythology of Melia.

Beam of the sun! O thou that seest afar, what
wilt thou be devising? O mother of mine eyes! O
star supreme, reft from us in the daytime! Why
hast thou perplexed the power of man and the way
of wisdom, by rushing forth on a darksome track?

ὀμμάτων Bergk⁴; τί πολύσκοπ᾽· ἐμήσαο μ᾽, ὦ μᾶτερ· ὀμμάτων
(cp. *Il.* xi 253, οἱ κακὰ μήσαο θυμῷ), "what didst thou devise
against me, thou source of·sight!", may also be suggested.

3 <τί δ᾽> Diehl: τύ γ᾽ s.

4 ἰσχύν τ᾽ ἀνδράσιν Blass (G–H, s): ἰσχὲν (ἰσχὺν vulgo)
κτανὸν ἀνδράσιν B.

5 ἐπίσκοτον; *v.l.* ἐπίσκοπον.
    ἀτραπὸν ἐσσυμένα J. G. Schneider: ἄτροπον ἐσσαμένα.

547

ἐλαύνεις τι νεώτερον ἢ πάρος;
ἀλλά σε πρὸς Διός, ἱπποσόα θεός,
ἱκετεύω, ἀπήμονα
εἰς ὄλβον τινὰ τράποιο Θήβαις,
10 ὦ πότνια, πάγκοινον τέρας·

ἀντ. α΄

  – ρα – ◡ ◡–◡◡– ◡◡–◡⏝

  – –◡– ◡– –◡ ◡–◡⏝

  ⏝ ὦνος –

  –, πολέμοιο δὲ σᾶμα φέρεις τινός,
14   ἢ καρποῦ φθίσιν,
  ἢ νιφετοῦ σθένος
15 ὑπέρφατον, ἢ στάσιν οὐλομέναν,
  ἢ πόντου κενέωσιν <ἄρ'> ἂμ πέδον,
  ἢ παγετὸν χθονός, ἢ νότιον θέρος
  ὕδατι ζακότῳ ῥέον,
  ἢ γαῖαν κατακλύσαισα θήσεις
20 ἀνδρῶν νέον ἐξ ἀρχῆς γένος;

ἐπ. α΄

ὀλοφύ[ρομαι οὐ]δέν, ὅ τι πάντων μέτα πείσομαι.

lines 22–33 lost, = ἐπ. α΄ 2–10, στρ. β΄ 1–3.

στρ. β΄

                  <μένει>
   ἐκράνθην ὕπο
  δαιμονίῳ τινί

6 ἐλαύνεις M (Diehl) ; v.l. '—νειν P (G–H, S), or —νει B.
7 ἱπποσόα θεός (or θοάς) Blass ; ἱπποσόα θοάς G–H, Diehl, S : ἵππους ζαθέας Schneidewin (ζαθόας Christ), ἵπποσθα θοὰς Dionys.
11–13 [ἢ]ρ' ἀ[τασθαλίαισι κοτεσσαμένα βροτῶν | πάμπαν μὲν οὐ θέλεις ἐξαλείψειν φάος | αἰ]ῶνος [ἀγνόν], πολέμοιο δὲ κτλ ? S.
13 πολέμοιο δὲ G–H (Diehl, S) : πολέμου δ' εἰ Hermann, σᾶμα Scaliger : πολεμοῦ δὶς ἅμα Dionys.

548

PAEAN IX

Art thou bringing on us some new and strange
disaster? Yet, by Zeus, I implore thee, thou swift
driver divine of steeds! do thou, O queen! change
this world wide portent into some painless blessing
for Thebes . . .

[Is it because, in thine anger at the presumptuous
sons of mortals, thou art unwilling utterly to blot
out the pure light of life?] [1]

But art thou bringing a sign of some war, or wasting
of produce, or an unspeakably violent snow-storm, or
fatal faction, or again, some overflowing of the sea
on the plain, or frost to bind the earth, or heat of
the south-wind streaming with raging rain? Or wilt
thou, by deluging the land, cause the race of men to
begin anew? I in no wise lament whate'er I shall
suffer with all the rest. [2]

By some might divine have I been prompted,

---

[1] A rendering of the proposal quoted in the Note on
lines 11–13.
[2] Verse rendering in Milman's *Agamemnon and Bacchanals*,
p. 188, and in F. D. Morice's *Pindar*, p. 21, ed. 1898.

---

16 <ἄρ'> Blass, ἄμ Hermann : ἀλλὰ Dionys.
18 ῥέον s ed. 1900 : ἱερὸν Dionys. ; διερὸν Scaliger.
19 θήσεις Barnes : θήσει.
21 ὀλοφύ[ρομαι οὐ]δέν Hermann.
33 <μένει?> S.

35 λέχει πέλας ἀμβροσίῳ Μελίας
ἀγανὸν καλάμῳ συνάγεν θρόον
μήδεσί τε φρενὸς ὑμετέραν χάριν.
λιτανεύω, ἑκαβόλε,
Μοισαίαις ἀνατιθεὶς τέχναισιν
40 χρηστήριον, [ὤπολ]λον, τ[εό]ν·
ἀντ. β΄
ἐν ᾧ Τήνε-
ρον εὐρυβίαν θεμίτ[ων ποτέ]
ἐξαίρετον προφά-
ταν ἔτεκ[εν λέχει]
κόρα μιγεῖσ'
Ὠκεανοῦ Μελία σέο, Πύθιε.
44 [τῷ] Κάδμου στρατόν
καὶ Ζεάθου πόλιν,
45 ἀκερσεκόμα πάτερ, ἀνορέας
ἐπέτρεψας ἕκατι σαόφρονος·
καὶ γὰρ ὁ πόντιος Ὀρσοτρίαινά νιν
περίαλλα βροτῶν τίεν,
Εὐρίπου τε συνέτεινε χῶρον . . .

1–21 = Pindar, Frag. *107 (74), from Dionys. Halic. *De
Demosthene*, 7, i 142 ed. Usener and Radermacher (1899), mss
BPM, discussed in 1845 in Hermann's *Opuscula*, viii 75–90.
In the *Oxyrhynchus Papyri*, v (1908), pp. 22, 73, 107, the first
strophe is represented by four letters in lines 9, 10, ολ above
οτ, the first antistrophe by about six words, but a subsequent
strophe and antistrophe are almost perfectly preserved.

35 Μελίας, cp. *P.* xi 4
40 [ὤπολ]λον τ[εό]ν ? G–H (s) ; [ἄντει]λον ? Diehl.   τ[όθ]ι
Bury, τ' [ὀπ]ί Blass.   44 Ζεάθου = Ζήθου.

PAEAN IX

hard by the immortal couch of Melia, to compose, for your sake, a noble strain with my flute, and with my fancy. I pray to thee, O Far-darter, while I devote to the Muses' arts thine oracular shrine, Apollo; there it was that Melia, the daughter of Ocean, wedded to thy couch, O Pythian god, bare mighty Tênerus, the chosen interpreter of thy decrees. Thou, O father with the unshorn locks, didst entrust to him the host of Cadmus and the city of Zêthus,[1] by reason of his prudent courage. For the Sea-god, who wieldeth the trident, honoured him above all mortals; and he hasted to the region of Eurîpus . . .

[1] *i.e.* the Thebans and Thebes. Zêthus and Amphîon were the twin sons of Zeus by Antiopê, daughter of the river-god, Asôpus. They avenged themselves on Lycus, the mortal husband of Antiopê, and on his second wife, Dircê, for the cruelties inflicted on their mother. After gaining possession of Thebes, they fortified it with a wall that rose to the music of the lyre which Apollo had given to Amphîon.

PINDAR

ΔΙΘΥΡΑΜΒΟΙ

The dithyramb, a word of obscure origin, is a song in honour of Dionysus. The primitive dithyramb was represented by Archilochus (c. 650 B.C.) and by Arion of Lesbos, who came to Corinth on the invitation of Periander; the old dithyramb (550–475 B.C.)

61 (33)

Τί δ' ἔλπεαι σοφίαν ἔμμεν, ᾇ <τ'> ὀλίγον
ἀνὴρ ὑπὲρ ἀνδρὸς ἴσχει;
οὐ γὰρ ἔσθ' ὅπως τὰ θεῶν βουλεύματ' ἐρευνάσει
βροτέᾳ φρενί, θνατᾶς δ' ἀπὸ ματρὸς ἔφυ.

Stobaeus, *Anth.* ii 4 Wachsmuth ; Clemens Alex. *Str.* v 726.

ΑΘΗΝΑΙΟΙΣ

75 (45)

This dithyramb, which was sung in the central mart of Athens, was probably composed for the Great Dionysia celebrated at the beginning

Δεῦτ' ἐν χορόν, Ὀλύμπιοι,
ἐπί τε κλυτὰν πέμπετε χάριν, θεοί,
πολύβατον οἵτ' ἄστεος ὀμφαλὸν θυόεντα
ἐν ταῖς ἱεραῖς Ἀθάναις
5 οἰχνεῖτε πανδαίδαλόν τ' εὐκλέ' ἀγοράν,

1 δεῦτ' *EFM²V* (BS) : ἴδετ' *PM¹* (Bergk). ἐν, Aeolic or Boeotian form of εἰς, as in *P.* ii 11, 86 ; v 38 ; *N.* vii 31.

DITHYRAMBS

DITHYRAMBS

by Lasus of Hermïone, by Simonides and Pratinas,
by Apollodorus and Agathocles, and their pupil,
Pindar; the middle dithyramb (475–400 B.C.), by
Melanippides, Bacchylides, and others. Among its
early homes were Naxos, Corinth, and Thebes.

Canst thou by searching find out God?

Why dost thou deem that to be wisdom, in which
one man in small measure excelleth another? For
man is not able with his human mind to search out
the counsels of the gods, but he was born of a mortal
mother.

2 ἴσχει L (s); ἰσχύει vulgo Stob.; ἔχειν Clemens.

FOR THE ATHENIANS

of spring. The festival included dithyrambic
contests between choruses of fifty members
each.

HASTE to the dance and send your glorious favour,
ye Olympian gods, who, in holy Athens, are march-
ing to the densely crowded incense-breathing centre
of the city,[1] and to its richly adorned and glorious

---

[1] The altar of the Twelve Gods, set up in the market-place
by Peisistratus, son of Hippias (Thuc. vi 54, 6).

PINDAR

ἰοδεταν λαχεῖν στεφάνων ταν τ' ἐαριδρόπων
    ἀοιδᾶν·
Διόθεν τέ με σὺν ἀγλαᾷ
ἴδετε πορευθέντ' ἀοιδᾶν δεύτερον
ἐπὶ τὸν κισσοδέταν θεόν,
10 τὸν Βρόμιον 'Εριβόαν τε βροτοὶ καλέομεν,
γόνον ὑπάτων μὲν πατέρων μελπέμεν
γυναικῶν τε Καδμεῖᾶν.

ἐναργέα τελέων σάματ' οὐ λανθάνει,
φοινικοεάνων ὁπότ' οἰχθέντος 'Ωρᾶν θαλάμου,
15 εὔοδμον ἐπάγηισιν ἔαρ φυτὰ νεκτάρεα.
τότε βάλλεται, τότ' ἐπ' ἀμβρόταν χέρσον.
    ἐραταὶ
ἴων φόβαι, ῥόδα τε κόμαισι μίγνυται,
ἀχεῖ τ' ὀμφαὶ μελέων σὺν αὐλοῖς,
ἀχεῖ τε Σεμέλαν ἑλικάμπυκα χοροί.

Dionys. Halicarnass. *de compositione verborum*, c. 22, i 99
and 180 ed. Usener, 1904.

6 λαχεῖν Usener (s) : λάχει *F*, λάχετε vulgo (B).
    ἐαριδρόπων *F* (s) : —δρέπ(τ)ων.
    ἀοιδᾶν : λοιβᾶν B.
9 τὸν om. Vat. (s). κισσοδέταν Rob. Stephanus : —δόταν
P (Usener), κισσομανῆ ? Usener ; *v.l.* —δαῆ s.
10 τὸν Βρόμιον 'Εριβόαν τε Usener : Βρ. ὅν τ' 'Ερ. Bergk (s) ;
(τ)δν Βρ. (τ)δν 'Ερ. mss ; τὸν Βρ. τὸν 'Ερ. τε B.
11 μελπέμεν B (s) : μέλπε *P* ; *v.l.* μέλπομεν.
12 Καδμ. followed in mss by ἔμολον (B) or Σεμέλαν.

DITHYRAMBS

mart, there to receive garlands bound with violets, and songs culled in the spring-time. And look upon me, who, with joyance of songs, am once more sped by Zeus into the presence of the ivy-crowned god, whom we mortals call Bromius and Eriboas, to celebrate the progeny of sires supreme and of Cadmean mothers.[1]

Clearly seen are the bright symbols of sacred rites, whensoever, at the opening of the chamber of the purple-robed Hours, the fragrant Spring bringeth the nectar-breathing plants. Then, oh then, are flung on the immortal earth the lovely tresses of violets, and roses are entwined in the hair; then ring the voices of songs to the sound of flutes; then ring the dances in honour of diadem-wreathed Semelê.[2]

[1] Zeus and Semelê, here treated as plurals, to give them additional dignity.
[2] Verse rendering in Milman's *Agamemnon and Bacchanals*, p. 185.

---

13 ἐναργέα τελέων σάματ' Usener (S) : — τεμεῶι τεμάντιν F, *v.l.* νεμέω or νεμέα μάντιν ; ἐν Ἀργείᾳ Νεμέᾳ B.

14 φοινικοεάνων Koch (S) : φοινικοεάων F, *v.l.* φοίνικος ἐανῶν ; φοίνικος ἔρνος B.

15 ἐπάγῃσιν Usener, ἐπάγῃσιν S : ἐπάγοισιν F, *v.l.* ἐπαΐωσιν.

18 ἀχεῖ τε F (S) ; ἀχεῖται τ' B ; *v.l.* οἰχνεῖ τ(ε).

19 ἀχεῖ τε Bergk (S) : οἰχνεῖ τε mss.

PINDAR

76 (46)

αἴ τε λιπαραὶ καὶ ἰοστέφανοι καὶ ἀοίδιμοι,
Ἑλλάδος ἔρεισμα, κλειναὶ Ἀθᾶναι, δαιμόνιον
πτολίεθρον.

Schol. Aristoph. Acharn. 674, *Nubes* 299; cp. *Acharn.* 636 f., *Eq.* 1329. δαιμόνιον πτολίεθρον in Schol. on Aristides, iii 341 Dindorf.

This fragment and the two following belong to a dithyramb composed in the spring of 474 B.C., in which Pindar eulogised Athens for the part she had lately played in the war against Persia. In gratitude for the eulogy the Athenians presented the poet with a gift of 10,000 *drachmae* (£400), and made him their *proxenus*, or representative, at Thebes (Isocr. xv 166). Later writers imply that the gift was an indemnity for a fine of 1,000 *drachmae*, which the jealous Thebans inflicted on their countryman for his praise of Athens (Aeschines Socr. *Ep.* iv 3, Eustathius' Life of Pindar, and Tzetzes on Hesiod, p. 104ᵇ). The first of these writers adds that a seated statue of the poet, with lyre and scroll, was placed in front of the *Stoa Basileios* at Athens.

On the date of this dithyramb, cp. Gaspar's *Chronologie Pindarique*, p. 99.

---

[1] It has sometimes been supposed that the epithet "violet-crowned" is intended to refer to "the amethystine hues of the garland of mountains that encompasses Athens" (Gildersleeve's *Hellas and Hesperia*, p. 40). But this interpretation,

77 (196)

. . . ὅθι παῖδες Ἀθηναίων ἐβάλλοντο φαεννὰν
κρηπῖδ' ἐλευθερίας.

Plutarch, *Themist.* c. 8, *de gloria Ath.* c. 7.

78 (225)

Κλῦθ' Ἀλαλά, Πολέμου θύγατερ,
ἐγχέων προοίμιον, ᾇ θύεται
ἄνδρες <ὑπὲρ πόλιος> τὸν ἱερόθυτον θάνατον.

Plutarch, *de gloria Atheniensium*, c. 7.

2 ᾇ θύεται Haupt, *Opusc.* i 313 (edd.); αἰθύεται schol.

DITHYRAMBS

The fame of Athens

Oh! the gleaming, and the violet-crowned,[1] and the sung in story; the bulwark of Hellas, famous Athens, city divine!

probably first suggested by the modern Greek historian, K. Paparrhigopoulos, must be limited to the "purple glow upon Hymettus," the *purpureos colles florentis Hymetti* (Ovid, *ars amat.* iii 687), together with the more or less purple colouring of the sea off the Piraeus, like the ἰοειδέα πόντον of *Il.* xi 298. It is only at sunset that this purple glow is visible, and it is peculiar to Hymettus alone of all the mountains which encircle the plain of Athens.

It therefore seems safer to connect the epithet with the "violet-twined garlands" mentioned in line 6 of the immediately preceding dithyramb, which was performed at Athens during the vernal Dionysia (this connection is recognised by Boeckh, Dissen, Donaldson, and Fennell). Simonides, in celebrating the dithyrambic victories of the Acamantid tribe at the same Dionysia, describes the Graces as making the victor famous, for the sake of the "violet-crowned Muses" (Frag. 150). The same epithet is repeatedly applied to festal divinities, such as Aphroditê, and the Muses and Graces, and to heroines of romance, such as Eurydicê. Thus, in using this epithet, Pindar may be regarded as personifying Athens as a divine or semi-divine being. See especially Mr. A. B. Cook's paper on *Iostephanos* in the *Journal of Hellenic Studies*, xx (1900) 1–13.

The battle of Artemisium

There, where the sons of Athens laid the bright foundation of Liberty.

A reference to the battle of Artemisium, 480 B.C.

Death for the father-land

Harken! O War-shout, daughter of War! prelude of spears! to whom soldiers are sacrificed for their city's sake in the holy sacrifice of death.

Aesch. *Pers.* 49, where the combination of the singular verb with the plural noun is noticed; ἀμφύετε Plutarch.

3 < ὑπὲρ πόλιος > Bergk (s).

PINDAR

ΘΡΑΣ[ΥΣ] ΗΡΑΚΛΗΣ Η ΚΕΡΒΕΡΟΣ. ΘΗΒΑΙΟΙΣ

στρ. α´

Π[ρὶν μὲν εἷρπε σχοινοτένειά τ᾽ ἀοιδὰ
διθ[υράμβων
καὶ τὸ σὰ[ν κίβδηλον ἀνθρώποισιν ἀπὸ
  στομάτων,
διαπέπ[τ]α[νται δὲ νῦν ἱροῖς ?] πύλα[ι κύ-
5 κλοισι νέαι· [σοφοὶ οἱ ? ε]ἰδότες
οἵαν Βρομίου [τελε]τὰν
καὶ παρὰ σκᾶ[πτ]ον Διὸς Οὐρανίδαι
ἐν μεγάροις ἵ[σ<τ>ά]ντι. σεμνᾷ μὲν
  κατάρχει
ματέρι πὰρ μ[εγ]άλα ῥόμβοι τυπάνων,
10 ἐν δὲ κέχλαδ[εν] κρόταλ᾽, αἰθομένα τε
δᾷς ὑπὸ ξαν[θα]ῖσι πεύκαις.

Fr. 79a (47)[1]

Fr. 79b (48)[2]

[1] Fr. 79a, Dionys. Halicarn. *De compos. verb.* c. 14: Clearchus in Athenaeus, x 455c, Aristoxenus, *ib.* xi 467a.
[2] Fr. 79a, b, Strabo, x 469.

1 εἷρπε Strabo, Athen. x ; ἧρπε Athen. xi, Dion. *F.* (*v.l.* ἧρχε *MV*, ἧριπε *EP*) ; ἔρπε (sGr).
σχοινοτένειά τ᾽ ἀοιδά (BSGr) : σχοινογονίας ἀοιδά Strabo, cod. Mosc.; σχοινοτενεῖα ατα οἶδα Dion. *P*, σχοινοτενῆ φωνήεντα Dion. *E*.
2 διθυράμβων Strabo, Dion. *EPMV* (sGr) ; -βου Dion. *F* (-βω Usener) ; om. Athen.
3 κίβδηλον Dion. *EF*, and Athen. (s) : κίβδαλον Dion. *PMV* (BGr). ἀνθρώποις or ἄνθρωποι Dion., Athen. x, ἀπὸ στομάτων Athen. xi (om. Strabo) ; ἀνθρώποισιν ἀπὸ στομάτων Hermann (BSGr).
4 διαπέπ[τ]α[νται δὲ] and πύλαι Sandys (Gr). Cp. *O.* vi 27. *N.* ix 2. νῦν Lobel. ἱροῖς ? Gr. [κύ|κλοισι Bury (Gr). Cp. Ar. *Ran.* 440, ἱρὸν ἀνὰ κύκλον, *Anth. P.* xiii 28, 9.
5 σοφοὶ οἱ ? Gr. 6 [τελε]τὰν Sandys.
8 ἵ[. .]ντι (ἱσάντι), corrected in margin into ἱστάντι.
σεμνᾷ — κατάρχει Gr ; σοὶ — κατάρχει Strabo, — καταρχαὶ Scaliger, Casaubon (BS), — κατάρχειν Hermann.

558

DITHYRAMBS

In olden days, there flowed from the lips[1] of men
the lay of the dithyrambs long drawn out,[2] with the
sibilant *san* discarded[3]; but now new portals have
been flung open for the sacred circles of the dance.
Wise are they that know what manner of festival of
Bromius the Celestials hold in their halls, hard by the
sceptre of Zeus.   In the adorable presence of the
mighty Mother of the gods, the prelude is the whirling
of timbrels[4]; there is also the ringing of rattles, and
the torch that blazeth beneath the glowing pine-
trees.[5]

[1] " Labebatur ex ore " Dissen.

[2] Cp. Hermogenes, *De Inventione*, iv 4 (of lengthy metres),
τὸ ὑπὲρ τὸ ἡρωϊκὸν σχοινοτενὲς κέκληται.

[3] An allusion to the ἄσιγμοι ᾠδαί, especially those of Lasus
of Hermionê, cp. Dion. Hal. *De Comp. Verb.* 14, " there are
writers who composed whole odes without a sigma, as is
proved by the passage in Pindar" (the present fragment),
and Athenaeus, 455ᶜ, Πίνδαρος πρὸς τὴν ἀσιγμοποιηθεῖσαν
(ἄσιγμον ποιηθεῖσαν?) ᾠδήν, and 467ᵃ; also Herodotus, i. 139,
" the Dorians call the letter *san*, but the Ionians *sigma*."

[4] Cp. Eur. *Hel.* 1362 f. and *Bacch.* pp. xxxii, 100, ed. Sandys.

[5] *fulvas taedas* (B), " yellow pine-brands"? (GR); " glowing
pine-trees" is confirmed by R. M. Dawkins, who explains it
by the ruddy glow of the tawny branches of the pine during
the Greek summer.

---

9. μάτέρι πὰρ μεγάλᾳ Gr: μᾶτερ πάρα μεγάλοι (v.l. -λαι)
Strabo; μᾶτερ μεγάλα, πάρα B (S).   ῥόμβοι edd.; ῥοίμβοι
Strabo.   τυπάνων (for τυμπάνων) Gr, κύμβαλων Strabo (BS).

10 κέχλᾱδ[εν] Sandys, 3rd pers. sing. of κέχλᾱδα, pf. of
χλάζω. Cp. *O.* ix 2, *P.* iv 179, Hesychius κεχληδέναι· ψοφεῖν.
-δ[ον] Gr (better sing. -δ[εν], or pl. -δ[αν] as in ἀπέσταλκαν);
καχλάδων Strabo (*sistrorum* Wilamowitz) s 1914; κεχλάδειν
(for κεχλαδέναι) Hermann (B S 1900).

ἐν δὲ Ναΐδων ἐρίγδουποι στοναχαί,
μανίαι τ' ἀλαλ[αί] τ' ὀρίνεται <ρι>ψαύ-
  χενι
σὺν κλόνῳ.

Fr.
208 (224)[1]

15 ἐν δ' ὁ παγκρα[τὴ]ς κεραυνὸς ἀμπνέων
πῦρ κεκίνη[ται, τό τ'] Ἐνυαλίου
ἔγχος, ἀλκάεσσά [τ]ε Παλλάδο[ς] αἰγὶς
μυρίων φθογγάζεται κλαγγαῖς δρακόντων.

ἀντ. ά

ῥίμφα δ' εἶσιν Ἄρτεμις οἰοπόλος ζεύ-
20 ξαισ' ἐν ὀργαῖς
βακχίαις φῦλον λεόντων ἀ[γροτέρων Βρομίῳ·
ὁ δὲ κηλεῖται χορευούσαισι κα[ὶ θη-
ρῶν ἀγέλαις. ἐμὲ δ' ἐξαίρετο[ν
κάρυκα σοφῶν ἐπέων

25 Μοῖσ' ἀνέστασ' Ἑλλάδι κα[ὶ] [γενεὰν ?
εὐχόμενον βρισαρμάτοις ο[ἶκόν τε Θήβαις,
ἔνθα ποθ' Ἁρμονίαν [φ]άμα γα[μετὰν
Κάδμον ὑψη[λαὶ]ς πραπίδεσ[σι λαχεῖν κεδ- ?
νάν· Δ[ιὸ]ς δ' ἄκ[ουσεν ὀ]μφάν,
30 καὶ τέκ' εὐδοξο[ν παρ'] ἀνθρώπο[ις Σεμέλαν.

Gr(enfell) and Hunt, *Oxyrhynchus Papyri*, xiii (1919),
no. 1604, text 34 f.; trans. and notes, 40 f.

[1] Fr. 208, Plutarch, *Symp. Q.* i 5, 2, vii 5, 4; *De def.
orac.* 14.

---

13 ὀρίνεται υψαύχενι pap., — ριψαύχενι, "an ancient variant,"
Gr. Plutarch, *Symp. Q.* i 5, 2 ὀρινομένων ἐριαύχενι, vii 5, 4
ὀρινόμενοι ριψ. *De def. orac.* 14 -ναι ριψ. (-νων ριψ s).
21 βακχειαις pap. (corr. Gr)。 ἀ[γροτέρων Sandys, Bury.
Βρομίῳ Bury] Gr

DITHYRAMBS

There, too, are the loudly sounding laments of the Naiads, and there the frenzied shouts of dancers are aroused, with the throng that tosseth the neck on high; there too hath been brandished the almighty fire-breathing thunderbolt (of Zeus), and the spear of Enyalius, while the war-like aegis of Pallas resoundeth with the hissings of countless serpents.

Meanwhile, lightly cometh the lone huntress Artemis, who in Bacchic revels hath yoked the brood of savage lions for Bromius, who is enchanted even by the dancing herds of wild beasts.

Me too hath the Muse raised up for Hellas as a chosen herald of wise words, who am proud that my race and my home are in Thebes the city of chariots, where of old the story telleth how Cadmus by high design won sage Harmonia as his wedded wife, who obeyed the voice of Zeus, and became the mother of Semele famed among men.

---

22 κα[ὶ θη]ρῶν Housman, Bury (Gr).

25 f. κα[ὶ γ]ε[νεὰν] — ο[ἰκόν τε]? Sandys; κα[λ]λ[ιχόρῳ] ὄ[λβον τε] Bury (Gr, the second letter after κα being a, δ, λ, or υ.

27 γα[μετὰν] Housman (Gr).

28 ὑψη[λαῖ]s Gr, or ὑψί[σται]s. [λαχεῖν κεδ]νάν (or ἀγ]νάν) Bury (Gr).

30 εὐδοξο[ν cp. O. i 70. παρ'] ἀνθρώπο[ις γενεάν] Bury (Gr, or Σεμέλαν, which is better, if we print γενεὰν in l. 25). 31, 32, begin with Διόνυσ[ε] and ματέ[ρος].

PINDAR

ΠΡΟΣΟΔΙΑ

The *Prosodia*, or "Processional Songs," were sung
to the accompaniment of the flute.

ΕΙΣ ΔΗΛΟΝ

(*a*) στρ.   87 + 88 (58)

Χαῖρ', ὦ θεοδμάτα, λιπαροπλοκάμου
  παίδεσσι Λατοῦς ἱμεροέστατον ἔρνος,
πόντου θύγατερ, χθονὸς εὐρείας ἀκίνητον τέρας,
  ἄντε βροτοὶ
Δᾶλον κικλήσκοισιν, μάκαρες δ' ἐν Ὀλύμπῳ
  τηλέφατον
5 κυανέας χθονὸς ἄστρον . . . .

  . . . .

  . . . .

ἀντ.

  . . . .

  . . . .

(*b*) ἦν γὰρ τὸ πάροιθε φορητὰ κυμάτεσσιν παντοδαπῶν
  ἀνέμων
ῥιπαῖσιν· ἀλλ' ἁ Κοιογενὴς ὁπότ' ὠδίνεσσι θυίοισ'
  ἀγχιτόκοις ἐπέβα νιν, δὴ τότε τέσσαρες ὀρθαὶ
  πρέμνων ὄρουσαν χθονίων,
10 ἂν δ' ἐπικράνοις σχέθον πέτραν ἀδαμαντοπέδιλοι
  κίονες· ἔνθα τεκοῖσ' εὐδαίμον' ἐπόψατο γένναν.

(a) Theophrastus in Pseudo-Philo, περὶ ἀφθαρσίας κόσμου, 23.
(b) Strabo x 485.

6 παντοδαπῶν Wilamowitz: παντοδαπῶν <τ'> Schneider
(edd.).

PROCESSIONAL SONGS

On Delos

Hail, O heaven-built isle, most lovely scion of the children of bright-haired Lêtô, O daughter of the sea, thou unmoved [1] marvel of the spacious earth, by mortal men called Dêlos, but by the blessed gods of Olympus known as the far-seen star of the dark-blue earth . . . [2]

[1] In contrast to the tradition (first found in Pindar) that it was a floating island until the visit of Lêtô. This seems better than the rendering "unshaken by earthquake" discussed in Smyth's *Greek Melic Poets*, p. 364 f. There was an earthquake in 490 B.C., in fulfilment of the oracle, κινήσω καὶ Δῆλον ἀκίνητόν περ ἐοῦσαν (Herodotus, vi 98).

[2] "Wie grossartig ist die Vorstellung, dass die Erde für den Blick der Götter eine blaue Fläche ist, wie ihr Himmel für uns, auf dem ihnen dann Delos, so klein sie ist, als ein heller Stern lieblich aufleuchtet. Wer an sprachlicher Kunst als solcher Gefallen findet, wird hier ein Juwel, einen seltenen Edelstein in reichster Fassung anerkennen" (Wilamowitz, *Sappho und Simonides*, 1913, p. 131).

For aforetime, that isle was tossed on the waves by all manner of whirling winds ; but, when Lêtô, the daughter of Coeüs, in the frenzy of her imminent pangs of travail, set foot on her, then it was that four lofty pillars rose from the roots of earth, and on their capitals held up the rock with their adamantine bases. There it was that she gave birth to, and beheld, her blessed offspring.

7 ἀλλ' ἁ Κοιογένης Schneider (edd.): αλλακαιογενης.
8 ἐπέβα νιν Porson (edd.): ἐπιβαίνειν.
9 ὄρουσαν S: ἀπώρουσαν.

PINDAR

ΑΙΓΙΝΗΤΑΙΣ ΕΙΣ ΑΦΑΙΑΝ

89ᵃ (59)

Τί κάλλιον ἀρχομένοισιν ἢ καταπαυομένοισιν,
ἢ βαθύζωνόν τε Λατὼ καὶ θοᾶν ἵππων ἐλάτειραν
ἀεῖσαι;

Schol. Aristoph. Equit. 1269.

Aphaia was a goddess worshipped in Aegina. Cp. Pausanias, ii 30, 3, "In Aegina, on the way to the mountain of the Pan-hellenic Zeus, there is a temple of Aphaia, on whom Pindar composed an ode for the Aeginetans." Aphaia was also worshipped in Crete, where she bore the names of

ΠΑΡΘΕΝΕΙΑ

Partheneia, or Virginal songs, were sung by girls to the accompaniment of the flute. These songs were always attended by the dance. The creator of this kind of composition was Alcman. Dionysius of Halicarnassus (*Dem.* c. 39, i 213 Usener) quotes, as examples of the "archaic and austere style," Aeschylus and Pindar, *with the exception of the*

95 (63)

'Ω Πάν, 'Αρκαδίας μεδέων, καὶ σεμνῶν ἀδύτων
    φύλαξ, . . .
Ματρὸς μεγάλας ὀπαδέ, σεμνᾶν Χαρίτων μέλημα
    τερπνόν.

Schol. Pyth. iii 139.

104ᵇ Schröder

οἱ μὲν περὶ τὸ Γαλάξιον τῆς Βοιωτίας κατοικοῦντες ᾔσθοντο τοῦ θεοῦ τὴν ἐπιφάνειαν ἀφθονίᾳ καὶ περιουσίᾳ γάλακτος·

MAIDENS' SONGS

For the Aeginetans.   On the goddess Aphaia

Is there any nobler theme for our commencing or
for our closing strains, than to sing the deep-zoned
Lêtô, and the goddess that driveth the swift steeds?

Britomartis or Dictynna.   She was sometimes identified
with the Greek Artemis.   Furtwängler (*Das Heiligthum der
Aphaia*, 1906) held that the great temple of Aegina was
dedicated, not to Zeus or Athena, but to Aphaia.   Cp.
Classical Review, xx 327.

MAIDENS' SONGS

Partheneia, adding that even these have a certain
nobility and dignity of style.   One of the species of
the *Partheneion* was the *Daphnephorikon*, an ode sung
at a festival celebrated by a procession bearing
branches of bay to the temple of Apollo at Thebes
or at Delphi.   (See below, p. 566.)

From a maiden's song to Pan

O Pan, that rulest over Arcadia, and art the
warder of holy shrines . . . thou companion of
the Great Mother, thou dear delight of the holy
Graces !

Dionysus, the giver of milk

They that dwell near Galaxion in Boeotia became
aware of the advent of Dionysus by the abundant
supply of milk :—

−∪− προβάτων γὰρ ἐκ πάντων κελάρυζεν,
ὡς ἀπὸ κρανᾶν φέρτατον ὕδωρ,
θήλεον γάλα· τοὶ δ' ἐπίμπλαν ἐσσύμενοι πίθους·
ἀσκὸς οὔτε τις ἀμφορεὺς ἐλίννεν δόμοις,
πέλλαι δὲ ξύλιναι πίθοι <τε> πλῆσθεν ἅπαντες.

104° Schröder
(1) *On Aeoladas,*
who is also the subject of the next poem.

. . . . οσ . . . . θείαις ερ-
. . . . διᾳ
5 μάντις ὡς τελέσσω
στρ.

ἱεραπόλος· τιμαὶ
    δὲ βροτοῖσι κεκριμέναι·
παντὶ δ' ἐπὶ φθόνος ἀνδρὶ κεῖται
ἀρετᾶς, ὁ δὲ μηδὲν ἔχων ὑπὸ σι-
10   γᾷ μελαίνᾳ κάρα κέκρυπται.
ἀντ.

φιλέων δ' ἂν εὐχοίμαν
    Κρονίδαις ἐπ' Αἰολάδᾳ
καὶ γένει εὐτυχίαν τετάχθαι
ὁμαλὸν χρόνον· ἀθάναται δὲ βροτοῖς
15   ἁμέραι, σῶμα δ' ἐστὶ θνατόν.
ἐπ.

ἀλλ' ᾧτινι μὴ λιπότε-
κνος σφαλῇ πάμπαν οἶκος βιαί-
    ᾳ δαμεὶς ἀνάγκᾳ,
ζώει κάματον προφυγὼν ἀνια-
20   -ρόν· τὸ γὰρ πρὶν γενέ-
    [σθαι τῷ θανεῖν ἴσον λέγω.]

MAIDENS' SONGS

" For, like fairest water from fountains, even so the
milk of the dams began to gush forth from all the
flocks ; and they hasted, and filled the jars ; and not
a single wine-skin or jug lingered in their homes, but
the wooden pails, and all the jars, were filled."

Plutarch, *Pyth. Or.* 29, p. 409 ; quoted without the name of
Pindar, to whom it was first ascribed by Schneidewin in 1834.

5 ξύλιναι πίθοι <τε> Wilamowitz (s) : ξύλινοι πίθοι.

On Aeoladas I

. . . that I may fulfil my duties as a prophet-priest.
The honours of mortals are diverse, but on every man
falleth the burden of envy for his merit ; while the
head of him that hath nought is hidden in dark
silence. In friendly wise would I pray to the child-
ren of Cronus that an unbroken prosperity may be
decreed for Aeoladas and his race. The days of
mortals are deathless, although the body die. Yet
he, whose house is not reft of children nor utterly
overthrown beneath the stroke of stern necessity,
liveth free from toilsome labour ; for the time
before birth I deem equal to death.

Grenfell and Hunt, *Oxyrhynchus Papyri*, iv (1904), **53** ;
ascribed to Pindar on the ground of style and diction.
Partheneia in Grenfell and Hunt, *Oxyrhynchus Papyri*, iv
(1904), No. 659 (1st cent. A.D.) pp. 53–60. Cp. Wilamowitz,
Gött. gel. Anz. (1904) 670 f. ; O. Schröder, *Berl. Phil. Woch.*
1904, 1476 f.; F. Blass, *Litt. Centralbl.* 1904, 929 ; Fraccaroli,
Rivista di Filologia, 1905, 365 f.

5 f. μάντις—ἱεραπόλος, cp. frag. 51ᵈ, ναοπόλον μάντιν.
8–10 Cp. *P.* xi 29 f.   12 Αἰολάδᾳ. cp. Parth. ii 9.
13 εὐτυχίαν pap. (G–H, S) : εὐτυχία Wilamowitz.
20 f. τὸ γὰρ πρὶν γενέσθαι [τῷ θανεῖν ἴσον λέγω] ? Wilamowitz ;
[ἐς τὸ μὴ συνάπτει] ? Schröder.

PINDAR

104ᵈ Schröder

(2) On Aeoladas

A poem in honour of Aeoladas, whose son,
Pagôndas (27 f.), commanded the Thebans at the
battle of Dêlium when they defeated Athens in 424
(Thuc. iv 91 f.). Aeoladas is also the theme of the
previous poem (104ᶜ). In the present poem, the
speaker is a maiden (26, 46); hence the poem has
been identified as one of the Παρθένεια, or choruses
for girls, and further, as one of the special group of
Παρθένεια known as Δαφνηφορικά, in which the
singers bore branches of bay (27 f., 73). The pro-
cession was headed by a noble youth of beautiful
form, both of whose parents were alive. The follow-
ing is proposed by Schröder as the pedigree of the

στρ. α΄
21 ‒◡‒◡◡ χρυσοπ[επλ ◡‒◡‒
  ‒δωμ‒◡ λέσης τ◡‒μ ε‒◡◡
  [ἥκε]ι γὰρ ὁ [Λοξ]ίας
  πρόφρων ἀθανάταν χάριν
25 Θήβαις ἐπιμίξων.
ἀντ. α΄
  ἀλλὰ ζωσαμένα τε πέπλον ὠκέως,
  χερσὶν ἐν μαλακαῖσιν ὄρπακ᾽ ἀγλαὸν
  δάφνας ὀχέοισα, παν-
  δόξον Αἰολάδα σταθμὸν
30 υἱοῦ τε Παγώνδα
ἐπ. α΄
  ὑμνήσω στεφάνοισι θάλ-
  -λοισα παρθένιον κάρα,

21 [χαῖρ᾽ ὦ Πιερὶ] χρυσόπε[πλέ μοι κόρα, | [αὐ]δῶμ[αι, τε]λέσαις
τ᾽ [ἐμὸν] μέ[λημ᾽ ἐΰ· ?] s ; ‒ ‒ πότνια ? Diehl, cp. I. vi 75.
568

MAIDENS' SONGS

On Aeoladas II

persons directly or indirectly mentioned in the
poem:—

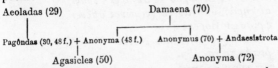

Here Agasicles, the grandson of Damaena, is the
παῖς δαφνηφόρος (ἀμφιθαλής). He is probably the
son of Pagôndas, and his cousin is the accomplished
daughter of Andaesistrota, a feminine name of a war-
like type, for which there is no known parallel; the
termination comes from στροτός, Boeotian for στρατός.

[Hail! O Pierian maiden robed in gold! I speak,
now that I have fitly discharged my duty.][1]

For Loxias hath gladly come to bring unto Thêbê
immortal glory.

But quickly girding up my robe, and bearing in
my delicate hands a splendid branch of bay, I shall
sing the all-glorious home of Aeoladas and of his
son Pagôndas, with my maidenly head gay with

[1] A rendering of the suggestion recorded in the Note on
l. 21.

---

22 μ[ηδ' ὀ]λέσῃ Diehl.
22-4 Cp. *P.* v 117 θεὸς πρόφρων τελεῖ δύνασαν.
23 ἥκει s, Wilamowitz.

σειρῆνα δὲ κόμπον
αὐλίσκων ὑπὸ λωτίνων
35 μιμήσομ' ἀοιδαῖς
στρ. β'
κεῖνον, ὃς Ζεφύρου τε σιγάζει πνοὰς
αἰψηράς, ὁπόταν τε χειμῶνος σθένει
φρίσσων Βορέας ἐπι-
σπέρχησ' ὠκύαλον Νότου
40 ῥιπάν τε ταράξῃ.
– – – φεν ⏑ – ⏑ –
– ạσι̅κ̅μ̣ . ζωννᾳ
στρ. γ'
πολλὰ μὲν τὰ πάροιθ[ε μέμνημαι καλά]
δαιδάλοισ' ἔπεσιν, τὰ δ' ἄ[λλ' ὁ παγκρατής]
45 Ζεὺς οἶδ', ἐμὲ δὲ πρέπει
παρθενήϊα μὲν φρονεῖν
γλώσσᾳ τε λέγεσθαι.
ἀντ. γ'
ἀνδρὸς δ' οὔτε γυναικός, ὧν θάλεσσιν ἔγ-
κειμαι, χρή με λαθεῖν ἀοιδὰν πρόσφορον
50 πιστὰ δ' Ἀγασικλέϊ
μάρτυς ἤλυθον ἐς χορὸν
ἐσλοῖς τε γονεῦσιν
ἐπ. γ'
ἀμφὶ προξενίαισι· τί-
μαθεν γὰρ τὰ πάλαι τὰ νῦν τ'

34 αὐλίσκων G–H etc. : λαισκων pap.
37 Cp. Sappho, 104, ὄρπακι βραδίνῳ.
38–40 ἐπισπέρχησ' — ταράξῃ P. Maas (s), cp. Od. v 304,
ἐτάραξε δὲ πόντον, ἐπισπέρχουσι δ' ἄελλαι : επισπερχης ωκναλον
τε ποντου. ιπαν εταραξε pap.; ἐπισπέρχῃ πόντου τ' ὠκύαλον ῥιπὰν
ἐμάλαξεν G–H, cp. Bergk, Poet. Lyr. Frag. 133, adespota,
ἐπερχόμενόν τε μαλάξοντας βίαιον πόντον ὠκείας τ' ἀνέμων ῥίπας.

garlands. To the notes of the lotus-pipe shall I mimic in song a siren-sound of praise, such as husheth the swift blasts of Zephyr; and whenever shivering Boreas speedeth on with strength of tempest, and stirreth up the swift rush of the South-wind . . .

Many are the fair deeds of old that I remember, while I adorn them in song, but the rest are known to Almighty Zeus alone: but for me, maidenly thought and maidenly speech are most meet. Neither for man nor for woman, whose children are dear to me, ought I to forget a fitting strain. As a faithful witness, have I come to the dance, in honour of Agasicles and his noble parents, and also by reason of our friendship. For, of old, as well as now, have

43 f. μέμνημαι καλά and ἄλλ' ὁ παγκρατής Wilamowitz (s).
46 f. μὲν . . . τέ, cp. O. vi 88 f.
50 f. πιστὰ—μάρτυς, cp. P. i 88, μάρτυρες ἀμφοτέροις πιστοί, and xii 27, πιστοὶ χορευτῶν μάρτυρες.
53 f. τίμαθεν γὰρ Wilamowitz (Diehl, s): τιμαθεντας pap.; τιμαθεῖσιν G–H, cp. I. iii 25 f.

55 ἀμφικτιόνεσσιν
ἵππων τ' ὠκυπόδων πολυ-
γνώτοις ἐπὶ νίκαις,

στρ. δ

αἷς ἐν ἀϊόνεσσιν Ὀγχη[στοῦ κλυ]τᾶς,
ταῖς δὲ ναὸν Ἰτωνίας ἀ[μφ' εὐκλε]ᾶ

60 χαίταν στεφάνοις ἐκόσ-
μηθεν, ἐν τε Πίσᾳ περὶ π – – ⏑ ⏑ – ⏓

Either 8 lines, or 8 lines + 15 of a whole triad, lost.

62 ῥίζα τε ⏑ – ⏓
[σε]μνὸν ἀν ⏑ ⏑ – ⏑ [Θή-
βαις] ἑπταπύλοισιν.

στρ. ε

65 ἐνῆκεν καὶ ἔπειτ[α δυσμενὴς χό]λος
τῶνδ' ἀνδρῶν ἕνεκεν μερίμνας σώφρονος
ἐχθρὰν ἔριν οὐ παλίγ-
γλωσσον, ἀλλὰ δίκας διδοὺς
π[ιστ]ὰς ἐφίλησεν.

ἀντ. ε

70 Δαμαίνας πα[ῖ, ἐναισίμ]ῳ νῦν μοι ποδὶ
στείχων ἅγεο· τὶν γὰρ εὔφρων ἕψεται
πρῶτα θυγάτηρ ὁδοῦ
δάφνας εὐπετάλου σχεδὸν
βαίνουσα πεδίλοις,

ἐπ. ε

75 Ἀνδαισιστρότα ἂν ἐπά-

58 ἐν ἀϊόνεσσιν Ὀγχηστοῦ, cp. *I.* i 33.
59 Ἰτωνίας = Ἀθάνας, cp. Bacchylides frag. 15 Blass, 11 Jebb, χρυσαίγιδος Ἰτωνίας—παρ' εὐδαιδαλον ναὸν ἐλθόντας κτλ. Her most famous shrine was probably that near Coroneia, which placed the head of the goddess on her silver coins.
61 περὶ π[ρώτων] or π[λείστου], Diehl.

they been honoured among their neighbours, both in
the famous victories of swift-footed steeds, victories
which adorned their locks with garlands on the
shores of renowned Onchestus, and by Itonia's
glorious fane, and at Pisa . . .

. . to seven-gated Thebes.

A jealous anger at their just ambition provoked a
bitter and unrelenting strife; but, giving loyal
satisfaction, it ended in friendship.

Son of Damaena¹ stepping forth with foot well-
omened, lead thou the march for me. First on the
road shalt thou be followed by thy happy daughter,
while she advanceth with her feet beside the leafy
branch of bay, she whom her mother, Andaesistrota,

65 ἐνῆκεν S : ἔθηκεν Wilamowitz.
66 μερίμνας σώφρονος cp. O. i 109 f. θεὸς . . . τεαῖσι μήδεται
. . . μερίμναισιν.
69 π[ιστ]ὰς : π[άσ]ας ? Diehl.
75 'Ἀνδ. Wilamowitz (S), ἂν Δαισιστρότα G–H (Diehl).

σκησε μήδεσ[ι ποικί]λο[ις]·
ἁ δ᾽ ἐρ[γ]ασί[αισιν]
μυρίων ἐ[χάρη καλα]ῖς
ζεύξα[ισά νιν οἴμων].

στρ. ϛ´

80 μὴ νῦν νέκτα[ρ ἰδόντ᾽ ἀπὸ κρά]νας ἐμᾶς
διψῶντ᾽ ἀ[λλότριον ῥόον] παρ᾽ ἁλμυρὸν
οἴχεσθον· ἐ – ◡ –

76 . . .]λᾳ[G–H.　　　76–79 and 81, restored by s.

ΥΠΟΡΧΗΜΑΤΑ

In the *Hyporchêma*, or dance-song, there was a
closer connexion between the dance and the words
than was usual in other kinds of choral lyric. It is
described by Plutarch as a link between the two arts
of poetry and dancing (*Quaest. Symp.* ix 15, 2,
p. 748[b]). It was accompanied by the flute, with or

ΙΕΡΩΝΙ

105 (71 + 72)

(a) Σύνες ὅ τοι λέγω, ζαθέων ἱερῶν ὁμώνυμε
　　πάτερ,
　　κτίστορ Αἴτνας·

(b) νομάδεσσι γὰρ ἐν Σκύθαις ἀλᾶται <μόνος>,
　　ὃς ἁμαξοφόρητον οἶκον οὐ πέπαται·

5 ἀκλεὲς <δ᾽> ἔβα *<ζεῦγος ἄνευθ᾽ ἀπήνας>.*

(a) Schol. Pind. *P.* ii 127, *N.* vii 1, Arist. *Aves* 927 with
scholia, and Strabo, vi 268.

(b) Arist. *Aves* 942 (with scholia). ἀκλεὴς δ᾽ ἔβα σπολὰς
ἄνευ χιτῶνος.

3 In Aristophanes' parody the line ends with Στράτων
(στρατῶν s, μόνος Hermann).

hath trained to all manner of skill, gladly linking
her with fair handiwork of many a kind.

Let not the twain, when they have seen the
nectar from my spring, stray in their thirst to
another stream,—a stream of brine.

30 νέκταρ, cp. *O.* vii 7 f.

DANCE-SONGS

without the cithara.   It was not confined to religious
subjects, as is clear from some of the following
fragments.   It is substituted for the encomiastic or
epinician ode, in the poem addressed to Hieron.
(See further in H. W. Smyth's *Greek Melic Poets,*
lxix–lxxv.)

TO HIERON OF SYRACUSE

MARK what I say to thee!   O namesake-father
of temples divine! founder of Aetna! for among
the Nomad Scythians, one is wandering all alone,
one who hath no wain-borne home; but the pair
hath gone inglorious without a mule-car.[1]

[1] It is said by the scholiast on the *Aves* of Aristophanes
that Hieron had given the mules with which he had won the
Pythian victory to his charioteer.   Pindar here gives Hieron
a hint that the mules were of little use without the chariot.

5 ἀκλεὴς ἔβα mss: ἀκλεὲς δ' ἔβα <ζεῦγος ἡμιόνων ἄνευ
ἅρματος>? Brunck ; ἀκλεὲς — <ζεῦγος ἄνευθ' ἀπήνας> Sandys.

PINDAR

106 (73)

Ἀπὸ Ταϋγέτοιο μὲν Λάκαιναν
ἐπὶ θηρσὶ κύνα τρέχειν πυκινώτατον ἑρπετόν·
Σκύριαι δ' ἐς ἄμελξιν γλάγεος
αἶγες ἐξοχώταται·
5 ὅπλα δ' ἀπ' Ἄργεος· ἅρμα Θηβαῖον· ἀλλ' ἀπ'
ἀγλαοκάρπου
Σικελίας ὄχημα δαιδάλεον ματεύειν.

Athen. i p. 28a, Eustathius, *ad Hom.* p. 1822, 5, schol.
Arist. *Pax* 73.

108ᵃ (75)

θεοῦ δὲ δείξαντος ἀρχὰν
ἕκαστον ἐν πρᾶγος εὐθεῖα δὴ
κέλευθος ἀρετὰν λαβεῖν,
τελευταί τε καλλίονες.

Epist. Socrat. 1 p. 610, 4.

142 (106)

θεοῦ δὲ δυνατὸν μελαίνας
ἐκ νυκτὸς ἀμίαντον ὄρσαι φάος,
κελαινεφέϊ δὲ σκότει
καλύψαι σέλας καθαρὸν
ἀμέρας.

Clemens Alexandrinus, *Strom.* v 708.

110 (76)

γλυκὺ δ' ἀπείρῳ πόλεμος· πεπειραμένων δέ τις
ταρβεῖ προσιόντα νιν καρδίᾳ περισσῶς.

Stobaeus, *Flor.* 50, 3 (πόλεμος ἀπείροισι), Schol. on *Il.* 11,
227, and Diogenianus iii 94 (γλυκὺς ἀπείρῳ).

576

DANCE-SONGS

The Sicilian mule-car

From mount Taÿgetus cometh the Laconian hound, the cleverest creature in chasing the quarry. The goats of Scyros are the best for milk ; arms are from Argos ; the chariot from Thebes. But it is from fruitful Sicily that you must seek the deftly-wrought mule-car.

2 τρέχειν Ath. (s): τρέφειν Eust.
3 γλάγους Eust., γάλακτος Ath.
5 ἀλλ' ἀπὸ τῆς schol. Arist., ἀπὸ τῆς Ath.

A good beginning

When, for any deed, a beginning hath been shown by God, straight indeed is the path for pursuing virtue, and fairer are its issues.

2 ἐν = ἐς.

An eclipse

God can cause unsullied light to spring out of black night. He can also shroud in a dark cloud of gloom the pure light of day.

Cp. *Paean*, ix, p. 546 f.

" Dulce bellum inexpertis "

To the inexperienced war is pleasant,[1] but he that hath had experience of it, in his heart sorely feareth its approach.

[1] " He jests at scars, that never felt a wound " (*Romeo and Juliet*, ii. 2).

109 (228)

τὸ κοινόν τις ἀστῶν ἐν εὐδίᾳ τιθείς
ἐρευνασάτω μεγαλάνορος Ἡσυχίας τὸ φαιδρὸν
    φάος,
στάσιν ἀπὸ πραπίδος ἐπίκοτον ἀνελών,
πενίας δότειραν, ἐχθρὰν <δὲ> κουροτρόφον.

Polybius, iv 31 ; Stobaeus, *Flor.* 58, 9.

111 (77)

ἐνέπισε κεκραμέν' ἐν αἵματι. πολλὰ δ' ἔμβαλ'
    ἕλκεα νωμῶν
τραχὺ ῥόπαλον, τέλος δ' ἀείραις πρὸς στιβαρὰς
    σπάραξε πλευράς,
αἰὼν δὲ δι' ὀστέων ἐραίσθη.

Erotianus, *gl. Harpocr.*, p. 49 Kl.

ΕΓΚΩΜΙΑ

ΘΗΡΩΝΙ ΑΚΡΑΓΑΝΤΙΝΩ
119 (84)

ἐν δὲ Ῥόδον καταοίκισθεν . . . . .
ἔνθεν ὁρμαθέντες ὑψηλὰν πόλιν ἀμφινέμονται,
πλεῖστα μὲν δῶρ' ἀθανάτοις ἀνέχοντες,
ἕσπετο δ' αἰενάου πλούτου νέφος.

Schol. *O.* ii 15 f.

1 καταοίκισθεν S : κατῴκισθεν.
2 ἔνθεν ὁρμαθέντες S : ἔνθεν δ' (or ἐν δ' or ἔνθ') ἀφορμαθέντες.

EULOGIES

Concord in the State

Let him that giveth tranquillity to the community of citizens, look for the bright light of manly Peace, when from out his heart he hath plucked hateful faction, faction that bringeth poverty, and is an ill nurse of youth.

Heracles and his club

He gave a draught blended with blood; and, wielding his rude club, he inflicted full many a wound, and, lastly, lifting it up, he rent asunder the sturdy flanks, and the marrow was crushed from the bones of the spine.

1 ἐμβαλ' ἕλκεα Heringa and Bergk (s): ἕλκεα πλευρὰς ἔμβαλε.

EULOGIES

ON THERON OF ACRAGAS

. . . and his ancestors [1] colonised Rhodes, and starting thence, they inhabit a lofty city,[2] where they offer many a gift to the immortals, and where they were followed by a cloud of ever-flowing wealth.

1 The ancestors of Thêrôn.
2 Acragas.

PINDAR

120 (85)

Ὀλβίων ὁμώνυμε Δαρδανιδᾶν,
παῖ θρασύμηδες Ἀμύντα.

Schol. *N.* vii 1 ; Dio Chrysost. *Orat.* ii 33 (ἐπώνυμε).

121 (86)

πρέπει δ' ἐσλοῖσιν ὑμνεῖσθαι . . . καλλίσταις
    ἀοιδαῖς·
τοῦτο γὰρ ἀθανάτοις τιμαῖς ποτιψαύει μόνον,
θνᾴσκει δὲ σιγαθὲν καλὸν ἔργον.

Dionys. Halicarn. *de Demosthene* 26, i 185 Usener.

122 (87)

Xenophon of Corinth, before competing for the
Olympic crown in 464 B.C., vowed that, in the event
of his success, he would devote a hundred courtesans
to the service of the temple of Aphroditê in that
city. On the occasion of the fulfilment of his

στρ. α΄

Πολύξεναι νεάνιδες, ἀμφίπολοι
Πειθοῦς ἐν ἀφνειῷ Κορίνθῳ,
αἴτε τᾶς χλωρᾶς λιβάνου ξανθὰ δάκρη
θυμιᾶτε, πολλάκι ματέρ' ἐρώτων οὐρανίαν πτά-
    μεναι
5 νόημα πὸτ τὰν Ἀφροδίταν,

580

EULOGIES

ON ALEXANDER, SON OF AMYNTAS

Namesake of the blessed Trojans, son of brave
Amyntas ! . . . [1]

[1] Alexander, son of Amyntas, was king of Macedonia in
505–455 B.C. He was compelled to submit to the Persians
in 480, but was really a friend of the Greek cause. He is
known as "Alexander the Philhellene." He is here described
as the namesake of Alexander (Paris), the son of Priam.

'Tis meet for the good to be hymned with fairest
songs . . . For this is the only tribute that vergeth
on the honours due to the immortals ; but every
noble deed dieth, if suppressed in silence.

3 σιγαθὲν Barnes (s): ἐπιταθὲν Dionys. ; ἐπιλασθὲν Sylbers
(B).

FOR XENOPHON OF CORINTH

vow, the following ode was sung in the temple
of the goddess, while the hundred women danced
to the words of the song. The same Olympic
victory was celebrated in the thirteenth Olympian
ode.

GUEST-LOVING girls ! servants of Suasion in wealthy
Corinth ! ye that burn the golden tears of fresh
frankincense, full often soaring upward in your souls
unto Aphrodîtê, the heavenly mother of Loves   She

581

PINDAR

στρ. β´
  ὑμῖν ἄνευθ᾽ ἐπαγορίας ἔπορεν,
  ὦ παῖδες, ἐρατειναῖς <ἐν> εὐναῖς
  μαλθακᾶς ὥρας ἀπὸ καρπὸν δρέπεσθαι.
  σὺν δ᾽ ἀνάγκᾳ πᾶν καλόν...

στρ. γ´
10 ἀλλὰ θαυμάζω, τί με λέξοντι Ἰσθμοῦ
  δεσπόται τοιάνδε μελίφρονος ἀρχὰν εὑρόμενον
     σκολίου
  ξυνάορον ξυναῖς γυναιξίν.

στρ. δ´
  διδάξαμεν χρυσὸν καθαρᾷ βασάνῳ.....
  ὦ Κύπρου δέσποινα, τεὸν δεῦτ᾽ ἐς ἄλσος
15 φορβάδων κουρᾶν ἀγέλαν ἑκατόγγυιον Ξενοφῶν
     τελέαις
  ἐπάγαγ᾽ εὐχωλαῖς ἰανθείς.

Athenaeus, xiii 573ᵉ.

6 ἄνευθ᾽ ἐπαγορίας Meineke (s) : ἄνωθεν ἀπαγορίας.
7 <ἐν> B.   10 Ἰσθμοῦ Casaubon (edd.) : ὁμοῦ Α.

ΘΕΟΞΕΝΩ ΤΕΝΕΔΙΩ
123 (88)

A poem in praise of Theoxenus of Tenedos, Pindar's
favourite, who was present at the poet's death in the
theatre, or more probably the gymnasium, at Argos.
He was the son of Hagêsilas, who has been identified

στρ. α´
  Χρῆν μὲν κατὰ καιρὸν ἐρώτων δρέπεσθαι, θυμέ,
     σὺν ἁλικίᾳ·

1 μὲν Hermann : με.

582

hath granted you, ye girls, blamelessly to cull on lovely couches the blossom of delicate bloom; for, under force, all things are fair.

Yet I wonder what the lords of the Isthmus [1] will say of my devising such a prelude for a sweet roundelay to be the companion of common women . . .

We have tested gold with a pure touchstone . . .

O Queen of Cyprus! a herded troop of a hundred girls hath been brought hither to thy sacred grove by Xenophon in his gladness for the fulfilment of his vows . . .

[1] The Corinthians.

ON THEOXENUS OF TENEDOS

with the father of Aristagoras, the counsellor of Tenedos who is the theme of the eleventh Nemean. (Cp. Wilamowitz, *Berlin Akad*. 24 June, 1909, pp. 829–839.)

RIGHT it were, fond heart, to cull love's blossom in due season, in life's prime; but whosoever, when

PINDAR

τὰς δὲ Θεοξένου ἀκτῖνάς ποτ' ὄσσων μαρμαριζοι-
    σας δρακείς
ὃς μὴ πόθῳ κυμαίνεται, ἐξ ἀδάμαντος
ἠὲ σιδάρου κεχάλκευται μέλαιναν καρδίαν

ἀντ. α΄
5 ψυχρᾷ φλογί, πρὸς δ' Ἀφροδίτας ἀτιμασθεὶς
    ἑλικοβλεφάρου
ἢ περὶ χρήμασι μοχθίζει βιαίως, ἢ γυναικείῳ
    θράσει
ψυχρὰν φορεῖται πᾶσαν ὁδὸν θεραπεύων.
ἀλλ' ἐγὼ <τᾶς> ἕκατι κηρὸς ὣς δαχθεὶς ἕλᾳ

ἐπ. α΄
ἱρᾶν μελισσᾶν τάκομαι, εὖτ' ἂν ἴδω
10 παίδων νεόγυιον ἐς ἥβαν.
ἐν δ' ἄρα καὶ Τενέδῳ Πειθώ τ' ἔναιεν
καὶ Χάρις υἱὸν Ἀγησίλα.

Athenaeus, xiii 564e, 601d.

2 ποτ' ὄσσων Wilamowitz: ὄσσων Ath.[1], προσώπων Ath.[2]
πρὸς ὄσσων Kaibel (s).
    μαρμαριζοίσας Ath.[2]: —ρυζούσας Ath.[1]; —ροιζοίσας s.
5 ἑλικογλ. s.

127 (236)

Εἴη καὶ ἐρᾶν καὶ ἔρωτι
χαρίζεσθαι κατὰ καιρόν· μὴ πρεσβυτέραν ἀριθμοῦ
δίωκε, θυμέ, πρᾶξιν.

Athenaeus, xiii 601c.

ΙΕΡΩΝΙ ΣΤΡΑΚΟΣΙΩ
125 + 126 (91 + 92)

τόν ῥα Τέρπανδρός ποθ' ὁ Λέσβιος εὗρεν
πρῶτος ἐν δείπνοισι Λυδῶν

584

once he hath seen the rays flashing from the eyes of
Theoxenus, doth not swell with desire, his black
heart, with its frozen flame, hath been forged of
adamant or of iron; and, unhonoured of brightly
glancing Aphrodîtê, he either toileth over hoarded
wealth, or, with a woman's courage, is borne along
enslaved to a path that is utterly cold.

But I, for the sake of that Queen of love, like the
wax of the holy bees that is melted beneath the
heat of the sun, waste away when I look at the
young limbs of blooming boys. Thus I ween that
even in Tenedos Suasion and Charm dwelt in the soul
of the son of Hagêsilas.[1]

[1] Cp. *N.* xi 11.

---

6 περὶ χρήμασι — βιαίως. Cp. Ar. *Eth.* i 3, ὁ χρηματιστὴς
(βίος) βίαιός τις ἐστιν.

7 ψυχρὰν Ath. (S), βληχρὰν ? S: ψυχὰν Schneider (B);
αἰσχρὰν Ahrens; σύρδαν Wilamowitz.

8 τᾶς ἕκατι Wilamowitz (S), τᾶσδ' ἕκατι Hermann; δεκα-
τιτας.   8 f. ἕλᾳ | ἱρὰν Bergk (S): ἐλεηρὰν.

Love

May we love, and yield to another's love, in season
due. In thy passion for that rite, deem it not, my
soul, more important than due measure.

TO HIERON OF SYRACUSE

(The *barbitos*), which, I ween, was first found long
ago by Terpander of Lesbos, when, in the banquets of

PINDAR

ψαλμὸν ἀντίφθογγον ὑψηλᾶς ἀκούων πηκτίδος. . .
μηδ᾿ ἀμαύρου τέρψιν ἐν βίῳ· πολύ τοι
φέρτιστον ἀνδρὶ τερπνὸς αἰών.

Athenaeus, xiv 635ᵇ˒ ᵈ, xii 512ᵈ. Ath. 635ᵈ shows that
this fragment refers to the *barbitos*; 635ᵉ, that the *pēctis* was
identical with the *magadis*; and 635ᵇ, that its notes were
an octave higher than those of the *barbitos*.

ΘΡΑΣΥΒΟΥΛῼ ΑΚΡΑΓΑΝΤΙΝῼ
124ᵃ˒ᵇ (89 + 239)

Addressed to Thrasybulus, son of Xenocrates of
Acragas, who was victorious at the Panathenaea.
Cp. *P.* vi 15, 44, and *I.* ii 1, 31.

στρ. α΄

(*a*) ᾿Ω Θρασύβουλ᾿, ἐρατᾶν ὄχημ᾿ ἀοιδᾶν
   τοῦτό <τοι> πέμπω μεταδόρπιον. ἐν ξυνῷ κεν
      εἴη
   συμπόταισίν τε γλυκερὸν καὶ Διωνύσοιο καρπῷ
στρ. β΄
   καὶ κυλίκεσσιν ᾿Αθηναίαισι κέντρον·
5 (*b*) ἁνίκ᾿ ἀνθρώπων καματώδεες οἴχονται μέριμναι
   στηθέων ἔξω· πελάγει δ᾿ ἐν πολυχρύσοιο πλούτου
στρ. γ΄
   πάντες ἴσον νέομεν ψευδῆ πρὸς ἀκτάν·
   ὃς μὲν ἀχρήμων, ἀφνεὸς τότε, τοὶ δ᾿ αὖ πλουτεῦν-
      τες
   —ἀέξονται φρένας ἀμπελίνοις τόξοις δαμέντες.

(*a*) Athenaeus, xi 480ᶜ; (*b*) 782ᵈ p. 19 Kaibel.

1 ὄχημ᾿ ἀοιδᾶν. Cp. Frag. 140ᵇ, 62.   2 <τοι> Boeckh.
6 ἔξω . . πολυχρύσοιο Mitscherlich (s) : ἔξωθεν . . πολυχρύσου
Ath.
7 ἴσον s : ἴσα Ath.   8 αὖ : οὐ s.

586

the Lydians, he heard the twanging of the shrill-toned *pêctis* sounding in unison with it.[1]

Nor let delight grow dim, while thou livest; know that for man the best of all things are days spent in delight.

[1] The *barbitos* and the *pêctis* were two ancient varieties of lyre, but the notes of the *barbitos* (a *lyra maior*) were an octave lower than those of the *pêctis*, and therefore better suited to accompany the voices of men singing at a banquet. Cp. Telestes, in Ath. 626ᵃ, ὀξύφωνοι πηκτίδων ψαλμοί.

TO THRASYBULUS OF ACRAGAS

A song for the end of a feast

I send thee, Thrasybulus, this car of lovely songs, to close thy banquet. At the common board, it may well be a sweet incentive to thy boon companions, and to the wine of Dionysus, and to the cups that came from Athens; what time the wearisome cares of men have vanished from their bosoms, and, on a wide sea of golden wealth, we are all alike voyaging to some visionary shore. He that is penniless is then rich, and even they that are wealthy find their hearts expanding, when they are smitten by the arrows of the vine.[1]

[1] We may compare with the above song a fragment of Bacchylides, translated as follows in Jebb's edition, p. 418 :—
"As the cups go swiftly round, a sweet subduing power warms the heart. . . . That power sends a man's thoughts soaring ;—straightway he is stripping cities of their diadem of towers,—he dreams that he shall be monarch of the world ;—his halls gleam with gold and ivory ;—over the sunlit sea his wheat-ships bring wealth untold from Egypt :—such are the raptures of the reveller's soul."

PINDAR

124ᶜ (94)

δείπνου δὲ λήγοντος γλυκὺ τρωγάλιον
καίπερ πεδ' ἄφθονον βοράν.

Athenaeus, xiv 641ᶜ.

128 (90)

χαρίτας τ' Ἀφροδισίων ἐρώτων,
ὄφρα σὺν Χειμάρῳ μεθύων
Ἀγαθωνίδᾳ βάλω κότταβον.

Athenaeus, x 427ᵈ.

3 Ἀγαθωνίδᾳ Wilamowitz : ἀγαθωνιθε.

ΘΡΗΝΟΙ

THE θρῆνος, or dirge, was a choral song of lamenta-
tion accompanied by the music of the flute.   Pindar,
in his dirges, dwells on the immortality of the soul,
and offers consolation to the mourner by describing

129 + 130 (95)

τοῖσι λάμπει μὲν σθένος ἀελίου τὰν ἐνθάδε νύκτα
      κάτω,
φοινικορόδοις τ' ἐν λειμώνεσσι προάστιον αὐτῶν
καὶ λιβάνῳ σκιαρὸν καὶ χρυσέοις καρποῖς βε-
βριθός. . . .

1 σθένος s : μένος Plutarch.
3 χρυσέοις καρποῖς Boeckh : χρυσοκάρποισι.

---

[1] The "incense-tree" of the upper world is the *Boswellia
thurifera* of Arabia Felix and the Soumali country (George
Birdwood, in *Linn. Trans.* 1869, part 3).

[2] It has been suggested that the manuscript reading,
χρυσοκάρποισι, used in Dioscorides, ii 210, of an ivy with
yellow berries, refers to the yellow-berried mistletoe, or the

DIRGES

The delights of dessert

When the banquet is ceasing, then sweet is dessert, though it follow the fullest feast.

The cottabus

. . . and (may I delight in) the graces of Aphrodisian Loves, that so, drinking deep with Cheimarus, I may fling the cottabus[1] in a contest with Agathônidas.

[1] A game depending on the dexterity with which the last drops of a cup of wine could be tossed into a metal bowl.

DIRGES

the progress of the soul through the future ages. After death, all receive their due reward, and the spirits of the just are purified, until they are free from all taint of evil.

Elysium

For them the sun shineth in his strength, in the world below, while here 'tis night; and, in meadows red with roses, the space before their city is shaded by the incense-tree,[1] and is laden with golden fruits[2] . . .

"Golden Bough" (W. R. Paton, in *Classical Review*, xxv, 1911, p. 205). But probably the "golden fruit" of the world below is not meant to be precisely identified. In the Islands of the Blest, Pindar places "golden flowers on shining trees" (*O.* ii 79), and, elsewhere, he compares himself to the dragon guarding the apples of the Hesperides, the παγχρύσεα μῆλα of Hesiod's *Theogony*, 355. The phrase quoted by Libanius is "guarding the golden apples of the Muses," Frag. 288 (121).

PINDAR

καὶ τοὶ μὲν ἵπποις γυμνασίοις <τε>, τοὶ δὲ πεσ-
σοῖς,
5 τοὶ δὲ φορμίγγεσσι τέρπονται, παρὰ δέ σφισιν
εὐανθὴς ἅπας τέθαλεν ὄλβος·
ὀδμὰ δ' ἐρατὸν κατὰ χῶρον κίδναται
αἰεὶ θύα μιγνύντων πυρὶ τηλεφανεῖ παντοῖα θεῶν
ἐπὶ βωμοῖς.
ἔνθεν τὸν ἄπειρον ἐρεύγονται σκότον
βληχροὶ δνοφερᾶς νυκτὸς ποταμοί . . .

Plutarch, *Consol. ad Apollon.* 35, p. 120.

4 ἵπποις γυμνασίοις τε Hermann (B): ἱππείοις γυμνασίοις
Plut. ; ἱππείαισί <τε> γυμνασίαις <τε> S.
7 αἰεὶ θύα Hermann (BS): ἀεὶ θύματα Plutarch.

131 (96)

. . . ὀλβίᾳ δραπόντες αἶσα λυσίπονον τελετάν.
καὶ σῶμα μὲν πάντων ἕπεται θανάτῳ περισθενεῖ,
ζωὸν δ' ἔτι λείπεται αἰῶνος εἴδωλον· τὸ γάρ ἐστι
μόνον
ἐκ θεῶν· εὕδει δὲ πρασσόντων μελέων, ἀτὰρ
εὐδόντεσσιν ἐν πολλοῖς ὀνείροις
δείκνυσι τερπνῶν ἐφέρποισαν χαλεπῶν τε κρίσιν·

Plutarch, *Consol. ad Apollon.* 35, p. 120, and *Romulus*, 28.

1 δραπόντες s: δ' ἅπαντες Plutarch.
τελετάν s (found in a Vatican ms by Rohde, *Psyche*,
ed. 2, ii 217n.): τελευτάν Plutarch (sc. μετανίσσονται B).

---

[1] By the "rite" is meant initiation into the Mysteries.
Cp. Frag. 137 (102), and *Homeric Hymn to Demeter*, 480–
482 : "Among mortal men, happy is he that hath seen these
things ; but he that is uninitiated in sacred rites (ἀτελὴς

DIRGES

Some of them delight themselves with horses and with wrestling; others with draughts, and with lyres; while beside them bloometh the fair flower of perfect bliss. And o'er that lovely land fragrance is ever shed, while they mingle all manner of incense with the far-shining fire on the altars of the gods.[1]

From the other side sluggish streams of darksome night belch forth a boundless gloom.

[1] Rendered in verse in Milman's *Agamemnon and Bacchanals*, p. 187, and in F. D. Morice's *Pindar*, p. 18; and partly translated at the close of Tennyson's *Tiresias* :—

"And every way the vales
Wind, clouded with the grateful incense-fume
Of those who mix all odours to the Gods
On one far height in one *far-shining* fire."

The survival of the soul

. . . having, by happy fortune, culled the fruit of the rite that releaseth from toil.[1] And, while the body of all men is subject to over-mastering death, an image of life[2] remaineth alive, for it alone cometh from the gods.[3] But it sleepeth, while the limbs are active; yet, to them that sleep, in many a dream it giveth presage of a decision of things delightful or doleful.

ἱερῶν), and hath no share in them, hath not the same lot when he lieth beneath the gloom of death."

[2] "The image of life" is the "soul." Here "the soul" is the psychic "double" in every man. It lives after the death of the body, cp. εἴδωλον *Od.* xi 83, ψυχὴ καὶ εἴδωλον xxiii 104. Pindar is the first to explain the immortality of the ψυχά by its divine origin (Smyth's *Greek Melic Poets*, p. 376).

[3] Lines 2-5 are the motto of Dr. James Adam's Praelection *On the Divine Origin of the Soul*, in "Cambridge Praelections" (1906), 29 f.

PINDAR

133 (98)

οἶσι δὲ Φερσεφόνα ποινὰν παλαιοῦ πένθεος
δέξεται, ἐς τὸν ὕπερθεν ἅλιον κείνων ἐνάτῳ ἔτεϊ
ἀνδιδοῖ ψυχὰς πάλιν·
ἐκ τᾶν βασιλῆες ἀγαυοὶ καὶ σθένει κραιπνοὶ σοφίᾳ
τε μέγιστοι
ἄνδρες αὔξοντ'· ἐς δὲ τὸν λοιπὸν χρόνον ἥρωες
ἁγνοὶ πρὸς ἀνθρώπων καλέονται.

Plato, *Meno*, p. 81ᵇ. Cp. E. S. Thompson's ed., pp. 120-5.

¹ Pindar's belief appears to be as follows : After the death
of the body, the soul is judged in Hades, and, if accounted
guiltless in its life on earth, passes to the Elysium in Hades
depicted in Frag. 129 (95). It must, however, return twice

134 (99)

εὐδαιμόνων
δραπέτας οὐκ ἔστιν ὄλβος.

Stobaeus, *Flor.* 103, 6.

136 (101)

ἄστρα τε καὶ ποταμοὶ καὶ
κύματ' <ἀγκαλεῖ σε> πόντου.

Aristides, ii 215 Bruno Keil.

<ἀγκαλεῖ σε ?> s.

137 (102)

ὄλβιος ὅστις ἰδὼν ἐκεῖνα
κοίλαν εἶσιν ὑπὸ χθόνα·

2 κοίλαν εἶσιν Heinsius (ʙ)   κοινὰ εἰς or εἰσ' Clemens ;
εἰσ' Bergk (s).

DIRGES

The spirits of just men made perfect

But, as for those from whom Persephonê shall
exact the penalty of their pristine woe, in the ninth
year she once more restoreth their souls to the upper
sun-light; and from these come into being august
monarchs, and men who are swift in strength and
supreme in wisdom; and, for all future time, men
call them sainted heroes.[1]

again to earth, and suffer two more deaths of its body (*Ol.* ii
68). Finally Persephonê releases it from the παλαιὸν πένθος
and it returns to earth to inhabit the body of a king, a hero,
or a sage. It is now free from the necessity of further
wanderings and passes at once to the Islands of the Blest
(Rohde's *Psyche* 499 f, quoted in Smyth's *Greek Melic Poets*,
p. 377). Cp. ii 204–222 of Rohde's second edition (1898).

The happiness of the blessed

The happiness of the blessed is no fugitive.

" Whom universal Nature did lament "

The stars and the rivers and the waves call thee
back.

The Eleusinian Mysteries

Blessed is he who hath seen these things before he
goeth beneath the hollow earth; for he understandeth

PINDAR

οἶδεν μὲν βιοτου τελευτὰν
οἶδεν δὲ διόσδοτον ἀρχάν.

Clemens Alex. *Strom.* iii 518 (περὶ τῶν ἐν Ἐλευσῖνι μυστηρίων). From a dirge in memory of an Athenian who had been initiated into the Eleusinian Mysteries,—possibly Hippocrates (son of Megacles, and brother of Cleisthenes, the Athenian legislator), the only known subject of any of Pindar's dirges (schol. on *P.* vii 18).

The above is Donaldson's arrangement of the frag-

139 (Bergk)

Ἔντι μὲν χρυσαλακάτου τεκέων Λατοῦς ἀοιδαί
ὥριαι παιανίδες· ἔντι <δὲ καὶ> θάλ-
λοντος ἐκ κισσοῦ στεφάνων Διονύσου
<διθύραμβον μ>αιόμεναι· τὸ δὲ κοιμίσσαν<το>
τρεῖς
<θεαὶ υἱῶν> σώματ᾽ ἀποφθιμένων·
5 ἁ μὲν ἀχέταν Λίνον αἴλινον ὕμνει,
ἁ δ᾽ Ὑμέναιον, <ὃν> ἐν γάμοισι χροϊζόμενον
<Μοῖρα> σύμπρωτον λάβεν,
ἐσχάτοις ὕμνοισιν· ἁ δ᾽ Ἰάλεμον ὠμοβόρῳ
νούσῳ πεδαθέντα σθένος·
9 υἱὸν Οἰάγρου <δ᾽> Ὀρφέα χρυσάορα. . .

Schol. Vat. Rhes. 895.

2 θάλλοντες (τέλλοντες). 3 διθ. κτλ Wilamowitz.
4 θεαὶ υἱῶν s. 5 ὕμνει Hermann (s) : ὑμνεῖν.
6 ὃν Hermann (s). 7 Μοῖρα Bergk.
8 ὠμοβόρῳ Schneidewin (Donaldson); ὠμοβόλῳ Hermann (s) : ὁμοβόλῳ.
9 Οἰάγρου schol. Pind. *P.* iv 313. <δὲ> Wilamowitz (s), <τε> Bergk. Ὀρφέα χρυσάορα schol. *Il.* xv 256 ; Frag. 187 f. Boeckh.

---

[1] Linus, Hymenaeus, and Iälemus were sons of Apollo by one or other of the Muses. Linus, the personification of

594

the end of mortal life, and the beginning (of a new life) given of god.

ment. That of Schröder is as follows :—

> ὄλβιος ὅστις ἰδὼν κεῖν'
> εἶσ' ὑπὸ χθόν'·
> οἶδε μὲν βίου τελευτάν,
> οἶδεν δὲ διόσδοτον ἀρχάν.

3 οἶδεν Donaldson : οἶδε S.

βιότου Lobeck, and Donaldson : βίου (S), cp. *I.* iii 25 (= iv 5).

Linus, Hymenaeus, Iálemus

There are lays of paeans, coming in due season, which belong to the children of Lêtô of the golden distaff. There are other lays, which, from amid the crowns of flourishing ivy, long for the dithyramb of Dionysus ; but in another song did three god-desses lull to rest the bodies of their sons.

The first of these sang a dirge over the clear-voiced Linus ; and the second lamented with her latest strains Hymenaeus, who was seized by Fate, when first he lay with another in wedlock ; while the third sorrowed over Iálemus, when his strength was stayed by the onset of a devouring malady.

But the son of Oeagrus, Orpheus of the golden sword[1] . . .

lamentation, was said to be his son by Terpsichorê or Euterpê, and the word αἴλινος, used for "a plaintive dirge," is supposed to be derived from αἰ Λίνον, "ah me for Linus" (Pausanias, ix 29, 8). Hymenaeus, son of Urania, is the god of marriage, who was invoked in the bridal song. Iálemus was a son of Calliopê, and his name is a synonym for "a dirge" or "lament." Orpheus was also described as a son of Calliopê. At the end of the above passage he is called a son of the (Thracian) Oeagrus, but (like Linus, Hymenaeus, and Iálemus) he is sometimes called a son of Apollo.

PINDAR

ΕΞ ΑΔΗΛΩΝ ΕΙΔΩΝ

140ᵃ (Schröder)

<καί>τοι προιδὼν αἶσαν ᾳ
ζοι τότ' ἀμφι. ουτ<u>α</u>τ.
25 Ἡρακλέης. ἁλίαι . . . .
ναὶ μολόντας . υ . . ης . . . . σϱεν
θονοι φύγον ον . . . . . .
πάντων γὰρ ὑπέρβιος αν . . σεφα
ψυχὰν κενεω[ν] εμε . . ρυϟ . α . .
30 λαῶν ξενοδαΐκτα βασιλ . . ?
ος ἀτασθαλίᾳ κοτέων θαμά,
ἀγχαγέτᾳ τε Δάλου
πίθετο παυσεν . . , ρμ . . ιαδες [τίεν]
γάρ σε, λιγυσφαράγων *[ἀν]τ[ί]νακ-
35   τα, Ἑκαβόλε, φορμίγγων.
μνάσθηθ' ὅτι τοι ζαθέας Πάρου ἐν
γυάλοις ἔσσατο ἄνακτι
βωμὸν πατρί τε Κρονίῳ
τιμάεντι πέραν Ἰσθμὸν διαβαίς,
40 ὅτε Λαομέδοντι πεπρωμένοι·
ἤρχετο μόροιο κᾶρυξ.
43 ἦ[ν] γὰρ τὸ παλαίφατον . . . . . ον
ἱκε συγγόνους
45 τρεῖς π . . εω . ν ϟεφαλαν . . ρ . . ται
ἐπιδ . . . . . . αιμα

Grenfell and Hunt, *Oxyrhynchus Papyri*, iii (1903) p. 13 f.

The subject of this poem is "the vengeance taken·by Heracles upon Laomedon" (G–H).

30 The "king who murders strangers" is Laomedon, cp. l. 40.

32 The "founder of Delos" is Apollo.

FRAGMENTS

FROM ODES OF UNCERTAIN CLASS

Apollo and Heracles

For he honoured thee, O Far-darter, that strikest
up the clearly sounding lyres. Remember that he[1] set
up an altar in the dells of holy Paros to thee, the
king, and to the honoured Father, son of Cronus, on
crossing to this side of the Isthmus, when, as a herald,
he began to tell of the doom fated for Laomedon.
For there was the ancient oracle . .

---

[1] Heracles.

---

33 τίεν s : . . ϛ .
34 ἀντίνακτα Sandys : . ντ . γαγτα. In Eur. *Bacch.* 80 we
have ἀνὰ θυρσόν τέ τινάσσων, and, in a fragment of the Greek
Anthology ?, τινάσσειν, applied to the νεῦρα κιθάρας, means
" to make the strings quiver by striking them." For ἀν- =
ἀνα- cp. the Pindaric ἀντείνειν, ἄντειλας, and ἀντιθέναι.
43 τὸ παλαίφατον, cp. *O.* ii 40.   44 ἷκε s : εἷκε.

PINDAR

140ᵇ (Schröder)

<pre>
55 'Ιων[ίδος ἀντίπαλον Μοίσας]
    ἀοιδ[άν τε κ]αὶ ἁρμονίαν
    αὐ[λοῖς ἐ]πεφράσατο
    Λοκρῶν τις, [οἵ τ' ἀργίλοφον]
    π[ὰρ Ζεφυρί]ου κολώ[ναν]
60 ν[αίονθ' ὑπὲ]ρ Αὐσονία[ς ἄκρας],
    λι[παρὰ πόλ]ις. ἄνθ[ηκε δὲ
    οἷον ὄχημα λιγ[. . . . . .]
    κες, οἷον παιήονα
    'Απόλλωνί τε καὶ [Μούσαις
65 ἄρμενον. ἐγὼ μ[ὰν κλύων]
    παῦρα μελιζομέν[ου, τέχναν]
    [γλώ]σσαργον ἀμφέπων,
    [ἐρεθίζ]ομαι πρὸς ἀοιδὰν
    [ἁλίο]υ δελφῖνος ὑπ[όκρισιν],
70 τὸν ἀκύμονος ἐν πόντου πελάγει
    αὐλῶν ἐκίνησ' ἐρατὸν μέλος.
</pre>

Grenfell and Hunt, *Oxyrhynchus Papyri*, iii (1903) p. 15 f.

55 'Ιων[ίδος ἀντίπαλον Μοίσας] ? s.

58 Λοκρῶν τις, Xenocrates (or Xenocritus) of Locri, cp. schol. *O.* x 17, k, . . . Λοκριστὶ γάρ τις ἁρμονία, ἣν ἀσκῆσαί φασι Ξενόκριτον τὸν Λοκρόν, Athen. xiv 625ᵉ, ἡ Λοκριστί· ταύτῃ γὰρ ἔνιοι τῶν γενομένων κατὰ Σιμωνίδην καὶ Πίνδαρον ἐχρήσαντό ποτε, καὶ πάλιν κατεφρονήθη, Plutarch, *De Musica*, 9, Ξενόκριτος ὁ Λοκρός, . . ἦσαν δ' οἱ περὶ — Ξενόκριτον ποιηταὶ παιάνων, 10 περὶ δὲ Ξενοκρίτου, ὃς ἦν τὸ γένος ἐκ Λοκρῶν τῶν ἐν Ἰταλίᾳ, ἀμφισβητεῖται εἰ παιάνων ποιητὴς γέγονεν . . ., also Westphal, *Griechische Harmonik* (1886), 209 ; Bergk, *Gr. Lit.* ii 229 f. ; and Wilamowitz on Timotheos, p. 103, 5.

58 f. οἵ — κολώναν quoted in schol. *O.* x 17, i (= Frag. 200 Bergk).

60 ν[αίονθ' ὑπὲ]ρ, for ναίουσ' ὑπὲρ: ν[άουσ' ὑπὲ]ρ G–H ν[άοντ' ὑπὲ]ρ Diehl ; ν[αίοντ'] <ὑπὲ>ρ s.

598

FRAGMENTS OF UNCERTAIN CLASS

Locrian music

As a rival to the Ionian music, song and harmony
with flutes were devised by one of the Locrians, who
dwell beside the white-crested hill of Zephyrium,
beyond the Ausonian foreland, a gleaming city; and
he dedicated it, as a chariot of clear song, as a
paean meet for Apollo and the Muses.

But I, while I hear him playing his few notes,
plying as I do a babbling art, vie with his lay,
like [1] a dolphin of the sea, whom the lovely sound
of flutes thrilled on the waters of the waveless
deep.

[1] ὑπόκρισιν, lit. "answering to," or "playing the part of";
for this adverbial use of the accusative, cp. δίκην and χάριν.

61 ἄνθ[ηκε δέ,] G–H (Diehl): ἀνθ[ώυξε δέ] S.

62 ὄχημα, Frag. 124, 1. ἐρατᾶν ὄχημ' ἀοιδᾶν. λιγ . . . κες,
λιγυαχές ? Diehl.

63 οἷον seems necessary after οἷον in line 62: ὁ . όν papyrus;
οἷον (edd.), "a *solitary* paean," which may perhaps be de-
fended by παῦρα μελιζομένου in l. 66.

64 Μούσαις or Χαρίτεσσιν Diehl.

69–71 ἁλίου — μέλος, Plutarch, *de soll. anim.* 36, δελφῖνι
Πίνδαρος ἀπεικάζων ἑαυτὸν ἐρεθίζεσθαί φησιν <ἁλί>ου δελφῖνος
ὑπόκρισιν, τὸν μὲν ἀκύμονος ἐν πόντου πελάγει αὐλῶν ἐκίνησ'
ἔρατον μέλος, cp. *Quaest. Symp.* vii 5, 2 (Pindar, Frag. 235
(259)).

70 τὸν μὲν Plutarch (Diehl): τὸν S.

PINDAR

141 (105)

θεὸς ὁ πάντα τεύχων βροτοῖς
καὶ χάριν ἀοιδᾷ φυτεύει.

Didymus Caecilius, *de Trinitate*, III i p. 320.

1 πάντα s: τὰ πάντα.

143 (107)

κεῖνοι γάρ τ᾽ ἄνοσοι καὶ ἀγήραοι
πόνων τ᾽ ἄπειροι, βαρυβόαν
πορθμὸν πεφευγότες Ἀχέροντος[1] . . .

Plutarch, (of the gods) *de superst.* c. 6; *adv. Stoicos*, c. 31; and *Amatorius*, c. 18.

[1] Cp. Bacchylides 60 (34), (of the gods) οἱ μὲν ἀδμᾶτες ἀεικελιᾶν εἰσι νόσων καὶ ἄνατοι, | οὐδὲν ἀνθρώποις ἴκελοι.

150 (118)

μαντεύεο, Μοῖσα, προφατεύσω δ᾽ ἐγώ.

Eustath. on *Iliad* i, p. 9.

152 (266)

. . . μελισσοτεύκτων κηρίων
ἐμὰ γλυκυρώτερος ὀμφά.

Cramer, *Anecd. Oxon.* i 285, 19.

153 (125)

δενδρέων δὲ νομὸν Διόνυσος πολυγαθὴς αὐξάνοι,
ἁγνὸν φέγγος ὀπώρας.

Plutarch, *de Iside et Osiri*, c. 35, *Qu. Symp.* ix 14, 4, and *Amatorius*, c. 15.

[1] νομὸν Heyne (edd.): νόμον in two passages of Plutarch (τρόπον in the third), but νομόν, "pasture-land," does not make as good sense as *γόνον, "produce"; cp. Anacreont. 58, 7, γόνον ἀμπέλου, τὸν οἶνον, and Pindar, *N.* ix 51, βιατὰν ἀμπέλου παῖδα.

FRAGMENTS OF UNCERTAIN CLASS

The gifts of God

God that doeth all things for mortals, even maketh grace to grow for song.

The felicity of the gods

But they, set free from sickness and eld and toils, having fled from the deeply sounding ferry of Acheron . . .

The Muse and the poet

Muse! be thou mine oracle, and I shall be thine interpreter.

"Sweeter than the honey-comb"

My voice is sweeter than the bee-wrought honey-combs.

Dionysus, the god of trees

May the field of fruit-trees receive increase from gladsome Dionysus, the pure sunshine of the fruit-time.[1]

---

[1] It is uncertain whether φέγγος is in apposition to Dionysus (so Dissen), or to the field of fruit-trees (so Boeckh). If we substitute for the *field* (νομὸν) the *produce* (γόνον) of the fruit-trees, the latter finds its fittest apposition in φέγγος, which, in that case, expresses the gleaming of the ripe fruit amid the green foliage : " May gladsome Dionysus give increase to the *produce* of the fruit-trees, the pure radiance of the fruit-time."

PINDAR

155 (127)

τί ἔρδων φίλος
σοί τε, καρτερόβροντα
Κρονίδα, φίλος δὲ Μοίσαις,
Εὐθυμία τε μέλων εἴην,
τοῦτ᾽ αἴτημί σε.

Athenaeus, v 191ᶠ.

157 (128)

ὦ τάλας ἐφάμερε, νήπια βάζεις
χρήματά μοι διακομπέων.

Schol. Aristoph. Nub. 223.

159 (132)

ἀνδρῶν δικαίων χρόνος σωτὴρ ἄριστος.

Dionysius Halicarn. de orat. ant. 2 (i 4, 20 Usener).

166 f (147 f)

(a) <ἀνδρ>οδάμαν<τα> δ᾽ ἐπεὶ Φῆρες δάεν ῥιπὰν
μελιαδέος οἴνου,
ἐσσυμένως ἀπὸ μὲν λευκὸν γάλα χερσὶ τραπεζᾶν
ὤθεον, αὐτόματοι δ᾽ ἐξ ἀργυρέων κεράτων πίνοντες
ἐπλάζοντο . . .

1 <ἀνδρ>οδ. Casaubon, -δάμαν<τα> B.
Φῆρες, Aeolic for Θῆρες, applied to the Centaurs in *Il.* i
268, ii 743 ; and, in the singular, Φήρ, to the Centaur Cheiron,
the "divine Beast" of *P.* iv 119, cp. iii 4.

FRAGMENTS OF UNCERTAIN CLASS

The poet's prayer

What shall I do to be dear unto thee, O loudly-thundering son of Cronus, and dear unto the Muses, and to be cared for by Jollity? This is my prayer to thee.

Silenus to the Phrygian hero, Olympus

Poor child of a day! you are childishly prating, in boasting to me of money.

Time, the champion of the Just

Time is the best of champions to the just.

The battle between the Centaurs and the Lapithae.

And when the Phêres[1] were aware of the overpowering aroma of honey-sweet wine, anon with their hands they thrust the white milk from the tables, and, drinking, unasked, out of the silver horns, began to wander in mind. But Caeneus,[2]

[1] The Centaurs, who fought with the Lapithae in Thessaly at the marriage feast of Pirithoüs the king of the Lapithae.

[2] One of the Lapithae, who was invulnerable. When he was belaboured with trunks of trees (as implied in the text), he stamped with his foot, and disappeared into the earth. On the invulnerability of Caeneus, cp. Ovid, *Met.* xii 206 f, 491.

PINDAR

(b) . . . ὁ δὲ χλωραῖς ἐλάταισι τυπεὶς
5 ὤχεθ᾽ ὑπὸ χθόνα Καινεὺς σχίσαις ὀρθῷ ποδὶ γᾶν.

(a) Athenaeus, xi 476ᵇ.
(b) Schol. Apollon. *Argon*. 7, Plutarch, *de absurd. Stoic. opin*. init.

5 ὑπὸ χθόνα Β : καταδὺς ὑπὸ γῆν Plutarch.

---

[1] Fir-trees were among the ordinary missiles, or weapons, of the Centaurs. Cp. Apollodorus, *Bibliotheca*, ii 5, 4 § 3, διὰ

168 (150)

δοιὰ βοῶν
θερμὰ πρὸς ἀνθρακίαν στέψεν, πυρὶ δ᾽ ἐκκαπύοντα
σώματα· καὶ τότ᾽ ἐγὼ σαρκῶν τ᾽ ἐνοπὰν <ἴδον>
ἠδ᾽ ὀστέων στεναγμὸν βαρύν·
ἦν διακρῖναι ἰδόντ᾽ <οὐ> πολλὸς ἐν καιρῷ χρόνος.

Athenaeus, x 411ᵇ.

1 δοιὰ Β : διὰ Ath.
2 πρὸς Β : δ᾽ εἰς Ath. στέψεν Β : στέψαν Ath. πυρὶ δ᾽ ἐκκα-
πύοντα Β, cp. *Il*. xxii 467, ἀπὸ δὲ ψυχὴν ἐκάπυσσεν : πυρὶ δ᾽
ὑπνόωντε Ath. ; πυρίπνοά τε Β.

169 (151)

νόμος ὁ πάντων βασιλεὺς
θνατῶν τε καὶ ἀθανάτων
ἄγει δικαιῶν τὸ βιαιότατον
ὑπερτάτᾳ χειρί. τεκμαίρομαι
5 ἔργοισιν Ἡρακλέος· ἐπεὶ Γηρυόνα βόας
Κυκλωπίων ἐπὶ προθύρων Εὐρυσθέος
ἀναιτήτας τε καὶ ἀπριάτας ἤλασεν.

Plato, *Gorgias*, 484ᵇ. Cp. *Laws*, iii 690ᵇ, x 890ᵃ, *Protag.*
337ᵈ, Herodotus, iii 38, and Aristides, ii 68.

7 ἤλασεν Ox. Vat. (S¹) : ἔλασεν vulgo (CS³).

604

struck by the green fir-trees,[1] cleft the ground with his foot, where he stood, and passed beneath the earth.

τῆς ὀσμῆς αἰσθόμενοι (τοῦ οἴνου), παρῆσαν οἱ Κένταυροι πέτραις ὡπλισμένοι καὶ ἐλάταις. When attacked by the Centaurs, Caeneus, "unconquered and unflinching passed beneath the earth," θεινόμενος στιβαρῇσι καταίγδην ἐλατῇσιν (Apollonius Rhodius, i 64). Cp. Ovid, *Met.* xii 509 f, "obrutus immani cumulo, sub pondere Caeneus aestuat arboreo, coniectaque robora duris fert umeris."

The gluttony of Heracles, (narrated by his host, Corônus, son of the Lapith, Caeneus)

Two warm bodies of oxen he set in a circle around the embers, bodies crackling in the fire ; and then I noted a noise of flesh and a heavy groaning of bones. There was no long time fitly to distinguish it.

4 διακρ. ἴδ. Bergk : ἴδ. διακρ. Ath. <οὐ> Coraës (s³). πολλὸν ἐν κραίρᾳ χράνος, "the foul mass in the skull," Verrall, *Journal of Philology*, ix 122.

Law, the lord of all

Law, the lord of all, mortals and immortals, carrieth everything with a high hand, justifying the extreme of violence.

This I infer from the labours of Heracles ; for he drave to the Cyclopian portals of Eurystheus the kine of Geryon,[1] which he had won neither by prayer nor by price.

[1] *I.* i 13 ; cp. Prof. E. B. Clapp in *Classical Quarterly*, viii (1914) 226-8.

PINDAR

172 (158)

Πηλέος ἀντιθέου μόχθοις νεότας ἐπέλαμψεν μυρίοις·
πρῶτον μὲν Ἀλκμήνας σὺν υἱῷ Τρώϊον ἂμ πεδίον,
καὶ μετὰ ζωστῆρας Ἀμαζόνος ἦλθεν,
καὶ τὸν Ἰάσονος εὔδοξον πλόον ἐκτελέσαις
5 εἷλε Μήδειαν ἐν Κόλχων δόμαις.

Schol. Eurip. *Androm.* 796, quoted to show that Euripides apparently followed Pindar in making Peleus accompany Heracles to Troy. The common account was that Heracles was accompanied by Telamon, as in *N.* iv 25, *I.* vi 27.

193 (205)

.... πενταετηρὶς ἑορτὰ
βουπομπός, ἐν ᾇ πρῶτον εὐνάσθην ἀγαπατὸς
ὑπὸ σπαργάνοις.

Vit. Vratisl. p. 2, 18 Drachmann. Cp. Plutarch, *Sympo*-. *Qu.* viii 1.

Pindar was born at the beginning of the Pythia, on the first day of which there was a solemn sacrifice of oxen.

194 (206)

κεκρότηται χρυσέα κρηπὶς ἱεραῖσιν ἀοιδαῖς·
εἶα τειχίζωμεν ἤδη ποικίλον
κόσμον αὐδάεντα λόγων·
<ὃς> καὶ πολυκλείταν περ ἐοῖσαν ὅμως Θήβαν
ἔτι μᾶλλον ἐπασκήσει θεῶν
5 καὶ κατ' ἀνθρώπων ἀγυιάς.

Aristides, T. ii 159 Bruno Keil.

2 εἶα *A*, εἶα W. Dindorf (Bergk, **8**) : οἶα vulgo **B**. τειχί-
ζωμεν *AS* (s) : —ζομεν *QUT* (Β). ποικίλων Bergk.

606

FRAGMENTS OF UNCERTAIN CLASS

The exploits of Peleus

The youth of god-like Peleus shone forth with countless labours. With the son of Alcmêna, first went he to the plain of Troy; and, again, on the quest of the girdles of the Amazon; and, when he had made an end of the famous voyage with Iason, he took Medea in the home of the Colchians.

5 ἐκ Κόλχων δόμων Bergk.

The birth of Pindar

It was the quadrennial festival (of the Pythian games) with its procession of oxen, when, as a dear infant, I was first cradled in swaddling-clothes.[1]

[1] Cp. first page of *Introduction.*

The praise of Thebes

For sacred songs a foundation of gold hath now been laid. Come! let us now build beauty of words, varied and vocal, thus making Thebes, which is already famous, still more splendid in streets belonging to gods as well as to men.

4 <ὃς> B. πολυκλείταν mss (Dindorf, S): πολύκλειτον vulgo.

PINDAR

195 (207)

Εὐάρματε χρυσοχίτων, ἱερώτατον ἄγαλμα, Θῆβα.

Schol. Pindar *P.* iv 25.

198

οὔτοι με ξένον
οὐδ' ἀδαήμονα Μοισᾶν ἐπαίδευσαν κλυταί
Θῆβαι.

Chrysippus περὶ ἀποφατικῶν c. 2.   First ascribed to Pindar
by Letronne in 1838.

199 (213)

Ἔνθα βουλαὶ <μὲν> γερόντων
καὶ νέων ἀνδρῶν ἀριστεύοισιν αἰχμαί,
καὶ χοροὶ καὶ Μοῖσα καὶ Ἀγλαΐα.

Plutarch, *Lycurg.* c. 21.

205 (221)

Ἀρχὰ μεγάλας ἀρετᾶς, ὤνασσα Ἀλάθεια, μὴ
πταίσῃς ἐμὰν
σύνθεσιν τραχεῖ ποτὶ ψεύδει . . . . . .

Stobaeus, *Flor.* xi 3 м (xi 18 н).

207 (223)

Ταρτάρου πυθμὴν πιέζει σ' ἀφανὴς
σφυρηλάτοις <δεσμοῖς> ἀνάγκας.

Plutarch, *consol. ad Apollon.* 6, p. 104.

208 (224)

μανίαι τ' ἀλαλαί τ' ὀρινομένων
ῥιψαύχενι σὺν κλόνῳ.

Plutarch, *Symp. Q.* i 5, 2. Now part of Dithyramb on p. 560.

FRAGMENTS OF UNCERTAIN CLASS

The patron goddess of Thebes

Thêbê, with the noble chariot, and with the golden tunic, our most hallowed pride !

The poet's pride in his Theban home

Verily, as no stranger, nor as ignorant of the Muses, was I reared by famous Thebes.

The praise of Sparta

. . Where old men's counsels and young men's spears are matchless, and choral dances also, and the Muse, and the Grace, Aglaïa.

A prayer to Truth

Queen of Truth, who art the beginning of great virtue, keep my good-faith from stumbling against rough falsehood.

The depth of Tartarus

The invisible depth of Tartarus presseth thee down with iron chains of necessity.

2 <δεσμοῖς> ἀνάγκας Bergk : ἀνάγκαις vulgo.

The madding dance divine

Frenzies and shouts of dancers driven wild together with the throng that toss their heads.

609

PINDAR

210 (229)

ἄγαν φιλοτιμίαν
μνώμενοι ἐν πολίεσσιν ἄνδρες
ἢ στάσιν, ἄλγος ἐμφανές.

Plutarch, de cohib. ir. 8, 457.

213 (232)

πότερον δίκᾳ τεῖχος ὕψιον
ἢ σκολιαῖς ἀπάταις ἀναβαίνει
ἐπιχθόνιον γένος ἀνδρῶν,
δίχα μοι νόος ἀτρέκειαν εἰπεῖν.

Plato, *Republic*, ii 365ᵇ, Cicero, *ad Atticum*, xiii 38, etc.
For the metaphor, cp. *I.* iv 45.

214 (233)

γλυκεῖά οἱ καρδίαν ἀτάλλοισα γηροτρόφος
συναορεῖ
'Ελπίς, ἃ μάλιστα θνατῶν πολύστροφον γνώμαν
κυβερνᾷ.

Plato, *Republic*, i 331ᵃ, etc.

220 (241)

τῶν οὔ τι μεμπτὸν
οὔτ᾽ ὦν μεταλλακτόν, ὅσ᾽ ἀγλαὰ χθὼν
πόντου τε ῥιπαὶ φέροισιν.

Plutarch, *Sympos. Qu.* vii 5, 3.

221 (242)

. . . ἀελλοπόδων μέν τιν᾽ εὐφραίνοισιν ἵππων
τιμαὶ καὶ στέφανοι, τοὺς δ᾽ ἐν πολυχρύσοις
θαλάμοις βιοτά·

2 τιμαί <τε> ? s.

610

FRAGMENTS OF UNCERTAIN CLASS

" The madding crowd's ignoble strife"

Men who, in the cities, are too eager for ambition, or for faction, that manifest woe . . .

2 πολίεσσιν Boeckh : πόλεσιν.

Does right fare better than wrong?

Whether the race of men on earth mounteth a loftier tower by justice, or by crooked wiles, my mind is divided in telling clearly.

Hope, the nurse of eld

With him liveth sweet Hope, the nurse of eld, the fosterer of his heart,—Hope, who chiefly ruleth the changeful mind of man.

" The earth is the Lord's, and the fulness thereof"

Nothing is to be disparaged, nothing to be made different, of all the boons of the glorious earth, and of the rushing sea.

" Sunt quos curriculo pulverem Olympico collegisse iuvat"

One man is gladdened by honours and crowns won by wind-swift steeds; other men by living in cham-

PINDAR

τέρπεται δὲ καί τις ἐπ' οἶδμ' ἅλιον ναὶ̈ θοᾷ
σῶς διαστείβων . . . .

Sextus Empiricus, *Hypotyp. Pyrr.* i 86.

4 σῶς omitted by s³.

222 (243)

. . . . Διὸς παῖς ὁ χρυσός·
κεῖνον οὐ σὴς οὐδὲ κίς,[1]
δάπτει <δὲ> βροτέαν φρένα κάρτιστον <κτεά-
νων.>

Schol. *Pyth.* iv 407.   Plutarch in Proclus *ad Hesiod. Opp.
et D.* 430.

[1] Cp. Theognis 451, τοῦ (χρυσοῦ) χροιῆς καθύπερθε μέλας
οὐχ ἅπτεται ἰὸς | οὐδ' εὐρώς, αἰεὶ δ' ἄνθος ἔχει καθαρόν.

227 (250)

νέων δὲ μέριμναι σὺν πόνοις εἱλισσόμεναι
δόξαν εὑρίσκοντι· λάμπει δὲ χρόνῳ
ἔργα μετ' αἰθέρ' <ἀερ>θέντα.

Clemens Alexandrinus, *Strom.* iv 586.

Boeckh ascribes the above passage to an Encomium, and
Schröder (with great probability) to an Epinician Ode.
Professor E. B. Clapp, however (*Classical Quarterly*, viii
(1914) 225), proposes to prefix it to Frag. 172 (158), which
is in the same metre, and has an echo of λάμπει in ἐπέλαμψεν.

3 <ἀερ>θέντα Boeckh (s), cp. *N.* viii 41, ἀρετὰ . . .
ἀερθεῖσα . . ., πρὸς ὑγρὸν αἰθέρα: λαμπευθέντα Clemens.

234 (258)

. . . ὑφ' ἅρμασιν ἵππος,
ἐν δ' ἀρότρῳ βοῦς· παρὰ ναῦν δ' ἰθύει τάχιστα
δελφίς·

612

bers rich with gold; and there is even one who rejoiceth in safely crossing the wave of the sea in a swift ship.

Man's mind devoured by gold,
which neither moth nor rust corrupteth

Gold is a child of Zeus; neither moth nor rust devoureth it; but the mind of man is devoured by this supreme possession.

3 <κτεάνων> B.

Labor omnia vincit

The ambitions [1] of youths, if constantly exercised with toil,[2] win glory; and, in time, their deeds are bathed in light, when lifted aloft to the air of heaven.[3]

[1] Keenness for victory in the games; cp. *O.* i 108, *P.* viii 82, *N.* iii 69.
[2] The toil of training and of contest; cp. *O.* v 15, xi 4; *N.* iv 1, vii 74, x 24; *I.* i 42, v 25, vi 11.
[3] Cp. *N.* viii 41, "the fame of glorious deeds . . . is borne aloft to the liquid air."

"Quam scit . . . exerceat artem."

The horse is for the chariot; the ox for the plough; while, beside the ship, most swiftly speedeth

PINDAR

κάπρῳ δὲ βουλεύοντι φόνον κύνα χρὴ τλάθυμον
[ἐξ]ευρεῖν . . .

Plutarch, de tranquill. anim. c. 13, virt. mor. c. 12.

249^b Schröder

πρόσθα μέν σ' Ἀχελωΐου τὸν ἀοιδότατον *εὐρεῖτα
κράνα, Μέλ[ανό]ς τε ποταμοῦ ῥοαὶ τρέφον
κάλαμον.

Grenfell and Hunt, *Oxyrhynchus Papyri* ii (1899) 64, schol.
of Ammonius on *Il.* xxi 195.

1 εὐρεῖτα Sandys, Doric gen. for εὐρρεῖταο (*Il.* vi 34), ρ often
remains single in Pindar : εὐρωπία pap. (G–H, S).

FRAGMENTS OF UNCERTAIN CLASS

the dolphin; and, to meet a boar that is meditating murder, you must find a stout-hearted hound.

3 βουλεύοντι (s), cp. Horace, *Carm.* iii 22, **7**, "verris obliquum meditantis ictum": *v.l.* βουλεύοντα (B).

Rivers "crowned with vocal reeds."

Thou, the most musical reed, wast aforetime nurtured by the spring of the fair-flowing Acheloüs, and by the streams of the river Melas.

2 κράνα Μέλανος Wilamowitz (s): κράναν ἕλικος G–H. Cp. Theophrastus, *Hist. Plant.* iv 11, 8, φύεται δὲ πλεῖστος (*sc.* ὁ κάλαμος) μεταξὺ τοῦ Κηφισοῦ καὶ τοῦ Μέλανος.

INDEX

PIND.

INDEX

INDEX

INDEX

INDEX

INDEX

INDEX

INDEX

INDEX

INDEX

INDEX

INDEX

INDEX

INDEX

INDEX

INDEX

INDEX